Principles of Financial Management

Principles of
Financial
Management

Haim Levy

Hebrew University, Jerusalem
University of Florida, Gainesville

Marshall Sarnat

Hebrew University, Jerusalem

PRENTICE HALL, Englewood Cliffs, N.J. 07632

Library of Congress Cataloging-in-Publication Data

LEVY, HAIM.
    Principles of financial management / Haim Levy, Marshall Sarnat.
        p.   cm.
    Includes index.
    ISBN 0-13-710054-X
    1. Corporations—Finance.   2. Business enterprises—Finance.
I. Sarnat, Marshall.   II. Title.
HG4026.L475   1988
658.1'5—dc19

British Library Cataloguing in Publication Data

LEVY, HAIM
    Principles of financial management
    1. Companies, Financial management.
    I. Title   II. Sarnat, Marshall
    658.1'5
    ISBN 0 13-709775-1

ISBN   0-13-710054-X

ISBN   0-13-709775-1

Printed in the United States of America

10 9 8 7 6 5 4 3 2 1

PRENTICE-HALL, INC., *Englewood Cliffs, New Jersey*
PRENTICE-HALL, INTERNATIONAL, UK., LTD., *London*
PRENTICE-HALL OF AUSTRALIA PTY., LTD., *Sydney*
PRENTICE-HALL CANADA, INC., *Toronto*
PRENTICE-HALL OF INDIA PRIVATE LIMITED, *New Delhi*
PRENTICE-HALL OF JAPAN, INC., *Tokyo*
PRENTICE-HALL OF SOUTHEAST ASIA PTE., LTD., *Singapore*
EDITORA PRENTICE-HALL DO BRASIL LTDA., *Rio de Janeiro*
PRENTICE-HALL HISPANOAMERICANA, S.A., *Mexico*
WHITEHALL BOOKS LIMITED, *Wellington, New Zealand*

For Iddo

Contents

10   Estimating Cash Flows   237

11   Special Topics and Risk Analysis in Capital Budgeting   258

PART V   Long-Term Strategy: Financing Decisions

Preface

Some of you may be familiar with the chronic complaint of the college professor, "I have found a book from which to lecture; now if I can only find one for the students to read." This book *is* for the students to read.

This is not a book about finance theory per se, nor does it set out to describe academic research. On the contrary, it is a book which deals with the major problems of corporate finance, explicitly from the viewpoint of the financial manager. However the book is a product of our underlying conviction that the modern theory of finance can (and does) provide useful guidelines for practical financial management.

It is a book about corporate financial decisions and how they are made. As such, it emphasizes the practical application of finance theory to actual problems in the uncertain environment which characterizes the business world. The book does not purport to solve all of the financial problems confronting the firm; however it is designed to help you *ask* the relevant questions at the proper time. Recognition of new problems in a changing environment, and developing the skills to deal with them, is a challenging but rewarding task. And as you will soon learn it can also be a lot of fun, just as writing this book has been for us.

If you have an eye for a graph and do not have an aversion to numerical examples you are well prepared to understand the text. Unnecessary complexities and mathematical formulations have been ruthlessly weeded out. All you really need is the desire to understand the logic of financial decisions and the common sense to want to learn more than common sense alone can teach you about them.

The book is completely self-contained; no rigid prerequisites beyond a reasonable secondary education are necessary, although some familiarity with elementary accounting and statistics can be helpful. But as we are risk-averse, each chapter contains a detailed summary, a review exercise (and answers), sample problems and their step-by-step solutions, a glossary of key terms (marked in bold face), questions, problems, and annotated suggestions for further reading. In addition, a computer disk is available which provides templates for those problems that have been designated as "computer problems". Finally, a study guide (Tom O'Brien, *Study Guide to Principles of Financial Management,* Prentice-Hall, 1988) includes additional insights, study material, and problems.

Financial management in practice and in theory is a dynamic, ever-changing subject. We have expended every effort to reflect these changes in the text. For example, the United States tax reform has had a significant impact on the substance of the theory of finance. Therefore old theorems have been discarded or replaced and the implications of the new tax environment for financial decision-making are spelled out. Similarly, important innovations have made deep inroads into the way we view traditional financing problems. The book is designed to help you enter, and learn to survive in, the colorful world of "green shoes," "white knights," "options," and "leveraged buyouts." Finally, the stock market collapse of October 19, 1987, a day that has come to be called "Black Monday," is examined in an appendix on the "Crash of '87." In short, everything you have wanted to know about modern financial management—but perhaps were afraid to ask.

A book like this is the result of the efforts of many people and, as a result, we have accumulated a long list of people whose help we want to acknowledge. Frank Cross, the University of Texas at Austin, wrote Chapter 2 on the business and tax environment. George Szpiro, Hebrew University, coauthored the Instructor's Manual and provided the software templates. Ghassem Homaifar, Middle Tennessee State University, compiled the Test Item File. Helpful comments and criticism were received from the following:

Seth C. Anderson, University of Alabama at Birmingham; David Dubofsky, Texas A & M University; Frank Hull, California State, Fresno; Dennis E. Logue, Dartmouth College/Georgetown University; Michael S. Long, University of Illinois at Chicago; David Loy, Illinois State University; Gershen N. Mandelker, University of Pittsburgh; Tom O'Brien, University of Connecticut; Michael S. Rozeff, University of Iowa; George Szpiro, Hebrew University; and James H. Vander Weide, Duke University.

In addition, special thanks are due to our good friend Henry Hirschberg who again served as midwife for this project; he deserves all of the credit but none of the blame. Dave Boelio, and especially Linda Frascino, also were extremely helpful in the early stages and saw the book through several drafts.

It is a real pleasure to acknowledge the expertise and good advice of the staff at Prentice Hall: Scott Barr, acquisitions editor; Sonia Meyer, production editor; Gary June, marketing manager; Janet Schmid, designer; and Jeannine Ciliotta, copyeditor.

We also wish to thank Nancy Weber, Judy Friedgut, and Hyla Berkowitz, who cheerfully typed the manuscript through its many drafts, and Marsha Harpaz and Debbie Ganthrope for correcting the page proofs.

This list is far from complete, but it would be remiss indeed not to mention our many colleagues at Hebrew University and at the University of Florida. We have picked their brains without mercy and much of what is good in this book reflects their comments and suggestions. Finally, thanks are due to the students at Hebrew University, University of Florida, New York University, and U.C.L.A. who served as a sounding board for much of the material.

1 | Financial Management and Strategy: An Overview

A business firm is confronted daily by many financial decisions—some important and others less so; some with long-run implications, and some which are crucial in the short run; some which are easily quantified, and others which must rest on judgment alone. The chapters that follow concentrate on the major strategic tradeoffs confronting a modern corporation. Should the firm expand into a new area or replace an ageing plant? How much risk should be incurred when making such decisions, and how should these investments be financed? Should the shareholder be paid a dividend? How should the firm's short-term assets and liabilities be managed? Taken together, these decisions shape the corporation's future growth and profitability, the value of the stockholders' stake in the firm, and incidentally, the compensation of its management team.

Thus, we view the finance function in terms of financial decision-making. As a result, this book deals with methods of analysis rather than dogma, with an emphasis on "learning by doing." With such an approach, financial management becomes a method for identifying and solving problems.

EVOLUTION OF THE FINANCE FUNCTION

The analytical approach to finance is a fairly recent innovation. The study of financial management has changed radically over the years. In its beginnings, at the turn of the century, the emphasis was on the legal intricacies of corporate organization and the details of the types of securities available to finance the firm's activities. This reflected the economic environment of the time. The end of the nineteenth century and the first decade of the twentieth coincided with the wave of mergers that created the great trusts.

1

John D. Rockefeller put together Standard Oil; the Dukes created the To-bacco Trust; and Andrew Carnegie set up U.S. Steel. These and numerous other mergers created a need to define and safeguard the rights of various classes of shareholders. To fill these needs, the academic study of finance concentrated on the legal basis for the mergers, expansions, and promotions of new firms that were sweeping the nation.

The Great Depression of the 1930s did not change the way finance was taught, but it did have a far-reaching impact on the choice of topics. The emphasis remained on types of securities and legal organization, but under the impact of the wave of bankruptcies that plagued the economy in the 1930s, the emphasis soon shifted from expansion to insolvency and reorga-nization. Designing a package of securities that could safeguard the privi-leges and rights of owners remained the primary objective of finance courses—but survival, rather than expansion, was now the name of the game.

Until the mid-1950s, finance remained a descriptive subject, usually taught from the viewpoint of an outside analyst. Problems of practical man-agement were largely ignored. This probably reflected the feeling that the formal study of finance offered little of practical value. An intellectual rev-olution, which had its roots in the need to solve logistic and other problems during World War II, provided the concepts and tools for creating the an-alytical problem-solving approach that today characterizes the study of fi-nance:

1. In the first half of the 1950s, the conceptual foundation was laid for the use of time-discounted methods of capital budgeting to determine the firm's capital investment decisions.

2. At the same time, *portfolio selection,* a valuable tool for the analysis of decisions under conditions of uncertainty, was forged and later applied to the analysis of the risky alternatives facing the firm. In addition, formal models for managing cash, receivables, inventories, and long-term assets were developed and refined.

3. In the first half of the 1960s, portfolio analysis was extended to the pricing of risky assets in general, and of common stock in particular.

4. In the 1970s methods for evaluating contingent claims, especially options, were developed and applied to corporate and financial invest-ments.

The availability of this arsenal of powerful analytical tools has left an indelible imprint on both the teaching and practice of finance. Whereas fi-nance formerly dealt almost exclusively with the supply of funds, the em-phasis has shifted to include the management of short-term and long-term assets as well.

THE ROLE OF THE FINANCIAL MANAGER

Given these changes, financial management can no longer be viewed solely in terms of finding ways to finance the firm's activities in the most efficient manner. A more appropriate definition of the functions of a modern financial management team is this:

1. *Determine* the costs and benefits of employing the firm's resources, both in the short and the long run.
2. *Locate* the sources of funds and determine their costs.
3. *Choose* the sources of funds and uses of resources that best achieve the firm's objectives.
4. *Evaluate* the risk and return involved in each activity.

The modern approach to finance as an academic discipline emphasizes the decision-making process within the firm. Such an approach more closely mirrors the activities of actual financial managers. Today, financial vice-presidents, controllers, and treasurers are vitally concerned with the use of resources and not just with finding the necessary means to finance these uses. They view themselves as part—and an important part at that—of the firm's decision-making team.

The evolution of the finance function has had an enormous impact on the place of financial management within the corporate hierarchy. Once, the financial manager was responsible for supplying the funds ("finance") to meet the goals and needs dictated by marketing and production planners. Today, a much more integrated approach to corporate decision-making explicitly recognizes the mutual interdependence of decisions relating to the "sources" and "uses" of corporate funds.

One result of this process has been greatly to increase the proportion of chief executives with financial (and legal) backgrounds. A second result has been the achievement of a broader diffusion of financial knowledge at lower levels within the firm. Today's marketing and production managers must have a good working knowledge of the financial implications of their operating decisions for the firm's goals.

THE GOALS OF THE FIRM

By its very nature, financial decision-making involves purposeful behavior, which implies the need for a goal—or what is much more likely, some combination of goals. In the absence of an objective, management would have no way to choose among alternative investment strategies and projects. But surely there is no need to tell the firm that $2 million is better than $1 million! Yet even this decision is not always that simple. For example, an investment strategy that promises $2 million, but with a risk of possible bankruptcy should the venture go sour, may not be preferable to a more conservative strategy that offers a payoff of only $1 million, but permits the firm's directors and shareholders to sleep soundly.

Once the complexity of the financial decision-making process is recognized, it is fairly easy to conjure up a large number of possible candidates for "the goal of the firm." A partial listing of some that have been mentioned at one time or another would include these:

1. Maximization of profits
2. Maximization of sales
3. Achieving a "satisfactory" level of profits
4. Achieving a target market share
5. Survival of the firm
6. Keeping employee turnover below some critical level
7. Stability of earnings

Listing possible corporate objectives is a nearly endless game, more likely to leave its players exhausted than enlightened. Profits, stability, market share, and so on all appear to influence decision-making, and many firms aim at some combination of these goals, although a firm usually cannot articulate the precise formula by which it combines or assigns weights to the various objectives. Despite the complexities of the decision process, however, a "goal" for corporate decision-making can be found to serve as an appropriate guide for critical financial decisions.

Although business motivation is admittedly a complicated topic, the first four objectives mentioned above (maximization of profits, sales maximization, satisfactory profits, and achieving a target market share) are each connected in some way with profitability. In this context, "market share" should be interpreted as a proxy for profits, since profits and market share often move together. The last three objectives (survival, employee turnover, and stability) place the emphasis on holding risk at tolerable levels. The two primary concerns of management thus appear to be profitability and risk.

MAXIMIZING STOCKHOLDERS' WEALTH

The goals of increasing profits and reducing risk appear to be contradictory because attempts to increase profits invariably involve greater risks. However, if the actual practice of business management is to be reflected accurately, a way must be found to combine profit seeking and risk reduction.

One way out of this dilemma is to assume that management takes as its goal the maximization of the market value of its shareholders' wealth. Equivalently, corporate objectives can be defined in terms of maximization of the market value (price) of its existing common stock. Anyone who has ever attended a board meeting is not likely to underestimate the ability of management to act in its own self-interest, and we are not suggesting that managers are altruists. Maximizing the financial well-being of the shareholders is not necessarily incompatible with managment's own interests. On the contrary, it is often a very effective strategy for achieving management's own objectives.

Stating corporate goals in terms of stock price combines the profitability and risk dimensions of alternative courses of action. Consider the case of two firms, A and B, with identical expected profits (say $1 per share of common stock). Now assume that firm B expects to earn its profit by a very risky undertaking, such as investing in an underdeveloped country, while firm A's expected proceeds come from relatively safe investments in government and public utility bonds. In such a case, the price (market value) of the common stock of firm A will be higher than that of firm B. Both companies offer investors the same expected future earnings, but firm B has a much higher risk.

The situation is more complex if we assume a more realistic case in which the risky venture also offers higher expected earnings. For example, suppose the firm can earn $1 per share with certainty, or $2 per share with a very high probability, but that there is also a small chance the venture will lead to bankruptcy. The decision in this case is not easy. Is the additional profit sufficient to offset the chance, however small, of going bankrupt? The answer depends on the market's evaluation of the risk-return tradeoff implicit in this venture. If the greater expectation of profit outweighs the increase in risk, we expect the price of the stock to rise if the project is undertaken. Conversely, for the case in which the risk outweighs the increase in expected profits, we expect the share price to fall. In the latter case, the project should be rejected.

PROFIT MAXIMIZATION vs. WEALTH MAXIMIZATION

The fact that almost every introductory economics text assumes the firm's goal is profit maximization raises a thorny question. Perhaps profit maximization and wealth maximization are really the same thing? The answer is No! The two approaches differ in three important respects: the investment horizon, the timing of returns, and the treatment of risk. Let us examine the question more closely.

Long-Run vs. Short-Run Profits

As a first step, we convert total corporate profits to earnings per share (EPS), where EPS is simply total profits divided by the number of shares outstanding.[1] Assume the firm earns $10 million and has 1 million shares outstanding. Its shareholders therefore have an EPS of $10. But profit maximization is a short-term concept, while wealth maximization emphasizes the long-term viewpoint. A firm can often increase its immediate profitability by foregoing an innovation or model change, or by reducing investment in research and development. But clearly these short-run savings may be offset by a future decline in sales and profits. Should this be the case, we expect a decline in the market price of the firm's shares even though current EPS has risen. Which strategy should the firm choose? A corporation is an ongoing organization. It is almost intuitively obvious that long-run profits, and not just those of a single year, are the relevant focus.

Timing of Returns

Stating corporate goals in terms of profit maximization also ignores possible differences in the time pattern of earnings. To illustrate this problem, assume that a firm is confronted with two alternative investment strategies. If it adopts strategy A, it will have an EPS of $10 per year for 10 years

Strategy A

Year	1	2	3	. . . 9	10
EPS	10	10	10	. . . 10	10

On the other hand, adopting investment strategy B yields the following stream of EPS:

Strategy B

Year	1	2	3	. . . 9	10
EPS	0	12	12	. . . 12	12

The first strategy gives an immediate increase in profits in the first year (EPS of $10 vs. an EPS of zero), but the second alternative increases the EPS in each of the remaining nine years. Which strategy is preferable?

Here again the profit maximization approach fails, since it does not consider the timing of earnings. Wealth maximization explicitly considers the impact of the timing of earnings on stock price. The technique of valuing a firm's stock by discounting the future cash flows, which will be developed in Part III, provides a model for reducing the stream of future returns

---

[1] For simplicity, we abstract here from the difficulties of arriving at a precise definition of EPS. For a more detailed discussion, see Chapter 4 and George Foster, *Financial Statement Analysis*, 2nd ed. (Englewood Cliffs, NJ: Prentice-Hall, 1986).

to some common denominator. This is essential if we are to make meaningful comparisons of alternative strategies.

Risk   As we have already noted, once the uncertainty of earnings is recognized, it is no longer obvious that a greater profit (no matter how you measure it) is preferable. Greater returns can be earned only by incurring greater risks. Recognizing the joint nature of risk and return, many firms indicate their concern with "stability of earnings" or "survival." Clearly, these objectives cannot stand alone; if the firm's goal is simply to survive, why not invest all of its resources in short-term government securities which guarantee a perfectly stable fixed income and therefore also guarantee survival?

The dual nature of corporate objectives—profitability and risk reduction—can be reconciled if we substitute wealth maximization for profit maximization. Firms that place greater emphasis on risk can be viewed as giving a very large weight to risk. Although this interpretation is inconsistent with the goal of maximizing profits, it is perfectly compatible with the goal of shareholder wealth maximization. Defining the goal of the firm in terms of the market value of its stock implies an effort on the part of management to seek an optimum tradeoff between risk and profitability. In this approach it is management's task to find that combination of profit and risk which maximizes shareholder wealth—that is, the market price of the firm's common stock. Moreover, this is consistent with the empirical evidence for the motivation behind corporate action.

MOTIVATING MANAGERS

It has long been felt that the separation of management from ownership in the modern corporation may affect corporate objectives. The delegation of decision-making authority from owners (the "principals") to managers (the "agents") has become the subject of what is now called **agency theory**. Agency theory deals with potential conflicts of interest between outside shareholders and management. Three major types of potential conflict have been identified:

agency theory
A theory that analyzes the major types of conflict of interest between shareholders and management.

1. Managers may use corporate resources to provide themselves with "perks" (superfluous executive jets, first-class air travel, etc.) or embark upon expansions (empire-building) that are not in the shareholders' best interests.

2. Managers may have shorter time horizons than shareholders. For example, managers may favor short-term projects with early returns at the expense of those that mature too late to influence their promotion.

3. Managers and owners may differ in their evaluation of risk.

In this context, two factors can be identified as effective means for reducing potential conflict between management and shareholders. First, owners may establish incentive compensation plans for executives that are tied to shareholders' objectives. Second, the ever-present threat of takeover (see Chapter 21) is often a powerful influence on managerial behavior.

The question of whether shareholders' economic welfare is or is not a principal concern of management is clearly an empirical question. One study[2] which examined the goals of a sample of 326 management-controlled firms in the United States over the period 1967–1975 indicates that maximization of stock price (shareholders' wealth maximization) is the dominant goal of such corporations.

Additional evidence supporting the wealth maximization hypothesis can be found in the growing tendency of firms to reward executives on the basis of stock price appreciation. Recognition that earnings per share often have very little impact on stock price has led some firms (for example, Sears Roebuck, Borden, Combustion Engineering, and Emhart) to tie their executive compensation plans to performance measures that create shareholder value in the form of higher prices for their common stock.[3] Historically, business objectives were usually stated in terms of return on investment (an approach that still lingers). Today, in a world marked by great uncertainty, it is being increasingly recognized that the ultimate goal of the corporation is the creation of shareholder value—the maximization of shareholder wealth.

PLAN OF THE BOOK

Expressing corporate objectives in terms of the market value of shareholders' equity places the valuation of securities at center stage. Throughout this book, corporate decisions will be evaluated in terms of the objective of shareholder wealth maximization. But this requires some knowledge of the economic environment in which the firm operates. The remaining chapters of Part I (Chapters 2 and 3) describe the environment for various forms of business organization, taxes, and financial markets, with special emphasis on the market for corporate securities.

In Part II, the firm's financial statements and the flow of accounting information, necessary for both short-term and long-term planning, are examined in some detail.

[2] Ali M. Fatemi, James S. Ang, and Jess H. Chua, "Evidence Supporting Shareholder Wealth Maximization in Management Controlled Firms," *Applied Economics,* February 1983. See also Robert F. Lanzillotti, "Pricing Objectives in Large Companies," *American Economic Review,* December 1958; and Wilber G. Lewellen, "Management and Ownership in the Large Firm," *Journal of Finance,* May 1969.

[3] *Business Week,* April 2, 1984, p. 67.

Part III focuses on the basic principles of valuation under conditions of uncertainty. The portfolio selection and capital asset pricing models, which form the foundation of much of the modern approach to financial problems, are examined, and the implications of these models for practical financial management are spelled out.

The three chapters of Part IV use the valuation approach to develop and apply the net present value rule to a wide variety of investment decisions. Project cash flows are defined, and methods for incorporating risk into the analysis are examined.

Part V is devoted to a firm's long-term financing strategy. The basic characteristics of equity and debt financing are identified in Chapters 12 and 13. The remaining chapters (Chapters 14, 15 and 16) are devoted to the firm's key long-term financing decisions: What is the best mix of debt and equity financing? How can the cost of these sources of capital be measured? Should the firm pay its shareholders a dividend?

Part VI is devoted to short-term financial strategy and examines the way in which a firm makes its ongoing decisions regarding the management of inventories and accounts receivable (Chapter 17), and cash (Chapter 18). The final chapter of this section (Chapter 19) considers the question of how these operations should be financed.

Part VII concludes the book by taking a long look at some of the specific issues that lie at the heart of much of the current debate over financial strategy. Hybrid securities, such as warrants, convertibles, and options, as well as lease financing, are examined in Chapter 20. Chapter 21 is devoted to mergers and acquisitions and gives the reader some insight into the colorful world of "white knights," "sharks," and "greenmail." The final chapter reminds us that as the world grows smaller, international financial management is likely to be one of the major concerns of financial managers in the next decade.

SUMMARY

Financial management, as a skill and as an academic area, has evolved over the years. Financial decisions imply the need to define a goal or objective for the firm, and there are several alternative goals. Although most firms probably have multiple objectives, the two most important factors appear to be profitability (or market share, which is highly correlated with profits), and risk ("stability" or "survival"). In the real world, the firm must consider risk as well as profits and therefore chooses that combination of risk and profit which is appropriate for its stockholders—not an easy task. A solution to this problem can be found by taking the maximization of the market value (price) of a firm's common stock as the goal for corporate decisions.

The rest of this book is devoted to spelling out the decision rules appropriate for a firm that takes the maximization of stock price as its goal. The organization of the book reflects this objective. Valuation models are developed and alternative financial decisions are evaluated in accordance with their expected impact on the market value of shareholders' equity— that is, on the market price of the firm's common stock.

REVIEW EXERCISE

Circle the correct word(s) to complete the sentence; see p. 11 for the correct answers.

1.1 During the beginning of the twentieth century financial management concentrated on the *mathematical/legal* basis for mergers, expansions, and formation of new firms.

1.2 Numerous mergers made it imperative to define carefully the *rights/size* of various classes of shareholders, and to safeguard their interests.

1.3 After the Great Depression, the emphasis in the study of finance shifted from expansion to *insolvency and reorganization/probability theory*.

1.4 During and after World War II, the concepts and tools were provided for the *epistemological interpretation of theory/analytical problem-solving* approach that now characterizes the study of finance.

1.5 Whereas finance formerly dealt almost exclusively with the supply of funds, today the emphasis has shifted to include *stockholders' voting rights/the management of short-term and long-term assets*.

1.6 The new approach to finance emphasizes the *internal decision-making process/outside constraints*.

1.7 The integrated approach to decision-making has made financial management *more/less* important.

1.8 The two primary concerns of management appear to be *market share and international diversification/profitability and risk reduction*.

1.9 Since the firm is an ongoing organization, it is obvious that profits *in the long run/in the first few years* are relevant.

1.10 Once the riskiness of a business is recognized, a greater profit is *always/not always* preferable.

1.11 Taking the maximization of wealth as the firm's goal permits us to *combine/split* the profitability and riskiness of alternative courses of action into *one/two* quantitative measure(s).

1.12 Defining the goal of the firm in terms of market value of the stock implies an effort on the part of management to seek *speculative gains in the market/an optimum tradeoff between risk and profitability*.

1.13 The ultimate goal of the firm is to maximize *return on investment/shareholders' wealth*.

QUESTIONS AND PROBLEMS

1.1 Goal of the firm. Inquire at a number of corporations in your city as to whether or not they have determined a set of stated objectives. Evaluate their answers. Does the absence of a fixed goal (or goals) necessarily indicate that the firm's actions are random?

1.2 Profit maximization vs. wealth maximization.   Compare profit maximization and stock price maximization. Which would you prefer as the goal for corporate decisions? Explain.

1.3 Goal of the firm.   In a recent study of 500 corporations, Professor Jack Skeptic found that not one firm mentioned maximizing shareholders' wealth as an objective. Most of the firms stressed profitability and risk as the key variables in their decisions. Discuss the implications of these findings for the assumption of shareholders' wealth as the goal of the firm.

1.4 Goal of the firm.   "We have no goals for the firm, we are too busy making money." Why might this be a perfectly acceptable motto for a corporate president? Why might this same motto be unacceptable for the authors of a text on financial management?

1.5 Risk and return.   Each of the following expects to earn $12 per share (all the shares cost $100). Rank them according to your preference as an investor, and explain your rankings.
   Oil exploration corporation
   Mutual fund (conservative)
   Mutual fund (aggressive)
   IBM
   Genetic engineering firm
   AT&T

Answers to Review Exercise

1.1 legal   **1.2** rights   **1.3** insolvency and reorganization
1.4 analytical problem-solving approach
1.5 the management of short-term and long-term assets
1.6 internal decision-making process   **1.7** more
1.8 profitability and risk reduction
1.9 in the long run   **1.10** not always   **1.11** combine, one
1.12 an optimum tradeoff between risk and profitability
1.13 shareholders' wealth

SUGGESTIONS FOR FURTHER READING

The evolution of the role of financial management and the development of the modern theory of corporate finance are surveyed by Michael C. Jensen and Clifford W. Smith Jr. in "The Theory of Corporate Finance: An Historical Overview," in *The Modern Theory of Corporate Finance* (New York: McGraw-Hill, 1983).

For a classic statement of the goals of the firm, see Nobel Laureate Herbert A. Simon's "On the Concept of Organizational Goal," *Administrative Science Quarterly*, June 1964.

Agency problems were introduced into the finance literature by Michael C. Jensen and William H. Meckling in "Theory of the Firm: Managerial Behavior, Agency Costs, and Ownership Structure," *Journal of Financial Economics*, October 1976.

For a detailed discussion of the implications of agency theory for financial management, see Amir Barnea, Robert A. Haugen, and Lemma W. Senbet, *Agency Problems and Financial Contracting* (Englewood Cliffs, NJ Prentice-Hall, 1985), and the *Midland Corporate Finance Journal*, Winter 1985.

2 | The Legal Environment, Business Organization, and Taxes

Forms of Business Organization
Federal Income Taxation
Individual Income Taxes
Corporate Income Taxes
Capital Investment and Depreciation

Financial management cannot be studied in a vacuum. Both theory and practice reflect the legal environment in which financial decisions are reached. Maximization of the value of owners' equity implies a knowledge of the basic legal and tax structure of the economy, since the value of an enterprise and its assets depend in a crucial way on the economy's legal and tax framework. The establishment and operation of business organizations in the modern American economy is profoundly affected by the legal environment. Financial decisions are no longer governed just by the marketplace—the framework of judicial decisions, statutes, and regulations created by governments has a crucial effect on business. In some decisions, legal factors may be paramount.

This chapter explores two of the most important categories of legal rules affecting businesses. First, it examines the varying forms of business organization available and the implications of each. Second, the chapter addresses the federal income tax as it affects business. Even with the recent reforms, tax considerations play a primary role in numerous financial decisions.

FORMS OF BUSINESS ORGANIZATION

The success of a business enterprise may hinge on the form of legal organization under which it operates. Traditionally, the common forms of business ownership include the sole proprietorship, the partnership, and the corporation. The choice of business structure is influenced largely by legal issues. Let us consider the advantages and disadvantages of the different forms of business structure.

Sole Proprietorship

sole proprietorship
A business that is controlled by one individual and that has no separate legal structure.

Many large corporations began as **sole proprietorships**, a very simple business structure where one individual controls the business personally, without the benefit of a separate legal structure. So far as the law is concerned, the business is completely identified with the proprietor. The vast majority (75%) of operating businesses are sole proprietorships, especially those in retail trade, agriculture, and services. Most sole proprietorships are quite small, and they account for a relatively low proportion of total monetary transactions in the United States. But the millions of sole proprietorships in existence testify to the advantages offered by this form of business organization. Foremost among them, especially for new businesses, is simplicity. Other forms of business organization require elaborate forms and fees and are governed by detailed legal strictures. Although a sole proprietorship may require some form of state operating license, little else is required, and the owner may save considerable cost and paperwork.

Sole proprietorships have other advantages as well. With few legal requirements, this type of organization offers the owner a unique degree of control and flexibility. The sole proprietorship may also have tax advantages, as we will see later in this chapter.

Counterbalancing these advantages are a number of potentially serious disadvantages. The most significant of these is unlimited liability. Because the sole proprietor *is* the company, he/she is liable for all debts and other liabilities resulting from the business, even at the risk of losing nonbusiness personal property. For example, if the company defaults on a loan, the sole proprietor may lose a home as well as a business. In recent years there has been a burgeoning of additional sources of business liability, such as product liability, so the sole proprietor today is at considerable risk.

A second problem faced by sole proprietors is difficulty in obtaining financing. The ability to borrow capital for expansion is limited by the proprietor's personal line of credit, and profitable expansion may have to be foregone. Sole proprietors may also have difficulty borrowing when the business has financial problems. Other disadvantages of sole proprietorships include lack of continuity. When the proprietor dies, so does the business, to the possible detriment of employees and heirs.

Partnership

partnership
An association of two or more persons conducting a business, sharing equally in managing and in profits.

A **partnership** is defined as an association of two or more persons conducting a business. Traditionally, all members of the partnership share equally in managing the enterprise and in profits. The United States has over a million functioning partnerships, most of them relatively small.

Partnerships offer a number of unique advantages. As opposed to sole proprietorships, they have an easier time obtaining financing, because the partners may pool their resources to obtain credit—the ability to borrow is backed up by their *combined* personal lines of credit. Like sole proprietorships, the partnership structure allows considerable management flexibility and may also have certain tax advantages.

Compared with corporations, partnerships suffer less government control and generally need not file any papers or formally adopt a specific organizational structure. Nevertheless, most partnerships are based on a written agreement among the partners that spells out their relative duties and rights. These agreements can be quite complex, especially for one of the more specialized forms of partnership.

limited partnership
A form of partnership in which some of the partners do not participate in management.

However, the partnership structure retains most of the disadvantages of the sole proprietorship. Overall partnership liability is unlimited and includes all the personal assets of the partners. This situation is ameliorated somewhat, though, as a consequence of the risk-sharing among partners. In addition, a different form of partnership, known as a **limited partnership**, can limit liability. An organization may include limited partners who invest money but do not participate in management. These partners risk only the amount they invest in the organization. The law places specific restrictions on this limited partnership structure, however, and all such partnerships must include at least one *general partner* who is subject to full personal liability.

Other disadvantages parallel those of sole proprietorships. The death or retirement of a partner automatically dissolves the organization, severely limiting continuity. Partnership interests typically cannot be transferred without the unanimous consent of other partners, which also limits owner flexibility and the ability to obtain new sources of capital.

Corporation

corporation
An independent legal business entity in which ownership is divided among stockholders.

The **corporation** is the best-known form of business organization and, unlike the others, is precisely defined by law. Corporations represent a small fraction of the total number of U.S. businesses, but have the lion's share of total receipts and profits. Corporations are typically larger and more closely regulated than other business structures.

Establishing a corporation is considerably more complex than setting up other forms of business organization. A remarkable number of legal requirements cover corporate ownership, including filing requirements, taxes, fees, and rules governing structure and ownership. Large corporations also usually have a complex internal structure.

Although the shareholders theoretically own the corporation, they generally have little influence on management. Some major corporations have thousands or even millions of shareholders. Shareholders are represented by a board of directors that exercises ultimate responsibility in many matters. Since many management decisions are beyond the capability of even the board of directors to supervise, many corporations are actually run by certain top management officials.

The corporate structure offers a number of substantial advantages to the businessperson. Paramount among these advantages is limited liability; because the corporation is recognized as an independent legal entity, liability generally extends only to corporate resources, and not to the personal assets of the owners. A significant exception exists, however, where the owners have undercapitalized the corporation; in this case creditors may "pierce the corporate veil" and reach individual assets.

A second important advantage of corporations is their ability to raise additional money for business expansion. Corporations may borrow money from conventional sources, based upon the company's own creditworthiness. In addition, corporations may raise money through equity financing. In this process, the company issues securities, known as *shares of stock*, for sale to the public. Purchasers become part owners of the corporation in proportion to their investment.

Other corporate advantages include relative ease and flexibility of transferability of ownership interest and continuity of existence even after the death or departure of the original owners. Corporations may also have some tax advantages, depending on the circumstances of the individual enterprise.

The corporate structure is not without its disadvantages, however. The complexity involved in forming a corporation may represent a considerable disadvantage, especially for a small or new business. Ongoing compliance costs may also be considerable, because certain corporate activities, such as the issuance of new securities, are governed by a large and complex body of regulatory law. The complex corporate structure also results in relative lack of management flexibility and control by the owners. Finally, corporations face a different tax situation, one that in some cases is much harsher than that for individuals.

There are no hard and fast rules regarding the best form of organization for a given enterprise. Each structure has its own unique advantages and disadvantages, all of which must be considered in setting up a business. But size is often an important consideration. For new businesses, especially relatively small ones, the sole proprietorship is probably preferable, so long as no major liability is contemplated. As the enterprise grows, its owners should consider altering the form of the business to a partnership or a corporation to reflect the new financial needs and risks of the operation.

FEDERAL INCOME TAXATION

The income of individuals and corporations is subject to taxes, both state and federal. When evaluating the financial value of an investment or other business action, a critical consideration is the usable income or appreciation derived for the company after taxes. Tax rates are high enough to be a major factor in business planning. The most significant tax is the federal income tax, both individual and corporate. The rules governing income taxes are extraordinarily complex; here we will summarize the most important financial aspects of this taxation.

INDIVIDUAL INCOME TAXES

Individual income taxes are best known as those paid by virtually all Americans on their salary income, offset by certain personal exemptions and deductions. Less well known is that the individual income tax applies to various businesses, depending on their organization. For many businesses, the individual income tax is considered preferable to the corporate business tax. The ultimate success of a business will depend in part on how well it adapts to tax considerations and whether it elects to be taxed under individual or corporate rules.

The Tax Reform Act of 1986 made wholesale changes in the federal income tax rules. A great many deductions and other benefits were eliminated, and rates were lowered. In so doing, the act shifted some of the tax load from individuals to corporations. Although it was intended largely to simplify the tax system, the complete implications of the new tax law are as yet unclear. What is clear is that financial decision-makers must take a completely new look at federal taxation and at the effects of the revised income tax system.

Coverage of Individual Income Taxation

Some types of businesses are covered by federal individual income taxes. Income from sole proprietorships and partnerships, in which the individual owners are ultimately responsible for all aspects of the business, are usually covered by individual taxes. The owners of these enterprises report income from the business on individual tax returns, along with whatever other sources of income they may possess.

In addition, some corporations, known as Subchapter S corporations, may elect to be taxed through individual income taxes. The Internal Revenue Code provides that a small business corporation meeting certain specific criteria may choose not to be taxed as a corporation, but rather to have all income passed through to the shareholders (whether actually distributed or not) and taxed as ordinary individual income. To qualify for this tax treatment, a corporation may have only one class of stock and no more than 35 shareholders, and at least 75% of corporate income must come from "active" business operations, among other technical requirements. Roughly one-fifth of American corporations have utilized this provision, which enables shareholders to receive the protection afforded by incorporation and yet retain the preferable tax treatment accorded individuals.

Types of Taxable Income

Virtually all conceivable sources of income for individuals are subject to federal individual income taxes. Wages and salary income, interest income, dividends on stock holdings, and other income from investments are all covered. Only a few sources of income, such as interest on certain tax-free state and local government bonds, are exempt from federal individual income taxation.

Also covered by the individual income tax are profits from the sale of property for a price higher than that originally paid. This form of income, known as *capital gains,* historically was treated differently from the other sources of "ordinary income" and taxed at a lower effective rate, since part of the long-term capital gains could be excluded from taxation. The 1986 Tax Reform Act, however, largely eliminated this preferred treatment of capital gains. No longer may part of the gain be excluded, and while some minor differences remain, the tax treatment for capital gains closely parallels that for other income sources. Of course, capital losses from the sale of business property at a lower price than originally paid may be used to offset income subject to individual income taxes.

Tax Rates   The various sources of an individual's income are taxed at progressive rates, meaning that the rate of taxation increases with the total amount of taxable income. The 1986 act reduced the number of different rates and the progressivity of the individual income tax. Before 1986, income could be taxed at rates as high as 50% for certain high-income taxpayers; after the reform, the highest tax bracket is 28%.

Once the new law is completely phased in, there will be only two tax rates—15% and 28%. The application of these rates varies somewhat with the individual's filing status—single, unmarried head of household, married filing joint returns, or married filing separate returns. For a single person, the first $17,850 of income will be taxed at 15%, and any additional income will be taxed at 28%. In addition, some higher-income taxpayers are subject to a 5% surtax designed to impose a 28% effective rate on *all* their taxable income. The new rates under the 1986 act are significantly lower than the preceding individual income tax rates; but a taxpayer's overall bill may not decline because the legislation also eliminated a number of important deductions.

Deductions and Other Tax Benefits   Before calculating individual income taxes, a taxpayer should consider the effects of various "tax benefits." Most such benefits are in the form of deductions. Allowable deductions authorize an individual to deduct certain expenditures from taxable income, and consequently reduce that individual's overall tax bill. A $1,000 deductible expense reduces the income subject to taxation by $1,000 and, for an individual in the 28% bracket, reduces the taxes owed by $280 (the amount that would be due in the absence of the deduction). Other rules permit certain tax exclusions for income exempted from taxation. By reducing the income subject to taxation, these exclusions have the same effect as deductions. However, the exclusion of the first $100 of qualified dividend income by an individual ($200 for a married couple) was repealed by the 1986 Tax Reform Act. The tax code also contains provision for some tax credits. A portion of child and dependent-care payments made by working parents can be used as tax credit, for example. Credits are expenditures that may be deducted directly from the taxes owed: A $1,000 credit reduces taxes owed by $1,000.

The individual income tax code provides for a variety of tax benefits, most of them in the form of deductions. The law provides an automatic standard deduction, but most businesspersons will prefer to itemize and take advantage of the full range of deductions. Deductible expenses include such expenditures as charitable contributions, state income and property taxes, and certain payments to retirement plans. The new act severely restricts employees' deducting business-related expenses, but for business owners most business expenses are still deductible. The notorious business entertainment deduction, used on occasion for business discussions during "three-martini lunches," is retained, but only 80% of the cost is now deductible. Historically, all interest payments were deductible from federal individual income taxes, but the 1986 legislation restricts this deduction to mortgage interest on first and second homes. Some interest on investment debts remains deductible, but only to the extent of investment income. Depreciation, discussed in detail below, is another significant business deduction.

Under the old tax law, a deduction could be used to offset almost any kind of income, regardless of its source. This system encouraged the growth of what are called *tax shelter investments.* They produced tax losses that could be applied against income from other sources. The 1986 law alters this by separating "passive" from "active" investments. A **passive investment** is one where the individual plays little or no role in managing the investment, a characteristic of most of the tax shelters attacked by Congress. Much rental real estate, for example, would be a passive investment. Under the new law, for taxpayers making over $100,000, passive investment losses can be deducted only from income from passive investments, not from active investment income. A high-income taxpayer who runs a computer business and has losses from a passive investment in cattle ranching may not use the ranch losses as deductions to offset the income from the computer business. This modification will undoubtedly have a major effect on investment strategies in the future. Another concern may be the repeal of *income averaging.* In the past, highly variable cyclical income sources could be averaged over several years to prevent an especially severe tax bill in any one year. This possibility is now eliminated.

passive investment
A tax shelter investment in which the individual plays little or no role in managing the investment.

Tax Calculation and Payment

Taxes are not deferred to the end of the tax year. For salaried employees, taxes are withheld every month. For self-employed business owners, estimated taxes must be paid quarterly. These individuals must make a good-faith estimate of the amount of taxes they will owe at the end of the year and send the government the proper share of that amount every three months.

To calculate an indivdual's annual taxes, we first must total all income received during the last tax year (usually the calendar year). This is that individual's **gross income.** The application of certain deductions, including

gross income
All income received during the last tax year.

adjusted gross income
Income that remains after certain deductions, including business deductions, have been applied.

taxable income
Income that remains after itemized deductions have been subtracted from the adjusted gross income.

business deductions, produces a lower **adjusted gross income.** From this, the taxpayer may deduct itemized deductions, yielding an amount called **taxable income.** IRS-provided tax schedules then permit the individual to determine the taxes applicable to this income level. After reducing this sum by any available tax credits, the taxpayer determines his or her tax liability.

Unfortunately, the calculations do not always end here. Congress has provided an alternative minimum tax that applies to some individuals who have an especially large number of deductions. This minimum tax existed before, but now it has been expanded. Elaborate rules govern the alternative minimum tax, but in simplified form, the taxpayer returns to the level of adjusted gross income, before itemized deductions. After taking a large exemption designed to help lower-income taxpayers, the individual takes 21% of this adjusted gross income. This figure is compared with the liability calculated earlier, and the higher of the two sums is owed to the government. This liability is then compared to the payments already made to the IRS, and the taxpayer files for a refund of taxes overpaid or submits a check for the remainder of taxes due.

CORPORATE INCOME TAXES

Corporations, like individuals, must pay substantial income taxes. But corporations, unless they qualify and elect subchapter S status, are taxed under very different income tax rules. Corporations face a disadvantage generally known as *double taxation*. First, income received by the corporation is taxed through corporate income taxes. If the remaining after-tax profit is distributed as dividends to shareholders, these distributions are taxed again on the recipients' individual income taxes.

Coverage of Corporate Income Taxes

In part to avoid double taxation many business owners remain as sole proprietorships or partnerships. These owners must be wary, however: The fact that a business is not classified as a corporation by state laws does not necessarily exempt it from corporate income taxes. The IRS will make its own independent determination of a company's status and may classify even an apparent partnership or sole proprietorship as a corporation for tax purposes, if the proprietorship has certain corporate "features" such as continuity of life, centralization of management, and free transferability of interests. Obviously, businesses organized as corporations under state laws are also subjected to the federal corporate income tax.

Types of Taxable Income

For enterprises subject to the corporate income tax, coverage is quite similar to that for individuals. Virtually every form of ordinary, or operating, income is subject to the federal tax, as is interest income. Corporate capital gains are also taxed. As is true for individuals, special capital gains treatment has been eliminated, and these revenues are taxed like other income.

Corporations do have one remaining advantage over individuals, though, in the treatment of dividend income. A corporation may own shares in other corporations and receive dividends. The corporation may, under corporate income tax rules, exclude 80% of these dividends received from its taxable income. Thus, the tax code favors certain corporate investments in the stock of other corporations. Of course, any dividends passed through to a corporations's shareholders are taxable on the shareholders' individual returns.

Corporate Tax Rates

The 1986 Tax Reform Act also lowered corporate income tax rates, though less than for individuals. Prior to 1986, corporate tax rates ranged up to 46% for large companies. Under the new legislation, rates are changed to the following schedule:

Taxable Income	Tax Rate
$50,000 or less	15%
$50,001–$75,000	25
Over $75,000	34

There is also an additional 5% tax on taxable corporate income in excess of $100,000, but that tax cannot be greater than $11,750. In effect, corporations with taxable income in excess of $335,000 pay a flat tax rate of 34%. Consider, for example, a corporation with a taxable income of $1,000,000. Its tax liability is as follows:

Taxable Income	Tax Rate	Tax Liability
First $50,000	15%	$7,500
Next $25,000	25	6,250
Next $925,000	34	314,500
Additional tax on income over $100,000 up to maximum of $11,750	5	11,750
Total tax liability		$340,000

For simplicity, we will apply a flat corporate tax rate of 34% in the numerical examples in this book.

All corporate income is subject to this rate structure. Consequently, although the tax rate on ordinary income went down, the effective tax rate on capital gains may rise for some corporations, because favorable treatment has been eliminated. Due to this and other changes, the federal government's total take from corporate income is expected to rise in the wake of the 1986 legislation. Some small businesses, however, may benefit from the changes. For others, opting for subchapter S status or other strategies for avoiding corporate income taxation now appears more promising.

Deductions and Other Tax Benefits

The 1986 legislation was especially hard on many corporate income tax benefits. The investment tax credit, designed to promote new American investment, was deleted altogether. Other credits and deductions were also limited, and new rules make takeovers and other corporate acquisitions less valuable from a tax standpoint. Expenses for business meals and entertainment are now only 80% deductible. New restrictions were placed on tax sheltering of foreign income.

But some important tax benefits were preserved in the new act. The tax credit for certain research and development expenditures was retained, although reduced from 25% to 20%. Many tax benefits for the oil and gas and timber industries remain. Interest payments on debts accrued to pay for business investments remain deductible. Significantly, dividends paid to shareholders, as before, are not deductible. Thus, the tax reform retains the financial bias for debt over equity financing of new expenditures. Similarly, corporations also retain some advantages over individuals under the new tax code. When corporate activity includes passive investments that yield losses to the corporation, such losses may be offset against even active sources of income.

Corporations have other tax advantages in the area of employee compensation. Corporations can provide a greater range of fringe benefits to shareholders or employees without incurring additional tax liabilities to those individuals. These benefits include some group term life insurance plans, disability insurance plans, reimbursement for some expenses, and discounts for corporate goods and services.

One important corporate tax benefit, retained but restricted by the 1986 act, involves corporate loss carryovers. When a corporation suffers a net loss in a given year, either from operating expenses or capital losses, it pays no taxes. Moreover, the amount of loss may, in some circumstances, be "carried" back 3 years or forward up to 15 years to other tax years to offset taxable income in those years. A company suffering a loss in 1987 thus can go back and recalculate its 1985 taxes, including the 1987 loss as a new deduction, and receive a refund for some of the 1985 taxes already paid. This provision offers considerable benefit to cyclical businesses. Individual taxpayers have no comparable opportunity.

Tax Calculation and Payment

Corporate taxes are calculated much like those for individuals. Total income is reported, and then deductions and other tax benefits are employed to obtain taxable income. Reference to government-supplied schedules then yields the corporate income tax liability for the year. Quarterly estimated tax payments also are expected of corporations.

As for individuals, an alternative minimum tax applies to corporations to prevent companies from escaping taxes with tax shelters. To calculate this potential liability, the company must ignore certain deductions, including depreciation. Companies then may take a $40,000 standard exemption, but must pay a 20% alternative minimum tax on all remaining income. The corporate alternative minimum tax strikes hardest at capital-intensive firms or emerging growth companies with large amounts of legitimate deductions.

Corporations should also beware of another tax code provision. Some companies refrain from paying dividends in part to permit their stockholders to avoid personal income taxes on those dividends. If the IRS decides that the purpose of this corporate accumulation of earnings is to enable stockholders to avoid income taxes, the accumulated earnings will be subject to penalty tax rates. This penalty applies to all amounts over $250,000 that are shown to be unnecessary to meet the reasonable needs of the business. Corporations with legitimate reasons for earnings accumulation are therefore free from this penalty provision.

CAPITAL INVESTMENT AND DEPRECIATION

Perhaps the most significant tax benefit accorded both individuals and corporations is the right to deduct depreciation when calculating taxable income. The substantial tax consequences of the depreciation of capital investments are critical considerations for financial decision-makers. The 1986 reform legislation preserves a depreciation deduction, but places new restrictions on its use in certain circumstances. Depreciation of business investments is available under both individual and corporate income taxes.

Depreciation operates as follows. Suppose a company invests in a new plant. The tax law presumes that this investment will decline in value over time, as the investment becomes outmoded or wears out. Accordingly, the law permits the company to deduct a certain percentage of the investment each year for depreciation suffered in the value of the investment. The cost of the actual depreciation or loss of value need not be proved.

Depreciation can be very significant to the financial manager. It shows up on corporate books and tax returns as a cost, reducing profits, but it involves no actual cash expense or outflow for the company. As such, depreciation is called a **noncash expense** of the firm. For a time, this expense or loss can actually represent a gain to the business. Because this "paper expense" is deductible, it reduces the tax liability of the enterprise and increases net after-tax revenues, thereby enhancing the corporate cash flow. Depreciation is one of the largest tax benefits available to business.

Tax law sets forth rigid rules for calculating depreciation. First, one must ascertain the depreciable life of the asset obtained—the number of years over which the asset's value may be depreciated. Originally, this in-

noncash expense
A business expense such as depreciation that involves no cash outlay.

volved an estimate of the actual useful economic life of the asset, but now this depreciable life is determined by uniform IRS specifications. This determination is made according to the 1981 Accelerated Cost Recovery System (ACRS), which specifies how much can be deducted each year. In addition to defining depreciable life, ACRS further authorizes the "front-loading" of deductions, enabling businesses to take a high proportion of deductions in the early years of the asset's service. Although ACRS was tightened in 1986, the system still provides many of the traditional benefits of depreciation.

The 1986 act extended the depreciable life of many business assets. Some examples of the new rules are summarized below:

- ☐ Certain special tools for use in the manufacture of rubber, plastic, or fabricated metal products—3 years
- ☐ Automobiles, trucks, computers, copiers, cargo containers—5 years
- ☐ Most machinery, equipment, and business furniture—7 years
- ☐ Certain public utility property—15 to 20 years
- ☐ Residential real property—27.5 years
- ☐ Commercial real property—31.5 years

Most of these periods are slightly longer than those under preceding tax legislation, which as we will see in subsequent chapters, operates to the detriment of the firm. Taxpayers also retain the option of stretching depreciation over a longer period, although this is seldom wise from a cost-benefit point of new.

Equipment   Once the depreciable life of the asset is ascertained, the taxpayer refers to IRS tables to determine the amount of deduction available in a given year. These tables yield recovery allowance percentages of initial value (called the "basis") that may be deducted from income. The percentage of asset value deductible for some sample types of depreciable property is determined according to the following schedule:

Recovery	Depreciable Life			
	3 Years	5 Years	7 Years	15 Years
1	33%	22.0%	14.28%	5.0%
2	45	32.0	24.49	9.5
3	15	19.2	17.49	8.5
4	7	11.5	12.49	7.7
5		11.5	8.93	6.9
6		5.8	8.93	6.2
7			8.93	5.9
8			4.46	5.9
9–15				5.9
16				3.0

These percentages are based on the assumption that the depreciable property is placed in service halfway through the first year.

Real Property The 1986 Tax Reform Act eliminated accelerated depreciation of new real property. Taxpayers now must use the *straight-line* method, which provides for the same percentage deduction every year over the depreciable life of the property. Thus, for commercial real property acquired after 1986 with a 31.5 year depreciable life, the taxpayer may write off approximately 3.14% of the real property's basis for each year in service. The old ACRS rules are still available for real property placed in service before the new legislation took effect.

Although depreciation provides considerable tax benefits to many businesses, owners must be aware of its potential costs. All depreciated property has a basis, which represents its value from the government's tax perspective. The basis of property declines in proportion to its depreciation. A $10,000 piece of property that is 50% depreciated has a basis of $5,000. Tax depreciation, though, may be a legal fiction, and the property may not actually decline in market value. If the property is sold for $12,000, the IRS considers the owner to have made a $7,000 profit which is taxable, thus recapturing the depreciation. Recapture may be avoided or postponed under some circumstances, but the principle involves substantial potential tax liabilities, and the financial decision-maker should be aware of these consequences when contemplating the sale of business assets. Such sales are often postponed until tax losses or other deductions are available to offset the liability from depreciation recapture.

SUMMARY

The value of an enterprise and its assets ultimately depends on the legal environment of business. The business organization selected for the enterprise can have a major bearing on its success. Even more important are tax considerations. Because only after-tax income is of actual benefit to the business, tax considerations, especially federal income tax considerations, are among the most important factors confronting a business's financial decision-makers.

REVIEW EXERCISE

Circle the correct word(s) to complete the sentence; see p. 26 for the correct answers.

2.1 Most sole proprietorships are quite *small/large*.

2.2 Sole proprietorships may find it *easy/difficult* to raise money.

2.3 Overall partnership liability is *limited/unlimited*.

2.4 Corporations are typically *smaller/larger* than other business structures, and are *more/less* closely regulated.

2.5 Shareholders in a corporation are represented by the *chief operating officer/ board of directors*.

2.6 The complex structure of corporations results in relatively *high/low* management flexibility.

2.7 Tax rates represent a *major/minor* factor in business planning.

2.8 The Tax Reform Act of 1986 shifted some of the previous tax load from *corporations to individuals/individuals to corporations*.

2.9 Small corporations meeting certain criteria may elect to be taxed through *individual income/value added* taxes.

2.10 The tax treatment of capital gains is now very *different from/similar to* other sources of income.

2.11 Most real estate income is considered *active/passive* income.

2.12 Taxes *are/are not* deferred to the end of the year.

2.13 Income of a corporation which is distributed as dividends may be *deducted/ taxed twice*.

2.14 Expenses on business meals are *not/80%* deductible.

2.15 Corporate interest payments on debts *are/are not* deductible.

2.16 Corporations *can/cannot* carry a loss forward or backward to offset taxes.

2.17 Depreciation *does/does not* involve a cash expense, but *does/does not* reduce profits.

QUESTIONS AND PROBLEMS

2.1 Define the following terms:
    a. Proprietorship   **b.** Partnership
    c. Corporation   **d.** Capital gains
    e. Depreciation   **f.** Tax benefit

2.2 List the advantages and disadvantages of organizing a firm as:
    a. A sole proprietorship   **b.** A partnership
    c. A corporation

2.3 If you were the loan officer of a bank, to whom would you prefer to loan money, a proprietorship or a partnership? Why?

2.4 Evaluate the following two quotations and compare your answers.
    a. "I own a share of General Motors Corporation, so I am entitled to tell the general manager how to run the firm."
    b. "I own 25% of Captain Motors Garage, so I am entitled to tell the general manager how to run the firm."

2.5 "I put all my money into a savings account, but I never buy stock in corporations. With all those liability suits, I could lose my shirt should the company be sued for damages." Do you agree? Why?

2.6 What were the principal changes introduced by the Tax Reform Act of 1986?

2.7 "Being a Subchapter S corporation gives me the best of both worlds." What does the president of a small corporation who said this mean?

2.8 **a.** A working mother whose income is taxed at 15% is allowed to deduct $300 of child care expenses from her income for tax purposes. By how much is her tax bill reduced? How does your answer change if her income is taxed at 28%?

b. The working mother is now told that the child care expenses can be used as a tax credit. How do your answers to part (a) change?

2.9 "We always invite our clients for a big splash. The government foots most of the bill anyway." Since 80% of the cost of the splash is deductible and the firm pays 34% tax on its tax income, how much of the $200 restaurant bill does the government foot?

2.10 What is meant by "double taxation"? Explain and give some examples.

2.11 You receive $200 in dividends and are in the 28% tax bracket. What is your *after-tax* dividend income?

2.12 A company receives $200 in preferred dividend income and is in the 34% corporate tax bracket. What is the firm's after-tax dividend? (*Hint:* Assume that the dividends qualify for exclusion.)

2.13 What effect do you think the Tax Reform Act of 1986 had on (a) the restaurant business, (b) corporate expenditures on research and development, and (c) investments abroad? Explain.

2.14 In what sense does the tax law reflect a bias in favor of debt over equity financing?

2.15 What is meant by a "loss carryover"?

2.16 "We do not want our shareholders to be taxed twice on the same income, so we retain all earnings and pay no dividends." Evaluate this statement.

2.17 How is depreciation similar to an ordinary expense? How is it different?

2.18 "The Tax Reform Act of 1986 extended the depreciable life of many business assets. That's great!" Is it, really? Why or why not?

2.19 "We wait until our cars are completely depreciated, and then sell them at the market price." Evaluate the tax implications of such a strategy.

Answers to Review Exercise

2.1 small   **2.2** difficult   **2.3** unlimited   **2.4** larger, more
2.5 board of directors   **2.6** low   **2.7** major
2.8 individuals to corporations   **2.9** individual income **2.10** similar to
2.11 passive   **2.12** are not   **2.13** taxed twice   **2.14** 80%
2.15 are   **2.16** can   **2.17** does not, does

SUGGESTIONS FOR FURTHER READING

Everything you always wanted to know about the 1986 Tax Reform Act, and more, can be found in: *A Complete Guide to the Tax Reform Act of 1986* (Englewood Cliffs, NJ: Prentice-Hall, 1986).

For a less demanding reference guide to tax problems, see *Introduction to Federal Taxation* (Englewood Cliffs, NJ: Prentice-Hall, annual).

3 | What Every Financial Manager Should Know About Security Markets and Interest Rates

Corporate financing decisions are made within a complex framework of financial institutions and intermediaries which together comprise the **capital market.** This market provides the mechanism for channeling savings into investment in productive facilities—that is, for allocating a nation's capital resources among alternative uses. In effect, the capital market provides an economy's link with the future. Current decisions regarding the allocation of capital resources are a major determining factor in tomorrow's output. In this chapter, we focus on the institutional framework of markets and intermediaries that constitutes the financial environment within which the firm must function. Special emphasis is given to a crucial element of a modern capital market, the market for *long-term* securities. (In Part VI of this book we examine the market for short-term securities in order to evaluate the firm's strategy for financing its short-term assets.) The chapter also focuses on the role of interest rates in the allocation of a country's financial resources among alternative uses. The major forces that determine interest rates are identified with special emphasis on the impact of inflation and investors' expectations on the level of both the short-term and long-term rates.

capital market
A complex framework of financial intermediaries that channels savings into investment in productive facilities.

THE FINANCIAL MARKETS

primary market for securities
The market in which newly issued securities are bought for the first time.

To place the capital market in proper perspective, it is useful to distinguish between the primary and secondary markets. The **primary market for securities** is the new issue market, which brings together the supply and demand for new capital funds. It is the market in which newly issued securities are bought for the first time. In this market, the principal source of funds is the domestic saving of individuals and nonfinancial businesses. The principal uses of funds are long-term financing of housing (mortgages), long-term investment of corporations, and borrowing by federal, state, and local governments.

secondary market for securities
The market in which securities are traded after they have been issued; the stock market.

Most individual investors are unfamiliar with the new issue market and its institutions.[1] For them, the capital market is synonymous with the **secondary market**—the stock market, or stock exchange, as it is also called. This is the market in which securities are traded *after* they have been issued. Like any other organized market, a stock exchange enables buyers and sellers to effect their transactions more quickly and cheaply than would otherwise be possible. However, because a stock market deals in existing securities rather than in new issues, its economic significance may be misunderstood.

The capital market channels savings into capital formation; hence its economic significance stems from the impact on the allocation of capital resources among alternative uses. But it is the new issue market which provides the funds to finance firms' capital investments. Transactions between individuals in outstanding securities do not provide additional financing to business firms. The secondary market, therefore, is *not* a source of funds for businesses to finance capital investments.

An analogy can be drawn from the automobile industry. The sale of new cars (new issues) by the automobile companies provides revenue to the companies; transactions in used cars (outstanding securities) in the resale car market do not. But just as the existence of a used car market increases consumers' willingness to purchase new cars, the stock market is an important factor affecting investors' willingness to acquire new issues of securities.

The basic economic function of a stock exchange is to provide greater liquidity for new security issues and to reduce the personal risk incurred by investors. The existence of a strong secondary market, in turn, broadens the supply of equity and long-term debt capital for the financing of business enterprises. For example, even though the investment in common stock is fixed for the life of the firm, the ability to shift ownership to others allows more individuals to participate in the long-term financing of companies. In a modern economy, with a well-developed secondary securities market, the fixed investment of firms is provided by a changing group of individuals. Many of these investors would not have been willing to commit their personal resources for the entire, or even a substantial part, of the life of the enterprise.

FINANCIAL INSTITUTIONS

In a highly developed capital market, a very large proportion of individuals' savings reaches its final destination *indirectly*. The savings of most individuals are channeled to an ultimate user, say a corporation desiring to finance an

[1] The new issue market is discussed in greater detail in Chapter 12.

expansion of its productive facilities, via a financial intermediary. Banks, pension funds, insurance companies, and mutual funds are examples of such financial intermediaries.

Types of Intermediaries

Commercial Banks.   Probably at one time or another, you have had dealings with a commercial bank. Historically, the commercial banking system has been the principal financial institution offering checking accounts, so the activities of these banks have a direct impact on the money supply. As a result, commercial banks have been subject to special control by the Federal Reserve System.[2] They accept a wide variety of demand and time deposits, and make these funds available to individuals and firms. Bank credit is typically short term (See Chapter 19), but commercial banks also provide a wide variety of financial services (mortgage loans, lease financing, and so on) to individuals and business firms.

Mutual Savings Banks.   These are savings banks located mostly in New York, New Jersey, and New England. Unlike the commercial banks, they do not accept demand deposits, but get their funds from savings accounts, money market accounts, and NOW (negotiable order of withdrawal) accounts, against which checks can be written. These funds are used to make long-term loans to individuals for housing, and to corporations.

Savings and Loan Associations.   Savings and loan associations (S & Ls) are very similar to mutual savings banks. They too offer their depositors a variety of savings, money market, and NOW accounts. Their principal use of funds takes the form of real estate mortgage loans to individuals. The S & Ls do not typically make loans to business firms.

Credit Unions.   These are cooperative savings associations, usually of people with some common bond—members of the same church or social group, employees of the same firm. The savings of credit members are made available to other members as consumer loans.

Life Insurance Companies.   The primary purpose of life insurance is to provide for the beneficiaries upon the death of the insured. Many policies, however, have a long-term savings (endowment) feature. Due to the nature of the business, insurance companies accumulate enormous amounts in anticipation of future payments. Some of these funds are loaned directly to individual corporations and the government; the remainder are invested via the capital market. To protect policyholders, the investment policies of life insurance companies are closely regulated. They are usually required by law

---

[2] Commercial banks are the only financial institutions which accept checking accounts (demand deposits). However, the trend to deregulation has permitted other financial institutions to offer "money market" accounts, and NOW (negotiable order of withdrawal) accounts which in effect are interest-earning checking accounts.

to purchase securities from an "approved list," or to observe the "prudent man" rule—invest only in high-grade conservative securities. One result of government intervention may have been to reduce the proportion of insurance savings channeled to the equity market.

Pension Funds.   One of the most striking developments of recent years has been the expansion of private pension plans. These are retirement funds, established by corporations for their workers, and usually administered by the trust departments of commercial banks or by life insurance companies. The ability to defer income taxes has greatly stimulated the growth of these funds. Both employer contributions, as well as the income earned by the funds, are exempt from federal income tax. The pensions themselves are taxable when paid. Pension fund managers invest primarily in securities, with heavy emphasis on corporate stocks. Unlike life insurance companies, the pension funds have been subject to less regulation of their investment policies.

Public pension plans are often subject to more stringent supervision. The largest pension fund is, of course, the federal government's Old Age, Survivors, Disability, and Health Insurance Scheme, or Social Security. Most of these funds are loaned to other federal agencies. The pension funds of state and local governments, however, are among the leading purchasers of corporate bonds.

Mutual Funds.   Mutual funds are investment companies that pool the resources of many individuals and invest them in a portfolio of securities. Unlike life insurance companies and pension funds, which invest in securities to meet assumed liabilities, investing itself is the primary function of a mutual fund. The funds often have varying objectives, and as a result their investment policies tend to differ. Today there are a great many stock funds, (growth, diversified, high tech) as well as balanced, internationally diversified, and money market funds. Investors who shop around long enough are likely to find whatever they are seeking, as there are literally hundreds of funds, with varying investment policies and objectives, to choose from.

Impact of Deregulation on Financial Institutions

Financial institutions have been subjected to relatively strict public regulation. They have been restricted as to the types of services they can offer, the maximum rate of interest that can be paid, and the assets in which they can invest. The primary motivating force behind this regulation has been the desire to protect the individuals whose savings are deposited in these institutions. But public regulation is not without cost. By its very nature, it impedes the free flow of capital, and therefore may impair the efficiency of the financial system.

The decade of the 1980s has witnessed a trend towards the *deregulation* of many financial services. Interest rate ceilings have been eliminated on many types of accounts, and financial institutions have been allowed to offer a wide variety of accounts and services. In many respects, we have entered the age of the financial supermarket, in which an individual can shop at one location for a complete array of financial services: checking and savings accounts, insurance, brokerage services, and so on.

The rise of the huge financial service corporation is exemplified by Sears, Roebuck and Company's Sears Financial Network. Sears owns Dean Witter (a leading stock brokerage firm), Allstate Insurance, Caldwell Banker (a national real estate brokerage company), Allstate Savings and Loan, its own credit card operation, and numerous other financial service businesses. Many other corporations have followed Sears' lead. American Express, Citicorp, and Transamerica are prominent examples of firms that have diversified in order to offer a variety of financial services.

THE STOCK MARKET

The secondary market, in which previously issued securities are traded, has special significance for today's financial manager. Here the price of a firm's stock, and hence the market value of the firm, is determined. As we noted in Chapter 1, there is a growing tendency to evaluate managerial performance in terms of its impact on the market value of shareholders' equity.

The Stock Exchange   Although regional stock exchanges exist in a dozen cities, the two largest organized markets are located very near each other in New York's financial district. These are the so-called Big Board and Little Big Board—the New York and American Stock Exchanges. Taken together, these two national exchanges account for almost 90% of the dollar volume of shares sold on registered exchanges. The NYSE is by far the biggest and the most important organized security exchange in the world. It is also the oldest security market in the United States, having been founded in 1792.

Common stock accounts for the bulk of transactions on the organized exchanges. However, the trade in options (see Chapter 20) has increased dramatically in recent years. Some indication of the growth of the securities market can be gleaned from the fact that on March 16, 1830, the dullest day in the history of the NYSE, only 31 shares were traded; 138 years later, on April 10, 1968, the Exchange recorded its first 20-million-share trading day. Today, 100-million-share days are nothing extraordinary.

The NYSE provides a meeting place for the demand and supply of securities, rather than for the buyers and sellers themselves. Trading in securities is limited to members, most of whom act as agents for the actual buyers and sellers. Since 1953, seats (that is, transferable memberships) on the NYSE have been limited to 1,366. A member may choose to trade on his own behalf (the so-called floor or registered traders), but if he does, he cannot carry customer accounts. Subject to the board's approval, members may also form a partnership or corporation with other individuals for the purpose of doing business with the public. Today, all the principal U.S. securities brokers are members of the Stock Exchange.

The privilege of trading on the NYSE is not a free good; it must be acquired, subject to the board's approval, through the purchase of a seat from one of the current members. The price of a seat is a good indicator of the risks of investment in general. At the crest of the stock market boom of the 1920s, a seat on the Exchange cost $500,000. By 1942, the price had fallen to $17,000. In the early 1960s, seats were again selling for more than $200,000. In 1979 they could be bought for as little as $40,000, but by 1981 the price of a seat was again over $200,000. In December 1986 the record was broken at $600,000; the current record was set twice, in April and in May of 1987, when the price soared to $1,100,000.

Placing an Order

Since active trading on the floor of the Stock Exchange is restricted to members, an investor who wants to purchase stock must first get in touch with a broker who will act as an agent. For simplicity, assume that the customer wants to purchase 100 shares of stock[3] in the Ford Motor Company. The customer must also stipulate the type or order, usually a *market* or *limit* order. A market order instructs the broker to buy (sell) the securities at the best obtainable price. A limit order, as its name implies, instructs the broker to buy (sell) the security at the limit price, or better. In the case of a purchase, this means to buy at the limit price, or below; in the case of a sale, to sell at the limit price, or above. (For example, an investor might instruct the broker to sell the stock at a price of *at least* $95 per share.) The customer's order is then relayed by telephone or computer to the broker's respresentative on the floor of the Exchange, who takes it to the area, or post, at which Ford stock is traded. The actual transaction is carried out by members of the Exchange, called *specialists*, who by their readiness to buy and sell Ford stock create a continuous market for that stock. After the transaction is concluded, a report is transmitted to the Exchange's computer center. Within seconds, the report is flashed to subscribers all over the country; if the investors are still at the broker's office, they can watch the report of the transaction projected electronically on a wall display panel.

Investors who feel confident about a stock's chances can purchase that stock. If the investors are particularly "bullish" about the stock, they might even borrow money to finance further purchases. This is called buying the stock *on margin*. But what about the proverbial bears, who think the price of a particular stock is going to fall significantly in the near future? If the bearish investors own the stock, they can sell it. But how can "bears" profit from

---

[3] The number of shares to be acquired has special significance in the securities business. Lower commissions are payable on shares purchased in *round lots*—that is, in multiples of 100 shares. Any fractional purchases or sales are considered *odd lots*, and an additional commission is charged on these transactions. For stocks whose unit prices are relatively high, 10 rather than 100 shares constitute a round lot.

short sale
The sale of stock borrowed from a broker and sold on the market at the current price.

a hunch, if they do not own the stock in question? The answer to this dilemma is to sell short. A **short sale** is defined as the sale of stock which an investor does not own. The investor must first *borrow* the stock (usually from a broker who acts as a go-between) and then sell it on the market, at the current price. Of course, the investor hopes to buy it back, at a lower price, in the future. But why should anyone lend stock to a short seller? The advantage to the lender is that the proceeds of the sale become available for investment during the interim period. Moreover, the lender is entitled to any dividends declared on the stock while it is out on loan.

Although the very term short sale smacks of speculation, these transactions are made for a variety of reasons, not all of them speculative. For example, an investor may *sell short against the box*, i.e., borrow a stock and sell it, even though he owns the stock himself. The "box" in this case refers to the short seller's safe deposit box. The motives for such a short sale are usually not speculative. For example, having made a profit in a particular stock in December, the owner may sell the stock short and then deliver her own stock to the lender to cover the short sale in January, thereby carrying the profit over to the next tax year. Short sales are used for a variety of hedging purposes by specialists and professional traders on the floor of the Exchange.

THE OVER-THE-COUNTER (OTC) MARKET

over–the–counter (OTC)
A secondary stock market made by brokerage houses.

In terms of number of companies (over 4,000), but not in terms of value, most common stock is traded **over-the-counter (OTC).** The organized security exchanges, such as the NYSE, operate a "continuous auction" market in which buy and sell orders flow in to the appropriate specialists more or less continuously. In the case of smaller firms, or infrequently traded stock, the process of matching buying and selling orders could become cumbersome. To avoid this problem, the brokerage houses themselves "make a market" in selected securities. They hold an inventory of securities they are willing to sell (at the offer or asked price). They also stand ready to buy these securities (at the *bid* price) from investors who wish to sell. The *spread* between the bid and asked prices provides the brokers' return on the transaction. The rather curious name "over-the-counter" derives from the fact that in the past, the shares were literally passed from the broker's safe to the investor's hands, "over the counter."

The National Association of Security Dealers

The National Association of Security Dealers is a self-regulatory organization charged by law with overseeing the over-the-counter market. Its members include virtually all U.S. broker-dealers serving investors. In 1971, the association introduced a system of automated quotations which uses computer and communication technology to provide quotations for OTC securities. In 1982, the National Market System (NMS) was introduced. The NMS provides sale quotations and volume figures for selected securities throughout the trading day. At the end of 1984, 1,180 securities were included in the NMS. The network of computer-linked brokerage houses has created a national market for those securities. The NMS is based on a computerized quotation system and multiple competing market makers—brokers who are prepared to buy or sell particular shares.

STOCK PRICE INDEXES

Almost all investors are concerned with general market trends, and not just with the particular securities they hold in their own portfolios. Today's financial manager must also keep abreast of the market, in order to interpret correctly the price movements of the company's stock. The financial manager will usually turn to one of the stock price indexes which are regularly published in the financial sections of all leading daily newspapers.

In 1965, the New York Stock Exchange introduced a comprehensive measure of the market trend. The *NYSE Composite Index* covers all listed stock. Changes in the index are printed on the ticker tape every half-hour. Four subgroups—industrial, transportation, utility, and finance—and their net changes also appear on the tape every hour. But despite the fact that the New York Stock Exchange is the nation's paramount securities market, this index is a relative newcomer to the financial scene. Many investors, and the general public as well, turn to a much better known indicator of market trends, the *Dow Jones Averages*.

In 1884, Dow, Jones and Company began publishing stock price averages in a daily newsletter that was later to become the *Wall Street Journal*. Today the company publishes four averages of the prices of selected stocks listed on the New York Stock Exchange: 30 industrials, 20 railroads, 15 utilities, and the composite average for all 65 stocks. These averages are reported regularly during trading days, and are sent out, at half hour intervals, over the Dow Jones News Service. The Dow Jones averages appear in *The Wall Street Journal*, and in the financial pages of leading newspapers all over the world.

The 30 industrials is the best known of the four averages. When the financial press reports new highs or lows for the D J average, the reference is invariably to the industrials. Figure 3.1 charts the Dow Jones industrial average since 1929. The industrial average is comprised of blue chip stocks: the 30 stocks represent a cross section of the most prominent and largest companies listed on the Exchange. These include AT&T, DuPont, General Electric, General Motors, Sears Roebuck, and U.S. Steel.

Standard & Poor's Corporation also publishes a well-known series of

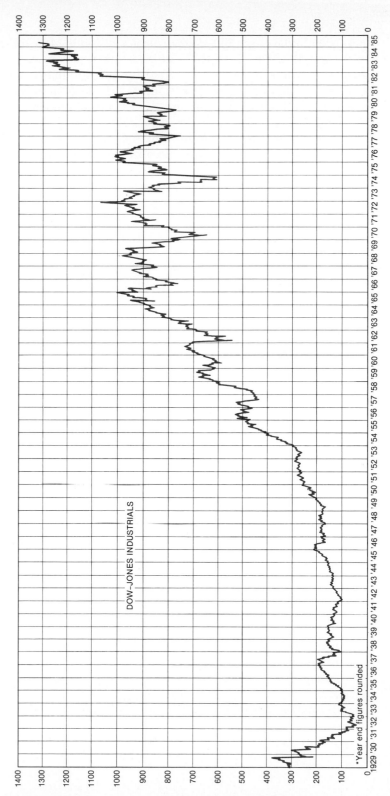

FIGURE 3–1   Dow Jones Industrials, 1929–1985   SOURCE: *Moody's Industrial Manual, 1985*

35

stock price indicators: 500 stocks composite index, 425 industrials, 25 rail-roads, and 50 utilities. All these indexes are reported regularly during the day by the various news services. A reader can find many other price indexes in the financial news media. For example, *The Wall Street Journal* also reports the options indexes of the Chicago Board of Options and the Chicago Mercantile Exchange.

A relatively new and important indicator is the *commodity price index*. This index represents the prices of contracts to buy and sell 12 commodities at a specified date. The commodities covered are cattle, coffee, copper, corn, cotton, gold, hogs, lumber, silver, soybeans, sugar, and wheat. The commodity index enables traders to compare the performance of their own holdings of commodity contracts with the general trend.

There are two main commodity indexes, the *spot* (or *cash*) index, and the *futures* index. The spot index represents the average price of the 12 commodities on a given day, divided by the average price on the previous day. Futures are contracts to deliver (or buy) a given commodity, at a fixed price, on a specified day in the future. The futures index represents the average price of the contracts to deliver the 12 commodities five months in the future. This index provides managers with an indication of the trend in raw material prices.

Stock Price Indexes Outside the United States

Stock price indexes are also calculated and published regularly for stock exchanges outside the United States. The following well-known indexes are published regularly by *The Wall Street Journal:*

Exchange	Index
London	Financial Times
Zurich	Credit Suisse
Frankfurt	Commerzbank
Paris	AGEFI
Amsterdam	ANP-CBS General
Brussels	Stock Index
Johannesburg	Johannesburg Gold
Tokyo	Nikkei Dow Jones
Hong Kong	Heng Seng
Singapore	Straits Times
Sydney	All Ordinaries
Toronto	300 Composite

In addition, the *London Financial Times* publishes stock indexes for Austria, Denmark, Italy, Norway, Spain, and Sweden, as well as the World Index, compiled by Capital International of Geneva.

MARKET EFFICIENCY

To fulfill its function as an allocator of capital effectively, the security market should be influenced solely by economic considerations. In such a market, current prices for a company's securities will reflect the investors' best estimate of the firm's anticipated profitability, and of the risks attached to these profits. Since rising stock prices attract investors, firms with relatively high levels of risk-adjusted profits will find it relatively easy to raise additional capital. Firms with low profitability, or excessive riskiness, will find it difficult, expensive, or on occasion even impossible to raise capital for expansion.

The Efficient Market Hypothesis

Efficiency in the stock market implies that all relevant information regarding a given stock is reflected in its current market price. Alternatively, we can characterize an efficient market as one in which a share's current price gives the best estimate of its true worth. In an efficient market, there are no bargains. It is impossible to gain from trading on the basis of generally available public information. Only "insiders" can consistently make money, as some of us have already learned from experience. What you and I know is already discounted by the market—it is already reflected in the stock's price. The weight of the empirical evidence strongly suggests that the U.S. securities market is efficient in this information sense.[4]

Efficient Markets and Financial Management

What does the existence of efficient markets imply for financial management? First and foremost, it means that the market is competitive, and that its prices are the best available estimates of a firm's future profitability. Despite the speculative nature of a modern security market and the randomness of its short-term price fluctuations, stock market evaluations still provide the best available benchmark for corporate financial decisions. Therefore, decision rules based on the attempt to maximize the market value of the firm (see Chapters 9–11) provide appropriate guides for managerial action. It also means that financial managers cannot be expected to "beat the market," in any meaningful sense, so long as they are limited to publicly available information. But this line of argument can be carried too far. Financial managers may be in a superior position to judge their own firms, or even other firms in the industry. The manager may also be in a position to bargain for better terms in the market. Finally, through innovation, the manager may be a "creator" of new information for the market.

The efficient market hypothesis must not be used as an excuse for in-

---

[4] As early as 1933, Alfred Cowles, an investment adviser himself, demonstrated statistically that choosing stocks by the flip of a coin (at random) was at least as good a strategy as following professional investment advice. See Alfred Cowles, "Can Stock Market Forecasters Forecast?" *Econometrica* 1, 1933.

action. Consider the case of the financial executive who turns to his son, a finance major, with the good news: "Son, I see a ten dollar bill on the sidewalk; should I pick it up?" Inebriated perhaps by the efficient market hypothesis, the son promptly replies: "No, Dad, if it were really there, surely it would already have been picked up by now!"

BOND MARKETS

Traded securities are not limited to equities. *Bonds*, debt instruments issued by corporations, central governments, and municipal and state authorities, are another important component of the security market. Most bonds promise investors periodic interest payments, usually every 6 months, and repayment of the principal upon maturity. The proportion of bonds in the total market value of listed securities increased from around 35% in the 1960s and the early 1970s to over 50% in the early 1980s. This reflects, among other things, a significant shift by U.S. corporations away from equity financing to a financing mix with a much higher debt component.

Unlike equities, only a small fraction of corporate bonds are listed on an organized exchange. Since bonds are usually traded in large blocks by institutional investors, such as pension funds and insurance companies, the over-the-counter mechanism is very convenient. Over 90% of bond transactions are made in the OTC market. There is also a significant difference in the pattern of listing of stocks and bonds on the different exchanges. Around 75 to 80% of the total listed common stock is traded on the New York Stock Exchange, but the NYSE accounts for only 35 to 40% of the total market value of listed bonds. This reflects the fact that the NYSE lists only corporate bonds. U.S. government, state, and municipal bonds are traded on the other exchanges.

THE BASIC CHARACTERISTICS OF INTEREST RATES

As we have already emphasized, the allocation of capital among alternative uses is the capital market's principal economic function. Like any other commodity in a free enterprise economy, capital is allocated by a price mechanism. The expected return (dividends plus capital gain) is the investor's incentive to provide additional equity financing. The interest rate is the price of borrowed capital. Chapter 7 discusses the return on common stock; here we examine the factors that influence the supply and demand for loans, which determines the level of interest rates.

FIGURE 3–2
Market Forces That
Determine Interest
Rates

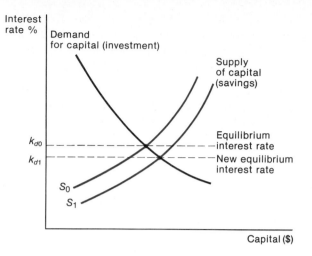

Forces
Determining
Interest Rates

To gain insight into the complex forces that explain the level of interest rates, we will make a few simplifying assumptions. These allow us to use the economists' simple, but very useful, framework of supply and demand curves. Assume a world in which there is neither risk nor inflation. Such a world would not only be a nice place to live in, but it also corresponds to the type of economy analyzed by one of the leading classical economists, Irving Fisher. Moreover, the results hold for a more complex economy in which inflation and risk exist.

Under the assumed conditions, the rate of interest will be determined by the interaction of two fundamental forces: (1) the supply of capital, which depends on the willingness of individuals to postpone consumption—that is, to save, and (2) the demand for capital, which depends on business opportunities for profitable investment. These two forces determine the effective rate of interest at that level which equates the supply with the demand. In the jargon of the economist, this rate of interest is the *equilibrium* rate, since it exactly balances the forces of supply and demand.

Figure 3–2 illustrates this model. The investment demand of firms declines from left to right. This signifies that they first execute their most profitable opportunities, and then move on to the less attractive ones. The supply curve, on the other hand, slopes upward. Savers require higher interest rates in order to induce them to postpone additional consumption. The interest rate that equates the demand and supply, k_{d0}, coincides with the intersection of the investment (demand) and savings (supply) curves. This rate just balances individuals' willingness to save with firms' willingness to invest.

What would happen if individuals became more thrifty, and decided to consume less and save more? This is illustrated in Figure 3–2 by a downward shift in the supply curve. At the former market interest rate, k_{d0}, individuals want to save more than firms are prepared to invest. The excess supply of funds drives down the interest rate to k_{d1}, at which a new equilibrium is reached. The fall in the interest rate from k_{d0} to k_{d1} is just sufficient to induce firms to increase their investments by the amount required to balance the public's increased desire to save.

Inflation and Interest Rates

real rates of interest
The rate of interest as measured in terms of constant purchasing power.

Since we have assumed the absence of inflation, the interest rates depicted in Figure 3–2 are the **real rates of interest;** that is, the rate of interest as measured in terms of constant purchasing power. The relationship between *nominal* and real interest rates can best be seen by examining a specific numerical example. Consider an individual who loans $100 for one year at a nominal interest rate of 8% and therefore expects to receive $108 (principal plus interest) at the end of the year. If consumer prices are expected to rise, the $108 at the end of the year will *not* represent an 8% increase in the lender's ability to buy goods and services. Assume, for example, that prices are expected to rise, on the average, by 6%. The investor gives up $100 at the beginning of the year and receives $108 at the end of the year. However, the $108 can purchase only $102 ($101.89 to be exact) worth of goods, in terms of beginning of year prices (108/106 × 100 = 101.89). Hence the *real* interest rate on this loan is

$$\text{real interest rate} = \frac{108}{106} - 1 = .0189 = 1.89\%$$

If we consider a more extreme case, in which prices are expected to rise by exactly 8%, the real rate is zero: (108/108) − 1 = 0. Should the rate of price increase *exceed* the money rate, the real interest rate would be negative. In such a case, individuals actually give up more current purchasing power than they receive at the end of year. In general, if the level of consumer prices is expected to rise, the money rate will be greater than the real rate. Conversely, in the unlikely event that prices are expected to fall, the real rate of interest exceeds the nominal rate.

Individuals save in order to increase their future consumption of goods and services. Strong expectations of inflation, therefore, undermine their willingness to loan money (buy bonds) at a *given* nominal interest rate. As a result, interest rates will tend to rise until the investing public is offered a return sufficiently high to provide the desired real rate of interest. In reality, however, all bondholders, and especially long-term bondholders, face the additional risk that realized inflation may turn out to be higher than was originally anticipated. In such instances the inflation premium, embodied in market interest rates, may prove insufficient to compensate them for unanticipated rises in the general price level.

The Inflation Premium

The nominal, or money, rate of interest is the actual rate observed in the market. If we relax the assumption of no inflation, the real rate will be lower than the nominal rate. The higher nominal rate reflects the expected rise in

inflation premium (IP)
A part of the nominal interest rate that reflects an anticipated rate of inflation.

consumer prices during the lifetime of the loan. The additional interest reflects the anticipated rate of inflation and is called the **inflation premium (IP)**. Such a premium is necessary because creditors (bondholders) suffer a real economic loss when consumer prices rise. Inflation reduces the purchasing power of the fixed nominal amounts (interest and return of principal) to which they are entitled. This creates a need for a rise in the interest rate in order to induce individuals to give up present money in return for a fixed amount of money in the future.

If we denote the real rate of interest by $k_{d\text{-real}}$, the inflation premium by *IP,* and the nominal rate on a government Treasury bill by $k_{\text{T-bill}}$, the relationship between the nominal and real rate is

$$k_{T\text{-}bill} = k_{d\text{-real}} + IP$$
$$\text{nominal rate} = \text{real rate} + \text{inflation premium}$$

Default Risk

It is now time to drop the unrealistic assumption of a riskless world. Real-life capital markets are highly uncertain, and as a result, interest rates will reflect the possibility that the borrower (issuer of a bond) will be unable to make the payments of interest and/or principal. In the case of government bonds we ignore such a possibility, since a government is not subject to *involuntary* insolvency in terms of its own currency. Although printing more money may lead to unpleasant economic consequences, it can always be done to meet *domestic* obligations. Hence the interest rate on government bonds of a given maturity can be taken as an indicator of the *default-free* rate of interest on such loans. With respect to corporate bonds, however, a significant credit risk does exist, and the investor is confronted with the problem of assessing the possibility of default. This default risk must then be weighed against the higher interest yields offered by corporate bonds.

Corporate bonds are rated regularly, by their default risk, from AAA, which applies to bonds of the best quality (lowest default risk), to D. The latter rating is assigned to firms that have already filed for bankruptcy. Lower ratings lead investors to demand higher interest rates on such bonds.[5] In 1985, the interest rates on various classes of bonds were:

U.S. Treasury	10.75%
AAA	11.37%
BBB	12.72%

The default risk premium (DP) is defined as the difference between the interest rates on Treasury and corporate bonds:

$$\frac{\text{default risk}}{\text{premium}} = \frac{\text{interest yield}}{\text{on corporate bond}} - \frac{\text{government}}{\text{bond rate}}$$

---

[5] Bond ratings are discussed in greater detail in Chapter 13.

A glance at the figures for 1985 shows that the default risk premium on AAA bonds was 0.62 percentage points ($11.37\% - 10.75\% = 0.62\%$).

Maturity Risk and Liquidity

liquid security
A highly marketable asset that can be converted to cash on short notice and without risk of capital loss.

A **liquid security**, or *asset*, is one that can be converted to cash on short notice, *and without risk of capital loss*. To be considered liquid, an asset must have two characteristics:

1. It must be highly marketable. In the case of a security, this means that an active market must exist, and that relatively large amounts of the security can be bought or sold without causing a large change in price. Such a market exists for many U.S. government securities.

2. The conversion of the asset to cash must be made without significant capital loss. Liquidity means that when such an asset is sold, it will fetch a price above, or at worst not very far below, its original purchase price. If there is any appreciable risk, the asset cannot be considered "liquid" in the full sense of the term.

maturity risk premium (MP)
A factor in bond interest rates that takes into account the risk of capital loss when interest rates rise.

The second characteristic, absence of risk, eliminates securities that have a significant risk of default. This leaves government bonds and those of some corporations with almost zero probabilities of default. But are *all* such bonds liquid? As we will see in Chapter 7, bond prices fall when market interest rates rise; moreover, the longer the bond's maturity, the greater the drop in price. Thus, even default-free government bonds contain an element of risk—the risk that a rise in the market interest rate will force bond prices down, thereby causing a capital loss to holders. Interest rates, therefore, will also reflect a **maturity risk premium** (MP). But in the case of maturity risk, the premium is greater the longer the maturity of the bond.

riskless interest rate (R_F)
The rate of interest on very short-term government securities, which can be converted to cash without significant risk.

The implications for liquidity are straightforward. Not all default-free bonds can be considered liquid assets. True, they have no default risk, but the long-term bonds do have significant maturity risk. Only very short-term government securities, such as Treasury bills, can always be converted to cash without significant risk of loss. The rate of interest on these short-term government securities will be considered the **riskless interest rate**, and will be denoted by R_F.

The Term Structure of Interest Rates

As we have seen, the interest rates on bonds, at any point in time, will differ chiefly for two reasons:

1. Differences in maturity risk premiums
2. Differences in default risk premiums

To focus on the interest-maturity relationship, we will center our attention on bonds that are identical in every respect but maturity. The family of outstanding U.S. Treasury issues provides a reasonable approximation.

At first glance, it would appear that liquidity considerations alone

term structure
The relationship between bond maturity and interest rates.

should be sufficient to determine the **term structure**—that is, the relationship between bond maturity and interest rates. Such an approach suggests that a premium will exist for giving up liquidity, so that the yield on long-term bonds will be higher than yield on shorter-term bonds. This *liquidity preference* explanation is often identified with the work of John Maynard Keynes, who viewed the rate of interest as the "reward for parting with liquidity."

In 1888, at the age of four and one half, Keynes was asked by his father what was meant by interest. The boy replied: "If I let you have a halfpenny and you kept it for a very long time, you would have to give me back that halfpenny and another too. That's interest".[6] Forty-eight years later, Keynes had not changed his mind: "The mere definition of the rate of interest tells us in so many words that the rate of interest is the reward for parting with liquidity for a specified period. For the rate of interest is, in itself, nothing more than the inverse proportion between a sum of money and what can be obtained for parting with . . . the money in exchange for a debt for a stated period of time".[7]

yield curve
A curve on a graph that shows the relationship of effective bond yields to bond maturity on a particular date.

This approach suggests that a graphic portrayal of the term structure will result in a continuously rising **yield curve**. Such a curve is illustrated in Figure 3–3, which shows the hypothetical relationship of effective bond yields to bond maturity on a particular date. Years to maturity are measured along the horizontal axis, and the interest rate is measured in percentages along the vertical axis.

Liquidity premiums are hard to identify, and even more difficult to measure. Moreover, the simplified liquidity conditions we have sketched here are *not* sufficient, in themselves, to account for all the observed time patterns of interest rates. Historically, three additional types of yield curves have been observed in the capital market. At various times, the yield curve has been (a) decreasing—the yields on long-term maturities lie *below* those

---

[6] R. F. Harrod, *The Life of John Maynard Keynes* (New York:Macmillan, 1951), p.8.
[7] John Maynard Keynes, *The General Theory of Employment, Interest and Money* (New York: Harcourt, Brace and Company, 1936), p. 167.

**FIGURE 3–3
A Rising Yield
Curve**

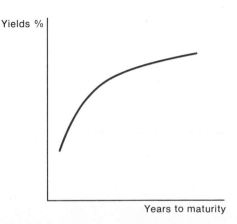

of short-term maturities; (b) "humped"—the yield curve rises between short- and intermediate-term bonds, and then declines for longer-term maturities; (c) stable—the yield curve remains flat, as the yields on short- and long-term securities are the same. These three additional varieties of yield curve are illustrated in Figure 3–4.

The yield curve is a simplified graphic representation of the term structure of interest rates, for a given risk class of securities, on a particular day. From time to time, the yield curve may change. No one type can be considered normal. Figure 3–5 gives two empirical examples. Figure 3–5a plots the yields of U.S. Treasury securities, against their maturities, as of the week ending July 27, 1984. On that date, the observed yield curve was, for the most part, upward-sloping. The yield on 1-year notes was 11.90%, rising to 13.15% for 20-year bonds; it was slightly less, 13.06%, for 30-year maturities. This relationship is reversed in Figure 3–5b, which plots the yield curve for the week ending July 3, 1981. On that day, the observed yield curve was downward-sloping. The interest rate on 1-year notes was about 15%, dropping to about 13 1/2%, on 30-year maturities.

The simple liquidity preference approach cannot account for the multiplicity of observed term structures. However, once we recognize the existence of expectations regarding future levels of interest rates, all types of yield curves—upward-sloping, downward-sloping, or stable—can be explained.

The "expectations" approach[8] to the term structure of interest rates is based on the observation that investors can make a long-term loan, or alternatively, a short-term one which then can be repeated over again. If future short-term rates were known with certainty, if there were no transaction

---

[8] Well-known variants of the expectations approach to the term structure were developed by many economists, including Keynes.

FIGURE 3—4
Alternative Forms of the Yield Curve

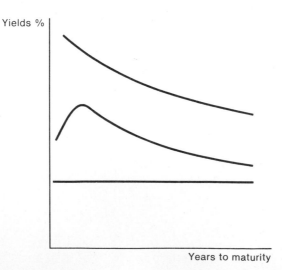

Yields %

Years to maturity

FIGURE 3–5a
Yield Curve, Week
Ending July 27,
1984   SOURCE: Board
of Governors, Federal
Reserve Bulletin.

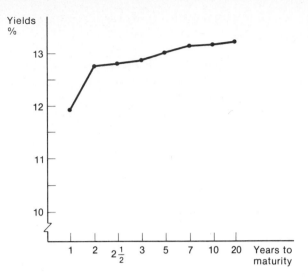

costs, and if investors were indifferent between long-term bonds and successive purchases of short-term bonds, the interest rate on the long-term bond would be exactly equal to the (geometric) average of the future short-term rates.

The following conclusions can be derived from the expectations model:

1. If at a point in time the future short-term rates are expected to remain unchanged, all long-term rates will equal the short-term rates. This is the case of a flat yield curve.
2. If the future short-term rates are expected to rise, the yield curve will be upward-sloping.

FIGURE 3–5b
Yield Curve, Week
Ending July 3,
1981   SOURCE: Board
of Governors, Federal
Reserve Bulletin.

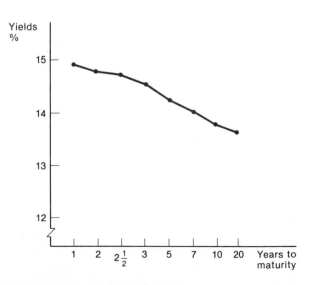

3. Conversely, if the future short-term rates are expected to fall, the yield curve will be downward-sloping.

By introducing expectations, all three types of yield curves—upward-sloping, flat, and downward-sloping, or for that matter, any combination of the three—can be explained.

In this context, we should note that no automatic mechanism exists to equalize the rates themselves. However, market forces do exist to keep the rates consistent with the hypothesis that the long-term rate will be equal to the average of the future short-term rates. For example, should the long-term rate *exceed* the average of expected future short-term rates, it would pay to borrow short, and buy a long-term bond. The increased demand for short-term loans would raise the short-term rate, while the increased demand for long-term bonds would raise their prices, thereby lowering their yields. This process would continue until the long-term rate again equals the average of expected future short-term rates.

The yield curve is a subject of considerable theoretical appeal, but it also has significance for financial management. At times of volatile changes in expectations, often due to a shift in inflationary pressures, the changes in long-term yields can be (and have been) dramatic. At such times, an understanding of the market forces underlying the term structure of interest rates is necessary for a rational financial strategy. Intuition is simply not sufficient to explain what often appear to be bewildering changes in bond prices and yields. For example, a sharp financial manager, taking advantage of a declining yield curve, should realize that the market "expects" future rates to fall. Under those circumstances, perhaps an investment in longer-term securities might be desirable, despite the fact that the current short-term rate exceeds the long-term rate.

SECURITY MARKETS OUTSIDE THE UNITED STATES

Stocks and bonds are issued by corporations and governments in all industrialized, and in some developing, countries. They are usually traded domestically on national exchanges. The market prices of listed securities on each exchange are, of course, quoted in the domestic currency of the country. This complicates comparison across countries, but the U.S. security market is, by far, the largest in the world, after adjusting for exchange rates. The U.S. securities market comprised nearly half of the world equity and bond market at the end of 1980. In other words, the size of the U.S. security exchanges matched all the exchanges in Europe, Asia, Canada, and Australia combined.[9]

---

[9] R. Ibbotson, C.R. Carr, and A.W. Robinson, "International Equity and Bond Returns". *Financial Analysts Journal.* July-Aug. 1982.

The proportion of bonds and stocks also differs across countries. On the whole, bonds have more importance abroad. While U.S. equities represent more than half of the world equity market, non-U.S. bonds predominate in the world bond market. This reflects the fact that debt financing by corporations is much more prevalent outside the United States. Although American corporations have increased their use of debt financing in recent years, they still finance mostly by equity (see Chapter 14). Japan is the largest foreign equity market; the United Kingdom is second. The leading countries in the bond market, outside of the United States, are Japan, Germany, and the United Kingdom. To sum up, the U.S. security market is the largest in the world, and Japan has the largest security market outside the United States. The leading markets in Europe are those of Germany and the United Kingdom.

SUMMARY

The *primary* market for new issues of securities is distinguished from the *secondary* market, or the stock market. The latter imparts greater liquidity to investment in long-term securities, such as common stock, by providing investors with a resale market for these securities. The New York Stock Exchange is the leading organized market; there is also an extensive over-the-counter (OTC) market in the United States.

Since financial investment is often carried out via an intermediary, the principal financial institutions play an important role. These include commercial banks, saving and loan associations, life insurance companies, pension funds, and mutual funds. In order to protect individuals' savings, the financial intermediaries have been subject to relatively strict public regulation. However, in recent years recognition of the costs of this intervention has led to *deregulation*. One important result of this new trend has been the rise of the so-called financial supermarkets, which offer a full line of financial services and accounts.

The United States market is by far the largest single security market in the world. Outside the United States, Japan, the United Kingdom, and Germany have the largest capital markets. Capital market trends are of special interest not only to investors, but to corporate financial managers as well. The financial press regularly reports price movements on the U.S. and world security markets. In addition, price quotations, and a composite index, are published for leading commodities.

An efficient market is one in which all relevant information is embodied in a security's price. As a result, stock market values can serve as useful benchmarks for corporate decisions and for the evaluation of managerial performance.

Several forces determine interest rates. The real rate is the rate of interest that would exist in the absence of inflation; it is measured in terms of *constant* purchasing power. The nominal rate, which is the rate actually observed in the market, is related to the real rate as follows:

$$\text{nominal rate of interest} = \text{real rate} + \text{inflation premium}$$

Thus, the nominal rate exceeds the real rate by an amount equal to the inflation premium. If the IP is zero (no rise in prices is expected), the nominal and real rates will be the same.

Interest rates reflect two additional considerations—*default risk* and *maturity risk*. Default risk stems from the chance that the borrower (or bond issuer) will default on either the payment of interest or the redemption of principal. Only government obligations are completely free of this risk. The interest rates on all other debt are subject to default risk, and therefore are higher by the amount of the required *default premium* (DP). Maturity risk affects all bonds, both government and corporate. It reflects the risk of a rise in market interest rates over the lifetime of the bond. Since the prices of outstanding bonds fall when market interest rates rise, the interest rate on bonds will also reflect a *maturity premium* (MP). Since the drop in price is greater the longer the maturity, longer-term bonds require higher premiums.

The interest rate on a typical corporate bond is equal to the real rate, adjusted for inflation, plus a risk premium that reflects the bond's maturity and default risk:

corporate interest rate = real rate + inflation premium + risk premium

The analysis of interest rates in terms of their required risk premiums can be used to define a liquid asset; that is, one which can be converted to cash quickly, and without loss. The rate of interest on very short-term government securities such as Treasury bills is an example of such an asset. Liquid assets have no default risk, very little maturity risk, and also adjust rapidly to expected inflation. The yield of short-term Treasury bills will be taken as an approximation of the *riskless rate of interest*, which plays a central role in the theory of finance. It will be denoted by the symbol R_F.

The term structure of interest rates can be examined using the concept of a *yield curve*. This curve is a simple graphic representation of the yields on a particular class of bonds, of varying maturity, on a particular date. At one time or another, the observed yield curve has been: (a) increasing; (b) decreasing; (c) "humped" (increasing up to a given maturity after which it declines); or (d) flat. No particular type can be considered normal. However, by explicitly considering investors' expectations regarding the future course of interest rates, all four relationships can be rationalized.

REVIEW EXERCISE

Circle the correct words to complete the sentence; see p. 50 for the correct answers.

3.1 The principal sources of funds in the primary market for securities are *foreign transfers/domestic savings* of consumers and nonfinancial businesses.

3.2 The principal uses of funds are long-term financing and housing, investments of corporations, and the *borrowing/lending* of state and local government.

3.3 A very *small/large* proportion of individual savings reaches the new issue market indirectly via a financial intermediary.

3.4 The stock exchange typically deals in *new issues/existing securities.*

3.5 The secondary market provided by the stock exchange *is/is not* an important factor inducing investors to acquire new securities.

3.6 *All investors/only members* can buy and sell on the floor of the NYSE.

3.7 *Lower/higher* commissions are payable on shares purchased in round lots.

3.8 A "short sale" is defined as the sale of stock which the investor *does/does not* own.

3.9 An investor who feels "bearish" about a stock will *buy it/sell it* short.

3.10 The equilibrium interest rate balances the individual's willingness to save with the firm's willingness to *take risks/invest.*

3.11 When inflation exists, the nominal interest rate is *lower/higher* than the real interest rate.

3.12 The lower the default risk, the *lower/higher* the interest rate.

3.13 Government bonds *are/are not* free of default risk, but *are/are not* necessarily completely riskless.

3.14 If short-term interest rates are expected to rise, the yield curve will be *downward/upward* sloping.

3.15 In an efficient market, current prices for a company's securities will reflect the *government's/investors'* best estimates of the firm's anticipated profitability and of the risks attached to these profits.

QUESTIONS

3.1 Define the following terms:
   a. Capital market
   b. Primary market; secondary market
   c. "NOW" account
   d. Mutual fund
   e. Financial supermarket
   f. Market order; limit order
   g. National Association of Security Dealers; National Market System
   h. Dow Jones averages
   i. An efficient stock market

j. Real interest rate; nominal interest rate

k. Default risk premium; inflation premium

l. Liquid asset

m. Rising, falling, constant, and humped yield curve

3.2 Distinguish between the primary and the secondary security markets.

3.3 What are the principal economic functions of a stock exchange?

3.4 Trace the activities undertaken by the various parties when an investor wishes to buy a share of, say, IBM stock.

3.5 How does a "bull" differ from a "bear" in assessment of the market?

3.6 What can a bear do if he doesn't own the stock he feels bearish about?

3.7 "I read all the relevant newspapers and trade journals, listen to the radio and watch TV, and have made a lot of money investing on the basis of the knowledge thus gained." Evaluate this statement.

3.8 What happens to interest rates if people consume more and save less of their income? (Use a graph to illustrate your answer.)

3.9 Evaluate the following statement: "The real rate of interest is always lower than the nominal interest rate."

3.10 Enumerate the factors that influence the nominal rate of return on a bond.

3.11 On January 1 your broker tells you that short-term interest rates are expected to stay constant during the next three years and then will fall for the following seven years. What shape will the yield curve have?

3.12 Do you expect long-term interest rates to fluctuate more or less than short-term rates? Explain.

Answers to Review Exercise

3.1 domestic savings   **3.2** borrowing   **3.3** large   **3.4** existing securities
3.5 is   **3.6** only members   **3.7** lower   **3.8** does not
3.9 sell it   **3.10** invest   **3.11** higher   **3.12** lower
3.13 are, are not   **3.14** upward   **3.15** investors'

SUGGESTIONS FOR FURTHER READING

A more comprehensive discussion of the institutional framework of the capital market and the role of financial institutions can be found in Herbert E. Dougall and Jack E. Gaumnitz, *Capital Markets and Institutions,* 5th ed. (Englewood Cliffs, NJ Prentice-Hall, 1986).

An excellent survey of market efficiency can be found in Eugene F. Fama, *Foundations of Finance* (New York: Basic Books, 1976), chap. 5.

For students with a historical bent, a brilliant description of stock market speculation, which is still well worth reading, can be found in John Maynard Keynes, *The General Theory of Employment, Interest, and Money* (New York: Harcourt, Brace and Company, 1936), chap. 12.

Interest rates in general, and the term structure in particular, are treated in greater depth by James C. Van Horne, *Financial Market Rates and Flows,* 2nd ed. (Englewood Cliffs, NJ: Prentice-Hall, 1984). Current data on bond yields are available in the monthly *Federal Reserve Bulletins.*

A useful collection of articles on the impact of inflation on capital markets can be found in Marshall Sarnat and Giorgio P. Szego (eds.), *Saving, Investment, and Capital Markets in an Inflationary Economy* (Lexington, MA: Ballinger, 1982).

4

The Accounting Framework as an Information System

In the same sense that mathematics is the "language" of modern physics, accounting can be considered to be the "language" of modern business. Boardroom walls are often covered with charts depicting the flow of funds, profitability ratios, and inventory turnover. Moreover, the jargon spoken by corporate directors is often peppered with accounting terms. If the valuation and decision models we develop in Parts III and IV are to be used for actual corporate strategy, managers must ensure that the firm's accounting system generates the required data inputs on costs, earnings, and financial stability.

In this chapter, we take a brief look at the basic accounting statements, and then examine some of the tools available to the financial manager for the analysis of those statements. The use of the information generated by these statements in financial analysis and decision-making is examined. The Appendix to this chapter illustrates how accounting information can be used to analyze and predict financial failure. Chapter 5 builds on this foundation and examines the dynamic problems of financial planning and forecasting.

THE EVOLUTION OF ACCOUNTING

Like most aspects of modern business studies, accounting has come a long way since the techniques of present day double-entry bookkeeping were developed out of the business practices of Italian merchants during the Renaissance. Initially, the accountant took business practices as given, and attempted to devise methods of measuring and portraying the impact of these practices on the profitability of the firm. The accountant did *not* tell the businessperson what to do.

Accounting has undergone a dramatic change during the past two decades. Today, it is viewed as an integral part of the decision-making process in which economic information is collected, interpreted, and then communicated to the relevant corporate decision-makers. The analysis of financial statements is part of an overall corporate *information system* which provides the data inputs for decision theories and models.

This information is transmitted both verbally and in writing. However, the reports are often restricted to the internal use of management. The firm also periodically issues accounting statements to its owners—that is, to its shareholders. These statements are external in the sense that they are widely distributed and therefore are also available to journalists, outside analysts, creditors, and potential investors. The most important of the external statements is the firm's annual report. In addition to much descriptive material, the annual report presents a quantitative record of the firm's activities during the year (the income statement), as well as a quantitative statement of its financial position at the close of the year (the balance sheet).

THE INCOME STATEMENT

income statement
An accounting statement that sets out in money terms the economic changes a firm has experienced during the year.

As we have already noted in Chapter 1, the goal of the firm can be viewed in terms of achieving the highest possible market value for its owners' equity (common stock). This, in turn, involves the weighing of potential profits against the risks incurred in earning them. One fundamental problem facing the accountant, therefore, is to determine and measure the profit (net income) realized by the firm during the year. This is the task of the **income statement**, which sets out in money terms the economic changes the firm has experienced during the year. Table 4–1 gives such an income statement for the Metro Manufacturing Company, a hypothetical firm which is a major producer of its own line of recreational equipment. Metro's net earnings before deducting interest and taxes (EBIT), or operating income as it is also called, amounted to $4,788,000.

The goal of the accountant is to come up with a defensible estimate of *net income*, that is, net profit after deducting interest and taxes. Net income was positive in the two years covered in Table 4–1, but fell sharply in the current year. Net earnings declined from $4,370,000 to $2,370,000. Despite this, Metro raised its annual dividend from $2.30 to $2.60 per share in the current year. In this context we should note that the recreational equipment industry, as a whole, showed a decline in earnings for that year, but the drop in industry earnings was proportionately somewhat less than was true of Metro. This raises serious questions regarding Metro's dividend policy (see Chapter 16). One possible explanation is that Metro viewed the decline in earnings as a temporary deviation from the long-term trend.

TABLE 4–1   Metro Manufacturing Company: Income Statement for Year Ending December 31 ($000)

	This Year	Previous Year
Net Sales	46,470	55,940
Expenses:		
Cost of goods sold (COGS)	37,505	42,230
Gross income	8,965	13,710
Depreciation	877	900
Sales and administrative expenses	3,300	3,126
Operating income (EBIT)	4,788	9,684
Interest expense	18	14
Net income before taxes	4,770	9,670
Taxes	2,400	5,300
net after-tax income	2,370	4,370
Distribution of net income		
To dividends	1,300	1,150
To retained earnings	1,070	3,220
Per Share Figures:		
Earnings per share (EPS)	4.74	8.74
Dividends per share	2.60	2.30

THE BALANCE SHEET

The income statement, which shows the economic changes of a business, must begin and end at definite points in time—usually the beginning and end of the year. The accountant attempts to show the opening and closing balances, in money terms, of the firm's economic assets and the various claims (of creditors and owners) against those assets. The statement that presents the assets and claims at the end of a given year is called the **balance sheet.** Table 4–2 gives the closing balance sheet for Metro at the end of the current year, and to facilitate comparison, the figures for the previous year as well.

balance sheet
An accounting statement, in money terms, of a firm's assets and claims against assets at the end of a given year.

The left-hand side of Metro's balance sheet shows the firm's assets in descending order of liquidity; that is, the amount of time required to convert them to cash. Those assets the firm expects to be able to turn into cash within one year (or during the normal operating cycle) are listed as *current assets.* The principal current assets are cash itself, marketable securities, receivables, inventories, and the prepayment of certain expenses, such as insurance. Conversely, Metro's plant and equipment, and other long-term investments, constitute its *fixed assets.*

In a similar fashion, the right-hand side of the balance sheet lists the claims against these assets according to the time in which they must be paid. Claims payable within one year (accounts payable and taxes) are called *cur-*

TABLE 4–2   **Metro Manufacturing Company: Balance Sheet as of December 31 ($000)**

	This Year	Previous Year
Current Assets		
Cash	967	725
Marketable securities	3,973	10,936
Accounts receivable	1,349	1,217
Inventories	5,975	5,633
Prepaid expenses	196	158
Total current assets	12,460	18,669
Fixed Assets		
Gross plant and equipment	23,354	17,540
Less: Depreciation reserves	6,493	5,616
Net plant and equipment	16,861	11,924
Investments and miscellaneous	1,394	1,239
Total Assets	30,715	31,832
Current Liabilities		
Accounts payable	6,831	6,436
Accrued taxes	2,788	5,978
Total current liabilities	9,619	12,414
Long-term Liabilities		
Long-term debt	1,643	1,035
Total liabilities	11,262	13,449
Equity		
Common stock ($10 par value shares)	5,000	5,000
Retained earnings	14,453	13,383
Total equity	19,453	18,383
Total Claims on Assets	30,715	31,832

rent liabilities; the firm's long-term debt, which is payable after more than one year, is a long-term liability. Finally there are the ownership claims of the firm's shareholders; these constitute its *equity,* or *net worth.* Strictly speaking, these claims are converted into cash only when the firm is liquidated.

The fundamental equation of accounting is the identity:

$$\textbf{assets = liabilities + shareholders' equity}$$

The equation reflects the underlying principle of accounting that against every asset there must exist a claim, either of an owner or of a creditor. The fundamental equality of assets and claims is shown graphically in Figure 4–1. The accounting identity can also be written in a form which emphasizes the fact that the equity, or net worth, represents the residual value of the assets, after the creditors' claims have been deducted:

$$\textbf{assets − liabilities = shareholders' equity}$$

FIGURE 4–1
Corporate Assets, Liabilities and Shareholders' Equity

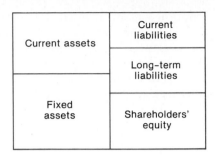

Current assets	Current liabilities
	Long-term liabilities
Fixed assets	Shareholders' equity

In the specific case of Metro, the equity is divided into two components: $5 million of common stock, which reflects the money raised when the shares were issued, and $14,453,000 of *retained earnings*. Retained earnings are the part of net income that was not paid out as dividends over the years, but was "saved" within the firm.

The changes in the firm's equity between balance sheet dates are shown in yet another account—the Statement of Retained Earnings (see Table 4–3). You can easily see the connection between the changes in the equity accounts (Table 4–3) and the distribution of net income in Table 4–1. Note, however, that the balance of retained earnings is a claim of stockholders *against* the firm's assets, and *not* an asset itself. The increase in equity has its counterpart in the increase in assets which results from the profitability of the firm's operations during the year. Clearly, one cannot write a check against retained earnings! For example, profits could set an all-time record, but the firm might still be short of cash at the end of the year. The amount of cash on hand at Metro at the end of the year was $967,000, and *not* the $14,453,000 of retained earnings.

TABLE 4–3   Metro Manufacturing Company: Statement of Retained Earnings for Year Ending December 31 ($000)

Beginning balance of retained earnings	$13,383
Plus: Net income for year	2,370
Less: Dividends	1,300
Balance of retained earnings at end of year	14,453

SOURCES AND USES OF FUNDS

The balance sheet provides a sort of snapshot of the firm's financial position at a given point of time—the end of the year in our example. But the firm also requires information, for itself and for its shareholders, regarding the changes in its financial position *between* balance sheet dates. On what activities were resources expended during the year? And what were the sources of financing for those expenditures? To answer these questions, the firm provides an analysis of the *flow of funds* during the year.

As a first step, we set out the change (increase or decrease) in each item of the balance sheet, and then classify the changes as *sources* or *uses* of funds:

Sources	**Uses**
Increase in a claim (liability or capital)	*Increase* in an asset
Decrease in an asset	*Decrease* in a claim (liability or capital)

The increase in a claim—for example, the increase in equity via a sale of additional stock, or taking an additional loan—provides a source of funds. Conversely, a decrease in an asset item—for example, from the sale of equipment, or running down of inventory—is also a source. An increase in an asset, such as the acquisition of new plant or equipment, is defined as a use of funds. Decreases in liabilities or capital, perhaps from redemption of debt or payment of dividends, are also classified as uses of funds.

Table 4–4 shows the changes in Metro's balance sheet accounts during the year classified according to this system. Note that this classification preserves the fundamental equality between assets and the claims against these

TABLE 4–4   Metro Manufacturing Company: Balance Sheet Changes during the Current Year ($000)

	Dec. 31 This Year	Dec. 31 Previous Year	Change Sources	Change Uses
Cash	967	725		242
Marketable securities	3,973	10,936	6,963	
Receivables	1,349	1,217		132
Inventories	5,975	5,633		342
Prepaid expenses	196	158		38
Gross plant and equipment	23,354	17,540		5,814
Accumulated depreciation*	6,493	5,616	877	
Investments and other assets	1,394	1,239		155
Accounts payable	6,831	6,436	395	
Accrued taxes	2,788	5,978		3,190
Long-term debt	1,643	1,035	608	
Common stock	5,000	5,000		
Retained earnings	14,453	13,383	1,070	
Total			9,913	9,913

* Since depreciation is a deduction from assets, the increase in this item is an increase in a "negative" asset and therefore is listed as a source.

assets. As a result, the balance sheet changes showing sources and uses are also equal. Total *sources* and total *uses* of funds, in our specific example, are the same—$9,913,000. The major use of funds was the acquisition of new plant and equipment, and the payment of an accrued tax liability. The sources of funds include the running down of assets (primarily short-term marketable securities), depreciation, and a modest increase in debt and retained earnings. With the notable exception of depreciation, most of these items are self-explanatory. Before going on to the preparation and analysis of a formal statement of sources and uses, we need to examine the role of depreciation as a "source" of financing.

Depreciation as a Source of Funds

depreciation
An estimate of that part of the dollar value of the property's economic capacity which has been used up during the year.

The deterioration in the use-value of a firm's long-term assets over time is called **depreciation.** The annual allowance for depreciation is an attempt by the accountant to estimate that part of the dollar value of the property's economic capacity which has been used up and therefore should be charged as an expense during the year in question. The depreciation allowance is *not* a cash outlay, like wages or taxes, but represents the gradual writing off of the asset's original cost over a number of income periods.

No one denies that depreciation is an expense. The deterioration of assets through use, corrosion, waste, breakage, or even just from the passage of time (obsolescence) is an observed fact of economic life. But depreciation raises an accounting problem because fixed assets, by definition, are not entirely exhausted during a single accounting period. As a result, the cost of using the asset must be absorbed through the operations of *all* the years in which it makes a contribution to earnings. This requires an estimate of the asset's useful life, and the proportion of that life which will be used up in any particular year.

A numerical example can help clarify what often appears to be a somewhat confusing practice. Consider the case of a textile manufacturer who decides to discard an old machine and replace it with a new high-speed model. Although the new machine costs $10,000, it increases the capacity of each spinner, reducing the unit cost of spinning. The new machine is expected to last 20 years, given normal maintenance, but the accountant feels that it is likely to become obsolete within 10 years. Thus, the machine's useful economic, as opposed to its engineering, lifetime is estimated at 10 years, after which it is expected to have no value at all. And since the accountant, in this instance, has no particular theory regarding the rate at which the new machine will be "used up," he applies a very common rule of thumb called *straight-line depreciation* (SLD). In SLD, the original cost of the machine is charged against profits in equal annual amounts. In this example, the annual depreciation allowance is $1,000 (the original cost of $10,000 divided by the expected lifetime of 10 years). This simplified calculation assumes a zero salvage value. If the machine can be sold for scrap at the end of 10 years at a price of $500, the annual depreciation allowance would be reduced to $950 (the original cost of the machine less the salvage value divided by 10).

The essential feature of the depreciation allowance is the fact that it does *not* constitute a cash outlay. It is an estimate, and very often a rough estimate, of the deduction from annual income necessary to reflect that year's share in the asset's overall economic cost. Today, the accountant has very little discretion with respect to depreciation because the IRS stipulates the acceptable depreciation schedules (see Chapter 2). Now in what sense can this annual allowance be considered a *source* of funds? The accountant reduces net income, and thereby retained earnings as well, by the amount of the annual depreciation allowance. Since depreciation is not a cash outflow, we "correct" the flow of funds statement by adding back the depreciation when estimating the contribution of earnings to the firm's sources.

This approach can also be justified by turning to a U.S. Supreme Court decision written by Louis Brandeis more than a half a century ago: "The theory underlying this allowance for depreciation is that by using up the plant a gradual sale is made of it. The depreciation charged is the measure of the cost of the part which has been sold."[1] As we have already pointed out, the sale of an asset is considered a source, rather than a use, of funds. Hence the depreciation allowance, which is not a cash outlay, must be added back to net income in order to approximate the cash flow from operations:

$$\text{Cash flow} = \text{net income} + \text{depreciation}$$

In the specific case of Metro this becomes:[2]

$$\text{Cash flow} = 2,370 + 877 = 3,247$$

Strictly speaking, sales revenue, and not depreciation, provides the firm with the resources needed to finance its operations. Should Metro's sales fall to zero, the cash throwoff from depreciation (apart from its effect on past and/or future tax liabilities) would also disappear.

Statement of Changes in Financial Position

We are now in a position to use the balance sheet changes from our worksheet (Table 4–4) to prepare the firm's statement of changes in financial position during the year (see Table 4–5). This statement is usually given a prominent place in the firm's annual report. The Statement of Changes in Financial Position is usually divided into two parts: (a) a presentation of sources and uses of funds; (b) an analysis of changes in working capital. The purpose of the statement of changes in financial position is to shed light on three fundamental issues relating to the year which is being examined:

1. What were the firm's sources of funds? That is, where did the funds come from?
2. How did the firm use the funds?

---

[1] See *U.S.* vs. *Ladey*, 274 U.S. 295, at 301 (1927).
[2] To save space, all figures in this and the following sections are in thousands of dollars.

TABLE 4–5   Metro Manufacturing Company: Statement of Changes in Financial Position during the Current Year

	Thousands of Dollars	Percent of Total
Sources of Funds:		
Net income	2,370	
Depreciation	877	
Funds provided by operations	3,247	45
Issue of long-term debt	608	8
Decrease in net working capital		
(see below)	3,414	47
Total sources	7,269	100
Uses of Funds:		
Additions to fixed plant and		
equipment	5,814	80
Increase in other fixed assets	155	2
Cash dividends	1,300	18
Total uses	7,269	100
Changes in Net Working Capital		
Increase (decrease) in current assets		
Cash	242	
Marketable securities	(6,963)	
Receivables	132	
Inventories	342	
Prepaid expenses	38	
Net increase (decrease) in current assets	(6,209)	
Increase (decrease) in current liabilities		
Accounts payable	395	
Accrued taxes	(3,190)	
Net increase (decrease) in current liabilities	(2,795)	
Net increase (decrease) in net working capital	**(3,414)**	

net working capital
The difference between current assets and current liabilities.

3. What was the net impact of the flow of funds on the firm's **net working capital** (NWC), which is defined as current assets minus current liabilities. An increase in NWC is usually interpreted as a sign of increased liquidity; decreases are viewed as a reduction in the firm's liquid position.

A closer look at Table 4–5 can help to determine the degree to which it actually answers these three questions.

1. Metro's sources of funds are clear: Forty-five percent came from operations (net income and depreciation), 8 percent from an increase in long-term debt, and the remaining 47 percent from a reduction in net working capital. One peculiarity should be mentioned. Table 4–4 listed the $1,070 change in retained earnings as a source. However, in Table 4–5 net income is listed as a source of funds from operations, and dividends paid are listed as a use. The change in retained earnings is omitted. But this comes to the same thing in the end, since net income (2,370) less dividends (1,300) exactly equals the 1,070 change in net earnings.

2. Similarly, the uses to which these funds were devoted are equally clear—82 percent went to finance the expansion of plant and equipment and other assets; the remaining 18 percent was used for the payment of cash dividends to shareholders.

3. Part three of the statement analyzes in detail the $3,414 decrease in net working capital during the year. Looking at the detailed statement of the changes in NWC, we see that the principal cause of the decrease can be traced to the reduction of almost $7 million in the firm's holdings of marketable securities.

The interpretation of the changes in financial position, as is true of the interpretation of any economic or accounting analysis, requires judgment and familiarity with the firm's operations. In the specific case of Metro, the decline in NWC should not be interpreted as an undesirable weakening of the firm's liquidity position. On the contrary, in this case the short-term marketable securities were held specifically for the purpose of financing expansion of plant and equipment. Selling them off merely means that the company carried out its original plan. In fact, a glance at the balance sheet (Table 4–2) shows that Metro still held almost $4 million of short-term securities at the end of the year. This suggests that the expansion of plant and equipment may be incomplete. In its annual report, this interpretation of the change in working capital would be emphasized. However, it does raise a question in the mind of the outside analyst, and therefore we will return to the question of the possible consequences of the reduction in net working capital.

TREND ANALYSIS

Many methods are available to help the analyst read and interpret a firm's financial statements. For example, a systematic statement of a firm's sources and uses of funds can shed light on the impact of its past activities on its current financial position. In addition, the percentage changes of individual balance sheet and income statement items can be presented. If for example, the previous year is set at a base of 100, the current year's results can be given as 100 *plus* the percentage change. This is called *trend analysis*. In the case of Metro, the current year's sales would be given an index of 83. This

**TABLE 4–6   Metro Manufacturing Company
Common Size Income Statement
(In percent)**

	This Year	Last Year
Net sales	100	100
Cost of goods sold (COGS)	80.7	75.5
Gross Profit Margin	**19.3**	**24.5**
Depreciation	1.9	1.6
Sales, administrative, and other operating expenses	7.1	5.6
Total expenses	9.0	7.2
Operating Profit Margin	**10.3**	**17.3**
Less: Interest	—	—
Net before taxes	10.3	17.3
Less: taxes	5.2	9.5
Net Profit Margin	**5.1**	**7.8**

reflects a 17% fall in sales relative to the preceding year ($46,470, as compared with $55,940). Alternatively, if last year's dividends ($1,150) are set at 100, current dividends ($1,300) receive an index of 113, which reflects the 13 percent increase in the current year's dividends.

Common size statements can also be prepared to help in the evaluation process. This is done by dividing each individual entry by the statement's total, and expressing the result in a percent. A common size balance sheet can easily be prepared by dividing each asset and liability by total assets (claims). A common size income statement can be formed by dividing each item by total sales. In the case of Metro, we have illustrated the common size approach in Table 4–6. The principal advantage of such an approach is to facilitate comparisons with other firms, or within the same firm over time.

WHO USES FINANCIAL STATEMENTS?

As we have just seen, the various financial statements prepared by the firm's accounting department convey important information regarding past performance and current financial position. In the remaining sections of this chapter, and in the following chapter, we will apply the tools of financial, economic, and statistical analysis to these statements in an effort to evaluate their implications for the future. Future earnings, and their riskiness, affect the market value of the firm's equity (see Chapter 7). Financial statement analysis is one way to help management, creditors, investors, and other interested parties gauge the probable impact of changes in corporate strategy on the firm's future performance and financial position.

This analysis serves corporate "insiders" (that is, management) as well as "outsiders" (investors, investment analysts, bankers, regulatory authorities). Special importance is attached to the analytical tools and indicators typically used by external analysts because their evaluations affect investors' willingness to supply the additional debt and equity capital needed to finance the firm's future activities. Financial ratio analysis is one of the oldest, and best-known, of the devices used by analysts to evaluate a firm's performance.

FINANCIAL RATIO ANALYSIS

ratio analysis
A method of interpreting a financial statement that focuses on comparisons among individual items.

For over a century, **ratio analysis** has been the principal method used to interpret financial statements. The use of ratios is designed to highlight the relationships among the individual items in a firm's financial accounts. Numbers by themselves are often worse than nothing—especially if they are large enough. Is $100 million of short-term debt a burden? Surely the answer depends, in a crucial way, on whether we are talking about a small firm such as Metro or a financial giant like AT&T. In this instance, a comparison with the firm's current assets would be helpful. Similarly, a $1 million inventory, which might prove the undoing of the local co-op bookstore, might be disastrously low for a large chain operation. Here, a comparison with total sales seems to be called for.

Comparison of Ratios

The need for comparison goes beyond the comparison of individual accounting items within the firm. Each individual ratio, in turn, must be compared with some benchmark in order to facilitate proper interpretation. There are no absolute standards by which a ratio can be judged. Two principal alternatives are available: cross-sectional analysis and time series analysis.

cross-sectional analysis
A method of financial analysis that compares the results of one firm to those of similar firms, or to an industry average.

In **cross-sectional analysis**, the results of one firm are compared to those of a similar firm, to a representative sample of firms, or to the industry average. Data on industry averages are published regularly by Dun & Bradstreet, Robert Morris Associates, the Federal Trade Commission, and various trade associations. Significant deviations from the industry average raise questions for further investigation, but they do not provide quick or easy answers. Each case must be carefully evaluated. For example, for many years IBM's debt policy deviated drastically from that of the industry. But it would be rash to conclude that IBM's greater reliance on debt financing was too risky, or necessarily wrong, simply because the other firms pursued a more conservative policy. A deviation from an industry average may reflect an innovative strategy of great merit, or management failure.

time–series analysis
A method of financial analysis in which the ratios within the same firm, over time, are evaluated.

In **time series analysis**, the ratios within the same firm, over time, are evaluated. Here again, the analyst must exercise caution when interpreting comparisons. For example, the comparison with some base year may suggest that the base year represents an "ideal," or "desirable," or "equilibrium" situation. However, this often is not the case. Deviations from past trends must be examined carefully before drawing any conclusions. But despite all the shortcomings, identifying breaks with past trends can be a useful test for management, as well as for the outside analyst. Careful monitoring of performance over time is a good method for checking on how a firm's long-term plans are progressing.

The comparison of ratios, either within the firm over time, or against external benchmarks, is designed to pinpoint questions that require further investigation. Significant deviations call for additional analysis. The mechanical calculation of ratios should never become a substitute for critical thinking and further analysis.

Classifying Ratios
Financial ratios can be classified in many ways; the only limitation appears to be the ingenuity of the analyst. One possibility is to classify the particular ratio by its source. Thus, for example, we would have:

1. Balance sheet ratios
2. Income statement ratios
3. Mixed ratios—ratios in which one item is drawn from the balance sheet, and the other from the income statement. (The ratio of inventory to sales is an example of such a mixed ratio.)

From the analyst's viewpoint, a classification in accordance with various aspects of the firm's operations is much more useful:

1. Liquidity ratios (short-term solvency)
2. Debt management ratios (long-term solvency)
3. Efficiency (turnover) ratios
4. Profitability ratios

LIQUIDITY RATIOS

The main objective of the use of liquidity ratios is to give the external analyst a rough measure of the firm's capacity to meet its short-term obligations. Financial managers have more refined tools to work with, such as detailed cash budgets (see Chapter 18). But liquidity ratios are very useful to a firm's short-term creditors, such as banks and suppliers. Their attention is usually focused on the relationship of the firm's liquid assets to its maturing liabilities. Two popular liquidity ratios are the current ratio and the quick (acid test) ratio.

Current Ratio   The *current ratio* is defined as the ratio of current assets to current liabilities. Recall that the difference between the two was defined above as *net working capital*. Current assets include all the firm's assets which are expected to be converted to cash during the year, or during the firm's operating cycle. They are usually considered the reserve out of which maturing short-term (one year or less) liabilities can be paid. It follows that a large current ratio constitutes a sort of safety margin for the firm's short-term creditors. Many analysts equate short-term solvency with the current ratio. This ratio is a measure of the firm's ability to meet its maturing obligations out of assets which will become available for this purpose during the normal course of the firm's operations.

The calculation of Metro's current ratio is as follows:

$$\text{Current Ratio} = \frac{\text{current assets}}{\text{current liabilities}} = \frac{12{,}460}{9{,}619} = 1.3$$

$$\text{previous year} = 1.5$$
$$\text{industry average} = 2.2$$

Metro's current ratio is noteworthy. First, it is significantly lower than the industry average. Second, in both years it was well below a traditional rule of thumb which states that a firm's current ratio should never be less than 2 to 1. This means that current assets should always be at least twice as large as current liabilities, which was not the case with Metro.

Today, modern financial analysis has made it clear that no hard and fast rule like 2 to 1 for the current ratio can be defended on logical grounds. Additional information is required in order to assess a firm's solvency. In Metro's case, most sales are to franchise outlets, and as a result are made virtually on a cash basis. Therefore, Metro's *receivables* are relatively low. Other things being equal, this reduces its current ratio. One way to increase the ratio would be to have Metro sell on credit, thereby creating accounts receivable. If the receivables are financed by long-term debt, the current ratio will rise. But would Metro really be better off, or more solvent?

The fall in the current ratio from 1.5 last year to 1.3 this year raises another question. This represents a substantial drop in liquidity as a result of the use of current assets to finance expenditures on plant and equipment. However, as we noted in the discussion of the flow of funds, the reduction in current assets (short-term marketable securities) was planned in advance. Moreover, the completion of Metro's expansion implies additional sales of securities in the future. This will have to be watched carefully, especially if revenues from sales continue to fall.

Metro's situation can be visualized in Figure 4–2. As long as current assets exceed current liabilities, the firm's net working capital (current assets *minus* current liabilities) will be positive and the current ratio, in turn, will be greater than 1. In essence, the shaded portion of the current assets is financed by long-term debt and equity, and the unshaded portion, by current liabilities. The use of short-term sources to finance the "fixed" or per-

**FIGURE 4–2
Net Working
Capital**

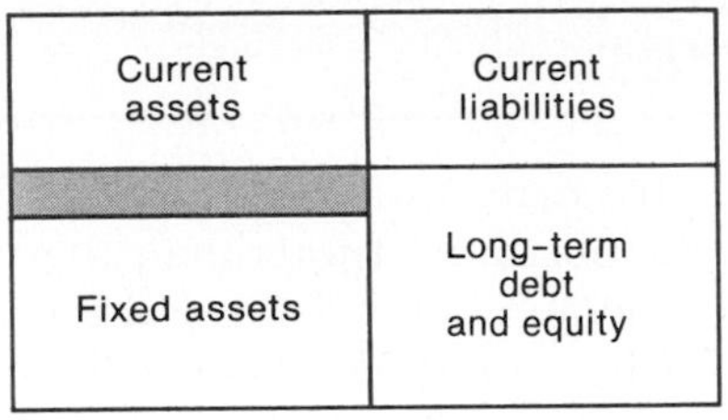

| Current assets | Current liabilities |
| Fixed assets | Long-term debt and equity |

manent part of working capital is risky and can lead to sleepless nights. For example, short-term loans have to be renewed periodically, and this exposes the firm to the risk that changes in financial conditions will make the renewal of loans difficult, or even impossible. Metro's net working capital is too low to be ignored, and will have to be watched very carefully as the plant expansion continues.

**Quick
(Acid Test)
Ratio**

The *quick ratio*, or *acid test* as some analysts call it, is calculated the same way as the current ratio, but after first deducting inventories and prepaid expenses, such as next year's insurance:

$$\text{Quick Ratio (Acid Test)} = \frac{\text{current assets} - \text{inventories} - \text{prepayments}}{\text{current liabilities}}$$

$$= \frac{6,289}{9,619} = 0.65$$

$$\text{previous year} = 1.04$$

$$\text{industry average} = 1.0$$

The so-called acid test reflects a feeling among many analysts that inventories and prepaid expenses cannot be relied upon to meet short-term obligations. The proposed measure focuses, therefore, on assets that can more easily be converted to cash. The quick ratio is a much stricter test of liquidity than the current ratio. However, the degree to which inventories can or cannot be considered liquid requires additional evidence. For example, are they comprised of unsalable merchandise from last year, or has the firm stockpiled raw materials due to favorable price trends? The need for further detail can also be seen by considering a firm with a large inventory of bathing suits in October, and whose liabilities fall due in November.

Once again we find Metro operating below the industry average, and below the traditional rule of thumb for the quick ratio. Traditional wisdom states that this ratio should never be less than 1 to 1. The decline in the ratio from 1.04 last year to 0.65 in the current year parallels the fall in the current ratio. But again, this is more of an indicator of the way Metro sells its product (no receivables) than evidence of financial weakness. However, it does emphasize Metro's dependence on the cash inflow from continued sales to meet its obligations. Any further decline in sales, without a reduction in inventories, could result in serious pressure on Metro's liquid reserves.

DEBT MANAGEMENT RATIOS

The use of debt financing has many aspects.[3] Firms may seek enhanced profits by earning more on the borrowed funds than they pay in interest. The use of debt also transfers some of the risks of the firm's operations from owners to creditors. A further advantage in debt financing stems from the fact that it typically does not affect the control of the firm. The purpose of long-term solvency analysis, using debt management ratios, is to determine the firm's ability to meet its overall debt burden—its payments of interest and principal.

The Debt Ratio   The ratio of total debt to total assets, or *debt ratio* as it is usually called, shows the proportion of the firm's assets that is provided by creditors. In a sense it measures the transfer of risk from owners to creditors. The smaller the proportion of assets provided by debt, the more secure a firm's creditors often feel. A lower debt ratio provides greater protection against loss should the firm be forced to liquidate.

In the case of Metro, the debt ratio is given by:

$$\text{Debt Ratio} = \frac{\text{total debt}}{\text{total assets}} = \frac{11,262}{30,715} = 37\%$$

$$\text{previous year} = \quad\quad 42\%$$

$$\text{industry average} = \quad\quad 50\%$$

Metro's debt ratio was 37% at the end of the current year. This represents a slight decline in the relative use of debt financing as compared with the preceding year. With creditors providing only a bit more than one-third of its total financing, Metro's use of debt is well below the industry average of 50%. If tax liabilities are ignored, Metro's use of debt is even more conservative. This is also confirmed by the fact that its interest-bearing debt (both long- and short-term) is very small for a firm of its size. This helps to explain what otherwise might appear to be a somewhat precarious short-term liquidity position. Given its low debt ratio, Metro is in a relatively strong position to increase its borrowing, both short- and long-term, should the need arise.

Times Interest   This is the ratio of earnings before interest and taxes (EBIT) to the interest
Earned[4]   charges. In the example of Metro, the times interest earned (TIE) ratio is given by:

$$\text{TIE Ratio} = \frac{\text{EBIT}}{\text{interest}} = \frac{4,788}{18} = 266$$

[3] Problems relating to debt strategy are discussed in Chapter 14.
[4] A more detailed discussion of the coverage of debt obligations occurs in Chapter 13.

Clearly, interest charges which are covered 266 times out of current earnings pose few problems. In fact, the principal question raised by the analysis is whether Metro might not consider additional debt financing in order to increase return on equity.

EFFICIENCY (TURNOVER) RATIOS

Efficiency or turnover ratios are usually composed of an entry from the income statement, such as sales, in the numerator, and an asset from the balance sheet, such as receivables, in the denominator. The purpose of these calculations is to pinpoint a particular aspect of the operational efficiency of a specific asset or group of assets.

Inventory Turnover This measure is defined as the ratio of cost of goods sold to inventory:

$$\text{Inventory Turnover} = \frac{\text{cost of goods sold}}{\text{inventory}} = \frac{37,505}{5,975} = 6.3 \text{ times}$$

$$\text{previous year} = 7.5 \text{ times}$$

$$\text{industry average} = 7.5 \text{ times}$$

Metro's ratio shows a decline in the utilization of inventories in the current year, presumably as a result of the decline in sales. How bad (if at all) is this slowdown in inventory turnover? Once again, we cannot answer the question raised by the ratio analysis without additional information. In this instance we would have to examine the composition of Metro's inventories. If the increase in inventories is of finished products which Metro was unable to move off the shelves fast enough, the rise represents a waste of resources. Should the examination reveal a planned increase in raw materials due to the expansion of plant, a very different conclusion would be called for. The ratio analysis may not provide a quick and easy answer, but it does raise the relevant questions.

We have defined the inventory turnover ratio in terms of *cost of goods sold;* however this ratio is sometimes defined as sales divided by inventory. We prefer cost of goods sold rather than sales in the numerator, since inventories are valued at cost. Similarly, many analysts prefer to use average, rather than end of period, inventory in the denominator. The latter refinement can be very important in firms with high degrees of seasonality. The use of December inventories of Good Humor ice cream bars may make an impressive inventory turnover figure, but would be a misleading estimate of the size of the average inventory over the entire year.

Accounts Receivable   A firm's credit policy is often appraised by calculating the *average collection period (ACP)* of its accounts receivable. This measure is computed for Metro in two stages:

$$1.\ \text{Average Daily Sales} = \frac{\text{annual sales}}{360 \text{ days}} = \frac{46,470}{360} = 129.08$$

$$2.\ \text{ACP} = \frac{\text{receivables}}{\text{average daily sales}} = \frac{1,349}{129.08} = 10.45 \text{ days}$$

$$\text{last year} \qquad 7.83 \text{ days}$$

$$\text{industry average} \quad 36 \quad \text{days}$$

The *ACP ratio,*[5] or "days sales outstanding" as it is sometimes called, is a measure of the average duration of accounts receivable—this is, the number of days that elapse (on the average) between the time a receivable is created and the date on which it is collected. This comes to slightly more than 10 days in the case of Metro, which confirms our earlier observation that Metro, for all practical purposes, sells its products virtually on a cash basis. This reflects the franchise nature of its particular business; the industry as a whole offers more liberal credit terms.

The average collection period can also be used to evaluate a firm's credit department by comparing the firm's stated credit terms with the ACP calculation.[6] Significant differences between the two may indicate: (a) inefficient collection methods; (b) deviation from management policy. For this purpose, credit sales, and not total sales, would be the more relevant figure. But many firms do not publish the breakdown between credit and cash sales. To facilitate interfirm comparisons, therefore, analysts usually use total sales data, since these data are available for all firms. The ACP is also an indicator of the liquidity of the firm's accounts receivable. Other things being equal, the shorter the collection period, the more liquid the receivables.

Other Turnover Ratios   Two less frequently used efficiency ratios refer to fixed and total assets, respectively:

$$\text{Fixed Asset Turnover} = \frac{\text{sales}}{\text{net fixed assets}}$$

In the case of Metro, this was

$$\frac{46,470}{16,861} = 2.76$$

$$\text{last year} = 4.69$$

$$\text{industry average} = 3.00$$

---

[5] The use of 360 days rather than 365 days is simply a convention that makes for somewhat easier calculations. Some analysts prefer to use 250 working days, rather than the calendar year, in the denominator.

[6] The "aging of accounts receivable," which is an alternative method for appraising the credit department, using internal data, is examined in Chapter 17.

$$\text{Total Asset Turnover} = \frac{\text{sales}}{\text{total assets}} = \frac{46,470}{30,715} = 1.51$$

$$\text{last year} = 1.76$$

$$\text{industry average} = 1.80$$

Clearly, these ratios reflect the specific character of Metro's manufacturing process. The degree of capital intensity of a metal manufacturer is far different from that of a whiskey distiller. In the case of asset turnover, therefore, comparison with industry averages is crucial. In this context, Metro's deviations from the respective industry averages do not appear unreasonable.

PROFITABILITY RATIOS

Up to this point we have used ratios to examine the firm's operations. The analysis of profitability, based on a firm's published accounting statements, presents the combined impact of liquidity, debt management, and operating efficiency on economic performance. Profitability ratios typically combine some measure of annual income in the numerator with the appropriate investment base given in the denominator. Profitability is a key input affecting investor decisions to provide the firm with additional capital. It is also one of the more important benchmarks used to evaluate managerial performance.

To facilitate the comparison of earnings between years (or between firms), the income statement can be presented on a *common size* basis. Table 4–6 (page 61) gives Metro's common size income statements for the current and preceding year. The common size statement expresses each entry as a percentage of total sales. As previously noted, Metro's sales declined by 17% relative to the preceding year. The common size statement is particularly helpful in evaluating the impact of the decline in sales on the structure of Metro's expenses.

Gross Profit Margin The decline in sales, as might have been expected, increased the proportion of expenses relative to sales. Cost of goods sold (COGS) comprised 80.7% of sales in the current year, as compared with 75.5% the year before. This reduced the gross profit margin from 24.5% to only 19.3% in the current year:

$$\text{Gross Profit Margin} = \frac{\text{sales} - \text{COGS}}{\text{sales}} = \frac{\text{gross profit}}{\text{sales}}$$

$$= \frac{46,470 - 37,505}{46,470} = \frac{8,965}{46,470} = 19.3\%$$

$$\text{previous year} = 24.5\%$$

$$\text{industry average} = 20.2\%$$

Operating Profit Margin

A similar result holds for other operating expenses. Depreciation and all other operating expenses rose relative to sales in the current year. As a result, Metro's operating profit margin also fell:

$$\text{Operating Profit Margin} = \frac{\text{operating profit}}{\text{sales}} = \frac{4,788}{46,470} = 10.3\%$$

$$\text{previous year} = 17.3\%$$
$$\text{industry average} = 10.8\%$$

Both the operating profit and the gross profit margins can be read directly from the common size income statement (Table 4–6).

Net Profit Margin

The net profit margin gives the percentage of each dollar of sales that remains after *all* expenses and taxes have been met. It represents the percentage contribution of each dollar of sales to the firm's net profits.

$$\text{Net Profit Margin} = \frac{\text{net after-tax income}}{\text{sales}} = \frac{2,370}{46,470} = 5.1\%$$

$$\text{previous year} = 7.8\%$$
$$\text{industry average} = 5.0\%$$

Metro's profit margin was 5.1% in the current year, down from 7.8% in the preceding year. These results also can be read directly from the bottom line of the common size income statement.

Like any ratio, all three profit margins (gross profit, operating profit, and net profit) must be compared with the relevant industry averages. Taken out of context, a profit margin conveys little; after all, you don't expect a supermarket and General Motors to have the same profit margins.

Return on Assets (ROA)

The *return on assets (ROA)*, or equivalently the *return on investment (ROI)*, is defined as the ratio of net after-tax income to total assets. It is the measure of the return on the firm's total resources.

$$\text{Return on Assets (ROA)} = \frac{\text{net after-tax income}}{\text{total assets}} = \frac{2,370}{30,715} = 7.72\%$$

$$\text{previous year} = 13.73\%$$
$$\text{industry average} = 9.00\%$$

Metro's return on assets fell, along with sales, from 13.7% to 7.7%. This result reflects the combined effects of the reduced profit margins and asset turnover following the sales decline. Since income is earned gradually over the year, an average of beginning and end of year assets is used by some analysts as the denominator of this ratio.

We have used net after-tax income as our measure of profits. However, when we want to concentrate on operating efficiency, interest charges can be excluded. This formulation uses earnings before the deduction of interest expense and taxes (EBIT) in the numerator:

$$\text{Operating Return on Assets} = \frac{\text{EBIT}}{\text{total assets}} = \frac{4{,}788}{30{,}715} \doteq 15.6\%$$

Return on Equity (ROE)

The return to common stockholders is given by this calculation:

$$\text{ROE} = \frac{\text{net after-tax income}}{\text{common equity}} = \frac{2{,}370}{19{,}453} = 12.2\%$$
$$\text{previous year} = 23.8\%$$
$$\text{industry average} = 16.0\%$$

If Metro had preferred stock outstanding, the preferred dividend would be deducted from the numerator and the preferred stock would be deducted from the denominator. Metro's *return on common equity* was 12.2%, just slightly more than one-half of the preceding year's figure. To put this figure in perspective, however, it must be compared with the industry average. In this context, Metro's return on equity was well *below* the industry average—12% as compared with 16% for the industry as a whole. Once again, this reflects the slump in sales. It also reflects the impact of Metro's plant expansion. It is reasonable to assume that some time might have been necessary to get the new plant fully on-line. Finally, the return on equity also reflects Metro's low level of long-term debt. The use of low-cost debt can often increase the return on common equity.

MARKET RATIOS

Many analysts introduce market values (e.g., stock prices) into the analysis of the company's accounts. Technically this does not present a serious problem, but as we will see in Part III, the interpretation of market value ratios is sometimes a difficult task. The importance of the use of market value stems from the fact that raising stock price, and not the percentage return on accounting equity, is the goal of the firm.

earnings per share of common stock (EPS)
A calculation in which total net earnings available to the common shareholders, after taxes, are divided by the number of shares outstanding.

Since the impact on stock prices is important to both investors and management, many firms provide per share calculations in their annual reports. One of the best known of these is the figure for **earnings per share of common stock (EPS).** EPS are total net earnings available to the common shareholder, after the payment of taxes, divided by the number of shares outstanding. Firms with preferred stock usually deduct the preferred dividends before calculating EPS. In the case of Metro, total after-tax earnings for the year were \$2,370,000; and since the company had 500,000 shares outstanding, net income per share (EPS) was \$4.74:

$$\text{EPS} = \frac{\text{net after-tax income}}{\text{number of shares outstanding}} = \frac{\$2{,}370}{500} = \$4.74$$

$$\text{previous year} = \$8.74$$

Price/Earnings (P/E) Ratio

price/earnings ratio (P/E)
A ratio applied to common stock that shows the price of a share relative to a firm's annual EPS.

Perhaps the most popular measure used by investors to evaluate a firm's common stock is the **price/earnings ratio (P/E):**

$$\text{P/E} = \frac{\text{market price per share}}{\text{earnings per share}} = \frac{\text{P}}{\text{EPS}}$$

The price/earnings ratio shows the price of a share relative to the firm's annual earnings. It represents, so to speak, the price of the share in terms of current earnings. Other things being equal, investors prefer to pay low prices for their investments, so a low P/E ratio should appeal to potential buyers of the stock. But as we will see in Chapter 7, this holds only in non-growth situations. Here too, it is essential to compare a firm's P/E ratio with the industry average.

Ratio of Market Value to Book Value

net worth–per share
Book value per share, or the sum of a firm's equity accounts divided by the number of shares outstanding.

Many analysts also compute the ratio of market value to book value:

$$\text{Market/Book ratio} = \frac{\text{stock price}}{\text{book value per share}}$$

The denominator of this ratio is **net worth—per share**, i.e., total equity as it appears in the balance sheet, divided by the number of shares outstanding. The net worth is the sum of the amounts paid to the firm by common shareholders (common stock plus surplus), and the retained earnings which have been reinvested on their behalf. The numerator reflects the market's estimate of the current value of these investments.

THE DUPONT SYSTEM

It is often convenient to summarize a company's ratio analysis using a type of chart developed by Dupont. Many variations are possible, and Figure 4–3 applies one version of the Dupont system to Metro Manufacturing.

The left-hand side of the figure builds up Metro's total costs, and then substracts costs and taxes from total sales to derive net income. Net income is then divided by sales to derive net profit margin, 5.1%. The right-hand side builds up the figure for total assets; it, in turn, is divided by sales to derive the total asset turnover, 1.51.

FIGURE 4–3
Dupont Chart

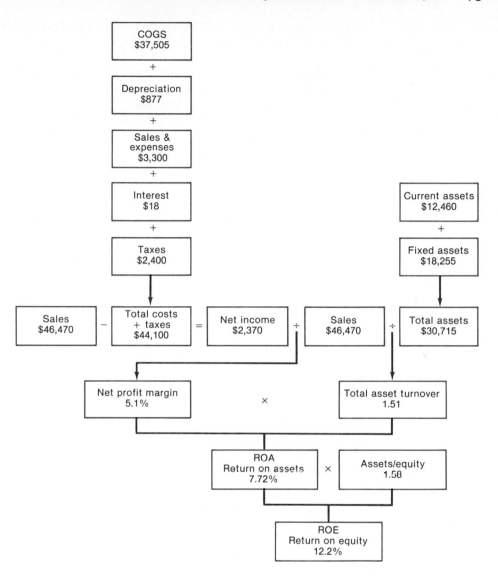

Net profit margin and total asset turnover are combined in the follow-ing equation to derive the *return on assets (ROA):*

$$\textbf{net profit margin} \times \textbf{asset turnover} = \textbf{return on assets}$$

$$\frac{\textbf{net income}}{\textbf{sales}} \times \frac{\textbf{sales}}{\textbf{total assets}} = \frac{\textbf{net income}}{\textbf{total assets}}$$

In the specific case of Metro, the equation becomes:

$$\text{ROA} = \frac{2{,}370}{46{,}470} \times \frac{46{,}470}{30{,}715} = \frac{2{,}370}{30{,}715}$$

$$\text{ROA} = 5.1\% \times 1.51 = 7.72\%$$

Metro earned, after taxes, about 5 cents on each dollar of sales. Since assets were turned over about 1.5 times during the year, this resulted in a net return on assets of 7.72%.

The figure goes on to show the return on equity (ROE) as the combined effect of the return on assets (ROA) and Metro's debt policy. Since 37% of Metro's assets are provided by creditors, the rate of return on assets must be multiplied by the so-called *equity multiplier*—the ratio of total assets to common equity:

$$
\begin{aligned}
\text{ROE} &= \frac{\text{net income}}{\text{assets}} \times \frac{\text{assets}}{\text{equity}} = \frac{\text{net income}}{\text{equity}} \\
&= \frac{2{,}370}{30{,}715} \times \frac{30{,}715}{19{,}453} \\
&= \quad 7.72 \quad \times 1.58 = 12.2\%
\end{aligned}
$$

The Dupont system is particularly helpful in showing the interaction between profit margin and asset turnover to derive the return on assets, as well as the interaction with debt policy to derive the return on equity.

ACCOUNTING EARNINGS VS. ECONOMIC EARNINGS

Much of the relevant information regarding a company's activities comes to us in the form of an accounting report, chiefly a balance sheet and an income statement. These reports are prepared in accordance with *accounting principles*, which often leads to significant differences between the accountant's estimate of past and current earnings, and that of the financial analyst or economist.

There are important conceptual differences between *accounting profits* and *economic profits*. Many of these differences reflect a basic disagreement regarding the definitions of income and costs, but they also reflect the very different objectives of the accountant and the economist. The accountant's primary concern is to measure past periodic (usually annual) earnings. In a way, the accountant is the firm's economic historian, albeit a very quantitative one. The economist, on the other hand, is solely concerned with the *future* stream of earnings over the expected life span of the firm; the periodic milestones, so vital to the preparation of a balance sheet, are of no particular interest.

The sympathies of the financial analyst tend to lie with the economist, since it is the estimation of future trends that provides the motivation for the analysis of the past. Although a complete adjustment of company reports to reflect economic profits is usually not possible, it is often desirable to make at least some rough adjustments, especially when comparing the performances of different firms.

Differences between accounting and economic profits arise from a number of sources. Some of the more important are these:

1. Economic analysis is based on the concept of *cash* flow, while a firm's accounts typically are kept on an *accrual* basis. This, of course, is a special case of the accountant's concern with the allocation of revenues and costs to specific years. The matching of costs and revenues which occupies much of accountants' time, and even more of their ingenuity, is not crucial to the economist. The latter can do without the one-year income statement, and replace it with a two-, or three-, or for that matter, with a life of the asset, income statement.

A major advantage of the cash flow approach is that it focuses on the *timing* of receipts and expenditures. Thus, the cash flow concept leads directly to the discounting of future earnings, which lies at the heart of modern financial analysis (see Chapters 6 and 7).

2. The economist and the accountant are not only in disagreement with respect to the *timing* of revenues and costs; they often do not agree on exactly what costs should be deducted, and from which revenues, when calculating net income. Owing to the quest for objectivity, the accountant tends to recognize only actual recorded historical costs and revenues. For example, while the economist assigns a cost of capital to the equity employed by the firm, the accountant recognizes only interest costs on debt capital.

economic depreciation
Depreciation measured by the difference in market values of an asset at the beginning and end of an accounting period.

3. Depreciation, on the other hand, is one non-outlay cost recognized by both accountants and economists. However, the way in which this cost is estimated by each differs. The accountant is concerned primarily with allocating the historical cost of the asset to particular years over its expected lifetime. Such an allocation is necessary if periodic income statements and balance sheets are to be drawn up. **Economic depreciation**, however, is measured by the difference in the market values of the asset at the beginning and end of the period. For the economist, the original cost of the asset is irrelevant.

4. For more than a century, economists, following the nineteenth-century English economist Jevons, have intoned, "Bygones are bygones." This view, that past costs (or *sunk* costs as they are often called) are irrelevant for all current evaluations and future decisions, is responsible for much of the divergence between the accounting and economic concepts of income.

5. Finally, inflation can have a distorting effect on the historical valuations made by the accountant. Many corporate assets are worth more today than what was originally paid for them. If you find this difficult to believe, just consider, for a moment, the current market value of a 30-year-old house in your neighborhood.

CAVEAT EMPTOR: LIMITATIONS OF RATIO ANALYSIS

Nowhere is the old Roman principle "Let the buyer beware" more appropriate than when applied to financial ratio analysis. The simplicity of the tools, and the ease of comparison within the firm or with industry averages, often lead to unwarranted complacency. Financial ratio analysis is one of the few fields of endeavor in which the widely discredited principle that a seller cannot be held responsible for the quality of the product still holds with alarming regularity. Almost all commercial financial analyses of actual companies carry an explicit disclaimer of responsibility for conclusions. Within the firm, executives carried away by enthusiasm for the point they are making often tend to overlook some of the serious shortcomings of the use of ratios:

1. A widely diversified firm, for example one with divisions operating in many different fields, may find the interpretation of overall company ratios difficult, if not impossible.

2. How should the absolute value of a particular ratio be evaluated? Is a high current ratio a good omen reflecting a high degree of safety, or is it a sign of misuse of the firm's assets? Too much cash in a world of high interest rates is wasteful; too little can, in some cases, lead to disaster.

3. Even if we agree on what constitutes a "good" result, some ratios may be strong while others are not. There remains the heroic task of trying to assign weights to the individual results in an attempt to assess overall performance.

4. Seasonality also hampers comparison. Ratios are calculated as of a particular date, usually the end of December. Hence it is important to compare the ratios with firms having similar seasonal patterns. After all, December may be a period of peak inventories for one firm, but a seasonal low for another.

5. The influence of specific dates can prove even more serious should the firm decide to "window dress" its accounts. For example, consider a firm with a current ratio of 2 to 1. If it pays back a bank loan *for one day*, on December 31, it can materially improve its current ratio, despite the fact that its cash balance actually went down. A numerical example makes this clear:

Current ratio on December 30	Repayment of loan	Current ratio on December 31
$\frac{16}{8} = 2:1$	4	$\frac{12}{4} = 3:1$

The temporary repayment of the loan reduces both the numerator and denominator by 4, but raises the current ratio from $2:1$ to $3:1$.

But what about a firm in a less favorable initial financial position? For example, what if its current ratio on December 30 is less than 1—say, 8/16 = 1/2. If the firm *takes a one-day loan on December 31*, it can increase its current ratio as follows:

Current ratio on December 30	One-day loan	Current ratio on December 31
$\dfrac{8}{16} = 0.5$	4	$\dfrac{12}{20} = 0.6$

Recall that in both cases the outside analyst sees only the end-of-year figure, and therefore can calculate only the December 31 ratios.

6. Using the industry average as a benchmark for comparison often provides an insufficient challenge for a firm's management. If your performance is average, it still means that roughly half of your competitors are doing better than you are.

But despite the serious shortcomings of the underlying accounting data, financial ratio analysis is often "the only game in town." Moreover, accounting ratios have been used successfully in a number of areas of major importance to the financial manager: (a) *credit analysis:* Accounting ratios have been used successfully to predict bankruptcy (see Appendix 4A); (b) *risk analysis:* The use of accounting ratios in risk analysis is particularly prevalent with respect to bond ratings (see Chapter 13).

SUMMARY

A firm's accounting information is used in the financial decision-making process, in particular four major financial statements: (a) income statement, (b) balance sheet, (c) statement of retained earnings, (d) statement of changes in financial position. Other necessary tools for financial analysis are the concept of the flow of funds, and the role of depreciation as a "source" of funds.

The basic tools of financial ratio analysis can be divided into five categories: (a) liquidity ratios, (b) debt-management ratios, (c) efficiency ratios, (d) profitability ratios, and (e) market ratios. The Dupont chart shows the interaction among the various ratios.

Ratio analysis is designed to raise, rather than answer, questions about a firm's performance. It is particularly useful for the analysis of a firm over time, or for comparison with other firms within the same industry. But like all financial tools, it must be used with caution.

There are some real differences between the accounting and economic concepts of income. Modern financial management rests on the economic concept of *cash flow*. Traditional financial ratio analysis is derived from accounting statements prepared on an accrual, rather than on a cash, basis. As a result, the ratios are often difficult to interpret. Another difficulty stems from the fact that financial management is concerned primarily with the future. In the next chapter we examine some methods for projecting financial ratio analysis into the future, so that it can be used as an aid for current decision-making.

APPENDIX 4A: | Predicting Financial Failure

One of the best known approaches to the problem of predicting financial failure is that of Edward Altman, who combines a number of financial ratios simultaneously in an effort to determine a firm's failure potential. This technique is called the Z-score model[1] and the weights given to each ratio are appropriate for manufacturing firms. The model is expressed as follows:

$$Z = 1.2X_1 + 1.4X_2 + 3.3X_3 + 0.6X_4 + 0.99X_5$$

where

X_1 = working capital/total assets
X_2 = retained earnings/total assets
X_3 = earnings before interest and taxes/total assets
X_4 = market value of preferred and common equity/total liabilities
X_5 = sales/total assets

Working Capital/Total Assets (X_1). The ratio of working capital (current assets less current liabilities) to total assets is a ratio which reflects liquidity and size characteristics. A firm that suffers continuing operating losses will find its working capital shrinking relative to its total assets.

Retained Earnings/Total assets (X_2). This ratio measures a firm's cumulative profitability over time. As such, it also reflects a firm's age. A young firm will have a low ratio, since it has not had the time to accumulate retained earnings. Hence the analysis is biased against young firms which have a greater chance of displaying a *low* retained earnings to total assets ratio than do older firms. But this accurately reflects the empirical evidence. The incidence of financial failure is significantly higher during firms' earlier years.

EBIT/Total Assets (X_3). This ratio measures the productivity of a firm's assets after abstracting from tax and financing effects. In essence, it measures a firm's earning power, which is the ultimate safeguard against financial failure.

Market Value of Equity/Total Liabilities (X_4). The numerator of this ratio is calculated by multiplying the number outstanding of each type of share (common and preferred) by their market prices. The denominator is the book value of current plus long-term liabilities. This ratio measures the degree to which the value of the firm can decline before it becomes insolvent. Since market value appears to provide a more effective predictor of bankruptcy, the market value of equity is substituted for the more commonly used book value of accounting net worth.

Sales/Total Assets (X_5). This turnover ratio measures a firm's ability to generate sales, and presumably reflects its ability to deal with competitive conditions.[2]

The interpretation of the Altman model is straightforward: The lower the Z-score, the higher a firm's failure potential. Any firm with a Z-score below 1.8 is considered a prime candidate for bankruptcy. To clarify the use of the model, we apply it, in Table 4A–1, to the data for the Metro Manufacturing Company. As can be seen from the table, Metro's Z-score is a robust 3.8185, comfortably above the critical value.

The Z-score model, or variants on the same theme, have been applied not only in the United States, but in many other countries as well, such as

---

[1] See Edward I. Altman, *Corporate Financial Distress* (New York: Wiley, 1983). Numerous variants of the Z-score model have been developed, but unlike the original model they are not in the public domain.

The weights assigned to each ratio were derived by Altman using multivariate discriminate analysis.

[2] Curiously, this ratio taken by itself is the least significant of the five; however, when combined with the other four, it ranks second in its contribution to the aggregate discriminating ability of the model.

TABLE 4A–1   Analysis of Metro Manufacturing Company Using the Z-Score Model

Ratio (1)	Value in Current Year (2)	Z-Score Model Coefficient (3)	Contribution to Z-Score (2) × (3) = (4)
X_1	$\dfrac{2,841}{30,715} = 0.0925$	1.2	0.1110
X_2	$\dfrac{14,453}{30,715} = 0.4706$	1.4	0.6588
X_3	$\dfrac{4,788}{30,715} = 0.1559$	3.3	0.5145
X_4^*	$\dfrac{19,453}{11,262} = 1.7273$	0.6	1.0364
X_5	$\dfrac{46,470}{30,715} = 1.5129$	0.99	1.4978
		Z-score	$\overline{\underline{3.8185}}$

* On the assumption that Metro's shares were selling in the market at book value.

Australia, Brazil, Canada, England, France, Germany, Ireland, Japan, and the Netherlands.[3] Although there is considerable variation among the scores of the different countries, in all cases the "failed groups" have much lower Z-scores than their "nonfailed" counterparts. And in all countries, the overall average Z-score of firms that subsequently failed is below the critical value of 1.8.

[3] See Edward I. Altman, "The Success of Business Failure Prediction Models: An International Survey," *Occasional Paper* No. 5, Salomon Brothers Center for the Study of Financial Institutions, Graduate School of Business Administration, New York University, 1983.

REVIEW EXERCISE

Circle the correct word(s) to complete each sentence; see page 86 for the correct answers.

4.1 An accountant can measure the realized profit during the last year by examining the *balance sheet/income statement*.

4.2 The statement which presents the assets and claims at the end of the year is called the *balance sheet/income statement*.

4.3 The left-hand side of the balance sheet sets out the firm's *assets/claims* in *ascending/descending* order of liquidity.

4.4 Current assets can be converted into cash within *one/two/three* years.

4.5 The right-hand side of the balance sheet lists the *assets/claims* against these *assets/claims* in *ascending/descending* order of liquidity.

4.6 Retained earnings are the part of net earnings which *are/are not* paid out as dividends.

4.7 In flow of funds analysis, increases in claims or decreases in assets are *sources/uses* of funds.

4.8 The depreciation allowance *is/is not* a cash outflow; it *is/is not* an expense.

4.9 Cash flow equals net income *plus/minus* depreciation.

4.10 Each financial ratio should *be presented in a graph/be compared to a benchmark.*

4.11 The calculation of ratios *is/is not* a substitute for further analysis.

4.12 A high current ratio is *always/not always* a sign of good management.

4.13 The accountant is usually concerned with measuring *past/future* earnings; the economist's concern is with *past/future* earnings.

QUESTIONS

4.1 Define the following:
a. Income statement; balance sheet
b. Current assets; current liabilities
c. Net working capital
d. Fundamental equation of accounting
e. Statement of changes in financial position
f. Straight-line depreciation (SLD)
g. Cash flow
h. Trend analysis; common size financial statements
i. The Dupont equations to derive return on assets and return on equity
j. "Window dressing"

4.2 Define the following financial ratios:
a. Current ratio; quick (acid test) ratio
b. Debt ratio; times interest earned (TIE) ratio
c. Inventory turnover; average collection period (ACP); fixed asset turnover; total asset turnover
d. Gross profit margin; return on assets (ROA); return on equity (ROE)
e. Earnings per share (EPS); price/earnings ratio

4.3 Rank the following assets in decreasing order of liquidity:
a. A plot of land
b. A Treasury bill
c. One share of IBM stock
d. 200 pounds of flour
e. A custom-made machine (paid for in full, but not yet delivered)

4.4 Evaluate the following statement by the chairman of the board in a speech at the annual stockholders' meeting: "Last year we showed an accounting loss. But there's nothing to worry about: After adding back depreciation, we were actually quite profitable."

4.5 Classify the following as sources or uses of funds:
a. Increase in inventory
b. Decrease in long-term debt
c. Decrease in retained earnings
d. Increase in receivables
e. Increase in payables
f. Decrease in plant and equipment
g. Decrease in cash

    h. Increase in accrued taxes
    i. Increase in common stock
    j. Decrease in marketable securities
    k. Increase in depreciation

4.6 Give the pros and cons of a low net working capital position.

4.7 How do cross-sectional analyses of accounting ratios differ from time series analyses?

4.8 What do the following ratios of the ABC Company imply? ("High" and "low" are relative to the industry average.)
    a. High current ratio and low quick ratio
    b. Low debt ratio and low "times interest earned" ratio (you may have to make some assumptions.).
    c. High gross profit margin, low operating profit margin, and high net profit margin
    d. Low return on assets and high return on equity

4.9 Explain the difference between accounting profit and economic profit.

4.10 List and explain the principal limitations of financial ratio analysis.

4.11 Explain the use of "window dressing" to improve the current ratio when the latter is (a) less than 1 and (b) greater than 1.

PROBLEMS

4.1 **Earnings per share.** Last year your company had sales of $1.6 million. Cost of goods sold and all other expenses amounted to $1.3 million. The corporate tax rate is 34%, and there are 200,000 shares outstanding. (a) What are the pretax and after-tax earnings per share? (b) What are the earnings per share if the corporate tax rate is 39%?

4.2 **Income statement.** Blue & White's sales amounted to $150,000. Cost of goods sold made up 80% of sales, and all other operating expenses amounted to 10% of sales. Blue & White is subject to a 34% corporate tax rate, and paid $40,000 in taxes. The company had a $50,000 loan outstanding. What interest rate did Blue & White pay on this loan? What is its net profit margin?

4.3 **Balance sheet.** A company has total assets of $93 million and liabilities of $55 million. What is the book value of the shareholders' equity?

4.4 **Balance sheet.** The Cornwall Corporation had current assets of $10,000 and net plant and equipment of $90,000 at the beginning of 1987. The company had no other assets. It had $30,000 of debt outstanding; the remainder of its assets were financed by equity. In 1987, Cornwall bought $50,000 worth of new equipment, and the annual depreciation allowance was $20,000 on the old equipment. Due to this purchase, current assets were decreased by $5,000. The debt ratio remained constant. Complete the 1987 balance sheet. How was the equipment purchase financed?

4.5 **Financial statements.** The following is the balance sheet of the Coldwater Company on December 31, 1986.

Cash		50
Marketable securities		150
Accounts receivable		200
Inventory		200
Plant and equipment	1,500	
Depreciation	500	
Net plant and equipment		1,000
Total assets		1,600
Accounts payable		150
Long-term debt		600
Common stock		250
Retained earnings		600
Total liabilities		1,600

During 1987 Coldwater earned net after-tax profits of $200, of which $150 were paid out as dividends. Accumulated depreciation rose by $60, $40 of marketable securities were bought, and accounts receivable increased by $100. A new machine was acquired for $120, and accounts payable increased. All other accounts in the balance sheet remained unchanged. (a) Set out the company's balance sheet as of December 31, 1987. (b) Prepare a Sources and Uses of Funds statement.

4.6   **Sources and uses of funds.**   (a) Classify the following changes in the balance sheet as sources or uses of funds: accounts receivable increased by $50,000; accounts payable increased by $35,000; gross plant and equipment increased by $75,000; accumulated depreciation increased by $18,000. (b) you are given the following additional information: net income for the year was $36,000; $28,000 was paid out as cash dividends; inventories decreased by $50,000; and accrued taxes increased by $14,000. Prepare a statement of Changes in Financial Position.

4.7   **Ratio analysis.**   The balance sheets and income statements of the Lester Corporation for the years 1985, 1986, and 1987 are given below.

The Lester Corporation: Balance Sheets (Millions of dollars)			
	1985	**1986**	**1987**
Inventories	50	50	60
Receivables	10	15	25
Prepaid expenses	10	12	18
Other current assets	60	63	52
Fixed assets	70	70	80
Total assets	200	225	235
Current liabilities	60	65	70
Long-term debt	70	80	85
Equity	70	75	80
Total liabilities	200	225	235

continued

The Lester Corporation: Income Statements (Millions of dollars)			
	1985	**1986**	**1987**
Sales	120	140	210
Cost of goods sold	90	100	160
Interest	20	25	25
Taxes	5	8	18
Earnings after interest and taxes	5	7	17

a. Compute the current ratio, quick ratio, net working capital, and the debt ratio for each of the three years.

b. Compute the profit margins and TIE ratio in each of the three years.

c. Compute the following mixed ratios: inventory turnover, average collection period, total asset turnover, return on assets, and return on equity for each of the three years.

4.8 Ratio analysis. A company's sales last year amounted to $1,168,000, and its average collection period was 10 days. This year sales rose by 9.4%, but the average collection period increased by 20%. Compute the accounts receivable in both years.

 4.9 Financial ratios, **computer problem.**

	Fortuna Corp.	Nanum Corp.	Sarula Corp.
Assets			
Current assets:			
Cash	780	290	480
Marketable securities	1,250	970	1,340
Accounts receivable	638	98	298
Inventories	4,876	2,154	987
Prepaid expenses	0	278	434
Fixed assets:			
Gross plant and equipment	12,567	4,398	6,566
Depreciation	3,200	876	1,250
Investments and misc. assets	2,864	421	870
Liabilities			
Accounts payable	455	612	129
Accrued taxes	128	0	63
Long-term debt	14,300	4,300	6,700
Other liabilities	1,215	324	728
Equity			
Common stock	3,000	2,000	1,500
Retained earnings	340	250	320
Other equity	337	247	285

continued

continued	Fortuna Corp.	Nanum Corp.	Sarula Corp.
Income Statement			
Sales	12,560	8,345	11,280
COGS	7,655	4,281	5,414
EBIT	3,430	2,089	1,867
Interest	1,523	976	1,111
Taxes	630	350	240

a. Compute the financial ratios for the three firms.

b. Compute the financial ratios on the assumption that each item in the financial statement of Fortuna is doubled; each item of Nanum is tripled; and those of Sarula are decreased by half. Compare your results with those of part (a).

4.10 Dupont chart.   Prepare Dupont charts for the three companies of problem 4.9. Note that "Prepaid expenses" are a current asset, and "Investment and misc. assets" are fixed assets. Depreciation for the current year amounts to 10% of accumulated depreciation; other operating expenses can be inferred from the income statement given in the previous problem.

PROBLEM FOR APPENDIX 4A

4A.1 What is Altman's Z-score for the three firms given in problem 4.9? Assume that the market value of equity is $4,200 for Fortuna, $2,850 for Nanum, and $2,430 for Sarula.

SAMPLE PROBLEM

SP4.1 Mr. Green spilled ink over the financial statements of Lavan Corporation. The information that is still readable is given below:

Lavan Corporation Income Statement	
Sales	2,500
Cost of goods sold	—
Other expenses	300
Earnings before interest and taxes	—
Interest on long-term debt	—
Taxes	—
After-tax earnings	—

continued

Lavan Corporation Balance Sheet	
Cash	50
Accounts receivable	—
Inventories	400
Plant and equipment (net)	2,000
Total assets	—
Accounts payable	—
Long-term debt	—
Common stock	—
Total liabilities and equity	—

In addition, the following is known:

☐   Inventory turnover = 5
☐   Average collection period = 29.2 days
☐   Accounts payable = 40% of accounts receivable
☐   Interest on long-term debt = 8.2%
☐   Tax rate = 34%
☐   Debt ratio = 36.6%

What is the net profit margin?

Solution to Sample Problem   SP4.1

Income Statement		
Sales	2,500	
Cost of goods sold	2,000	(a)
Other expenses	300	
Earnings before interest and taxes	200	(b)
Interest on long-term debt	80	(i)
Taxes	40	(j)
After-tax earnings	40	(k)

Balance Sheet		
Cash	50	
Accounts receivable	200	(c)
Inventories	400	
Plant and equipment (net)	2,000	
Total assets	2,650	(d)
Accounts payable	80	(e)
Long-term debt	970	(f)
Common stock	1,600	(h)
Total liabilities and equity	2,650	(g)

a. Inventory turnover = cost of goods sold/inventory. Cost of goods sold = inventory turnover × inventory = 5 × 400 = 2,000.

b. Earnings before interest and taxes = sales − COGS − other expenses
$$= 2,500 - 2,000 - 300 = 200$$

c. Collection period = accounts receivable/(sales/365). accounts receivable
= collection period × (sales/365) = 29.2 × (2,500/365)
= 29.2 × 6.85 = 200.

d. Total assets = cash + receivables + inventories + plant and equipment
$$= 50 + 200 + 400 + 2,000 = 2,650$$

e. Accounts payable = 40% of accounts receivable = 0.4 × 200 = 80.

f. Long-term debt = debt ratio × total assets = 0.366 × 2,650 = 970.

g. Total liabilities and owners' equity = total assets = 2,650.

h. Common stock = total liabilities and owners' equity − debt − accounts
payable = 2,650 − 970 − 80 = 1,600.

i. Interest = long-term debt × interest rate = 970 × 8.2% = 80.

j. Taxes = 34% on earnings after interest = 34% × (EBIT − interest)
= 34% × (200 − 80) = 0.34 × 120 = 41

k. Net earnings = EBIT − interest − taxes = 200 − 80 − 41 = 39.
Hence the net profit margin is 1.6 percent (39/2,500 = 1.6%).

**Answers
to Review
Exercise**

4.1 income statement   **4.2** balance sheet   **4.3** assets, descending
4.4 one   **4.5** claims, assets, descending   **4.6** are not   **4.7** sources
4.8 is not, is   **4.9** plus   **4.10** be compared to a benchmark
4.11 is not   **4.12** not always   **4.13** past, future

SUGGESTIONS FOR FURTHER READING

The conceptual foundations of financial analysis are examined in many accounting textbooks. Comprehensive reviews can be found in: George Foster, *Financial Statement Analysis*, 2nd ed. (Englewood Cliffs, NJ: Prentice-Hall, 1986), and Baruch Lev, *Financial Statement Analysis: A New Approach* (Englewood Cliffs, NJ: Prentice-Hall, 1974).

Annually updated ratios are published by Dun & Bradstreet, *Key Business Ratios*, New York, annual edition; and Robert Morris Associates, *Annual Statement Studies*, Philadelphia, annual edition.

The application of financial ratio analysis to the prediction of financial failure was pioneered by these researchers: Edward I. Altman, "Financial Ratios, Discriminant Analysis and the Prediction of Corporate Bankruptcy," *Journal of Finance*, September 1968; William Beaver, "Financial Ratios as Predictors of Failure," *Empirical Research in Accounting: Selected Studies, 1966*, Supplement to vol. 4, *Journal of Accounting Research;* and Meir Tamari, "Financial Ratios as a Means of Forecasting Bankruptcy," *Management International Review*, Vol. 4, 1966.

The difference between accounting and economic income has been the subject of countless books and articles, but a short and readable proposal to eliminate most of the differences is given by Robert N. Anthony in "Accounting Rates of Return: Note," *American Economic Review* (March 1986), pp. 244–46.

5 Financial Forecasting and Planning

Anyone who claims he can predict the future is lying—even if he thinks he is telling the truth.

Anon

From time immemorial, people have tried to predict (and influence) the future, and the ability to do so was often ascribed to the possession of magical powers. A typical method was to try to connect, or correlate, certain events or signs from the past with events in the future. Roman priests, for instance, thought that the intestines of a sacrificed animal were an indicator of coming events, and gypsies still believe that the shape of tea leaves left in a cup can be used to predict the future. Astrologers are convinced that the configuration of stars at a certain date, definitely a foreseeable event, can be connected with other, less foreseeable events (that is, less foreseeable only for those of us who are not well versed in astrology). The most recent descendants of this line of priests, magicians, witches, and other claimants to supernatural powers are today's econometricians and statistical analysts. Fortunately, their techniques are not as esoteric as those of the Roman priests. In fact, many are common knowledge to anyone who has had a basic course in statistics. In this chapter we describe and apply some of these methods to the problem of financial forecasting, with special emphasis on the short term—that is, on next year.

BENEFITS OF FORECASTING

Almost all firms forecast their future needs for funds. The real question is not whether to forecast, but rather how systematic and detailed the projections should be. Like any forward planning exercise, financial forecasting requires time, energy, and cooperation with nonfinancial executives. And like any other use of a firm's resources, the time and effort invested in making the forecasts must be weighed against the prospective benefits.

Control

The forecast provides an effective device for management control. It is helpful in discovering, and dealing with, significant deviations from corporate plans. For example, forecasted levels of sales may serve as checkpoints against which actual results can be compared; and if necessary, existing plans can be revised or amended.

Pretesting

Forecasting future fund requirements allows management to simulate, in advance, the financial impact of various programs *before* making a binding commitment of resources. At times, this can be crucial. Funds are not unlimited, and often plans have to be recast to conform with the firm's financial resources, and not the other way around. This is obvious when major projects are involved, but sometimes even a group of diverse small needs can have a disastrous *cumulative* effect on the firm's financial position.

Raising Additional Capital

Effective forecasting can facilitate the raising of needed funds in at least two ways:

1. The advance warning provided by the forecast is useful in negotiating with suppliers of capital, especially in those instances in which the raising of the capital requires time—for example, a new issue of shares.

2. Neither commercial nor investment bankers like to be taken by surprise. Even the most hardened bank loan officer tends to be impressed by a financial executive who presents the firm's financial requirements *before* they are actually needed. Lenders' confidence in management is a delicate commodity, and its importance should not be overlooked.

FORECASTING USING PRO FORMA FINANCIAL STATEMENTS

Toward the end of the financial year, or at some time earlier, the top management of most companies would like to have an estimate of what next year's income statement and balance sheet will look like. This is crucial if plans are to be made in an orderly manner. Personnel needs to know how many people to hire, Purchasing may want to negotiate for quantity discounts on raw materials, Accounting will want to have enough cash on hand at the time it is required, Budgeting needs to know how many additional machines will be required, and so on.

The most commonly used method to forecast next year's financial statements are *pro forma* balance sheets and income statements using the **percentage of sales method.**

The Percentage of Sales Method

percentage of sales method
A method of forecasting a company's financial statement that involves estimating key balance sheet items at some specified future date.

The pro forma financial statements are based on a forecast of key balance sheet items at some specified future date. Four major steps can be identified in the preparation of these statements:

1. Estimate alternative levels for next year's sales.
2. Identify the items that depend directly on sales and calculate the relationships for each sales forecast.
3. "Plug the holes" by estimating those items which are not directly related to sales and were not estimated in step 2.
4. Balance the balance sheet. This requires deciding how the firm's activities are to be financed.

STEP ONE: The first step consists of identifying the items in the financial statements that are directly related to sales. Next, the value of these items as a percentage of the year's sales is computed. Table 5–1 shows the income statement and balance sheet of Metro Manufacturing for the current year as they were given in Chapter 4. Whenever applicable, we also give in the right-hand column of the table the coefficients that will be used as the basis for the percentage of sales method. These figures have been expressed as a percentage of the year's sales; hence the name of the method. For example, Labor and Materials (the cost of goods sold) are expected to comprise 80.7% of sales; Inventories are expected to remain 12.9% of sales; and so on. Items not directly related to sales are left blank and marked N/A for "not applicable."

STEP TWO: The next step is to estimate next year's sales. At this stage of the process it is likely to be no more than a crude guess. Often three such estimates—optimistic, reasonable, and pessimistic—are given. Then the items in the income statement are related to these sales forecasts, using the percentage coefficients from Table 5–1. This has been done in Table 5–2, which presents *projected figures* for next year based on the three alternative sales forecasts. For example, in the pessimistic case, Labor and Materials are projected as 80.7% of $48,000, or $38,736.

STEP THREE: The next step is to "plug" figures into the "holes" (denoted by N/A) which have been left in the projected financial statements. These items are not directly related to sales revenue; for example, Depreciation, Plant and Equipment, and Liabilities. To plug these holes, further information is needed. What investments in equipment are planned for the next year? Given our use of straight-line methods, what will next year's allowance for depreciation be? How will all of this affect the tax bill?

TABLE 5–1   Metro Manufacturing Company

Income Statement for Current Year

	Thousands $	Percentage of Sales
Net Sales	46,470	**100.0**
Expenses: Labor and materials (COGS)	37,505	80.7
Depreciation	877	N/A
Other expenses	3,300	**7.1**
Operating Income (EBIT)	4,788	N/A
Interest	18	.4
Taxes	1,622	N/A
Net After-Tax Income	3,148	N/A

Balance Sheet for Current Year

	Thousands $	Percentage of Sales
Assets		
Cash	967	**2.1**
Marketable securities	3,973	N/A
Accounts receivable	1,349	**2.9**
Inventories	5,975	**12.9**
Prepaid expenses	196	**.4**
Total current assets	12,460	N/A
Gross plant and equipment	23,354	N/A
Less depreciation reserves	6,493	N/A
Net plant and equipment	16,861	N/A
Investment and misc. assets	1,394	N/A
Total Assets	30,715	N/A
Claims on Assets		
Accounts payable	6,831	**14.7**
Accrued taxes	2,788	N/A
Total current liabilities	9,619	N/A
Long-term debt	1,643	N/A
Equity:		
Common stock	5,000	N/A
Retained earnings	14,453	N/A
Total equity	19,453	N/A
Total Claims on Assets	30,715	N/A

STEP FOUR: Finally, we must determine how current operations and the proposed capital expansions will be financed (either by debt or by equity). An answer to this question is also needed to ensure that the projected balance sheet actually balances.

To illustrate this process, we shall make some assumptions about the items in steps three and four. The most important of these are that $547 of next year's estimated profit will be retained within the firm, thereby increasing retained earnings to $15,000, and that the remaining deficit will be financed by a new issue of long-term debt. Table 5–3 shows the complete projected financial statements, which are usually called *pro forma* financial

TABLE 5–2   Metro Manufacturing Company

Projected Income Statement for Next Year

	Scenarios		
	Pessimistic	Reasonable	Optimistic
Net Sales	48,000	52,000	60,000
Labor and materials (COGS)	38,736	41,964	48,420
Depreciation	N/A	N/A	N/A
Other expenses	3,408	3,692	4,260
Operating Income (EBIT)	N/A	N/A	N/A
Interest	192	208	240
Taxes	N/A	N/A	N/A
Net After-Tax Income	N/A	N/A	N/A

Projected Balance Sheet for Next Year

	Scenarios		
	Pessimistic	Reasonable	Optimistic
Assets			
Cash	1,008	1,092	1,260
Marketable securities	N/A	N/A	N/A
Accounts receivable	1,392	1,508	1,740
Inventories	6,192	6,708	7,740
Prepaid expenses	192	208	240
Total current assets	N/A	N/A	N/A
Gross plant and equipment	N/A	N/A	N/A
Less depreciation reserves	N/A	N/A	N/A
Net plant and equipment	N/A	N/A	N/A
Investments and misc. assets	N/A	N/A	N/A
Total Assets	N/A	N/A	N/A
Claims on Assets			
Accounts payable	7,065	7,644	8,820
Accrued taxes	N/A	N/A	N/A
Total current liabilities	N/A	N/A	N/A
Long-term debt	N/A	N/A	N/A
Equity:			
Common stock	N/A	N/A	N/A
Retained earnings	N/A	N/A	N/A
Total equity	N/A	N/A	N/A
Total Claims on Assets	N/A	N/A	N/A

statements. These statements provide management with an important tool for planning its capital requirements.

Refining the Estimates   Here we have simplified the process of preparing the pro forma statements in order to focus attention on the underlying logic. Clearly, many refinements can be, and often should be, made when forecasting individual balance sheet items:

1. *Receivables.* The ratio of receivables to sales can be adjusted to account for planned changes in credit policy.

TABLE 5–3   Metro Manufacturing Company

Pro Forma Income Statement for Next Year

	Scenarios		
	Pessimistic	Reasonable	Optimistic
Net Sales	48,000	52,000	60,000
Labor and materials (COGS)	38,736	41,964	48,420
Depreciation	850	850	850
Other expenses	3,408	3,692	4,260
Operating Income (EBIT)	5,006	5,494	6,470
Interest	192	208	240
Taxes (34%)	1,637	1,797	2,118
Net After-Tax Income	3,177	3,489	4,112

Pro Forma Balance Sheet for Next Year

	Scenarios		
	Pessimistic	Reasonable	Optimistic
Assets			
Cash	1,008	1,092	1,260
Marketable securities	4,000	4,000	4,000
Accounts receivable	1,392	1,508	1,740
Inventories	6,192	6,708	7,740
Prepaid expenses	192	208	240
Total current assets	12,784	13,516	14,980
Gross plant and equipment	25,000	25,000	25,000
Less depreciation reserves	7,000	7,000	7,000
Net plant and equipment	18,000	18,000	18,000
Investments and misc. assets	1,000	1,000	1,000
Total Assets	31,784	32,516	33,980
Claims on Assets			
Accounts payable	7,065	7,644	8,820
Accrued taxes	3,000	3,000	3,000
Total current liabilities	10,065	10,644	11,820
Long-term debt	1,719	1,872	2,160
Equity:			
Common stock	5,000	5,000	5,000
Retained earnings	15,000	15,000	15,000
Total equity	20,000	20,000	20,000
Total Claims on Assets	31,784	32,516	33,980

2. *Inventory and Cash Balances.* A projected increase in sales may not re-quire a proportional increase in inventory or in cash balances. Often important economies of scale can be exploited when a firm expands its operations (see Chapters 17 and 18).

3. *Accounts Payable.* The estimate can be improved by preparing a detailed schedule of purchases and estimating the terms that will be offered by suppliers. Here again, if we are to increase our purchases, we may be in a better position to negotiate better credit items. This, in turn, will decrease the projected ratio of payables to sales.

RATIO ANALYSIS OF PRO FORMA STATEMENTS

How should these pro forma financial statements be interpreted? One way is to apply the technique of financial ratio analysis, described in Chapter 4, to the pro forma financial statements. Table 5–4 summarizes the results of this analysis.

Liquidity.   In all three sales forecasts—pessimistic, reasonable, and optimistic—a decline in the current ratio from 1.3 to 1.27 is expected. The picture is somewhat different with respect to net working capital. The latter is expected to decrease only in the case of the pessimistic forecast.

Long-term Debt.   Metro's projected ratio of long-term debt to total assets is also expected to rise in the two more favorable sales forecasts.

Fixed Asset Turnover.   Here too Metro is projecting a more efficient use of fixed assets if the favorable sales forecasts materialize. However, the ratio of sales to fixed assets is expected to fall in the case of the pessimistic forecast.

Profitability.   Metro's net profit margin on sales, its net return on assets (ROA), and the net return on equity (ROE) are all expected to rise even in the most pessimistic of the forecasts. (Clearly, we would want to check the economic arguments underlying these projections.) Especially noteworthy is the rise in ROE, from 16.18% to 20.56%, should the optimistic forecast prove correct. The projected profitability ratios clearly show the importance of the sales forecast for Metro's future financial position.

The astute reader will have noticed that neither the inventory turnover nor average collection period of receivables were discussed. This is not an oversight. Both inventories and accounts receivable were estimated in the

TABLE 5–4   **Metro Manufacturing Company Selected Ratios from the Pro Forma Financial Statements**

Ratio	Current Year	Scenarios		
		Pessimistic	**Reasonable**	**Optimistic**
Current ratio	1.30	1.27	1.27	1.27
Net working capital	$2,841	$2,719	$2,872	$3,160
Debt ratio	0.37	0.37	0.39	0.41
Fixed asset turnover	2.76	2.67	2.89	3.33
Profit margin	6.77	6.62	6.71	6.85
Return on assets (ROA)	10.25	10.00	10.73	12.10
Return on equity (ROE)	16.18	15.89	17.45	20.56

pro forma balance sheet as fixed percentages of sales. The same holds true for cost of goods sold. Thus, when dividing cost of goods sold (or sales) by inventories in order to compute the turnover, the results simply reflect the method used to forecast the inventories in the pro forma balance sheet. The analysis of such a ratio may therefore be subject to the charge of circular reasoning. The same argument holds for the average collection period of receivables. One solution is to drop the simple assumption that the percentage relationship is stable. In many instances, the forecaster will probably wish to substitute different percentages in the various projections to reflect more accurately the impact of increases in sales on inventory and credit policy.

To sum up, Metro's pro forma financial statements look quite reasonable, and indeed they provide a fairly good picture, considering the limited effort expended in their preparation. This approach, however, has some serious shortcomings. The pro forma balance sheet estimates fund requirements as of a particular date; it tells us nothing about interim needs. A firm's projected financial statements are not a substitute for the detailed forecasting of cash flows. The latter, however, is essentially a short-term (month-to-month, or week-to-week) problem of cash management, and therefore is discussed in Part VI of this book (Chapter 18).

The simple percentage of sales method is most useful when detailed information is lacking, so that projections have to be made on the basis of limited information. For example, consider a firm that asks itself how much additional financing will be needed, should sales double next year. A projection using the percentage of sales method is a very good *first step*, but it really can not be expected to provide comprehensive answers to all of our questions.

FORECASTING USING STATISTICAL METHODS

The pro forma financial statements depend on the level of projected sales. Even the cautious approach of giving three alternative estimates is not satisfactory. In view of the importance of the sales forecast, most financial managers will demand more reliable estimates than someone's best guesses. In this section we describe a more sophisticated approach using statistical methods. Of course, other items of the financial statements can also be forecast in the same manner. The simple percentage of sales method should not be used whenever statistical estimation will give a better picture. For example, next year's raw material prices, and not just sales, might be estimated from statistical data. However, the interrelationships among different items must always be kept in mind. A new production line might have to be built for every additional 100,000 units of sales; or, for example, while the size of the board of directors stays constant, independent of sales, the salaries of the members may not.

If it is known that the size of one variable depends on the size of another, statistical **regression analysis** can be used to help us make predictions about one variable, based on the behavior of the others. When one of the variables is time, we are forecasting in the true sense of the word. This is known as *time series analysis*. In this chapter, we will illustrate the general problem of estimating the relationship between any two variables.

regression analysis
A method of statistical analysis used to make predictions about one variable when the behavior of the others is known.

Curve Fitting

Consider a supermarket chain with a number of outlets. First, we collect data on sales area and annual sales for each outlet. Common sense suggests that the magnitude of sales is probably greater the larger the sales area. But what is the exact form of the relationship? And how can we express it mathematically? As a first step, we plot the data for each outlet in a coordinate system. Figure 5–1 presents such a scatterplot. Each point represents the amount of sales and sales area for each outlet. We can immediately see that in this case, our intuition was correct; sales tend to be higher, the larger the selling area. However, we often wish to be more precise about the relationship. For this purpose, C. F. Gauss,[1] the great nineteenth-century mathematician, invented the method known as *least squares*.

Goodness of Fit

The problem Gauss wanted to solve was to find the line that fits best through a group of points. Actually this problem has two related aspects. Before finding the best straight line, we must first define what is meant by "best." Intuitively, an obvious definition of the best line is the one that cuts through Figure 5–1 in such a way as to minimize the sum of the distances between

[1] Gauss was one of the great geniuses in the history of mathematics. Curiously, one of his most amazing intellectual achievements took place when he was 3, when he corrected a mistake in his father's bookkeeping.

**FIGURE 5–1
Relationship of
Sales to Floor
Space**

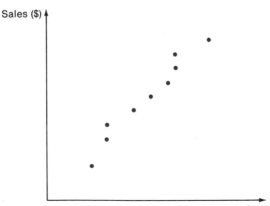

Sales ($)

Floor space (square feet)

the line and all the scatterpoints. However, in this instance intuition is misleading. Any straight line that offsets the positive deviations against the negative ones would be considered an excellent fit. Thus, one could have a perfectly good fit as long as the points above the line were about as far off the line as the points below, independent of the absolute size of the deviations. This consideration led Gauss to define the measure of the goodness of fit as the *sum of the squares* of the distances between the points and the line in question. In this case, the deviations are squared and therefore are all positive; hence the smaller the squared deviations, the better the fit.

The Method of Least Squares

Having decided on a measure of goodness of fit, it was just a small step for Gauss to find the exact formula for the line that actually minimizes the sum of the squared deviations; hence the name *least squares*. The line he was looking for has this form:

$$y = a + bx$$

where y is the dependent variable (in our example, sales) which is to be explained by the independent variable, x (in our example, sales area). Least squares regression analysis is designed to help us find the values for a and b which result in the line with the best fit (with the smallest sum of the squared deviations). The expressions Gauss computed for the two coefficients, a and b, are [2]

$$b = \Sigma xy - \bar{x}\Sigma y \div (\Sigma x^2 - \bar{x}\Sigma x)$$
$$a = \bar{y} - b\bar{x}$$

where $\bar{x}$ and $\bar{y}$ denote the means for all observed values of the independent and dependent variables, and Σx, Σy, and Σxy stand for the summation of all xs, ys, and xys, respectively. Note that a is the intercept on the y axis, and b is the slope of the linear regression line, $y = a + bx$.

The least squares formula has the advantage of being easy to calculate. Table 5–5 gives hypothetical observations for two variables, x and y. Using the least squares formula, the coefficients a and b are:

$$b = \frac{6{,}465 - 23.7(216)}{4{,}594 - 23.7(142)} = 1.1$$
$$a = 36 - 1.1\,(23.7) = 10.0$$

The least squares regression line is given by the equation

$$y = 10 + 1.1x$$

---

[2] The coefficient b is the ratio of the covariance of x and y to the variance of x. An equivalent formula, which can be used to find b, is

$$b = \frac{\Sigma xy - n\bar{x}\bar{y}}{\Sigma x^2 - n\bar{x}^2}$$

where n is the number of observations.

TABLE 5–5   A Numerical Example

Number of Observations	Observed Values				
	x	y	x^2	y^2	xy
1	30	44	900	1,936	1,320
2	18	26	324	676	468
3	51	67	2,601	4,489	3,417
4	7	12	49	144	84
5	24	31	576	961	744
6	12	36	144	1,296	432
Total	142	216	4,594	9,502	6,465
Mean	23.7	36	765.7	1,583.7	1,077.5

coefficient of determination (R^2)
A statistical measure that tells what percentage of the variation of the data from their mean is explained by the regression line.

Often we would like to know how "good" our regression line really is. Does it explain a little or a lot of the behavior of the dependent variable? In other words, is it likely to be useful for prediction?

A simple measure can be used to answer this question. It is called the **coefficient of determination**, and is usually known as **R square**, or simply R^2. This coefficient provides a quantitative measure of the goodness of fit of the regression line. It tells us what percentage of the variation of the data points from their mean is explained by the regression line. For example, an R square of 1 would mean that all the variation is explained by the regression line. In such a case, all the data points would lie exactly on the regression line. An R^2 of, say, 0.80 means that 80% of the deviation of the dependent variable, in our case y, from its mean is explained by the regression line; the remaining 20% would have to be accounted for by other factors, or are just random "noise."

In the numerical example given in Table 5–5, the R square is 0.86; that is, 86% of the variation around the mean is explained by the regression line.[3]

FORECASTING SALES

We can demonstrate the use of regression analysis by applying it to Metro's need for a forecast of next year's sales of leisure vehicles. Table 5–6 sets out selected economic data collected by Metro's marketing division for the 12

---

[3] The formula for the coefficient of determination is

$$R^2 = \frac{[\Sigma xy - \bar{x}\Sigma y]^2}{(\Sigma x^2 - \bar{x}\Sigma x)(\Sigma y^2 - \bar{y}\Sigma y)}$$

Applying the formula to the numerical example of Table 5–5, we have

$$R^2 = \frac{[6,465 - (23.7)216]^2}{[4,594 - (23.7)142][9,502 - (36)216]}$$

$$= \frac{(1,345.8)^2}{(1,228.6)(1,726)} = .86$$

years preceding the forecast. Now assume that Metro wants to use these data to forecast next year's sales of leisure vehicles. To get a grasp of the overall picture, even before any calculations, we plot the data of Table 5–6 in Figure 5–2.

We then use a ruler to trace straight lines through the data points, and we mark the points where we believe next year's values will lie. This simple but helpful method is often called "eyeballing" and provides the following estimates:

Sales	$1,700 million
Gross national product	$3,150 billion

Of course, these estimates are not exact. Good forecasts are usually available for such important economic variables as GNP; however, for the purpose of our example, we will use the figures above.

Now let us be a little more sophisticated in our forecast of sales and compute the relationship between the sales of leisure vehicles and the other economic variable. We can, for example, predict next year's demand as a function of our forecast GNP, rather than simply projecting sales on the basis of the market's performance of the last few years. Applying the method of least squares, we define sales in millions of dollars as the dependent variable, and gross national product in billions of dollars as the independent variable. The regression equation is then

$$\text{sales} = -210 + 0.58 \text{ (GNP)}$$
$$R \text{ square} = 0.99$$

If we now insert the previously estimated value for next year's GNP into the formulas, the sales forecast is as follows:

$$\text{forecast sales} = \$ 1.617 \text{ million}$$

TABLE 5–6   Sales and GNP

Year	Sales of Leisure Vehicles ($ million)	GNP ($ billion)
1	$ 400	$ 993
2	430	1,078
3	480	1,186
4	550	1,326
5	620	1,434
6	690	1,549
7	790	1,718
8	900	1,918
9	1,020	2,164
10	1,160	2,418
11	1,360	2,633
12	1,530	2,938

FIGURE 5–2
Annual Sales
and GNP

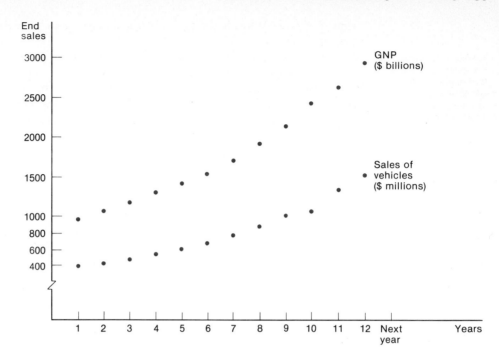

The coefficient of determination, R^2, is very high, which would indicate a very good fit. However, one must be extremely cautious when interpreting such regression equations.[4] A good rule to follow is to never compute regressions without first having a theory about why the dependent variable (sales in our example) should depend on the independent variable (GNP).

SENSITIVITY ANALYSIS AND ELECTRONIC SPREADSHEETS

To this point we have seen how a pro forma balance sheet can be prepared using the percentage of sales method, and how selected items of the financial statements can be forecast using regression analysis. Both methods rely on certain assumptions. For example, the percentage of sales method depends on the assumed sales for next year. The regression analysis depends on the values of the coefficients a and b. In this section, we consider questions of this type: What happens to projected profits if sales turn out to be 10% less

---

[4] Naive forecasting may result in very high values for R^2. This is often due to the fact that many variables tend to grow together over time. Hence caution should be exercised in interpreting regression results.

than forecast? What is the demand for leisure vehicles if the regression coefficient *b* turns out to be 1.2 instead of 1.1?

sensitivity analysis
A method of analysis that examines the sensitivity of the results to changes in initial assumptions.

One method for handling such questions is called **sensitivity analysis.** It examines the sensitivity of the results to changes in the initial assumptions. First, the way the item in question influences the result is determined; then we make alternative assumptions about the item, and observe the impact on the initial result. If large changes in an assumption have only a small effect on the results, we say that the result is *robust* (insensitive) with respect to that assumption. In such cases, there is no need to expend a great deal of effort on refining the assumption. The opposite conclusion holds for the case in which even slight changes in an assumption lead to drastic changes in results. Here the result is very sensitive to the assumption, and therefore it often pays to make a maximum effort to refine the initial assumptions.

Sensitivity analysis can be illustrated by a numerical example using the net earnings entry of the pro forma income statement given in column 1 of Table 5–7. Net after-tax earnings have been projected as $12,540. What happens to net earnings when we change one of the underlying assumptions?

Case A: Should sales rise 20% more than forecast, to $120,000, net earnings would increase by slightly more than 20% to $15,180 (see column 2 of Table 5–7).

Case B: Should the cost of goods sold rise from 80% to 85% of sales, net earnings would drop by 26% to $9,240 (see column 3 of Table 5–7).

Case C: Should interest payments increase by 50% to $1,500, net after-tax earnings would fall to $12,210, which is a decrease in profits of only 2.5% (see column 4 of Table 5–7). In this case, we have little incentive to expend great effort on improving the forecast of interest rates.

TABLE 5–7   Pro Forma Income Statements for Next Year

	Original Estimate (1)	Increase in Sales (2)	Increase in COGS (3)	Increase in Interest (4)
Sales	$100,000	$120,000	$100,000	$100,000
COGS	80,000	96,000	85,000	80,000
Interest	1,000	1,000	1,000	1,500
Earnings before taxes	$ 19,000	$ 23,000	$ 14,000	$ 18,500
Taxes (34%)	6,460	7,820	4,760	6,290
Net after-tax earnings	$ 12,540	$ 15,180	$ 9,240	$ 12,210

One difficulty with sensitivity analysis is the need for numerous computations, especially when many variations in assumptions have to be explored, or when a number of assumptions must be changed simultaneously. Luckily, many computer software packages perform sensitivity analyses in seconds, no matter how many assumptions are changed. These programs, or *electronic spreadsheets* as they are usually called, consist of a matrix of columns and rows. Each cell has to be filled by the analyst with a number, or with a formula that links the numbers from other cells. When one cell is changed, all other cells which depend on it are automatically changed.

Tables 5–8 and 5–9 give a numerical illustration of how this is done. In cell B3, the sales forecast ($100,000) is entered, and in cell B4 we enter the cost of goods sold in percent (80%); in B5 we enter interest payments ($1,000), and in B6 the tax rate (34%). In B7 we enter the formula that expresses net earnings in terms of cells B3, B4, B5, and B6.

$$B8 = \left[\frac{100 - B4}{100} \times (B3) - B5 \right] \left[1 - \frac{B6}{100} \right]$$

The resulting net income is $12,540 in Table 5–8.

Now we can change assumptions as easily as pressing buttons. For example, let us increase the sales forecast to $117,500, decrease cost of goods sold to 78.2%, increase interest payments by 50% to $1,500, and change the tax rate to 40%. The new matrix (Table 5–9) is displayed on the computer screen in a fraction of a second: Net earnings have risen to $14,469. Should you want to try another set of assumptions, just type them in and let the computer do the work!

TABLE 5–8   Sample Computer Output: Pro Forma Income Statement

B3 Sales	$100,000
B4 COGS (%)	80
B5 Interest	1,000
B6 Tax rate (%)	34
B8 Net Earnings	**$ 12,540**

TABLE 5–9   Sample Computer Output: Sensitivity Analysis

B3 Sales	$117,500
B4 COGS (%)	78.2
B5 Interest	1,500
B6 Tax Rate (%)	40.0
B8 Net Earnings	**$ 14,469**

SUMMARY

Forecasting a firm's future fund requirements has many advantages:

1. It permits the pretesting of the implications of various programs before the actual commitments are made.
2. By providing advance notice of fund needs, forecasting is useful in negotiating loans and planning new issues of securities.
3. Forecasts provide useful benchmarks for the evaluation and control of actual operations.

The percentage of sales method is one method for preparing pro forma balance sheets and income statements. The following operations are required:

1. Alternative levels of next year's sales are estimated.
2. The relationship of items directly related to sales is specified and applied to each sales forecast.
3. Items not directly related to sales are estimated.
4. The pro forma balance sheet is "balanced" by specifying how the firm's projected operations are to be financed.

Statistical techniques can be used to improve the forecasts. One such method is least squares regression, which we defined and applied to the problem of forecasting sales. Computers can now be used to facilitate the sensitivity analysis of pro forma financial statements.

REVIEW EXERCISE

Circle the correct word(s) to complete each sentence; see p. 110 for the correct answers.

5.1   Anyone who claims he can predict the future *is/is not* lying, even if he thinks he is telling the truth.

5.2   Forecasted levels of sales can be compared with *market share/actual sales* and existing plans can be revised.

5.3   When using the percentage of sales method to project financial statements, the first step consists of *reducing/identifying* the items in the financial statements which are directly related to *sales/current assets*.

5.4   Expenses for labor *are/are not* directly related to sales; depreciation *is/is not* directly related to sales.

5.5   When estimating next year's sales, *only one/more than one* estimate *is/are* usually given.

5.6 When using the percentage of sales method to forecast cost of goods sold and receivables, inventory turnover and collection period *can/cannot* be correctly interpreted.

5.7 Regression analysis can help us make predictions if it is known that the size of one variable *depends/does not depend* on the size of the other.

5.8 The measure of the "goodness of fit" of a regression line is a function of the *distance/square of the distance* between the data points and the regression line.

5.9 A coefficient of determination equal to one signifies *an awful/a perfect* fit.

5.10 A value of 0.8 for the R^2 means that *20/80* % of the variation is explained by the regression equation.

5.11 One *should/should not* compute regressions without a theory of why the dependent variable depends on the independent variable.

5.12 If a large change in an initial assumption has only a small effect on the result, the latter is said to be *sensitive/robust* with respect to the assumption.

5.13 Electronic spreadsheets consist of a *mattress/matrix* of columns and rows.

5.14 When one cell in an electronic spreadsheet is changed, all the other cells which depend on it *must also be changed/change automatically.*

QUESTIONS

5.1 Define the following terms:
   a. Percentage of sales method   b. Circular reasoning
   c. Regression analysis   d. R square or R^2
   e. Electronic spreadsheet   f. Robust result
   g. Pro forma financial statement

5.2 Give some reasons why a firm would want to spend time and money to forecast the future.

5.3 Which items in an income statement and a balance sheet can typically be forecast using the percentage of sales method?

5.4 How do you forecast the items in the income statement and the balance sheet which are *not* directly related to sales?

5.5 Which financial ratios can be applied in a meaningful manner to financial statements that have been forecast using the percentage of sales method? Why can't the remaining ratios be analyzed?

5.6 Why doesn't the line that cuts through a scatterplot so as to minimize the sum of the distances of the scatterpoints to the line represent the best regression line? How can this dilemma be resolved?

5.7 "In our company we have a computer program that regresses everything on everything. The equation which results in the highest R square is then used for forecasting." Evaluate this statement.

5.8 Your company's computer is down. Joe, the executive trainee, is sitting at a table, squinting with one eye and pushing a ruler around the scatterplot. Do you fire Joe for coming to work drunk? Explain.

5.9 You have performed a time series regression analysis. The value for R^2 is 0.99. Are you satisfied? Explain.

5.10 CompuCast has built a model to forecast sales. It contains 12 explanatory variables. The next step is to get forecasts of the explanatory variables. You are given until 8:00 A.M. tomorrow to come up with something. Given this time constraint, how would you go about this assignment?

5.11 You are asked to make up an advertisement for an electronic spreadsheet. Explain in a few sentences how it works, in a way that can be understood by someone who has had no more than high school math.

PROBLEMS

5.1 Percentage of sales method. The following is a simplified income statement of the Janner Corporation.

Janner Corporation
Income Statement for This Year

Sales	2,200
Materials	1,650
Labor	220
Other expenses	110
Interest	55
Taxes	56
Net income	109

Use the percentage of sales method to derive the pro forma income statement for next year, on the assumptions that interest payments stay constant, that the corporate tax rate is 34%, and that:

a. Sales increase to $2,500. **b.** Sales fall to $1,800.
c. Sales fall to zero. **d.** Sales rise to $12,600.
e. Evaluate your results for (c) and (d) above.

5.2 Additional funds required. The financial vice president of Q&P Enterprises is thinking about how to finance next year's funds requirements. He knows that cash and marketable securities correspond to 6% of sales, accounts receivable correspond to 10% of sales, and inventories to 30%. No new fixed assets will be bought next year (they currently amount to $2,000,000), but depreciation will be $300,000. "This takes care of the asset side," he thinks to himself, "but how about liabilities and equity?" All he knows is that accounts payable are expected to be 12% of sales, long-term debt is currently $1,000,000, there is $500,000 of common stock outstanding, and $100,000 of retained earnings have been accumulated. He expects sales to reach $1,000,000 next year, with a net profit margin of 10%; half of the net profit will be paid out as dividends.

a. What are the funds requirements for next year? Prepare a pro forma balance sheet, under the constraint that no additional debt will be raised.

b. Answer question (a) on the optimistic assumption that sales will reach $1,200,000.

c. Answer question (a) on the pessimistic assumption that sales will reach only $800,000.

5.3 Pro forma financial statements. The current income statement and balance sheet of the Candy Computer Corporation are given below. In addition, the following facts are known: labor, materials, other expenses, cash, accounts receivable, accounts payable, and inventories all vary in proportion with sales. Depreciation stays at the current level. The corporate tax rate will be raised to 40%. Half of the net after-tax income will be distributed as dividends. A $12,250 investment in equipment is planned, of which 20% will be financed by retained earnings and 40% by additional long-term debt. The latter will carry the same interest rate as the current loan. Some common stock may also be issued. Miscellaneous assets will remain at their current level.

Candy Computer Corporation
Income Statement

Sales	100,000
Labor	30,000
Materials	50,000
Depreciation	4,000
Other expenses	5,000
Interest	3,000
Taxes	2,400
Net income after taxes	5,600

Candy Computer Corporation Balance Sheet

Assets		Liabilities	
Cash	2,000	Accounts payable	12,000
Accounts receivable	6,000	Long-term debt	30,000
Inventories	12,000	Common stock	20,000
Total current assets	20,000	Retained earnings	13,000
Plant and equipment	50,000	Total liabilities	
Less depreciation	(10,000)	and equity	75,000
Miscellaneous assets	15,000		
Total assets	75,000		

a. Prepare a pro forma income statement and balance sheet for next year on the assumption that sales rise by 50%.

b. Prepare a pro forma income statement and balance sheet for next year on the assumption that sales rise by 100%.

c. Prepare a pro forma income statement and balance sheet for next year on the assumption that sales remain constant.

5.4 Regression analysis. An athlete runs the 100-meter dash in 11.7 seconds. She runs 110 meters in 12.8 seconds, 120 meters in 13.9 seconds, and 90 meters in 10.6 seconds. Use the techniques of eyeballing and of linear regression to estimate the following:

a. How long will it take her to run 100 yards (1 yard = 91.7 centimeters)?

b. How long will it take her to run 130 meters?

c. How long will it take her to run the marathon (42 km, 195.77 m)?

d. What's wrong with the result in part (c)?

5.5 Regression analysis. The following table shows the shelf space for five competing products in a supermarket, and the corresponding daily sales:

Product	Shelf Space (sq ft)	Sales ($)
K	12.0	11,160
S	13.6	12,648
F	8.7	8,091
W	21.9	20,367
T	18.1	16,833

A new product called M is to receive 16.2 square feet of shelf space. What is your estimate of the sales of M? (Solve the problem without the help of a computer.)

5.6 Sensitivity analysis. The table below shows the pro forma income statement of the Apex Corporation:

Apex Corporation
Pro Forma Income
Statement

Sales	140,000
Labor	90,000
Materials	30,000
Other expenses	4,500
Interest	5,500
Taxes	3,400
Net income	6,600

All figures except depreciation, interest, and taxes can be computed as a percentage of sales. What is the impact of each of the following changes on net income?

a. The corporate income tax is lowered to 30%.

b. Cost of materials falls to 15% of sales.

c. "Other expenses" double.

d. Depreciation rises to $8,000.

e. (a) and (b) together.

f. (a) and (b) and (c) together.

g. (a) and (b) and (c) and (d) together.

5.7 Pro forma financial statements. The table below gives the income statement and balance sheet for the Violet Company for the year 1987 (all figures in thousands of dollars). The following information is also known: Sales for the four preceding years were $102, $118, $138, and $162, respectively, and this trend is expected to continue through next year. However, an optimistic estimate would put sales 5% above this estimate; a pessimistic estimate would put it 5% below the trendline. Fixed expenses are expected to increase to $20 next year, and depreciation will amount to 6 ⅔% of net plant and equipment. Annual interest charges will be 10% of long-term loans outstanding at the beginning of the year. Because of problems with suppliers, management has decided to raise the level of inventories to 40% of sales. It is management's aim to hold the debt ratio constant. A decision on the amount of common stock to be issued must be made in advance, and the firm has decided to base such a decision on the "realistic" sales forecast. Should sales be higher (optimistic case) or lower (pessimistic case), the level of debt will be adjusted accordingly. All profits are reinvested. For simplicity, assume that the Violet Company is exempt from all taxes. Prepare pro forma income statements and balance sheets for the pessimistic, realistic, and optimistic assumptions.

The Violet Company Income Statement 1987

Sales	180
COGS: Labor and materials	45
Fixed expenses	15
Depreciation	10
Administration	9
Interest	2.8
Net income	8.2

The Violet Company Balance Sheet

Assets	
Cash	12
Marketable securities	24
Accounts receivables	27
Inventories	45
Gross plant and equipment	200
Accumulated depreciation	(80)
Net plant and equipment	120
Other assets	18
Claims on Assets	246
Accounts payable	20
Long-term debt	32
Common stock	128
Retained earnings	66
Total claims on assets	246

5.8 Regression analysis, computer problem. Dugan Consultants have been asked to analyze the following data:

Observations	Sales $	TV Spots	Radio Spots	Newspaper Advertisements
1.	25,638	23	54	126
2.	106,567	83	189	212
3.	99,234	79	154	200
4.	212,506	186	402	445
5.	54,612	39	88	101
6.	182,345	154	388	392
7.	175,777	151	389	375
8.	201,372	176	406	438
9.	321,987	245	449	576
10.	43,213	37	78	56

Dugan decided to run three regressions to determine how each factor (TV, radio, and newspapers), taken by itself, seems to influence sales.

a. What is the regression equation, with TV spots as the independent variable? What is the goodness of fit? Other things being equal, what sales can be expected without any TV spots? What sales can be expected for each additional TV spot?

b. Answer question (a) for radio spots.

c. Answer question (a) for newspaper advertisements.

SAMPLE PROBLEMS

SP5.1 Mr. Green of Lavan Corporation (see Sample Problem, Chapter 4) has once again spilled ink over the financial statements. But this time he has last year's income statement and balance sheet available. Help Mr. Green fill in the blanks (inkspots) using the percentage of sales method wherever possible.

Income Statement	1985	1986
Sales	2,500	3000
Cost of goods sold	2,000	—
Other expenses	300	—
Earnings before interest and taxes	200	—
Interest on long-term debt	80	—
Taxes	40	—
After-tax earnings	40	—
Balance Sheet	50	—
Cash		
Accounts receivable	200	—
Inventories	400	—
Plant and equipment (net)	2,000	2200
Total assets	2,650	—
Accounts payable	80	—
Long-term debt	970	—
Common stock	1,600	—
Total liabilities and equity	2,650	—

Footnotes to 1986 financial statements: (a) No new common stock was issued, but additional——[inkblot] long-term debt has been taken on. (b) Average interest on long-term debt during 1986 increased to 8.57%. (c) The corporate tax rate was 34%.

SP5.2 You have been provided with the following data about the study habits and the grades of a group of students:

Student	Hours Spent Studying	Grade Received on Exam
Michael	6	83
Susan	8	84
Eve	5	75
George	3	99
Joe	7	89
Frederika	1	65

a. Alice intends to study for 6 hours. Using the data above, what grade can she expect to receive?

b. How many more grade points can she expect to receive if she studies an additional hour?

c. Sarah doesn't intend to spend any time studying. What grade can she expect?

d. How good is the "fit"?

Solutions to Sample Problems

SP5.1

Income Statement	1985	1986	
Sales	2,500	3,000	
Cost of goods sold	2,000	2,400	(80% of 3,000)
Other expenses	300	375	(12.5% of 3,000)
Earnings before interest and taxes	200	225	(remainder)
Interest on long-term debt	80	110	(2)
Taxes	40	39	(3)
After-tax earnings	40	71	(remainder)
Balance Sheet			
Cash	50	60	(2% of 3,000)
Accounts receivable	200	240	(8% of 3,000)
Inventories	400	480	(16% of 3,000)
Plant and equipment (net)	2,000	2,200	
Total assets	2,650	2,980	(sum of the above)
Accounts payable	80	96	(3.2% of 3,000)
Long-term debt	970	1,284	(1)
Common stock	1,600	1,600	(1)
Total liabilities and owner's equity	2,650	2,980	(same as total assets)

1. As per footnote (a) of the financial reports, the increase in total assets was financed by long-term debt (except for the additional accounts payable). New total assets = 2980 = new liabilities and owners' equity = accounts payable + common stock + long-term debt = 96 + 1600 (unchanged) + long-term debt. Long-term debt = 2980 − 96 − 1600 = 1284.

2. As per footnote (b), interest is now 8.57% of 1284 = 110.

3. As per footnote (c), taxes are 34% of before-tax income: 0.34(115) = 39.

SP5.2 We use regression analysis to solve this problem. The grade is the dependent variable (y), hours spent studying is the independent variable (x). The following worksheet can facilitate the calculations.

	x	y	x^2	y^2	xy
Michael	6	83	36	6,889	498
Susan	8	84	64	7,056	672
Eve	5	75	25	5,625	375
George	3	99	9	9,801	297
Joe	7	89	49	7,921	623
Frederika	1	65	1	4,225	65
Sum	30	495	184	41,517	2,530
Mean	5	82.5			

$$b = (\Sigma xy - \bar{x}\Sigma y)/(\Sigma x^2 - \bar{x}\Sigma x) = [2,530 - (5)495]/[184 - 5(30)]$$
$$= (2,530 - 2,475)/(184 - 150) = 55/34 = 1.62$$
$$a = \bar{y} - b\bar{x} = 82.5 - 1.62(5) = 82.5 - 8.1 = 74.4$$
$$R^2 = (\Sigma xy - \bar{x}\Sigma y)^2/(\Sigma x^2 - \bar{x}\Sigma x) \times (\Sigma y^2 - \bar{y}\Sigma y)$$
$$= [2,530 - (5)495]^2/[184 - (5)30] \times [41,517 - 82.5 \times 495]$$
$$= (55)^2/[34(679)] = 3025/23,086 = 0.13$$

Hence the regression equation is $y = 75.4 + (1.62)x$.

a. Alice can expect to receive a grade of $74.4 + (1.62)6 = 84.1$.

b. An additional hour of studying would result in 1.62 additional grade points.

c. Sarah, who would study zero hours, could expect to receive a grade of 74.4.

d. Since R^2 is 0.13, only 13% of the variation of the grade from its mean is "explained" by the time spent studying. Other factors, such as students' ability, are more important explanatory variables in this case.

Answers to Review Exercise

5.1 is   5.2 actual sales   5.3 identifying, sales   5.4 are, is not
5.5 more than one, are   5.6 cannot   5.7 depends
5.8 square of the distances   5.9 a perfect   5.10 80
5.11 should not   5.12 robust   5.13 matrix
5.14 change automatically

SUGGESTIONS FOR FURTHER READING

On the problems posed by financial planning, see Robert N. Anthony, *Planning and Control Systems: A Framework for Analysis* (Cambridge MA: Graduate School of Business, Harvard University, 1965).

For the application of formal models to corporate planning, see Willard T. Carleton, Charles L. Dick, Jr., and David H. Downs, "Financial Policy Models: Theory and Practice," *Journal of Financial and Quantitative Analysis,* December 1973; and Willard T. Carleton and J. M. McInnes, "Theory, Models and Implementation in Financial Management," *Management Science,* September 1982.

As emphasized in the text, the sales forecast lies at the heart of the planning process. For a discussion of the financial implications of the sales forecast, see Judy Pan, Donald R. Nichols, and O. Maurice Joy, "Sales Forecasting Practices of Large U.S. Industrial Firms," *Financial Management,* Fall 1977.

6

Time Value of Money and Interest Rates

How often have you heard the expression "time is money"? What does it mean to you? To the financial manager, the expression "time is money" has special significance for the determination of the firm's investment and financing decisions. This significance stems from the fact that a dollar received "tomorrow" is not equivalent to a dollar in hand "today." And since the typical capital investment decision invariably involves the comparison of present outlays with future benefits, problems relating to the *timing* of receipts and outlays lie at the very heart of the evaluation of capital investment decisions. Similarly, long-term financing decisions obligate the firm to make a series of future payments. Once again, the proper evaluation of such decisions depends, *inter alia,* on our ability to make meaningful comparisons of cash flows which occur at different points of time.

This chapter examines the significance of the time value of money for financial decision-making. We introduce the basic concepts of *future value* and *present value,* and apply them to a variety of financial problems and to the calculation of the rate of interest.

THE TIME VALUE OF MONEY

A typical financial decision often involves the comparison of present outlays and future benefits. To focus attention on the implications of the time value of money for financial decision-making, we initially assume that the costs and benefits of alternative investment proposals are known with certainty. But even if the size of the relevant cash flow is known, we must still pay attention to its timing.

Consider the following example of a project which requires an immediate investment of $1,000, and which returns $1,100, with certainty, exactly 1 year later. Does it pay to make such an investment? That is, does it pay to give up $1,000 today in order to receive $1,100 one year from now? Our answer depends on the *alternative use* we have for the $1,000. If, for example, we assume that 12% interest can be earned by depositing the $1,000 in a bank, the value of the deposit at the end of the year will be $1,120. And since $1,120 exceeds $1,100, the proposed investment is *not* desirable. On the other hand, if the bank pays only 8% interest, the value of the account at the end of the year will be $1,080. Since $1,080 is less than $1,100, the proposal is to be preferred over the bank account—assuming, of course, that both alternatives have the same risk.

Clearly, an intelligent decision requires the comparison of alternatives; and it is the fact that money can always earn a positive return that lends importance to the time dimension of many financial decisions. A dollar given up today is *not* the equivalent of a dollar received in the future, as long as there exists the alternative of earning a positive return during the interim. This is the financial manager's interpretation of the saying "Time is money."

FUTURE VALUE

future (compounded) value
A value that results from the application of compound interest to a present amount of money.

The **future value** or **compounded value,** as it is also called, results from the application of compound interest to a present amount of money. In the example above, the future value at the end of one year of a $1,000 bank deposit earning 12% interest was $1,200.

The formula for calculating future values can be illustrated by considering the following example:

Assume you deposit one dollar (principal) in the bank. What is the value of the deposit at the end of the year, if the bank pays 10% interest? In our example using a 10% interest rate, the future value of the deposit at the end of the year is,

$$FV_1 = 1(1 + .10) = 1 + .10 = \$1.10$$

that is, 1 dollar of principal, plus 10 cents of interest income. More generally, the formula for future value can be defined as follows:

future value = principal + interest income

If we denote the relevant interest rate by the letter k, the principal by the letter P, and the value of the deposit at the end of the year by FV_1, we get,

$$FV_1 = P + kP$$

which can be rewritten as

$$FV_1 = P(1 + k) \tag{6.1}$$

What is the future value of the deposit at the end of 2 years? As we have already seen, its value at the end of the first year is \$1.10. In the second year, an additional 10% will be earned on the \$1.10. Therefore

$$FV_2 = 1.10 + .11 = \$1.21$$

where FV_2 denotes the value of the deposit at the end of 2 years. In symbols:

$$FV_2 = P(1 + k)(1 + k)$$
$$= P(1 + k)^2$$

In general, the value of the deposit at the end of n years is

$$FV_n = P(1 + k)^n \tag{6.2}$$

Of course, the future value formula (Eq. 6.2) is a special version of the general formula for compound interest over time. As such, it can be applied to any amount of money, using any interest rate. Thus, if we want to know the future value to which P dollars will accumulate when compounded annually for n years, we can write:

$$FV_n = P(1 + k)^n \tag{6.3}$$

where k denotes the appropriate interest (compounding) rate.

In a world of electronic computers, the calculation of compounded future values has been reduced to the mechanical reading of numbers from a table or from a hand calculator. Using the compound interest formula (in Eq. 6.3), we can easily generate the data of Table 6–1, which gives the value of $(1 + k)^n$ for alternative values of k and n.[1] The future value of any initial amount can be found by multiplying that amount by the relevant future value interest factor *(FVF)* from Table 6–1. In our previous example, we assumed a 10% compounding rate and a 5-year time horizon. The corre-

---

[1] More complete financial tables of both future and present value are given in the appendix at the end of the book.

TABLE 6.1   Compounded Future Value of \$1

Years Hence	1%	2%	3%	4%	5%	6%	7%	8%	9%	10%
1	1.010	1.020	1.030	1.040	1.050	1.060	1.070	1.080	1.090	1.100
2	1.020	1.040	1.061	1.082	1.102	1.124	1.145	1.166	1.188	1.210
3	1.030	1.061	1.093	1.125	1.158	1.191	1.225	1.260	1.295	1.331
4	1.041	1.082	1.126	1.170	1.216	1.262	1.311	1.360	1.412	1.464
5	1.051	1.104	1.159	1.217	1.276	1.338	1.403	1.469	1.539	1.611
6	1.062	1.126	1.194	1.265	1.340	1.419	1.501	1.587	1.677	1.772
7	1.072	1.149	1.230	1.316	1.407	1.504	1.605	1.714	1.828	1.949
8	1.083	1.172	1.267	1.369	1.477	1.594	1.718	1.851	1.993	2.144
9	1.094	1.195	1.305	1.423	1.551	1.689	1.838	1.999	2.172	2.358
10	1.105	1.219	1.344	1.480	1.629	1.791	1.967	2.159	2.367	2.594

**FIGURE 6–1
Future Value
of One Dollar
for Selected
Interest Rates.**

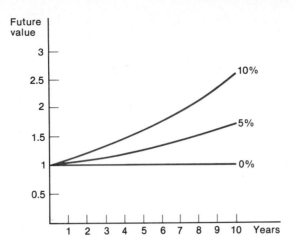

sponding future value factor, 1.611, is found in line 5 of the 10% column of Table 6–1; the future value of $1000 at the end of 5 years is $1,611:

$$1,000(FVF_{10\%,5yr}) = 1,000(1.611) = \$1,611$$

where the subscripts 10% and 5 yr denote the compounding rate and time horizon, respectively.

The future value formula can be illustrated by using a simple graphic device. Figure 6–1 shows the growth of one dollar over time, at various interest rates. The graph itself was constructed from the data in Table 6–1. The table and the graph show that the higher the rate of interest (compounding rate), the higher the rate of growth of the original principal. Money invested at 10% grows at a constant (compounded) rate of 10% per year; money invested at a lower interest rate grows at a slower rate, and so on. Note that a zero interest rate implies a zero growth rate; the future value of one dollar remains unchanged.

CALCULATING FUTURE VALUE:
INTRAYEAR COMPOUNDING

To this point we have considered only annual compounding, but all of us have probably been puzzled, at one time or another, by the bewildering variety of interest rates banks and savings and loan associations offer on deposits. In addition to an array of toasters, casseroles, and alarm clocks, many thrift institutions offer a *stated interest rate,* which is compounded *semi-annually, quarterly,* of even *daily.* To make sense out of the various offers, we must adjust the future value formula to reflect alternative assumptions regarding the frequency of compounding.

For a given interest rate, the greater the frequency with which interest is compounded, the higher the future value of the deposit, so that the investor is better off.

Semi-annual Compounding

Consider the following example: An individual deposits $100 in a bank for 1 year at a stated annual interest rate of 6%. The value of the account at the end of the year will be 100(1 + .06) = $106. Now, suppose the interest is compounded *twice* a year. In this case, the value of the deposit at the end of the year is given by:

$$100\left(1 + \frac{.06}{2}\right)\left(1 + \frac{.06}{2}\right) = 100\left(1 + \frac{.06}{2}\right)^2 = \$106.09$$

The only difference between this calculation and the previous one is that, in this instance, the bank credits the account with $3 interest after 6 months have elapsed. During the next 6 months, the investor earns 3% on $103 (rather than 3% on $100), or $3.09. The economic meaning of compounding within a given period is that the bank pays interest on the principal *plus* the accumulated interest up to the compounding date.

Now consider a 2-year example, but again with semi-annual compounding, and a stated interest rate of 6%. Table 6–2 shows the relevant calculations. As the table shows, the deposit will have grown to $112.55 at the end of 2 years, compared with $112.36 with annual compounding.[2]

Quarterly Compounding

Quarterly compounding is similar to semi-annual; the only difference is that it involves four compounding periods during the year (every 3 months). In this case, one-fourth of the stated annual interest rate is paid at the end of each quarter.

---

[2] $100 (1.06)^2 = \$112.36$. The slight discrepancy between this result and that of Table 6–1 (100(1.124) = $112.40) is a result of rounding. Such rounding discrepancies will be ignored.

TABLE 6–2   Future Value of Deposit of $100 at 6% Interest Compounded Semi-annually over Two Years*

Period	Beginning Principal (1)	Semi-annual Interest Rate Factor (2)	Future Value [(1) × (2) = (3)] (3)
6 months	$100.00	1.03	$103.00
1 year	103.00	1.03	106.09
18 months	106.09	1.03	109.27
2 years	109.27	1.03	112.55

* At a 6% annual interest rate.

Again, assume that $100 is deposited for 2 years, at a stated interest rate of 6%. In this instance, however, the interest is to be compounded quarterly, or every 3 months. Table 6–3 shows the relevant calculations. The value of the account at the end of 2 years is $112.65, or slightly higher than the result obtained assuming semi-annual compounding, $112.55 (see Table 6–2).

The General Formula for Intrayear Compounding

The results above can be generalized for deposits at any maturity and compounding period. If we let m denote the number of times interest is compounded within a year, k the stated interest rate, n the number of years, and P the principal, the formula for annual compounding (Eq. 6.3) can be written as

$$FV_n = P(1 + k/m)^{m \times n} \tag{6.4}$$

When $m = 1$, Eq. 6.4 is identical to Eq. 6.3, as it should be.

Using Eq. 6.4, the future value of deposits of any maturity (n), for any compounding period (m), and for any stated interest rate (k) can easily be calculated on many pocket calculators. For example, the future values of a $100 deposit at the end of n years are given by the following formulas:[3]

Annual compounding: $\qquad 100\,(1 + k)^n$

Semi-annual compounding: $\qquad 100\left(1 + \dfrac{k}{2}\right)^{2n}$

Quarterly compounding: $\qquad 100\left(1 + \dfrac{k}{4}\right)^{4n}$

---

[3] The maximum end-of-year value is achieved should the bank compound continuously:

$$FV_1 = Pe^k$$

where e denotes the base of the natural logarithm. In our specific example, the terminal value of the deposit is, at the end of 1 year, $100 \times e^{0.06} = 106.18$.

TABLE 6–3   Future Value of Deposit of $100 at 6% Interest Compounded Quarterly over Two Years*

Period	Beginning Principal (1)	Quarterly Interest Rate Factor (2)	Future Value [(1) × (2) = (3)] (3)
3 months	$100.00	1.015	$101.50
6 months	101.50	1.015	103.25
9 months	103.25	1.015	104.57
1 year	104.57	1.015	106.14
15 months	106.14	1.015	107.73
18 months	107.73	1.015	109.34
21 months	109.34	1.015	110.98
2 years	110.98	1.015	112.65

* At a 6% annual interest rate.

Monthly compounding: $100 \left(1 + \dfrac{k}{12}\right)^{12n}$

Daily compounding: $100 \left(1 + \dfrac{k}{365}\right)^{365n}$

Figure 6–2 graphs the value of the deposit as a function of the frequency of compounding, and of the time the deposit is held. In this particular example, we have assumed an interest rate of 12%. However, it is worth noting that for short periods, and for low interest rates, the differences induced by the various compounding methods are negligible. In general, the higher the interest rate and the longer the deposit is held, the greater is the impact of the compounding methods. Thus, when a bank declares that the annual interest of, say, 6% is compounded several times a year, this is tantamount to *raising* the stated interest rate.

If you have not done so before, now is probably a good time to invest in a pocket calculator. But to test your understanding, not to mention your patience, use Table 6–1 to calculate the future value of a $100 deposit for 2 years at 6% interest compounded semi-annually. Applying our formula, we find the answer by looking at the 3% column of line 4. Recall that there are

FIGURE 6–2
Future Value of $100 Received in the _n_th Year Compounded by 12%

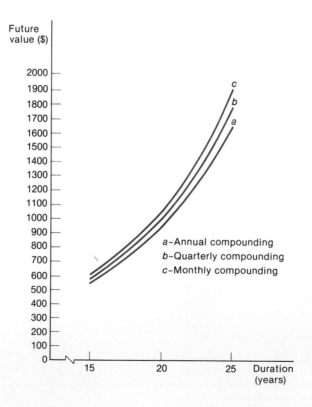

a–Annual compounding
b–Quarterly compounding
c–Monthly compounding

four compounding periods during the 2 years, and that the 6% interest rate must be divided by 2 for semi-annual compounding. The future value factor of one dollar is 1.126, so that the value of the $100 deposit, at the end of 2 years, is

$$FV_2 = 100(1.126) = \$112.60$$

This is the same result (except for rounding) we obtained by applying the compound interest formula. But how would you like to solve for a 2-year deposit, at 6% interest, with *daily* compounding? You need a bigger table of future values—or perhaps it really *is* time to buy that calculator.

FUTURE VALUE OF A MIXED SERIES

Until now we have dealt only with the future value of a given sum, but the general approach can easily be applied to a series of payments.

Assume that you are offered the following alternatives:

1. Receive the following three annual payments at the end of each of the next 3 years:

$$
\begin{aligned}
\text{First receipt} &= C_1 = 300 \\
\text{Second receipt} &= C_2 = 400 \\
\text{Third receipt} &= C_3 = 500 \\
\text{Total} &\quad\ \ \$1{,}200
\end{aligned}
$$

2. Receive a single lump sum payment of $1,000 today.

Which alternative do you prefer? Clearly, the first alternative offers more than $1,000; $1,200 > $1,000, (the sign > indicates "greater than"). In a world in which money earns no interest, the stream of three payments would be preferable to the smaller lump sum.

What happens if we assume that the relevant interest rate which can be earned is 10%. (For simplicity, we assume annual compounding.) To compare the two alternatives, they must first be brought to a common denominator. One solution is to calculate the future value of each strategy at the end of 3 years. The alternative which promises the greatest terminal value is the better of the two.

The future value of the lump sum payment presents no problem. Applying Eq. 6.3, we have:

$$FV_3 = P\,(1 + k)^3$$
$$FV_3 = 1{,}000(1.10)^3$$

From Table 6–1 (line 3 in the 10% column), we identify the relevant future value factor:

$$FV_3 = 1,000(FVF_{10\%,3yr})$$
$$FV_3 = 1,000(1.331) = \$1,331$$

Thus, the value of the $1,000 lump sum payment is $1,331 *at the end of 3 years.*

The mixed series of payments can be handled in a similar fashion by applying the appropriate future value factor to each of the receipts. In general, the future value of a series of annual receipts $C_1, C_2 \ldots C_n$ can be found by applying the formula for the future value of a single sum to each one of the receipts, and then adding them up:

$$FV_n = C_1 (1 + k)^{n-1} + C_2 (1+k)^{n-2} + \ldots + C_{n-1} (1+k) + C_n \quad (6.5)$$

Note that the first year's receipts are compounded forward for $n-1$ years, the second for $n-2$, and so on. Since the last sum C_n is received only at the end of the last year, it is added in without any interest. Figure 6–3 illustrates this procedure.

Now let us return to our specific example: $C_1 = 300$, $C_2 = 400$, $C_3 = 500$, and $k = 10\%$. From Table 6–1 we find the appropriate compounding factors and calculate the future value:

$$300(1.21) = \quad 363$$
$$400(1.10) = \quad 440$$
$$500(1.00) = \quad \underline{500}$$
$$\text{Future value} = 1,303$$

Thus, the future value of this series of payments is $1,303. Since $1,303 < \$1,331$ the lump sum is preferable to the series of annual receipts, and this is true despite the fact that the sum of the three payments ($1,200) exceeds the lump sum ($1,000). Once the time value of money is considered, the early receipt of the lump sum is more than sufficient, in this case, to offset the greater magnitude of the series of receipts.

FIGURE 6–3
Future Value
of Mixed
Cash Flow

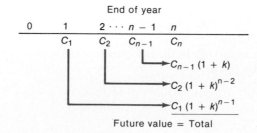

FUTURE VALUE OF AN ANNUITY

ordinary annuities
A series of fixed payments received at the end of each period.

annuity due
An annuity in which payments are made at the beginning of each period.

Now consider the special case of a series of payments in which all payments are equal: $C_1 = C_2 \ldots = C_n = C$. An *annuity* is a series of fixed payments over a given number of periods. The payments are usually received at the end of each period; such annuities are called **ordinary annuities,** or *deferred payment* annuities. Occasionally payments are made at the beginning of each period; this type of annuity is called an **annuity due.** Since the common practice, in finance, is to make payments at the end of each period, we focus on ordinary annuities.

Suppose an insurance company offers to pay you $1,000 a year for 3 years, or a single lump sum payment today. If the annuity is to be compared with the lump sum payment, we must again bring them to a common denominator. In the case of an annuity, the calculation of its future value is even easier than for a mixed series of payments. Figure 6–4 on page 122 illustrates the process assuming an interest rate of 6% ($k = 6\%$).

The future value of the annuity is found by applying the future value factors from the 6% column of Table 6–1 to each annuity payment:

$$1,000(1.124) = 1,124$$
$$1,000(1.060) = 1,060$$
$$1,000(1) \quad\;\; = 1,000$$
$$FV = 3,184$$

In any n period annuity, each individual payment, in say period t, is compounded forward ($n - t$) times. In our specific example $n = 3$, and therefore the first payment is compounded forward for two periods, the second payment is compounded for one period, and the last payment, which is received on the last day of the 3 year period, is simply added in without interest. Thus, the future value of an n year annuity, of C dollars per year, at an interest rate equal to k, can be written as:[4]

$$FVA_{k,n} = C\sum_{t=1}^{n} (1 + k)^{n-t} \tag{6.6}$$

In our specific example:

$$FVA_{6\%,3\text{yr}} = 1,000(1.124 + 1.060 + 1) = 3,184$$

[4] The general formula for the future value of a $1 annuity is

$$\sum_{t=1}^{n}(1 + k)^{n-t}$$

Summing the geometric progression contained in this equation yields the equivalent formula:

$$\frac{(1 + k)^n - 1}{k}$$

This equation was used to generate the data of Table 6–4.

FIGURE 6—4
Future value
of an Annuity

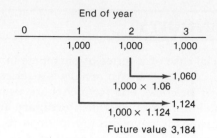

The numbers in the parentheses are the relevant future value factors from Table 6–1. The calculation of future values can be simplified by using Table 6–4 which sets out the future value of annuity factors (FVAF). In line 3 of the 6% column, we find 3.184. Hence, the future value of our 3-year annuity of $1,000 per period at 6% interest can be calculated directly from Table 6–4:

$$FVA = C(FVAF_{6\%,3yr})$$
$$= 1,000(3.184) \tag{6.7}$$
$$= \textbf{3,184}$$

We can also use these results to handle the infrequent case of an *annuity due,* an annuity in which payments are received at the beginning of each period. This simply means that the payment becomes available one period earlier than in the case of an ordinary annuity. In terms of our previous example, we have an extra period's interest for each payment. Eq. 6.7 can be written as follows:

$$\text{future value of annuity due} = C\ (FVAF_{6\%,3yr})\ (1\ +\ k)$$
$$= 1,000(3.184)\ (1.06) \tag{6.8}$$
$$= 3,375$$

TABLE 6—4   Future Value of Annuity Factors (FVAF)

n	1%	2%	3%	4%	5%	6%	7%	8%	9%	10%
1	1.000	1.000	1.000	1.000	1.000	1.000	1.000	1.000	1.000	1.000
2	2.010	2.020	2.030	2.040	2.050	2.060	2.070	2.080	2.090	2.100
3	3.030	3.060	3.091	3.122	3.152	3.184	3.215	3.246	3.278	3.310
4	4.060	4.122	4.184	4.246	4.310	4.375	4.440	4.506	4.573	4.641
5	5.101	5.204	5.309	5.416	5.526	5.637	5.751	5.867	5.985	6.105
6	6.152	6.308	6.468	6.633	6.802	6.975	7.153	7.336	7.523	7.716
7	7.214	7.434	7.662	7.898	8.142	8.394	8.654	8.923	9.200	9.487
8	8.286	8.583	8.892	9.214	9.549	9.897	10.260	10.637	11.028	11.436
9	9.368	9.755	10.159	10.583	11.027	11.491	11.978	12.488	13.021	13.579
10	10.462	10.950	11.464	12.006	12.578	13.181	13.816	14.487	15.193	15.937
11	11.567	12.169	12.808	13.486	14.207	14.972	15.784	16.645	17.560	18.531
12	12.682	13.412	14.192	15.026	15.917	16.870	17.888	18.977	20.141	21.384
13	13.809	14.680	15.618	16.627	17.713	18.882	20.141	21.495	22.953	24.523
14	14.947	15.974	17.086	18.292	19.598	21.015	22.550	24.215	26.019	27.975
15	16.097	17.293	18.599	20.023	21.578	23.276	25.129	27.152	29.361	31.772

THE RELATIONSHIP OF PRESENT VALUE
TO FUTURE VALUE

Present value is the other side of future value. The latter, as we have just seen, shows the value of a sum, or a series of sums, at some future date. Present value shows the value *today* of some amount (or series of amounts) that will be received in the future. The process of moving back in time is called *discounting,* and it is the mirror image of compounding. The interest rate used in discounting will again be denoted by *k,* but it will be called the **discount rate.**

discount rate (k)
An interest rate used in discounting.

present value (PV)
The value today of some amount (or series of amounts) that will be received in the future.

It requires only a minor extension of the future value formula to derive the formula for **present value (PV).** Dividing both sides of Eq. 6.3 by $(1 + k)^n$ and writing PV in place of P, we get

present value = future value ÷ (1 + discount rate)^n

or

$$PV = \frac{FV_n}{(1 + k)^n} \qquad (6.9)$$

which can be read as the present value of FV_n dollars received at the end of n years. This is perhaps the less familiar formula for *discounting* future sums to their present values, and is, as we have just seen, the other side of the compound interest formula.

If we assume that the discount rate is 10%, the present value (PV) of one dollar to be received at the end of 1 year is

$$PV = \frac{FV_1}{1 + k} = \frac{1.00}{1.10} = \$0.909$$

that is, the present value of one dollar, received at the end of 1 year, is 91 cents. Similarly, the present value of one dollar, received at the end of 2 years, is equal to 83 cents:

$$PV = \frac{FV_2}{(1 + k)^2} = \$0.826$$

The line of reasoning behind the formula is straightforward. Given the alternative of earning 10% with certainty, individuals should never offer (invest) more than $909 to obtain $1,000 with certainty at the end of 1 year. If they pay more, say $920, they could have reached a higher future value by depositing the $920 in the bank for 1 year at 10%:

$$\$920 (1 + 0.10) = \$1,012 > 1,000$$

Alternatively, we can apply the present value formula directly by noting that:

$$PV = \frac{1,000}{1.10} = 909 < 920$$

The present value of $1,000, received 1 year hence, is only $909, which is less than the proposed investment outlay of $920. Therefore, the proposed investment is not worthwhile. Modern time-discounted methods for evaluating investment projects are straightforward applications of this future value–present value relationship (see Chapter 9).

CALCULATING PRESENT VALUES

The actual calculations can be reduced to a very simple procedure by using a table of present value such as Table 6–5. The present value formula for any sum of money, C_t, to be received at the end of any year t, can be written

$$PV = C_t \left(\frac{1}{1+k} \right)^t$$

where k denotes the relevant discount rate.

The expression in parentheses is the appropriate *discount factor (DF)* required to reduce the future receipt to its present value. Thus, if we assume a 10% discount rate ($k = 10\%$), the discount factors for sums received in years 1 to 3 are:

$$(DF_{10\%,1\text{yr}}) = \frac{1}{1+k} = \frac{1}{1.10} = .909$$

$$(DF_{10\%,2\text{yr}}) = \left(\frac{1}{1+k} \right)^2 = \left(\frac{1}{1.10} \right)^2 = .826$$

$$(DF_{10\%,3\text{yr}}) = \left(\frac{1}{1+k} \right)^3 = \left(\frac{1}{1.10} \right)^3 = .751$$

These discount factors can be read off directly from the 10% column of Table 6–5. The subscripts 1, 2, and 3, denote the year in which the dollars are received. They also indicate the relevant line (year) in the present

TABLE 6.5   Present Value of $1

Years Hence	1%	2%	4%	5%	6%	8%	10%
1	.990	.980	.962	.952	.943	.926	.909
2	.980	.961	.925	.907	.890	.857	.826
3	.971	.942	.889	.864	.840	.794	.751
4	.961	.924	.855	.823	.792	.735	.683
5	.951	.906	.822	.784	.747	.681	.621
6	.942	.888	.790	.746	.705	.630	.564
7	.933	.871	.760	.711	.665	.583	.513
8	.923	.853	.731	.677	.627	.540	.467
9	.914	.837	.703	.645	.592	.500	.424
10	.905	.820	.676	.614	.558	.463	.386

value table. Thus, $DF_{(10\%,1yr)}$ is found by taking the discount factor appearing in line 1 of the 10% column of the present value table. $DF_{(10\%,2yr)}$ is found by taking the factor appearing in line 2 of the same column, and so on for later years.

The impact of the discounting process is illustrated graphically in Figure 6–5, which plots the present value of one dollar to be received in future years. Given the discount rate (for example, $k = 5\%$), the present value of a dollar declines the longer we have to wait to receive it. Similarly, the present value of a dollar to be received in any given year declines as the discount rate is raised. In the first instance this relationship reflects the fact that, given the time value of money, there is a price (in terms of foregone interest) to be paid for waiting. The longer the waiting period, the greater the loss of income, and therefore the greater too the decline in present value. The second relationship reflects the fact that, given the waiting period, the decline in present value will be greater for higher discount rates.

Present Value of a Mixed Series

Most investment proposals involve the comparison of the value of a series of receipts with the required initial outlay. The present value formula for a single year can easily be extended to such a series of receipts.

Consider an investment opportunity which offers C_1 dollars in the first year, C_2 dollars in the second, and C_3 dollars in the third year. The required investment outlay today is I_0 dollars. Clearly, the simple comparison of the sum of future net receipts with the initial outlay involves the comparison of apples with oranges. Since money has a time value, the dollars to be received in more distant years have a smaller value than those to be received in earlier years.

**FIGURE 6–5
Present Value
of One Dollar
for Selected
Discount Rates**

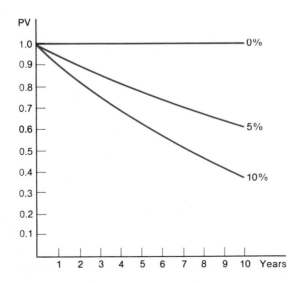

If we assume that the appropriate discount rate is k, we can apply Eq. 6.9 to a mixed stream of receipts in order to reduce the annual receipts to their present values. The formula for the present value of a mixed series of receipts can be written as follows:

present value of a mixed series = sum of present values

$$PV = C_1\left(\frac{1}{1+k}\right) + C_2\left(\frac{1}{1+k}\right)^2 + C_3\left(\frac{1}{1+k}\right)^3 \tag{6.10}$$

or alternatively,

$$PV = C_1(DF_{k,1}) + C_2(DF_{k,2}) + C_3(DF_{k,3})$$

The actual calculation is illustrated in Table 6–6 using the following numerical example: $k = 10\%$, $C_1 = 400$, $C_2 = 600$, $C_3 = 500$.

Total undiscounted cash receipts are $1,500, but their present value is only $1,234. What is the meaning of this reduction from $1,500 to a present value of $1,234? An explanation can be found by considering the relationship of *present* to *future* value. First write the future value of the series of three receipts at the end of 3 years. Using Eq. 6.5, we get:

$$FV = C_1(1.10)^2 + C_2(1.10) + C_3$$
$$FV = 400(1.21) + 600(1.10) + 500 = 1,644$$

As we can see from Figure 6–6, the future value formula reflects the fact that the $400 received in the first year can be invested, at 10%, for 2 years, while the $600 received in the second year can be invested for 1 year. Now calculate the *present value* of $1,644,

$$PV = 1,644 \, (DF_{10\%,3yr})$$
$$= 1,644(.751)$$
$$= \$1,234.64$$

Except for a rounding difference, the present value of $1,644 is *equal* to the present value of the series of receipts. In this manner, the present value calculation automatically reflects the alternative use of money. It follows, that if we are required to invest more than $1,234 (say, $1,300) in

TABLE 6.6   A Numerical Example

Year (t)	Net Receipt (S)	Discount Factor DF		Present Value of Cash Flow
1	400	.909		363.60
2	600	.826		495.60
3	500	.751		375.50
			Total	1,234.70
	Less Initial Outlay (I_0)			−1,000.00
			NPV	+234.70

FIGURE 6–6
Future Value
of Cash Flow

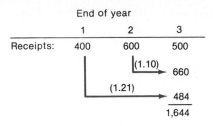

order to receive the above series of receipts, we should refuse. Given the alternative of earning 10%, a terminal value greater than $1,644 can be reached by investing the $1,300 for 3 years at 10%:

$$1,300(1.10)^3 = 1,300(1.331) = 1,730.30 > 1,644$$

Present Value
of an Annuity

In the case of an annuity (uniform annual receipts), the present value calculation can be further simplified by using Table 6–7, which is merely a summation of the relevant annual discount factors of Table 6–5. To find the present value of a 5-year, one-dollar annuity at 10% discount, we multiply one dollar by the discount factor of an annuity (DFA) appearing in line 5 of the 10% column of Table 6–7. This is 3.791, which is a summation of the first five factors in the 10% column of Table 6–5. The calculation can be illustrated by considering the example of a 3-year annuity of $400 per year and assuming that $k = 10\%$:

present value of annuity = fixed annual receipt × sum of the discount rates
$$PV = \$400(DFA_{10\%,3\text{yr}}) \qquad (6.11)$$
$$994.8 = \$400(2.487)$$

The calculation is illustrated in Figure 6–7.

Should you buy such an annuity, for say, $1,000? Surely, you would be better off if you forego the annuity. The present value of the purchase price

TABLE 6.7   Present Value of an Annuity of $1

Years	1%	2%	4%	5%	6%	8%	10%
1	0.990	0.980	0.962	0.952	0.943	0.926	0.909
2	1.970	1.942	1.886	1.859	1.833	1.783	1.736
3	2.941	2.884	2.775	2.723	2.673	2.577	2.487
4	3.902	3.808	3.630	3.546	3.465	3.312	3.170
5	4.853	4.713	4.452	4.329	4.212	3.993	3.791
6	5.795	5.601	5.242	5.076	4.917	4.623	4.355
7	6.728	6.472	6.002	5.786	5.582	5.206	4.868
8	7.652	7.325	6.733	6.463	6.210	5.747	5.335
9	8.566	8.162	7.435	7.108	6.802	6.247	5.759
10	9.471	8.983	8.111	7.722	7.360	6.710	6.145

FIGURE 6–7
Present Value
of Annuity

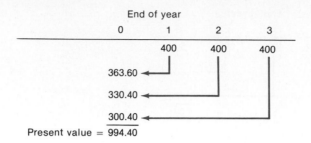

($1,000) is greater than the present value of the stream of benefits ($994.80). But what would be your decision if the discount rate representing the alternative use of money was less than 10%—say, 5%? In this instance, the present value of the annuity is $1,089.20, and the offer should be accepted:

$$400(2.723) = \$1,089.20 > \$1,000$$

Present Value
of Annuity Due

Figure 6–7 can also help us understand the case of the present value of an annuity due—the rare case of an annuity in which the payments are made at the beginning of the year. In such an annuity, the cash flow would be shifted one year to the left: 400 would appear under year 0, year 1, and year 2; zero would be entered for the third year. We therefore modify Eq. 6.11 as follows:

$$\text{Present value of annuity due} = 400(DFA_{10\%,3yr}) (1 + .10)$$

The present value calculation is

$$400(2.487) = 994.80(1.10) = \$1,094.28$$

Since each payment is received at the beginning instead of the end of the year, or one year earlier, this form of annuity has a greater present value than its ordinary counterpart.

CALCULATING PRESENT VALUE: INTRAYEAR DISCOUNTING

For simplicity we have presented the discussion of present value in terms of annual *discounting*. Discounting more than once in a given period is the counterpart of the frequency with which interest is compounded. What is the value of $100 received one year from now? If the discount rate is 10% and we assume annual discounting, the present value is equal to $90.91,

$$\left(\frac{100}{1 + .10}\right) = 90.91$$

But if the cash flow is discounted *twice* a year, the present value is smaller, only $90.70

$$\frac{100}{\left(1 + \frac{.10}{2}\right)^2} = 90.70.$$

In general, the present value of $100 received n years from now, and discounted m times a year, is

$$100\left(1 + \frac{0.10}{m}\right)^{mn}$$

In Table 6–8 the present value of $100 received at the end of n years is calculated for several alternative assumptions regarding the frequency of compounding. These figures confirm that an increase in the frequency of compounding *decreases* the present value.

TABLE 6.8 **Present Value of $100 Received in the** nth Year Discounted at 12%

	Year			
	1	5	10	20
Compounded Annually	89.3	56.7	38.2	10.4
Compounded Quarterly	88.8	55.4	30.6	9.4
Compounded Monthly	88.7	55.0	30.2	9.2

CALCULATING INTEREST RATES

The present value formulas are based on the general principle of compound interest and therefore can also be used in the calculation of interest rates.

Example 1: 1-Year Loan.   A bank offers to loan you $100 for 1 year and asks for $106 in return. What is the rate of interest on the loan? Clearly we can answer without hesitation (and in fact without calculation) that the interest rate is 6%. However, in order to clarify our thinking and to pave the way for handling more complicated loans, we define the **rate of interest** as the discount rate which equates the present value of the loan repayment(s) to the amount received. Hence we solve the following equation for the appropriate discount factor:

$$(DF_{k,1})106 = 100$$
$$(DF_{k,1}) = \frac{100}{106} = .943$$

A glance at line 1 of Table 6–5 shows that .943 lies in the 6% column, which confirms our intuition that the rate of interest on the loan in question is indeed 6%.

Example 2: 3-Year Loan.   The same bank also offers to lend you $100 for 3 years, but requires you to sign a note agreeing to repay $119.05 at the end of 3 years. Before making a decision, you want to know the rate of interest on the loan. In this instance intuition is *not* sufficient, but our formula quickly solves the dilemma. Once again, solve the *PV* equation for the appropriate discount factor:

$$(DF_{k,3})119.05 = 100$$
$$(DF_{k,3}) = \frac{100}{119.05} = .840$$

Turning again to Table 6–5, we glance along line 3 (recall it is a 3-year loan) until we come to .840, which lies in the 6% column. Thus, the rate of interest on the 3-year loan is also 6% per year. The need for a present value table reflects the basic fact that we live in a world of *compound interest.*

Example 3: A Development Loan.   You are contemplating the possibility of moving your plant to a new location, and are offered a development loan of $100,000 to be repaid in 10 equal[5] installments of $13,586.96 at the end of each year. This seems like an awful lot of money; you will be repaying the $100,000 loan plus more than $35,000 in interest. However, before making up your mind, first determine the rate of interest on the 10-year loan. Since we are confronted with 10 *equal annual payments*, the formula for the present value of an annuity can be used:

$$(DFA_{k,10})13,586.96 = 100,000$$
$$(DFA_{k,10}) = 7.360$$

Turning to Table 6–7, we find the discount factor, 7.360, in the 6 percent column of line 10. Hence, once again the rate of interest on the 10-year development loan is 6% per year.

Example 4: A Different Development Loan.   Now assume that the authorities decide to give you a break and require you to pay back only $12,500 per year over 10 years for the same $100,000. Clearly you are better off. But by how much has the rate of interest been reduced? Applying our formula, we have

$$(DFA_{k,10})12,500 = 100,000$$
$$(DFA_{k,10}) = 8$$

---

[5] In cases of unequal payments, the interest rate is calculated by a process of trial and error. For details, see the discussion of rates of return in Chapter 9.

A glance at Table 6–7 suffices to show that the factor 8 lies somewhere between 4% and 5% and, by inspection, somewhat closer to 4% than to 5%. If that is sufficient, OK, but a couple of punches on an appropriate pocket calculator[6] will give you a more exact answer: 4.28%.

INTEREST RATES WITH INTRAYEAR COMPOUNDING

All our loan examples have assumed annual compounding, but as we have already noted above, numerous intrayear compounding alternatives are often offered by banks and other financial institutions. In the United States and in some other countries, lenders are required by law to publish the effective annual rate of interest represented by their particular loan arrangements. Still, it may be useful to be able to check on them and to calculate the true annual rate yourself.

Eq. 6.4 above showed the general equation for compounded future value:

$$FV_n = P \left(1 + \frac{k}{m} \right)^{mn}$$

The expression $\left(1 + \frac{k}{m} \right)^{mn}$ is sufficient, for our purposes, to convert the

stated interest rate, k, into its effective annual rate for any compounding period.

Let's return to our previous example of a 6% interest rate, but assume that the interest payments are to be compounded semi-annually. What is the annual interest rate? Applying Eq. 6.4, we get the future value of one dollar:

$$\left(1 + \frac{.06}{2} \right)^2 = (1.03)\,(1.03) = 1.0609$$

and the annual interest rate is given by:

$$(1.0609 - 1)100 = 6.09\%$$

[6] Alternatively, you can derive a close approximation by using Table 6–7 and a technique known as linear interpolation:

STEP ONE: From Table 6–7. Calculate the difference between the DFAs for 4% and 5%: 8.111 − 7.722 = .389.

STEP TWO: Find the difference between your calculated DFA (8.000) and the DFA for 5% (7.722): 8.000 − 7.722 = .278.

STEP THREE: Divide the result of step 2 by that of step 1: .278 ÷ .389 = .715.

STEP FOUR: The calculated DFA represents 71.5% of the distance between 4% and 5%, and the interest rate given by 5% minus .715% = 4.29%, which is very close to the true rate.

If interest is to be compounded quarterly, we get:

$$\left(1 + \frac{.06}{4}\right)^4 = (1.015)^4 = 1.0614$$

and the annual interest rate is 6.14%.

AMORTIZATION OF LOANS

The concepts of future and present value are general and have numerous uses. In this section we focus on one of the more important applications, the amortization of loans.

The present value of an annuity of, say, C dollars per year can be written as:

$$PV = C(DFA_{k,n}) \tag{6.12}$$

Should we want to determine the equal annual amounts required to repay the principal and interest on a loan contract or mortgage, we solve Eq. 6.12 for C:

$$C = \frac{PV}{DFA_{k,n}} \tag{6.13}$$

If we substitute known values of PV, n, and k, the equal annual amounts can easily be found.

Assume that you want to determine the equal annual payments required to service a 3-year loan of $10,000 at 8% interest. Applying Eq. 6.13, we get:

$$C = \frac{10,000}{2.577} = 3,880.48$$

Table 6–9 shows the repayment schedule for this loan, assuming that the three annual payments of $3,880.48 are made at the end of each year. Note

TABLE 6–9   Loan Amortization for $10,000 Loan at 8% Interest and 3-Year Repayment Period

End of Year	Beginning of Year Principal (1)	Loan Repayment (2)	Payments Interest .08 × (1) (3)	Payments Principal (2) − (3) (4)	Balance of Loan Outstanding (1) − (4) (5)
1	$10,000.00	3,880.48	800.00	3,080.48	6,919.52
2	6,919.52	3,880.48	553.56	3,326.92	3,592.60
3	3,592.60	3,880.48	287.41	3,593.07	0*

* The slight discrepancy of 47 cents is due to rounding.

that the interest component of the annual payment declines over time, while the payments of the return of principal increase. This holds for all equal annual payment loans, since the interest component becomes smaller as the fixed rate is applied to a declining outstanding principal.

The Rule of 72   Finally, just in case you get caught without your calculator or PV tables you may want to recall a popular rule of thumb which requires neither. It is often convenient to get a quick idea of how rapidly the value of an investment will double. A simple rule, which is easy to remember, is this: "Divide 72 by the interest rate." For example, 72 divided by 8 is 9, which means that money invested at 8% doubles in approximately 9 years. A glance at Table A-1 in the Appendix can confirm the usefulness of the rule of 72. For example, money invested at 6% compounded doubles in about 12 years.

SUMMARY

One of the basic building blocks of financial analysis is the time dimension involved in the concepts of future and present value. The following are the key formulas for these concepts:

future value = principal + interest income

or

$$FV_n = P\,(1 + k)^n$$

where FV_n is the compounded future value at the end of n years, P is the principal, and k is the appropriate compounding rate.

future value of a series of receipts = sum of future values

or

$$FV_n = C_1\,(1 + k)^{n-1} + C_2\,(1 + k)^{n-2} + \ldots + C_{n-1}\,(1 + k) + C_n$$

Future value of an annuity:

$$FVA_{k,n} = C \sum_{t=1}^{n} (1 + k)^{n-t}$$

where C is the fixed annual receipt.

present value = future value ÷ (1 + discount rate)^n

or

$$PV = \frac{FV_n}{(1 + k)^n}$$

The actual calculation of present value can be greatly simplified by using a table of present value:

$$PV = (DF_{k,n})FV_n$$

where PV denotes present value.

present value of a series of receipts = sum of present values

or

$$PV = \sum_{t=1}^{n} \frac{C_t}{(1 + k)^t}$$

where C_t denotes the receipt in year t.

Once again, for an annuity, the actual calculation can be simplified by using the present value of an annuity table:

$$\begin{matrix} \textbf{present value of} \\ \textbf{an annuity} \end{matrix} = \begin{matrix} \textbf{fixed annual} \\ \textbf{receipt} \end{matrix} \times \begin{matrix} \textbf{sum of appropriate} \\ \textbf{discount rates} \end{matrix}$$

In symbols:

$$PV = C(DFA_{k,n})$$

where C is the fixed value of the annuity, and $DFA_{k,n}$ is the appropriate discount factor.

The present value formulas were also used to derive the formula for calculating compound interest for loans of varying maturity. In addition, the impact of changing the compounding (discounting) periods was determined. Other things being equal, an increase in the frequency of compounding increases the future value of a given sum and decreases the present value of a fixed receipt in a given future year.

REVIEW EXERCISE

Circle the correct word(s) to complete each sentence; see p. 139 for correct answers.

6.1 A typical financial decision involves the comparison of present *inflation/outlays* and future *benefits/inflation*.

6.2 A dollar received today *is/is not* the equivalent of a dollar received in the future.

6.3 The future value of a sum of money invested at a *constant/zero* interest rate is constant.

6.4 The greater the frequency with which interest is compounded, the *lower/higher* will be the future value of a bank deposit.

6.5 In the case of quarterly compounding, the bank credits the account with the interest every *3/4* months.

6.6 An annuity is a series of *variable/fixed* payments over a given number of years.

6.7 In the case of an annuity due, the payments become available 1 month *earlier/later* than in the case of an ordinary annuity.

6.8 The process of moving back in time is called *compounding/discounting*.

6.9 Present value is the future value in period *n* *multiplied by/divided by* 1 plus the discount rate, raised to the power *n*.

6.10 Given the discount rate, the present value of a dollar *rises/declines* the longer we have to wait for it.

6.11 The rate of interest is defined as the *discount rate/compounding rate* which equates the present value of the loan repayments to the amount originally received.

6.12 When amortizing a loan, the interest component of the annual payment *rises/declines* over time, while the return of principal component *increases/decreases* over time.

6.13 The rule of 72 says: Divide 72 by the interest rate and the result tells you how many years it takes for your money to *double/treble*.

QUESTIONS

6.1 Define the following terms:
  a. Principal
  b. Future value
  c. Present value
  d. Annuity
  e. Annuity due
  f. Compounding, discounting
  g. Intrayear compounding
  h. Amortization of a loan

6.2 What does the 1 stand for in the future value formula, $FV = (1 + k)^n$?

6.3 Janet tells you: "I have just changed banks. I am now going to one which has a monthly compounding period, even though it pays ¼% less than my previous bank, which compounded annually." Under what circumstances has Janet done the correct thing?

6.4 Bank A pays 12% interest on your deposit and compounds semi-annually. Bank B pays 11.77%. What is the compounding period for bank B which will make you prefer it to bank A?

6.5 Assume you are going to receive the following stream of payments during the next 50 years: $1000 today; starting next year, you will receive 7.5% over and above the previous year's amount. Assume further that the appropriate discount rate is 7.5%. What is the present value of this stream of payments? (Answer without the use of either present value tables or a calculator.)

6.6 "In order to compute the present value, I simply add the cash flows." What assumption are you making?

6.7 You have just computed the future value of a stream of inflows and outflows for the next 25 years, on the assumption that all payments and receipts take place at the end of the year, using a 9.5% discount rate. Now your boss tells you that all payments and receipts will take place at the beginning of the year. What do you do?

6.8 Can the present value tables in this book be used for semi-annual compounding? Explain.

6.9 Show the mathematical relationship between the present value and the future value of one dollar.

6.10 Evaluate the following statement: "I do not like amortization of loans, since one has to repay the principal sooner than for conventional loans. In the latter, only interest is paid each year; the principal is repaid only at the end of the last year."

6.11 *(Optional: for computer hackers)* Write a computer program that prints out the following tables for interest rates between 1% and 25% (at 0.5% increments) and for 1 to 25 years:
  a. Present value of $1
  b. Future value of $1
  c. Present value of an annuity of $1 per year
  d. Future value of an annuity of $1 per year

PROBLEMS

6.1 **Future value.** Jane invests $10 in bank A, $20 in bank B, and $30 in bank C. How much money will she receive 1 year, 2 years, 3 years, 5 years, and 10 years from now, if the annual interest rate is 4%, 6%, 12%, or 24%? (Show your answer in tabular form.)

6.2 **Intrayear compounding.** Jane has just found out that bank A compounds its interest semi-annually, bank B compounds quarterly, and bank C uses monthly compounding. How does this affect your answer to the previous question?

6.3 **Future value of a mixed series.** Milson & Co. forecast the following net receipts for the years 1988 to 1991 (in thousands of dollars): 1988, $1,250; 1989, $1,430; 1990, $1,680; 1991, $1,715. Assume that all cash flows take place at the end of the year.
  a. What is the future value of the cash flow if the compounding rate is 10%?
  b. What is the future value of the cash flow if the compounding rate is 12%?
  c. What is the future value of the cash flow if the compounding rate is 8%?

6.4 **Future value of an annuity.** Patricia Peterson, financial manager of Milson & Co., is thinking to herself: "Wouldn't it be nice to have the same cash flow each year, instead of having to deal with a mixed series?"
  a. With one constraint that the future value of the cash flow remains unchanged, what constant annual cash flow will Milson have to generate? Assume a compounding rate of 10%.
  b. What is your answer if the compounding rate is 12%?
  c. What is your answer if the compounding rate is 8%?

6.5 **Present value.** Jim invests $5 in bank A, $8 in bank B, and $13 in bank C. What are the present values of the investments if he deposits these amounts for 1 year, 2 years, 3 years, 5 years, and 10 years, at 4%, 6%, 12%, or 24% interest? (Show your answer in tabular form.)

6.6 **Intrayear discounting.** Jane has just told Jim that bank A compounds interest semi-annually, bank B compounds it quarterly, and bank C uses a monthly compounding period. How does this affect your answer to the previous question?

6.7 Present value of a mixed series.   Take another look at Milson & Co. of problem 6.3.

  a. What is the present value of the cash flow, if the discount rate is 10%?
  b. What is the present value of the cash flow, if the discount rate is 12%?
  c. What is the present value of the cash flow, if the discount rate is 8%?

6.8 Present value of an annuity.   Milson & Co. would like to compute the annuities that would leave the present values of the cash flows unchanged. Can you help? Use discount rates of 8%, 10%, and 12%. (*Hint:* If you have already solved problem 6.4, there is no need to use present value tables or a calculator.)

6.9   A local savings and loan association offers to loan you $2,560. The terms of the loan require you to pay back $2,850 two years from now.

  a. What interest rate is the S&L charging?
  b. The bank manager has changed her mind; she wants to receive the $2,850 at the end of the first year. What interest are you being charged now?

6.10 Present value, future value.   The Woolesley Company expects the following sales during the next 6 years (all receipts are assumed to take place on the last day of the year):

Year:	1	2	3	4	5	6
Receipts:	7,500	12,680	8,350	15,230	16,000	18,300

Woolesley also expects the following costs during the next 6 years (all outlays are incurred on the *first day* of the year):

Year:	1	2	3	4	5	6
Outlays:	6,200	10,700	8,200	13,700	14,800	17,200

Assume a discount rate of 8%.

  a. What is the present value of the firm's cash flow? (Cash flow is defined simply as sales receipts minus outflows.)
  b. What is the future value of the cash flow?

6.11 Annuities.   Life & Health Insurance Company offers you the following plan: During the next 30 years you pay $2,000 at the end of each year. Starting at the end of year 31, you (or your heirs) will receive a pension for the following 15 years. The discount rate used by the company to calculate your pension is 5%.

  a. What is the size of your annual pension?
  b. If you could take a one-time lump sum payment at the end of year 35 instead of the pension, how high would the *equivalent* lump sum payment have to be?

6.12 Annuities.   Life & Health offers you a plan similar to that in the previous problem. It offers a pension of $10,000 per year, for 15 years, starting at the end of year 31. The discount rate is 5%.

a. What is the annual amount you will be required to pay during the next 30 years?

b. What is the equivalent lump sum that you would be willing to pay today in order to receive the pension?

6.13 Annuities.   John has won a lawsuit against the Smith Company. The terms are the following: He will receive a stream of payments for 12 years, starting at $1,600 at the end of this year. The subsequent payments will grow by 14.5% each year. John and Smith agree to settle the whole affair today with a lump sum payment. They agree on a discount rate of 6%. What payment does John receive?

6.14 Amortization of loans.   The Waterfalls Bank agrees to loan you $150,000 for 8 years. It charges an 8% interest rate and wants you to pay equal amounts each year, on the condition that after the eighth payment you will have paid all the interest and will have repaid the entire principal.

a. What are the yearly payments?

b. Prepare a table that shows the interest component and repayment of the principal component of each payment.

6.15 Amortization of loans.   The First International Bank also agrees to loan you $150,000. Its loan agreement specifies that you pay $25,000 at the end of each year for 8 years. What interest rate does this bank charge? Prepare a table which shows the payments and repayment of principal components of each year's payment to the bank.

6.16 Computer problem, present value.   Compute the present values of the following projects:

	Net Cash Receipt at the End of Year					Discount	Compounding
Project	1	2	3	4	5	Rate	Frequency
A	12,345	15,898	9,419	23,987	17,823	7.356%	annual
B	3,789	33,451	11,098	17,634	21,333	9.024%	quarterly
C	16,234	786	9,234	21,899	24,445	6.384%	monthly
D	41,567	212	455	1,211	234	11.023%	weekly
E	11,345	0	0	12,876	0	13.059%	daily

SAMPLE PROBLEM

SP6.1 A salesman from Stevenson Insurance Company would like to sell you the following plan: You pay $15,000 at the end of each year for the next 10 years. Starting at the end of year 25, you (or your heirs) will receive a yearly pension of $25,000 for 15 years. The discount rate is 6%. Do you accept the offer?

Solution To Sample Problem

SP6.1 The answer depends on the comparison of two annuities: (a) A 10-year annuity of $15,000 (outflow): present value = 15,000 ($DFA_{6\%,10}$) = 15,000(7.36) = 110,400; (b) A 15-year annuity of $25,000 (inflow): present value = 25,000 ($DFA_{6\%,15}$) = 25,000(9.712) = 242,800. However, the second annuity's present value was calculated for the *beginning* of year 25. So we still have to discount the result (242,800) back to year 0: present value = 242,800/(1 + .06)^{24} = 242,800 × (0.247) = 59,972. Hence the present value of the outflow (110,400) is greater than the present value of the inflow (59,972). The offer should be rejected.

Answers To Review Exercise

6.1 outlays, benefits   **6.2** is not   **6.3** zero

6.4 higher   **6.5** 3   **6.6** fixed   **6.7** earlier

6.8 discounting   **6.9** divided by   **6.10** declines

6.11 discount rate   **6.12** declines, increases   **6.13** double

SUGGESTIONS FOR FURTHER READING

The derivations of the present value formulas are given in most textbooks on the mathematics of finance. See, for example, Robert Cissell, Helen Cissel, and David C. Flaspohler, *Mathematics of Finance* (Boston: Houghton-Mifflin, 1978).

To get the most out of your pocket calculator, consult the owner's manual. See, for example, Texas Instruments, *Professional Business Analyst Guide,* which is based on the BA-55 financial calculator.

7 | Valuation of Stocks and Bonds

Chapter 6 established the basic principle that money has a *time value*. The concept of *present value*, which rests on this same principle, is very general, and can be used to value investments in both financial and real assets. In this chapter, we examine the principal factors that determine the value of financial assets. The market forces which determine financial values are of interest to any investor, but they are of special concern to financial managers. Recall, in this context, that Chapter 1 established the proposition that all major corporate decisions should be evaluated in terms of their impact on the value of the firm's common stock. Since firms typically raise capital in two major forms, debt and equity, it is crucial that financial managers understand the forces that affect the market value of securities. The concept of present value is used to develop the basic valuation model for both bonds and stocks. The value of these securities depends on the size and timing of their future cash flows and the degree of risk. In the case of common stock, special attention is also paid to the important growth property of such securities. To this end, a dividend valuation model is spelled out for cases of constant (and of limited) growth in the future stream of dividends.

THE BASIC VALUATION MODEL

The valuation of any asset, real or financial, depends on the cash flow it generates over its economic life. In terms of the analysis in Chapter 6, the value of an asset is simply the discounted present value of its expected future cash flows:

$$V_0 = \frac{CF_1}{1 + k} + \frac{CF_2}{(1 + k)^2} + \ldots + \frac{CF_n}{(1 + k)^n} \qquad (7.1)$$

where

V_0 = the asset's current value—i.e., its value at time zero

CF_t = the expected cash flow from the asset in period t

n = the asset's economic life—the period during which cash flows are generated

k = the discount rate

Using the present value notation of Chapter 6, this formula can be rewritten as:

$$V_0 = CF_1 (DF_{k,1}) + CF_2(DF_{k,2}) + \ldots + CF_n(DF_{k,n}) \qquad (7.2)$$

The present value approach rests on three basic principles:

1. Only *cash flows* are relevant for the valuation process. The emphasis on the actual receipt of the cash flow is essential in order to reflect the time value of money properly.
2. Value depends on the *future;* past flows are irrelevant for the valuation process. It is the asset's *expected* cash flow that determines its current value.
3. The discount rate used in the valuation model must reflect the asset's risk—the degree of uncertainty attached to the future cash flow. The greater the risk, the higher the appropriate discount rate.

Once all the variables are known, it takes only a few minutes to compute Eq. 7.2. The valuation of assets, however, is not a simple matter. Estimating future cash flows and determining appropriate discount rates are intellectually challenging and time-consuming tasks. In fact, the remainder of this book is concerned, for the most part, with little else. Practical valuation is not likely to become an exact science because it rests on the skills and judgment of the financial analyst or manager. With this in mind, we might add a fourth valuation principle: "It is better to be approximately right than exactly wrong."

BOND VALUATION

bond
A legal contract by which the borrower agrees to pay the lender a series of interest payments and to repay the original principal.

Broadly speaking, firms finance capital investment projects with debt or with equity (funds provided by, and belonging to, the firm's owners). We first examine the valuation process for bonds, which are a very important form of corporate long-term debt.

A typical **bond** is a legal contract by which the borrower (debtor) agrees to pay the lender (creditor, in this instance the bondholder) a series of interest payments, and to repay the original principal *(face value,* or *par value)* when the bond matures. Since the bondholder receives the stream of benefits over a number of years, the bond's current value (price) can be found by using the present value formula. For the moment, we leave aside many of the details of bond payments, such as semi-annual interest payments or serial redemptions of principal over a number of years.

$$P_0 = \text{bond price} = C\left[\sum_{t=1}^{n}\left(\frac{1}{1 + k_d}\right)^t\right] + M\left[\left(\frac{1}{1 + k_d}\right)^n\right] \qquad (7.3)$$

$$= C\,(DFA_{k_d,n}) + M\,(DF_{k_d,n}) \qquad (7.4)$$

where

P_0	= the bond's current market price
C	= the coupon interest paid at the end of year, in dollars
$DFA_{k_d,n}$	= discount factor for annuity
$DF_{k_d,n}$	= discount factor of sum received in year n
M	= the bond's redemption value upon maturity
n	= the year in which the bond matures
k_d	= the *market* interest rate (yield) on this type of bond; the subscript d denotes debt

A numerical example can help clarify bond valuation. Assume a 20-year bond with a par value of $1,000, which pays $60 in interest at the end of each year. At the end of the 20th year the bond matures, and the face value of $1,000 is returned to the investor. We also assume that the market interest rate for such a bond is 8% (k_d = 8%).

Given the current observed market interest rate of 8% for new bonds of this type, the appropriate discount factors are

$$(DFA_{8\%,20}) = 9.818$$
$$(DF_{8\%,20}) = 0.215$$

Applying Eq. 7.4, the current market price of the bond is $804.08:

$$P_0 = 60\,(9.818) + 1,000\,(.215) = 589.08 + 215 = \$804.08$$

The value of the bond, $804.08, is below its face value. This reflects the fact that the 6% coupon ($60 per $1,000 of par value) will yield the required market rate of 8% only at the lower purchase price of $804. Hence the bond will sell at a *discount* from par value.

If the market interest rate had been lower than the coupon rate of 6%, say 4%, the value of the bond would be higher than its par value—in this instance, $1,271.40:

$$P_0 = 60\,(13.590) = 1,000\,(.456) = 815.40 + 456 = \$1,271.40$$

The rise in the bond's price can readily be explained. Since the market rate is only 4%, every rational investor would like to buy a 6% coupon bond at par value. However, the increased demand for the bonds drives up their price until they also yield the market interest rate of 4%. But this implies a price of $1,271.40 for the bond in question, so that the bond will sell in the market at a *premium* over par.

In the special case in which the market interest rate just equals the bond's coupon rate, in this example 6%, the bond will sell *at par*—that is, for a price of $1,000:

$$P_0 = 60 \ (11.470) + 1,000 \ (.312) = 688.20 + 312 = \$1,000$$

The forces of supply and demand determine the appropriate interest yield, (k_d), for the bond in question. And as we pointed out in Chapter 3, this rate will reflect the risk premium necessary to cover default and maturity risks. Since a bond's cash flow (the stream of interest payments) and redemption of principal at maturity are known in advance, the required market interest rate determines the bond's price.

CALCULATING THE INTEREST RATE ON BONDS

Bond yields are important to investors. More often than not, bonds are purchased for their long-term return. An insurance company, for example, is concerned with the *long-term* return that can be earned on bonds currently purchased, since this return is an important factor influencing the terms the company is able to offer new clients. Similarly, a firm that finances part of a long-term project by issuing bonds will be concerned with the interest cost over the entire life of the debt.

yield to maturity (YTM)
The interest rate earned on a bond purchased at its current market price and held until maturity.

The present value formula can also be used to determine interest rates. The interest rate on a bond is called its **yield to maturity (YTM),** or simply *yield*. It is the rate of interest investors will earn if they purchase the bonds at their current market price (P_0) and hold them until maturity. In this instance, we plug in the bond price (P_0), and solve Eq. 7.3 for the interest yield, k_d.

Consider the bond in our previous example: $60 annual interest, par value of $1,000, and redemption upon maturity at the end of 20 years. What is the yield to maturity of such a bond, if the asking price is $470.38? From Eq. 7.3 we have

$$470.38 = 60 \left[\sum_{t=1}^{n} \left(\frac{1}{1 + k_d} \right)^t \right] + 1,000 \left[\left(\frac{1}{1 + k_d} \right)^n \right]$$

or equivalently

$$470.38 = 60 \ (DFA_{kd, \ 20}) + 1,000 \ (DF_{kd, \ 20})$$

The bond's yield is unknown, but we can find k_d by trial and error.[1] Since the bond is being offered at a deep discount from par at $470.38, the

---

[1] Alternatively, the yield can be readily calculated on many "business" calculators.

yield must be considerably higher than the coupon interest rate of 6%. As a first approximation, we try the discount factors for 10% interest:

$$60(8.514) + 1,000 (.149) = 659.84$$

The present value of the cash flow is greater than purchase price (659.84 > 470.38). Hence we must try a higher interest rate. If we use the discount factors for 14%, we get:

$$60 (6.623) + 1,000 (.973) = 470.38$$

which is exactly equal to the purchase price. Thus, the bond's yield to maturity (YTM) is 14%.

What we have called the interest rate on a bond, k_d, can now be defined more precisely as its yield to maturity. In our specific example:

$$k_d = YTM = 14\%$$

Interest Rate Risk

Market interest rates fluctuate for a wide variety of economic reasons. For example, the demand for funds by corporations rises and falls with the phases of the business cycle; a firm's default risk may change; expectations of inflation are subject to change. A glance back at Eq. 7.3 will verify that an *inverse relationship* exists between interest yields and bond prices. Yields rise when bond prices fall, and vice versa. This relationship can best be seen by considering the rate of interest on a **perpetuity**, that is, a bond whose principal is not redeemable. The famous British consols, issued to help finance the Napoleonic wars, in the early nineteenth century, are an example of this type of bond.

perpetuity
A bond whose principal is not redeemable.

The present value of a perpetuity[2] is a special case of Eq. 7.3, in which the discount factor of an annuity is equal to $1/k_d$

$$P_0 = C (1/k_d) = C/k_d \qquad (7.4a)$$

where

C = the coupon interest
k_d = the bond's yield
P_0 = the bond's current price

Solving (7.4a) for the bond's annual yield, we get:

$$k_d = \frac{C}{P_0}$$

Thus, for a perpetuity the yield is found by dividing the annual interest coupon *(C)* by the bond's market price.

Once again, this formula confirms that the higher the price of the bond, the lower the yield, and vice versa. Since the interest coupon is fixed

[2] The formula for the present value of an annuity is derived in Appendix 7A at the end of the chapter.

for the life of the contract (in the case of a perpetuity, forever), fluctuations in the *market's required yield* must induce changes in the price of the bond. For example, consider a 6% nonredeemable bond which was originally issued at a price of 100. Applying Eq. 7.4a, we have:

$$P_0 = 100 = \frac{C}{k_d} = \frac{6}{0.06}$$

Now assume that, for any number of reasons, the market rate of interest on bonds of a similar type rises to 8%. This means that new bonds, which by definition are perfect substitutes for the outstanding bonds, are now being offered at 8%. Investors will not be willing to buy (or hold) the old bonds, unless their yield is equalized to that of the new bonds. However, this can occur only if the old bonds' price falls sufficently to raise their yield to 8%:

$$P_0 = \frac{6}{0.08} = 75$$

In this instance, the outstanding bonds' price must fall to $75. Conversely, should the market interest rate (on identical bonds) fall, say to 4%, the price of the outstanding bonds will rise to $150. At a price of $150, the yield on the old bonds is also 4%:

$$P_0 = \frac{6}{0.04} = 150$$

$$k_d = \frac{6}{150} = 0.04 = 4\%$$

law of one price
The principle that in an efficient capital market identical products cannot sell at different prices.

These results reflect a special case of the **law of one price.** This is the fundamental principle that in a perfectly efficient capital market in which all relevant information is freely available, identical products cannot sell at different prices. Of course, in practice tax considerations, transactions costs, and other market imperfections prevent the exact equalization of prices (yields). These deviations are usually small and do not alter the underlying adjustment mechanism. In fact, were it not for the need to adjust yields, there would be very little reason for the prices of government bonds, which have no default risk, to fluctuate. A drastic fall in U.S. government bond prices does not imply a weakening of confidence in the government's ability to meet its obligations; it is the result of a rise in market interest rates. The latter, for example, might reflect a more restrictive monetary policy, an increase in the demand for credit, or any number of other causes.

interest rate risk (maturity risk)
A risk taken by investors that interest rates will rise and the market price of currently held bonds will fall.

The inverse relationship between interest rates and bond prices is important for both individual and institutional investors. Clearly a rise in interest rates implies the availability in the market of higher yields on bonds. But as we have already noted, the rise in interest rates is a mixed blessing. Investors who hold previously issued bonds suffer a "loss" due to the fall in the market price of these older bonds. This **interest rate risk**, or **maturity risk**, is vitally important for financial management.

For convenience, we used above the example of a nonredeemable bond to illustrate the relationship between bond prices and interest yields. When bonds with different maturities are considered, another systematic relationship between prices and yields can be found. This relationship is illustrated in Table 7–1, which shows the prices of 6% coupon bonds, of varying maturities, for alternative market interest rates. Note that the bond price equals 100, for all maturities, when the market rate is assumed to be 6%. However, should the market rate of interest rise, the drop in price is greater for bonds of longer maturity. Thus, a rise in the market rate from 6% to 8% causes the price of a 1-year bond to fall from $100 to $98.15. In this instance, the fall in price is less than 2%. In the case of a 20-year bond, the price drops almost 20% (from $100 to $80.41). Conversely, the windfall gain, in the event of a fall in interest rates, is again greater for the longer-term bonds.

From Table 7–1 it is clear that the risk exposure on bonds of longer maturities is greater than on those which are close to maturity. This is illustrated graphically in Figure 7–1, which plots the relationship between bond price and the market interest rate for a 1-year and a 20-year bond. The steeper slope of the long term curve is the measure of the enhanced risk.[3]

The reason for the greater sensitivity of the longer-term bonds can be explained intuitively. Assume that the market interest rate doubles, from 6% to 12%. What is the impact of such a rise on the current price of a bond that has one year to maturity (line 1 of Table 7–1)? Its price falls to $94.66,

[3] This always holds true for bonds selling at par and also over a wide range of bonds which sell at a discount.

TABLE 7–1   Price of a $100, 6% Coupon Bond at Alternative Market Rates of Interest, by Maturity* (In Dollars)

Years to Maturity	Market Rate of Interest			
	4%	6%	8%	12%
1	101.97	100.00	98.15	94.66
2	103.82	100.00	96.40	89.84
3	105.55	100.00	94.86	85.61
4	107.28	100.00	93.37	81.83
5	108.91	100.00	92.06	78.32
8	113.50	100.00	88.48	70.21
10	116.27	100.00	86.56	66.10
15	122.21	100.00	82.85	59.17
20	127.14	100.00	80.41	55.22
30	134.55	100.00	77.44	51.63
40	139.56	100.00	76.15	50.56
50	142.30	100.00	75.50	50.12

* Coupon interest is assumed to be payable at the end of the year.

FIGURE 7–1
Price of a 1-year and 20-year 6% Coupon Bond for Alternative Market Interest Rates

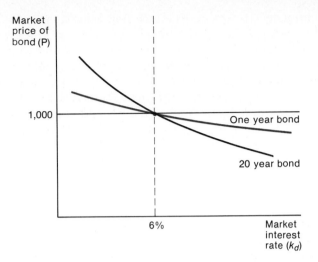

for at that price the expected return on the bond is 12%. An investor who acquires the bond for $94.66 will earn $11.34 ($6 in interest plus a capital gain of $5.34). The capital gain is the difference between the maturity value and the current price ($100 − $94.66 = $5.34). Together, they provide the required 12% rate of return:

$$11.34/94.66 = 0.12 = 12\%$$

But what happens with a longer-term bond? Here too, investors expect a capital gain at maturity from the difference between the redemption value and the discounted purchase price. But the longer they have to wait until the date of maturity, the smaller is the *present value* of the capital gain. Hence the current price of the longer-term bonds must fall farther in order to achieve the 12% return.

Similar considerations apply to a fall in the market interest rate. In this instance, the current price of the bond will rise above its current redemption value, creating a capital loss for potential investors. The loss reflects the difference between the (above par) current price paid for the bond and the par value received upon redemption. Here too, the longer-term bond's price will be more sensitive to the fall in interest rates because of the influence of present value. As a result, a greater rise in the price of the longer-term bonds is required to achieve a given reduction in yield.

Bond Valuation with Semi-annual Compounding

Because of the sensitivity of current bond prices to fluctuations in the market interest rate, bonds typically sell in the market at a *discount* (below par value) or at a *premium* (above par value). This complicates the calculations of yields somewhat, but they can readily be handled, even by a simple hand calculator, or by the trial and error method.

Another complication arises from the need to compound bond interest semi-annually. In practice the cash flow from a typical bond is more complicated than Eq. 7.3 suggests. Interest coupons are usually paid semi-annually, and the redemption of principal is often prorated over a number of years. Even so, the calculation of bond yields is still a relatively simple matter. In the past, detailed bond tables were used to eliminate all the tedious arithmetic necessary to calculate the yield. Today, the fat volumes of bond tables have given way to electronic calculators and computers.

Even if you lose your computer program, a slight modification of Eq. 7.3 can deal with the valuation of bonds when interest is paid twice a year. From Chapter 6 we know that three minor changes in the valuation formula are required to reflect such intrayear compounding:

1. The semiannual interest coupon must be divided by 2: $C/2$.
2. The number of periods is calculated by multiplying the years to maturity by 2: $2n$.
3. The semiannual interest rate is defined as the annual rate divided by 2: $k_d/2$.

Inserting these changes into Eq. 7.3, we derive the following equation for determining the price of a bond that pays interest every 6 months:

$$P_0 = \frac{C}{2}\left[\sum_{t=1}^{2n}\left(\frac{1}{1 + k_d/2}\right)^t\right] + M\left(\frac{1}{1 + k_d/2}\right)^{2n} \tag{7.5}$$

Consider an example of a $1,000 bond ($M = 1,000$) which pays annual interest of $100 ($C = 100$), and matures in 15 years ($n = 15$). Assuming a market interest rate of 8% ($k_d = 8\%$), its price is $1,171:

$$P_0 = 100\,(DFA_{8\%,15}) + 1,000\,(DF_{8\%,15})$$
$$= 100\,(8.560) + 1.000\,(.315)$$
$$= 856 + 315 = 1,171$$

Now assume that the same bond pays interest semi-annually. In this case, $C/2 = 50$, $2n = 30$, and $k_d/2 = 4\%$. Applying Eq. 7.5, we find that the bond price becomes $1,172.60:

$$P_0 = 50\,(DFA_{4\%,30}) + 1,000\,(DF_{4\%,30})$$
$$= 50\,(17.292) + 1,000\,(.308)$$
$$= 864.60 + 308 = 1,172.60$$

In this particular case, receiving the interest payments earlier (semi-annually) offsets the higher discount rate. As a result, the price of the bond with semi-annual compounding is slightly higher than with end-of-year interest payments.[4]

---

[4]Note that $(1 + k/2)^2$ is greater than $(1 + k)$. It is not always possible to detect these small differences in price when using PV tables because of rounding.

STOCK VALUATION

Unlike the case for most bonds, the return on common stock (dividends and capital gains) is highly uncertain, and can change from period to period. It is the size of the return and the degree of risk which together determine the value of a share of stock to an investor. We will first examine two traditional methods for evaluating common stock, net asset value and valuation using price/earnings ratios, before applying the basic valuation formula (Eq. 7.1) to equities. The detailed analysis of the risk-return tradeoff is deferred to Chapter 8.

Net Asset Value Approach

net asset value (book value)
A company's total net assets divided by the total number of shares outstanding.

Net asset value, or **book value** as it is also called, is derived from the accounting identity (see Chapter 4). The book value of net assets is defined as total assets minus total liabilities. But this, of course, is also the definition of net worth, or the book value of the firm's equity. Book value per share is easily calculated by dividing the number of shares into total net assets (or net worth).

Consider the following example. On December 31, 1987, the Mobility Oil Corporation had total assets of $6,872 million and total liabilities of $2,800 million and hence a net worth of $4,072 million. The company had 101.3 million shares of common stock outstanding, so that the calculation of book value per share becomes:

$$\frac{\$4,072 \text{ million}}{101.3 \text{ million}} = \$40.20 \text{ per share}$$

But although the book value approach is deceptively easy, it is a very unreliable measure of economic value. As a result, stocks often trade at prices that have little relationship to the book value of their net assets. This is not surprising. As we emphasized in Chapter 4, accounting practice deviates significantly from economic concepts, so there is little reason to suppose that accounting and economic valuations will be similar. One example should be sufficient. Say that Mobility Oil has a plant which has a net value in its balance sheet of $50 million, but which today is worth double that amount on the open market. This extreme difference between accounting and economic values might reflect any number of causes: a rise in property value due to inflation, a change in local zoning laws, or perhaps even the discovery of oil under the basement.

In general, basing valuation on asset values is a poor substitute for the valuation of cash flows because (a) Not all of a firm's valuable assets appear in the balance sheet; quality of management, or a 10-year contract to supply widgets to General Motors, for example, do not. (b) Not all assets that do appear in the balance sheet have economic value—for example, an inventory of buggy whips.

The Price/Earnings Multiplier

Many financial analysts use some variant of the price/earnings ratio to value a firm's stock. Assume a company with an EPS of $10 and a share price of $100; the price/earnings ratio (price/EPS) is 10. This is also called the **earnings multiplier.** If we multiply current earnings by 10, we derive the market price of $10.

earnings multiplier
The reciprocal of the P/E ratio, that is, share price divided by the EPS.

Despite their popularity, price/earnings ratios are particularly difficult to interpret, except in the economically uninteresting case of constant growth (see below). Low multipliers mean that current earnings are reasonably priced, which is a desirable attribute, but they may also reflect a poor outlook for future earnings. High earnings multipliers, on the other hand, mean that current earnings are being priced high, which is undesirable from the investor's viewpoint. But the high P/E ratio may also reflect excellent growth prospects, which investors value highly.

Some analysts attempt to overcome this difficulty by calculating the price/future earnings ratio:

price/future earnings
Ratio of current share price to expected EPS.

$$\textbf{price/future earnings} = \frac{\text{current price}}{\text{expected EPS}}$$

But this brings us back to the need to value the shares by the present values of their future cash flows.

APPLYING THE PRESENT VALUE MODEL[5]

The present value concept can also be used to define a valuation model for a firm's common stock. As we have already pointed out, a security's market value (or price) is given by the present value of the cash flow to its owner, in this case the shareholder.

Components of the Cash Flow

The cash flow of a common stock has two principal components: (1) The shareholder receives **cash dividends;** (2) if the shareholder can sell the stock at a higher price than he or she originally paid, he or she will enjoy a **capital gain.** Should the price fall, the shareholder will suffer a capital loss. However, people rarely buy a common stock whose price is expected to fall, so we can safely assume that investors in common stock *expect* to earn a capital gain in addition to dividends.

cash dividend
The part of a company's profits that are distributed to shareholders in the form of cash.

capital gain
The increase in the value of a share of stock between the time it is bought and the time it is sold.

[5] This chapter concentrates on the principles underlying the application of the concept of present value to the valuation of common stock. For a discussion of other important features of equities, see chapter 12.

**The Market
Capitalization
Rate**

**market
capitalization rate
(required rate of
return)(k_e)**
*The discount rate
on common stock.*

Since the investment in common stock is usually a much riskier venture than the investment in a bond, the market rate of interest is not the appropriate discount rate for the expected stream of dividends and capital gains. In general, investors will require a higher rate of return on stock, thereby raising the discount rate. We will refer to this discount rate as the **market capitalization rate**, or the **required rate of return** on equity (k_e). (The factors determining the required return will be discussed in more detail in Chapter 8.)

**Present Value
of the Cash
Flow**

In order to derive the valuation formula, we first take a look at the formula for the rate of return on common stock. For simplicity, consider an investor who holds the stock for only 1 year:

$$\text{rate of return} = \frac{\text{cash flow}}{\text{purchase price}}$$

or in symbols:

$$k_e = \frac{D_1 + (P_1 - P_0)}{P_0} = \frac{D_1 + P_1}{P_0} - 1 \tag{7.6}$$

where

P_0 = current market price
P_1 = the share's price at the end of the year, and therefore ($P_1 - P_0$)
    = the expected capital gain
D_1 = the first year dividend (for simplicity only we assume it is paid at the end of the year)
k_e = the expected rate of return (the market capitalization rate); the subscript e denotes equity

If we let $D_1 = \$10$, $P_1 = 105$, and $P_0 = 100$, we get:

$$k_e = \frac{10 + 105}{100} - 1 = 0.15 = 15\%$$

Thus the expected 1-year rate of return on a common stock that offers a $10 dividend, a capital gain of $5 (105 − 100 = 5), and that has a current market price of $100 is 15%.

Now let us apply the present value principle. Turning Eq. 7.6 around and rearranging the terms, we derive the formula for the price of a common stock when held for 1 year:[6]

$$P_0 = \frac{D_1 + P_1}{1 + k_e} \tag{7.7}$$

---

[6] Equation (7.5) can be written as:

$$1 + k_e = \frac{D_1 + P_1}{P_0}, \text{ so that}$$

$$P_0 = \frac{D_1 + P_1}{1 + k_e}$$

What happens if we extend the holding period to 2 years? Once again, investors will be looking at dividends plus the possibility of a capital gain. However, in this instance the cash flow is given by a 2-year dividend stream plus the proceeds from the sale of the stock at the end of the second year:[7]

$$P_0 = \frac{D_1}{1 + k_e} + \frac{D_2 + P_2}{(1 + k_e)^2}$$

where

D_2 = the expected dividend at the end of second year

P_2 = the expected market price at the end of the second year

Thus the current price of a share of common stock remains the present value of the expected cash flow (dividends and capital gain) even if the stock is held for more than 1 year.

Present Value of Dividends

The period over which an investor is assumed to hold the stock in question can easily by extended. If we assume, for example, a holding period of 3 years, the present value formula becomes:

$$P_0 = \frac{D_1}{1 + k_e} + \frac{D_2}{(1 + k_e)^2} + \frac{D_3 + P_3}{(1 + k_e)^3}$$

Note that as the holding period is extended, the expected market price recedes into the future. If we extend our holdings into the very distant future, say 100 years, the value of the stock becomes the present value of the stream of dividends over 100 years, plus the *present value* of the sale price of the stock at the end of 100 years. But since the discount factors for the distant future are very small, the influence of the capital gain can be ignored. For example, if we assume a 10% market capitalization rate, the discount factor to be applied in year 100 is only 0.0073%. The present value of each $1000 expected to be received at the end of 100 years is only 7 cents. And should the required rate of return (capitalization rate) be higher—say 15%—the discount factor is even smaller (in this instance 0.000085%).

If we extend the investment horizon *indefinitely* (that is until infinity) the influence of the capital gain disappears altogether. In this case, the val-

---

[7] The formula is derived by plugging in the valuation formula for next year's price:

$$P_1 = \frac{D_2 + P_2}{1 + k_e}$$

Hence,

$$P_0 = \frac{D_1 + P_1}{1 + k_e} = \frac{D_1}{1 + k_e} + \frac{D_2 + P_2}{(1 + k_e)} \cdot \frac{1}{(1 + k_e)}$$

and

$$P_0 = \frac{D_1}{1 + k_e} + \frac{D_2 + P_2}{(1 + k_e)^2}$$

uation formula for common stock is given by the *present value of the expected stream of dividends:*

$$P_0 = \frac{D_1}{1 + k_e} + \frac{D_2}{(1 + k_e)^2} + \ldots + \frac{D_n}{(1 + k_e)^n} + \ldots$$

$$P_0 = \sum_{t=1}^{\infty} \frac{D_t}{(1 + k_e)^t} \qquad (7.8)$$

where: the sign ∞ indicates infinity. Some readers may feel uncomfortable with the dividend formula because it seems to ignore capital gains. But remember: The capital gain element disappears as the investment horizon is extended indefinitely into the future.

ZERO GROWTH

In the simple case in which the dividend is not expected to grow over time, a common stock is valued as if it were a preferred stock. In such a case, each year's dividend is the same as the next's:

$$D_1 = D_2 = D_n = \ldots = D$$

$$P_0 = \frac{D}{1 + k_e} + \frac{D}{(1 + k_e)^2} + \ldots + \frac{D}{(1 + k_e)^n} + \ldots + \frac{D}{(1 + k_e)^{\infty}}$$

Applying the formula for a perpetuity, we get:[8]

$$P_0 = \frac{D}{k_e} \qquad (7.9)$$

Turning this around, we get

$$k_e = \frac{D}{P_0} \qquad (7.10)$$

That is, the market capitalization rate is equal to the *dividend yield.*

$$\frac{D}{P_0}$$

Consider, for example, a firm that is expected to pay a dividend of $1.90 forever, and that has a current market price of $9.50. The market capitalization rate is 10%:

$$k_e = \frac{D}{P_0} = \frac{1.90}{19.00} = 10\%$$

---

[8] The derivation of the formula is given in Appendix 7A. Since a preferred stock typically pays a constant dividend, formulas (7.9) and (7.10) are also appropriate for preferred stock.

CONSTANT GROWTH

Fortunately for investors, the typical firm retains a proportion of its earnings each year which is then reinvested. This permits the firm to grow. The yearly reinvestment of earnings produces a stream of dividends that grows over time.[9] If, for simplicity, we assume that earnings (and dividends) are expected to grow at a constant rate of g percent per year, the price (present value) of a share of common stock can be expressed by the formula:

$$P_0 = \frac{D_1}{k_e - g} \qquad (7.11)$$

where D_1 is the expected dividend at the end of the first year.

The market capitalization rate is:

$$k_e = \frac{D_1}{P_0} + g \qquad (7.12)$$

Thus, for the case of constant growth, the capitalization rate is equal to the dividend yield *plus* the expected growth rate of future dividends.

The growth model can be used to approximate the appropriate market capitalization rate for equity. Consider a firm whose expected dividend is $1.90, with a market price of $9.50. If the dividend is expected to grow at a constant rate of 5% per year, the market capitalization rate can be estimated by applying Eq. 7.12:

$$k_e = \frac{1.90}{9.50} + .05 = 25\%$$

Approximating the capitalization rate by adding a constant growth rate to the dividend yield is deceptively simple. Although it often provides a very useful rule of thumb, some warnings may be in order:

1. Only the future dividends on *existing* shares affect the current price (present value). Dividends paid in the future on shares subsequently issued to new investors do not create value for *existing* shareholders. Therefore, it is the stream of future dividends on existing shares that must be estimated.

2. The riskiness of individual companies differs greatly from one to another. In Chapter 8 we will spell out a method for incorporating these risk differentials into the valuation process.

---

[9] The derivation of this formula is given in Appendix 7A.

GROWTH FOR A LIMITED PERIOD

The dividend growth model is based on the assumption that dividends (and earnings) will grow at the constant rate g forever. But in the typical case a firm cannot earn extraordinarily high profits *forever*. As new firms enter a highly profitable industry, extraordinary returns will tend to disappear. Even in the case of a firm that earns extraordinary profits due to an invention, the underlying patents have finite lives. Hence, one should consider the possibility of a reduction in the future growth rate when applying the dividend valuation model.

A simple formula is available to handle situations in which extraordinary growth is not expected to last forever. Assume, for example, that dividends (and earnings) are expected to grow at a "super growth" rate g_1, for $n - 1$ years, after which they will continue to grow at some normal rate, g_2. In such a case, the price of the stock is equal to the:[10]

$$
\boxed{\begin{array}{c} \text{present value} \\ \text{of dividends} \\ \text{during the} \\ \text{supergrowth period} \end{array}} \quad + \quad \boxed{\begin{array}{c} \text{present value} \\ \text{of dividends} \\ \text{during the normal} \\ \text{growth period} \end{array}}
$$

SUMMARY

Chapter 1 established the proposition that a firm's financial strategy should be guided and judged by its impact on the value of a firm's equity. In Chapter 6 the technique of present value was used to evaluate future cash flows. In this chapter the present value principle was extended to derive valuation models for a firm's securities—bonds and stocks.

The present value approach stipulates that only future cash flows should be considered in the valuation process, and that the discount rate should reflect the asset's risk.

The general valuation formula for any asset, real or financial, is the discounted present value of its expected cash flow:

$$
V_0 = \frac{CF_1}{1 + k} + \frac{CF_2}{(1 + k)^2} + \ldots + \frac{CF_n}{(1 + k)^n}
$$

---

[10] For this case the valuation equation is given by,

$$
P_0 = \sum_{t=1}^{n} \frac{D (1 + g_1)^{t-1}}{(1 + k_e)^t} + \frac{D(1 + g_1)^{n-1}}{(1 + k_e)^n} \times \frac{1 + g_2}{k_e - g_2}
$$

The same formula can be used to estimate the capitalization rate by solving for k_e, using the method of trial and error, (or an appropriate computer program). For additional details, see chapter 15.

or

$$V_0 = CF_1(DF_{k,1}) + CF_2(DF_{k,2}) + \ldots + CF_n(DF_{k,n})$$

The basic valuation formula is then applied to the determination of bond prices. In the case of a bond, the cash flow is usually comprised of a series of interest payments *(C)* plus the repayment of the principal upon redemption *(M)*:

$$\text{bond price} = P_0 = C\,(DFA_{k_d,n}) + M\,(DF_{k_d,n})$$

where k_d is the market interest rate on the bond, or its yield to maturity *(YTM)*, as it is also called. Given a bond's cash flow and its current market price, the present value equation can be solved for *YTM*.

In the special case of a perpetuity, a nonredeemable bond, the present value formula becomes:

$$\text{bond price of perpetuity} = p_0 = C/k_d$$

and its yield is

$$k_d = C/P_0$$

Bond prices fluctuate in response to changes in market interest rates, so they usually sell in the market either at a discount (below per value) or at a premium (above par value):

1. When the going market rate is above a bond's stated rate of interest (the coupon rate), it sells at a *discount.*
2. When the going market rate is below the coupon rate, the bond sells at a *premium.*
3. When a bond's coupon rate equals the going market rate, the bond's market price equals its par value.
4. Increases in market interest rates cause the prices of outstanding bonds to fall.
5. A fall in the market rate induces a rise in the prices of outstanding bonds.
6. The sensitivity of bond prices to a given change in the market interest rate is greater, the farther away the bond's maturity.

Unlike a bond, the return on a common stock is very uncertain, and is subject to change from period to period. Two rules of thumb have traditionally been used to value common stock: (a) net asset value (book value of the equity), and (b) price/earnings ratios. Both methods are based on accounting values, and suffer from the fact that accounting and economic concepts of asset value, cost, and revenue are rarely the same. As a result, they are difficult to interpret.

One solution to this problem is to apply the basic present value model to the valuation of common stock. As a first step, we defined the following concepts:

$$\text{cash flow of a stock} = \text{dividends } (D) + \text{capital gain}$$
$$\text{price (value) of a stock} = \text{present value of its cash flow}$$

$$P_0 = \frac{D_1}{1+k_e} + \frac{D_2}{(1+k_e)^2} + \ldots + \frac{D_n + P_n}{(1+k_e)^n}$$

where k_e is the market capitalization rate and n is the assumed holding period.

By extending the investment holding period indefinitely into the future, the current price of common stock can be viewed as the present value of its expected dividends:

$$P_0 = \sum_{t=1}^{\infty} \frac{D_t}{(1+k_e)^t}$$

In the case of nongrowth, or a constant dividend stream, this becomes

$$P_0 = \frac{D}{k_e}$$

and the market capitalization rate (k_e) is given by the current dividend yield:

$$k_e = \frac{D}{P_0}$$

In the case of a constant annual growth rate (g) which is expected to continue indefinitely into the future, the dividend growth model can be defined as:

$$P_0 = \frac{D_1}{k_e - g}$$

and the market capitalization rate equals the expected dividend yield plus the annual growth rate:

$$k_e = \frac{D_1}{P_0} + g$$

In the case of an exceptionally high growth rate for a limited period followed by a return to a normal growth rate, the price of the stock is equal to

present value of dividends during the supergrowth period	$+$	present value of dividends during the normal growth period

With these basic concepts in mind, we turn in the next chapter to the problem of estimating the crucial impact of risk on the valuation process.

APPENDIX 7A | Derivation of the Dividend Valuation Model

ZERO GROWTH

The stock valuation model with zero growth (with a constant dividend) can be derived by applying the formula for the present value of a perpetuity:

$$P_0 = \frac{D}{(1 + k_e)} + \frac{D}{(1 + k_e)^2} + \ldots + \frac{D}{(1 + k_e)^\infty} \quad (7A.1)$$

where

D = the constant expected dividend

k_e = the market capitalization rate

Eq. 7A.1 can be rewritten as

$$P_0 = \frac{D}{1 + k}\left[1 + \frac{1}{1 + k_e} + \frac{1}{(1 + k_e)^2} + \ldots \right]$$

The expression within the brackets is an infinite geometric series with a common factor or $1/(1 + k_e)$.

Applying the formula for the summation of a geometric series, we get

$$P_0 = \frac{D}{1 + k_e}\left[\frac{1}{1 - \left(\frac{1}{1 + k_e}\right)}\right] = \frac{D}{k_e}$$

Rearranging terms, we can solve for the market capitalization rate:

$$k_e = \frac{D}{P_0}$$

CONSTANT GROWTH

Consider the more realistic case in which firms retain some proportion of their annual earnings and distribute the rest as dividends. If we denote current net earnings per share (after deduction of depreciation, interest, and taxes) by E, and the current cash dividend per share by D, the current dividend is given by

$$D = (1 - b)E$$

where b denotes the fraction of annual earnings which the firm reinvests $(0 < b < 1)$. It is clear from this definition that if the firm follows a policy of reinvesting a *fixed proportion* of its annual earnings, dividends in the following years will *not* remain constant. This can be seen from the following calculation of the earnings available for distribution in the next year. Assume that the firm earns an average rate of return (R) on the reinvested portion of the previous year's earnings. Hence, the expected earnings (E_1) are

$$E_1 = E + RbE = E(1 + bR)$$

If the firm follows a policy of paying out a fixed proportion $(1 - b)$ of its annual earnings as a dividend, the expected dividend (D_1) becomes:

$$D_1 = (1 - b)E_1 = (1 - b)E(1 + bR)$$

or

$$D_1 = D(1 + bR)$$

In the second year, the earnings available for allocation equal the earnings of the year 1 plus the additional earnings on the investments financed out of the retention of part of the previous year's earnings. Thus the level of EPS in the second year will be

$$E_2 = E_1 + E_1 bR$$

which can be written as

$$E_2 = E(1 + bR) + bE(1 + bR)R$$

This, in turn, can be written as

$$E_2 = E(1 + bR)(1 + bR) = E(1 + bR)^2$$

Hence, the dividend in the second year becomes

$$D_2 = (1 - b)E(1 + bR)^2$$

or

$$D_2 = D(1 + bR)^2$$

This same process can be continued in years 3, 4, and so on. Thus, it can be shown that given the fixed investment policy, the dividend will continue to increase from year to year at the rate bR. If we assume that the firm retains 50% of its earnings ($b = 0.5$) and earns 10% on the average on new investments ($R = 10\%$), the dividends will grow at a 5% rate each year ($bR = 0.5 \times 0.10 = 0.05$). We shall denote this constant growth rate by the letter g.

Having identified the components of the dividend flow, we can compute the present value of the future dividend stream using the required rate of return k_e as the discount rate:

$$P_0 = \frac{D(1+g)}{1+k_e} + \frac{D(1+g)^2}{(1+k_e)^2} + \frac{D(1+g)^3}{(1+k_e)^3} + \ldots$$

$$(7A.2)$$

The equation is an infinite geometric series with the common factor $(1 + g/1 + k_e)$. Rewriting Eq. 7A.2 yields[1]

$$P_0 = \frac{D(1+g)}{1+k_e}\left[1 + \left(\frac{1+g}{1+k_e}\right) + \left(\frac{1+g}{1+k_e}\right)^2 + \ldots\right]$$

hence,

$$P_0 = \frac{D(1+g)}{1+k_e} \times \frac{1}{1 - \left(\frac{1+g}{1+k_e}\right)}$$

which reduces the dividend growth model:[2]

$$P_0 = \frac{D(1+g)}{k_e - g} = \frac{D_1}{k_e - g} \qquad (7A.3)$$

[1] Note that $bR < k_e$ constitutes a necessary condition for the convergence of the geometric series. Since, in general, $b < 1$ (that is, dividends are paid), R can be greater or smaller than k_e.
[2] The dividend growth model is associated with the work of Myron Gordon and is often called the Gordon growth model.

REVIEW EXERCISE

Circle the correct word(s) to complete each sentence; see p. 163 for correct answers.

7.1 The value of an asset is simply the discounted present value of its *assets/ expected future cash flow.*

7.2 A bondholder receives a series of interest payments over a number of years; the original principle is returned when *the bond matures/the firm defaults.*

7.3 Whenever the market interest rate is higher than the coupon interest rate, the bond sells at a *discount from/premium over* par value.

7.4 The yield to maturity is the rate of interest an investor could earn if he or she purchases the bond *at a premium/at its current market price* and holds it *until maturity/for one year.*

7.5 The higher the price of a bond, the *lower/higher* is the yield.

7.6 A rise in long-term interest rates causes the price of a bond to *rise/fall.*

7.7 The risk exposure on bonds which are close to maturity is *greater/smaller* than those which have a long time to maturity.

7.8 The book value of net assets is defined as total assets minus *equity/total liabilities.*

7.9 Basing the valuation of stock on asset value is a *good/poor* substitute for the valuation of cash flows.

7.10 A common stock's market price can be viewed as the *present value/future benefits* of the cash flows to its owners.

7.11 The cash flow of a common stock has two principal components: *coupon interest plus inventory gains/dividends plus capital gains.*

7.12 Investment in common stock is usually a *much riskier/less risky* venture than investment in a bond.

7.13 Typically, investors will demand a *lower/higher* rate of return on common stock than on bonds, thereby *lowering/raising* the discount rate.

7.14 If one is willing to hold a common stock indefinitely, the influence of the capital gain *becomes larger/disappears*.

7.15 A firm *can/cannot* keep growing at the same rate forever.

QUESTIONS

7.1 Define the following terms:
  a. Bond
  c. Face value
  e. Coupon interest
  g. Stock
  b. Redemption value
  d. Market capitalization rate
  f. Yield to maturity

7.2 Winthrop & Co. has had a very erratic dividend history. Paul Winthrop Jr, the senior vice-president, claims, however, that "past flows are irrelevant for the valuation process." Evaluate Mr. Winthrop's statement.

7.3 Explain how the forces of supply and demand determine bond yields.

7.4 "When I want to invest my money in a riskless asset, I buy U.S. Treasury bonds; the Treasury will never let me down." Do you agree with this strategy? Explain.

7.5 Marcia Brown just bought a $1,000 bond. "I don't care what happens to interest rates, since I am guaranteed 6% of my investment. I will get $60 per year in any case." Under which circumstances is Marcia Brown correct?

7.6 "A given set of observed interest yields implies a particular set of bond prices." Appraise this statement.

7.7 In recent years, the yield on short-term government bonds has often been above the long-term rate. Can you offer an explanation for the observed pattern of yields?

7.8 The Acme Engineering Company has worked for years to establish itself in the machine-tool industry. It has a large and loyal clientele, and the company has a good reputation with banks and suppliers. Acme now wishes to issue equity. Its plant, equipment, and inventories are worth $350,000. There are no other assets, but the company owes the bank $150,000.
  a. What is Acme's book value?
  b. How might its economic value differ from its book value?

7.9 The following exchange took place in a class on corporate finance:

Ted:	"A high price/earnings multiplier is good."
Instructor:	"You're right, Ted."
Nancy:	"A low price/earnings multiplier is good."
Instructor:	"You're right, Nancy."
Fred:	"But surely they can't both be right; they said the opposite things."

Instructor: "You know what, Fred? You're also right."

Who is right? Explain.

7.10 Under which conditions is the market capitalization rate equal to the dividend yield?

7.11 "I don't care about capital gains or losses; all that matters to me is dividends." What does this person intend to do with the shares?

7.12 "Supergrowth firms cannot sustain such growth for a long time. This is why I personally prefer companies whose dividends grow only moderately, say by 5% a year, but who keep this pace up forever." Evaluate this statement.

PROBLEMS

7.1 **Bond valuation.** You have just bought a bond for $500 which pays $45 interest at the end of each year for 16 years. At the end of the 16th year the principal is also repaid. Assume that the market rate of interest (discount rate) is 4%.

   a. What is the net present value of this investment?

   b. Assume that the bond in part (a) sells at a 5% discount (for $475). How does your answer change?

7.2 **Stock valuation.** What is the maximum price you would be willing to pay for a share of common stock that is paying a $1.80 annual dividend, if you expect the dividend to grow at a rate of 7% in perpetuity and your required rate of return is 10%?

7.3 **Growth stock.** Two chemical corporations are essentially in the same business, and therefore have the same risk and the same required rate of return. One of the corporations has a stable earnings and dividend record; in fact, it pays out all its earnings as dividends. The other company uses a different management strategy, and as a result its earnings and dividends increase annually. The current dividend is $5 per share for both corporations. The stable corporation's stock trades for $40 per share, whereas the price of the "growth" stock is $50.

   a. Estimate the market's required rate of return for these two stocks.

   b. What is the constant future growth rate that is implied by these data?

7.4 **Stock valuation.** A stock that you bought for $100 in January 1987 paid a $8 dividend in December 1987. On December 31, 1987, its price was $120.

   a. Calculate the rate of return on your investment.

   b. The 1987 inflation rate was around 9%. What was the *real* rate of return on your investment?

7.5 **Bond valuation.** Consider a 9% nonredeemable bond which was originally issued at a price of $1,000. What happens to its market price if the market rate of interest on bonds of this type (assume that interest is paid annually at the end of each year):

a. Falls to 6%.

b. Rises to 12%.

c. Rises to 13%.

7.6 Bond valuation.

a. What is the price of a 6% $1,000 bond with a 10-year maturity if the market rate of interest falls to 4%?

b. How does your answer change if there are only 3 years left to maturity?

c. What is the price if the market interest rate rises to 9%, and there are 8 years left to maturity?

d. How does your answer change if there are only 3 years left to maturity?

(Again, assume that interest is paid at the end of each year.)

7.7 Bond valuation. You own a 6% bond with 1 year left to maturity. Redemption value of the bond is $100. Interest rises to 8%.

a. What is the market price of the bond today?

b. How does your answer change if the market interest rate falls to 5%?

7.8 Bond valuation. A bond with a face value of $1,000, an 8% interest coupon (payable at the end of the year), and 6 years to maturity sells at a $50 premium. What is the current market interest rate on 6-year bonds?

7.9 Bond valuation. A bond with a face value of $1,000 and a 10% interest coupon (payable at the end of the year) has 3 years left to maturity. Currently, interest on 3-year bonds is 11%. What is the market value of the bond?

7.10 Bond valuation, semi-annual compounding. What is the market value of the bond in the previous question if interest is received semi-annually?

7.11 Stock valuation. Nancy Weber has purchased one share of Snowcroft & Co. Dividends are expected to be $1.50 per share 1 year from now, $1.80, 2 years from now, and $2.10 after 3 years. At the end of the 3 years, the share will be sold for $24. Assume that all of the above is known with certainty, and that the appropriate discount rate is 11%.

a. How much should Nancy pay for the share?

b. How much should she pay if the discount rate is 4%?

7.12 Dividend valuation model. Dividends on Boland's stock are currently $1 per share and are expected to stay constant. The market capitalization rate is 7.35%.

a. How much are you willing to pay for one share of Boland's stock?

b. How does your answer change if the market capitalization rises to 8.25%?

c. What is the implied market capitalization rate if Boland's shares sell for $21.45?

7.13 Constant growth model. How do your answers to the previous problem change if Boland's dividends are expected to increase by 5% each year?

 7.14 Bond valuation, computer problem. Compute the current market value of the following bonds:

	Face Value ($)	Coupon Rate (%)	Years to Maturity	Compounding Frequency	Interest Yield on Similar Bonds
A	1,000	65	8	semi-annual	6.35
B	1,200	78	14	quarterly	9.125
C	500	36	4	annual	3.875
D	2,000	105	2	semi-annual	5.010

SAMPLE PROBLEMS

SP7.1 What is the current market price of a $1,000 bond which has an 8% coupon rate and 6 years to maturity? Assume that the current interest rate for 6-year loans of similar risk is 10%.

SP7.2 What is the market capitalization rate for a common stock which has a current market price of $20, and whose dividend next year is expected to be $2 per share? Assume that the market expects the dividends to grow by 5% thereafter.

Solutions to Sample Problems

SP7.1 The current market price is the present value of the cash flows. In this case the cash flows are a 6-year annuity of $80 per year (a coupon rate of 8% on a $1,000 bond = $80), and the return of the principal (face value: $1,000) in the sixth year. The discount factor is 10%, since this is what can be earned if the money is invested in other bonds of similar risk.

present value of an annuity of $80 for 6 years $\qquad = 80(DFA_{6\ yr,10\%})$

$\qquad\qquad\qquad\qquad\qquad\qquad\qquad\qquad\qquad\qquad\qquad = 80(4.355) = 348.40$

present value of $1000 received 6 years from now $\quad = 1,000(DF_{6\ yr,10\%})$

$\qquad\qquad\qquad\qquad\qquad\qquad\qquad\qquad\qquad\qquad\qquad = 1,000(0.564) = 564$

present value of the bond is the sum of the two amounts $= 348.40 + 564$

$\qquad\qquad\qquad\qquad\qquad\qquad\qquad\qquad\qquad\qquad\qquad\qquad = \$912.40$

SP7.2 The market capitalization rate can be approximated by $k_e = (D_1/P_0) + g$. In this particular case, next year's dividend is $2 per share, $(D_1 = 2)$, and is expected to grow by 5% per year thereafter $(g = 0.05)$. The market price of the stock is $20 $(P_0 = 20)$. Therefore, the market capitalization rate (k_e) is 15%: $k_e = (2/20) + .05 = .10 + .05 = .15$.

Answers to Review Exercise

7.1 expected future cash flow   **7.2** the bond matures

7.3 discount from   **7.4** at its current market price, until maturity

7.5 lower   **7.6** fall   **7.7** smaller   **7.8** total liabilities

7.9 poor   **7.10** present value   **7.11** dividends plus capital gains

7.12 much riskier   **7.13** higher, raising   **7.14** disappears

7.15 cannot

SUGGESTIONS FOR FURTHER READING

The valuation of securities is dealt with in much greater detail in investment textbooks. See for example, Nancy L. Jacob and R. Richardson Pettit, *Investments* (Homewood, IL: Irwin, 1984); William F. Sharpe, *Investments*, 3rd ed. Englewood Cliffs, NJ: Prentice-Hall, 1985); and Seha M. Tinic and Richard R. West, *Investing in Securities: An Efficient Market Approach* (Boston: Addison-Wesley, 1979).

The original work on the development of the dividend growth model was done by John B. Williams, *The Theory of Investment Value* (Cambridge, MA: Harvard University Press, 1938); Myron J. Gordon and Eli Shapiro, "Capital Equipment Analysis: The Required Rate of Profit," *Management Science*, October 1956; and Myron J. Gordon, *The Investment, Financing and Valuation of the Corporation* (Homewood, IL: Irwin, 1962).

8 | Risk and Return

Risk and uncertainty lie at the very heart of a firm's financial decisions. The formal treatment of risk, however, can be quite complicated; hence we preferred to explore the basic methods of valuation first, in Chapter 7. In this chapter we examine the relationship between the two key determinants of the value of a firm's common stock: risk and return. Although the discussion focuses on the individual investor in securities, the conclusions hold for the investments of the firm as well. The analysis is carried out first for a single investment held in isolation, and then for a portfolio of securities. The results of the portfolio analysis are then applied to the capital market as a whole. Throughout this book we have taken the maximization of the market value of the sharcholders' equity as the goal of the firm. This, in turn, implies the need for a formal model which can explain share prices in terms of risk and return. To this end, the capital asset pricing model (CAPM), which underlies much of the modern theory of finance, is defined and the concept of beta risk is derived.

RETURN ON INVESTMENT

In the preceding chapter, the rate of return based on an investment in a share of common stock over some period of time t was defined as

$$k_e = \frac{D_t + (P_t - P_{t-1})}{P_{t-1}} = \frac{D_t + P_t}{P_{t-1}} - 1 \qquad (8.1)$$

where

k_e = the rate of return
P_t = the price (value) of the stock at time t
P_{t-1} = the price (value) of the stock at time $t - 1$
D_t = the cash dividend, assumed to have been paid at the end of time t

Thus the return on the stock reflects both the dividend received and the capital appreciation (if any) during the period.

Consider, for example, a share of stock in the ABC Corporation which sold for $50 at the beginning of the year, paid a dividend of $2 per share on the last day of the year, and sold for $62 on that same day. The rate of return to an investor in ABC stock was:

$$k_e = \frac{2 + 62}{50} - 1 = 28\%$$

It is often convenient to express this rate of return formula in a slightly different form:

$$k_e = \frac{\text{value of investment at end of period}}{\text{initial investment outlay}} - 1 \qquad (8.2)$$

The initial investment outlay at the beginning of the year is the market price of the share. The value of the investment at the end of the year is the share's market price at the end of the year *plus* the dividend.

We turn now to a more complicated example of a stock which sold for $35 at the beginning of the year, paid a dividend of $1.50 per share on the last day of the year, *split* 2 for 1 in July of that year, and sold for only $17.75 on the last day of the year. What is the rate of return on the stock? The initial value is clearly $35; but the end-of-period value is certainly *not* $17.75. Due to the split in July, our hypothetical investor holds *two* shares at the end of the year for every one owned at the beginning. Moreover, the investor received a dividend of $1.50 on *each* of the two shares held, since the stock split occurred before the dividend was declared.[1] Thus the end-of-period value of the investment is *$38.50* [2(17.75) + 2(1.50)] = *$38.50*, and the rate of return is 10%:

$$\text{rate of return} = \frac{38.50}{35.00} - 1 = 10\%$$

---

[1] Stock splits and stock dividends are discussed in greater detail in Chapter 16.

WHAT IS RISK?

As we emphasized in Chapter 7, the value of any asset depends on the *estimate* of its future cash flow. But future returns can usually be estimated only tentatively. As a result, investors rarely have very precise expectations regarding the future return that will be derived from a particular security.

Certainty Formally, we can distinguish between two states of expectation: certainty and risk (uncertainty). Strictly speaking, perfect *certainty* refers to cases in which expectations are single-valued; that is, the prospective return is viewed in terms of one particular outcome, and not in terms of a range of alternative possible returns. We will also use certainty to describe those situations in which investors' expectations regarding future returns lie within a very narrow range. But do such investments actually exist outside the realm of textbooks? At first glance, it may appear that no investment could possibly yield a perfectly certain income stream, but on reflection we can find several illustrations.

For example, suppose you decide to invest in a 3-month Treasury bill. The exact return you will receive upon redemption (at the end of 3 months) on short-term[2] Treasury bills can be calculated with absolute certainty. After all, the government can always, as a last resort, print the money needed to meet its obligations. Thus, we simply ignore the small probability of a revolution, or of a war, which might destroy the existing monetary system. Similarly, if we are willing to ignore the remote possibility of bankruptcy or financial default of such giants as General Motors and AT&T, the short-term notes of these companies can also be considered, for all practical purposes, as investments yielding perfectly safe returns.

Investment companies and mutual funds often invest relatively large proportions of their assets in such low-risk assets, but most firms invest in productive rather than in financial assets. As a result, most firms are typically confronted by risky investment alternatives. Although the opportunity to invest in Treasury bills exists for all investors, this opportunity is irrelevant for the long-term investment of most firms. Since the stockholder can readily acquire the riskless assets directly, there would be little incentive for an individual to invest in the shares of a company which in turn invested a *significant* proportion of its equity in riskless assets.

---

[2] Perfectly certain assets must be short-term because of the impact of interest rate fluctuations on long-term securities; see Chapter 7.

Risk   The term *risk,* or equivalently *uncertainty,* will be used to describe an investment opportunity whose return is *not* known in advance with absolute certainty, but for which an array of alternative outcomes, and their probabilities, are known. In other words, a risky investment is one for which only a *distribution* of returns is known. The distribution, in turn, may have been estimated on the basis of objective or purely subjective, probabilities.

An example of such a frequency distribution is given in Table 8.1, which shows the historical record of the returns from a hypothetical investment over the past 40 years. The data of Table 8–1 were then used to prepare the histogram in Figure 8–1. Historical data of this sort are often available for financial investments, and can be used in current investment decisions. But even when a long record of past returns is available, the decision to invest remains complex. There often may be no reason why the future distribution should resemble the distribution in the past. Before arriving at a decision, all the factors that might indicate future changes in this distribution must be carefully weighed. Moreover, even if the distribution is expected to remain unchanged, realizing a high return (the right-hand side of the histogram) or a loss (the left-hand side of the histogram) in any particular year is largely a matter of chance.

Individuals (or firms) with a lot of experience, or those who are confronted with repetitive investments that are renewed every few years, are faced with situations similar to the one portrayed in Figure 8–1. However, more often than not one has little or no past experience to draw upon. This is often the case when investments in newly issued securities are being considered for which no relevant historical data can be found to serve as a guide

TABLE 8–1   An Example of a Frequency Distribution of Returns

Profit*	Frequency (Number of years)
−30.00 to −20.01	2
−20.00 to −10.01	3
−10.00 to − 0.01	5
0.00 to 9.99	10
10.00 to 19.99	9
20.00 to 29.99	6
30.00 to 39.99	3
40.00 to 49.99	2
Total	40

* To facilitate comparison, the returns are expressed as percentages.

FIGURE 8–1
Histogram
of Returns

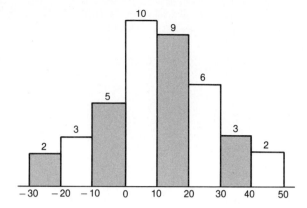

for current decisions. With respect to such investments, decisions must be based solely on subjective probabilities—that is, on purely personal judgments regarding the chances of gain or loss.

MEASURING RISK: SINGLE ASSETS

If the analysis of risk is to be meaningful, a way must be found to translate uncertainty into operational decision rules. There are many ways to incorporate risk into decision problems, but common to almost all approaches is the need to develop an index that *directly* reflects the investment's risk.[3] Although today the word "risk" has come to mean "hazard" or "danger of loss," the Latin word *risicum* had some positive connotations. In this earlier form, risk referred to chance or luck—both good and bad. Modern investment analysis has returned to the original meaning of risk, identifying it with the dispersion of returns from the expected return—with possible deviations, both positive and negative, from the mean.

One widely used method of risk analysis utilizes the *expected* (mean) *return* to indicate an investment's anticipated profitability, and the *variance* (or standard deviation) as an indicator of its risk.

Expected
Return

expected return
The arithmetic average of the possible outcomes, weighted by their probabilities.

The **expected return** of an investment is given by the arithmetic average of the possible outcomes, weighted by their probabilities. Consider, for example, an investment which offers a 50% chance of earning a net profit of $1,000, a 25% chance of breaking even, and a 25% chance of a $400 loss.

---

[3] The implications of combining projects into portfolios are spelled out below.

The *expected return* of the investment is the weighted average of the three possible outcomes; in this example, $400:

$$E = 0.5(1,000) + 0.25(0) + 0.25(-400) = 400 \qquad (8.3)$$

where

E = the expected (mean) return.

Variance and Standard Deviation

Since we identify risk with the uncertainty of the outcome, it is a natural extension of this line of thinking to measure an investment's risk by the variance (standard deviation) of its returns, which measures the dispersion of returns around their mean value. The variance provides information on the extent of the deviations of the possible return from the expected return.

To determine the variance, which we denote by σ^2, we first calculate the deviation of each possible outcome (x_i) from the expected value ($x_i - E$). We then "square" the deviations and multiply each squared deviation by P_i, the probability of getting each outcome, x_i. The variance is the summation of all these products and serves as a measure of the distribution's variability.

Since the distribution of future returns is measured in dollars, the dimension of variance is "dollars squared," which of course is economically meaningless. Therefore, we take the square root of the variance and obtain the **standard deviation** (σ). The standard deviation also measures the distribution's variability, but has the further advantage of being given in terms of dollars. But despite this difference in dimensions, if investment A is more risky than investment B (if A has a larger variance), its standard deviation must also be greater.

standard deviation (σ)
The square root of the variance—that is, the dispersion around their mean value—of an investment's returns.

For the purpose of ranking investments by their risk, we can thus use the variance or standard deviation interchangeably. One might legitimately ask: If we want a risk index in terms of dollars, rather than in dollars squared, why raise all terms to the second power in the first place? Note that the sum of the positive and negative deviations from the mean is, by definition, *always* equal to zero. This explains the necessity to "square" the deviations before adding them.

In practice, the actual calculation of the variance is somewhat easier if the following formula is used:

$$\text{variance} = \sigma^2 = \sum_{i=1}^{n} P_i x_i^2 - E^2 \qquad (8.4)$$

To illustrate, let's calculate the expected value and the variance of the following distribution:

Profit in Dollars (x_i)	Probability of Occurrence P_i
80	1/2
100	1/4
200	1/4

The expected value is given by

$$E = P_1x_1 + P_2x_2 + P_3x_3 = 1/2(80) + 1/4(100) + 1/4(200) = \$115$$

and the variance is

$$\sigma^2 = \sum_{i=1}^{3} P_ix_i^2 - E^2 = 1/2(80^2) + 1/4(100^2) + 1/4(200^2) - 115^2$$

$$= 15,700 - 13,225 + 2,475$$

The *standard deviation*, which is defined as the square root of the variance, is given by[4]

$$\sigma = \sqrt{2,475} = 49.75$$

RISK PREFERENCES

Three distinct possibilities regarding investors' attitudes toward risk can be identified:

1. **Risk aversion.** An investor may be risk-averse and therefore will demand a *risk premium* (additional return) in order to enter into a risky venture.
2. **Risk neutrality.** An investor may be *indifferent* to risk—does not demand an additional return to enter into a risky investment.

---

[4] This method of calculation is very simple even for relatively large problems; the reader can verify that calculating the variance from its basic definition gives the same results, but the calculations are somewhat more tedious:

$$\sigma^2 = \sum_{i=1}^{3} P_i(x_i - E)^2 = 1/2(80 - 115)^2 + 1/4(100 - 115)^2 + 1/4(200 - 115)^2$$

$$= 1/2(1,225) + 1/4(225) + 1/4(7,225) = 2,475$$

Once again, the standard deviation is 49.75:

$$\sigma = \sqrt{2,475} = 49.75$$

3. **Preference for risk.** Some investors are *risk-takers*. Such individuals would be willing to accept a lower return for the chance to gamble; other things being equal, they would pay a premium, if necessary, to enter into a risky endeavor.

The empirical evidence clearly indicates that most investors in the capital market are risk-averse. Therefore, throughout the book we will assume that risky investments must offer higher returns than their more certain counterparts.

Table 8–2 gives the historical record of the average annual rates of return on various investments in the United States for the period 1926–1981. The riskiness of these investments, as measured by their dispersion (standard deviation), is also shown and portrayed graphically. The data confirm the hypothesis of risk-aversion: the greater the risk incurred, the higher the return on the security. This can be seen by examining the distribution of returns. The investment in common stock was more profitable, on the average, than the investment in bonds, but common stockholders also faced a higher probability of large deviations from the mean. We return to this risk-return tradeoff below, but for the time being it is sufficient to note that riskier investments imply higher required market rates of return (capitalization rates).

TABLE 8–2   Average Annual Rates of Return on Alternative Investments 1926–1981

	Annual Rate of Return*	Risk†	Distribution
Common stocks	9.1%	21.9%	
Long-term corporate bonds	3.6	5.6	
Long-term government bonds	3.0	5.7	
U.S. Treasury bills	3.0	3.1	

* Geometric mean.
† Standard deviation.

SOURCE: R. Ibbotson and K. Sinquefield, *Stocks, Bonds, Bills and Inflation,* The Financial Analysts Research Foundation, 1982.

THE MEAN-VARIANCE RULE

A very popular decision rule has been developed by Harry Markowitz for evaluating risky investments on the basis of their expected return and variance (or standard deviation).[5] The expected return-variance, or mean-variance, rule (also referred to as the *E–V rule*) can be defined as follows: Security A will be preferred to security B, if one of the following combinations holds: (1) Expected return of A is at least as high as the expected return of B, *and* the variance of A is less than the variance of B; or (2) expected return of A exceeds that of B, *and* the variance of A is at most as high as that of B.

In symbols, the E-V rule implies a preference for *A*, if either of the following holds:

$$E(A) \geq E(B) \text{ and variance (A)} < \text{variance (B)}$$
$$E(A) > E(B) \text{ and variance (A)} \leq \text{variance (B)}$$

Since the variance and standard deviation rank risk the same, the E-V rule holds for the standard deviation as well.

To illustrate the application of the E-V rule, consider the example of the two securities whose distributions of returns are given in Table 8–3. Both securities A and B have the same expected return:

$$E(A) = 1/2(1,000) + 1/2(3,000) = 2,000$$
$$E(B) = 1/2(0) \quad + 1/2(4,000) = 2,000$$

The variance of A is 1,000,000:

$$\sigma^2(A) = 1/2(1,000 - 2,000)^2 + 1/2(3,000 - 2,000)^2 = 1,000,000$$

Hence the standard deviation of A, which is the square root of the variance, is 1,000.

$$\sigma(A) = \sqrt{1,000,000} = 1,000$$

---

[5] See his pioneering article "Portfolio Selection," *Journal of Finance,* March 1952.

TABLE 8–3

	Investment A		Investment B	
	Net Return ($)	**Probability**	**Net Return ($)**	**Probability**
	1,000	1/2	0	1/2
	3,000	1/2	4,000	1/2
Expected return	2,000		2,000	
Standard deviation	1,000		2,000	

Similarly, the variance and standard deviation of B are 4,000,000 and 2,000, respectively:

$$\sigma^2(B) = 1/2(0 - 2,000)^2 + 1/2(4,000 - 2,000)^2 = 4,000,000$$

and

$$\sigma(B) = \sqrt{4,000,000} = 2,000$$

If we apply the Markowitz mean-variance (or mean standard deviation) criterion, we can confirm that security A is preferred to security B. Both have the same expected return (2,000), but B is the more risky of the two.

The importance of the E-V criterion stems from the fact that it can be derived from underlying risk attitudes. Assume, for example, that returns are *normally distributed* (bell-shaped) so that the mean and the variance provide us with all the relevant information about their distribution. In this case, the E-V criterion is optimal for *all* risk-averse investors.[6]

normal distribution
A symmetrical, bell-shaped curve on a graph.

A **normal distribution** is characterized by a bell-shaped curve; see, for example, Figure 8–2. The most important feature of a normal distribution is its symmetry; the left-hand of the curve, up to the peak, is a mirror image of the right-hand side. As a result, the areas under each half of the curve are the same, and therefore the probability of achieving a given point on the right-hand side has its exact counterpart on the left-hand side. Another important feature of this type of distribution is that it is completely specified by the mean and the standard deviation (variance). For example, given the mean and standard deviation, the possibilities of achieving returns which deviate by 1, 2, or 3 standard deviations from the mean are indicated on the graph in Figure 8–2.

----

[6] In the case of normal distributions, the E-V criterion ensures the maximization of investors' expected utility.

**FIGURE 8–2
A Normal
Distribution**

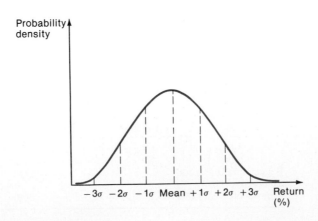

MEASURING RISK BY THE COEFFICIENT OF VARIATION

Even when we restrict ourselves to single assets, using the variance (or standard deviation) as an indicator of risk can sometimes be misleading. Clearly, the larger the variance of earnings, the larger the chance that the actual return will deviate significantly from the expected return. In some cases, however, the expected return may be so large that the security can be considered relatively safe, even if it has a large variance.

The expected return and the standard deviation of two hypothetical investments are given in Table 8–4. As can be seen, the expected return of B is $500, which is significantly larger than the expected return of A, which is only $100. Can we say with assurance that B should be preferred to A? Although B is the more profitable of the two, on the average, it is also the more risky. Its standard deviation is 25, compared with a deviation of only 10 for A. Thus, the mean-variance (or the mean-standard deviation) rule cannot discriminate between the two, and therefore we cannot determine which proposal is preferable.

This simple example illustrates one of the major drawbacks of using the standard deviation (or variance) as a risk index. Intuitively it seems that most investors will prefer B, even though the E-V rule does not indicate a clear-cut preference for B over A. And, as we will see, this is one instance in which our intuition, rather than our arithmetic, should be relied upon. B's profitability more than compensates for its greater variability. For example, should the return of B deviate by 4 standard deviations[7] to the left-hand side of its distribution (a very pessimistic result), while the return of A deviates by 4 standard deviations to the right side (a very optimistic outcome), an individual would still be better off with investment B. Even if this very unlikely combination of deviations should occur, the return on B would still be $400 [500 − 4(25) = 400], compared with A's return of only $140 [100 + 4(10) = 140].

This simple example shows that when returns are *not* distributed normally (symmetrically), the standard deviation (or variance) may not always provide an appropriate measure of risk. To overcome this shortcoming,

---

[7] The chance of such a large deviation occurring is extremely small. For example, if the distribution is normal, the probability of such a deviation is only 0.003%.

TABLE 8–4

	Expected Profit	Standard Deviation	Coefficient of Variation (σ/E)
Investment A	100	10	0.10
Investment B	500	25	0.05

coefficient of variation
A statistical indicator of risk in which the standard deviation is divided by the expected return.

some business analysts have advocated that the **coefficient of variation:**

$$c = \sigma/E$$

be used instead of the standard deviation as the measure of an investment's risk. The coefficient of variation is defined as the standard deviation divided (normalized) by the expected return. And indeed, if we replace the standard deviation by the coefficient of variation in our numerical example, intuition is vindicated: B is clearly preferable to A. Looking back at Table 8–4, we note that B has both a *higher* expected return and a *lower* coefficient of variation. Thus, if we employ the expected return-coefficient of variation rule, it follows that an investor will be better off with B rather than A.

Does the replacement of the standard deviation by the coefficient of variation overcome all the difficulties encountered in measuring risk? Unfortunately, the answer is No. Although the coefficient of variation can serve as a better measure of risk in some instances, it by no means resolves *all* the problems relating to risk. This is illustrated in Table 8–5, which shows the relevant data for another two hypothetical investments. Again, the E-V rule cannot distinguish between the two proposals; investment B is the more profitable, but is also the more risky. Nor does the expected return-coefficient of variation rule help resolve the issue. The coefficient of variation of B is also larger than that of A (1/2 as compared with zero). Thus neither the expected return-standard deviation criterion nor the expected return-coefficient of variation criterion can distinguish between the two proposals. Despite this, upon a little reflection, common sense alone is sufficient to indicate that investment B is preferable to investment A. Every rational individual would choose security B rather than security A, because even the *worst* possible outcome of investment B ($5) is higher than the return offered by alternative A ($2).

TABLE 8–5

	Investment A		Investment B	
	Profit	**Probability**	**Profit**	**Probability**
	2	1	5	1/2
			15	1/2
Expected return (E)		2		10
Variance (σ^2)		0		25
Standard deviation (σ)		0		5
Coefficient of variation (σ/E)		0		1/2

The expected values of proposals A and B are given by $1 \times 2 = \$2$, and $1/2 \times \$5 + 1/2 \times \$15 = \$10$, respectively. Similarly, the variance of the two proposals is given by:

$$1(2 - 2)^2 = 0 \text{ for A}$$

and

$$1/2(5 - 10)^2 + 1/2(15 - 10)^2 = 25 \text{ for B}$$

Clearly, decision-makers must exercise considerable caution when using either of these two popular measures of investment risk if paradoxical choices are to be avoided when considering non-normal distributions.[8] The evaluation of risk is itself a risky business. But like risk-taking, the rewards of risk analysis can be substantial.

IMPROVING THE RISK-RETURN RELATIONSHIP BY DIVERSIFICATION

To this point we have ignored the old maxim, "Don't put all of your eggs in one basket." In the preceding sections, risk was discussed for the assumption that it could be explained and measured in terms of individual investments. In what follows we explore the concept of risk in a more realistic setting that takes into account the interaction among investments.

PORTFOLIO RISK AND RETURN

In the preceding sections of this chapter, we calculated the expected return and the variance (standard deviation) for a single security. The extension of this analysis to portfolios is straightforward.

Portfolio Return The expected return on a portfolio of securities is the weighted average of the expected returns of the individual securities making up the portfolio. The weights are equal to the proportion of each security in the portfolio:

$$E_p = W_1E_1 + W_2E_2 \ldots + W_nE_n$$

which can also be written as

$$E_p = \sum_{i=1}^{n} W_iE_i \qquad (8.5)$$

[8] The precise conditions under which each of the alternative risk measures provides the appropriate decision criterion are given in Haim Levy and Marshall Sarnat, *Portfolio and Investment Selection* (Englewood Cliffs, NJ: Prentice-Hall, 1984). Briefly, if distributions are normal, the E-V criterion is optimal and no such paradoxes are possible. If the distributions are log-normal, the mean-coefficient of variation rule is appropriate. In cases in which the shapes of the distributions are not known, judgment must be exercised to avoid paradoxical results.

where

E_p = expected return on the portfolio

E_i = expected return of security i

W_i = the proportion of security i in the portfolio; of course, the proportions must add up to 100% ($\Sigma\, W_i = 1$)

Correlation   The relationship between the fluctuations of two securities can materially affect the fluctuations (riskiness) of a portfolio that combines the two. Consider an individual who has invested part of his money in the construction industry. Since profits in this industry fluctuate strongly, he may be interested in investing another part of his money in a different industry to help stabilize his return. This stabilization can be facilitated by investing in an industry whose profits fluctuate, either independently or negatively, with those of the construction industry. By doing this, the investor can achieve a more stable average return. When the return on one type of stock is relatively low the return from the other stocks presumably will be relatively high, and vice versa. The degree to which diversification stabilizes the return depends on the strength of this relationship between the two securities.

The degree to which the returns of the securities fluctuate together, or in opposite directions, is called *correlation:* its statistical measure is called the **coefficient of correlation,** and will be denoted by the letter R. The coefficient lies between -1 (perfect negative correlation) and $+1$ (perfect positive correlation; see Figure 8–3). When R lies between zero and one, the relationship between the two returns is positive; and the closer we approach unity, the stronger the relationship. The returns on the stock of two automobile manufacturers, such as Ford and General Motors, can be expected to display a strong positive correlation. When $R = 1$, there exists a perfect positive correlation. When R lies between zero and minus one the relationship is negative; the smaller the R, the stronger the negative correlation. Bonds and common stocks provide an example of securities whose returns

coefficient of correlation
A statistical measure of the relationship between returns of securities and/or portfolios.

**FIGURE 8–3
Examples of
Perfect Correlation**

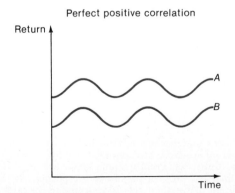

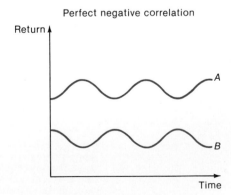

are negatively correlated. In the extreme case in which $R = -1$, we have a perfect negative correlation.

The correlation coefficient is closely related to another quantitative measure of the relationship between security fluctuations—the covariance.[9] The covariance has a positive value when the returns of the two securities are both above (or both below) their respective expected values. However, the covariance is negative if the two securities tend to disperse from their expected values in opposite directions.

Portfolio Variance

If we assume zero correlation between two securities, the portfolio variance is

$$\text{portfolio variance} = \sigma_p^2 = W_1^2\sigma_1^2 + W_2^2\sigma_2^2 \tag{8.6}$$

The general formula for "two-security" portfolios, when the correlation is not zero, includes a third term which reflects the degree to which the individual returns tend to fluctuate together:

$$\text{portfolio variance} = \sigma_p^2 = W_1^2\sigma_1^2 + W_2^2\sigma_2^2 + 2W_1W_2R_{1,2}{}^{\sigma_1\sigma_2} \tag{8.7}$$

where $R_{1,2}$ denotes the coefficient of correlation between the returns of the two securities making up the portfolio, and σ_1 and σ_2 are the standard deviations of each security. When the correlation coefficient ($R_{1,2}$) is assumed to be zero the entire third term disappears, and therefore does not appear in the calculation of the portfolio variance.

Underlying the modern approach to risk and uncertainty is the idea that risk cannot be measured correctly for each individual security alone. This can be illustrated by considering an individual who can invest (say $100) in one of the two securities, A or B; or alternatively, can diversify the investment by putting half of her resources in A and the other half in B. To emphasize the portfolio effect, the distribution of the returns on security A is assumed to be *identical* to the distribution of returns on security B (see Table 8–6).

If our hypothetical individual invests the entire $100 in one security (either A or B), there is an equal chance of earning $30 or losing $20. Whichever security is chosen, the *expected return* is $5 and the risk, as measured by the standard deviation, is 25.

---

[9] The correlation coefficient is related to the covariance, as follows:

$$\text{Cov}_{x,y} = (R_{x,y})\,\sigma_x\sigma_y$$

where

$\text{Cov}_{x,y}$ = the covariance between security x and security y

σ_x and σ_y = the standard deviations of security x and security y

$R_{x,y}$ = the correlation coefficient between the two securities.

Using this relationship, the portfolio risk formula can also be written as follows:

$$\sigma_p^2 = W_1^2\sigma_1^2 + W_2^2\sigma_2^2 + 2W_1W_2\text{cov}_{1,2}$$

TABLE 8–6   **Distribution of Returns for $100 Investment in Two Identical Securities**

	Security A		Security B	
	Return	**Probability**	**Return**	**Probability**
	−20	1/2	−20	1/2
	30	1/2	30	1/2
Expected return		5		5
Variance		625		625
Standard deviation		25		25

Now, what are the relevant expected portfolio return and risk should she decide to diversify her holdings in a portfolio comprised of $50 of A and $50 of B? The answer depends on the *statistical relationship* between the two distributions. For simplicity, let us assume that the income streams of the two securities are statistically *independent*. In other words, the correlation between the returns from the two securities is zero. In such a case, the probability of getting any pair of returns from the two projects is equal to the product of their individual probabilities. For example, the *joint probability* that she will lose 20% on both investments is 1/4 [(1/2)(1/2) = 1/4]. Thus, by putting $50 in each security, she has only a 25% chance of losing $20. Her total loss, in this case, is $10 on A plus $10 on B, because she invested only $50 in each security.

Using this approach, we can calculate the probability distribution of the returns on a *mixed portfolio* comprised of equal proportions of securities A and B (see Table 8–7). The expected return on such a portfolio is $5; that is, the same as for each of the individual securities:

$$E_p = 1/2(5) + 1/2(5) = 5$$

The portfolio variance, however, is only one-half of the variance of the individual securities; 312.5 compared with 625:

$$\sigma_p^2 = W_1^2\sigma_1^2 + W_2^2\sigma_2^2$$
$$= (1/2)^2(625) + (1/2)^2(625)$$
$$= 1/4(625) + 1/4(625) = 312.5$$

In addition to the extreme results (+30 and −20) which are attainable for each of the single investments, the portfolio provides an intermediate result (+5) as well. Since the two alternatives are independent events, the probability of earning $5 results from a 1/4 chance that A will lose 20% while B earns 30%, and from a 1/4 probability that A will earn 30% while B loses 20%. Thus, the diversified portfolio *reduces* the dispersion of outcomes. The chances of suffering a major loss (−$20) or a maximum gain (+$30) are lowered from a 50% chance for each single security to a 25% chance for the

TABLE 8–7   Distribution of Returns for a Mixed Portfolio: $50 in Security A and $50 in Security B

	Return	Probability
	−20	1/4
	+ 5	1/2*
	+30	1/4
Expected return		+5
Variance of return[†]		312.5
Standard deviation		17.7

* Since the two alternatives are independent events, the probability of earning $5 results from a 1/4 chance that A will lose 20%, while B earns 30%, and from a 1/4 probability that A will earn 30%, while B loses 20%.
[†] The variance is given by $1/4(-25)^2 + 1/4(+25)^2 + 1/2(0) = 312.5$. The standard deviation is $\sqrt{312.5} = 17.7$.

mixed portfolio. Moreover, this risk-reduction property of portfolio diversification exists even though we have assumed that the two securities have *identical* earnings and risk characteristics.

THE GAINS FROM DIVERSIFICATION

It is clear from Eq. 8.7 and the example given in Table 8–7 that combining securities in a portfolio can reduce portfolio risk. Although the expected return on a portfolio is the weighted average of the expected return of each security, the portfolio risk is *not* simply a weighted average of the individual variances (or standard deviations). When securities are combined in a portfolio, risk is reduced because some of the fluctuations offset each other. This reduction in risk can occur as long as the securities are not perfectly (positively) correlated. The degree of risk reduction, however, depends on the statistical correlation between the income streams of the different investments. The lower the correlation, the greater the potential gain from risk diversification.

To quantify this relationship, let us assume the following expected returns, variances, and standard deviations for two hypothetical securities, A and B:

A	B
$E_1 = 10$	$E_2 = 20$
$\sigma_1^2 = 100$	$\sigma_2^2 = 900$
$\sigma_1 = 10$	$\sigma_2 = 30$

The expected returns and variances for portfolios of varying proportions, and for five alternative assumptions regarding the degree of correlation between returns, are given in Table 8–8. The data show that the lower the coefficient of correlation, the greater the reduction in the portfolio variance. For example, if we choose the proportions W_1 and W_2, which minimize the variance,[10] in this case $W_1 = 75\%$ and $W_2 = 25\%$, the minimum portfolio variance falls from 225, in the case of perfect positive correlation, to 0 when the returns display perfect negative correlation, when $R = -1$:

$$\sigma^2 = W_1^2\sigma_1^2 + W_2^2\sigma_2^2 - 2W_1W_2\sigma_1\sigma_2$$
$$= 9/16(100) + 1/16(900) - 2(3/4)(1/4)(10)(30)$$
$$= \frac{900 + 900 - 1{,}800}{16} = 0$$

It is noteworthy that with the exception of the case of perfect negative correlation, portfolio risk cannot be reduced to zero.

In reality, the returns on investments are *not* perfectly correlated, pos-

---

[10] The minimum variance is found from the following formula:

$$\frac{W_1}{W_2} = \frac{\sigma_2}{\sigma_1}$$

In our example,

$$\frac{W_1}{W_2} = \frac{30}{10}$$

so that $W_1 = 3W_2$. From the fact that the portfolio proportions must add to 1, we have

$$3W_2 + W_2 = 1$$
$$W_2 = .25, \text{ and}$$
$$W_1 = 1 - W_2 = .75$$

In general, diversification will reduce the minimum attainable variance if the correlation coefficient is less than the ratio of the smaller standard deviation to the larger one.

TABLE 8–8   Expected Return and Variance of "Two Security" Portfolios for Selected Correlation Coefficients

Proportion of Portfolio Invested in Security A (%)	Expected Return on Portfolio*	Variance of Returns for Alternative Correlation Coefficients[†]				
		+1	+1/2	0	-1/2	-1
0	20	900	900	900	900	900
20	18	676	628	580	532	484
40	16	484	412	340	268	196
60	14	324	252	180	108	36
75	12.5	225	169	112	56	0
100	10	100	100	100	100	100

* The mean is independent of R_{AB} and is obtained from the formula $E_p = W_1E_1 + W_2E_2$
[†] The formula for the variance is $\sigma_p^2 = W_1^2\sigma_1^2 + W_2^2\sigma_2^2 + 2W_1W_2R_{1,2}\sigma_1\sigma_2$.

itively or negatively. In most cases, some positive correlation, reflecting general economic conditions, exists. At best the security returns may have zero or slightly negative correlations. As a result, portfolio diversification helps to stabilize the returns, but does not entirely eliminate the fluctuations (variance) of investment returns. In general, diversification reduces, but does not eliminate, risk. However, this does not mean that the individual should seek diversification at any cost. The fact that two securities have a low degree of correlation is not, in itself, sufficient cause to combine them in a portfolio. The decision to diversify is more complex; it depends on expected return as well as on the correlation between returns.

An alternative way to reduce fluctuations is to increase the number of different securities included in the portfolio. For any given correlation coefficient, portfolio risk (variance) is reduced as additional securities are added to the portfolio. Empirical research has shown that this diversification effect approaches a limit. Virtually all the significant benefits of diversification (risk reduction) are reached when randomly chosen portfolios containing 15 to 20 securities are chosen (see Figure 8–4). As the figure shows, the bulk of the risk reduction (reduction of the portfolio variance) is achieved by relatively small portfolios.

THE CAPITAL ASSET PRICING MODEL (CAPM)

Throughout the book we have taken the maximization of the market value of the shareholders' equity as the goal of the firm. A direct implication of this assumption is that the firm should choose its investment program and financing policy so as to maximize the price (value) of its common stock. In other words, we need a decision rule which can tell us what a security's required expected return should be, given its risk. This in turn requires some sort of model of the forces (risk and return) which influence and determine

FIGURE 8–4
Relationship of risk to portfolio size

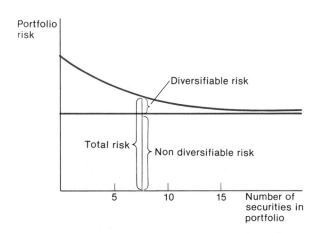

capital asset pricing model (CAPM)
A model of market equilibrium based on mean-variance portfolio theory.

stock prices. The most widely used model that relates risk and return is the **capital asset pricing model (CAPM)**, which is based explicitly on mean-variance portfolio theory. This model provides a powerful tool for analyzing relationships between risk and return, and important insights into the basic risk-return tradeoffs that characterize almost all financial decisions. We will first apply the CAPM framework to the analysis of the risk-return relationship in the security market.

A modern security market is a complex mechanism incorporating thousands of decision variables, and therefore any attempt to gain insight into the workings of such a market requires a high degree of abstraction. For this purpose, the fascinating world of brokers, specialists, speculators, and market tips must be ruthlessly shunted aside in order to focus on the all-important relationship between risk and expected return. To this end, the CAPM assumes that securities are traded in a hypothetical "perfect" capital market with the following characteristics:

1. *Risk aversion.* Investors are risk-averse and reach their decisions using the E-V rule.

2. *Information.* All relevant information is freely available to all investors. All investors therefore have the same expectations regarding the future returns and variances of all securities.

3. *Investment horizon.* There is a uniform investment period for all investors. This means that all decisions are assumed to be made at a particular point in time, and all investments are held for the same period.

4. *Costs.* The model assumes *no* transactions costs or taxes.

5. *Interest rate.* All investors can borrow or lend any amount of money, in the relevant range, without affecting the interest rate. In other words, there is no default risk.

These assumptions permit the building of an equilibrium model of the capital market. This in turn provides important insights into the crucial risk-return tradeoff and the way in which the equilibrium values of risk assets in general, and of common stock in particular, are determined.

Basing the analysis of the risk-return relationship on a market equilibrium model raises an almost obvious objection. The very essence of a security market is that prices fluctuate continuously. In more technical jargon, there is no equilibrium in such a market, or if there is, it is never reached! How then can the CAPM, which is explicitly a model of market equilibrium, be used to determine and explain the value of securities? In this context, it may be instructive to recall the well-known analogy drawn from dog racing in which the dogs go around the track chasing a mechanical rabbit. "Equilibrium" is reached only when one of the dogs catches the rabbit—but this *never* happens. Even so; knowledge of the existence of the rabbit (equilibrium) is vital when we attempt to predict or explain the otherwise rather peculiar behavior of the dogs.

DIVERSIFIABLE vs. NONDIVERSIFIABLE RISK

In the earlier sections of this chapter we used the mean-variance theory to derive an index of *portfolio risk*. The variance, or equivalently the standard deviation, of portfolio returns is the appropriate measure of portfolio risk. The CAPM offers additional insight into the measurement of the risk of a single asset. Using the CAPM, the riskiness (σ^2) of any *individual* security (or asset) can be divided into two parts:

total security risk (σ^2) = diversifiable risk + nondiversifiable risk

nonsystematic risk
That part of a security's risk that can be eliminated by combining it in a diversified portfolio.

Diversifiable Risk.   The first component is that part of a security's risk which can be eliminated by combining it in a diversified portfolio. The diversifiable component is also called **nonsystematic risk**, since no systematic relationship exists between this portion of a security's risk and general market fluctuations.

systematic risk
That part of a security's risk that cannot be eliminated by including it in a diversified portfolio.

Nondiversifiable Risk.   The nondiversifiable component of a security's risk, the part of the risk which *cannot* be eliminated by including the security in a diversified portfolio, is usually called the **systematic risk**. The latter stems from general market fluctuations, or from that component of a security's risk which reflects the relationship of·its fluctuations to those of the overall market. It is this nondiversifiable portion of the risk which gives rise to the risk premium. In the CAPM, the nonsystematic risk requires no such premium, since it can always be eliminted through diversification.

THE CONCEPT OF BETA

As we have seen, the variancc is a measure of risk. However, in the case of a two-security portfolio, risk reflects the correlation between the two securities, as well as their individual variances (see Eq. 8.7). When portfolios are comprised of many securities, the risk of each individual security depends on its correlation with all the others. Thus, if there are n securities, all of the correlation coefficients must be taken into account when evaluating risk, and this is very complicated. The CAPM avoids this complication by providing a single measure of a security's risk, called **beta.** The CAPM not only provides an appropriate index of risk for an *individual* security, but also allows us to assess the significance and impact of the two risk components (diversifiable and nondiversifiable risk) on investors' decisions.

beta risk
The contribution of a security to the overall risk of the market portfolio.

Given the assumptions of the CAPM, the following equilibrium condition will hold between the risk and the expected return (E_i) of a security:

$$E_i = R_F + \frac{E_m - R_F}{\sigma^2_m} \text{ cov } (x_i, x_m) \qquad (8.8)$$

where

E_m	= the expected return on the market in general
σ_m^2	= the variance of the aggregate market portfolio
R_F	= the riskless interest rate
cov (x_i, x_m)	= the covariance between the returns of security i and the return on the *market portfolio* (on a portfolio which includes all the securities in the market)

The **covariance** measures the relationship between the fluctuations of any security and the market portfolio. If it is positive, their prices tend to move together; if it is negative, the price of the first tends to fall when the market rises and vice versa. Thus the expected return of each security reflects the pure riskless interest rate plus a *risk premium* which is related to that security's contribution to the overall risk (variance) of the aggregate market portfolio. From the formula, we see that the *higher* the association between the return on the individual security and the return on the market, the greater the required risk premium.

We define a security's *beta risk* as its contribution to the overall risk (variance) of the market portfolio:

$$\text{beta}_i \equiv \beta_i = \frac{\text{cov } (x_i, x_m)}{\sigma_m^2}$$

Thus the degree of riskiness of an *individual* security can be approximated by the ratio of its covariance with the market to the fluctuations (variance) of the market as a whole. Beta provides a measure of the very important *nondiversifiable (systematic)* component of a security's risk. The higher a security's beta (other things being constant), the higher its nondiversifiable risk.

THE SECURITY MARKET LINE (SML)

Within the CAPM framework, only nondiversifiable risk gives rise to a need for a risk premium. No investor will be willing to pay a premium to avoid that part of the risk which can be diversified away. If we substitute beta for Cov $(x_i, x_m)/\sigma_m^2$ in Eq. 8.8, we get the following linear relationship between risk and return:

$$E_i = R_F + (E_m - R_F) \text{ beta}_i \qquad (8.9)$$

This linear relationship between the expected return of each risky security and its beta risk is called the **security market line (SML)**. Figure 8–5 illustrates the linear relationship between expected return and the security's beta risk. A glance at the security market line of Figure 8–5 shows that if beta is equal to 1, the security has the same risk as the market portfolio: If beta =

$$E_i = R_F + (E_m - R_F) \cdot 1 = E_m$$

**FIGURE 8–5
The Security
Market Line (SML)**

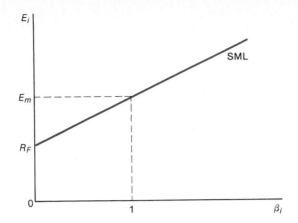

0, the ith security makes a zero contribution to the market portfolio's risk, and therefore the expected return on the security is equal to the riskless rate R_F. In general, E_i increases linearly with increases in beta; the higher a security's nondiversifiable risk (the higher its beta risk), the greater will be its expected return.

CALCULATING BETA IN PRACTICE

In order to apply the capital asset pricing model, a method must be found for estimating each firm's *future* beta. Although beta might be estimated solely on the basis of subjective beliefs, it is common practice to use historical data to estimate future betas. However, if the historical relationship between the rates of return on a given security and the rates of return on the market portfolio are expected to be materially different in the future, the observed past relationship must be modified to reflect such changes.

The beta risk coefficient can be estimated by using statistical methods[11] to determine the relationship between a security's returns and the return on the market portfolio. The latter is usually approximated by taking some index of the return on common stocks in general such as the S&P 500 stock index. A hypothetical example of the results of such an analysis is given in Figure 8–6, which shows the regression line of x_i on x_m, or the **characteristic line**, as it is usually called. The 10 dots represent the 10 annual plots of the relationship between the individual security's rate of return and that of the market portfolio. The slope of the regression line, in this case 1.6, is the measure of the security's beta. A second characteristic line, denoted as beta $= 1$, has a slope of 45°, and is appropriate for any security having the *same*

characteristic line
A regression line that shows the relationship between an individual security's rate of return and that of the market portfolio.

[11] See Appendix 8A.

FIGURE 8–6
**Examples of
"Characteristic
Lines"**

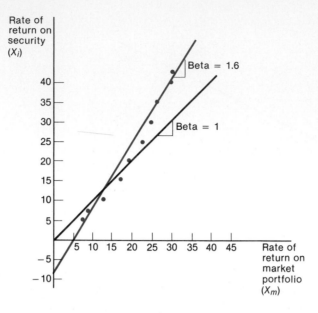

risk as the market portfolio. The return on such a security fluctuates, on average, in the same way as the market as a whole.

The concept of a characteristic line also suggests the possibility of classifying companies by their systematic risk. Stocks having a beta greater than one ($\beta > 1$) are classified as **aggressive stocks.** They go up faster than the market in a bull, or rising, market, but fall faster in a bear, or falling, market. Stocks with betas smaller than one ($\beta < 1$) are **defensive;** their returns fluctuate less than the market as a whole. Stocks with betas equal to unity are **neutral stocks**, since they fluctuate, on the average, along with the market.

The classification of stocks by beta risk is illustrated in Table 8–9. Using the regression technique and substituting the average return on all New

aggressive stocks
*Stocks having beta
risks greater than one;
their returns fluctuate
more than the market
as a whole.*

defensive stocks
*Stocks with beta risks
smaller than one; their
returns fluctuate less
than the market as a
whole.*

neutral stocks
*Stocks having beta
risks equal to one;
they generally fluctuate
along with the market.*

**TABLE 8–9   Selected Stocks Classified
by Beta Coefficients**

Defensive Stocks ($\beta < 1$)	
Abbott Laboratory	0.42
General Telephone	0.60
Greyhound Corporation	0.62
R.H. Macy Corporation	0.65
Union Carbide Corporation	0.92
Aggressive Stocks ($\beta > 1$)	
Bethlehem Steel	1.37
Hooper Chemical	1.43
Cerro Corporation	1.67
Medusa Portland	1.86
Conalco, Inc.	3.44

York Stock Exchange stocks for the market portfolio, betas were derived using the historical rates of return for a sample of firms over a 20-year period. The betas of the defensive stocks ranged from 0.42 for Abbott Laboratory to 0.92 for Union Carbide. With respect to the aggressive securities, Bethlehem Steel had a beta of 1.37, and the highest beta was 3.44 for Conalco.

Although it was originally developed for the security market, the CAPM also provides some important insights into the capital investment process of firms. Applied to individual projects, the appropriate discount rate is given by the riskless interest rate plus a premium which is determined by the projects' nondiversifiable (systematic) risk. However, in an extremely imperfect market in which investors hold only single-security portfolios, the variance remains the appropriate risk measure. Clearly, the truth lies somewhere between these two extreme assumptions.[12]

SUMMARY

A risky, or uncertain, investment is defined as one whose monetary return is not known with perfect certainty, but for which an array of alternative returns and their (objective or subjective) probabilities are known. One popular method for evaluating risky investments is the mean-variance (E-V) rule.

Despite its widespread use, the variance (standard deviation) does not always provide a meaningful definition of risk. As a result, decision-makers must exercise considerable caution when using this popular measure of investment risk if errors are to be avoided. In some instances the *coefficient of variation*, the standard deviation divided by the expected value, can be substituted as a measure of risk. However, in any case the proper measure of an individual security's risk can only be given within the context of portfolio analysis.

In general, risk can be reduced by combining individual securities in a portfolio; the degree of risk reduction depends on the degree of correlation among returns and the number of securities included in the portfolio. The lower the correlation or the larger the number of securities included in the portfolio, the greater the potential gains from diversification.

Building on the portfolio analysis, the basic principles of the capital asset pricing model (CAPM) are set out. This model assumes a perfect capital market in which investors hold fully diversified portfolios. This assumption permits us to define a number of important concepts:

1. The CAPM divides a security's risk into two components. The *diversifiable* component, or *nonsystematic risk*, is the part of the security's risk which

[12] The application of the CAPM to capital budgeting is discussed in detail in Chapters 11 and 15.

can be eliminated by combining it in a portfolio. The *nondiversifiable* component, or *systematic risk*, is that part which cannot be eliminated through portfolio diversification.

2. The beta coefficient, an index of a security's systematic risk, is the ratio of its covariance with the market portfolio to the variance of the market portfolio:

$$\text{beta} \equiv \beta_i = \frac{\text{cov}(x_i, x_m)}{\sigma_m^2}$$

3. The security market line (SML) shows the linear relationship between expected return and risk: $E_i = R_F + (E_m - R_F)\,\text{beta}_i$.

Risk lies at the very heart of the corporate decision-making process. With this in mind, we turn in Chapter 9 to the problem of evaluating a firm's capital investments.

APPENDIX 8A: | Estimating Beta

The method for estimating beta can be illustrated using the hypothetical data of Table 8A–1, which shows the rates of return for an individual security and for the market portfolio during the period 1978–87. If we also assume that the risk-free interest rate is constant, and equal to r percent per year, a security's beta can be estimated on the basis of the historical data using the following regression equation:

$$x_{it} = \alpha + \beta_i x_{mt} + e_t$$

where:

X_{it} = the rate of return on the ith security in year t

x_{mt} = the rate of return on the market portfolio in year t

α = the vertical intercept of security i

e_t = the residual error about the regression line

β_i = index of ith security's systematic risk

The estimate of the systematic risk, denoted by $\hat{\beta}$; is given by the standard formula:

TABLE 8A–1

Year	Rate of Return on Security (1) x_t	Rate of Return on Market Portfolio (2) x_m	(2) × (2) x_m^2	(1) × (2) $x_i x_m$
1978	5.2	7.4	54.8	38.5
1979	7.3	8.2	67.2	59.9
1980	10.1	12.3	151.3	124.2
1981	15.4	16.9	285.6	260.3
1982	19.8	19.1	364.8	378.2
1983	24.9	22.5	506.3	560.3
1984	29.7	25.1	630.0	745.5
1985	35.2	26.4	697.0	929.3
1986	40.1	29.8	888.0	1,195.0
1987	42.6	30.3	918.1	1.290.8
Total	230.3	198.0	4,563.1	5,582.0
Mean	23.0	19.8		

$$\hat{\beta}_i = \frac{\text{cov}(x_i, x_m)}{\sigma_m^2} = \frac{\sum\limits_{t=1}^{10} (x_{it} - \bar{x}_i)(x_{mt} - \bar{x}_m)}{\sum\limits_{t=1}^{10} (x_{mt} - \bar{x}_m)^2}$$

where $\bar{x}_i$ and $\bar{x}_m$ denote the arithmetic annual average rate of return on the ith security and market portfolio, respectively, and 10 represents the number of years in this specific example.

Employing some algebraic manipulation, this equation can be rewritten as:

$$\hat{\beta}_i = \frac{\sum\limits_{t=1}^{10} x_{it}\, x_{mt} - 10\, \bar{x}_i\, \bar{x}_m}{\sum\limits_{t=1}^{10} x_{mt}^2 - 10\, \bar{x}_m^2}$$

Using the data from Table 7–6, we obtain an estimate of the security's future beta, $\hat{\beta}_i = 1.6$:

$$\hat{\beta}_i = \frac{5582.0 - (10 \times 23 \times 19.8)}{4563.1 - 10 \times 392} = \frac{1028}{643.1} = 1.6$$

In this example we used hypothetical figures to calculate the beta. In practice, actual data on rates of return of the security would be used, and a stock market index, such as the S&P 500, would be used as a proxy for the market portfolio. (The S&P index, which provides a measure of the rate of return on a well-diversified portfolio consisting of 500 selected stocks, is considered to be representative of the market as a whole.)

REVIEW EXERCISE

Circle the correct word(s) to complete each sentence; see p. 197 for correct answers.

8.1 Perfect certainty refers to cases in which expectations are *single valued/multivalued.*

8.2 A risky investment is one for which only a *present value/distribution* of returns is known.

8.3 The expected return of an investment is given by the *geometric/arithmetic* average of the possible outcomes, weighted by their probabilities.

8.4 An investment's risk can be measured by the *variance/frequency* of its returns.

8.5 Variance provides information on the extent of the deviations of possible returns from *zero/expected return.*

8.6 The dimension of the standard deviation is *dollars/dollars squared.*

8.7 Risk-averters *demand/pay* a premium to enter a risky venture.

8.8 Risk-lovers *demand/pay* a premium to avoid a risky endeavor.

8.9 Most investors in the capital market are risk-*averse/neutral/loving.*

8.10 In general, risky investments must offer *higher/lower* returns than nonrisky ones.

8.11 If the expected return on stock A is equal to the expected return on stock B, and the variance of A is *lower/higher* than the variance of B, then A will be preferred to B.

8.12 The expected return on a portfolio of securities is the *straight/weighted* average of the expected returns of the individual securities.

8.13 The degree to which the returns of the securities fluctutate together is called *variance/correlation.*

8.14 Portfolio variance *does/does not* depend on the correlation between the returns of securities.

8.15 If two securities have identical earnings and risk characteristics, their combination into a portfolio *may/may not* reduce the risk.

8.16 One way to reduce fluctuations in the portfolio returns is to *reduce/increase* the number of different securities included.

8.17 The nonsystematic risk of a security *can/cannot* be eliminated by combining the securities in a portfolio.

8.18 A security's beta risk is its contribution to the overall risk of *Treasury bills/the market portfolio.*

8.19 The security market line shows the relationship between securities' expected returns and their *variance/beta risk.*

8.20 Aggressive stocks go up (fall) *slower/faster* than the market.

QUESTIONS

8.1 Define the following terms:

a. Distribution	**b.** Subjective probability
c. Expected return	**d.** Variance
e. Standard deviation	**f.** Risk-averse, risk-neutral, risk-loving
g. Diversifiable	**h.** Systematic risk
i. Portfolio	**j.** Security market line

8.2 Are government T-bills completely riskless?

8.3 Plot the frequency distribution of the grades you received last year.

8.4 Why is variance measured in "squared dollars"? How can this problem be resolved?

8.5 "We have problems deciding between investment projects. When risk is measured by the variance, project A is less risky, but when the standard deviation is used, project B is less risky." Comment on this statement.

8.6 Are you a risk-averter, a risk-lover, or risk-neutral? Give examples from your own experience to substantiate your claim.

8.7 Can you think of an example in which every investor will prefer project A to project B even though project A is very risky, while project B has no risk?

8.8 "If most investors were risk-averse, there would be very few investors in the capital market. Therefore, we conclude that most people are risk-lovers." Do you agree? Explain.

8.9 "The replacement of variance or the standard deviation by the coefficient of variation does not overcome all the difficulties encountered in measuring risk." Give a numerical example to support this statement.

8.10 "I use a simple arithmetic average to compute the return on my portfolio." What can you infer about the composition of that portfolio?

8.11 Given the assumption of zero correlation between two securities, the portfolio variance can be computed as a weighted average of the individual variances. What weights should be used?

8.12 Given the assumption of zero correlation, can the standard deviation of a portfolio be computed as a weighted average of the individual standard deviations?

8.13 Evaluate the following statement: "One can get rid of all risk, if only it were possible to build a big enough portfolio."

8.14 Why, according to the CAPM, does the market require no risk premium to offset a security's nonsystematic risk?

8.15 Give examples of pairs of companies, or industries, whose returns are
    a. Positively correlated
    b. Uncorrelated
    c. Negatively correlated

PROBLEMS

8.1 **Expected value, variance, standard deviation.**   The following sales data are available for the Jackson Company: During the past 2 years Jackson had 35 weeks with sales of $12,000, 26 weeks with $14,000, 21 weeks with $8,000, 8 weeks with $16,000, 2 weeks with $18,000, 5 weeks with $6,000, and 3 weeks with $4,000. (Each year Jackson & Co. closes for two weeks in the summer.)
    a. Draw the frequency distribution of weekly sales.
    b. Compute the expected sales, the variance, and the standard deviation.

8.2 **Expected return, variance, standard deviation.**   Compute the expected return, variance, and standard deviation for the following securities:

	Return in Year				
	1	**2**	**3**	**4**	**5**
Security A	7.5	6.3	9.0	12.1	8.6
Security B	10.1	9.9	3.2	0	4.5
Security C	2.4	8.8	11.0	14.4	12.0

8.3 **Mean-variance rule.**   Mark Wilson makes his financial choices according to the E-V rule, but must choose a single security. He is faced with the following investment alternatives:

Alternative	Expected Return	Variance
A	12%	6.5
B	8%	13.0
C	10%	8.1
D	11%	7.8

    a. Which alternative will he choose?
    b. A new alternative has become available with an expected return of 13% and variance of 7.5. How does your answer change?

8.4 **Mean variance rule.**   Jack Graham studies the yearly reports of the Gamma, Delta, and Epsilon Corporations. He wants to buy stock in only *one* of these corporations and will decide according to the M-V rule. Which stock do you think he is going to buy?

	Return in Year		
	1	**2**	**3**	
Gamma	12%	6%	11%	11%
Delta	7	12	13	12
Epsilon	9	11	7	8

8.5 Portfolio return.   Consolidated Mutual Fund owns five stocks. The following table gives the details of the portfolio:

	Amount Invested	Expected Return	Variance
Stock A	$17,000	12%	8.5
Stock B	35,000	6	4.5
Stock C	21,000	8	6.0
Stock D	16,000	15	12.6
Stock E	11,000	7	6.2

What is the expected return of the portfolio?

8.6 Portfolio variance.

a. What is the expected return and the variance of a portfolio made up of stocks A and B of the previous question, if the coefficient of correlation is 0.6? (Assume that the amounts invested are the same as in the previous question.)

b. What is the expected return and the variance of a portfolio made up of stocks C and D of the previous question, if the coefficient of correlation is −0.3? (Assume that the amounts invested remain the same.)

c. What is the expected return and the variance of a portfolio made up of stocks D and E of the previous question, if their returns are statistically independent? (Assume that the amounts invested remain unchanged.)

8.7 Portfolio variance.   What are all the possible returns of a portfolio comprised of $5,000 of RTA stock and $5,000 of S&P stock. Assume the following data on the returns of each individual stock:

RTA	+5% with probability 70%	+ 8% with probability 30%
S&P	−2% with probability 20%	+12% with probability 80%

The returns of RTA and S&P are statistically independent; that is, the correlation coefficient is zero.

8.8 Diversification. Henry Brown is evaluating two stocks with the following expected returns and variances:

	Eta	Zeta
Expected return	8%	11%
Variance	6	8

What is the expected return and variance of a portfolio made up of equal amounts of Eta and Zeta if the coefficient of correlation is
a. 1   **b.** 0.5
c. 0   **d.** −0.5
e. −1

8.9 Diversification. Henry Brown is still evaluating the two stocks, Eta and Zeta. He knows now, however, that the coefficient of correlation between their returns is 0.8. What is the expected return and the variance of a portfolio made up of the two stocks if the proportion invested in Eta is:
a. 10%   **b.** 30%
c. 50%   **d.** 70%
e. 90%   **f.** 100%

8.10 CAPM. What is the expected return on a security with a beta of:
a. .75   **b.** 2.80
c. −0.35   **d.** −0.65
e. 3.55
In your answer, assume that the risk-free rate of interest is 6% and the return on the market is 12%

8.11 Beta. What are the betas of the securities with the following expected returns, if we assume that the risk-free interest rate is 3.5% and the return on the market is 9%?
a. Expected return = 5%   **b.** Expected return = 2.5%
c. Expected return = 15%   **d.** Expected return = 6%
e. Expected return = 9%   **f.** Expected return = 3.5%
g. Expected return = 23%

8.12 Security market line.
a. Plot the expected returns of the securities of problem 8.11 against their betas.
b. Draw a line through these points. What do the y-intercept and the slope of this line indicate?

8.13 Beta, computer problem. Compute the betas of the following stocks:

	Return in year					
	1	2	3	4	5	6
Stock A	11.41	8.13	14.08	7.24	6.35	8.41
Stock B	9.98	11.03	12.44	9.12	7.65	7.88
Stock C	10.01	9.99	11.22	8.12	7.09	8.88
Market portfolio	10.11	10.48	12.31	8.61	7.92	8.02

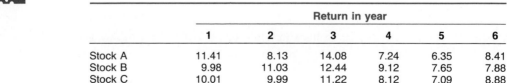

8.14 **Expected return, variance, standard deviation, computer problem.** Compute the expected return, variance, and standard deviation for the three stocks and for the market portfolio of problem 8.13.

SAMPLE PROBLEMS

SP8.1 What is the expected return, variance, and standard deviation of the stock of Jefferson Labs, whose returns for the last four years are given below:

Year	Return
1984	12%
1985	8
1986	6
1987	14

SP8.2 Assume that the risk-free rate of interest is 5% and the return on the market portfolio is 9%. What are the expected returns for securities, according to the CAPM, which have betas of 0, 0.8, 1, and 2.5, respectively?

Solutions to Sample Problems

SP8.1 The expected return can be computed as the weighted average of the previous years' returns, where the weights are the probabilities of each outcome. In our case, each outcome takes place only once, so the probability of each is 25%.

expected return = .25(12%) + .25(8%) + .25(6%) + .25(14%) = 10%

The variance is defined as the weighted average of the squared deviations of the outcomes from the expected return:

$$\text{variance} = .25(12 - 10)^2 + .25(8 - 10)^2 + .25(6 - 10)^2$$
$$+ .25(14 - 10)^2$$
$$= .25(2)^2 + .25(2)^2 + .25(4)^2 + .25(4)^2$$
$$= .25(4 + 4 + 16 + 16) = 10$$

The standard deviation is the square root of the variance:

$$\text{standard deviation} = \sqrt{10} = 3.16$$

SP8.2 According to the CAPM, the security market line gives the relationship between a security's beta risk and its expected return. Hence:

$$E_i = R_F + (E_m - R_F)\,\beta_i$$

Substituting 5% for R_F and 9% for E_m, we get:

For $\beta = 0$: $E_i = 5\% + (9\% - 5\%)0 = 5\%$
For $\beta = 0.8$: $E_i = 5\% + (9\% - 5\%)0.8 = 8.2\%$
For $\beta = 1.0$: $E_i = 5\% + (9\% - 5\%)1 = 9\%$
For $\beta = 2.5$: $E_i = 5\% + (9\% - 5\%)2.5 = 15\%$

**Answers
to Review
Exercises**

8.1 single valued   **8.2** distribution   **8.3** arithmetic   **8.4** variance

8.5 expected return   **8.6** dollars   **8.7** demand   **8.8** demand

8.9 averse   **8.10** higher   **8.11** lower   **8.12** weighted

8.13 correlation   **8.14** does   **8.15** may   **8.16** increase

8.17 can   **8.18** the market portfolio   **8.19** beta risk   **8.20** faster

SUGGESTIONS FOR FURTHER READING

Risk diversification and portfolio analysis are treated at greater depth in Haim Levy and Marshall Sarnat, *Portfolio and Investment Selection* (Englewood Cliffs, NJ: Prentice-Hall, 1984); Gordon J. Alexander and Jack C. Francis, *Portfolio Analysis,* 3rd ed. (Englewood Cliffs, NJ: Prentice-Hall, 1986); and Edwin J. Elton and Martin J. Gruber, *Modern Portfolio Theory and Investment Analysis* (New York: Wiley, 1981).

Critical evaluations of the empirical evidence and of the interpretation of the CAPM can be found in Richard Roll, "A Critique of the Asset Pricing Theory's Tests, Part I," *Journal of Financial Economics,* March 1977.

Readable surveys of the risk-return literature are given by Franco Modigliani and Gerald A. Pogue, "An Introduction to Risk and Return," *Financial Analysts Journal,* March–April 1974 and May–June 1974; and Richard A. Brealey, *An Introduction to Risk and Return from Common Stocks* (Cambridge, MA: MIT Press, 1969).

9 | The Net Present Value Rule and Capital Budgeting

Companies invest in a large variety of real assets—a plant in West Virginia to produce a new product, new equipment to replace an obsolete manufacturing facility in California, or a new research laboratory in Texas. The aggregate investment on new plant and equipment involves very large sums of money. In 1986, planned business expenditures on new plant and equipment amounted to almost $400 billion.[1] These current capital expenditures, which help determine the size and composition of tomorrow's output, have great social significance. They are also crucial to the investing firm and its shareholders. In large measure, the company's future is irrevocably determined by today's investment decisions. For the individual firm, investment, or *capital budgeting* decisions, as they are usually called, are one of the most demanding challenges facing the management team. In such decisions, the firm commits some of its present resources in the hope of securing a stream of future benefits. Hence the timing of receipts and outlays, and not just their magnitude, must be considered when evaluating investment proposals.

In Chapter 7, the universal valuation principle based on present value was established using financial investments—bonds and common stock—as examples. In this chapter, the present value technique is applied to the evaluation of a firm's capital investments—for example, in new plant and equipment. The net present value rule is defined and its superiority is demonstrated by comparing it with alternative decision criteria: internal rate of return, profitability index, payback and accounting rates of return. These methods are also of interest in themselves, since they are used by many firms in actual practice.

---

[1] See *Economic Report of the President*, Washington, DC, 1986.

CAPITAL BUDGETING: AN OVERVIEW

A systematic approach to capital budgeting requires:

a. The formulation of a long-term strategy and goals
b. The creative search for, and identification of, new investment opportunities
c. The estimation and forecasting of current and future cash flows
d. A set of decision rules that can differentiate acceptable from unacceptable alternatives
e. The building of a suitable administrative framework capable of transferring the required information to the decision level
f. The controlling of expenditures and the careful monitoring of project implementation

Figure 9–1 shows a highly simplified flowchart for a typical investment proposal. The emphasis is on the importance of feedback from operating results both for control and for the planning of new projects. The flowchart assumes that the firm employs a formal capital budget based on intensive financial planning. Practice, however, is far from uniform, even among the medium-sized and large firms that typically budget their capital expenditures. Length of budget period, definition of projects, evaluation techniques, and administrative procedures vary greatly from firm to firm.

Many firms divide their efforts between a long-term planning budget, which rarely exceeds 5 years, and a short-term 1-year capital budget. The former is usually general in nature and often indicates areas of future interest, rather than specific investment proposals. For example, the rough order of magnitudes of planned investment in fixed assets such as land, buildings, and machines is projected by divisions, by product line, or by manufacturing process. The short-term budget is more specific and includes the final estimates for an actual proposed project. It is this budget that provides the cornerstone for the control of capital expenditures. With the possible exception of firms of very moderate size, some sort of short-term budget is essential if management is to monitor and control capital expenditures.

Although there are no hard and fast rules, most firms apply formal capital budgeting procedures only to those projects in which a significant period of time (usually more than 1 year) elapses between the initial investment outlay and the receipt of the project's final benefits. The procedures, however, can apply to the investment in any asset—accounts receivable, inventory, and so on.

Many firms also limit their formal capital budgeting procedures to relatively large expenditures. This constraint is necessary if management time (a resource in short supply in most firms) is to be used economically. The board of directors, or a capital appropriations committee, is usually unwill-

FIGURE 9–1
Project Planning

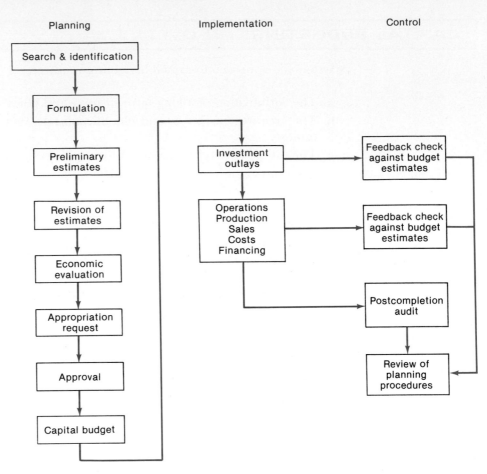

ing to discuss the merits of a proposed switch to electric pencil sharpeners, despite the fact that the benefits are expected to accrue over a number of years. Of course, the concept "relatively large" has no precise meaning outside the particular problem at hand. Clearly, a definition of "large" that is good for General Motors may not be appropriate for the local ice cream parlor.

Long-term Goals   A systematic approach to capital investment decisions requires the formulation of a set of long-term goals which can serve as a guide for managerial decisions. As we noted in Chapter 1, we assume throughout the book that management is concerned with maximizing the market value (price) of the firm's common stock. For the purposes of capital budgeting, this means that management will be concerned with both the expected returns and the risks incurred on its capital investments. Of course, many investment projects cannot be described completely in terms of monetary costs and benefits; for example, a new cafeteria for workers, or an executive dining room. However, even in these cases, a systematic calculation of the profitability of alternative investments can provide a benchmark for evaluating intangible benefits.

Generating Investment Proposals

Another prerequisite for efficient capital management is so obvious that it is often overlooked. A good investment proposal is not just born—someone has to suggest it! In the absence of a creative search for new investment opportunities, even the most sophisticated evaluation technique may be worthless. In addition, someone within the firm must be willing to listen to such proposals. In other words, a method must exist for transferring proposals to the decision level. The best method for identifying new investment opportunities differs from industry to industry, and from firm to firm. A large chemical plant or an electronics manufacturer is likely to have a well-equipped research and development division charged with the task of finding economically feasible and attractive uses for sophisticated new products or processes. In a small machine shop, the search for investment possibilities may be less structured. It often takes the form of an employee suggestion box, or informal discussions during a coffee break.

Depending on the size and organization of the firm, requests for investment funds are made by heads of operating divisions or departments, often in conjunction with research and planning units. These requests are usually based on market research, technical engineering studies, cost analyses, methods studies, employee suggestions, and so on.

investment
The laying out of money to expand current facilities or create new ones.

From the viewpoint of capital budgeting, a broad interpretation of the term **investment** is desirable. The search for opportunities should include the acquisition of *existing* production and marketing facilities by means of a merger with another company, as well as the expansion of the company's own facilities or the creation of an entirely new division. The problems created by business mergers are sufficiently different and important to warrant separate treatment (see Chapter 21). In many large companies, a staff of trained specialists concentrates on discovering and analyzing the benefits and costs of potential corporate acquisitions. The need for such a staff reflects the complex legal, tax, financing, and accounting aspects of these mergers.

Forecasting Cash Flows

From the very inception of a proposal, the project's expected costs and revenues must be estimated. Often the rough preliminary estimates prepared when the project is first defined have to be revised and refined before it is incorporated in the firm's formal budget. Finally, on the eve of the actual decision, these revised estimates must be presented in the form of an *appropriation request*. The relevant engineering, marketing, and financial data must be gathered from departments and divisions throughout the firm. In the final stage, many of the cost estimates will be replaced by the actual bids from supplying companies, which include fixed prices. However, the timing and size of future cash flows, of course, usually remain uncertain throughout the budgeting process, and for that matter, over the course of the project's life. But the proper estimation of cash flows is so vital that we devote the next chapter to this important problem.

The Administrative Framework

Successful capital budgeting requires an administrative framework that facilitates the gathering and transfer of relevant information on alternative courses of action. This is necessary for decision-making, as well as for the control of expenditures. Such a framework requires a uniform set of procedures and forms that can be used to check project estimates for accuracy and against budget limits. In general, capital budgeting is a multifaceted activity that demands a high degree of cooperation among various departments. At one stage or another, marketing, engineering, production, accounting, and financial personnel are likely to be involved in the preparation of the capital budget. Final approval of all major capital expenditures, however, usually rests with the company's board of directors.

The Post-Completion Audit

The post-completion audit of capital investment projects is one stage of the decision-making process that is often neglected. Strictly speaking, the audit is not part of the decision-making process, since it refers to implemented projects. However, systematic evaluation of past decisions can often improve current decision-making. Past errors can be analyzed by department, by personnel, or by type of expenditure. These data are often extremely valuable in revising current forecasting and evaluation methods.

The post-audit is a necessary management tool. Unlike the Hollywood movies of the 1930s, even the best-laid plans of management may not ensure a happy ending. Although past mistakes cannot be undone, a careful analysis of the deviation of actual from planned performance may prevent history from repeating itself. For example, if investment outlays are consistently underestimated by 10 percent, a rule of thumb correction of that order of magnitude may be called for. In general, the post-audit can be a sobering and rewarding experience for the decision-maker.

The post-audit has two principal objectives: (a) to improve forecasts, and (b) to improve operations. In both instances, financial executives, who after all are people just like everyone else, tend to improve their performance when they know they are being monitored. It's a little like striving to meet a deadline, or running a race against the clock. But exploiting the post-audit in practice is a tricky business. A number of pitfalls must be avoided:

1. Care must be exercised to differentiate between controllable and uncontrollable events. Executives should not be credited because a competitor's plant burned down—unless, perhaps, they were responsible for the fire. Nor should managers be fired because their long-term projections failed to forecast the world oil crisis of the mid-1970s.

2. There is also some danger that too strenuous an application of the auditing principle may make executives overly cautious. Executives may become so risk-averse that they will be reluctant to recommend risky projects.

3. Finally, by the time the audit reveals the errors of the vice-president in charge of planning, that gentleman may have become the corporation's president, or perhaps even secretary of defense. Here we must take a hint from Dostoevsky and make sure "the punishment fits the crime." It is unreasonable to chop off the head of the nearest executive just because it happens to be within reach.

THE NET PRESENT VALUE RULE

decision rule
A rule that differentiates acceptable from unacceptable alternatives in capital investment decisions.

The administrative framework is designed to help the firm make capital investment decisions that are in its shareholders' best interests. But such decisions do not just pop out of a feasibility study or capital budget; they require a **decision rule** which can differentiate acceptable from unacceptable alternatives. Moreover, the decision rule must be compatible with corporate objectives. The net present value rule is a decision criterion that meets this test.

By now you know that money has a time value. As a result, cash flows over time must be reduced to a common denominator if meaningful comparisons are to be made (see Chapter 6). In the context of capital budgeting, this means that the evaluation of project cash flows requires the comparison of the present value of future receipts with today's investment outlay. The net present value (NPV) method of evaluating a firm's capital investments can be defined as follows:

$$\text{NPV} = \frac{CF_1}{1 + k} + \frac{CF_2}{(1 + k)^2} + \ldots + \frac{CF_n}{(1 + k)^n} - I_0 \qquad (9.1)$$

or equivalently

$$\text{NPV} = CF_1(DF_{k,1}) + CF_2(DF_{k,2}) + \ldots + CF_n(DF_{k,n}) - I_0$$

where

CF_t = the net cash flow expected in year $t(t = 1,2, \ldots, n)$
I_0 = the initial investment outlay
k = the appropriate market capitalization rate, that is the opportunity cost of using capital for risky projects
$DF_{k,t}$ = the discount factor for year t $(t = 1,2, \ldots, n)$
n = the project's economic lifetime, in years

The calculation of a project's NPV is straightforward:

STEP 1:   Use the present value table, or a calculator, to find the present value (PV) of each year's expected net cash receipt—expected cash revenues less expected cash outlays.

STEP 2: Sum the present values to get the total PV of the expected future cash flow.

STEP 3: Deduct the initial investment outlay (I_0) to derive the project's net present value (NPV).

STEP 4: Accept or reject the proposal.

Before step 4 can be carried out, a *decision rule* must be set. Given the goal of maximizing stock price, the following decision rules should be adopted:

☐ *If NPV is positive, accept the project.*
☐ *If NPV is negative, reject the project.*

The firm should execute only projects that promise a *positive* NPV; proposals with negative NPVs should be rejected. This decision rule can be derived directly from the assumption that the firm wishes to maximize the market value of its owners' equity (stock price).

So long as the firm uses a discount rate which reflects the alternative return that can be earned in the capital market on investments of similar risk, the market will translate increases in NPV into increases in share price. By accepting a project with a postive NPV, the firm obtains an expected future cash flow with a higher present value than the investment outlay. As a result of this net gain, the expected dividend stream also rises, thereby increasing the current value (price) of the firm's common stock. In a sense, the NPV calculation replicates the valuation process for the firm's stock (see Chapter 7). Hence, maximizing NPV and maximizing the value of equity come to the same thing.

This result depends on the choice of discount rate. Project cash flows must be discounted using the appropriate **opportunity cost of capital**—that is, a discount rate that reflects the alternative rate of return which the shareholders can earn if they were to invest the funds themselves in securities of equal risk.[2] Correctly applied, the NPV decision rule results in an optimal choice of projects. Under the assumed conditions, no other group of projects can be found that will increase the value of the firm.

opportunity cost of capital
A discount rate that reflects the alternative rate of return that shareholders could earn if they themselves invested project funds in securities of equal risk.

[2] Chapter 15 examines in detail the methods used to estimate the cost of capital.

TABLE 9–1   Calculation of NPV with Alternative Discount Rates

Discount Rate	PV of Cash Flow		Less the Outlay Investment	NPV
	120(1)	= 120	−100	20
10%	120(.909)	= 109	−100	9
20%	120(.833)	= 100	−100	0
30%	12(.769)	= 92	−100	(−8)

FIGURE 9–2
Example of an NPV Profile

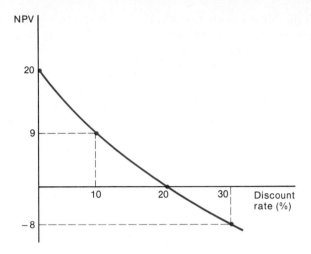

A Graphic
Representation
of NPV

NPV profile
A graph that shows a project's net present value at alternative discount rates.

A project's NPV depends solely on the size and timing of the cash flow, the investment outlay, and the discount rate. This dependence can be "visualized" by using a simple graphic device called the **NPV profile.** Consider an example of a $100 investment that generates a net receipt of $120 at the end of one year. Table 9–1 calculates the project's NPV using four alternative discount rates—zero, 10%, 20%, and 30%. The data in Table 9–1 identify four points on Figure 9–2, which graphs the project's NPV for these four discount rates. The remaining points of the NPV profile have been sketched in.

For a zero discount rate ($k = 0$), the discount factor is 1, ($DF_{0,n} = 1$). This reflects the fact that in a world without a profitable alternative use for money, a dollar received tomorrow *is equal* to a dollar received today. Therefore, the NPV is simply the algebraic sum of the stream of *undiscounted* net receipts, minus the initial investment outlay ($120 - 100 = 20$). When $k = 10\%$, the NPV is positive, ($+9$); conversely, for $k = 30\%$, the NPV is negative, (-8). If the discount rate is set equal to 20 percent, the project's NPV is zero.

From the complete diagram we can see that the project in question has a positive NPV at all discount rates below 20%. Its NPV is negative for discount rates above 20%. Thus, it should be accepted if and only if the opportunity cost of capital, k, is below 20%.

INTERNAL RATE OF RETURN

Corporate executives often prefer to discuss investment decisions in terms of the *percentage* return on investment. Fortunately, Figure 9–2 offers us a way to meet this need. As we have already noted, a discount rate of 20%

reduces the NPV of our hypothetical project to zero. But this is precisely the definition of the project's rate of return. It is intuitively obvious that a 1-year investment with an expected cash receipt of $120 and an initial outlay of $100 represents a 20% rate of return:

$$\text{rate of return} = \frac{120 - 100}{100} = \frac{120}{100} - 1 = 20\%$$

In symbols:

$$\text{rate of return} = \frac{CF_1}{I_0} - 1$$

So far so good, but realistically, most projects have cash flows that are received over a number of years, and therefore the multiperiod rate of return should reflect compound interest.

Recall the discussion of bond valuation and interest rates. Now we derive the time-discounted version of the rate of return, which we call the **internal rate of return (IRR)**. For 1-year projects, the IRR is the same as the simple rate of return. Denoting the IRR by the letter R, we have:

internal rate of return (IRR)
That discount rate which equates the present value of expected cash flow with initial investment outlay.

$$R = \frac{CF_1}{I_0} - 1 \quad \text{or} \quad 1 + R = \frac{CF_1}{I_0}$$

Rearranging terms, we get

$$I_0 = \frac{CF_1}{1 + R}$$

In the general case of projects with durations greater than 1 year, the IRR formula becomes:

$$I_0 = \frac{CF_1}{1 + R} + \frac{CF_2}{(1 + R)^2} + \ldots + \frac{CF_n}{(1 + R)^n} \tag{9.2}$$

where R again denotes the internal rate of return.

The *internal rate of return* is defined as that rate of discount which equates the present value of the expected cash flow with the initial investment outlay. An alternative and equivalent definition is that rate of discount which reduced the NPV of the expected cash flow to zero:

$$\frac{CF_1}{1 + R} + \frac{CF_2}{(1 + R)^2} + \ldots + \frac{CF_n}{(1 + R)^n} - I_0 = 0 \tag{9.2a}$$

Calculating the IRR: Constant Cash Flow

When the cash flow is constant ($CF_1 = CF_2 = CF_n$), the IRR can be calculated using the present value table for an annuity:

STEP 1:   Use Eq. 9.2 to find the *critical value* of the discount factor needed to equate the present value of the expected receipts to the initial investment outlay:

$$CF(DFA_{k,n}^{*}) = I_0$$

where the asterisk (*) denotes the critical value of the discount factor. The critical value of the discount factor can be found by dividing the initial investment outlay (I_0) by the fixed annual cash receipt (CF):

$$(DFA_{k,n}^{*}) = I_0 / CF$$

STEP 2:   The IRR is found by looking along the appropriate line (year) of the present value table for an annuity until the column which includes the critical discount factor is reached. The *discount rate* of this column is the project's IRR.

Now let's apply the formula to the following numerical example:

$$CF = \$20 \text{ per year}$$
$$n = 7 \text{ years}$$
$$I_0 = \$120$$

First we find the critical discount factor:

$$DFA_{k,7}^{*} = \frac{I_0}{CF} = \frac{120}{20} = 6$$

A glance at line 7 of the present value of an annuity table shows that 6.002 (which is approximately equal to 6) appears in the 4% column. The annuity's IRR, therefore, is 4 percent.

Calculating the IRR: Fluctuating Cash Flow[3]   An annuity is a very special case of project cash flows. Clearly, the annual net cash receipts need not, and very often are not, uniform. The general case of nonuniform cash receipts requires an iterative or "trial and error" solution. The computation procedure is as follows:

1. Choose a discount rate at random, and calculate the project's NPV.
2. If the NPV is positive, choose a *higher* discount rate and repeat the procedure; if the NPV is negative, choose a *lower* discount rate and repeat the procedure.
3. That discount rate which reduces the NPV to zero is the IRR, and the procedure is completed.

Table 9–2 gives a numerical example of the procedure for calculating the IRR when the cash flow is not constant.

---

[3] For most projects, the IRR can be calculated by hand in a few minutes, but where necessary, standard computer programs are available to facilitate the calculations. In the special case of a 2-year project, the IRR can also be found directly by applying the formula for a quadratic equation.

TABLE 9–2   Calculation of IRR for a Hypothetical Project

Year	Net Cash Flow	Discount Factor	Present Value of Cash flow
First Iteration: 8% Discount Rate*			
1	452	0.926	418.6
2	500	0.857	428.5
3	278	0.794	220.7
		PV of receipts	1,067.8
		Less: Initial outlay	−1,000.0
		NPV	**+67.8**
Second Iteration: 15% Discount Rate			
1	452	0.870	393.2
2	500	0.756	378.0
3	278	0.658	182.9
		PV of receipts	954.1
		Less: Initial outlay	−1,000.0
		NPV	**−45.9**
Final Iteration: 12% Discount Rate			
1	452	0.893	403.6
2	500	0.797	398.5
3	278	0.712	197.9
		PV of receipts	1,000.0
		Less: Initial outlay	−1,000.0
		NPV	**0**

STEP 1: Applying the factors for an 8% discount rate, the NPV of the project is positive (+67.8). Therefore, a higher discount rate (smaller discount factors) is required if the NPV is to be reduced to zero.

STEP 2: A 15% discount rate is chosen. This results in a negative NPV (−45.9). Now we require a discount rate that is lower than 15%, but higher than 8%.

STEP 3: The discount rate that reduces the NPV to zero is 12%. Thus 12%, by definition, is the project's IRR.

Unlike the NPV, which can be positive or negative depending on the discount rate used, a project's IRR is fixed, once and for all, and independent of the discount rate. Because of this, the IRR decision rules must take the opportunity cost of using capital—that is, the discount rate (k)—explicitly into account:

☐ *If the IRR is greater than k, accept the project.*
☐ *If the IRR is less than k, reject the project.*

We ignore the possibility that the IRR will be exactly equal to the discount rate, for in that case the firm would indifferent to the project.

THE MEANING OF IRR AND NPV

If you remember the discussion of interest rates in Chapter 6, you probably have already realized that the IRR formula is the same as that for the compounded rate of interest. This can easily be verified by considering the following 2-year project:

$$I_0 = \text{initial investment outlay} = 200$$
$$CF = \text{annual net receipt} = 123$$
$$n = \text{project's lifetime} = 2 \text{ years}$$

To calculate the project's IRR, we first find the critical discount factor:

$$(DFA_{k,2}^{*}) = 200/123 = 1.626$$

A glance at line 2 of the present value table for an annuity shows that the factor 1.626 appears in the 15% column; so the project's IRR is 15%. Common sense suggests that if we borrow the money needed to finance the project from a bank at less than 15%, a profit will be made. That is, we will be able to pay the interest and repay the principal out of the project's proceeds and still have money left over. Should the bank demand more than 15% interest the cash flow from the project will be insufficient, and a loss will be incurred. If the interest rate is 15% (that is, exactly equal to the project's IRR) we will just break even, since the cash flow will just cover the interest and repayment of principal.

To check this line of reasoning, assume the bank charges 15% interest. Table 9–3 shows the relevant cash flows between the firm and the bank. At the end of the first year, the firm pays the bank 15% interest on its loan of $200—that is, $30. But since the firm earned $123 from the project, it uses the remaining $93 to reduce its bank loan. At the end of the second year, the interest payment is only $16 (15% on an outstanding balance of $107). After paying the interest out of the project's second-year cash flow, $107 remains. This amount is just sufficient to repay the outstanding balance of the loan. We leave it to you to verify that had the bank charged a higher rate of interest, say 20%, the proceeds from the project would *not* have been sufficient to meet all the firm's payments to the bank.

TABLE 9–3 Cash Flows Between Firm and Bank to Repay Loan

	First Year	Second Year
Cash inflow from project	123	123
To bank:		
Interest payments	30	16
Repayments of principal	93	107
Loan outstanding beginning of year	200	107
Loan outstanding end of year	107	0

FIGURE 9–3
Example of NPV
Profile

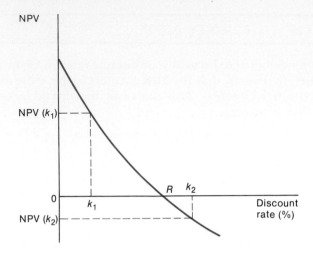

The IRR can also be used to provide an intuitively appealing economic rationale for the NPV rule. Figure 9–3 shows the general NPV profile for a typical investment project. Recall that the intercept with the horizontal axis, point R, denotes the project's IRR. (By definition R is the discount rate that reduces the project's NPV to zero). If we assume a discount rate equal to k_1, the project's NPV is measured by the height of the line connecting k_1 with the NPV profile. The NPV is positive in this case, and the project should be accepted. If we assume a discount rate equal to k_2, the line connecting that discount rate to the NPV profile lies in the negative part of the diagram, and the project's NPV is negative. In such a case, the project should be rejected. A glance at Figure 9–3 shows that the NPV is positive for *all* discount rates to the left of R, and negative for *all* discount rates to the right of R. This means that if the NPV is to be positive, the IRR must exceed the discount rate (opportunity cost of capital). Conversely, when the NPV is negative, the cost of capital must exceed the IRR.

Thus, both the NPV and IRR lead to identical accept-reject decisions: If the NPV criterion is fulfilled, the IRR criterion must also be satisfied, and vice versa. This also permits a restatement of the NPV rule in terms of the internal rate of return. Only projects that offer an IRR greater than the cost of the capital employed should be accepted. This is the exact equivalent of the statement that only projects with a positive NPV should be accepted.

NPV vs. IRR: MUTUALLY EXCLUSIVE PROJECTS

Up to this point we have assumed a simplifed world in which all projects are economically *independent* of one another—that is, the selection of a particular project does not preclude the choice of the other. Given this assumption, both NPV and IRR rules lead to identical accept-reject decisions.

Once we drop the assumption of independence[4] and recognize the fact that it is often impossible to undertake all investment opportunities, a direct confrontation between the two time-adjusted methods of profitability analysis cannot be avoided. When the acceptance of one project effectively precludes the acceptance of another, we will refer to them as being *mutually exclusive*. Such mutually exclusive alternatives crop up often in a modern business enterprise. Both a five-story apartment building and a ten-story office building cannot be built on the same plot of land. Similarly, the purchase of an IBM computer precludes the alternative of *leasing* the same computer. When you locate your manufacturing plant near sources of raw materials, this may often mean that it cannot be located close to the market. The early identification of mutually exclusive alternatives is crucial for logical screening of investments. Much effort, even more patience, and often a great deal of money are wasted when two divisions of the same firm independently develop and evaluate projects that are only later recognized as mutually exclusive.

The problems raised by mutually exclusive investments are illustrated by the following two examples:

	Initial Investment Outlay	Net Cash Receipt
Project A	10,000	12,000
Project B	15,000	17,700

Since both projects have one-year durations, their IRRs can be calculated directly, without recourse to present value tables:

$$IRR_A = \frac{12,000}{10,000} - 1 = 0.20 = 20\%$$

$$IRR_B = \frac{17,700}{15,000} - 1 = 0.18 = 18\%$$

Assuming a 10% cost of capital, the NPVs of the two projects are $908 and $1,089:

	Net Cash Flow (1)	Discount Factor (2)	Initial Outlay (3)	NPV (1) × (2) − (3)
Project A	12,000	0.909	10,000	908
Project B	17,700	0.909	15,000	1,089

[4] We have also assumed that all projects have *conventional cash flows*—that the initial investment outlay is followed by a stream of positive net annual receipts. This assumption will be relaxed later in the chapter.

If the proposals are independent, both A and B will be accepted, using either the NPV or the IRR rules, which is as it should be. However, if the firm is forced to choose between them—for example, if they are *mutually exclusive* alternatives—*which* of the two projects should be accepted? In such a case, the decision rule becomes crucial.

	IRR	NPV
Project A	**20%**	908
Project B	18	**1,089**

If the firm uses the NPV criterion, project B will be chosen, since it has the higher NPV (1,089 > 908). However, should the firm use the IRR criterion, project A, which has the higher IRR (20% > 18%), will be preferred.

This paradoxical result reflects the fact that the two decision criteria do not necessarily *rank* projects the same. In the case of independent proposals, ranking is not important. The firm is indifferent as the "order" in which projects are accepted, because the acceptance of one does not preclude the acceptance of the other. However, in the case of mutually exclusive proposals, ranking becomes crucial. Only one of a group of mutually exclusive alternatives (presumably that with the highest rank) can be executed.

To clarify the difference in ranking, we have drawn the NPV curves for each of the projects above in Figure 9–4. The ranking by their internal rates of return is constant: 20% always exceeds 18%. On the other hand, the

FIGURE 9–4
NPV Profiles
of Two Mutually
Exclusive Projects

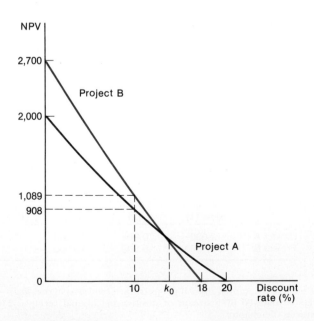

ranking by net present values is not fixed. The NPV ranking depends on the cost of capital.

For discount rates greater than k_0, no contradiction arises: both the IRR and the NPV methods rank project A first. However, for discount rates that are smaller than k_0, the two methods result in different rankings. Project B has the higher NPV, but project A has the higher IRR. In general, if the two functions intersect in the positive quadrant of the diagram, and such is the case in Figure 9–4, the dominance of one project over another by the NPV rule will not be absolute. There exists a range of values for k in which contradictory rankings can arise.

WHY NPV LEADS TO BETTER INVESTMENT DECISIONS

We now turn to the task of providing an intuitively appealing argument for preferring the NPV ranking. Differences in the ranking of projects by the two methods may arise for a variety of reasons, but they can be classified into two principal categories: (a) effects of project size, and (b) effects of timing of cash flows.

Differences in the Scale of Investment

Clearly there is no need, and in fact little chance, that two mutually exclusive proposals will be of the same size. In the real world one project often has a much larger initial outlay than its alternative. Since the firm is concerned with *both* the percentage return and the size of the investment on which this percentage is earned, we will show that the NPV decision is superior.

Consider, for example, a firm that is examining the mutually exclusive alternatives, A and B, producing the same product. The two alternative projects have the following cash flows in years 0 to 5:

	0	1	2	3	4	5
Alternative A	−50,000	17,000	17,000	17,000	17,000	17,000
Alternative B	−32,000	12,000	12,000	12,000	12,000	12,000

Both alternatives have a 5-year life, but alternative A, which generates a larger net inflow ($17,000 per year), also involves a larger investment outlay ($50,000). If we assume that the appropriate discount rate for projects of this type is 8%, which of the two alternatives should the firm accept?

As a first step, calculate the IRR and NPV for each of the two projects. Using the present value table for an annuity, the IRR of each project is easy to calculate.

$$\text{Alternative A: } (DFA^*_{k,5}) = \frac{50,000}{17,000} = 2.941; \text{ IRR}_A = 20.8\%$$

$$\text{Alternative B: } (DFA^*_{k,5}) = \frac{32,000}{12,000} = 2.667; \text{ IRR}_B = 25.4\%$$

In the case of alternative A, the critical discount factor lies between the 20% and 21% columns of the present value table; the critical discount factor for the second alternative lies between 25% and 26%. Alternatively, we can use a pocket calculator or desk computer and derive the IRR to any desired degree of exactitude.[5]

The NPV calculation uses the DFA for $k = 8\%$ and $n = 5$ years:

Alternative A: 17,000 (3.993) − 50,000 = 17.881
Alternative B: 12,000 (3.993) − 32,000 = 15.916

The results of our calculations show that both projects are acceptable using either the NPV or the IRR rules. The IRRs of both alternatives exceed the discount rate, and both projects have positive net present values. However, as we have assumed that the two projects in question are mutually exclusive, the firm must choose the best alternative, because only one can be accepted. Recall that the firm is considering two alternatives producing the same product, and therefore only one can be accepted. We simply cannot sell the same product to the same customer twice!

	IRR	NPV
Alternative A	20.8%	**17,881**
Alternative B	**25.4%**	15,916

The need to choose the best alternative focuses attention on the crucial importance of ranking. Using the IRR rule, alternative B with a 25.4% rate of return is preferable to alternative A, which has a smaller IRR (20.8%). However, if the NPV rule is applied project A should be chosen, since it has the larger NPV.

What is the underlying reason for this difference in the ranking of the alternatives? Figure 9–5 graphs the NPV profiles of the two alternatives. As can be seen from the diagram, the two NPV curves intersect at a discount rate of 12%. The diagram can be interpreted as follows: Given the necessity of choosing between the two projects, alternative A will be preferred to B if the cost of capital is below 12%. The opposite result holds if the cost of capital is above 12%. In fact, for discount rates above 20.8%, only alternative B is acceptable; the NPV of A becomes negative after that point.

---

[5] A close approximation of the IRR can also be found by simple interpolation; see Chapter 6, footnote 6.

FIGURE 9–5
NPV profiles of two mutually exclusive projects

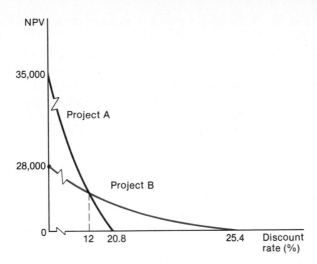

So much for the arithmetic of capital budgeting. But how can we provide an intuitively understandable explanation for the fact that the NPV method gives priority to project A at discount rates below 12%, despite that project's relatively low rate of return? One way to clarify this somewhat paradoxical result is to examine the *incremental cash flow* such a choice represents. As Table 9–4 shows, choosing the larger alternative (A) is equivalent to choosing the smaller alternative (B) *plus* an additional investment of $18,000, on which $5,000 will be earned each year for 5 years. The internal rate of return on this "incremental cash flow" is 12%.

$$A \text{ minus } B: (DFA^*_{k,5}) = \frac{18,000}{5,000} = 3.600; \text{ IRR } = 12\%$$

Since we have assumed a cost of capital of $k = 8\%$, this incremental cash flow represents a profitable opportunity. Therefore, the larger project, which incorporates this additional cash flow, should be accepted.

Conversely, if we assume a cost of capital greater than 12%, it does not pay to make the additional commitment of resources, and the hypothetical incremental project $(A - B)$ should be rejected. Thus, if the cost of capital is greater than 12%, the firm should choose the smaller project, B. But again this is precisely what the NPV method prescribes. For costs of capital larger

TABLE 9–4   Cash flow of Two Mutually Exclusive Projects

	0	1	2	3	4	5
Alternative A	−50,000	17,000	17,000	17,000	17,000	17,000
Alternative B	−32,000	12,000	12,000	12,000	12,000	12,000
A minus B	−18,000	5,000	5,000	5,000	5,000	5,000

than 12%, the NPV of project B is greater than the NPV of project A (see Figure 9–5).

By *automatically* examining and comparing the incremental cash flows against the cost of capital, the NPV method ensures that the firm will reach the optimal *scale* of investment. The IRR criterion, which is expressed in percentages rather than in absolute dollar values, ignores this important aspect of an investment decision. Put in the crudest terms, the IRR method will always prefer a 500% return on $1 to a 20% return on $100. To most of us (assuming a discount rate below 20%), the optimal solution is to take advantage of both opportunities, but where a choice between the two must be made, few would argue in favor of the IRR solution. Most individuals, as is true of most firms, have financial goals that are set in terms of money, and not in terms of percentages. Since present values are expressed in absolute values and rates of return are not, the NPV rule, and not the IRR, should be applied when making mutually exclusive choices among alternatives of different size.[6]

Differences in the Timing of the Cash Flow

But what about projects that have the same initial outlay? Can the IRR be used when mutually exclusive projects of the *same size* are being compared? In such cases, will the NPV and IRR always rank these projects in the same order?

The following example shows that even if projects have identical initial outlays, the IRR and NPV rankings may differ.

	Initial Outlay	First Year Cash Flow	Second Year Cash Flow
Project C	100	20	120.00
Project D	100	100	31.25
C minus D	0	−80	88.75

Assuming a cost of capital of 10%, the NPV and IRR for two projects, C and D, which have the same initial outlay, are:

	NPV	IRR
Project C	**17.3**	20%
Project D	16.7	**25%**
C minus D	0.6	10.9%

[6] One could, of course, use a *modified* IRR which examines the incremental cash flows among all mutually exclusive alternatives, but this can become a tedious procedure.

Here again, a contradiction between the rankings arises. The NPV ranks project C first, while the IRR gives first priority to project D, even though both projects have identical initial outlays. In this instance, we cannot use the scale of investment argument to justify the NPV preference for project C. However, we can still use the same incremental cash flow technique.

Assume for the moment that a firm uses the IRR criterion. If C and D are mutually exclusive, project D will be accepted and project C will be rejected, using the IRR. Before accepting project D, it is legitimate to ask whether or not it is worthwhile to add the (hypothetical) incremental investment C minus D. Since the IRR of the incremental investment is 10.9%, which exceeds the cost of capital (10%), the hypothetical project should be accepted. But once again this is tantamount to accepting project C—that is, the alternative with the higher NPV.

This result is illustrated graphically in Figure 9–6. For discount rates below 10.9%, the incremental investment C minus D is acceptable. This coincides with the range of discount rates over which project C has the higher NPV. Thus even when initial investment outlays are the same, the two methods can still give contradictory rankings because, as Figure 9–6 shows, their NPV profiles may still intersect. In general, such an intersection can occur even if the projects have the same initial outlays, and even the same lifetimes, so long as they do not also have identical annual cash flows. (If they did, the projects themselves would be identical.) Any difference in the size, or timing, of the cash flow can potentially cause a difference in the rankings of projects by the two methods.

But how can we justify the use of the NPV rule when differences in the scale of investment do not exist? The answer lies in the element of time value that is so crucial to investment analysis. Although *both* the NPV and the IRR take the time value of money into account, the time adjustment made by the IRR is incorrect. The NPV formula discounts future receipts using the appropriate opportunity cost of the funds invested—that is, the

**FIGURE 9–6
NPV profile of
incremental cash
flow**

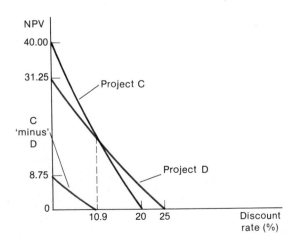

opportunity cost of capital, which we have denoted as k. The IRR method also discounts future receipts, but it uses the projects' own internal rates of return, R. Since R must be greater than k if the project is to be accepted, the IRR method incorrectly penalizes the receipts of more distant years by using *too high* a discount rate. Intuitively one can easily see that it may not appear worthwhile to wait, even for a windfall, if the cost of waiting is thought to be much higher than it really is.

Nonconventional Cash Flows

conventional investment project
An investment project in which the initial outlay is followed by a stream of net cash receipts.

nonconventional projects
Investment projects that have cash flows with more than one change of sign; that is, in which the initial outlay is followed by a stream of net cash receipts, which in turn are followed by another net cash outflow.

To this point we have implicitly assumed that all projects have "conventional" cash flows. When we relax this assumption, the NPV approach has an additional technical advantage over IRR.

A **conventional investment project** is one in which the initial outlay is followed by a stream of net cash receipts of the form: $- +$, or $- + + +$. . .; or, if the outlay takes place over a number of years, $- - + + +$. . . . Some numerical examples of conventional cash flows are given in Table 9–5. Projects A, B, C, and D are conventional. As can be seen from the table, their cash flows have *only one change* of sign: for example, $-/+$, or $-/+ + +$, or $- -/+ +$.

Nonconventional projects have cash flows with *more than one* change of sign. Projects E and F of Table 9–5 are examples of nonconventional projects. Nonconventional cash flows can arise for a variety of reasons. For example, any project with "termination costs" has a cash flow of the type $-/+ + + +/-$. The initial investment outlay is followed by a stream of positive net receipts, but a net cash outflow occurs at the end of the project due to the cost of closing it down. Such projects are *nonconventional*. Their cash flows have *two* changes in sign: the first following the initial investment, and the second in the terminal year. An example of such a project is provided by a strip mining or quarrying project in which the company is required by law to restore the physical appearance of the site after the supply of ore or stone has been exhausted. Nonconventional cash flows can also result from

TABLE 9–5   Conventional and Nonconventional Cash Flows*

Project	Year					
	0	1	2	3	4	5
Conventional Cash Flows						
A	−100	+110	. . .	. . .	. . .	. . .
B	−200	. . .	. . .	. . .	+250	. . .
C	−1,000	+400	+400	+ 400	+400	+400
D	−150	−100	+ 80	+ 100	+ 50	+175
Nonconventional Cash Flows						
E	−1,000	+500	+500	+ 500	+500	−200
F	−1,000	+800	+800	−1000	+800	+800

* Net outlays are entered as negative figures.

the purchase of a machine that generates a positive cash flow for a number of years, after which it must be overhauled. Following the outlay, it again generates a stream of net cash receipts.

The existence of nonconventional cash flows raises a technical problem with respect to the use of the IRR (see Appendix 9A). When projects with more than one change in sign are considered, a proposal's IRR may not exist—or if it does, it may not be unique. Each additional change in sign may result in an additional IRR solution. Thus a nonconventional project, with *two* changes of sign, may have *two* internal rates of return. And if the cash flow has three changes of sign, we might find as many as three rates of return for the same project. Fortunately, nonconventional projects do not present a problem for the NPV method. The NPV model can easily be applied to any cash flow, independent of the number of changes of sign (see Appendix 9A).

The Superiority of the NPV Rule

To sum up, although both NPV and IRR are equivalent decision criteria with respect to independent conventional projects, they do not rank projects in the same order. This difference in ranking, as we have seen, becomes crucial in mutually exclusive situations in which the best proposal out of two or more alternatives must be chosen. NPV provides the better decision rule for the following reasons:

1. NPV reflects the *absolute* size of the alternatives in question; the IRR does not. This is a point in NPV's favor, since the firm is concerned with the absolute market value of its owners' equity (stock price).

2. NPV assumes that the time value of money is equal to its opportunity cost, and therefore discounts future receipts using the appropriate market capitalization rate. The IRR formula implicitly assumes the time value of money to be equal to the project's own IRR. Once again this is a point in NPV's favor, because the opportunity cost is the theoretically correct discount rate to use when reducing future cash flows to their present value. In general, the use of IRR applies too high a discount rate to future cash flows.

3. NPV is not only theoretically superior to the IRR, but also has important technical advantages. When nonconventional cash flows are considered, more than one IRR may be found for a single project.

4. Theoretically correct decision rules are often difficult to calculate and impractical to apply. The NPV decision criterion, however, is an exception. In all respects it is less complicated and easier to apply than the alternative IRR method. One is tempted, therefore, to add to the list of advantages the fact that the NPV is more easily calculated. Clearly this is factually correct, but in a world of electronic calculators and sophisticated desk computers, ease of calculation is no longer relevant for most business decisions.

NPV vs. IRR: A RECONCILIATION WITH BUSINESS PRACTICE

Despite the theoretical advantages of NPV, empirical studies of actual business practice often reveal a managerial preference for IRR. Thus, even in the face of the theoretical difficulties, IRR has remained popular with many practitioners. It should be recalled in this context that the theoretical shortcomings of the IRR method relate only to mutually exclusive choice situations. With respect to many (and perhaps most) capital expenditure decisions, the IRR is not inferior to NPV. But even though it gives good results in most cases, why should management prefer the IRR when an even better method is available? Moreover, as we have already noted, the use of IRR cannot be justified on the grounds of simplicity. On the contrary, the IRR is actually somewhat more difficult to calculate than the NPV; moreover, it is plagued on occasion by the technical problem of multiple rates.

The popularity of the IRR is in part psychological. It probably reflects a very strong, but perhaps subconscious, preference for measures of profitability which are stated in terms of percent. "Everyone knows what 10% means; what the devil is a positive net present value?" But this intuitive appeal of the IRR cannot alter the fact that mutually exclusive decisions must be made by the NPV, and not the IRR, rule.

OTHER COMPETITORS OF THE NPV RULE

Now that we are convinced of NPV's superiority, this may be a safe place to pause and consider some other decision rules which have been proposed, and used, by many firms. We first consider a variant of the NPV, the profitability index, and then go on to consider two popular "rule of thumb" measures which are used to reach investment decisions: the accounting rate of return and payback.

The Profitability Index

profitability index
The present value of a project's expected cash flow divided by its initial investment outlay.

One popular variant of the NPV criterion is the **profitability index,** which is defined as the present value of a project's expected cash flow divided by its initial investment outlay:

$$\text{profitability index} = \frac{\text{present value of expected cash flow}}{\text{initial investment outlay}} = \frac{PV}{I_0}$$

The following decision rule is associated with the profitability index:

- ☐ *Accept the project, if the index is greater than 1.*
- ☐ *Reject the project, if the index is less than 1.*

In the case of independent projects, the profitability index and the NPV rule reach the same acceptance-rejection decisions. If a project's NPV is positive, its profitability index will also be greater than 1.[7]

Many business executives find the profitability index more intuitively appealing than the NPV criterion. The statement that a project's NPV is 2 million is not sufficiently clear. As we have already noted, many people prefer a *relative* measure of profitability. By dividing the project's present value by its initial outlay, say $10 million, the profitability index ($12 million/$10 million = 1.2) provides a measure of profitability in more readily understandable terms. It seems only a small step to convert the index of 1.2 to 20%.

But here too, problems may arise when mutually exclusive alternatives are considered. One advantage of NPV in mutually exclusive choose situations stems from the fact that it reflects the *absolute* size of alternative investment proposals. The profitability index converts the NPV criterion into a *relative* measure. Like the IRR, the profitability index is a pure number that no longer reflects differences in investment size. As a result, it re-creates the very paradox the NPV criterion is designed to avoid. Consider, for example, the following two *mutually exclusive* proposals:

	Present Value of Cash flow (PV)	Initial Investment Outlay (I_0)	NPV	Profitability Index (PV)/(I_0)
Project A	$100	$50	$50	**2.0**
Project B	$1,500	$1,000	**$500**	1.5

Using the profitability index, project A, which has an index of 2, should be preferred. But it is clear that a firm which desires to maximize its absolute present value, rather than percentage return, should prefer project B. The NPV of project B ($500) is greater than the NPV of project A ($50). Thus, while the profitability index may be a useful tool for expository purposes, it should not be used as a decision rule when mutually exclusive projects of different size are being considered.

Accounting Rate of Return

One of the more pervasive facts of economic life has been the continued widespread use of a variety of shortcut rules of thumb to evaluate capital investment projects. Actual business practice suggests that the only effective limit on the number of different methods employed has been the ingenuity

---

[7] IF NPV > 0, we necessarily have NPV $= PV - I_0 > 0$, and therefore, $PV > I_0$. Dividing both sides by I_0 we get $PV/I_0 > 1$; that is, the profitability index is also greater than 1. Thus, if a project is acceptable by the NPV rule, it must also be acceptable by the profitability index.

of management in devising additional variants of existing profitability measures. But despite differences in detail, almost all the popular rules of thumb fall into one of two broad classes: (undiscounted) accounting rates of return and payback measures.

accounting rate of return (ARR)
A rate of return calculated by dividing a proposal's expected annual net profit by the average investment outlay.

One widely used measure of investment profitability is the **accounting rate of return (ARR).** This rate of return is calculated by dividing a proposal's expected annual net profit (after deducting depreciation) by the *average* investment outlay:

$$\text{accounting rate of return} = \frac{\text{expected net annual profit}}{\text{investment outlay}/2}$$

Consider the following project:

Initial investment outlay (I_0)	= $1 million
Expected annual net receipts (CF) (before deducting depreciation)	= $250,000
Economic lifetime (n)	= 10 years
Annual straight-line depreciation (D)	= $100,000

The ARR is 30%:

$$\text{ARR} = \frac{\text{CF} - \text{D}}{I_0/2}$$

$$\text{ARR} = \frac{250,000 - 100,000}{500,000} = 30\%$$

The ARR has some very obvious defects:

1. The accounting rate neglects the *timing* of receipts—that is, no provision is made for discounting the future cash flows. As a result, profitability is overstated. In this particular example, the project's "true" rate of return (its IRR) is 21.4%, *not* 30%!

2. The accounting rate of return ignores fluctuations in cash receipts over time. Needless to add, this measure is particularly inappropriate where cash flows are expected to change significantly over the life of the project.

As its name implies, the ARR is still popular with some accountants. However, a glance at a modern accounting text suffices to show that NPV and IRR have already provided a serious challenge to the older methods. The ARR's main advantage lies in its simplicity and ease of calculation, but these are difficult arguments to support.

Payback   Many firms still use a simple payback formula as their index of a project's desirability. The **payback** is defined as the number of years required to re-

payback
The number of years required to recover the initial investment outlay out of a project's expected future cash flows.

cover the initial investment outlay out of the project's expected future cash flows. For example, if a project requires an initial outlay of $1 million and is expected to generate a net cash flow of $250,000 per year for, say, 10 years, it has a *4-year* payback. Had the expected annual cash flow been $500,000, the payback period would be 2 years, and so on for any combination of investment outlay and cash receipts.

If we assume that all projects have equal annual receipts (as in the above examples), the payback can be calculated from the following formula:

$$\text{payback} = \frac{\text{initial investment outlay}}{\text{annual cash receipt}} = \frac{I_0}{CF}$$

In the more general case, in which receipts are expected to fluctuate over time, the payback is calculated by summing the receipts until the initial investment outlay is covered. Table 9–6 shows the cash flows of two hypothetical projects, A and B. The former has a payback period of 3 years; summing the annual receipts of project B gives a somewhat larger payback of 5 years for that proposal.

Ranking projects by the payback criterion is simple and straightforward. The shorter the project's payback, the more desirable is the proposal. The payback formula also has some very obvious and serious shortcomings:

1. Like the ARR, the formula for payback does not discount future returns.[8]

2. Perhaps even more important, it concentrates attention solely on the receipts *within* the payback period; receipts in later years are ignored. Thus, project A of Table 9–6 has a shorter payback than project B, and therefore would be ranked ahead of B. This preference for project

---

[8] Some of the shortcomings of this method can be overcome by using a discounted payback based on the present values of future receipts.

TABLE 9–6   Cash Flows of Two Hypothetical Projects

	Project A	Project B
Investment outlay	1,000,000	1,000,000
Net cash flow		
First Year	500,000	400,000
Second year	400,000	300,000
Third year	100,000	100,000
Fourth year	0	100,000
Fifth year	0	100,000
.	.	.
.	.	.
.	.	.
Tenth year	0	100,000

A holds despite the fact that its internal rate of return is *zero,* while that of B is positive!

3. Finally, the method offers no insight into how the critical maximum payback acceptance criterion can be set. Should all projects with a 3-year payback (or less) be accepted, or should the maximum acceptable payback be 5 years?

Upon reflection, the payback criterion is not primarily a measure of profitability. After all, Table 9–6 shows that a project with a zero IRR can have a perfectly respectable payback (3 years in the case of project A). It would be extremely naive to assume that any businessperson would be willing to accept such a project, which promises only the return of the initial investment. It is more likely that at least part of the payback's popularity lies in its relationship to risk analysis. Demanding shorter required paybacks is like raising the required discount rate on a risky project. Moreover, this criterion's concentration on the returns of early years may be viewed by many managers as an advantage, especially if they have an aversion to making long-term forecasts. In this context, the short payback periods required by some firms may be an indication of their planning horizons—a rough measure of how far they are willing to forecast future cash flows.

Use of Rules of Thumb: A Reconciliation with Business Practice

Despite their very obvious defects, a majority of business firms probably still employ such simple rules of thumb, although more and more larger firms have been making the transition to time-discounted measures of investment worth (see Table 9–7). One reason for the persistence of the use of payback is that some firms assume cash flows with equal annual receipts. In such cases, this simple rule of thumb often provides a close approximation of the accept-reject decisions that would have been reached using modern time-

TABLE 9–7   Project Evaluation Techniques

Technique	Percentages Used in			
	1976*	1970†	1964†	1959†
Discounting (IRR, NPV or profitability index)	66	57	38	19
Accounting rate of return	25	26	30	34
Payback or payback reciprocal	9	12	24	34
Qualitative methods		5	8	13
	100	100	100	100

* Based on primary evaluation technique used.
† Only most sophisticated method reported was counted.

Sources: For the years 1970, 1964, and 1959: Thomas Klammer, "Empirical Evidence of the Adoption of Sophisticated Capital Budgeting Techniques," *Journal of Business,* July 1972. For 1976, Lawrence J. Gitman and John R. Forrester, Jr., "A Survey of Capital Budgeting Techniques Used by Major U.S. Firms," *Financial Management,* Fall 1977.

discounted methods. However, when more sophisticated techniques are used to forecast the components and timing of the cash flow, the use of time discounted methods becomes an imperative for rational decision-making.

Considerable evidence exists that most of the industrial firms that used the payback rule operated in the range of project durations and profitability in which the rule of thumb provided a reasonably close estimate of projects' true profitability.[9] Almost all of the researchers who reported on the use of payback comment on the fact that firms demanded relatively short payback periods and applied the rule to projects of rather long duration. But these are precisely the conditions (high profitability and long economic life) which ensure a very close approximation of the payback decisions to those of the IRR or NPV. This helps to explain why many successful business firms used the simple payback method in the past. It may also explain why some still persist in its use today, even in the face of the overwhelming theoretical arguments in favor of time discounting.

SUMMARY

Capital investments are usually distinguished from current expenditures by two principal features: (a) such projects are relatively large; (b) a significant period of time (more than one year) elapses between the initial investment outlay and the receipt of benefits.

The systematic approach to capital budgeting decisions requires: (a) the formulation of long-term goals; (b) the creative search for new investment opportunities; (c) the estimation of current and future cash flows; (d) a suitable adminstrative framework; (e) the careful monitoring and control of the project after its acceptance.

Finally, a set of decision rules is required which can differentiate acceptable from unacceptable alternatives. Two types of decision rules are associated with two time-discounted decision models, NPV and IRR. Although both criteria give equivalent results with respect to independent conventional projects, they do not rank projects the same. This difference in ranking becomes crucial in mutually exclusive choice situations—that is, when the firm must choose the best proposal from two or more alternatives. NPV provides the more appropriate criterion for the following reasons:

1. NPV reflects the *absolute* size of the projects; the IRR does not.
2. NPV uses the opportunity cost of capital as the discount rate; the IRR discounts the future using the project's own IRR.
3. NPV is not only theoretically superior to the IRR, but also has important technical advantages. When nonconventional cash flows are con-

[9] For a detailed analysis, see Haim Levy and Marshall Sarnat, *Capital Investment and Financial Decisions,* 3rd ed. (Englewood Cliffs, NJ: Prentice-Hall International, 1986), chap. 8.

**Summary Table:
Contrasting NPV
and IRR Rules**

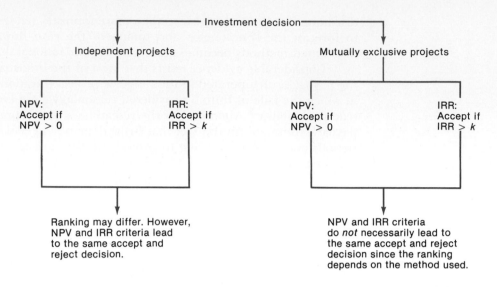

sidered, a solution for the project's IRR may not exist; in other instances, more than one IRR may be found for a single project.

To sum up, NPV provides an optimal (best possible) decision criterion for capital budgeting decisions.

Three other decision criteria are the profitability index, the accounting rate of return (ARR), and the payback.

$$\text{profitability index} = \frac{\text{present value of cash flow}}{\text{initial investment outlay}}$$

$$\text{ARR} = \frac{\text{average annual net profit}}{\text{total investment}/2}$$

$$\text{payback} = \frac{\text{initial investment outlay}}{\text{annual cash receipt}}$$

If future cash flows are expected to fluctuate, the payback is calculated by summing the annual receipts until the initial investment outlay is covered.

APPENDIX 9A: | Nonconventional Cash Flows

As we noted in the text, nonconventional cash flows can lead to some paradoxical results when the IRR criterion is applied:

1. The project's IRR may not exist!
2. the project may have more than one IRR.

Consider the following nonconventional cash flow:

	Period		
	0	**1**	**2**
	+100	−200	+150

What is the IRR of this project? Should it be accepted, assuming the cost of capital is, say, 10%?

Anyone who attempts to solve for the IRR by trial and error will expend most of his patience, as well as all of his computer budget. However, he will not succeed. The reason is simple; the IRR for this project does not exist! This can be seen by solving the following formula analytically:

$$100 - \frac{200}{(1 + R)} + \frac{150}{(1 + R)^2} = 0$$

Dividing through by 100 (for simplicity only) and denoting $1/(1 + R)$ by x, we derive the following quadratic equation:

$$1.5^2 - 2x + 1 = 0$$

The values of x which solve this equation are called the *roots* of the equation. If at least one real root exists, we can safely assert that there are values of x (hence values of R) which equate the NPV to zero. But if we cannot find real values of x which equate the formula to zero, this is tantamount to asserting that the IRR does not exist. Using the conventional formula for solving a quadratic equation, we get:[1]

$$x_1 = \frac{2 - \sqrt{4 - 4(1.5)}}{3} = \frac{2 - \sqrt{-2}}{3}$$

$$x_2 = \frac{2 + \sqrt{4 - 4(1.5)}}{3} = \frac{2 + \sqrt{-2}}{3}$$

Since the square root of -2 is an imaginary rather than a real number, the IRR is also imaginary in this case. This is clear from Figure 9A–1, which graphs the NPV of this nonconventional project as a function of the discount rate. At a zero discount rate the NPV is simply the algebraic sum of the

---

[1] In general, a quadratic equation $ax^2 + bx + c = 0$ has two roots which we denote by x_1 and x_2. That is to say, if we substitute either x_1 or x_2 in the equation above, the value of the equation is equal to zero. x_1 and x_2 can be found by applying the standard formula:

$$x_1 = \frac{-b - \sqrt{b^2 - 4ac}}{2a}$$

and

$$x_2 = \frac{-b + \sqrt{b^2 - 4ac}}{2a}$$

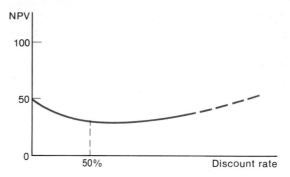

FIGURE 9A–1   NPV profile of nonconventional project

cash flow: $100 - 200 + 150 = 50$. As the discount rate approaches infinity, the NPV approaches 100. Between these values, the curve is U-shaped but always positive; that is, there is no positive discount rate at which the NPV becomes zero. As Figure 9A–1 shows, the project in question is acceptable, by the NPV criterion, at any cost of capital. Despite this, the IRR rule cannot be applied, since the IRR for such a project does not exist! Nor is this merely an intellectual curiosity; such nonconventional cash flows are generated whenever a contract which calls for an advance payment is being evaluated.

MULTIPLE RATES OF RETURN

In general, the IRR equation is an n degree polynomial of the form:

$$\frac{S_1}{1 + R} + \frac{S_2}{(1 + R)^2} + \ldots + \frac{S_n}{(1 + R)^n} - I_0 = 0$$

and therefore has n roots; that is, n values of R which solve the equation. However, if the cash flow is conventional, only one of these values of R is a real number; the other $n - 1$ roots are imaginary numbers which, while of importance in higher mathematics, have no economic meaning. In this sense we can say that a conventional project has a unique (real) rate of return, since the NPV function of such a proposal crosses the horizontal axis of a diagram such as Figure 9A–1 *once and only once*. If the project is nonconventional—that is, we are confronted by a cash flow which has more than one change in sign–the number of real solutions for the IRR of such a proposal can vary[2] from zero to n. In our previous example we examined a case of a nonconventional, but economically meaningful, project that has no real IRR; we turn now to an example of a nonconventional project that has more than one real IRR.

Consider the following problem: A firm has an old machine that will produce a net return of $770 at the end of the first year and $332 at the end of the second year. The current market value of this machine is zero. The firm is weighing the alternative of replacing the old machine with a new one that costs $100, but that will produce a net return of $1000 at the end of the first year and only $200 at the end of the second year. The replacement problem requires the evaluation of the *incremental* cash flow stemming from the decision. The necessary data are summarized below:

		Cash Flow	
		Year 1	Year 2
New machine	−100	1000	200
Old machine		770	332
Incremental flow*	−100	+230	−132

* Cash flow of new machine minus cash flow of old machine.

Should the firm replace the old machine? Using the IRR rule, we must first solve the following equation for R:

$$-100 + \frac{230}{1 + R} - \frac{132}{(1 + R)^2} = 0$$

Dividing through by 100 and denoting $1/(1 + R)$ by x, the following must hold:

$$1.32x^2 + 2.3x - 1 = 0$$

Solving this equation by formula yields two real roots:

$$x_1 = \frac{-2.3 - \sqrt{5.29 - 5.28}}{-2.64} = \frac{1}{1.1}$$

[2] The maximum number of real solutions is equal to the number of sign changes in the cash flow; see D. Teichroew, A. A. Robichek, and M. Montalbano. "An Analysis of Criteria for Investment and Financing Decisions under Certainty," *Management Science*, January 1965.

and since

$$x = \frac{1}{1 + R}$$
$$R_1 = 10\%$$

Similarly

$$x_2 + \frac{-2.3 + \sqrt{5.29 - 5.28}}{-2.64} = \frac{1}{1.2}$$

and since

$$x = \frac{1}{1 + R}$$
$$R_2 = 20\%$$

Now, for the sake of argument, assume that our firm's cost of capital is 15%. Should the old machine be replaced? The IRR rule breaks down in such a case, since contradictory answers are indicated depending on which rate of return is chosen:

$$R_1 = 10\% < 15\%; \text{ don't replace}$$
$$R_2 = 20\% > 15\%; \text{ replace}$$

Moreover, we have no way of discriminating between the two solutions.

The dilemma can be resolved by examining Figure 9A–2 which plots the NPV profiles of the cash flows of the new machine and the old machine, as well as the incremental cash flow of the replace-

FIGURE 9A–2   NPV profiles of new and old machines

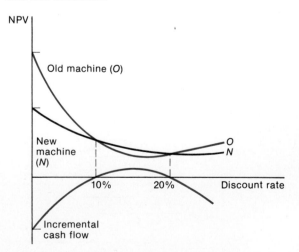

ment decision. The dual rate of return reflects the fact that the NPV functions of the old and new machines intersect twice at discount rates of 10% and 20%. These rates are also, by definition, the internal rates of return on the incremental cash flow, since they equate the NPV of the two alternatives. Applying the NPV rule to the diagram, we note that for costs of capital between 10% and 20%, the NPV of the new machine is greater than the NPV of the old machine, and as a result the NPV of the incremental cash flow is positive over this range as well. Thus for these discount rates, the replacement is worthwhile. However, firms with cost of capital below 10% or over 20% should not replace the old machine.

REVIEW EXERCISE

Circle the correct word(s) to complete each sentence; See p. 236 for correct answers.

9.1 Firms should always execute projects which offer a *positive/negative* net present value, and reject those proposals which have *positive/negative* net present values.

9.2 A project's internal rate of return can be defined as the rate of discount which equates the present value of the stream of net receipts with the *initial outlay/rate of interest.*

9.3 To compute the IRR, choose a discount rate at random and calculate the NPV; if the NPV is positive, choose a *lower/higher* discount rate and repeat.

9.4 From the graph of an investment's NPV profile, it is clear that a project's NPV is positive only if the discount rate is *lower/higher* than its IRR.

9.5 If it is not possible to implement two investment projects simultaneously, they are said to be *mutually exclusive/complements.*

9.6 If all investment projects are *mutually exclusive/economically independent,* both the NPV and the IRR rules lead to identical accept or reject decisions.

9.7 In the case of *independent/mutually exclusive* projects, ranking becomes crucial.

9.8 When using the IRR and the NPV rules, differences in ranking may arise because of differences in: (a) the *scale of investment/tax rates;* (b) the *timing of cash flows/government regulations.*

9.9 These differences in ranking can be explained intuitively by considering the *incremental/nominal* cash flow.

9.10 The IRR criterion, which is expressed in terms of *dollars/percent* rather than in terms of *dollars/percent,* does not reflect differences in the size of investments.

9.11 The IRR method *always/sometimes* prefers a 500% return on $1 to a 20% return on $100.

9.12 By nonconventional cash flows we mean cash flows which have *only one/more than one* change of sign.

9.13 When considering projects with more than one change in sign, a proposal's IRR *always exists/may not exist.*

9.14 The profitability index *reflects/does not reflect* differences in the size of investments.

9.15 The accounting rate of return *accounts for/neglects* the timing of receipts.

9.16 The payback method has obvious defects: It *discounts/does not discount* future returns, and it concentrates solely on the receipts within the payback period; receipts in later years are *discounted/ignored.*

QUESTIONS

9.1 Define the following terms:

a. Net present value   b. Internal rate of return

c. Incremental cash flow   d. Mututally exclusive

e. Conventional cash flow   f. Profitability index

g. Accounting rate of return   h. Payback period

9.2 If the NPV is positive when using a discount rate k, the IRR must exceed the discount rate k. Explain.

9.3 Technical problems may arise when the IRR is applied to so-called nonconventional cash flows. Explain.

9.4 Assess the following statement: The IRR method uses the project's own rate of return to discount the future, thereby penalizing the receipts of more distant years.

9.5 Evaluate the following statement of the vice-president for marketing of a chain of retail outlets: "Since our outlets are all of equal size and require the same initial investment, we can use the IRR method to rank the desirability of new locations."

9.6 Mr. Stone-Rich III is a billionaire. "I can use the IRR method to evaluate investment projects, since there is no need for rankings: I invest in each project which has a IRR greater than the discount rate." Is Mr. Stone-Rich III correct? Explain.

9.7 How can the incremental cash flow reconcile the IRR and the NPV rules?

9.8 The NPV and IRR criteria always lead to the same decisions when projects are independent. Prove this statement.

9.9 The NPV and IRR may lead to different decisions when the projects are mutually exclusive. Explain.

9.10 Why does the NPV rule provide the better decision rule?

9.11 Under what assumptions will the IRR and NPV methods rank all projects in the same order? (*Hint:* Use a graph to prove your answer.)

PROBLEMS

9.1 **Mutually exclusive investments: differences in scale.** Joe Stevens has a lease for the next 5 years on a plot of land next to a highway. He would like to open either a pizza parlor or a hot dog stand on this property. The following are the anticipated cash flows for each alternative in years 0–5:

	0	1	2	3	4	5
Pizza parlor	−20,000	7,000	7,000	7,000	7,000	7,000
Hot dog stand	− 6,000	2,450	2,450	2,450	2,450	2,450

    a. Calculate the net present value of the pizza parlor and the hot dog stand, using a 10% discount rate.

    b. Calculate the IRR for each of the projects.

    c. Which alternative should Joe Stevens choose according to the IRR criterion? Which according to the NPV criterion?

    d. Show the hypothetical cash flow pizza parlor minus hot dog stand and calculate its NPV and IRR. Use this result to "defend" the NPV decision.

    e. Graph the NPV of each project (including the project pizza parlor minus hot dog stand) as a function of the discount rate.

9.2 **Mutually exclusive investments: differences in scale.** Consider the following two mutually exclusive investment opportunities:

	Year					
	0	**1**	**2**	**3**	**4**	**5**
Project A	−97,400	34,000	34,000	34,000	34,000	34,000
Project B	−63,200	24,000	24,000	24,000	24,000	24,000

    a. Calculate each project's net present value and internal rate of return. (Assume that the appropriate discount rate is 8%.)

    b. Which of the two would be chosen according to the IRR criterion? According to the NPV criterion?

    c. How can you explain the differences in rankings by the two methods?

9.3 **NPV, IRR, and profitability index.** The Crown Corporation owns a building in Center City. If it is renovated, the building can be used for offices or as a residence. In either case, after 2 years, the building will have to be renovated again. The following table shows the relevant cash flows, years 0, 1, 2:

	0	**1**	**2**
Residential	−25,000	16,750	14,250
Offices	− 5,000	4,750	2,250

    a. Calculate the net present values, internal rates of return, and the profitability indexes, assuming an 8% discount rate.

    b. What should the Crown Corporation do according to each of the three methods?

    c. How can you explain the differences in rankings given by the NPV criterion and the profitability index? Which of the two methods is the best one?

    d. Calculate the internal rate of return of the incremental project "residential minus office." Does it confirm your answer to part (c)? Explain.

9.4   NPV profile. For each of the following three projects:

a. Calculate the net present value using a 16% discount rate.

b. Calculate the internal rate of return.

c. Graph the NPV of each as a function of the discount rate. (*Hint:* Calculate three points and draw the remaining segments of the curve (in freehand), and check your graphic answer with the answer to question (b).

		Year			
	0	1	2	3	4
Project A	−800	350	350	350	100
Project B	−70	40	25	25	25
Project C	−20,000	2,000	8,000	14,000	4,466

9.5   NPV vs. IRR: timing of cash flow. The Rose Company is considering the following two mutually exclusive investment proposals: Proposal A: Initial outlay of $200,000 and receipts of $50,000 in the first year and $250,000 in the second year. Proposal B: Initial outlay of $200,000 and receipts of $190,000 in the first year and $91,000 in the second year.

a. Calculate each project's IRR and net present value. (Assume a cost of capital of 10%.)

b. Which of the two projects would be chosen according to the NPV rule? According to the IRR criterion?

c. How can you explain the difference in rankings given by the NPV and the IRR methods in this case? (Use the incremental cash flow A minus B in your explanation.)

d. How does your answer to part (c) change if you use the incremental cash flow B minus A?

e. How would your answers to parts (a)–(d) change if you assume that the cost of capital is 16%?

9.6   NPV vs. IRR. PART 1: Assume the following two mutually exclusive investment projects:

		Year	
	0	1	2
Project R	−20,000	23,600	—
Project S	−20,000	—	26,000

a. Calculate each project's net present value, assuming a cost of capital of 8%, and its internal rate of return.

b. Rank the projects according to each of the two methods.

c. How can you explain the difference in rankings given by the NPV and the IRR methods in this case?

PART 2: You are now confronted with the following two mutually exclusive investment opportunities:

	Year				
	0	1	2	3	4
Project T	−10,000	—	—	—	20,740
Project S	−20,000	26,000	—	—	—

a. Calculate each project's net present value, assuming a cost of capital of 8%, and its internal rate of return.
b. Rank the projects according to each of the two methods.
c. How can you explain the difference in rankings in this case?

PART 3: **(a)** In view of your answers to parts 1 and 2 above, which of the two methods, in your opinion, provides the optimal decision in each of the cases? Explain and defend your choice.
b. How would you qualify your answers in the absence of mutual exclusiveness—that is, if the projects are economically independent?

9.7 NPV profile: loan.   You are offered a choice between an outright gift of $500 or a $3,500 interest-free loan to be paid back at the end of each year in seven equal installments of $500 each.
a. Which alternative would you prefer? Explain your decision.
b. Under what circumstances would you reverse your choice? (Use a graph to illustrate your answer.)

9.8 Meaning of decision rules.   National Resources Corporation is evaluating the possibility of opening one new plant in either Montana or Wyoming. The planning department has carried out an initial feasibility study, with the following results: *Montana:* An initial investment outlay of $1,000,000 is needed. This will then generate an annual cash flow of $90,000 during the next 100 years. *Wyoming:* The initial investment amounts to $400,000, and this will generate an annual cash flow of $50,000 during the next 100 years. Assume that the relevant discount rate is 10%. Which location should be preferred? Answer without the use of present value tables.

9.9 Alternatives to the NPV rule.   For each of the following projects, calculate the accounting rate of return, the payback period (reciprocal), and the internal rate of return. (Use straight-line depreciation.) Project A: Initial investment of $5,000 and annual net receipts of $1,000 for 10 years. Project B: Initial investment of $5,000 and annual receipts of $1,000 for 20 years. Project C: Initial investment of $5,000 and annual net receipts of $1,000 for 40 years. Compare your results.

9.10 Alternatives to the NPV rule.   For each of the following projects, calculate the ARR, the payback period (reciprocal), and the IRR. (Use straight-line depreciation.) Project D: Initial investment of $40,000 and annual net receipts of $6,000 for 10 years. Project E: Initial investment of $40,000 and annual net receipts of $12,000 for 10 years. Compare your results.

9.11 Computer problem.   Compute the NPV (using a 6% discount rate) and the internal rate of return for each of the following projects:

	Year				
	0	1	2	3	4
Alpha	−15,367	6,239	9,843	3,729	1,009
Beta	−21,493	11,723	0	0	16,286
Gamma	− 3,209	0	243	2,931	123
Delta	−56,999	31,398	24,276	11,101	621

APPENDIX 9A PROBLEMS

9A.1 Consider the following cash flows:

	Year		
	0	1	2
Project K	250	−350	150
Project L	−30	60	−50

a. Calculate the internal rate of return and the net present value (at a discount rate of 12%) for each project.
b. Plot the NPV profile for each project as a function of the discount rate. Explain your results.

9A.2 Consider the following cash flows:

	Year		
	0	1	2
Project U	− 600	1,950	−1,500
Project V	375	−2,100	2,400
Project W	−1,500	750	−9,000

a. Calculate each project's NPV and IRR (assume a discount rate of 10%).
b. Plot each project's NPV profile as a function of the discount rate. Indicate the intercepts on both axes.
c. What is the economic meaning of the IRR when a project has two rates of return?

9A.3 Your examination of a project reveals that it has two internal rates of return: 10% and 30%. Assume that the cost of capital is 15%. Should the firm accept the project? Explain your answer. (*Hint:* Use a graph of the NPV profile.)

SAMPLE PROBLEMS

SP9.1 You are confronted with the following three projects:

	Year					
	0	**1**	**2**	**3**	**4**	**5**
Project X	−500	50	50	50	50	550
Project Y	−500	132	132	132	132	132
Project Z	−500	—	—	—	—	806

    a. Calculate the net present value of each of the projects, assuming a 10% discount rate, and rank the projects.

    b. Calculate the net present value of each of the projects, assuming a 6% discount rate, and rank the projects.

    c. Calculate the net present value of each of the projects, assuming a 15% discount rate, and rank the projects.

SP9.2 Calculate the internal rate of return for each of the projects, and rank them by IRR.

SP9.3 What is the payback period for a project that requires an initial investment of $2,000 and has receipts of $1,000 for 5 years? What is its payback period if the receipts are $1,000 for only 2 years? What can you conclude about the payback criterion?

Solutions to Sample Problems

SP9.1 a. We compute the NPV with the formula derived in the text.

Project X

$$NPV = -500 + 50/1.1 + 50/(1.1)^2$$
$$+50/(1.1)^3 + 50/(1.1)^4 + 550/(1.1)^5$$
$$= -500 + 45.45 + 41.32 + 37.56 + 34.15 + 341.50$$
$$\cong 0.00$$

Project Y

$$NPV = -500 + 132/1.1 + 132/(1.1)^2$$
$$+132/(1.1)^3 + 132/(1.1)^4 + 132/(1.1)^5$$
$$= -500 + 120 + 109.09 + 99.17 + 90.16 + 81.96$$
$$\cong 0.00$$

Project Z

$$NPV = -500 + 806/(1.1)^5 = -500 + 500 \cong 0.00$$

Since the NPV of all three projects is 0 when discounted at 10%, they are all ranked the same at that discount rate.

    b. Using a 6% discount rate, and computing in the same manner as above, we get: Project X: NPV = 84.25, project Y: NPV = 56.03, project Z: NPV = 102.29. Hence, at a 6% discount rate, project Z is preferred to project X, which in turn is preferred to project Y.

c. Again, we compute the NPV in the same manner as above, this time discounting at 15%: Project X: NPV = -83.80, project Y: NPV = -57.25, project Z: NPV = -99.28. Thus, discounting at 15%, project Y has the smallest negative NPV; project Z with the largest negative NPV is the least desirable project.

SP9.2 The IRR is defined as the discount rate which equates the NPV to zero. Since the NPV for all three projects is zero when discounted at 10% (see above), the IRR is 10% for all three projects.

SP9.3 The payback period tells us how many years it takes to recoup the initial investment. Since in both cases the investment is $2,000 and the receipts are $1,000 in the first year and $1,000 in the second year, we have recouped our investment after the second year. Hence the payback period is 2 years in both cases. We conclude that the payback period is not a good measure of profitability, since it fails to distinguish between the two projects despite the fact that one of them has a zero IRR.

Answers to Review Exercise

9.1 positive, negative   **9.2** initial outlay   **9.3** higher   **9.4** lower

9.5 mutually exclusive   **9.6** economically independent

9.7 mutually exclusive   **9.8** (a) scale of investment; (b) timing of cash flows

9.9 incremental   **9.10** percent, dollars   **9.11** always

9.12 more than one   **9.13** may not exist   **9.14** does not reflect

9.15 neglects   **9.16** does not discount, ignored

SUGGESTIONS FOR FURTHER READING

Capital budgeting is examined in greater detail by: Harold Bierman, Jr., and Seymour Smidt, *The Capital Budgeting Decision,* 5th ed. (New York: Macmillian, 1980), John J. Clark, Thomas J. Hindelang, and Robert E. Pritchard, *Capital Budgeting,* 2nd ed. (Englewood Cliffs, NJ: Prentice-Hall, 1984), and Haim Levy and Marshall Sarnat, *Capital Investment and Financial Decisions,* 3rd ed. (Englewood Cliffs, NJ: Prentice-Hall International 1986).

Useful collections of articles dealing with various aspects of capital budgeting are given by: Stephen H. Archer and Charles A. D' Ambrosio, *The Theory of Business Finance: A Book of Readings,* 2nd ed. (New York: Macmillan, 1976); and Stewart C. Myers, *Modern Developments in Financial Management* (New York: Praeger, 1976).

Finally, readers who are somewhat skeptical about optimal decision rules might want to look at Chapter 8 of the Levy and Sarnat book, *Capital Investments and Financial Decisions.*

10 | Estimating Cash Flows

Having reviewed the basic principles of the present value rule, we turn in this chapter to the practical application of the present value approach to a firm's capital investment decisions.

Modern investment analysis using the present value approach is based on the evaluation of cash flows. In the preceding chapter alternative decision criteria were analyzed on the assumption that the annual cash flows are known. No attempt was made to determine how the receipts and outlays should be defined and estimated. The importance of accurate projections of future costs and revenues, cannot be overemphasized. Effective capital budgeting in practice implies the careful estimation of the cash flows engendered by each project if appropriate investment decisions are to be made. This chapter examines the types of problems that arise when the NPV model is applied to actual cash flows. The principles underlying the definition of a project's after-tax cash flow are explained and applied to the estimation of project cash flows in a variety of different situations.

CLASSIFYING PROJECTS

The *capital budgeting* process is a complex activity of vital importance to the firm. Capital investment decisions can often be facilitated by first classifying a project by one or more of its salient characteristics. Such a procedure can help the firm to develop standardized estimation and administration procedures for handling particular classes of proposals. Classification is especially helpful in the following cases: (a) When the accuracy of cost-revenue estimates varies widely. This depends on the type of investment proposal being considered: for some types, no quantitative forecast is possible; for others, costs can be estimated within relatively narrow bounds. (b) When the definition and methods for estimating future cash flows differ significantly. This can be especially important in a conglomerate firm that pursues many different lines of activity. (c) When a project has an impact beyond its direct money return. The firm may desire to give such projects priority, or special consideration, when examining their desirability.

Of course, the "best" classification scheme for some firms may be not to classify projects at all. This is the practice in many small companies in which the executives are familiar with almost all aspects of the projects under consideration.

The grouping of projects into different categories often simplifies the decision process, but it should be emphasized from the outset that no magic formula exists: Each company has to adopt the classification system best suited to its needs. Three typical examples of corporate practice are the classification of investment proposals by size, by type of benefit, and by degree of dependence.

Classification by Project Size

The amount of cash, or other scarce resource, needed to implement a project is a useful way of differentiating investments. For example, a firm may give separate treatment to "major projects," which are defined as initial expenditures of over $1 million. Another may apply formal capital budgeting procedures to expenditures in excess of $100,000; smaller projects may be exempted from formal approval. Similarly, projects can be classified by the type of scarce resources used: land, key management personnel, floor space, and so on.

Classification by Type of Benefit

Benefits can arise from cost reduction, expansion of sales of existing products, expansion into new lines of activities, risk reduction, or social overhead investments designed to improve general working conditions. Hot showers for workers, improved antipollution facilities, and perhaps even a contribution to the community welfare fund are examples of the latter type of investment.

An alternative classification might be (a) projects that do not alter business risk—these include replacement using unchanged production methods and expansion of existing business; and (b) projects that change business risk—these include replacement using new technologies and expansion into new product lines or activities.

Classification by Degree of Dependence

Interdependence between investment projects can arise for several reasons:

1. It may be technically impossible to undertake both project A and project B. Such investments were referred to in Chapter 9 as being *mutually*

exclusive, since the acceptance of one effectively precludes the acceptance of the other.

2. If the decision to adopt one investment project increases the expected benefits from a second project, the proposals are said to be **complements.** For example, the construction of a water recycling facility may have a positive impact on the profitability of a number of other projects.

3. If the acceptance of one project decreases the profitability of a second project, they are called **substitutes.** Thus, when a large razor blade manufacturer such as Gillette contemplated the introduction of stainless steel blades, the forecasted revenue from the sale of new blades was offset, in part, by a decline in the expected sales of its conventional blades. No such consideration hampered Wilkinson Ltd., the English firm which first introduced stainless steel blades. Presumably Wilkinson assumed that the proceeds from razor blade sales were *economically independent* of the revenue from its other line of ceremonial swords. (The company ignored the possibility that naval officers who previously had shaved with their Wilkinson sabers would now switch to Wilkinson blades, thereby decreasing the replacement demand for the former.)

4. The above-mentioned types of economic dependence must be distinguished from another type of interrelationship, *statistical dependence.* Two projects are said to be statistically dependent when increases (decreases) in the benefits from the one are accompanied over time by an increase (decrease) in the benefits of the second. Thus, the revenues from two lines of luxury goods, for example, caviar and Cadillacs, are likely to fluctuate together over time (see Chapter 8).

Clearly many other classifications are possible. Some firms assign a priority rating to alternative proposals; classifying projects as "urgent," "required," "desirable," and so on. Others classify investment alternatives by the location of the projects within the firm or within a division. The various classification schemes are *not* mutually exclusive; a firm can, and many do, use all of the above-mentioned classifications at one stage or another of the capital budgeting process.

complements
Investment projects in which the adoption of one increases the expected benefits of others.

substitutes
Investment projects in which the adoption of one decreases the profitability of a second.

CASH FLOWS vs. ACCOUNTING FLOWS

Modern investment analysis rests on the principle that projects should be evaluated on the basis of their cash flows, and not on the accounting concepts of income and expense. The cash flow principle can be clarified by considering an extreme example. Assume that a shipyard signs a contract to supply an oil tanker to the Universal Oil Company in 1989. The contract is signed in 1987, and Universal pays an advance of $20 million to help finance the project. No profit from this contract will have an impact on the shipyard's reported profit in 1987 or in 1988. Only in 1989, when the tanker is delivered to Universal, will the profit (or loss) generated by this transaction be reflected in the shipyard's accounts. The $20 million received in 1987 does not affect the accounting revenues of the project. From the viewpoint of reported accounting earnings, the shipyard's decision to undertake such a project would not be influenced by the receipt of the advance payment. But this does not make economic sense. In practice, a firm will always prefer, other things being equal, to receive as large a cash advance as possible, thereby reducing the cost of financing the project. In order to reflect this important dimension of the decision process, modern time-adjusted investment criteria are based on cash, rather than accounting, inflows and outlays. Hence, the exact timing of each component of the cash flow must be determined accurately if a proposal's full economic impact is to be gauged correctly.

The difference between the cash flow and accounting concepts can also be illustrated by considering the case of trade credit. Let us assume that the annual sales in 1988 of the ABC Company are $100,000, and that the company's policy is to offer 2-year payment terms to customers. The accounting department of ABC will report gross revenues of $100,000 for the year. Now suppose that the total cost of producing and selling the product in question is $80,000, and that this outlay also occurs in 1988. The company's balance sheet for 1988 will include an entry *accounts receivable* of $100,000, and its income statement will report a profit of $20,000. However, from the viewpoint of capital budgeting, the impact on NPV is considerably smaller. Since the outlay of $80,000 occurs in 1988, no adjustment is required. For simplicity, we assume that the costs are incurred on the first day of the year. The revenues from sales, however, will be realized only in 1990—that is, 2 years later. The calculation of the "cash flow" profit, therefore, is as follows:

1988	1989	1990
−80,000	—	+100,000

Obviously, the accounting and the cash flow profits are the same only for the unrealistic case of a zero discount rate. At all positive discount rates, the cash flow profit will be smaller. For example, if we assume a 10% discount rate, the calculation of the discounted value of the profit is:

$$\text{NPV} = \$100,000(DF_{10\%,2}) - \$80,000$$
$$= \$100,000(0.826) - \$80,000 = \$2,600$$

Thus the contribution to NPV is $2,600, and not $20,000. And as we have already shown in Chapter 9, the NPV of cash flows is the appropriate decision criterion if the market value of the owners' equity is to be maximized.

THE INCREMENTAL PRINCIPLE

The cash flow principle by itself is not sufficient to resolve all the conceptual difficulties that plague the estimation of a project's costs and benefits. Even if we are committed to using cash flows, questions can arise regarding the inclusion (or exclusion) of some costs, even though they are clearly cash outlays.

For example, suppose the Pacific Electric Company is considering an investment in a new power unit. The gross cash inflows from this unit are expected to be $100,000 per year, while the annual cash outflows for fuel, labor, and so on are expected to be $75,000. In addition, the company's cost accounting department estimates that overhead costs of $20,000 per year should be charged to the new power unit. These costs include the new project's share in managerial salaries, general administrative expenses, and so on. For simplicity, we assume that those **overhead costs** include $10,000 of fixed costs—that is, costs which will be incurred even if the project is *not* implemented. An example of such a cost would be the fraction of the company president's salary allocated to the new power unit. The remaining $10,000 is assumed to be *variable;* these costs will be incurred *only* if the project is adopted. The cost of insuring the new power unit is an example of such a cost. Finally, it has been estimated that the company's net receipts from its other power units will decrease by $5,000 per year if the new power unit is installed.

Table 10–1 summarizes the information on the receipts and outlays of the proposed project. Clearly the annual cash receipts of $100,000 are part of the project's cash flow, but it is not equally clear that all four types of outlays listed in the table should be deducted when calculating the project's annual net cash flow. In general, the *fixed* overhead expenses should *not* be deducted from the project's receipts because they do not represent a cash outflow which is generated by the decision to invest in the new power unit. By definition, these fixed costs (president's salary, and so on) will remain the same whether or not the new investment is made. Therefore, they should not be "charged" against the project. Variable overhead costs and the direct

overhead costs
Project costs that include managerial salaries, general administrative expenses, and other fixed costs.

TABLE 10–1	Annual Receipts and Outlays of New Power Unit (In Dollars)
Annual inflow	100,000
Annual outflow	
Fuel, labor, etc.	75,000
Fixed overhead	10,000
Variable overhead	10,000
Decrease in net receipts from other power units	5,000

costs (fuel, labor, and so on) should be deducted, since they do represent additional outlays incurred as a result of the decision to invest in the new unit.

The last item of Table 10–1, the decrease in net receipts elsewhere in the firm, must also be deducted. Applying the incremental cash flow principle, this is a (negative) cash flow that occurs as a direct result of the decision to invest in the new unit. The fact that the change in the cash flow takes place with respect to other power units, or in another department, is irrelevant; in capital budgeting, we seek to measure the net change in the firm's *total cash flow*. Thus, the new project's impact on the cash flows of existing units is germane to the investment decision, and therefore should be reflected in the estimated cash flows of the new unit. When Ford or General Motors develops a new model car, the company is sensitive to the possibility that the new model may compete with existing models. A very "successful" new car that drastically reduces revenues from the sales of existing models might prove a disaster. Only when projects are evaluated on the basis of the overall cash flows generated by the decision to invest can we be certain that their true impact is reflected in the profitability calculation.

Now let's turn to some additional examples. For some projects, the opportunity cost of using the limited services of key personnel may have to be estimated, especially if their involvement in the project creates a need to hire additional people elsewhere in the firm. Despite the difficulties involved, a careful analysis of the costs of transferring existing assets (both human and physical) to the new project must be made in order to ensure that the return to the firm as a whole is reflected in the NPV calculation.

Consider, for example, the case of a firm that is evaluating a project which, among other things, requires 10,000 cubic feet of cold storage space. Assume also that the firm has 20,000 cubic feet of suitable storage space available, only half of which is currently being used for the firm's other products. Under the circumstances, what storage cost (if any) should be assigned to the proposed project? The answer to this question is not simple.

opportunity cost
The income generated by the alternative use of an asset that is foregone when a new project is adopted.

On the surface at least, it appears that storage costs should *not* be charged to the project. The firm already has the storage space available, and therefore no additional cash outflow is incurred. But suppose the firm can rent out this space—say at a net annual rental of $20 per cubic foot. If the new project is adopted, the firm suffers an annual loss of alternative income of $200,000. In such a case, the **opportunity cost** of using the storage space (that is, $200,000) should be subtracted from the annual cash inflow of the new project. The opportunity cost of using any asset is measured by the income foregone—the income that could have been generated in the asset's best alternative use.

The problem becomes more complicated if we assume, for some reason, that the firm cannot rent the unused storage space to outsiders. In this instance, it would seem that excess capacity exists (recall that only 10,000 cubic feet is currently being used). In the absence of any alternative use, the storage space's opportunity cost is zero, and therefore no storage cost should be charged to the new project. However, if we are concerned with a project whose economic life is 10 years, we must examine the possible alternative uses for the storage space over the entire period. If, for example, we expect the excess capacity to disappear after the second year due to the expansion of the firm's other activities, the cost of acquiring additional storage space in the third and later years must be charged to the project under consideration. In such a case, the storage cost is zero for the first two years, and positive from the third year onward.

WORKING CAPITAL

The NPV calculation deducts the present value of the investment outlays from the present value of the annual cash flows. In addition to fixed assets (buildings, machinery), implementation of the project often requires an increase in working capital (cash, inventories, receivables). Consider the following hypothetical example (for simplicity, we assume a world without taxes).

$$
\begin{aligned}
I_0 &= \text{initial investment outlay in fixed assets} &&= \$100,000 \\
W &= \text{investment in additional working capital} &&= \$\ 25,000 \\
CF &= \text{annual net cash receipts} &&= \$\ 35,000 \\
&\quad \text{(cash receipts less cash expenses)} \\
I_n &= \text{salvage value of fixed assets} &&= \$\ \ 2,000 \\
n &= \text{economic life of the project} &&= 5 \text{ years} \\
k &= \text{the discount rate} &&= 10\%
\end{aligned}
$$

salvage value
The value of fixed assets at the end of a project.

Table 10–2 gives the cash flow for this project. Note that at the end of the project's expected duration, the **salvage** (market) **value** of the fixed assets

TABLE 10–2   Project Cash Flow (In thousands of dollars)

	Year					
	0	1	2	3	4	5
Net annual receipts	—	35	35	35	35	35
Initial investment (depreciable assets)	(100)					2
Investment in working capital	(25)					25
Net cash flow	(125)	35	35	35	35	62
Present value at 10%	(125)	31.815	28.910	26.285	23.905	38.502
Net present value = **$24.417**						

and the total amount of working capital are added to the cash flow of that year. Adding the salvage value reflects the fact that the fixed assets may still have some value at the end of the project. Adding the working capital to the cash flow at the end of the project reflects the fact that termination of the project releases the *entire* amount of funds previously tied up in working capital.

An alternative, and fully equivalent, way of handling the investment in working capital would be to exclude working capital from the initial investment outlay and to charge each year's cash flow with the *imputed cost*. Table 10–3 gives the cash flow of the project using the imputed cost of working capital approach. Each year the amount of working capital (25,000) is multiplied by the cost of capital (10%), and the resulting product ($2,500) is deducted from the annual cash flow. In both approaches the project's NPV is the same (except for a rounding difference) because the two methods are equivalent. The present value of the stream of imputed costs is exactly equal to the difference between W and $W/(1 + k)^n$.[1]

Both methods are equivalent—but remember, use one or the other, not both! The first method is simpler, but the imputed cost method has the advantage of greater flexibility. This is important for projects in which the

---

[1] The annual imputed cost is given by
$$-(kW) = [-(.10)\ \$25,000)] = \$-2,500$$
And the present value of the stream of imputed costs is
$$-\$2,500\ (DFA_{10\%,5})$$
$$-\ \$2,500(3.791) = -9,477$$
But except for a rounding error, this is exactly the same result obtained when we deduct the initial investment in working capital *(W)* and add back its present value at the end of the fifth year:
$$-W + W/(1 + k)^5 =$$
$$-\ \$25,000 + 25,000(DF_{10\%,5}) =$$
$$-\$25,000 + 25,000(.621) = -9,475$$

TABLE 10–3 Project Cash Flow (In Thousands of Dollars)

	Year					
	0	1	2	3	4	5
Net annual receipts	—	35	35	35	35	35
Imputed cost of working capital	—	(2.5)	(2.5)	(2.5)	(2.5)	(2.5)
Initial investment (depreciable assets)	(100)					2
Net cash flow	(100)	32.5	32.5	32.5	32.5	34.5
Present value	(100)	29.543	26.845	24.408	22.198	21.425
Net present value = **$24.419**						

amount of working capital tied up by the project varies over the years. The procedure for applying the imputed cost of working capital is as follows:

STEP 1:   Calculate the appropriate imputed cost each year by multiplying that year's working capital by the discount rate.

STEP 2:   Enter the imputed costs as deductions to the cash flow in the appropriate years.

STEP 3:   Calculate the project's NPV as usual.

Finally, we should note that part of the working capital is often provided by suppliers' credit. The calculation of the required working capital should be *net* of such credits. For example, a typical calculation of the additional investment in working capital required by a project might look like this:

Increase in cash balances	$ 10,000
Increase in inventories	$100,000
Increase in accounts receivable	$ 50,000
Total increase in working capital	$160,000
Less:	
Increase in accounts payable	
(Supplier's credit)	$ 30,000
Required working capital	**$130,000**

In such a case, $130,000 and not $160,000 would enter the NPV calculation. The remaining $30,000 of the investment in working capital will be financed by credit granted by suppliers. In all cases, note that we are speaking of the *increment* to working capital due to the acceptance of the project in question, and *not* the accounting entries in the firm's balance sheet. The latter reflect the operation of the company as a whole. Here we are concerned with isolating the cash flows of the particular project that is being evaluated.

DEPRECIATION

There still remains the question of how to handle the depreciation of the project's physical assets. Suppose, for example, that the ABC Company acquires a machine which costs $10,000, has an expected economic life of 10 years, and is expected to produce a net annual cash inflow of CF dollars. The cash flow for such a machine can be written as follows:

Years				
0	1	2	3. . .	10
(10,000)	CF	CF	CF. . .	CF

The problem confronting the company's accountant is how to allocate the project's revenues and expenses to particular years in order to estimate the annual net profit in the report to the shareholders. To do this, the accountant must first calculate that part of the machine's original purchase price which is used up each year. The most popular solution to this problem is to divide the original cost of the machine by its expected economic life, thereby deriving the annual depreciation allowance. This depreciation allowance is then deducted from the annual receipts when calculating the accounting profit for the year. Because it allocates an equal proportion of the machine's total cost to each year, this type of calculation is called **straight-line depreciation,** or **SLD** for short. In our example, the annual depreciation expense using the straight-line method is $1,000 (10,000/10 = 1,000), and the firm's *pretax annual profit* is *CF* minus $1,000.

straight-line depreciation (SLD)
A method of calculating depreciation that allocates an equal portion of a physical asset's total cost to each year.

The deduction of the depreciation allowance is a compromise between reality and the legal requirement to calculate an annual profit figure. However, when evaluating the profitability of a proposed capital investment using the NPV approach, we ignore interim profits and consider the project's entire life as a single decision unit. In capital budgeting the allocation of costs to particular years is ignored, and attention is focused on project cash flows at the precise time they are expected to occur.

Since the machine in question is to be purchased and paid for at the project's outset, $10,000 is deducted from the NPV calculation at the outset, instead of deducting a depreciation allowance of $1,000 in each of the next 10 years. The two alternative ways of handling the initial investment outlays are equivalent only for the unrealistic case of a zero discount rate. In general, the two methods differ. In the NPV approach, we deduct the initial investment outlay when it is incurred because it is an actual cash flow. Since the investment cost is fully taken into account, accounting depreciation is *not* deducted from the annual net receipts *(CF)*. Deducting an annual depreciation allowance would, in effect, *double count* the investment cost.

IMPACT OF CORPORATE TAXES

To this point we have emphasized that investment decisions should be based on cash flows. Accounting conventions—for example, those affecting the allocation of depreciation expense over time—have been ignored. However, the accounting treatment of individual cost items, including depreciation expense, does influence the measurement and timing of net income. Therefore, accounting conventions also affect the size and timing of corporate income tax payments, which of course are actual cash outflows. Moreover, because corporate taxes do *not* affect all investments to the same degree, project cash flows must always be expressed on an after-tax basis if meaningful comparisons are to be made.

Corporate taxes are a cash outflow and must be taken into account when evaluating a project's desirability. Suppose, for simplicity, that the corporate tax rate is $T\%$; the annual cash flow (before deducting depreciation) is CF, and the annual straight-line depreciation allowance is D. As noted earlier, depreciation is not an actual cash outflow and therefore is *not* subtracted from the annual cash flow. However, the tax deductibility of depreciation decreases the firm's tax liability and therefore the impact of depreciation is an element to be considered when calculating the company's *after-tax cash flow*.

The net after-tax cash flow equals the pretax cash flow (CF) minus taxes, where taxes are $T\%$ of the firm's taxable income:

$$\text{after-tax cash flow} = \text{pretax cash flow} - \text{corporate taxes}$$
$$ATCF = CF - T(CF - D) = (1 - T)CF + TD$$

where $T =$ the corporate tax rate, and D is the annual depreciation allowance, and TD is the depreciation tax shield.

The after-tax cash flow is central to all financial decision problems, and can be derived as follows:

STEP 1:   Calculate the project's net income by subtracting the depreciation allowance (D) from the pretax cash flow (CF).

STEP 2:   The tax rate (T) is then applied to the net income to derive corporate taxes.

STEP 3:   Deduct corporate taxes from the pretax cash flow, thereby deriving the *after-tax cash flow.*

Table 10–4 shows the following numerical example of the calculation of the after-tax cash flow:

Annual cash flow (CF) (cash revenues less cash expenses)	$= \$400$
Corporate tax rate (T)	$= 34\%$
Initial investment outlay (I_0)	$= \$1,000$
Project's lifetime (n)	$= 10$ years
Annual straight-line depreciation (D)	$= \$100$

As can be seen Table 10–4, the after-tax cash flow is $298:

$$ATCF = CF - T(CF - D)$$
$$ATCF = 400 - (.34)300 = \mathbf{\$298}$$

We can easily verify that the same result can be obtained using the depreciation tax shield *(TD):*

$$(1 - T)CF + TD = (.66)400 + (.34)100 = \mathbf{\$298}$$

If we assume that the relevant after-tax discount rate is equal to 10%, the project's NPV can be calculated as follows:

$$(DFA_{10\%,10})298 - 1000 = (6.145)298 - 1000 = \mathbf{\$831}$$

TABLE 10—4   Example of After-Tax Cash Flow

1. Annual pretax cash flow (CF)	400
2. Depreciation allowance (D)	100
3. Net income before tax [line (1) minus line (2)]	300
4. Corporate taxes [34% × line (3)]	102
5. After-tax cash flow [line (1) − line (4)]	**298**

An additional tax factor should be mentioned. If a firm's equipment is expected to have any salvage value at the end of the project's lifetime and this value exceeds the equipment's book value (original sales price less accumulated depreciation), a corporate tax liability will be incurred on the profit (net of all removal costs) from the sale of such equipment. Of course, the proceeds from the sale and any tax payment will appear at the end of the last year of the project's life. As a result, their present values tend to be small in relation to the project's NPV. However, when contemplating the replacement of machinery at the beginning or in the middle of a planned project, the impact of the proceeds from such sales can be significant. Tax payments generated by such sales can be crucial to the decision, and should not be overlooked.

Assume that a firm expects to be able to sell one of its machines at the end of its tenth year for $60,000 after paying all the removal costs of the equipment. The machine originally cost $1 million, but by the end of the 10 years will have been fully depreciated; its book value will be zero. Since the net proceeds from the sale ($60,000) exceeds the equipment's (zero) book value, the firm will have to pay taxes on the $60,000 of recaptured depreciation.

$$\$60,000 - 0 = \$60,000$$

Applying the 34% tax rate, the firm will have to pay $20,400 (.34 × 60,000 = 20,400) in taxes on the "profit" from the sale.[2] As a result, the calculation of the net salvage value of the equipment, which will be added to the project's terminal cash flow at the end of year 10, is $39,600:

Proceeds from sale of equipment	$60,000
minus taxes on sale	$20,400
Net salvage value	**$39,600**

---

[2] Starting with the 1987 tax year, corporate long-term capital gains are to be taxed as ordinary income, and are subject to a maximum tax rate of 34%. Prior to the 1986 tax reform capital gains were taxed at a special corporate rate of 28%.

Investment Tax Credit

From time to time the U.S. government, and the governments of many other countries, have offered a tax credit on the acquisition of certain kinds of capital equipment.[3] The purpose of such tax credits is to provide an incentive for new corporate investment. The investment credit is usually set as a percentage of the cost of the capital equipment—for example, 10% for qualifying assets. It works as follows. Assume a firm is contemplating a project that entails the purchase of $100,000 of new equipment with an expected duration of 10 years. If the equipment qualifies for the investment credit, the firm will be able to deduct $10,000 from its tax bill. So long as the company has a current tax liability exceeding $10,000, the effective cost of the new equipment is reduced to $90,000, which serves as an added incentive to make the investment. Although practice varies, we will assume that in order to avoid "double benefits," the tax authorities force the firm to reduce the value of the asset for depreciation purposes by the amount of the tax credit. For example, if the firm uses straight-line depreciation, the annual depreciation allowance is $9,000:

$$\frac{(.90)I_0}{10} = \frac{90,000}{10} = 9,000$$

The investment credit can be clarified by considering the following numerical example:

Project duration (n)	= 10 years
Corporate tax rate (T)	= 34%
Cost of capital (k)	= 5%
Annual net receipt (CF_t)	= $14,000
Initial investment (I_0)	= $100,000
Annual depreciation $(SLD) = D_t$ (without the tax credit)	= $10,000
Annual depreciation $(SLD) = (.90)D_t$ (with the tax credit)	= $9,000

The annual after-tax cash flow *without* the 10% tax credit is

$$(1 - T)CF_t + TD = (.66)14,000 + (.34)10,000 = \$12,640$$

and the project's NPV is

$$NPV = \$12,640\ (DF_{5\%,10}) - \$100,000$$
$$= 12,640(7.722) - 100,000 = -2,394$$

Since the NPV is negative, the project is unacceptable and the new equipment will not be purchased. But what happens to this particular decision if a 10% investment credit is granted? The annual after-tax cash flow becomes:

$$(1 - T)CF_t + (.90)TD$$
$$(.66)\$14,000 + (.34) \$9,000 = \$12,300$$

The project's NPV, taking the investment credit into account, is now positive:

$$NPV = 12,300(7.722) - 90,000 = \$4,981$$

Since the NPV is positive, the project is acceptable, and the new equipment will be purchased.

Accelerated Depreciation

As we have already noted, the primary function of accounting depreciation is to allocate an asset's original cost over the period of its useful life. For tax purposes, a firm should try to depreciate its assets in the shortest possible period, since by doing so it will enjoy the tax benefits at an earlier date. To avoid any misunderstanding, note that "accelerating" the depreciation allowance does *not* affect the actual economic depreciation of the assets. It neither lengthens nor shortens the asset's useful economic life. Thus, no matter what method of depreciation is used, the total cost that will be written off will be the same. But of course this does not hold for its present value: Faster cost writeoffs imply higher present values for the depreciation tax shield, and therefore increase the project's NPV.

The size of the annual depreciation allowance depends on the depreciation method employed, as well as on the proposal's lifetime. The Internal Revenue Service (IRS) establishes the minimum number of years to be used in calculating depreciation for tax purposes for various classes of assets. For example, from 1981 to 1985, U.S. firms had to comply with the rules for the **accelerated cost recovery system (ACRS).** The 1986 Tax Reform Act overhauled these rules. All depreciable property (excluding real property) is assigned a recovery period (life expectancy) of 3, 5, 7, 10, 15, or 20 years, and a depreciation percentage to be applied to each recovery year (see Chapter 2).

accelerated cost recovery system (ACRS)
IRS rules governing the minimum number of years to be used in calculating depreciation of physical assets.

SUMMARY

This chapter has examined the problems that arise when the NPV model is applied to actual cash flows. In order to facilitate the capital budgeting process, there are a number of methods for classifying projects. For example, projects can be classified (a) by size, (b) by type of benefit, and (c) by degree of dependence.

The interdependence of cash flows can take many forms:

1. Projects are *mutually exclusive* if the implementation of one project precludes the implementation of another.

2. Projects are *complements* if the decision to adopt one increases the benefits from another.

3. Two projects are *substitutes* if the acceptance of one proposal decreases the benefits from the second.

4. Projects are *statistically dependent* if increases (decreases) in the benefits of the one *over time* are accompanied by increases (decreases) in the benefits of the second.

Modern investment analysis rests on the evaluation of cash flows. There are real differences between conventional accounting concepts of income and expense and their cash flow counterparts. Of special importance are the timing of receipts and outlays and the handling of fixed and variable costs. *Fixed costs* are those costs which will be incurred by the firm even if the project in question is not implemented. *Variable costs* are those which will be incurred by the firm only if the project in question is implemented. When evaluating a project's NPV, only the variable costs are considered.

In general, a project's cash flow should reflect all the cash flows generated by the investment decision, independent of whether they occur in the department in question or elsewhere in the firm. Here the concept of opportunity cost plays a role. The *opportunity cost* of using any resource is measured by the income that could have been generated by that resource in its best alternative use.

Since the investment outlay must be deducted when calculating a project's NPV, we need to follow the principles underlying the definition of investment outlay. The investment outlay should include any required increase in working capital, as well as the outlay for fixed assets. There are two equivalent methods for handling working capital: (a) imputing an annual cost to the required working capital in each year, and (b) adding the working capital to the initial investment outlay and then adding it back to the cash flow at the end of the project's life.

The NPV analysis deducts the actual cash outlay on fixed assets from the project's cash flow, rather than accounting depreciation, which is not a cash flow. In fact, if depreciation is also deducted, this would in effect *double count* the investment cost. Depreciation, however, does affect the calculation of a project's after-tax cash flow:

$$\text{after-tax cash flow} = \text{pretax cash flow} - \text{corporate taxes}$$
$$ATCF = CF - T(CF - D)$$
$$= (1 - T)CF + TD$$

where T = the corporate tax rate, D is the annual depreciation allowance, and TD is the depreciation tax shield.

Two additional factors affecting projects' after-tax cash flows are the investment tax credit and accelerated depreciation.

In the next chapter, we build on this foundation and consider some refinements of the basic NPV model, and the impact of risk on the decision process.

REVIEW EXERCISE

Circle the correct word(s) to complete each sentence; see p. 257 for correct answers.

10.1 The grouping of projects into different categories often *negates/simplifies* the decision process.

10.2 If the acceptance of one project increases the profitability of a second project, they are said to be *substitutes/complements*.

10.3 Modern investment analysis maintains that *accounting profits/cash flows* are appropriate for the NPV calculations.

10.4 A new project's impact on the cash flow of existing projects *is/is not* germane to the investment decision.

10.5 For the calculation of cash flows, fixed overhead expenses *should/should not* be deducted from the project's receipts.

10.6 When estimating the cash flow of a proposed project, opportunity costs *should/should not* be taken into consideration.

10.7 The investment outlay for a project *includes/excludes* the required change in working capital, which will be *added back/deducted* at the end of the project.

10.8 Depreciation *is/is not* an actual cash outlay and *should/should not* be deducted from the net receipts when calculating a project's NPV.

10.9 Corporate taxes *are/are not* a cash outflow.

10.10 In order to compute the corporate tax, we calculate the project's net income by *subtracting/adding* the depreciation allowance *from/to* the pretax cash flow.

10.11 To derive the after-tax cash flow, we subtract taxes from *pretax cash flow/net income*.

10.12 An investment tax credit *reduces/increases* the effective cost of an asset.

10.13 A firm should try to depreciate its assets in the *longest/shortest* possible period.

10.14 Accelerated depreciation *does/does not* affect the actual economic depreciation of an asset, but it *does/does not* affect a project's net present value.

QUESTIONS

10.1 Define the following terms:
   a. Accounting profit   **b.** Incremental cost
   c. Opportunity cost   **d.** Complementary projects
   e. Substitute projects   **f.** Depreciation allowance
   g. Accelerated depreciation

10.2 Under which circumstances will accounting profits equal cash flow profits?

10.3 Give two examples for each of the following types of investments:
   a. Mutually exclusive projects   **b.** Complementary projects
   c. Substitute projects   **d.** Independent projects

10.4 Mr. Jones is offered the opportunity to invest $2,000 in order to receive a return of $2,280 at the end of one year. "I refused to make the investment," Jones said. "I had only $400 of my own, and for a $1,600 loan which I would have had to take, the bank wanted 10% interest. Thus, my net return would have been only $2,120. Would you be satisfied with a 6% return these days?" Appraise the statement.

10.5 When Ms. Milford, the manager of a new computer unit, made her feasibility report on the new unit, she didn't include her salary. "I am not a new worker in the company," Ms. Milford said. "I used to be the manager of the laboratory, and my deputy there took my place." Appraise Ms. Milford's logic.

10.6 Assume that the duration of a project is 10 years. Most of the equipment will serve 10 years, but a few machines will last for only 5 years, while the buildings will last for approximately 20 years. How is the cash flow affected by these facts?

10.7 "In the calculation of NPV, depreciation is not deducted from the net cash flow, despite the fact that depreciation is a real economic cost, and is recognized as such by the tax authorities." Evaluate this statement.

10.8 "Taxes can't be all bad. Any increase in the corporate tax rate, T, will increase the value of the depreciation tax shield, thereby improving the profitability of the project." Evaluate this statement.

10.9 "In order to evaluate an investment project, we add the increase in working capital to the initial investment outlay and then charge each year's cash flow with the working capital's imputed cost." Do you agree? Explain.

10.10 Evaluate the following statement: "I want to use my car for as long as possible and am therefore not interested in accelerated depreciation."

10.11 Fulton & Co. is adding a new product to its line. The new product increases the workload of the marketing department by 5%. Under which circumstances should some or all of the additional cost be allocated to the new product?

10.12 "Working capital is added back at the end of the project without deducting any interest. We could have invested the same amount in the bank and at least have earned some interest on it." Evaluate this statement.

PROBLEMS

10.1 **Cash flows.**   Show the cash flows generated by the following activities:
   a. Developing a new product requires an investment of $800,000. This product will generate annual receipts of $250,000 for the next 6 years.
   b. A firm invests $3 million in a new projects and expects annual receipts of $600,000 for the first 3 years, and $900,000 during the last 5 years.
   c. Evelyn Smith borrows $5,000 from the bank. This loan is repayable in seven equal annual installments of $650 each.
   d. An investment of $7,500 in new equipment is expected to generate annual receipts of $45,000 for 4 years starting at the end of the third year.
   3. A firm takes a 3-year loan of $100,000, which is to be repaid at the end of the fourth year in a lump sum of $130,000.

10.2 **Allocating costs to the cash flow.**   The Portland Company is considering opening a new loading dock. In order to do so, the company must purchase

$280,000 worth of new equipment. The gross annual receipts are expected to be $250,000, and the annual costs of the new unit are as follows:

Direct labor cost	$65,000
Fuel	40,000
Electricity	17,000
Direct administrative cost	25,000
Fixed overhead expense	26,000
General administrative cost (pro rata share of office expenses)	29,000

In addition, it has been estimated that the company's net receipts from its other loading docks will decrease by $25,000 per year when the new unit is installed. Construct the net annual cash flow for the investment in the new loading dock. Explain your calculations.

10.3 After-tax cash flow.   Assume an economic life of 8 years for Portland's new equipment (see the previous problem) and that it is to be depreciated using the straight-line method over 5 years. The corporate tax rate is 34%, and the after-tax cost of capital is 10%. Should Portland open the new loading dock? (*Hint:* You may want to make some additional assumptions.)

10.4 After-tax cash flow.   The Aston Company has acquired a new lathe for $66,000, which is to be depreciated in 11 years according to the straight-line method. The lathe's economic life is 13 years, during which it produces an annual cash flow (cash revenue minus cash expenditures) of $13,000 per year. The corporate tax rate is 34%.
a. What is the after-tax cash flow?
b. Assuming an after-tax cost of capital of 5%, was it worthwhile to invest in the new lathe?

10.5 After-tax cash flow.   The Green Box Company is considering buying special equipment, with an economic life of 8 years, for $200,000. The annual pretax cash flow generated by this equipment is expected to be $40,000. Assume that the corporate tax rate is 46%, and the after-tax cost of capital is 8%
a. Show the after-tax cash flow of the project assuming straight-line depreciation.
b. Should the firm buy the equipment? Support your answer.
c. Does your answer to part (b) change if the cost of capital is assumed to be 6%?

10.6 Impact of change in tax rates.   The administration has lowered the corporate tax rate from 46% to 34%. How do your answers to the previous problem change?

10.7 Integrative.   In 1980 the Western Metals Company (WMC) was forced to discontinue the operations of its Export Division owing to the closing of the foreign market for its particular product. While it would have been possible to sell limited amounts of the product on the local market, a careful feasibility study showed that such limited production could be carried on only at a loss, even if fixed costs were ignored. As a result of this study, production of the item was discontinued.

In 1987 it not only became possible to export the item again, but in much larger amounts. To permit the expanded scale of production, WMC would have to acquire two additional machines. The cost of the two machines was $400,000 and $300,000, and the machines had expected economic lives of 4 and 5 years, respectively. The company's production manager also pointed out that the division's old equipment had been transferred to the Maintenance Department, and it would now be necessary to return it to the Export Division. While the book value of the old equipment was zero, the production manager estimated its market value at $150,000. He also stated that when the old equipment is transferred, WMC will have to acquire additional used equipment to replace it in the Maintenance Department. He estimated the cost of this equipment at $200,000. The production manager estimated that the old equipment still had a useful economic life of 4 years. The expected receipts of the Export Division from the expanded scale of production were estimated at $600,000 per year. Annual expenses were estimated as follows:

Raw materials	$40,000
Salaries	$60,000
Other expenses	$20,000
Fixed expenses of the company (120% of salaries)	$72,000
Straight-line depreciation	$160,000
Total	$352,000

Renewed production would also require an additional $500,000 for working capital—principally inventories of raw materials and finished goods. Assume that the cost of capital (minimum required rate of return) is 15% and that the company does *not* pay taxes. Write a report to the president of WMC on the economic feasibility of reopening the Export Division.

SAMPLE PROBLEMS

SP10.1 The Fortuna Boat Company builds fishing boats to order. In 1986 the firm examined a proposal for building 10 fishing boats for a large client. The receipts and outlays during the project's first year were expected to be $500,000 and $300,000, respectively. The terms of the contract allow the client to pay only 40% of the total receipts in the first year, 30% in the following year, and the remainder in the next year. Assume the outlays are paid out immediately on the first day of the year, and that the cost of capital is 12%.

  a. Calculate the project's accounting profit.
  b. Calculate the project's cash flow profit.

SP10.2 The Northern Company is considering introducing a new product line. The required investment outlay is $550,000 this year. The investment will be depreciated on a straight-line basis over 5 years; the economic life of the equipment is also 5 years. The expected net receipts (after deducting variable costs) are $120,000 for the next 2 years, and $250,000 in the third, fourth, and fifth years. The share of fixed overhead expenses imputed to be the new product line is $30,000 for the first 2 years and $40,000 thereafter. The corporate tax rate is 34%. Calculate the project's cash flow.

Solutions to Sample Problems

SP10.1 a. The project's expected accounting profit is:

$$500,000 - 300,000 = \$200,000$$

b. Because receipts will be spread over three years, the expected cash flow of the project is

	Year			
	0	**1**	**2**	**3**
which equals:	−300,000	500,000 × .4	500,000 × .3	500,000 × .3
	−300,000	200,000	150,000	150,000

Therefore, the expected cash flow profit is

$$-300,000 + 200,000/(1 + .12) + 150,000/(1 + .12)^2 + 150,000/(1 + .12)^3$$
$$= -300,000 + (200,000) \times .893 + (150,000) \times .797 + (150,000) \times .712$$
$$= -300,000 + 178,600 + 119,550 + 106,800 = \$104,950$$

SP10.2 The pretax inflows and outflows are as follows:

	Year						
	0	**1**	**2**	**3**	**4**	**5**	**6**
Cash flow	−550,000	120,000	120,000	250,000	250,000	250,000	250,000

In order to compute taxes, we first compute the annual depreciation allowance, which is then deducted from cash receipts to derive the taxable income. Since the straight-line method is used, we get annual depreciation of $550,000/5 = $110,000 for the next 5 years.

	Year						
	0	**1**	**2**	**3**	**4**	**5**	**6**
Cash flow	−550,000	120,000	120,000	250,000	250,000	250,000	250,000
Depreciation		110,000	−110,000	−110,000	−110,000	−110,000	0
Net income before taxes		10,000	10,000	140,000	140,000	140,000	250,000

Taxes are deducted from net income at a rate of 34%, to derive after-tax net income:

	Year					
	1	2	3	4	5	6
Income before taxes	10,000	10,000	140,000	140,000	140,000	250,000
Taxes (34%)	−3,400	−3,400	−47,600	−46,600	−47,600	−85,000
After-tax net income	6,600	6,600	92,400	92,400	92,400	165,000

But to derive the after-tax *cash flow*, depreciation must be added back to net income:

	Year						
	0	1	2	3	4	5	6
Net income after tax		6,600	6,600	92,400	92,400	92,400	165,000
Plus depreciation		110,000	110,000	110,000	110,000	110,000	0
After-tax cash flow	−550,000	116,600	116,600	202,400	202,400	202,400	165,000

Answers to Review Exercise

10.1 simplifies   **10.2** complements   **10.3** cash flows   **10.4** is
10.5 should not   **10.6** should   **10.7** includes, added back
10.8 is not, should not   **10.9** are   **10.10** subtracting, from
10.11 pre-tax cash flow   **10.12** reduces   **10.13** shortest
10.14 does not, does

SUGGESTIONS FOR FURTHER READING

Some important tax aspects of capital budgeting are examined by: S. Davidson and D.F. Drake, "Capital Budgeting and the 'Best' Tax Depreciation Method, *Journal of Business,* October 1961; and N. Dopuch and S. Sunder, "FASB's Statements on Objectives and Elements of Financial Accounting: A Review," *Accounting Review,* January 1980.

A comprehensive explanation of the 1986 tax reform is given in *A Complete Guide to the Tax Reform Act of 1986,* Prentice-Hall, 1986.

11 | Special Topics and Risk Analysis In Capital Budgeting

The NPV model is a very versatile tool. In the preceding chapter we saw how it can be applied to the evaluation of the cash flows of new investments. This chapter deals with the practical application of the NPV model and risk analysis. The present value approach is applied in a number of special situations. Most firms, at one time or another, are confronted with the problem of replacing worn-out or obsolete equipment. The use of a variant of the basic NPV model that can help the firm establish an optimal equipment-replacement strategy is defined. Inflation also has an impact on a firm's capital investments. Two alternative methods are presented for estimating net present values under inflationary conditions. Many firms face a constraint on the total amount of funds available for investment. With this in mind, the NPV model is adapted to the evaluation of projects when capital is "rationed." We then illustrate how formal methods of risk analysis and computer methods can be applied within the general NPV framework. Finally, the logic of alternative methods for making risk-adjustments is examined.

EQUIPMENT REPLACEMENT DECISIONS

Almost every firm is confronted, at one time or another, with the problem of establishing an equipment replacement policy. The decision of when to replace equipment is one that can be handled using the NPV model. To focus on the problem at hand, we assume a world without taxes—or alternatively, that all the figures here have been calculated on an after-tax basis.

Consider a machine that costs $10,000, has a 5 year life expectancy, and generates a *net* cash inflow of $5,000 a year. The firm is faced with the alternative of using the machine for the entire 5 years or selling it before the 5 years are up and replacing it with a new machine. Assume also that the market value of the old machine at the end of each year is expected to be:

Market Value of Old Machine

Year	Value
1	$8,000
2	7,000
3	6,000
4	2,000
5	0

On the basis of this information, the firm seeks to determine the *optimal replacement period;* but this requires the prior construction of the appropriate cash flow for each alternative course of action. Assuming a discount rate of 10% and the machine being sold at the end of the first year, the net present value of this alternative (NPV_1) is given by:

$$NPV_1 = -10,000 + \frac{5,000}{1.1} + \frac{8,000}{1.1} = \$1,817$$

Similarly, if the machine is sold after 2, 3, 4, or 5 years, the following NPV calculations are generated:

$$NPV_2 = -10,000 + \frac{5,000}{1.1} + \frac{5,000}{(1.1)^2} + \frac{7,000}{(1.1)^2} = \$4,462$$

$$NPV_3 = -10,000 + \frac{5,000}{1.1} + \frac{5,000}{(1.1)^2} + \frac{5,000}{(1.1)^3} + \frac{6,000}{(1.1)^3} = \$6,941$$

$$NPV_4 = -10,000 + \frac{5,000}{1.1} + \frac{5,000}{(1.1)^2} + \frac{5,000}{(1.1)^3} + \frac{5,000}{(1.1)^4} + \frac{2,000}{(1.1)^4} = \$7,216$$

$$NPV_5 = -10,000 + \frac{5,000}{1.1} + \frac{5,000}{(1.1)^2} + \frac{5,000}{(1.1)^3} + \frac{5,000}{(1.1)^4} + \frac{5,000}{(1.1)^5} = \$8,955$$

These calculations can be misleading. While it is true that using the machine for 5 years yields the highest net present value ($NPV_5 = \$8,955$), this does *not* necessarily mean that the optimal decision is to replace after 5 years. Since we are seeking the optimal strategy over time, different policies for *equal economic horizons* must be compared. For example, if we want to compare a 2-year replacement policy with a policy of replacing equipment every 4 years, the shorter cash flows must be repeated for another 2-year period if the comparison is to make economic sense.

In replacement problems, the cash flows of alternative policies over *equal* time periods must be considered. Otherwise, the calculation discriminates against short replacement policies. In the example above, one might compare all five alternative replacement policies up to a common horizon of, say, 60 years. Thus the policy to replace every year would be repeated 60 times, the policy to replace every 2 years would be repeated 30 times, and so on. But this can be a cumbersome problem indeed!

Uniform Annuity Series (UAS)

uniform annuity series (UAS)
The annuity whose present value equals the NPV of the investment project in question.

Another and more efficient way to deal with the replacement of equipment is to find the **uniform annuity series (UAS)** for each alternative replacement strategy and then choose the policy that has the highest UAS. The UAS is defined as the annuity whose present value equals the NPV of the investment project in question. Applying the present value factor for an annuity, we have:

$$NPV = UAS(DFA_{k,n})$$

Hence

$$UAS = \frac{NPV}{(DFA_{k,n})} \qquad (11.1)$$

Suppose that strategy A has a net present value of $200 and a 10-year duration. Assuming a 9% discount rate, its UAS is $31.16:

$$UAS_A = \frac{200}{6.418} = \$31.16$$

Similarly, if strategy B has a net present value of $100 and its duration is only 2 years, its UAS is $56.85:

$$UAS_B = \frac{100}{1.759} = \$56.85$$

Of course the two alternatives could be compared by repeating the 2-year strategy 5 times. However, there really is no need to do this: The UAS converts the NPV to an equivalent annual cash flow that can be compared up to any desired horizon. The UAS approach immediately shows that the shorter strategy is preferable. It yields a cash flow equivalent to an *annuity* of $56.85. The 10-year strategy has a UAS of only $31.16, and therefore is inferior. The NPV of the 2-year strategy is $100 and its UAS for 2 years is a cash flow of $56.85. Since it can be repeated every 2 years, each replication creates an NPV identical to the original—net present value of $100 and a cash flow of $56.85 each year. Thus, we obtain an *annuity* of $56.85. The other project earns a higher NPV of $200 every 10 years, but its equivalent equal annual cash flow is only $31.16. Therefore, the project with the shorter life has a higher NPV on a *comparable basis*—namely, for all equal durations.

Now we are in a position to solve our original machine replacement problem. Recall that the firm is trying to determine the *optimal* (best possible) strategy for replacement, and that we have already calculated the net present values for the five alternative replacement policies:

- [ ] $NPV_1 = \$1,817$, for 1-year replacement
- [ ] $NPV_2 = \$4,462$, for 2-year replacement
- [ ] $NPV_3 = \$6,941$, for 3-year replacement
- [ ] $NPV_4 = \$7,216$, for 4-year replacement
- [ ] $NPV_5 = \$8,955$, for 5-year replacement

Since the assumed discount rate was 10%, the UAS for each replacement policy can readily be calculated from Eq. 11.1. All that remains is to choose the replacement strategy with the highest UAS.

Using the appropriate values of $(DFA_{10\%,n})$ for each alternative replacement policy in Eq. 11.1, we get:

- [ ] $UAS_1 = 1,817/0.909 = 1,998.90$ for a 1-year replacement policy
- [ ] $UAS_2 = 4,462/1.736 = 2,570.28$ for a 2-year replacement policy
- [ ] $UAS_3 = 6,941/2.487 = 2,790.91$ for a 3-year replacement policy
- [ ] $UAS_4 = 7,216/3.170 = 2,276.34$ for a 4-year replacement policy
- [ ] $UAS_5 = 8,955/3.791 = 2,362.17$ for a 5-year replacement policy

The UAS approach easily identifies the optimal strategy: replacement every 3 years.

PROJECTS WITH UNEQUAL LIVES

Essentially, equipment replacement is a case of mutually exclusive alternatives of unequal duration. Therefore, it would appear, on the surface at least, that the method of "repeating" project cash flows until they are the same economic life, or the UAS model, can be used for any investment project of unequal duration. Nothing could be further from the truth! The equalization of time horizons and the equivalent alternative method of finding the uniform annuity series are appropriate methods if, *and only if*, the relevant projects can be repeated. As we have just seen, such an assumption is appropriate for technical problems such as finding the optimal replacement period. However, it would be a very unrealistic assumption for evaluating alternative ways to build a new chemical plant designed to produce a new product that, due to obsolescence and competition, has an expected economic life of less than a decade.

In general, the NPV calculation ignores any differences in projects' duration; the NPVs are calculated for the number of years each project is expected to generate its cash flow. Take, for example, the case of a company which is comparing the desirability of investing in a new product (A) which has an economic lifetime of only 5 years with the alternative of investing in a more conservative product (B) which has a longer expected lifetime, say 10 years. The present value of the cash flow in the first alternative would be calculated for 5 years *only;* the present value of the second alternative's cash flow would be calculated for 10 years:

Cash Flow of Two Products

Product	Years										
	0	1	2	3	4	5	6	7	8	9	10
A	$-I_0$	CF_1	CF_2	CF_3	CF_4	CF_5	—	—	—	—	—
B	$-I_0$	CF_1	CF_2	CF_3	CF_4	CF_5	CF_6	CF_7	CF_8	CF_9	CF_{10}

The product with the higher NPV is the preferred alternative.

INFLATION AND CAPITAL BUDGETING

Significant inflationary pressure in the 1970s and first half of the 1980s, even in some of the highly industrialized countries of North America and Western Europe, again focused attention on the financial and economic implications of a rapidly rising price level. Although inflation subsided in the mid-1980s, there can be no guarantee against a resurgence of inflationary pressure. As a result, it is no longer prudent to ignore the potential impact of inflation on financial decision-making.

Real vs. Nominal Values The key to understanding the way inflation affects cash flow analysis is to keep in mind the distinction, made in Chapter 6, between *real* and *nominal* magnitudes. As with any measure of profitability, special care must be exercised when applying the NPV criterion to project cash flows under inflationary conditions. For simplicity only, consider the case of a "neutral" inflation in which sales, labor costs, prices of raw materials, and so on all rise at the same rate.

Now assume that the real discount rate in the absence of inflation (k_R) is 10%, so that an investment of $100 will be attractive only if the cash flow at the end of the year is more than $110. The *real* net present value of a project that offers exactly $110 at the end of the year is, by definition, zero:

$$NPV = \frac{110}{1.1} - 100 = 0$$

or equivalently, using the NPV table

$$NPV = 110(DF_{10\%,1}) - 100$$
$$= 110(.909) - 100 = 0$$

If the cash flow in the absence of inflation is greater than $110, the project's *real* NPV is positive, and it should be accepted.

Now suppose that all prices and costs are expected to rise by 20% per year. What is the *minimum* required cash flow that will induce the firm to accept the project? Since the critical cash flow, in the absence of inflation, is $110, the minimum required *nominal* cash flow, given an annual inflation rate of 20%, must be ($110) (1.20) = $132. In other words, the cash flow must increase by 20% in order to preserve the project's previous NPV in *real* terms. Thus, for a 20% inflation rate, the minimum required nominal cash flow is $132, but the real value remains $110. Dividing 132 by 1.2 gives us 110. Any net receipt in excess of $132 will generate a positive *real* NPV.

Two Methods for Handling Inflation

A project's net present value, in an inflationary environment, can be measured in either of two ways: real analysis or nominal analysis.

Real Analysis. The nominal cash flows are first "deflated"—that is, reduced to real terms, and then present values are calculated using the *real* discount rate. Now reconsider the project which offers a return of $132 at the end of the year for an immediate outlay of $100. We continue to assume a 20% rate of inflation, and a required minimum return on investment of 10% in *real* terms.

Clearly the NPV of such a project is zero in real terms:

$$\text{NPV} = \frac{132/1.20}{1.1} - 100 = \frac{110}{1.1} - 100 = 0$$

Nominal Analysis. The *same* result can be reached using the nominal cost of capital to discount the nominal cash flows. Using the nominal approach, the end of year cash flow remains $132, but the real discount rate of 10% is adjusted to nominal terms. As we have pointed out, an investor who desires a 10% *real* return in a world of 20% inflation will demand a nominal return, k_n, equal to 32%.

$$k_n = (1.10)\,(1.20) - 1 = 1.32 - 1 = 32\%$$

The 32% discount rate reflects the fact that investors who receive $132 at the end of the year in return for a $100 outlay at the beginning of the year get only $110 worth of purchasing power. Hence, if they wish to preserve the 10% real return, they must demand a 32% nominal return just to remain in the same place.

Once again, the NPV of such a project is zero, but this time the calculation is in nominal terms:

$$\text{NPV} = \frac{132}{(1.2)(1.1)} - 100 = \frac{132}{1.32} - 100 = 0$$

Comparing the Two Methods

As we have just seen, cash flows can be discounted in nominal or in real (constant purchasing power) terms. If it is correctly done, shifting from one method to the other will not affect a firm's investment decisions. Project analysis can be carried out either in terms of current (nominal) or real (constant) dollars. But we should emphasize that the project's NPVs will be the same under both methods if, *and only if*, the real discount rate is applied to the constant dollar cash flows, or the appropriate nominal rate is used to discount the nominal cash flows.

The implications of this analysis for capital budgeting are straightforward. In evaluating its investment opportunities, the firm makes forecasts of future revenues and costs, both of which reflect a forecast of the rate of inflation as well. Hence the appropriate discount rate to be used in discounting such a cash flow is the nominal cost of capital. Alternatively, the firm could project into the future *current* prices and costs—base its cash flow forecast on the relationship between current prices and costs, without an upward adjustment for inflation. Using this approach, the appropriate discount rate would be the *real* cost of capital.

CAPITAL RATIONING

To this point, we have made the implicit assumption that the capital necessary to finance a given investment project is always available to the firm—at some cost, of course. And it is this cost of capital which constitutes the appropriate discount rate for evaluating cash flows. In this section we change our viewpoint somewhat in order to focus on a problem that confronts many firms. For these firms, the amount of capital that can be invested in any time period is more or less fixed, independent of the capital market. Their capital budgeting problem involves the allocation of scarce resources among competing and economically desirable projects, not all of which can be carried out due to a capital (or other) constraint. This problem is usually referred to as **capital rationing.**

capital rationing
The allocation of a fixed amount of capital among competing and economically desirable projects.

Despite its name, a capital rationing situation can arise for a variety of reasons, not all of which are concerned with the capital market per se. Of course, some far-reaching imperfection in the capital markets may preclude the raising of additional debt, and/or equity, beyond some stipulated amount. But more often than not, the restriction on the supply of capital reflects *noncapital* constraints or bottlenecks within the firm. For example, the supply of key personnel necessary to carry out the projects may be severely limited, thereby restricting the dollar amount of feasible investment. Considerations of management time may preclude the adoption of programs beyond some level. For example, the board of directors may insist on reviewing and approving all major projects, thereby limiting the number of projects that can be implemented in any one year.

Of course, it might be argued that such constraints on a firm's freedom to invest should more properly be called labor or management constraints rather than capital constraints. But whatever their origin, all these restrictions limit the maximum amount of investment that can be undertaken by the firm. For simplicity it is convenient to discuss the problems that can arise from such complex situations *as if* a capital constraint on the total amount of investment funds had been imposed. This approach avoids the necessity of discussing the difficult problems of labor management relations or of technology, which in reality are often the underlying causes of the need to ration capital.

A First Approximation

Consider the example of a firm faced with a variety of investment proposals and a *fixed investment budget*. Use these assumptions:

1. The timing and magnitude of the cash flows of all projects are known.
2. The cost of capital is known (independent of the investment decisions under consideration), so that the present values of all the projects are also given.
3. All projects are strictly independent; the implementation of one project does not affect the costs and benefits of some other project.
4. The total investment outlay of all those projects that have a positive NPV *exceeds* the firm's budget constraint.

Given these assumptions, the capital rationing problem is how to choose a subset of desirable projects such that the total investment outlay does not exceed the firm's fixed budget. A solution to this dilemma can be found by using the following procedure:

1. Rank all projects with positive NPVs by their profitability index—by the ratio of present value to initial investment outlay.
2. Select projects from the top of the list until the fixed budget is exhausted.

An Improved Approach

The approach to capital rationing above has one great advantage: The procedure is simple and easy to understand. However, it has one particularly glaring defect. The projects' NPVs are calculated in advance using a discount rate which, due to the budget constraint, does not necessarily reflect the opportunity cost of the capital invested.

This line of reasoning is illustrated in Figures 11–1a and 11–1b, which graph the projects confronting the firm. For simplicity, the projects are drawn in both diagrams as a continuous curve, in descending order of internal rates of return. Figure 11–1a assumes an unconstrained "perfect" capital market in which the firm can raise any amount of capital required at a cost of k_0; that is, there is no problem of capital rationing. The supply of funds is portrayed by the horizontal line drawn at the level of the cost of capital, k_0.

FIGURE 11–1
Firm's Demand and Supply of Capital

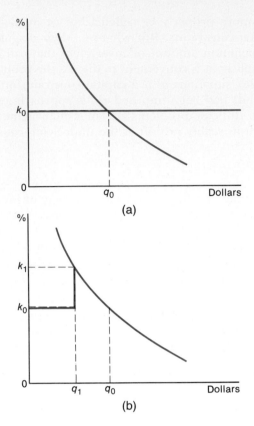

(a)

(b)

The firm implements all projects with a positive NPV (those with an IRR greater than k_0). The total initial outlay is denoted by $0q_0$. Figure 11–1b assumes that for some reason or other the firm is *constrained* to a total outlay of $0q_1$ dollars. Although the capital funds up to that amount are still made available at a cost of k_0, it is apparent from the diagram that the opportunity cost of the budget constraint is now k_1, which is considerably higher than k_0. If we add one dollar to the budget, the firm will earn k_1 and not k_0 on the additional investment. Hence the opportunity cost of funds, which we have defined in terms of foregone income, is measured by the IRR of the *marginal* project; that is, the last one which can be implemented without overshooting the fixed budget.

Given this insight, an improved method for selecting projects under capital rationing can be found:

STEP 1:   Calculate the projects' NPVs using the *market* cost of capital, k_0.

STEP 2:   Sum the investment outlays required to implement those projects which have positive NPVs, and compare this total outlay with the budget constraint.

STEP 3:   If the total outlay required exceeds the fixed budget, choose a higher discount rate and repeat steps 1 and 2.

STEP 4:   Proceed by trial and error until a discount rate is found such that the total outlay on those projects that still have positive NPVs does *not* exceed the budget constraint.

Even this approach to the rationing problem is a second-best solution. The optimal solution would be to remove the budget constraint and implement all the projects which have positive NPVs at the *market* cost of capital, k_0. In the long run additional personnel can be trained, top management can be recruited, or authority can be delegated, thereby removing the investment bottlenecks. But investment decisions have to be made *now*. It is of little solace to be told that somewhere over the rainbow lies a better world in which all the required human and capital resources are always available. For many firms, the most pressing problem is how to function within the existing constraints. Admittedly all such solutions are only second best, in the sense that the firm can always improve its situation by eliminating the constraint. But that takes time, and as you know by now, time is also a scarce resource.

APPLYING RISK ANALYSIS IN CAPITAL BUDGETING

In Chapter 8, we focused on the principles of risk measurement in an attempt to determine the fundamental properties of some of the better-known risk indexes and decision rules. With this theoretical background to build on, we turn now to the no less important problems that arise when risk analysis is applied in actual practice. We first consider that subset of firms which are able to apply the relatively sophisticated techniques of risk analysis *directly* to project cash flows.

Simulation Analysis

The various measures of risk and return which have been proposed share an important characteristic: All the indexes and decision rules require the prior assignment of a probability to each of the investment's possible outcomes. One straightforward way to handle this problem is to assign probabilities to different outcomes in terms of a project's net present value. These probabilities may be objective or subjective, or what is probably more often the case, some mixture of objective information regarding the possible outcomes with a large measure of subjective judgment.

In order to improve the process by which the probabilities are assigned, recall that a project's NPV is a sort of summary of the proposal's prospects which is based on forecasts of sales, market prices, costs, and so on. Once we recognize the underlying roots that determine the NPV the risk analysis becomes considerably more complex, because a probability distribution must be assigned to each of the relevant economic factors. For example, probabilities might be assigned to market size, selling price, market growth rate, and market share. Similarly, separate probability distributions can be built up for operating costs, fixed costs, expected duration, and size of investment outlay.

The probability distribution of the NPV, in turn, is derived from the distributions of the underlying real economic factors. Of course, the larger the number of factors considered, the more difficult it becomes to derive the NPV distribution. However, such an analysis of the basic factors that determine the project's NPV is necessary if the estimate of the project's chances of success or failure is to be improved.

Sensitivity Analysis

sensitivity analysis
A method of evaluating project risk that involves making the best estimate of a project's NPV and then checking the sensitivity of the NPV to errors in the estimation of revenues and costs.

Having clarified somewhat the underlying concepts of risk, we turn in this section to a practical way of handling project risk. Probably the most common method of evaluating uncertainty in practice is **sensitivity analysis.** In such an analysis, the firm makes its best estimate of the project's NPV, and then checks the sensitivity of the NPV to errors in the estimation of revenues and costs. For example, what happens to the NPV should the estimate of the annual revenues turn out too high, say by 5% or by 10%? If a small error proves critical, in the sense that the NPV becomes negative, the project is considered very risky. After all, small estimation errors are very likely to occur. On the other hand, suppose that for errors in the range of 1% to 15% the NPV remains positive. In this instance the NPV is relatively *insensitive* to errors in the estimate of future cash flows, and therefore, the project will be considered to have low risk. Even if one overestimates the revenue by as much as 14%, the project's NPV is still positive.

Sensitivity analysis can be illustrated by a numerical example. Consider a project with zero initial outlay (renting or leasing a machine) and the annual gross revenue and costs that are given in Table 11–1. Let us further assume that the proposal's economic duration is 10 years ($n = 10$) and that the cost of capital is 10% ($k = 10\%$). The firm's best estimate of the project's NPV is

$$\text{NPV}_0 = (DFA_{10\%,10})10 = (6.145)10 = \$61.5 \text{ million}$$

where DFA = the appropriate discount factor for a 10-year annuity and 10% discount rate.

TABLE 11–1   Best Estimate of Future Annual Cash Flows ($millions)

Gross revenue (R)	100
Costs:	
Labor(C_1)	10
Energy (C_2	60
Materials (C_3)	5
Other (C_4)	5
Total annual costs (ΣC_j)	80
Annual income (before tax)	20
Tax (at 50%)	10
Net annual after-tax income	10

The NPV for this project can be rewritten in a more general form as follows:

$$NPV_0 = (DFA_{10\%,10})(1 - T)R - (DFA_{10\%,10})(1 - T)C_1 - (DFA_{10\%,10})$$
$$(1 - T)C_2 - \ldots \text{ and so on}$$

where R denotes revenue, C denotes costs, and T is the corporate tax rate.

This approach allows the firm to examine the sensitivity of the NPV to changes in revenue or in each of the cost components. For example, suppose there is an error of $y\%$ in the estimate of the revenue (R), but there is no change in any of the other cost components. We obtain a new estimate of the project's net present value, NPVy, which is given by:

$$NPVy = NPV_0 + (DFA_{10\%,10})(1 - T)R_y$$

If y is greater than zero, the new estimate, NPVy, will be higher than the basic NPV_0. If y is less than zero, the opposite will hold and the new NPVy will be smaller than NPV_0. In a similar manner, the sensitivity of the project's profitability to errors in the estimates of each of the cost components can be examined.

Table 11–2 presents the results of the sensitivity analysis. The table gives the new NPV; that is, the NPV after a change of $y\%$ has been made in one of the components. For example, if revenue is reduced by 10%, the NPV drops from $61.5 million to $30.7 million. However, a 10% increase in energy costs (component C_2) decreases the NPV from $61.5 to $43 million.

An examination of the sensitivity matrix permits the firm to reach a number of conclusions relating to the project's riskiness:

1. Even if the gross revenue is overestimated by as much as 20%, the NPV is still positive.

TABLE 11–2   **Sensitivity Analysis of the NPV* of the Hypothetical Project ($millions)**

Estimation Error (y)	Revenue (R)	Labor Cost (C_1)	Energy Cost (C_2)	Material Cost (C_3)	Other Costs (C_4)
−50%	−92.2	76.8	153.6	69.2	69.1
−40%	−61.4	73.7	135.1	67.6	67.6
−30%	−30.7	70.7	116.8	66.1	66.1
−20%	0.0	67.6	98.3	64.5	64.5
−10%	30.7	64.5	79.9	63.0	63.0
0	**61.5**	**61.5**	**61.5**	**61.5**	**61.5**
+10%	92.9	58.4	43.0	59.9	59.9
+20%	122.9	55.3	24.6	58.4	58.4
+30%	153.6	52.2	6.2	56.8	56.8
+40%	184.4	49.2	−12.3	55.3	55.3
+50%	215.1	46.1	−30.7	53.8	53.8

* $NPV_0 = \sum_{t=1}^{10} \dfrac{10}{(1.1)^t} = \$61.5$ million

2. The price of energy may go up in the future, but as long as the price rise is 33% or less, the project remains profitable.

3. The project's desirability is not seriously affected by the other cost components.

Figure 11-2 summarizes the sensitivity of the project to changes in revenue *(R)* and in each of the cost components. From the diagram we can see that changes in each of the cost components, C_1, C_3, and C_4, have only a minor impact on NPV. (The lines corresponding to these cost items are relatively flat.) On the other hand, the lines for R and C_2 are relatively steep. The firm would be well advised to take greater pains when predicting these two items, because an error could mean serious losses.

The linear property of the sensitivity relationship has two principal advantages: (a) By extending the lines, the firm can consider estimation errors up to any level it considers relevant, without additional calculation; (b) errors in various components can be combined. For example, suppose that sales are overestimated by 10%. If the firm sells less, it also consumes about 10% less energy. A reduction of 10% in revenue decreases the NPV from $61.5 million to about $30 million (point *A* of Figure 11-2), but the parallel reduction in energy costs (C_1) increases the NPV from $61.5 million to about $80 million (point *B*). The net effect of the reduction in revenue, therefore, would be a decrease in the NPV of about $10 million. In this case, the project remains profitable; its NPV is still positive.

Electronic Spreadsheets   For illustration purposes, we have assumed simple relationships among the various items in the sensitivity analysis. For example, if revenue or a cost

FIGURE 11-2
Graphical Sensitivity Analysis of the NPV of the Hypothetical Project

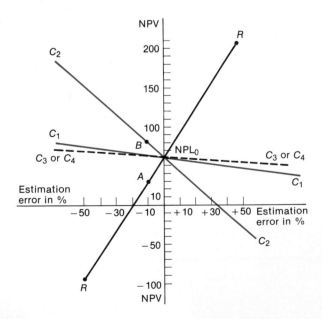

item changes in one year, it changes in all years—that is, all cash flows are of the equal-annual variety. The availability of microcomputers and finance-related software packages makes such simplification unnecessary. *Electronic spreadsheets* are offered by a wide variety of companies under different names and with somewhat different features.

If you try to conduct a more complex sensitivity analysis in the traditional way, it is useful to work with a large sheet of paper, a pencil, and a good eraser. You would divide the sheet up into, say, 10 columns, one for each year, or you could even divide the sheet into yearly columns for the next 20 years, or into 52 weekly columns (provided wide enough paper can be found). Across the top of this sheet you would write the appropriate headings for each column (1988, 1989, and so on). Each line would also be labeled—Revenue, Labor Costs, Energy Costs. Thus a matrix is created into which the estimates can be entered. The real work starts now: What happens to NPV if revenue remains stable for 2 years, and then is expected to rise by 10 percent per year after that? What happens if energy costs fall by 10% a year? Before the electronic age, the eraser would now come into use. The old figure would be taken out, the new figures would be entered, and the results recomputed. This can be quite tedious and quite difficult, especially if many changes need to be made simultaneously. And it is good management practice to consider and try as many realistic options as possible.

Electronic spreadsheets operate on the same principle; a matrix is created on the computer into which figures (and text) can be entered, and then altered; however, the results are now recomputed almost instantly, and without an effort on the user's part. In our example, its use permits easy simulation of a large variety of assumptions relating to revenues and costs. In particular, there is no longer any need to make the simplifying assumptions regarding the manner in which costs and revenues can change. And the revenue and cost items can be broken down into as many subdivisions as management deems desirable.

ADJUSTING THE DISCOUNT RATE FOR RISK

An alternative way to incorporate risk into the decision-making process is to include it in the discount rate for calculating the NPV. In this approach, each project is characterized by a *single* indicator of investment worth—that is, its *risk-adjusted* net present value. In this instance the project's NPV contains an *implicit* factor which reflects the project's risk. No attempt is made to express the risk of each proposal or portfolio of proposals explicitly.[1] The greater the risk, the higher the adjusted discount rate, and therefore the lower the project's risk-adjusted NPV. The difference between the risk-ad-

---

[1] The rule of thumb adjustment to the discount rate is conceptually equivalent to the more sophisticated techniques based on the discounting of certainty–equivalent cash flows. See Haim Levy and Marshall Sarnat, *Capital Investment and Financial Decisions,* 3rd Edition, Prentice Hall, Englewood Cliffs, N.J., 1986.

justed discount rate and the riskless interest rate is an index of the required *risk premium.*

Consider an investment proposal that requires an initial outlay of $100 and provides an equal probability of earning a net annual cash flow of $50, or $150, for 10 years. Its expected (mean) annual cash receipt is $100:

$$\frac{1}{2} \times \$50 + \frac{1}{2} \times \$150 = \$100$$

If we assume a 5% riskless rate of interest, the *unadjusted* NPV of this proposal is $672.20:

$$\$100 \ (7.722) - \$100 = \$772.20 - \$100 = \$672.20$$

where 7.722 is the appropriate discount factor for an annuity, assuming a 5% discount rate and a 10-year cash flow. However, since the future cash flow is *not* known with certainty, the firm requires an additional return, say of 5%, to compensate for the risk. Therefore it calculates the project's NPV using a 10% discount rate. In this case, the *risk-adjusted NPV* is only $514.50:

$$\$100 \ (6.145) - \$100 = \$614.50 - \$100 = \$514.50$$

Thus, even though the project's expected NPV is $672.20, the firm values the proposal, due to its risk, at only $514.50.

Now suppose we hold the average receipt constant at $100 but increase its variability. For example, suppose that for the same $100 initial outlay there is a second project which provides an equal probability of receiving an annual cash flow of either $200 or nothing for 10 years. Note that the expected (mean) annual cash flow of this project is also $100. But since the second project has a higher variance, we can assume that the required risk premium will also be larger—say, 15%. Hence the risk-adjusted discount rate will be 20% (5% riskless interest rate plus 15% risk premium). For this project, the risk-adjusted NPV is only $319.20:

$$\$100 \ (4.192) - \$100 = \$419.20 - \$100 = \$319.20$$

where 4.192 is the appropriate present value coefficient for a 20% discount rate and 10 year cash flow. Thus the higher the variance, the greater the discount rate, and hence the lower the risk-adjusted NPV. The critical problem, of course, is to decide by how much the discount rate should be increased. One way to do this is to apply the CAPM.

USING THE CAPM TO ADJUST THE DISCOUNT RATE

In Chapter 8, we introduced the capital asset pricing model (CAPM). This model analyzes the relationship between risk and return. Although the CAPM was developed with the security market in mind, it is applicable, in principle, to any asset. Under a set of restrictive assumptions regarding the behavior of investors and the efficiency of the capital market, the total risk of any security (or asset) is divided into two parts:

total risk = diversifiable risk + nondiversifiable risk

For assets traded under conditions that fulfill the CAPM restrictions, the diversifiable portion of an asset's risk can be eliminated by diversification. The nondiversifable component is that portion of the asset which remains even after combining it in a completely diversified portfolio. Beta (β) is the index of an asset's nondiversifiable risk—that portion of an asset's variance which gives rise to the risk premium in the CAPM framework.

Applying the CAPM, the required (expected) return on any asset is a linear function of its beta risk:

$$E_i = R_F + (E_m - R_F) \, \beta_i \tag{11.2}$$

where

E_i = the required (or expected) return on asset i

R_F = the riskless rate of interest

E_m = the required (or expected) return on the market in general

β_i = the appropriate beta risk coefficient of asset i

If you are willing to assume that the assets corporations invest in (new production equipment, marketing facilities, and computers) are also traded in perfectly efficient markets, under conditions which approximate the assumptions of the CAPM, Eq. 11.2 can be applied to corporate investment projects:

$$k_j = R_F + (E_m - R_F) \, \beta_j \tag{11.3}$$

where

k_j = the required (expected) return on project j

β_j = the appropriate beta risk coefficient for project j

The implications of the CAPM for capital budgeting are as follows: In a perfectly efficient capital market, combining the cash flows of investment projects does not necessarily create opportunities for risk diversification over and beyond what was previously possible for individual (and institutional) investors. In such a market, portfolio diversification and corporate risk diversification are perfect substitutes. The diversifiable portion of the corporate risk can be eliminated *indirectly* by the investors themselves when building their portfolios. Thus, given the assumptions of the CAPM, each project would be evaluated solely in terms of its own expected return and nondiversifiable risk. The appropriate discount rate is equal to the risk-free interest rate plus a premium that depends only on the *project's* beta risk.

Applying the CAPM directly to individual projects is, as we will see, difficult; but it does help explain some extreme cases that have plagued capital budgeting theory. For example, should a firm consider the possibility of investing in riskless bonds, the required rate of return is reduced to $k_j = R_F$; that is, to the interest rate itself. Because the covariance between the return on a riskless bond and the return on the market portfolio is zero, such an investment's beta is also zero. Equation 11.2 becomes:

$$k_j = R_F + (E_m - R_F) \times 0 = R_F$$

If, however, a project's beta is 1, the required rate of return is the same as the expected return on the market, E_m:

$$k_j = R_F + (E_m - R_F) \times 1 = E_m$$

Thus, the required rate of return on a project whose returns fluctuate exactly like the market as a whole is the same as the expected return on the market portfolio. Moreover, for projects whose returns fluctuate *inversely* with the market, the required rate of return may be *less* than the riskless interest rate, once their superior risk-reducing properties are recogized. In conclusion, the higher a project's nondiversifiable risk (beta), the higher the required rate of return (k_j). The remainder of the project's variance, which results from random fluctuations that are not systematically associated with the market, can be ignored.

As we noted in Chapter 8, Eq. 11.3 also defines a security market line (SML). Figure 11–3 portrays the SML, as defined by Eq. 11.3. All points along the SML shows combinations of risk and return that fulfill Eq. 11.3. All points above the SML have expected IRRs which are greater than that required by the CAPM: $\text{IRR}_j > k_j$. As a result, such projects have positive NPVs when k_j is the discount rate, and therefore should be accepted. Project A in Figure 11–3 is an example. Given its beta risk, the project's expected IRR is greater than the required return implied by the SML. Conversely, all points that lie below the SML have expected IRRs that are lower than k_j. Hence such projects have negative NPVs and should be rejected. Project R in Figure 11–3 is an example. Given its beta risk, the SML implies a required rate of return greater than IRR_R.

The logic of the CAPM is very appealing. Consider the case of an oil company that must evaluate risky oil drilling projects, the investment in new marketing facilities, such as tankers or pipe lines, as well as the replacement of existing refinery facilities as they wear out. Although all the projects are to be implemented by the same firm, they differ significantly in risk. It follows that they should be evaluated using discount rates which reflect the

FIGURE 11-3
Applying the SML in Capital Budgeting

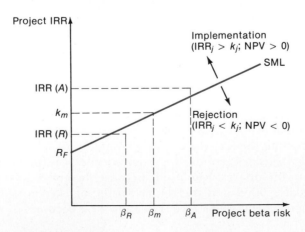

differential risk of the projects in question. One way out of this dilemma is to apply the CAPM directly to the individual projects themselves.

Unfortunately, the CAPM's assumptions simply do not hold for most corporate assets:

1. Many corporate assets are not traded in perfectly efficient competitive markets, or for that matter, even on organized exchanges.
2. It is unlikely that investors in these assets have reasonably complete information on all the relevant aspects affecting expected returns and risks.
3. Corporations usually cannot borrow money, within the relevant range, without affecting the interest rate.
4. Finally, estimating the market return from a portfolio of corporate assets seems a heroic task indeed.

As a result, estimating the risk-adjusted discount rate for individual projects is a tricky business. In fact, one empirical study reported that only 2% of the firms surveyed used the CAPM to estimate the discount rate.[2] In actual practice, almost all firms tend to use a discount rate that reflects the firm's average risk (see Chapter 15), plus a rule of thumb adjustment where necessary.

SUMMARY

This chapter deals with the practical application of the NPV model and risk analysis.

In equipment replacement problems, the cash flows of alternative strategies must be considered over equal time periods. However, bringing all the cash flows to a common horizon can be cumbersome. To get around this problem, replacement can be analyzed using the *uniform annuity series* (UAS). The UAS is defined as the equivalent annuity whose NPV equals that of the replacement policy in question:

$$\text{UAS} = \frac{\text{NPV}}{(DFA_{k,n})}$$

The *optimal replacement policy* is the one which results in the highest UAS.

Two alternative methods are presented for calculating net present values under inflationary conditions: (a) *Real analysis:* Here the nominal cash flows are first reduced to *real* terms and the NPV is calculated using the real discount rate—the firm's minimum required rate of return in terms of constant purchasing power. (b) *Nominal analysis:* The same NPV can be reached

[2] See M. E. Blume, I. Friend, and R. Westerfield, *Impediments to Capital Formation* (Philadelphia: The Wharton School, Rodney L. White Center, December 1980).

using nominal cash flows and a discount rate that reflects the firm's minimum required rate of return in nominal terms. Project analysis can be carried out using either the nominal or the real approach. And as long as the inflation adjustment of the cash flows and discount rate is consistent, the two approaches are equivalent.

Capital rationing deals with capital budgeting decisions that have to be made subject to a constraint on the total amount of funds available for investment. Two approaches to this problem are these:

1. All projects which have positive NPVs are ranked by the ratio of their present values to the required investment outlay. Projects are then selected in descending order of profitability until the fixed budget is exhausted.

2. The discount rate is raised until the total investment outlay on projects that have positive NPVs (using the higher discount rate) no longer exceeds the fixed budget constraint.

Simulation is a method for improving the estimate of the probability distribution of a project's NPV by examining the distributions of the underlying economic factors.

Many firms try to resolve some of the riskiness of projects by determining the sensitivity of the project's NPV to changes in the major components of the cash flow. Sensitivity analysis allows the firm to concentrate on those components which can potentially have a major impact on its decision to implement or reject the proposal.

Electronic spreadsheets are a very useful tool for analyzing the impact of alternative assumptions on a project's NPV. Using a spreadsheet permits the simulation of a large variety of assumptions regarding project revenues and costs. There is no need for simplifying assumptions, and the analysis can be as detailed as management deems necessary.

Many firms still prefer the adjustment of the discount rate to the more sophisticated method of directly estimating the probability distributions of individual projects. One such indirect method of adjusting NPV calculations for risk is raising the discount rate.

The CAPM can also be used in capital budgeting. In this approach a project's discount rate is a function of its beta risk:

$$k_j = R_F + (E_m - R_F) \text{ beta}$$

where

k_j = the discount rate of project j

R_F = the riskless interest rate

E_m = the return on the market

Although the logic of the CAPM is very appealing, serious reservations exist in relation to its suitability for capital budgeting. Unfortunately, the CAPM's underlying assumptions do not always hold for corporate assets. (We return to this important question in Chapter 15.)

REVIEW EXERCISE

Circle the correct word(s) below to complete the sentences; see p. 283 for the correct answers.

11.1 In replacement problems the cash flows of alternative policies over *the lifetime/equal time periods* must be considered.

11.2 The uniform annuity series (UAS) is defined as the annuity whose present value equals the *net present value/replacement value* of the alternative in question.

11.3 The UAS is appropriate if, and only if, the relevant alternatives can be *undertaken once/repeated*.

11.4 Under neutral inflation all costs increase at *the same rate/an accelerated rate*.

11.5 Shifting from the real analysis to the nominal analysis of cash flows *does/does not* necessarily affect the investment decision.

11.6 The capital rationing problem is *always/not always* due to restrictions on the supply of capital.

11.7 If the NPV of a project remains positive, even for large errors in the assumptions, the NPV is said to be *sensitive/insensitive* to errors in the assumptions.

11.8 A firm *should/need not* invest much time and money to forecast those factors to which the result is insensitive.

11.9 Electronic spreadsheets permit the *neglect/simulation* of a large variety of assumptions relating to costs and revenues.

11.10 Risk *can/cannot* be included in the decision-making process by incorporating it in the discount rate.

11.11 The smaller the risk, the *higher/lower* will be the adjusted discount rate, and therefore the *higher/lower* will be the project's risk-adjusted NPV.

11.12 According to the CAPM, part of the contribution of a project to the firm's variance *can/cannot* be ignored.

11.13 For projects whose returns fluctuate inversely with the market, the required rate of return may be *more/less* than the riskless interest rate.

11.14 The CAPM assumptions *do/do not* hold for many corporate assets.

QUESTIONS

11.1 Define the following terms:
- **a.** Uniform annuity series (UAS)
- **b.** Neutral inflation
- **c.** Capital rationing
- **d.** Sensitivity analysis
- **e.** Sensitive/insensitive (robust)
- **f.** Electronic spreadsheet

11.2 Explain why the UAS method and the method of repeating project cash flows until they have the same economic life give equivalent results.

11.3 "In countries with very low inflation, for example Switzerland, real cash flows are approximately equal to nominal cash flows." Do you agree? Explain.

11.4 Under what conditions can the real analysis method and the nominal analysis method of handling inflation lead to different investment decisions?

11.5 "We have more than enough capital; therefore the capital rationing problem is not relevant for us." Do you agree with this statement?

11.6 Enumerate and describe the steps that can be used to select projects when the size of the capital budget is limited.

11.7 Under what circumstances can a project's required rate of return (discount rate) be less than the riskless rate of interest?

11.8 Set up the income statement of a fictitious company. To which items do you expect the net after-tax income will be sensitive? To which will it not be sensitive?

11.9 Derive the formula which shows how changes in the items of the income statement of the previous question's fictitious company are translated into changes in the net after-tax income.

11.10 (Only if you have an electronic spreadsheet) Set up the template for the fictitious company's income statement and perform a sensitivity analysis.

11.11 Give examples of income statement items whose relationship to net income is nonlinear.

11.12 When is it appropriate to adjust the discount rate for risk using the CAPM? How does this method differ from other methods of adjusting the discount rate for risk?

11.13 Jack Forster is thinking of putting up money for his first investment project. Why might it be inappropriate for him to use the CAPM to adjust the discount rate for the risk of alternative proposals?

PROBLEMS

11.1   Equipment replacement.   The Pelem Lock Company is using a new lathe which costs $120,000, has a 6-year life, and generates a net annual cash inflow of $42,000. The firm is faced with the alternative of using the lathe for the next 6 years, or selling it before the 6 years are up and replacing it with a new lathe. The company's financial vice-president asks you to determine the optimal replacement period. You are given the following information regarding the market value of the lathe:

End of Year	Market Value of Old Lathe
1	$100,000
2	85,000
3	75,000
4	60,000
5	32,000
6	6,000

Assume a 6% cost of capital, and answer the following questions (ignoring corporate taxes):

a. What is the optimal replacement policy for the firm?

b. How would your answer to part (a) change if the lathe generated a net annual cash inflow of $60,000?

c. What would your advice be to the finance manager if the lathe generated a net annual cash inflow of $24,000

11.2 **Equipment replacement.** The United Cooling Company is using a machine with a life expectancy of 5 years. The company is considering its replacement, and for this purpose has gathered the following data:
The purchase price of a new machine is $97,000. The market price of the machine and the operating expenses, at time t, are estimated as follows:

Year	Market Value at End of Year	Operating Expenses
1	$70,000	$16,000
2	60,000	20,000
3	50,000	27,000
4	35,000	36,000
5	5,000	42,000

Note: The price for the last year is the salvage value. The operating expenses are calculated gross of depreciation and interest. Assume that technological changes are not expected and therefore operating expenses and equipment prices will remain constant over time. Assume also that the cost of capital is 15%, and that there are no taxes.

a. On the assumption that the company considers only the possibility of purchasing new equipment, what is the optimal replacement policy?

b. What is your answer to part (a) if there is no possibility of selling used equipment?

c. (Optional) On the assumption that the company also considers the possibility of buying used equipment, what is the optimal replacement policy? (Assume there are no commissions on buying and selling, and therefore the buying price is equal to the selling price of used equipment.)

11.3 **Inflation.** Mr. Brockaw wants to know the real interest rate he paid during the last year on a $6,000 loan he took from the bank on January 1. At that time, the Consumer Price Index (CPI) stood at 176. On December 31 of the same year the CPI was 193, and the loan repayment of $9,500 fell due.

a. What was the nominal interest on the loan for the year?

b. What was the inflation rate during the year?

c. What was the real interest rate on the loan?

11.4 **Inflation.** The Consolidated Chain is considering a 5-year loan of $100,000 from a local bank. Interest payments are $10,000 after the first year, $12,000 after the second and third years, $11,000 after the fourth year, and $20,000 after the fifth year. At the end of the fifth year the principal must also be repaid. The annual rate of inflation is expected to be 3% for the first 3 years and 5% thereafter.

a. From the bank's standpoint, what is the nominal interest rate on the loan?

b. What is the real value of the interest payments each year?

c. What is the real interest rate on the loan? (*Hint:* Recall that the interest rate was defined in Chapter 6 as the IRR of the loan's cash flow.)

d. Do your answers to parts (a) and (c) change if we adopt the viewpoint of the borrower rather than the bank? Explain.

11.5 **Capital rationing.** The Marathon Corporation is faced with the following investment opportunities:

Project	Investment	Net Cash flow			
		Year 1	Year 2	Year 3	Year 4
A	15,000	6,000	4,000	3,000	8,000
B	18,000	3,000	10,000	4,000	5,000
C	9,000	5,000	0	0	8,000
D	11,000	0	8,000	1,000	4,000
E	14,000	13,000	0	0	6,000
F	10,000	3,000	3,000	4,000	4,000

Assume that all projects have similar risk, and that there are no other possibilities to invest. The market cost of capital is 5%.

a. If Marathon has $35,000 available for investment, which projects should be chosen?

b. If Marathon has $45,000 available for investment, which projects should be chosen?

c. If Marathon has $55,000 available for investment, which projects should be chosen?

d. If Marathon has $65,000 available for investment, which projects should be chosen?

11.6 **Sensitivity analysis.** John Elton is considering opening a boutique to sell extravagant clothing. The initial investment outlay is $40,000, which can be depreciated over 4 years on a straight-line basis. Sales are estimated at $150,000 each year, the cost of goods sold is 60% of sales, and variable administration and overhead expenses amount to 20% of sales. The corporate tax rate is 34%. After 3 years John Elton would be able to sell his assets for 25% of the initial investment. The appropriate discount rate is 6%.

a. Should John Elton invest in this venture?

b. How does your answer change if the cost of goods sold rises to 70%?

c. How does your answer change if administration and overhead rises to 30%?

d. How does your answer change if the corporate tax rate is raised to 44%?

e. How does your answer change if resale value of his assets rises to 35% of the initial investment? (Capital gains are taxed at the 34% rate.)

f. How does your answer change if the discount rate rises to 8%?

g. To which factors is the NPV of this venture sensitive? To which items is it insensitive?

11.7 **Computer problem.** Set up a template for the previous problem, and examine the sensitivity of the result to *simultaneous changes* in more than one variable.

11.8 **Risk adjustment.** The Melkor Tool Company is examining the following project: The initial outlay is $400,000 and the net annual cash flow for the next 10 years is $60,000, with a probability of ⅔, and $150,000, with a probability of ⅓. Assume a 7% riskless interest rate. What is the risk premium (in terms of the discount rate) required by the firm, if you know that the project has a risk-adjusted NPV of $35,000?

11.9 Risk adjustment, CAPM. The Hartford Conglomerate has widely diversified business interests, and their assets reflect this fact. Michelle Stratford, the financial vice-president, has the task of reviewing the following economically independent investment projects. She is asked to give an opinion, by tomorrow morning, as to which projects should be accepted. She decides to use the CAPM. The riskless rate of interest is 4%, and the expected return on the market is 9%.

Project	Beta Risk	Initial Investment	Net Cash flow in Year			Residual Value at End of year 3
			1	2	3	
A	0.5	$17,000	$ 6,000	8,000	$6,000	$2,000
B	1.5	15,000	6,000	8,000	6,000	2,000
C	2.2	33,000	13,000	19,000	9,000	7,000
D	0.8	9,000	3,000	4,000	6,000	2,000
E	1.0	12,000	5,000	5,000	0	5,000

a. Write a report to the president giving your evaluation.
b. Is the use of the CAPM approach appropriate in this instance? Explain.

11.10 Equipment replacement, computer problem. Mary Crown drives a cab in the city. She is trying to determine the optimal replacement period for her cab. The car she is considering costs $8,650 (this new car price is assumed to stay constant over the years). The following table shows the net income per year (after all expenses) that she expects to earn with a cab which is n years old. Assume that all income is received on the last day of the year. The table also shows the resale value of the cab at the end of each year. The cost of capital is 7.675% (assume a world without taxes).

Year	Net Cash Flow	Resale value
1	28,650	$6,995
2	27,120	5,420
3	25,980	4,570
4	24,070	3,770
5	21,990	3,215
6	19,720	2,425
7	17,530	1,660
8	16,990	870
9	16,240	15

What is the optimal replacement period?

SAMPLE PROBLEMS

SP11.1 At the beginning of 1987, "Ye Olde Printe Shoppe" is evaluating the introduction of a modern laser printer which costs $11,000 and has an economic life of 3 years. The market price for used printers and the net cash receipts, at the end of each year, are as follows:

	Market Price	Net Receipts
1987	$7,000	$6,000
1988	3,000	5,000
1989	0	4,000

Assuming a discount rate of 10%, what is the optimal replacement period? (Note that the firm does not consider buying a used printer.)

SP11.2

a. You are paying 12% interest on a 1-year loan. You expect inflation to be 4% during that year. What is the nominal rate of interest? What is the real rate of interest?

b. At the end of the year the Consumer Price Index (CPI) stands at 147 (at the beginning of the year it was 150). How do your answers change?

Solutions to Sample Problems

SP11.1 The net present value of a printer which is sold after n years is computed as:

$$NPV_n = -\text{ investment } + \text{ PV of net receipts } + \text{ PV of printer when sold}$$

If the printer is sold after 1 year, we get

$$NPV_1 = -11,000 + 6,000/1.1 + 7,000/1.1 = -11,000 + 5,454.54 + 6,363.63 \qquad = 818.18$$

Similarly, we compute the NPV assuming the sale of the printer after 2 years:

$$NPV_2 = -11,000 + 6,000/1.1 + 5,000/(1.1)^2 + 3,000/(1.1)^2$$
$$= -11,000 + 5,454.54 + 4,132.23 + 2,479.34 \qquad = 1,066.11$$

If the printer is sold after 3 years, we get:

$$NPV_3 = -11,000 + 6,000/1.1 + 5,000/(1.1)^2 + 4,000/(1.1)^3 + 0$$
$$= -11,000 + 5,454.54 + 4,132.23 + 3,005.26 \qquad = 1,592.03$$

However, the "Shoppe" does not just sell the printer after n years, since it wants to stay in business, the printer must also be replaced every n years. Hence, the alternatives must be reduced to a "common denominator." As the text explains, the UAS method does just that. The annuities (UAS) which are equal to the net present values of the three replacement options ($n = 1, 2,$ or 3) are as follows:

For replacement after 1 year:

$$\text{UAS} \times (.909) = 818.18$$
$$\text{UAS} = 818.18/.909 \qquad\qquad = 900.09$$

For replacement after 2 years:

$$\text{UAS} \times (1.736) = 1{,}066.11$$
$$\text{UAS} = 1{,}006.11/1.736 \qquad\qquad = 614.12$$

For 3-year replacement:

$$\text{UAS} \times (2{,}487) = 1{,}592.03$$
$$\text{UAS} = 1{,}592.03/2.487 \qquad\qquad = 614.12$$

The UAS for $n = 1$ year has the highest value, and therefore the machine should be replaced every year.

SP11.2 a. Since the nominal interest rate is 12% and the inflation rate is 4%, the real interest rate is computed as follows:

$$\text{real interest rate} = \frac{1 + \text{nominal rate}}{1 + \text{inflation rate}} - 1$$

$$= \frac{1 + 0.12}{1 + 0.04} - 1 = 7.69\%$$

b. Inflation is usually defined in terms of the percentage change in the consumer price index (CPI). In this case, the CPI decreased by 2%:

$$\text{inflation rate} = \frac{\text{CPI at year end}}{\text{CPI at the beginning of the year}} - 1 = \frac{147}{150} - 1 = -2\%$$

In this case the real interest rate is computed as follows:

$$\text{real interest rate} = \frac{1 + \text{nominal rate}}{1 + \text{inflation rate}} - 1$$

$$= \frac{1 + 0.12}{1 - 0.02} - 1 = 14.29\%$$

Answers to Review Exercise

11.1 equal time periods **11.2** net present value **11.3** repeated
11.4 the same rate **11.5** does not **11.6** not always **11.7** insensitive
11.8 need not **11.9** simulation **11.10** can **11.11** lower, higher
11.12 can **11.13** less **11.14** do not

SUGGESTIONS FOR FURTHER READING

Equipment replacement and capital rationing are discussed in greater detail in the Bierman and Smidt and Levy and Sarnat texts cited in Chapter 9.

An interesting analysis of the impact of inflation on corporate financial management can be found in Part IV of Edward I. Altman and Marti G. Subrahmanyam (eds.), *Recent Advances in Corporate Finance* (Homewood, IL: Irwin, 1985).

The theoretical foundations of applying the CAPM to capital budgeting are examined by Mark E. Rubinstein,

"A Mean-Variance Synthesis of Corporate Financial Theory," *Journal of Finance*, March 1973.

Risk-adjusted discount rates are discussed in much greater detail by A. A. Robichek and Stewart C. Myers, "Conceptual Problems in the Use of Risk-Adjusted Discount Rates," *Journal of Finance*, December 1966; and Eugene F. Fama, "Risk-Adjusted Discount Rates and Capital Budgeting under Uncertainty," *Journal of Financial Economics*, August 1977.

12

Common Stock and Investment Banking

E nterprising archeologists have uncovered the existence of trading associations among merchants , sanctioned by the sovereign, in the Assyrian Empire almost two thousand years before the Common era. In ancient Rome, "shares" in mines, in ships, and in so-called caravan companies were not only issued, but perhaps were traded on rudimentary exchanges. But if we seek to find the more immediate roots of today's profit-seeking corporations, it is to the sixteenth-century English joint stock companies that we usually turn. This type of association, under royal charter, was used to develop international trade; the best-known example was the giant East India Company. From the standpoint of financial management, the most significant aspect of the joint stock company, and of the modern ccorporation which evolved from it, is the fact that this type of organization is a separate legal entity. As a result, a careful line must always be drawn between the corporation's assets and liabilities, and the rights and obligations of the individuals (shareholders, bondholders) who have claims against those assets. This chapter is devoted to the main features of common stock and how it is issued; bonds and preferred stock are the subject of Chapter 13.

DEFINITION OF CAPITAL STOCK

A firm's capital stock is the *evidence of ownership;* hence, the fortunate holder of 2% of General Motors common stock is the owner of 2% of GM's net assets (total assets *less* the claims of debtholders). For convenience, the capital contributed to the corporation is divided into unit amounts, called *shares* of common stock.

Table 12–1 shows the stockholder's equity section of the Lester Cor-

TABLE 12–1   The Lester Corporation Stockholders' Equity Account, as of December 31, 1987 ($000)

Common stock* (Par value $1)	9,244
Additional paid-in capital	19,886
Total paid-in capital	29,130
Retained earnings	145,025
Total equity (net worth)	174,155

*Authorized capital is 30 million shares.

authorized share capital
The maximum number of shares a corporation is allowed to issue.

issued capital
Shares of stock outstanding.

par value
The nominal value of a stock, bond, etc., fixed at the time of its issue.

total paid-in capital
The sum of the par value of all outstanding shares and the additional paid-in capital from the sale of shares at prices above par.

poration's 1987 balance sheet. In 1986, Lester's shareholders voted to increase the number of shares which could be issued to 30 million. Thirty million dollars represents the **authorized share capital**—that is, the maximum number of shares that can be issued. In terms of the 1987 balance sheet, this means that Lester could issue an additional 20,756,000 shares. But if circumstances should call for the issue of additional stock beyond that amount, the shareholders can always vote to increase the firm's authorized capital.

As of the end of 1987, Lester had actually issued only 9,244,000 shares. These shares constitute **issued capital**, or shares *outstanding*. Each share has a **par value** of $1, which sets the legal limit of a shareholder's liability for the corporation's debts. However, there is no legal obligation to establish a par value for stock, and many cases of no par value shares can be found. In the unlikely event that the firm should sell shares *below* par value, any purchaser would be personally liable for the difference between the issue price and the par value in the case of bankruptcy. Since common stock is almost invariably sold at a price that exceeds its par value, this consideration has no economic significance.

Lester is no exception. Over the years, shares were sold at prices above par, and as a result, *additional paid-in-capital* of $19,886,000, which represents the premium of issue price over par value, appears in Table 12–1. Thus, **total paid-in-capital** at the end of 1987 was $29,130,000 ($9,244,000 of par value *plus* $19,886,000 of additional paid-in-capital).

To clarify our understanding of these differences, let's assume that Lester decides to sell an additional 100,000 shares at a price of $25 per share. The authorized share capital clearly permits such an issue, and if it is successful, the following entries will appear in the equity account:

1. Common stock is increased by $100,000 (100,000 shares times $1 of par value);
2. The additional paid-in capital account is increased by $2,400,000 ($2,500,000 minus $100,000).

Since Lester normally pays out only part of its earnings as dividends, the equity account of Table 12–1 also reflects the cumulative amount of

retained earnings
That part of a corporation's net profits which is reinvested in the business rather than being paid out as dividends.

retained earnings—in this instance, $145,025,000. Retained earnings are credited to stockholders' equity because the common shareholders are the residual owners of the corporation, and therefore have a legal claim to its net profits. At the end of 1987, total shareholders' equity was $174,155,000. This is also equal to the firm's net assets (total assets minus liabilities). Since Lester had 9,244,000 shares outstanding, *book value* per share was $18.84.

$$\text{book value per share} = \frac{\text{total stockholders' equity}}{\text{shares outstanding}}$$

$$= \frac{\$174,155,000}{9,244,000} = \$18.84$$

Treasury Stock

Now assume that, for one reason or another, Lester decides to repurchase some of its own stock in the open market. Specifically, 50,000 shares are purchased at an average market price of $22. In this instance stockholders' equity would be reduced by $1,100,000 ($22 × 50,000 = $1,100,000). A *negative* entry, **treasury stock** *at cost*, is entered at the bottom of the account. As a result, total shareholders' equity is reduced to $173,055,000 ($174,155,000 *minus* $1,100,000 = $173,055,000). These changes are summarized in Table 12–2, which shows the company's equity account after the repurchase of the shares.

treasury stock
Shares that have been repurchased and retired by the firm.

Other Types of Stock

Lester has also authorized 400,000 shares of preferred stock, none of which have been issued. As we will see in the next chapter, preferred stock is a hybrid security combining features of both debt and equity. However, depending on the circumstances, a firm may also issue more than one type of common stock. The different types are usually designated as Class A, Class B, and so on. The use of different types of common stock permits the corporation to vary one or more of the shares' characteristics. For example, Class A might have full voting rights, while other classes have diminished voting power, or no vote at all. One example of this type of "discrimination" can be found in new firms that issue *founders' shares* to the firm's promoters.

TABLE 12–2   The Lester Corporation Stockholders' Equity Account after Repurchase ($000)

Common stock* (Par value $1)	9,244
Additional paid-in capital	19,886
Retained earnings	145,025
	174,155
Less: Treasury stock at cost†	1,100
Total equity (net worth)	173,055

* Authorized capital is 30 million shares.
† 50,000 shares at $22 per share.

These shares are often given exclusive voting rights for a specified number of years. A special class of stock with diminished rights to dividends might also be created.

STOCKHOLDERS' RIGHTS

If we ignore exceptional cases and the special prescriptions of various state laws, the rights of the stockholders of American corporations can be grouped into three categories: management, property, and fundamental contract changes.

Rights to Management   The stockholders have a fundamental right to elect the corporation's directors, and it is through the elected board of directors that the owners manage the business. Although the managers of small corporations frequently own most of the firm's shares, the holdings of managers of large publicly owned corporations are usually small relative to those of the nonmanagerial shareholders. In addition to the right to elect the corporation's directors, the stockholders also have the right to inspect the firm's books, and to approve certain extraordinary transactions such as the sale of important properties.

In recent years attention has been focused on the problem of corporate control. "Proxy fights," in which a group of interested parties, or a single investor, solicit the voting rights of shareholders, appear regularly in newspaper headlines. The transfer of a shareholder's voting rights to another party is called a **proxy**, and typically management has little trouble in obtaining such proxies from a majority of its stockholders. However, when stockholders are dissatisfied with management's performance, or during a *takeover bid* (see Chapter 21) in which an outside group tries to gain control of the firm, vigorous and sometimes successful bids have been made by outside groups to solicit proxies.

proxy
The transfer of a shareholder's voting rights to another party.

Since corporate elections can be crucial, it is worth noting that two principal methods, majority voting and cumulative voting, can be used to elect a firm's directors.

majority voting
A method of electing a firm's directors in which each director is elected separately, each shareholder casting one vote for each share owned.

Majority Voting.   Under the **majority voting** system, each director is elected separately, and the shareholders cast one vote for each share owned. As a result, the shareholders who control a majority of the outstanding stock can elect *all* the corporation's directors. The minority shareholders cannot elect any directors, and therefore they are not represented on the board. Assume, for example, that a corporation which uses majority voting is electing five members to the board, and there are 1 million shares outstanding. If management controls more than 50 percent of the voting rights, for example, 51 percent, it can vote the 510,000 shares for each of the five preferred candidates (A, B, C, D, and E). The minority shareholders can cast at most only 490,000 votes for each of their candidates (say, G, H, I, J, and K). Each of management's candidates receives 510,000 votes; each minority candidate receives 490,000 votes. Thus, the entire management slate—A, B, C, D, and E—is elected.

cumulative voting
A joint method of electing directors in which shareholders can cast all their votes for a single candidate or divide them among a number of candidates.

Cumulative Voting.   In firms whose charters stipulate **cumulative voting,** the directors are elected jointly. Individual shareholders can cast all of their votes (number of shares owned *times* number of directors to be elected) for a single candidate, or divide their votes among a number of candidates. Cumulative voting makes it possible for minority interests to obtain representation on the board. This can be seen from the cumulative voting formula:

$$NR = \frac{D \times S}{B + 1}$$

where

NR = number of shares required to elect a desired number of directors. (If NR is a fraction, round up; if not, add 1.)

D = number of directors you seek to elect

S = total number of voting shares outstanding

B = total number of directors to be elected to the board

Now assume that 10 positions are open on the board, and there are 100,000 shares outstanding. If a group of investors wants to be sure of electing two directors, how many shares must they control? Applying the formula, we find that 18,182 shares are required to ensure the election of two directors:

$$NR = \frac{2 \times 100,000}{11} = 18,182$$

By splitting *all* of its cumulative votes between two candidates, the group can ensure a 20% representation on the board. Of course, if the group is ready to take a chance, it might attempt to stretch its votes and divide them among a larger number of candidates. But if the group wants to be certain of the result, the formula should be followed. Under the majority voting system, the group would be unable to elect even one representative, so long as a competing group controls a majority of the voting shares.

Rights to Property   Although most stockholders view their investment in common stock as a source of potential capital gain, their holdings are also a source of current income. However, once control has been delegated to the directors, the stockholders have a right to receive their share of the profits *only* if the board declares a dividend. Despite this, all the profits, including retained earnings, "belong" to the stockholders. If and when they are distributed, the dividends *must* go to the stockholders. Moreover, should the firm wind up its affairs, be sold, or merge with another firm, each stockholder has the right to receive his or her proportionate share of the corporate property.

Right to Approve Major Changes

In addition to the right to manage the corporation, to receive dividends (when declared), and to receive a proportionate share of the property of the corporation when it is sold, the stockholders also have the right to approve any changes in the corporation's charter and bylaws. Thus, the stockholders have the right to prevent the use of corporate resources for purposes other than those stipulated in its charter. In addition, the stockholders must be consulted whenever the corporation wishes to issue additional shares.

The Preemptive Right

Subject to restrictions by state statutes or the provisions of the corporate charter, the stockholders have the *preemptive right* to purchase, if they wish, any new stock issued by the firm. But despite the fundamental importance of this right, many states allow a majority of shareholders to annul the preemptive right.

The preemptive right is often of considerable value. First, it ensures that the existing stockholders will not automatically lose control of the corporation when a new issue takes place. The right to subscribe to any new issue allows the existing shareholders to preserve their proportionate share in the control of the firm. The preemptive right also protects stockholders from any dilution of value. Consider a case in which, for one reason or another, the directors decide to issue additional stock at a price *below* the market value of the corporation's net assets. Despite this, each new share has an *equal* claim to dividends and the residual value of the corporate assets. In such circumstances, the preemptive right to purchase the underpriced shares is essential if existing stockholders are to be insured against loss.

Consider the case of the Catalina Corporation, which has 100,000 shares outstanding, with a market price of $10. The market value of the firm is $1 million (100,000 shares *times* $10 equals $1 million). Now assume that the firm issues an additional 20,000 shares, which are sold for $5 each. Following the sale, the market value of the firm is $1,100,000 but the price of each share is $9.17. (Dividing the market value by the total number of new and old shares outstanding we have: $1,100,000/120,000 = $9.17). The new shareholders have made a windfall gain; the shares that cost them only $5 each are worth $9.17 immediately after the issue. But their *gain* is the old shareholders' *loss!* The old shareholders suffer a loss of 83 cents per share due to the fall in price following the new issue ($10.00 *minus* $9.17 = 83 cents). The preemptive right is designed to prevent such abuses.

ISSUING COMMON STOCK

A corporation can raise additional equity capital in a number of ways. There are three basic alternatives: (a) private placement, (b) public issue, and (c) privileged subscription.

Private Placement

private placement
A new issue of common stock in which the entire issue, or a substantial part, is taken up by a single investor or limited number of investors.

In a **private placement,** the entire, or a substantial part, of the new issue is taken up by a single, or limited number, of investors. Private placements of securities are usually made to large institutional investors such as pension funds and insurance companies. Typically, these investors acquire the securities as a long-term investment—that is, *not* for early resale. The principal advantage of the private placement lies in the fact that it permits the issuing firm to avoid the costly process of filing a registration statement with the Securities and Exchange Commission (SEC). But to prevent abuse, the SEC restricts the resale of privately placed securities. Sale of the stock within 2 years of acquisition is usually interpreted by the SEC as evidence that the original issue was not a private placement. Since resale is often a prime consideration for the investor in common stock, private placements are more frequently used for bonds. Here large institutional investors are often willing to give up liquidity, if other favorable terms can be obtained (see Chapter 13).

Public Issue

going public
A corporation's first public issue of common stock.

The alternative to a private placement is a public issue or a privileged subscription. In a *public issue*, the shares are offered for sale to the general public in what is also called a *general cash offer*. If this is the firm's first public issue, we speak of the corporation **going public**.

Privileged Subscription

rights offering
A privileged subscription in which stockholders are permitted to subscribe to their pro rata share of a new issue or sell it on the open market.

Although many corporate charters grant their stockholders the preemptive right to subscribe to all new security offerings, in practice the preemptive right is usually limited to new issues of common stock, convertibles, and voting preferred shares; new debt issues are excluded. Similarly, the preemptive right does not apply to issues of stock made in conjunction with a merger, or to stock issued to employees as part of a compensation plan; nor does it apply to the reissue of treasury stock.

If the shareholders have the preemptive privilege to subscribe to the new shares, the firm must first offer them directly to its existing shareholders. In such a *privileged subscription*, the stockholders are given the prior opportunity to subscribe to their pro rata share of the new issue. In many instances these prior rights are transferable; in such cases, we speak of a **rights offering**. In a rights offering, each shareholder is permitted to subscribe to a certain number of new shares. The terms of the offer are printed on a certificate called a *right*, and each shareholder receives one "right" for every share currently held. A rights offering differs from an ordinary privileged subscription in that these "rights" are transferable and therefore can be sold by the shareholders on the open market. (The economic logic underlying a rights offering is discussed in detail in Appendix 12A.)

APPROVAL BY THE BOARD OF DIRECTORS

The first step in the rather complicated process of raising new equity is to obtain formal approval for the new issue from the board of directors. As we have already noted, unless sufficient authorized capital exists, an extraordinary meeting of the firm's stockholders may also be required to approve the necessary increase in authorized capital. To ensure greater flexibility, many firms make it a habit always to keep on hand a large unused "reserve" of authorized (but as yet not issued) capital.

SECURITIES REGULATION

Securities and Exchange Commission (SEC)
The federal agency that regulates new security issues and the trading of securities in secondary markets.

In the United States and in many countries, both the primary new issues market and the secondary security markets (stock exchanges and the over-the-counter market) are subject to public regulation. The history of regulation in the United States goes back to the Securities Act of 1933 and the Securities and Exchange Act of 1934. The primary purpose of this public regulation has been the protection of investors. To this end, the **Securities and Exchange Commission (SEC)** demands *full disclosure* of all material facts regarding securities in both the primary and secondary markets, and seeks to prevent the manipulation of security prices.

The SEC is charged with the regulation of new security issues, as well as the trading in outstanding securities. All security exchanges are regulated by the SEC. In addition, companies whose shares are traded on the organized exchanges are required to file periodic reports. The SEC also controls the security dealings of corporate "insiders" such as officers and major shareholders, all of whom must file reports on their personal transactions. The SEC supervises the use of proxies in corporate voting as well.

The Securities Act of 1934 also empowers the Board of Governors of the Federal Reserve System to regulate credit extended by banks and brokers to customers for the purchase of securities. The Fed stipulates the *margin*—that is, the minimum cash down payment a credit customer must make when purchasing a security; only the balance can be advanced by the broker. For example, an 80% margin requirement means that the customer's initial equity in the purchase of, say, $10,000 of common stock must be at least $8,000. Only $2,000 can be financed by loans.

The regulation of new issues applies to all issues of $500,000 or more, except private placements. Generally, a registration statement must be filed with the SEC. Very small issues and loans maturing within 9 months are exempted from this requirement. The SEC then has 20 days to study the document, to ask for additional information, and to determine if there are omissions or misrepresentations. During this *waiting period* the securities cannot be offered for sale. In practice, the waiting period can be much longer, especially for those issues which, for one reason or another, the SEC finds undesirable. In such cases, the SEC's demands for additional information are numerous and often continue over a relatively long period of time.

Regulation is a controversial subject. The supporters of full disclosure argue that the provision of information to investors is a necessary condition for efficient markets. Holders of the opposite view are also interested in efficient markets, but want these markets to take care of themselves. They argue that the costs of intervention outweigh the benefits, and therefore take as their motto the old Roman saying *caveat emptor*—let the buyer beware.

The Prospectus

red herring
A preliminary prospectus of a stock offering that contains all relevant information except the offer price.

During the waiting period, a *preliminary prospectus*, called a **red herring**, with all the relevant information except the offer price, may be published. The red herring carries the warning that it does *not* purport to offer the securities for sale. After registration, a final version of the prospectus, which includes the offer price and any changes the SEC has required, is sent to potential purchasers.

A sample prospectus is given in Appendix 12B. The reader should note that publication of the prospectus does not mean that the SEC has "approved" the new issue. On the contrary, an examination of the prospectus of Grow Group, Inc., in Appendix 12B reveals the SEC's explicit disclaimer: "These securities have not been approved or disapproved by the Securities and Exchange Commission." All parties who actually prepared the prospectus (the company's directors, officers, accountants, appraisers, underwriters, and so on) are legally responsible for its contents. Should it contain misrepresentations or omit material facts, purchasers of the securities who suffer a loss can sue for damages. If those accused are convicted, severe penalties, including a jail sentence may be imposed.

tombstone advertisement
Publication of the members of the underwriting syndicate from whom a full prospectus can be obtained.

In addition, a so-called **tombstone** advertisement which lists the members of the underwriting syndicate from whom the full prospectus can be obtained is published. Figure 12–1 presents a typical tombstone advertisement for the common stock of Great Western Financial Corporation.

Shelf Registration: SEC Rule 415

Rule 415
An SEC rule that permits firms to file single registration statements covering financing plans over a period of up to 2 years.

Preparing a formal registration statement for every security issue is often time-consuming and expensive. In 1983, the SEC issued **Rule 415**, which permits firms to file a single registration statement covering financing plans over a period of up to 2 years. During this period, securities can be issued when desired with almost no additional paperwork. This option is called *shelf registration*, perhaps to indicate that the firm keeps the securities handy—"on the shelf," so to speak.

Rule 415 has introduced a degree of flexibility that previously did not exist:

1. Once the financing plan has been registered, securities can be issued quickly on very short notice.

All of these securities having been sold, this announcement appears as a matter of record only.

4,000,000 Shares

Great Western Financial Corporation

Common Stock

Lehman Brothers
Shearson Lehman/American Express Inc.

Merrill Lynch Capital Markets

Salomon Brothers Inc

Atlantic Capital Corporation	The First Boston Corporation	Bear, Stearns & Co.
Sanford C. Bernstein & Co., Inc.	Alex. Brown & Sons Incorporated	Dillon, Read & Co. Inc.
Donaldson, Lufkin & Jenrette Securities Corporation	Drexel Burnham Lambert Incorporated	Goldman, Sachs & Co.
Hambrecht & Quist Incorporated	E. F. Hutton & Company Inc. Kidder, Peabody & Co. Incorporated	Lazard Frères & Co.
Montgomery Securities	Morgan Stanley & Co. Incorporated	PaineWebber Incorporated
Prudential-Bache Securities	Robertson, Colman & Stephens	L. F. Rothschild, Unterberg, Towbin
Smith Barney, Harris Upham & Co. Incorporated		Swiss Bank Corporation International Securities Inc.
UBS Securities Inc.	Wertheim & Co., Inc.	Dean Witter Reynolds Inc.
Allen & Company Incorporated	A. G. Edwards & Sons, Inc.	Oppenheimer & Co., Inc.
Rothschild Inc.		Thomson McKinnon Securities Inc.
Arnhold and S. Bleichroeder, Inc.	BHF Securities Corporation	Cazenove Inc.
EuroPartners Securities Corporation		Robert Fleming Incorporated
Kleinwort, Benson Incorporated		Sogen Securities Corporation

Samuel Montagu & Co. Limited

J. Henry Schroder Wagg & Co. Limited

October, 1984

FIGURE 12–1 **Tombstone Advertisement for Great Western Financial Corporation**

2. It permits the firm to break up an issue into smaller components that can be issued over a period of time.

3. Rule 415 is especially attractive to firms that want to take advantage of short-term swings in market conditions.

4. Finally, shelf registration facilitates competition among investment bankers for the firm's business. In effect, the firm can contact a number of underwriters and sell off part of its overall issue at the "best offer."

Rule 415 was introduced in the wake of the high volatility of interest rates in the United States during the early 1980s. Shelf registration has been especially popular with bond issuers; it is less appropriate for equities. With respect to common stock, a firm often prefers an ongoing connection with the investment banker who, as we shall see, provides a wide variety of valuable services.

CHOOSING AN INVESTMENT BANKER

investment banker (underwriter)
A firm which buys new stock issues from corporations and sells them to the public.

In actual practice, the firm usually contacts an **investment banker, or underwriter**, when it is still only contemplating the new issue. If we are talking about an established corporation, it probably will already have a relationship with the investment banker who handled its previous security issues. In the case of a firm that is "going public," issuing securities for the first time, several elements, in addition to the general reputation of the investment banker, will influence its choice:

☐ Is the issue appropriate for the underwriter in question? If we are issuing shares, we do not want an investment banker who specializes in bonds, and vice versa.

☐ Some underwriters specialize in public utilities; others will not handle what they consider "speculative" issues.

☐ Is the issue too large (or too small) for this investment banker to handle?

☐ Does the underwriter in question have Canadian or international connections?

syndicate
Participating bankers organized by the originating house to help sell a large issue.

The investment banker serves as the middleman between the public and the issuing corporation. The most common practice with respect to public issues is for one or more investment bankers to buy the issue outright from the corporation. If the issue is large, the *originating house* may form a **syndicate** comprised of other participating bankers to help sell the issue.

Table 12–3 gives the names of the most active U.S. underwriters, in terms of the number and dollar value of issues managed, in 1985. An indi-

TABLE 12–3   **Leading Underwriters of Corporate Securities, 1985***

		$ Volume (millions)	No. of Issues
1	Salomon Brothers	$26,387.1	437
2	First Boston	20,270.0	417
3	Merrill Lynch	16,574.7	366
4	Goldman Sachs	15,661.2	283
5	Drexel Burnham Lambert	11,465.0	217
6	Morgan Stanley	10,035.2	205
7	Shearson Lehman Brothers	9,948.1	287
8	Kidder, Peabody	4,126.5	150
9	Paine Webber	3,173.7	113
10	Smith Barney, Harris Upham	2,141.5	80
11	Prudential-Bache Securities	1,600.8	90
12	E.F. Hutton	1,490.1	73
13	Bear Stearns	1,486.8	68
14	Dean Witter Reynolds	1,463.2	67
15	Dillon Read	1,318.4	19
16	Lazard Freres	870.3	24
17	Rothschild, Unterberg, Towbin	731.7	37
18	Donaldson, Lufkin & Jenrette	565.8	34
19	Alex. Brown & Sons	509.4	41
20	Montgomery Securities	369.4	21
21	Dominion Securities Pitfield	357.5	8
22	Edward D. Jones	337.6	39
23	Robinson-Humphrey	319.2	23
24	Wertheim	297.3	12
25	Keefe, Bruyette & Woods	289.5	17

* Includes Robinson-Humphrey.
Leading Managers are given a double share of the issue.

SOURCE: *Institutional Investor*, March 1986, p. 155.

cation of the relative importance of various underwriters can also be gleaned by examining their relative position on the tombstone. Other things being equal, "room at the top" is reserved for the more important houses. Thus, in Figure 12–1 the names of the *syndicate managers*, in this case Lehman Brothers, Merrill Lynch Capital Markets, and Salomon Brothers, appear at the top of the advertisement. Following the syndicate managers, participating underwriters are listed alphabetically within brackets, starting with the "major" participants. A notable exception to the alphabetical rule is First Boston Corporation. First Boston usually insists on being listed first or second after the managers, and therefore appears before Bear, Stearns in Figure 12–1.

THE ROLE OF THE UNDERWRITER

In addition to selling the issue, the underwriter provides a variety of services, not all of which will always be utilized by every issuing firm. Depending on the circumstances, the investment banker may serve as an *advisor* to the firm on legal and other aspects of the issue. In this capacity, the investment house may help decide on the type of security to be issued and the price to be charged the public. In a sense, the underwriter helps reconcile the objectives of the issuing company with the needs of investors. The investment banker may also help in the preparation of the registration forms and prospectus, and often represents the firm before the SEC and other regulatory bodies.

In addition, the underwriter is often perceived by investors as a sort of "certifier" of the information contained in the prospectus. Since the investment banker has access to "insider information," its agreement to underwrite the security issue grants a sort of certification that the issue price is consistent with this information. In a manner of speaking, the investment banker "backs the issue" with its own reputation and standing within the investment community.

The most important service rendered by the underwriter is as an *insurer* of the issue's success. The originating house (or group) buys the issue for less than the offering price, thereby "undertaking" the risk that the issue or part of the issue may remain unsold. The *spread* between the price paid by the underwriter to the firm and the offer price to the public provides the underwriter's margin. This serves to compensate for the services rendered—insurance, advice, certification, and marketing the issue. Of course, the greater the risk, the larger the spread.

flotation (issuing) cost
The cost to a corporation of issuing new stock as reflected in the spread between the stock price paid by the underwriter to the firm and the offer price to the public.

The underwriting services can always be waived; the firm could gamble that the securities will sell, and save a substantial part of the **flotation** or **issuing cost.** But like all corporate financial decisions, the costs and benefits of insuring the issue must be weighed. The penalties for mistakes are very high. An offering that does not sell may lead to costly postponements (or even cancellations) of investment projects, difficulties in meeting fixed payments, or recourse to expensive alternative sources of financing.

The underwriting fee reflects the value of the services rendered, and is usually set by direct negotiation between the firm and the investment banker. However, government bonds and the securities of utility holding companies are exceptions to this practice. For these issues, the underwriter is selected by a **competitive bid.**

competitive bid
Process by which sealed bids are received from investment banks.

best efforts basis
A type of underwriting in which the investment banker serves as selling agent for the issuing firm.

In some cases, especially where the securities in question are very risky, the underwriter may agree to accept the issue only on a **best efforts** (or *agency*) **basis.** In this case, the investment banker (for a fee) serves as adviser, helps to design the security, and provides the selling organization; however, it does not insure the issuing firm against the risk that the securities will not be sold. Another extreme position is to accept the issue on an *all or none* basis. Here the deal with the underwriter will not go through unless the entire issue is sold at the offering price. These special constraints reflect the underwriter's principal worry—being left with unsold shares. Finally, in the case of a rights issue, the underwriter typically accepts the issue on a **standby basis.** In a standby agreement, the underwriter is paid a fee in return for which it agrees to purchase any part of the issue that remains unsubscribed.

standby basis
Agreement by the underwriter to buy any stock that remains unsubscribed.

SETTING THE OFFER PRICE

unseasoned issue
A corporation's first public issue.

seasoned issue
An offering of shares that are already traded on the market.

In setting the offer price for a new stock issue, it is convenient to differentiate between two types of public issues. A corporation's first public issue is called an **unseasoned issue.** If it is offering shares that are already traded in the market, we speak of a **seasoned issue.** Of course, in the latter case the firm may decide on a *rights issue* to its shareholders, but the pricing of such issues is so different that we devote a separate section (Appendix 12A) to these subscriptions.

In a seasoned public issue, the shares' current market price provides guidelines for setting the offer price. Typically the price will be set slightly below the market benchmark, since a degree of *underpricing* is usually considered necessary to induce the market to absorb the new issue. Although the degree of underpricing of a seasoned equity issue is usually less than 1%, this can amount to a considerable sum of money. For example, in a $50 million issue, even underpricing by a half percent could "cost" the existing shareholders a quarter of million dollars. In the case of *unseasoned* issues, setting the offer price is much more difficult. Here the underwriter must make an educated guess as to the market's evaluation of the stock's value. The empirical evidence suggests that such shares are often issued at a very substantial discount (from 15 to 25%) of their true market value.

In both types of public issue, the underwriter tries to reduce uncertainty by fixing the final offer price as late as possible, usually on the last day of registration. Even so, it is clear that a potential conflict of interest exists between the issuing firm and its investment banker. Underpricing is an additional hidden cost of a new issue which raises the cost of capital to the firm (see Chapter 15). The underwriter, on the other hand, has a strong incentive to push the offer price as low as possible to ensure that the securities will be taken up by investors.

green shoe clause
An arrangement between an issuing firm and an underwriter that gives the underwriter a short-term option to buy a fixed amount of additional shares at the offer price.

Most underwritten equity issues by industrial corporations include a so-called **green shoe clause.** This arrangement gives the underwriting syndicate a short-term option (usually 30 days) to buy a fixed amount of additional shares at the offer price. The need for such an option stems from the underwriters' practice of "overselling" an issue. Like some airlines, the underwriting syndicate often accepts subscriptions for more than the entire issue in order to compensate for the possibility that some purchasers may renege at the last moment. The sample prospectus in Appendix 12B contains a typical green shoe option: "The Company has granted the underwriters a 30-day option to purchase up to 50,000 additional shares of Common Stock solely to cover over-allotments. . . ."

The existence of a green shoe option offers a further incentive to the underwriter to underprice the new shares. Other things being equal, the value of the green shoe to the underwriter (and conversely its cost to the issuing firm) rises when the shares are priced below their market value.

COST OF SECURITY ISSUES

Floating a new issue of securities is an expensive proposition. The process involves the firm's management, legal counsel, accountants and auditors, as well as an investment banker. In addition to the administrative and legal expenses, the firm also must decide whether or not to insure all or part of the new issue with an underwriter. Table 12–4 provides some insight into the average size of the administrative and underwriting costs for new issues of common stock. First, it is clear from the data of Table 12–4 that flotation costs are substantial. Second, because of the existence of fixed costs which must be incurred regardless of the amount of money raised, and the lower risk of many of the larger well-known firms, the percentage of flotation cost in small issues is much higher than for larger issues. For example, total costs absorbed almost 14% of the gross proceeds of public equity issues which were smaller than $1 million. These same costs comprised only 4% of the gross proceeds of very large new issues (over $100 million). These very significant cost differentials must be kept in mind by the corporate financial manager.[1] Clearly, new security issues should *not* be made in small doses. However, a firm cannot change the economic facts of life; if it is relatively small, not well known, or has a high risk profile, it will have to incur greater proportional flotation costs.

1 The existence of economies of scale has been reconfirmed by a number of recent empirical studies; see, for example, the Spring 1986 issue of the *Midland Corporate Finance Journal.*

TABLE 12–4   **Issue Costs as a Percent of Proceeds for Registered Issues of Common Stock During 1971–1975**

Size of Issue, Millions of Dollars	General Underwritten Cash Offers			Underwritten Rights Issues		
	Underwriters' Compensation, Percent	Other Expenses, Percent	Total Cost, Percent	Underwriters' Compensation, Percent	Other Expenses, Percent	Total Cost, Percent
0.50 to 0.99	7.0	6.8	13.7	3.4	4.8	8.2
1.00 to 1.99	10.4	4.9	15.3	6.4	4.2	10.5
2.00 to 4.99	6.6	2.9	9.5	5.2	2.9	8.1
5.00 to 9.99	5.5	1.5	7.0	3.9	2.2	6.1
10.00 to 19.99	4.8	0.7	5.6	4.1	1.2	5.4
20.00 to 49.99	4.3	0.4	4.7	3.8	0.9	4.7
50.00 to 99.99	4.0	0.2	4.2	4.0	0.7	4.7
100.00 to 500.00	3.8	0.1	4.0	3.5	0.5	4.0
Average	5.0	1.2	6.2	4.3	1.7	6.1

SOURCE: C. W. Smith, "Alternative Methods for Raising Capital: Rights Versus Underwritten Offerings," *Journal of Financial Economics,* 5: 273–307 (December 1977), table 1, p. 277.

LISTING ON AN EXCHANGE

Having "gone public," a firm has the option of listing its shares for trading on a securities exchange. If the company is sufficiently large, it might even consider seeking a listing on the New York Stock Exchange.

Just as individual investors are precluded from actively buying and selling on the floor of the NYSE unless they are members (see Chapter 3), only the securities of a "listed" company are eligible for trading. To be listed on the NYSE, a company must meet certain qualifications, and also be willing to keep the investing public informed of the progress of its affairs. Although each case is determined on its own merits, the following minimum requirements have been laid down:[2]

1. Demonstrated earning power under competitive conditions of $2.5 million before federal income taxes for the most recent year prior to listing, and $2 million pretax for each of the preceding 2 years.
2. Net tangible assets of $16 million; however, greater emphasis is placed on the aggregate market value of the common stock.
3. A total of $18 million in market value of publicly held common stock.
4. A total of 1,100,000 common shares must be publicly held.
5. At least 2,000 shareholders must be round-lot shareholders—that is, owners of 100 or more shares. Alternatively, there must be 2,200 stockholders, together with an average monthly trading volume of 100,000 shares.

In addition, it was the policy of the Exchange until recently not to list nonvoting common stock. As a result, almost all of the common stocks listed on the exchange have the right to vote.[3]

The principal advantage of listing are these:

☐ Listing on the NYSE enhances a security's marketability and collateral value.

☐ It facilitates and may lower the cost of additional equity financing.

☐ The availability of a continuous "objective" valuation of the firm's shares is often very advantageous to the shareholders, as well as to the corporation, when a merger or other acquisition requiring an exchange of stock is contemplated.

☐ Listing on the NYSE often increases the number of shareholders and provides a great deal of free advertising for the company; the activities,

---

[2] The listing requirements are taken from New York Stock Exchange *Fact Book 1985*.

[3] In 1985, a committee appointed to review exchange policy with respect to voting rights recommended that the exchange allow the trading of dual class common stock in certain situations.

announcements, and periodic earnings reports of listed corporations are all newsworthy items for the financial pages of the nation's leading newspapers.

The disclosure required by the Exchange is not without costs, and it can prove an embarrassment to a corporation experiencing financial difficulties. In addition, the advantages of listing to the corporation and its shareholders are difficult to substantiate. The emergence of a national over-the-counter market (see Chapter 3) probably means that most of the advantages are also obtainable in the OTC.

SUMMARY

This chapter has been devoted to the problems that arise when a firm raises additional equity capital. Several alternative classifications of a firm's capital are these:

☐ *Authorized share capital*, which is the maximum number of shares which can be issued
☐ *Par value of common stock*, which is given by the number of shares actually issued valued at their par value
☐ *Total paid-in capital*, shares which have been authorized, and actually issued, valued at their issue price
☐ *Treasury stock*, the shares which have been repurchased and retired by the firm

A firm's common stockholders have a number of fundamental rights. The stockholders have the right to elect the corporation's directors, inspect the firm's accounts, and approve certain extraordinary expenditures. Two alternative election systems, *majority voting* and *cumulative voting,* are used. The latter is of special significance because it permits the representation of minority stockholders on the board of directors. The stockholders are the residual owners of the corporation's property and retained earnings. However, they have a right to receive their share of the profits only if the board declares a dividend. The shareholders have the right to approve major changes, such as new issues of additional shares. The latter is often stipulated explicitly in the form of a *preemptive* right to subscribe to any new share issue in proportion to their existing holdings.

In general, the firm can raise additional equity by public issue, privileged subscription, or private placement. In a public issue, or general cash offer as it is also called, the shares are offered to the general public. A corporation making its initial public offering is said to be "going public."

A privileged subscription gives existing stockholders the prior right to subscribe to the new issue. If the privilege is transferable (if it can be sold on the market), the issue is called a *stock rights offering* (see Appendix 12A).

In a private placement, part or all of the shares are taken by a single investor or by a limited number of investors. Private placements are usually made to major financial institutions such as pension funds and life insurance companies.

Both the primary and secondary security markets are subject to regulation by the Securities and Exchange Commission (SEC). The SEC requires full disclosure of all material facts. In a new issue, this means that a registration statement must be prepared and filed with the SEC. Only then can a formal offer to sell the securities (prospectus) be issued.

To ensure the success of a new issue, the firm often employs the services of an *investment banker (underwriter)*. (1) The investment banker serves as an advisor on legal and other aspects of the new issue; (2) The investment banker helps to design the issue and provides the marketing network for its sale; (3) By lending its name to the issue, the underwriter also implicitly serves as a sort of "certifier" of the reasonableness of the stipulated offer price; (4) Finally, the most important service rendered by the underwriter is as an insurer of the issue's sale.

Issuing securities is a time-consuming and expensive process. An examination of the flotation costs for common stock issues suggests the existence of economies of scale in the capital market. In general, larger issues have a lower percentage of flotation costs.

APPENDIX 12A | Stock Rights

A privileged subscription, in which the firm's shareholders are able to sell their preemptive right to purchase the new shares, is called a *rights offering*. In such an issue, each shareholder is permitted to buy a certain number of new shares. The terms of the offer are printed on a certificate call a *right;* each stockholder receives one such *right* for every share that he or she currently holds.

The economic logic underlying the use of rights can best be understood by considering a simplified, but realistic, example. Table 12A–1 shows the fi-

nancial data of the Midwest Corporation. The company's net after-tax earnings are $10 million, and since it has 1 million shares outstanding, earnings per share (EPS) are $10. Its stock sells for $100 (price/earnings ratio of 10 to 1), so that the firm's total market value is $100 million. (For simplicity, we assume Midwest has no debt.)

Assume Midwest decides to raise an additional $25 million of common stock by means of a rights offering to its existing shareholders, at a price of $50 per share. The decision to raise $25 million, and the *subscription price* of $50 per new share, determines the *allocation ratio*—that is, the number of rights required to purchase one new share. Since each existing share gets one right certificate, this also determines the number of old shares needed to subscribe to one new share.

STEP 1: Divide the subscription price into the total amount to be raised in order to get the number of new shares to be issued:

TABLE 12A–1	Midwest Corporation: Selected Financial Data before the Rights Offering
Number of shares outstanding	1,000,000
Market price of a share ($)	100
Total market value of equity ($)	100,000,000
Net after-tax earnings ($)	10,000,000
Earnings per share ($)	10
Price/earnings ratio	10

$$\frac{\text{number of new shares}}{\text{to be issued}} = \frac{\text{money to be raised}}{\text{subscription price}}$$

$$= \frac{\$25 \text{ million}}{\$50} = 500{,}000 \text{ shares}$$

STEP 2:   Divide the number of new shares to be issued into the number of shares currently outstanding in order to get the *allocation ratio*—the number of rights required to subscribe to one new share:

$$\frac{\text{allocation}}{\text{ratio}} = \frac{\begin{array}{c}\text{number of rights}\\\text{required}\\\text{to purchase}\\\text{a new share}\end{array}}{} = \frac{\text{old shares}}{\text{new shares}}$$

$$= \frac{1{,}000{,}000}{500{,}000} = 2$$

Thus a shareholder must surrender to the firm 2 "rights" plus an additional $50 in order to subscribe to 1 new share. Had the subscription price been set higher, say at $70, 2.8 rights would be needed to obtain 1 new share; had the subscription price been set lower than $50, less than 2 rights would be needed to purchase a new share (see Table 12A–2). Alternatively, shareholders can sell their "rights" to someone else, who in turn will use these rights to buy shares from the firm at the subscription price of $50.

We have now gained some insight into the mechanics of a rights offering. Given the decision to raise $25 million, Midwest can reach its financing objective by alternative combinations of *subscription price* and *allocation ratio*. Table 12A–2 shows a number of such combinations. Notice that the firm considers only subscription prices which are *below* the current market price ($100), because no rational investor will use the "right" to buy shares at a price above the current market price.

HOW RIGHTS AFFECT SHARE PRICE

Now that we know a bit about the mechanics of a rights offering, we have to face a question that has probably already popped into your mind. Clearly the right to purchase a stock at a discount from its market value must be worth something. It is possible that we have finally discovered the proverbial

TABLE 12A–2   Examples of Possible Combinations of Subscription Prices and Allocation Ratios for Midwest's Issue.

Alternative Subscription Prices (P_s)	Number of Rights Required to Purchase One New Share (Allocation Ratio)* (N)
$90	3.6
80	3.2
70	2.8
60	2.4
50	2.0
40	1.6
30	1.2
20	0.8
10	0.4

* Calculated from the formula:

$$N = \frac{\text{numbers of old shares}}{\text{money to be raised}/P_s} = \frac{1{,}000{,}000}{25{,}000{,}000/P_s}$$

"golden goose," or what the finance profession refers to as a "free lunch"? On the surface, it would appear that if the old shareholders can convince management to set the subscription price low enough, a windfall gain is assured. But golden geese and free lunches have an awkward tendency to disappear in the cold light of reality. And, as we will now see, rights offerings are no exception.

FORMULAS FOR RIGHTS OFFERINGS

What will be the price of the firm's shares after the rights offering? And what price will the rights themselves command in the market? If we ignore transaction costs and assume a perfectly competitive capital market, the theoretical value of a right will depend on the difference between the rights-on price and the ex-rights price. *Rights-on* refers to the price of the old shares *before* the right to subscribe to the new shares is removed. The *ex-rights* price refers to the shares' market price *after* the new issue; that is, *after* the right to subscribe has been removed.

The formula for the theoretical value of a right is:

$$\text{value of right} = \frac{\text{rights-on price} - \text{subscription price}}{N + 1}$$

or

$$V_R = \frac{P_c - P_s}{N + 1} \qquad (12A.1)$$

where

P_c = the rights-on price

P_s = the subscription price

N = the allocation ratio, or the number of rights required to subscribe to 1 new share

V_R = the theoretical value of 1 right

In our numerical example of Midwest, we have

$$V_R = \frac{100 - 50}{3} = \$16.67$$

Using the same symbols, the theoretical formula for the ex-rights price of the stock, P_x, becomes:

$$P_x = \frac{NP_c + P_s}{N + 1} \qquad (12A.2)$$

$$= \frac{2(100) + 50}{3} = \$83.33$$

The theoretical formulas state that the ex-rights price of Midwest's shares will fall to $88.33 after the new issue, and that the market price of each right, should the stockholder wish to sell it, will be $16.67.

But what mechanism in a competitive market ensures that prices will not deviate substantially from their theoretical values? In our example, the ex-rights price of the shares (after exercise of the rights) will be $83.33 and the rights will have a market value of $16.67. The proof is straightforward. Any investor can obtain a share of Midwest during the subscription period *either* by purchasing 2 rights on the market and adding to this the subscription price of $50, or by purchasing a share, ex-rights, on the open market. Should the ex-rights price be higher than $83.33—say $85—it will pay investors to purchase rights and add the subscription price, since a share obtained in this way costs less than $85; similarly, should the ex-rights price

of the share be less than $83.33—say $80—it would pay an investor to buy the new shares directly in the market rather than purchase the rights. The market will be in equilibrium when the value of the right is just equal to the difference between the rights-on price and ex-rights price of the stock.

$$\text{value of right} = \text{rights-on price} - \text{ex-rights price}$$

or in our example:

$$\text{value of right} = \$100 - 83.33 = \$16.67$$

DO SHAREHOLDERS GAIN FROM LOW SUBSCRIPTION PRICES?

If market forces ensure that share prices will not deviate substantially from the theoretical relationship, they also effectively eliminate any "free lunch." Whatever the shareholders "gain" from a lower subscription price, they "lose" from the fall in the ex-rights price of the shares.

Consider an investor who held 10 shares of Midwest prior to the rights offering. The total market value of his holdings was $1,000. What is the value of his holdings after the rights offering? If he sells his rights, he receives $166.67 (10 rights times $16.67 = $166.67). In addition, he still owns the 10 shares that are now worth $833.33 (10 shares times $83.33 = $833.33). As long as the market is in equilibrium, and the value of the rights and the ex-rights price of the shares conform to their theoretical values (Eqs. 12A.1 and 12A.2), the total market value of his investment remains unchanged at $1,000.

Value of Holdings after the Rights Offering

10 shares at $83.33 each	$ 833.33
Plus proceeds from sale of	
10 rights at $16.67 each	166.67
Total value of investment	$1,000.00

Thus, in a competitive capital market, the shareholders neither gain nor lose by selling their rights.

What happens should our investor decide to exercise his rights and subscribe to the new shares? Before the rights offering he owned 10 shares, which gave him the right to purchase 5 new shares for a subscription price of $50. (Recall the allocation ratio is 1 new share for each 2 rights). After the offering, he holds 15 shares which are worth $1,250 (15 times $83.33 = $1,250). If we deduct the subscription price he paid for the 5 new shares ($50 times 5 = $250), we once again find no change in the net value of his investment.

Value of Holdings after the Rights Offering

15 shares at $83.33	$ 1250
Less additional investment	250
	$1,000

Again the investor neither gains nor loses from the rights offering.

APPENDIX 12–B   A sample prospectus appears on pages 307-311

REVIEW EXERCISE

Circle the correct word(s) to complete the sentences; see p. 314 for the correct answers.

12.1 The holders of a company's stock have a claim to a proportional part of the company's *total/net* assets.

12.2 A share's par value *has great/is of no* economic significance.

12.3 Common shareholders have a legal claim only to a company's *net profits/dividends*.

12.4 Retained earnings are credited to *assets/stockholders' equity*.

12.5 "Cumulative voting" makes it *possible/impossible* for minority interests to obtain representation on the board.

12.6 The stockholders *do/do not* have the right to prevent the use of corporate resources for purposes other than those stipulated in the charter.

12.7 The preemptive right to purchase any new stock issued by the firm *protects/does not protect* the stockholder from dilution of value.

12.8 Private placements *avoid/do not avoid* the costly process of registering the issue with the SEC.

12.9 The publication of a prospectus *means/does not mean* that the SEC has approved the new issue.

12.10 The most common practice with respect to public issues is for investment bankers to *float/buy* the issue from the corporation outright.

12.11 The most important service rendered by the underwriter is as an *investor in/insurer of* the issue's success.

12.12 For a "seasoned" issue, the offer price will be set slightly *below/above* the market benchmark.

12.13 Underwriters have a tendency to *underestimate/exaggerate* the degree of underpricing.

12.14 The value of a "green shoe" to the underwriters *rises/falls* when the shares are priced below their market value.

12.15 In the new issue market for securities, there exist *considerable/no* economies of scale.

12.16 *All/Only listed* securities can be traded on the NYSE.

12.17 Listing on the NYSE *reduces/enhances* a security's marketability.

12.18 An empirical study has shown that flotation costs are *lowest/highest* for public issues and *lowest/highest* for non-underwritten rights issues.

QUESTIONS

12.1 Define the following terms:
- **a.** Treasury stock
- **b.** Par value
- **c.** Paid-in capital
- **d.** Cumulative voting
- **e.** Underwriter
- **f.** Seasoned issue
- **g.** Green shoe
- **h.** Going public
- **i.** Tombstone advertisement
- **j.** Red herring

12.2 Joe Mason bought 10 shares of common stock at par when Major Dynamics first went public 12 years ago. When Major Dynamics issued more common stock last year, Janet Wilson bought 10 shares, but paid $5 over par. Who owns a larger share of the company, Joe Mason or Janet Wilson?

12.3 How can the owners of common stock influence the management of the company?

12.4 Explain the difference between majority voting and cumulative voting. Which is more advantageous to minority groups? Why?

12.5 Which abuse does the preemptive right prevent? Give a numerical example.

12.6 What is the advantage to the issuing corporation of raising equity capital by private placement?

12.7 What services do underwriters perform?

12.8 How can an investment banker ensure an issue's success?

12.9 "Our company's decision on the final offer price is based exclusively on the advice of our investment banker." Do you agree with such a policy?

12.10 Why is the cost of a "green shoe" to the issuing firm smaller when the shares are priced above their market value?

12.11 "We only raise the amount of money which is needed right away. If it turns out we need more, say in 6 months, we can always float another offering." Do you agree? Explain.

12.12 What is the logic behind the NYSE's listing requirements?

12.13 What are the advantages of listing to the corporation? Can you think of any disadvantages?

500,000 Shares

GROW GROUP, INC.

Common Stock

($.10 Par Value)

The Common Stock is listed on the New York Stock Exchange.   On June 4, 1980, the last reported sale price of the Common Stock on the New York Stock Exchange was $11⅛ per share.

THESE SECURITIES HAVE NOT BEEN APPROVED OR DISAPPROVED BY THE SECURITIES AND EXCHANGE COMMISSION NOR HAS THE COMMISSION PASSED UPON THE ACCURACY OR ADEQUACY OF THIS PROSPECTUS. ANY REPRESENTATION TO THE CONTRARY IS A CRIMINAL OFFENSE.

	Price to Public	Underwriting Discounts(1)	Proceeds to the Company(2)
Per Share	$11.125	$.75	$10.375
Total(3)	$5,562,500	$375,000	$5,187,500

(1) The Company has agreed to indemnify the Underwriters against certain civil liabilities, including certain liabilities under the Securities Act of 1933, as amended.   See "Underwriting".

(2) The proceeds are before deduction of expenses payable by the Company estimated at approximately $390,000.

(3) The Company has granted the Underwriters a 30-day option to purchase up to 50,000 additional shares of Common Stock solely to cover over-allotments, exercisable at the above per share price to the public, less the above underwriting discounts.   If and to the extent such option is exercised, the total price to the public, underwriting discounts and proceeds to the Company will be increased proportionately. See "Underwriting".

The shares are being offered by the Underwriters subject to prior sale, when, as, and if delivered to and accepted by the Underwriters, and subject to approval of certain legal matters by counsel.   It is expected that delivery of the shares will be made against payment therefor on or about June 12, 1980 at the offices of Drexel Burnham Lambert Incorporated, 60 Broad Street, New York, New York.

Drexel Burnham Lambert
INCORPORATED

Blyth Eastman Paine Webber
INCORPORATED

June 5, 1980

AVAILABLE INFORMATION

The Company is subject to the informational requirements of the Securities Exchange Act of 1934 and in accordance therewith files reports and other information with the Securities and Exchange Commission. Information as of particular dates concerning the Company's directors and officers, their remuneration, options granted to them, the principal holders of securities of the Company and any material interest of such persons in transactions with the Company, is disclosed in proxy statements distributed to stockholders of the Company and filed with the Commission. Such reports, proxy statements and other information can be inspected and copied at the offices of the Commission at Room 6101, 1100 L Street, N.W., Washington, D.C. or at its Regional Offices located at Room 1228, Everett McKinley Dirksen Building, 219 South Dearborn Street, Chicago, Illinois 60604; Room 1100, Federal Building, 26 Federal Plaza, New York, New York 10007; and Suite 1710, Tishman Building, 10960 Wilshire Boulevard, Los Angeles, California 90024. Copies of such material can be obtained at prescribed rates from the Public Reference Section of the Commission at 500 North Capitol Street, N.W., Washington, D.C. 20549. The Company's Common Stock is listed on the New York Stock Exchange and the Company's Convertible Subordinated Debentures are listed on the American Stock Exchange; and reports, proxy material and other information concerning the Company may be inspected at the offices of the New York Stock Exchange, 20 Broad Street, New York, New York 10005 and the American Stock Exchange, 86 Trinity Place, New York, New York 10006.

IN CONNECTION WITH THIS OFFERING, THE UNDERWRITERS MAY OVER-ALLOT OR EFFECT TRANSACTIONS WHICH STABILIZE OR MAINTAIN THE MARKET PRICE OF THE COMMON STOCK OF THE COMPANY AT LEVELS ABOVE THOSE WHICH MAY OTHERWISE PREVAIL IN THE OPEN MARKET. SUCH TRANSACTIONS MAY BE EFFECTED ON THE NEW YORK STOCK EXCHANGE OR OTHERWISE. SUCH STABILIZING, IF COMMENCED, MAY BE DISCONTINUED AT ANY TIME.

PROSPECTUS SUMMARY

The following summary is qualified in its entirety by the detailed information and financial statements appearing elsewhere in this Prospectus.

The Company

Grow Group, Inc. believes that, based on revenues, it is the second largest manufacturer of specialty chemical coatings and general purpose or trade paints in the United States, excluding companies which are divisions, subsidiaries or affiliates of other corporations. The Company is also a producer of a broad line of other specialty chemical products. The Company's products are sold nationally to commercial and industrial users and the general public through its own sales force, independent distributors and dealers and 82 Company owned outlets. The Company has acquired the rights to two patented processes (the Enviro-Spray™ self-pressurizing aerosol type dispensing system and the Thermaljet™ cooking system) which are nearing pilot scale commercial production. Neither process has yet generated any revenues for the Company and there is no assurance that these processes will achieve market acceptability or profitable operations.

The Offering

Security Offered	500,000 shares of Common Stock (excluding up to 50,000 shares which may be sold pursuant to an over-allotment option)
Common Stock Outstanding	At May 31, 1980: 3,242,504 shares; pro forma for this offering (excluding any over-allotment shares): 3,742,504 shares (in each case net of treasury shares)
Use of Proceeds	Approximately $2,500,000 will be used for capital expenditures for machinery and equipment and for working capital for the Enviro-Spray and Thermaljet processes. The balance will be used to reduce short-term indebtedness, approximately $2,100,000 of which was incurred to provide financing for the development of these processes.
Listing	New York Stock Exchange (symbol GRO)
1979-1980 Price Range	Through June 4, 1980: $16½-$7¾ (as adjusted)
Last Sale Price	On June 4, 1980: $11⅛

Selected Consolidated Financial Information(a)

(In Thousands Except Per Share Amounts)

	Year Ended June 30					Nine Months Ended March 31	
	1975	**1976**	**1977**	**1978**	**1979**	**1979** (Unaudited)	**1980** (Unaudited)
Revenues	$ 92,897	$ 99,866	$177,390	$190,126	$215,382	$153,971	$167,255
Net Income	1,389	2,045	3,805	4,089	4,577	2,635	2,978
Net Income Per Share(b):							
Primary	$.61	$.91	$1.30	$1.35	$1.49	$.85	$.88
Fully Diluted	.53	.77	1.21	1.10	1.22	.71	.74
Dividends Per Share(b):							
Cash	$.26	$.27	$.29(c)	$.36	$.42	$.31	$.33
Stock	5%	5%	5%	5%	5%	5%	5%

(a) See "Management's Discussion and Analysis of Consolidated Statements of Income—Estimated Results for the Three Months Ending June 30, 1980" below.

(b) The net income per share and cash dividends per share have been adjusted for stock dividends.

(c) Includes fourth quarter dividend of $.09 (as adjusted) declared and paid after June 30th.

THE COMPANY

The Company formulates and produces a broad line of specialty chemical coatings, and sells these products and a line of thinners and other chemical products to commercial and industrial users and retail outlets. The Company also formulates and produces general purpose or trade paints, which are marketed through dealers and Company owned outlets, and distributes wallcoverings.

The Company is comprised of operations that have been acquired since 1961. The most significant acquisition was in June 1976, when the Company, through its Devoe & Raynolds Company, Inc. subsidiary, acquired the assets of the Trade Sales and Marine Divisions of Celanese Coatings & Specialties Company, a subsidiary of Celanese Corporation.

In recent years the Company has been looking into other technologies as a means of further diversifying its business. In this regard, the Company has acquired the rights to two patented processes which have been under study by the Company over the past couple of years. The Enviro-Spray aerosol type dispensing system utilizes the *in situ* production of carbon dioxide as the pressurizing agent instead of fluorocarbon or hydrocarbon propellants, and the Thermaljet system is a new process for cooking beef and other food products. (See "Use of Proceeds" and "Business—Grow Ventures Corporation" below.)

The Company was organized under the laws of the State of New York in 1950. The Company's principal executive offices are located at 200 Park Avenue, New York, New York 10017, and its telephone number is (212) 599-4400. The term "Company" as used herein refers to Grow Group, Inc. and its subsidiaries and divisions, unless the context otherwise requires.

USE OF PROCEEDS

The Company intends to use approximately $2,500,000 of the net proceeds from the sale of the shares of Common Stock offered hereby, estimated at approximately $4,798,000 ($5,316,000 if the over-allotment option is exercised in full), in connection with bringing the Enviro-Spray and Thermaljet processes into commercial production. The balance of the net proceeds, approximately $2,298,000, will be used to reduce short-term indebtedness, approximately $2,100,000 of which was incurred to provide financing for the development of these ventures.

As more fully described in "Business—Grow Ventures Corporation" below, the Company has authorized the expenditure of $2,500,000 to be applied towards bringing the Enviro-Spray and Thermaljet processes into limited scale commercial production. Such funds will be obtained from the proceeds of this offering and are expected to be spent through June 30, 1981 to acquire machinery and equipment and for continued research and development, field and market tests, advertising and promotion and working capital. Pending utilization, such funds will be applied to further reduce short-term indebtedness or invested in short-term money market instruments.

Neither process is presently in commercial production, nor has either generated any revenues for the Company. The Company estimates that the $2,500,000 budget will be adequate to achieve the proposed pilot scale commercial production, but there is no assurance that such production can be achieved within such budget. Even if the proposed pilot scale commercial production and the additional field and market testing indicate potential market acceptability and the Company decides to bring either or both processes into full scale commercial production, there is no assurance that the Company would be able to achieve profitable operations for either venture. If for any reason the Company's Board of Directors should determine at any time in the future that continued investment in one or both of these processes is not warranted, any proceeds of this offering which have not then been spent will be used by the Company for general corporate purposes.

The balance of the net proceeds, together with any proceeds from the exercise of the over-allotment option, will be used by the Company to reduce short-term indebtedness (see "Capitalization" below). In addition to the funds borrowed with respect to the ventures, such debt was incurred by the Company for working capital and other corporate purposes, and the Company anticipates it will incur additional debt from time to time subsequent to this offering for such purposes and for possible acquisitions. Although the Company continually reviews possible acquisitions, there can be no assurance that any acquisitions will be made.

CAPITALIZATION

The capitalization of the Company at March 31, 1980, and as adjusted to give effect to the sale by the Company of the 500,000 shares of Common Stock offered hereby, was as follows:

	Outstanding	As Adjusted
	(In thousands)	
Short-Term Debt:		
Notes payable to banks (prime interest rate)	$ 8,700	$·6,402
Long-Term Debt:		
Non-convertible debt:		
Notes payable to insurance companies:		
6½% to 9¾% payable $.8 million in 1981, $1.8 million in 1982 and 1983 and $2.7 million annually thereafter	$28,607	$28,607
Bank borrowings and other debt:		
6¾% Industrial Development Revenue Bonds, due in varying amounts through 2002	2,240	2,240
Other notes payable, 6% to 12.3%, $2.4 million collateralized by land, buildings and equipment at March 31, 1980	2,884	2,884
Convertible subordinated debt:		
5¼% convertible subordinated debentures, due September 15, 1987	3,337	3,337
Total Long-Term Debt ($1.3 million due within one year)	37,068	37,068
Redeemable Preferred Stock—par value $1 per share (redemption value $100 per share):		
Series F, L and M (aggregate redemption value $4.4 million)	44	44
Applicable paid-in capital	4,340	4,340
Total Redeemable Preferred Stock	4,384	4,384
Stockholders' Equity(1):		
Non-Redeemable Preferred Stock—par value $1 per share (liquidating value $100 per share):		
Series A, B, C and H (aggregate liquidating value $1.2 million)	12	12
Common Stock—par value $.10 per share:		
Authorized 15,000,000 shares, issued 3,139,471 and 3,639,471 shares	314	364
Less treasury stock at cost (7,056 shares)	(40)	(40)
Paid-in capital	21,896	26,644
Retained earnings	9,128	9,128
Total Stockholders' Equity	31,310	36,108
Total Long-Term Debt, Redeemable Preferred Stock and Stockholders' Equity	$72,762	$77,560

(1) The number of shares to be outstanding does not include 50,000 shares of Common Stock which may be issued on exercise of the over-allotment option (see "Underwriting" below) or 110,089 shares issued from April 1, 1980 through May 31, 1980 upon conversion of convertible securities and exercise of options. A total of 1,408,000 (1,369,000 as of May 31, 1980) shares of Common Stock were reserved for issuance on conversion of convertible debentures and convertible preferred stock and for exercise of options, of which 574,000 (564,000 as of May 31, 1980) shares were reserved for issuance on conversion of the preferred stock. The Company has recently reached an agreement in principle to acquire another company in exchange for two new series of convertible preferred stock (see "Description of Capital Stock—Conversion Rights" below). The issuance of the Common Stock offered hereby will not affect the conversion prices of the convertible securities and options, nor the number of shares reserved for issuance upon the conversion or exercise of such securities. The Series A, B, C and H Preferred Stock contain optional redemption provisions. See "Description of Capital Stock" below and Note D(a) to Financial Statements for information respecting restrictions on the payment of cash dividends on the Common Stock.

(2) For further information regarding preferred stock, debt, stock options, leases and other commitments, see Notes D, E, F and H to Financial Statements.

PROBLEMS

12.1 Book value. Afton Enterprises has 500,000 $2 par value shares outstanding. Additional paid-in capital amounts to $12,500,000, and $14,600,000 of retained earnings appear in the balance sheet.

a. What is the book value per share?

b. Assuming that all shares were sold at the same price, what was their issue price?

c. Can you figure out the market price per share?

12.2 Book value. An additional issue of 100,000 shares of common stock has been authorized by Afton Enterprises (see problem 12.1). They are sold for $60 per share.

a. What accounting entries must be made in the balance sheet?

b. What is the book value per share after the issue?

12.3 Treasury stock. Mr. Justin is a major shareholder of Afton Enterprises and owns 50,000 shares of the total 600,000 shares of common stock outstanding. Afton's management is bothered by this concentration of ownership and would like to buy him out. They offer Mr. Justin $65 per share.

a. Assuming Mr. Justin accepts the offer, what does the balance sheet look like after the repurchase?

b. What is the book value of the outstanding shares, after Mr. Justin sells his shares to the company?

12.4 Voting rights. The Smog Corporation is holding an election to its board. There are 90,000 voting shares outstanding, and eight directors are to be elected. A group of ecologically minded shareholders would like to have at least one director on the board who will defend their interests. How many votes do they need to make certain he will be elected

a. under the majority voting system?

b. under the cumulative voting system?

QUESTIONS AND PROBLEMS APPENDIX 12A

12A.1 Define

a. allocation ratio   **b.** rights-on

c. ex-rights

12A.2 With which of the following statements do you agree?

a. In an efficient competitive market a shareholder gains from a rights offering.

b. The fall in the price of a share when it goes ex-rights does not represent a loss in investment value.

c. The rights offering is equivalent to a new public issue priced at book value.

Explain.

12A.3 Southwest Corporation decides to raise $2.1 million by a rights offering. There are 300,000 shares outstanding; their market price is $48 per share. The company sets the subscription price at $35.

a. What is the allocation ratio?

b. How does your answer change if the subscription price is set at $42?

12A.4. What are the theoretical values of the rights and the theoretical ex-rights price of the shares in the previous problem if the subscription price is set at:

a. $35?   **b.** $42?

SAMPLE PROBLEMS

SP12.1 The Ridges Corporation is authorized to issue 150,000 shares of common stock at a par value of $2 and manages to sell them at $18 per share. What entries have to be made in the balance sheet?

SP12.2 The following is the stockholders' equity account of National Movers:

Equity Account	
Stock	350,000
Additional paid-in capital	3,000,000
Retained earnings	1,900,000
Total equity	5,250,000

Common stock was issued twice: when the company was founded 25,000 shares were issues and sold at par, and 5 years later 150,000 additional shares of common stock were sold.

a. What is the par value of the company's common stock?
b. What is the book value of a share of common stock?
c. At what price were the additional 150,000 shares sold?

Solutions to Sample Problems

SP12.1 Since the par value of the newly issued shares is $300,000 ($2 × 150,000 = $300,000), the entry "Common stock" is increased by $300,000. The remainder of the issue's proceeds is credited to "Additional paid-in capital":

total proceeds = 150,000 × $18 = $2,700,000

total proceeds − common stock = additional paid-in capital

$2,700,000 − $300,000 = $2,400,000

SP12.2 a. "Common stock" equals the number of shares issued times their par value. Hence:

$$\text{par value} = \text{common stock/number of shares issued}$$

175,000 shares have been issued (25,000 at the time of the company's founding, and 150,000 five years later). The "Common stock" account shows $350,000. Therefore

$$\text{par value} = \$350,000/175,000 = \$2$$

b. Book value per share is defined as total equity divided by the number of shares:

$$\text{book value} = \text{total equity/number of shares}$$

Since total equity is $5,250,000, we get

$$\text{book value} = \$5,250,000/175,000 = \$30$$

c. Additional paid-in capital is defined as the excess of receipts over the shares' par value. Since the first issue of 25,000 shares was sold at par, the additional paid-in capital stems solely from the second issue of 150,000 shares. Thus, the excess over par per share is

$$\text{additional paid-in capital/number of shares in second issue} = \\ \$3,000,000/150,000 = \$20$$

It follows that the shares were sold at par + $20, or $22.

Answers to Review Exercises	**12.1** net	**12.2** is of no	**12.3** net profits	**12.4** stockholders' equity

Answers to Review Exercises

12.1 net   **12.2** is of no   **12.3** net profits   **12.4** stockholders' equity

12.5 possible   **12.6** do   **12.7** protects   **12.8** avoid

12.9 does not mean   **12.10** buy   **12.11** insurer of

12.12 below   **12.13** exaggerate   **12.14** rises   **12.15** considerable

12.16 only listed   **12.17** enhances   **12.18** highest; lowest

SUGGESTIONS FOR FURTHER READING

For comprehensive studies of investment banking, see I. Friend, J. Longstreet, M. Mendelson, E. Miller, and A. Hess, *Investment Banking and the New Issues Market* (Cleveland: World Publishing Company, 1967); and Ernest Bloch, *Inside Investment Banking*, (Homewood, Ill: Dow-Jones-Irwin, 1986.)

Flotation costs of new equity issues are estimated empirically by Clifford W. Smith, "Alternative Methods for Raising Capital: Rights Versus Underwritten Offerings," *Journal of Financial Economics*, December 1977; and Robert S. Hansen and John M. Pinkerton, "Direct Equity Financing: A Resolution to a Paradox," *Journal of Finance*, June 1982.

The new issues market for public utility stocks is examined by Dennis E. Logue and Robert A. Jarrow, "Negotiation vs. Competitive Bidding in the Sale of Securities by Public Utilities," *Financial Management*, Autumn 1978;

and Richard H. Pettway and Robert C. Radcliffe, "Impacts of New Equity Sales Upon Electric Utility Share Prices," *Financial Management*, Spring 1985.

The pros and cons of public regulation of securities markets are discussed by Irwin Friend, "Economic and Equity Aspects of Securities Regulation," in Robert F. Lanzillotti and Yoram C. Peles (eds.), *Management Under Government Intervention: A View From Mount Scopus* (Greenwich, CT: JAI Press, 1984); and Gregg Jarrell, "The Economic Effects of Federal Regulation of the Market for New Security Issues," *Journal of Law and Economics*, December 1981.

The impact of SEC Rule 415 is examined empirically in Norman H. Moore, David R. Peterson, and Pamela P. Peterson, "Shelf Registrations and Shareholder Wealth: A Comparison of Shelf and Traditional Equity Offerings," *Journal of Finance*, June 1986.

13 | Fixed Income Securities: Long-Term Debt and Preferred Stock

"Variety is the spice of life," as we are often told, and the long-term financing of a modern corporation is a good example of this dictum. In practice, an often bewildering array of long-term debt instruments and preferred stocks confronts the financial manager. In this chapter, we examine the principal features of these long-term alternatives. After a brief discussion of the advantages and disadvantages of debt financing, the terms and conditions of long-term bonds are explained and compared with those of long-term loans. The protective and retirement provisions which are typically built into bond contracts are analyzed and the use of financial ratio analysis and agency ratings to assess bonds' investment quality is discussed. Attention is also given to the role played by various types of bonds, for example, mortgage bonds, in the allocation of risk. Similarly, the function of preferred stocks, which are a hybrid type of financing that combines many of the features of debt and equity, is examined. Since the decade of the 1980s has witnessed far-reaching changes in corporate debt strategy, attention is also focused on the innovations which have inundated the capital market in recent years. In this context special attention is given to inflation which appears to have been a primary stimulus for change.

LONG-TERM DEBT: VIEWPOINT OF THE FINANCIAL MANAGER

Different securities affect the allocation of risk, income, and control within the firm differently. Long-term debt has a leverage effect (see Chapter 14) which on average may help the firm increase stockholders' income; however, it also increases the variability of net earnings and the risk of default. With respect to control, there is no dilution of ownership and control when bonds are issued, since bondholders typically do not receive voting rights. The advantages and disadvantages to the corporation of using long-term debt can conveniently be summarized as follows:

Advantages of Debt Financing

1. The bond is a relatively low-risk security, and therefore the after-tax cost of debt is lower, and often substantially lower, than equity financing (see Chapter 15). This reflects the fact that the bondholders' claim is limited to a *fixed* rate of interest, and that the interest cost is deductible for tax purposes.
2. Typically there is no sharing of control when debt is issued.
3. Debt is not permanent; the firm can adjust its financing program to meet expected and unanticipated changes, and therefore debt permits greater flexibility.

A firm's debt capacity is limited; if stretched beyond a point, taking on more debt may not be possible. Because of this, firms rarely push borrowing to the limit. A reserve of unused borrowing power is a handy thing to have if unforeseen contingencies arise. This is especially true if a serious slump in the market should make the flotation of equity temporarily impossible.

Thus, from the viewpoint of the firm, debt financing has the following advantages: relatively low cost, no sharing of control, tax advantages due to deductibility of interest, and greater flexibility.

Disadvantages of Debt Financing

1. The use of long-term debt increases financial risk (see Chapter 14).
2. The fixed interest payments and maturity date of a bond issue create a burden on the firm's financial resources, which in extreme cases can lead to default and bankruptcy.
3. The protective provisions demanded by bondholders often restrict management's freedom of action (see below).

LONG-TERM DEBT: VIEWPOINT OF THE INVESTOR

Bonds are sold to the public, or the debt issue can be placed privately with one or more financial institutions. As is true of any financial asset, the investor is concerned with the return and the risk. Typically, bond investors receive a fixed interest income with relatively little risk; however, they exercise little or no control over the corporation's decisions. The reduced risk stems from the fact that the bondholders have a prior contractual claim to the firm's earnings, and in case of liquidation, to its assets as well.

CHARACTERISTICS OF LONG-TERM BONDS

In practice, long-term corporate debt has many different features. The various features of a modern bond issue have emerged in response to real economic needs. To understand the economic function of the various provisions of a debt contract, we will focus initially on some of the more important alternatives open to a firm that has decided to issue long-term bonds.

Indenture

indenture
A document specifying the detailed provisions of a bond issue.

The formal agreement between the issuing company and the bondholders is called the **indenture.** This is a document specifying the detailed provisions of the bond issue (rate of interest, dates of payment, and so on, as well as any restrictions on the company. Unlike a stock certificate, the bond indenture is very detailed, and is often several hundred pages long! For example, the indenture includes a complete description of any property that is pledged. The indenture also fixes the method of redemption—for example, redemption of a fixed proportion of the issue each year—and so on.

The indenture is an integral part of the *prospectus* of a bond issue, and as such is subject to review by the Securities and Exchange Commission. The SEC checks to make sure that all provisions of the indenture are met before the corporation is permitted to sell the new securities to the public.

Trustee

trustee
A person or institution that represents the interests of bondholders over the lifetime of an issue.

Bondholders' interests are represented over the lifetime of the issue by the **trustee** designated in the indenture to act on their behalf. A large bank usually serves as the trustee of the bond issue. The duties and responsibilities of the trustee are set out in the Trust Indenture Act of 1939. These include: (a) certifying the legality of the bond contract at the time of issue; (b) insuring that all the provisions of the indenture are carried out; and (c) initiating action on behalf of the bondholders in case the company defaults on any of its obligations, or payments, to those bondholders.

PROTECTIVE PROVISIONS

The issuing company can, and often does, enhance the investment quality of its bonds by introducing a number of protective provisions into the bond indenture. However, the presence of such provisions does not guarantee strength, nor does their absence necessarily indicate weakness. On the contrary, very large corporations such as AT&T are often able to forego many of the protective provisions without impairing the quality, or credit rating, of the bonds.

Perhaps the most popular means of modifying the risk of a bond issue is tne inclusion of a *pledge of assets* clause in the indenture. *Mortgage bonds,* for example, have priority over other debtors with regard to the mortgaged assets. Risk may also be reduced by including a *negative pledge*—for example, a limitation on the creation of additional debt with prior or equal status to the bonds in question.

The realities of bankruptcy proceedings have led to a de-emphasis on the various collateral provisions. The assets of a modern corporation are often highly specific. The very fact of bankruptcy suggests that the present value of the future earnings that can be derived from the assets, and therefore their value, is likely to be very low. As a result, the market value of the pledged assets often has an unfortunate tendency to shrink drastically during bankruptcy, so that the holders of defaulted bonds are only rarely compensated in full. But even in cases where a substantial proportion of the debt can be recovered, the legal processes often stretch over a number of years.

Recognition of the limited protection that asset pledges afford has led to the inclusion of clauses designed to protect the bondholder by means of restrictions placed on the corporation's activities subsequent to the bond issue. Restrictions may be placed on the size of dividend payments to common stockholders if certain minimum standards regarding the size of earned surplus or working capital are not met. A minimum current ratio requirement and certain early retirement provisions may also be included. If the company fails to fulfill any of these provisions, the trustee may call for the immediate redemption of the bonds.

RETIREMENT PROVISIONS

serial bonds
A bond issue in which a given number of bonds matures periodically.

As we have already noted, the bond indenture stipulates the method and timing of redemption payments. In the case of **serial bonds,** a given amount of an issue matures periodically. For example, if we assume that $100 million of 20-year serial bonds is issued in 1987, 5% of the original issue ($5 million) might mature each year. Note that the *average* maturity of the bonds is 10 years, but by purchasing these bonds selectively, investors can choose any maturity they desire. More often than not, bonds mature on the same date, but a **sinking fund** provision is almost invariably included in the indenture. Such a provision stipulates that the issuing corporation will make periodic sinking fund payments for the purpose of retiring the bond issue.

sinking fund
Periodic payments made by an issuing corporation to retire a bond issue.

Many variants exist: The bonds to be retired may be purchased on the open market, or drawn at random and purchased at a fixed call price (see below), or the sinking fund may be left with a trustee until the final redemption date. In the case of early redemption, the actual bonds that will be retired often cannot be identified in advance. This can prove inconvenient to the investor. Consider an investor who, acting on expectations of future interest rate movements, acquired the bonds to increase the average maturity of her bond portfolio, only to have them called for sinking fund redemption at a time when interest rates have fallen. This disadvantage must be weighed against the protection from default which the sinking fund affords.

Call Provision

call
The right of a company to repurchase its securities at a given price during the period that they are outstanding.

The **call** feature gives the company the right to repurchase its securities at a given call price during all, or part, of the period that the bonds are outstanding. The call price itself is almost invariably fixed above par, with the price declining according to a scale, fixed in advance, as the maturity date approaches. Clearly the call privilege has value to the issuing company. Should interest rates decline, the company will be able to retire older and presumably high-interest-bearing issues at a fixed price, using the proceeds of a new lower-interest-bearing issue for this purpose. The company's willingness to take advantage of this privilege depends on the prices (yields) of the bonds, the call price, and flotation costs. Thus, the value of the call privilege to the firm depends on its expectations regarding the direction and magnitude of future fluctuations in interest rates. The greater the expectation of a fall in interest rates, the greater the call provision's value to the firm.

Just as clearly, the call privilege is a *disadvantage* for investors, with the degree of disadvantage again depending on the call price, flotation costs, and the course of future interest rates. Given a fixed call price, for instance 106% of par value, there exists an upper limit to an investor's potential capital gain. No matter how steep the fall in interest rates, the market price of the bond cannot rise much above the call price of 106. Beyond that price (plus a premium to cover flotation costs), the company is likely to exercise its privilege of repurchasing the bonds. But as we have stressed so often, there are no "free lunches" in the capital market. When interest rates are considered high—for example at cyclical peaks—the issuing firm will have to offer higher yields to induce investors to accept a given call privilege. Similarly, investors will press for higher call prices, and/or for the deferment of the call privilege for a maximum number of years after issue.

BOND RATINGS

bond rating
An estimate of a bond's investment quality and its risk of default.

Most investors lack the time, the inclination, or the ability to attempt an independent assessment of the investment quality of the myriad of corporate bonds available in the market. One way out of this dilemma is to consult the **bond ratings** regularly published by agencies that seek to evaluate the quality of a firm's outstanding bonds. The best-known measures of bond quality are the ratings published by Moody's and Standard & Poor's. These ratings reflect the agency's estimate of the bonds' investment quality, and provide a subjective measure of its default risk. Although each agency publishes its own definition of the meaning of the ratings, no explicit explanation of the actual method used in calculating them is provided.

Table 13–1 gives the risk categories used by Moody's and Standard & Poor's. Moody's, for example, rates corporate bonds from Aaa, "gilt edge" bonds of minimal credit risk, to D, which includes bonds of a speculative nature. This category includes bonds that are already in default, or offer only minimal assurance that obligations will be met in the future. Standard & Poor's uses the same principle but a slightly different notation, with AAA designating its highest rating. Bonds included in the two highest categories (triple A and double A) have the lowest default risk. Bonds rated Baa or better by Moody's (or triple B or better by Standard & Poor's) are classified as *investment grade*. Many financial institutions must hold only bonds of investment grade.

TABLE 13–1   Bond Ratings

	Investment Grade		Substandard	Speculative
	Highest Quality	High Quality	Substandard	Speculative
Moody's	Aaa Aa	A Baa	Ba B	Caa to D
S & P	AAA AA	A BBB	BB B	CCC to D

Table 13–2 gives Moody's key to its bond ratings. From the results of statistical attempts to predict a bond's rating solely on the basis of quantitative measures, it would appear that the agencies exercise considerable qualitative judgment. Table 13–3 gives some sample corporate bond ratings as of February 1986.

TABLE 13–2   Key to Moody's Bond Ratings by Default Risk

Aaa	Bonds which are rated Aaa are judged to be of the best quality. They carry the smallest degree of investment risk and are generally referred to as "gilt edge." Interest payments are protected by a large or by an exceptionally stable margin, and principal is secure. While the various protective elements are likely to change, such changes as can be visualized are most unlikely to impair the fundamentally strong position of such issues.
Aa	Bonds which are rated Aa are judged to be of high quality by all standards. Together with the Aaa group they comprise what are generally known as high-grade bonds. They are rated lower than the best bonds because margins of protection may not be as large as in Aaa securities or fluctuation of protective elements may be of greater amplitude or there may be other elements present which make the long-term risks appear somewhat larger than in Aaa securities.
A	Bonds which are rated A possess many favorable investment attributes and are to be considered as upper medium grade obligations. Factors giving security to principal and interest are considered adequate but elements may be present which suggest a susceptibility to impairment sometime in the future.
Baa	Bonds which are rated Baa are considered as medium grade obligations i.e., they are neither highly protected nor poorly secured. Interest payments and principal security appear adequate for the present but certain protective elements may be lacking or may be characteristically unreliable over any great length of time. Such bonds lack outstanding investment characteristics and in fact have speculative characteristics as well.

Ba	Bonds which are rated Ba are judged to have speculative elements: their future cannot be considered as well assured. Often the protection of interest and principal payments may be very moderate and thereby not well safeguarded during both good and bad times over the future. Uncertainty of positions characterizes bonds in this class.
B	Bonds which are rated B generally lack characteristics of the desirable investment. Assurance of interest and principal payments or of maintenance of other terms of the contract over any long period of time may be small.
Caa	Bonds which are rated Caa are of poor standing. Such issues may be in default or there may be present elements of danger with respect to principal or interest.
Ca	Bonds which are rated Ca represent obligations which are speculative in a high degree. Such issues are often in default or have other marked shortcomings.
C	Bonds which are rated C are the lowest-rated class of bonds and issues so rated can be regarded as having extremely poor prospects of ever attaining any real investment standing.

SOURCE: *Moody's Investors Services, Inc.*

Clearly these agency ratings affect a corporation's ability to raise additional long-term debt:

1. Generally speaking, a lower rating, which signifies higher default risk, translates into higher interest costs to the firm because investors demand a higher premium to offset this additional risk.

2. Institutional investors, who make up the bulk of the bond market, are very sensitive to the bond ratings. Many such investors are precluded by law or by custom from investing in bonds with ratings below "investment grade"—that is, below Baa.

3. This institutional sensitivity has led many regulated institutional investors to hold only very high grade bonds in their portfolios. Such strategy minimizes the probability that a fall in a bond's rating below Baa will force the institution to sell them off in a very thin market. As a result, the number of potential purchasers tends to shrink as we consider successively lower grades of bonds.

TABLE 13–3   Sample Bond Ratings as of February 1986

Bond Issuer	Rating
Anaconda Debentures 1993	Aaa
General Motors Acceptance Corp.	
Debentures 2006	Aa
J.C. Penny 1991	A
Pan Am World 1994	B
Vagabond Hotels 1995	Caa
White Motor 1993	C

SOURCE: *Moody's Bond Record,* February 1986.

The impact of these forces on the bond market creates very significant yield differentials on bonds of different quality. Table 13–4 lists the interest yields and risk premiums on long-term government bonds, and on two classes of long-term corporate bonds (Aaa and Baa) for the years 1978–1986. The data in Table 13–4 are also plotted in Figure 13–1.

Throughout the period, yields rose systematically as we consider bonds of higher default risk (that is, bonds with lower agency ratings). The early 1980s were characterized by relatively high inflation, which led investors to demand (and obtain) significantly higher yields on all classes of bonds. Long-term U.S. government bonds that yielded less than 8% on the average in 1978 gave investors a yield of almost 13% in 1981. The enhanced uncertainty of this inflationary period also translated into a sharp rise in the default risk premiums on both classes of corporate bonds. For example, the risk premium on Baa bonds increased 2.5 times from 1978 to 1982.

Used as an initial screening device, agency ratings have some obvious advantages, especially for the investor who is concerned with avoiding speculative securities. However, a high agency rating at time of issue does not constitute a guarantee that the bonds will retain their initial quality (and therefore their rating) until redemption.

Independent Analysis

Financial managers are often concerned with predicting the ratings of their bonds because the high correlation between bond ratings and bond yields enables them to estimate the risk premium required on the bonds. In some instances, action might be taken to change some of the financial dimensions of the firm in order to improve its agency rating. Using the agency ratings as a starting point, the analyst (or investor) can carry out an independent evaluation of the creditworthiness of the corporate securities in question us-

TABLE 13–4   Yields* and Default Risk Premiums on Bonds (In percent)

	Long-Term Government (Default-free) (1)	Aaa Corporate Bonds (2)	Baa Corporate Bonds (3)	Risk Premiums	
				Aaa (4) = (2) − (1)	Baa (5) = (3) − (1)
1978	7.89	8.73	9.45	0.84	1.56
1979	8.74	9.63	10.69	0.89	1.95
1980	10.81	11.94	13.67	1.13	2.86
1981	12.87	14.17	16.04	1.30	3.17
1982	12.23	13.79	16.11	1.56	3.88
1983	10.84	12.04	13.55	1.20	2.71
1984	11.99	12.71	14.19	0.72	2.20
1985	10.75	11.37	12.72	0.62	1.97
1986†	8.19	9.14	10.37	0.95	2.18

* Annual average.
† Week ending May 30, 1986.

SOURCE: *Federal Reserve Bulletin*, various issues.

Figure 13—1
Bond Ratings,
Yields, and Default
Risk Premiums,
1978 and 1982

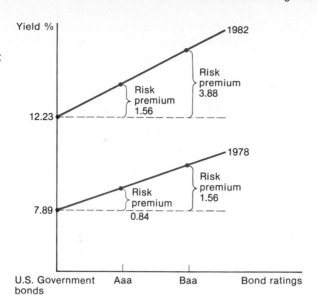

ing the tools of financial ratio analysis. Essentially this requires an estimate of the probability of default on payments of interest or principal. The outside analyst is rarely in a position to acquire all the data required for such an analysis, but even when limited to the data of firms' financial statements, some useful rule-of-thumb tests can be carried out.

The number of possibilities is quite large, but we will restrict ourselves to the more widely used financial ratios. The most popular measure of ability to pay is the *times interest earned ratio (TIE)* or *interest coverage ratio:*

$$TIE = \frac{\text{carnings before interest and taxes (EBIT)}}{\text{total bond interest}}$$

For example, if we assume the following hypothetical financial data: EBIT, $1,000,000, interest payments, $250,000, the TIE ratio is 4. In other words, the firm's interest obligation is "covered" 4 times by pretax earnings. The problem is slightly more complicated if several classes of bonds (for example, senior bonds with priority over a junior issue) are outstanding. In such cases, care must be exercised to ensure that the comparative strengths of the two issues are assessed correctly. In our example, if we assume that the firm's annual interest obligations were as follows: interest on senior bonds, $200,000, interest on junior bonds, $50,000, the average ratio of all interest obligations, as we have already seen, is 4. If the inappropriate *prior deductions* method is employed, we find that the coverage of the senior bonds, taken alone, is 1,000,000/200,000 = 5. If we then deduct the senior interest from earnings, the coverage of the remaining junior bonds becomes $800,000/ 50,000 = 16.

Such an approach implies that the junior bonds are much better protected than the senior obligations, which does not make economic sense. A better approach is to examine the coverage ratio of the senior bonds as above, followed by an examination of the coverage ratio of the *cumulative combination* of the senior and junior obligations. In our example, the coverage of the senior obligation is, as before, 5:

$$\frac{\$1,000,000}{\$200,000} = 5$$

Using the *cumulative method,* the coverage of the junior bonds is only 4:

$$\frac{\$1,000,000}{\$200,000 + 50,000} = 4$$

Since the firm incurs an obligation to redeem the principal of the bonds as well as to pay the interest, many analysts prefer to use a *total coverage ratio* or *burden coverage ratio,* which relates the firm's pretax earnings to the combined principal and interest payments:

$$\text{burden coverage ratio} = \frac{\text{earnings before interest and taxes (EBIT)}}{\text{interest} + \text{principal payment}/(1 - T)}$$

where T = the appropriate corporate tax rate. The tax adjustment is necessary since redemptions of principal, unlike interest payments, are *not* deductible for tax purposes. The firm must first pay its corporate tax bill and then redeem the principal of the bonds out of net *after-tax* earnings. If we assume a 34% corporate tax rate and annual principal payments of $200,000, the amount of *pretax* earnings necessary to meet the redemption obligation is 200,000/(1 − 0.34) = $303,030, and the burden coverage ratio is

$$\text{burden coverage ratio} = \frac{\$1,000,000}{\$250,000 + \$303,030} = 1.8$$

A similar line of reasoning applies to preferred dividend payments, which also are not deductible for tax purposes. The effective burden of $175,000 of annual preferred dividends, in terms of pretax income, is $175,000/(1 − 0.34) = $265,152, and the burden coverage ratio becomes 1.2:

$$\text{burden coverage ratio} = \frac{\$1,000,000}{\$250,000 + \$303,030 + \$265,152} = 1.2$$

Of course this type of ratio analysis provides only a rough rule of thumb calculation of the firm's ability to meet its fixed charges out of current income. A more comprehensive analysis would require an examination of the firm's cash and capital budgets, but these data are not generally available to the external analyst. Moreover, no absolute standard is available to assess the ratios. We have no objective standard that can be used to determine the adequacy of a burden ratio of, say, 2 to 1, except to compare it with other companies within the industry or with industry averages. However, where the ratios are available over a long period of time, they can also be usefully compared within the same company in order to discern any trends in the firm's financial position.

Similarly, ratio analysis can be applied to various other balance sheet items in order to get a rough idea of a firm's liquidity (see Chapter 4). The firm's net working capital (current assets minus current liabilities) can be examined over time and compared with that of other firms; the current ratio (current assets divided by current liabilities) also provides a rough measure of the firm's ability to pay its current debt out of its current assets. And finally, some idea can be gained of the protection afforded to holders of prior claims in case of insolvency by examining the firm's capital structure.

ALTERNATIVE DEBT INSTRUMENTS

Bonds can be classified in a variety of ways, each method depending on some particular characteristic. The two most common classification schemes are types of security offered or industry affiliation of the issuing firm (industrial, transportation, public utility). Classification by type of security is the more illuminating of the two methods, especially from the viewpoint of a firm faced with the decision of what type of bond to offer to the public.

Mortgage Bonds

mortgage bond
A bond secured by a lien on specific assets.

Securing debt by some sort of lien or claim on physical property appears to be almost as old as civilization itself: Archeologists have uncovered a deed listing an olive press as security for a debt executed in Mesopotamia more than 5,400 years ago. Today we call a bond secured by a lien on specific assets a **mortgage bond**. Like the familiar home mortgage, the value of the mortgaged property, in most cases, exceeds the amount of the debt by some reasonable margin of safety. In the event of default, the trustee may foreclose and sell the property, the proceeds of which are used to compensate the mortgage bondholders. Should the proceeds from the sale of the mortgaged assets prove insufficient, the mortgage bondholders have an equal claim, along with the corporation's general creditors, to the firm's other assets.

second mortgage bonds
Bonds that have a secondary claim on a mortgaged property.

Bonds that have a secondary claim to the same property may also be issued by the firm; such bonds are called **second mortgage bonds**. In this case, the senior bondholders must be fully compensated, out of the proceeds from the sale of the mortgaged property, *before* the holders of the junior lien can be compensated.

after-acquired property clause
A stipulation in a mortgage bond that the present mortgage covers not only existing property but all assets subsequently acquired by a corporation.

A mortgage bond may also contain an **after-acquired property clause** which stipulates that the present mortgage covers not only the existing property, but all assets subsequently acquired by the corporation as well. Such a clause enhances the security of the bond from the investors' viewpoint, but seriously limits management's freedom.

closed-end
Refers to mortgage that stipulates that additional bonds secured by the same property cannot be issued.

open-end
Refers to mortgage that permits a firm to issue additional bonds under the same lien.

The mortgage may also be **closed-end** or **open-end**. A closed-end mortgage stipulates that additional bonds, secured by the same property, cannot be issued; hence the corporation can issue new mortgage bonds only by pledging additional assets. An *open-end* mortgage, as the name implies, permits the firm to issue additional bonds under the same lien. This gives management a greater degree of flexibility regarding future financing, but might prove detrimental to the existing mortgage bondholders. A compromise is often reached by issuing a *limited open-end* mortgage. This type of mortgage bond permits the additional issue of bonds up to some predetermined limit—for example, the total value of bonds outstanding under the lien may be restricted to, say, 50 percent of the property's original value.

Finally, it pays to remember that the value of the best of assets has a tendency to depreciate drastically in the case of financial failure. Thus, even the most protected of creditors—holders of a hypothetical closed-end first mortgage, with an after-acquired property clause—are not assured of recovering in full. The ultimate test of a bond's quality rests squarely on the earning power of the corporation over the duration of the issue—that is, on the ability of the corporation to meet its obligations out of current operating income.

Equipment Obligations

equipment trust certificates
First liens against a company's equipment sold by a trust company to the public.

Another form of secured bond is created by a special type of leasing arrangement commonly employed by railroads and airlines. In order to raise funds at favorable rates, these companies pledge their essential equipment—rolling stock and aircraft. Although the legal arrangements are often complicated, a simplified example based on the so-called Philadelphia plan will suffice to show the underlying logic of equipment financing. A railroad places an order for rolling stock with a manufacturer; at the same time, an arrangement is made with a trustee (usually a trust company) to pay three-quarters of the purchase price, with the railroad paying the remainder out of its own funds. Title to the equipment passes to the trustee, and **equipment trust certificates**, which in effect represent a first lien against the equipment, are sold to the public up to the amount paid by the trust company for the equipment. The title to the equipment remains with the trustee, which in turn *leases* the rolling stock to the railroad.

The advantage of this form of financing lies in the legal status of the certificates, and their collateral, in case of bankruptcy. Since the rolling stock is *owned* by the trustee, the court, at whose direction the railroad is now being operated, has no jurisdiction over the equipment. (From the standpoint of collateral, the equipment trust certificates are similar to an automobile loan.)

Moreover, since the equipment (rolling stock, locomotives) is essential to the operation of the railroad, the present value of the equipment is, in almost all cases, greater than the amount of certificates outstanding. As a result, the receiver who operates the line will make every effort to meet all the obligations of the lease agreement. However, even if the railroad should repudiate this lease, the trustee can usually sell the equipment to another line for an amount at least equal to the face value of the certificates outstanding. It is the great strength of the underlying collateral which has permitted even relatively weak railroads to finance their investment in equipment, at very low rates, by means of trust certificates.

Debentures

debenture
A bond that is not secured by a direct pledge of specific property.

A **debenture** refers to a bond which is not secured by a direct pledge of specific property. Such a bond simply represents a promise to pay interest and principal at given times and therefore, in event of default, the holder of a debenture is considered a general creditor. Debentures are often protected in the indenture by the inclusion of a negative pledge which precludes the corporation from granting prior liens against its property. Debentures are often issued by firms such as AT&T, whose creditworthiness is especially strong, or by manufacturing and commercial companies, whose assets cannot be considered suitable long-term collateral because they are not fixed or because they are very specific to the particular company.

Subordinated Debentures

subordinated debentures
Bonds that are placed in a secondary position with respect to specific classes of debts.

The quality of unsecured long-term bonds can be further reduced by issuing them as **subordinated debentures**—that is, bonds that are placed in a secondary position with respect to specific classes of debts. In the event of liquidation, such bondholders would receive compensation only after the senior creditors named in the indenture have been paid in full. However, in practice, especially in cases of complex reorganizations, the courts have been known to deviate from this rule.

Obviously, issuing subordinated debt has an advantage for the firm's senior debt holders. Consider a hypothetical case in which a firm is liquidated for $900,000, but has outstanding $600,000 of straight debentures, $600,000 to trade creditors, and $600,000 of subordinated debentures. Each of the three classes of creditors is entitled to an equal one-third share of the proceeds from liquidation—that is, $300,000 each. However, if the subordinated bonds are secondary to the straight debentures, their claim passes to the straight debentures, so that the latter are entitled to $600,000. Hence the final allocation is $600,000 payment in full to the straight debentures, $300,000 to the trade creditors, and *nothing* to the subordinated bondholders. If $1,200,000 had been realized from the liquidation, the allocation would have been as follows: $600,000 to the straight debentures ($400,000 plus $200,000 from the subordinated debentures' share); $400,000 to the trade creditors, and $200,000 to the subordinated debentures.

In this way, the subordinated debt enhances the position of the senior debt at the expense of the holders of the subordinated debentures. The latter are often issued in corporate reorganizations in which the firm's debt holders have no recourse other than to accept the lesser of two evils—a subordinated position in the reorganized company, or bankruptcy proceedings.

In one sense, subordinated debt is very much like preferred stock, ranking as it does after other debt but before the ownership interest. However, we must emphasize that default on subordinated debt can force bankruptcy; failure to pay preferred dividends cannot. A major reason for issuing this type of debt rather than preferred stock often reflects tax considerations; the interest on subordinated debt is tax deductible, preferred dividends are not.

Income Bonds

income bond
A bond the interest payments on which depend on their actually being earned by the issuing corporation.

An **income bond** is the weakest form of debt a corporation can issue. As the name implies, the interest payment on such bonds depends upon its actually being earned by the corporation, although the indenture does stipulate that the principal be paid at a specified time in the future. These bonds are a hybrid that places the holders in a relatively weak position. As a result, income bonds are most frequently found in the financial structures of railroads emerging from receivership and bankruptcy. Such bonds are also issued to a firm's creditors in exchange for their old bonds during reorganization. In order to increase their appeal, the interest sometimes is cumulative (if not paid, the obligation "accumulates," to be paid at a future date if earned). However, income bonds have never been very popular with investors. As one investment banker has put it, income bonds, which so often have been issued during financial stress or corporate reorganizations to investors with no better alternative than to accept them, have "the smell of death" about them.[1]

BOND INNOVATIONS

The decade of the 1980s witnessed far-reaching changes in corporate debt financing. The widespread innovations that characterized the bond market had many causes. However, the principal stimuli for change appear to have been:

1. The upsurge of inflation and the volatile interest rates that accompanied it;
2. Changes in the tax structure;
3. Changes in public regulation;
4. Perhaps academic research on efficient capital markets.

Inflation and Bond Financing

The rapid rise in consumer prices during the 1970s and early 1980s had a significant impact on the bond market. Interest rates on bonds and on competing money market investments, such as bank certificates of deposit,

[1]Quoted by Merton H. Miller, "Debt and Taxes," *Journal of Finance,* May 1977.

soared. Corporations were often dissuaded by these very high rates from borrowing "long" and locking themselves into high interest costs for 20 to 30 years. Investors, on the other hand, were often reluctant to lend their money at even relatively high *fixed* interest rates because of the expectation that the rate of inflation might accelerate. The financial community responded to the challenge of inflation by changing the terms of traditional financing contracts and introducing new types of debt instruments.

Since the end of the 1960s, industrial, and later public utility, issuers of long-term debt typically have been required to offer greater call protection to investors. A 10-year guarantee that bonds will not be recalled for redemption replaced the typical 5-year guarantee of the pre-inflation era. Similarly, during periods in which short-term interest rates rose above the long-term rate, some corporations offered their bonds on a **delayed-settlement basis**. This is an agreement which stipulates that delivery of part of the bonds to the investors would be delayed, say 6 months, thereby permitting the investors—almost invariably institutions—to earn the higher short-term money market rates for an additional half-year before committing their funds for the longer term. Such a provision is especially attractive to the investor who expects both long- and short-term interest rates to decline in the near future.

Another innovation induced by inflation was the introduction of **floating-rate or variable-rate bonds**. These bonds offer investors a fixed interest rate for, say, 6 months. In the second and later periods, the interest rate is pegged at one or more percentage points above the average Treasury bill rate. To enhance their marketability, these variable-rate notes can usually be redeemed for the full face amount at the end of 2 years.

delayed-settlement basis
An agreement that delays the delivery of some bonds to investors, thereby permitting investors to earn high short-term interest on funds earmarked for the purchase of the bonds.

floating-rate (variable-rate) bonds
Bonds whose interest rate is adjusted during its lifetime if interest rates rise.

Index Bonds

When uncertainty regarding the purchasing power of money becomes very great, investors may become unwilling to acquire fixed-income securities unless an explicit purchasing power guarantee is added to the contract. The worldwide inflation following World War II created a demand for investments whose interest and/or principal were linked to various price indexes. Such purchasing power guarantees have become quite common in countries suffering from an unstable price level (for example, Brazil and Israel). In Great Britain, the double-digit inflation of the mid-1970s led the government to introduce Index-Linked National Savings Certificates for investors of pensionable age.

The principle underlying purchasing power guarantees can be illustrated by a simple numerical example. Assume that investors are offered a 6% 1-year $100 bond with both interest and principal *linked* to the cost-of-living index. Now assume that the consumer price index *doubles* during the year. The bondholders receive $212, rather than $106, at the end of the year. Had prices risen by 50 percent they would have received $159, and of course if the consumer price index had remained unchanged, each bondholder would have received $106 at the end of the year. In all three cases, the investor is assured a *real* return of 6 percent, independent of the degree of inflation:

$$\frac{106}{100} - 1 = 6\% \qquad \frac{159}{150} - 1 = 6\% \qquad \frac{212}{200} - 1 = 6\%$$

Zero Coupon Bonds

zero coupon bonds
Deep discount bonds that have no interest coupon.

deep discount bonds
Bonds issued with very low interest coupons and selling at prices far below par.

Changes in the tax laws have always been a motivating factor for financial innovation. A good example of the influence of tax legislation on bond financing is provided by **zero coupon bonds**. These bonds are an extreme case of a **deep discount bond**—a bond issued with a very low interest coupon, and therefore selling at prices far below par. By definition, a zero coupon bond is the most deeply discounted bond, since it has no interest coupon at all. In such a case the investor's return results solely from the gain in the value of the bond.

Initially, deep discount bonds had a special appeal to issuers, since they required little or no periodic cash outlays, while some tax benefits due to the writing off of the discount could be obtained annually. Subsequent legislation, however, eliminated the tax advantage.

Changes in Public Regulation

cocktail bonds
Global bonds denominated in terms of currency baskets such as the IMF's SDR or the ECU.

Financial deregulation has been another major motivating force for innovation in the capital market. With respect to bonds, perhaps the most significant stimulus was provided by the introduction of SEC Rule 415 (see Chapter 12), which permits the continuous new issue of securities, under certain circumstances, over a period of up to 2 years. Rule 415 led to yet another innovation, the *global* bond issue. For example, the greater flexibility and speed of issue provided by Rule 415 means that a corporation can more easily decide to switch its financing strategy from domestic to Eurobond markets. The issuing firm's ultimate decision depends on the terms offered by the competing markets. In addition, numerous variants in bond denominations have been introduced. These are the so-called **cocktail bonds**, which are denominated in terms of currency "baskets" such as the International Monetary Fund's SDR (Special Drawing Rights), or ECU (the European Currency Unit). In such issues, interest and principal are defined in terms of the weighted average of currencies making up the particular "basket."

TERM LOANS

term loan
A long-term loan from a financial institution to a corporation in which the borrower agrees to pay interest and principal.

Not all corporate long-term debt is raised by bond issues; long-term loans are also made to corporations by financial institutions. A **term loan** is an agreement to pay interest and principal, but unlike a bond issue, the loan and its conditions are a product of direct negotiation between the borrower and the lending institution, usually a bank. The principal nonbanking financial institutions making term loans to corporations are insurance companies, pension funds, the Small Business Administration, commercial finance companies, and equipment manufacturers. Depending on the economic situation, the duration of such loans has varied. In recent years, maturities of from 3 to 15 years have been common, but shorter maturities (2 to 5 years), as well as longer maturities of 20 to 30 years, have been observed. The longer-term loans are usually made by insurance companies.

Advantages of Term Loans

Term loans have three principal advantages over a comparable bond issue: greater speed, more flexibility, and lower costs. Because a term loan is negotiated directly with the lender, the provisions can usually be worked out more quickly. Term loans have the further advantage of permitting a greater degree of flexibility should a need to amend some provision arise. In the case of a term loan, only one lender has to be convinced should the firm wish to alter one of the provisions of the original agreement due to a change in economic conditions. In a widely held bond issue, securing such agreement is considerably more difficult. The term loan also has significant cost advantages over a public bond issue, since such loans are exempt from SEC registration requirements. Finally, in the case of a small firm, a public bond issue may simply be out of the question.

Loan Repayment

amortized term loan
Refers to the repayment of term loans in equal monthly, quarterly, or annual amounts over the period of a loan.

Term loans are usually **amortized**—that is, they are repaid in equal monthly, quarterly, or annual amounts over the period of the loan. This form of repayment protects the lender against the possibility that the borrowing corporation will not make adequate provision to retire the loan during its lifetime. This can be especially important in the case of an equipment loan. Here the loan repayment schedule is usually geared to the equipment's productive lifetime, so that the payments can be made out of the cash flows resulting from its use.

The terms of repayment are flexible. In some cases repayment may be delayed for a number of years—perhaps until the factory which is being financed comes into full production. In other cases, there may be a large final payment at the termination. These are the so-called balloon or bullet payments. In effect, such a provision increases the effective duration of the term loan in question. In an extreme case, in which the periodic payments are for interest only, the final balloon payment is the entire principal of the loan. As with bonds, the lending institution, in such instances, might insist on some sort of sinking fund provision.

Collateral Requirements and Other Restrictions

As is true of any bank loan (see Chapter 19), term loans may or may not be secured by a lien against the firm's property. The collateral may take the form of a mortgage on fixed assets, or the loan may be covered by the continuous pledge of current assets, such as marketable securities and accounts receivable. In many cases, however, term loans are unsecured debt. To protect the lender, restrictions are often imposed on management's freedom of action. Minimum levels for working capital, net worth, and interest coverage ratios may be set. Moreover, management may be restricted with regard to dividend payments. In the case of very small companies, the lending institution may even require the firm to insure the lives of senior management personnel or even provide personal guarantees for the loan.

The Default Trigger

default trigger
A restriction in a term loan that gives the lender the right to call the entire loan.

Perhaps the most far-reaching restriction is the lender's right to call the loan, or "trigger" a default. Hence the name **default trigger**. The right to call the entire loan is particularly important in cases where losses are eroding the borrowing company's assets, and the lender wants to force repayment before the deterioration goes any further. If the company cannot repay the loan, the bank has a legal claim to the assets.

In practice, the default trigger is rarely pulled. If the firm cannot meet its obligations, the result is bankruptcy, which is a time-consuming and very costly legal procedure for the lender as well as for the borrower. In effect, if the trigger will induce default, the loan is rarely recalled. In such cases, the lending institution uses the potential threat to force the borrowing company back to the bargaining table so that the terms of the loan can be revised. For example, the interest rate may be renegotiated and additional collateral provided in return for the lender's agreement to continue the loan.

The Interest Rate on Term Loans

The interest rate on a term loan may be variable or fixed for the duration of the loan. Because of the volatility of interest rates in recent years, variable interest rates, which are set as a number of percentage points above the prime lending rate, have become common. This helps to avoid the risk of locking the participants into a particular long-term interest rate. When the prime rate changes, the interest rate on the outstanding balance of the term loan also changes. In all cases, the interest rate on the term loan will usually be very close to the rate on a bond of comparable risk and maturity.

PREFERRED STOCK

Stock issues with a formal preference over common stock can be found in England as early as the sixteenth century, but, there was no general use of preferred stock in the United States until the end of the nineteenth century, when the industrial trusts were being formed and the railroads reorganized. In recent years, many preferred shares which are convertible into common stock have been issued, especially in connection with mergers and acquisitions.

Preferred stock gives the shareholders the right to receive their dividends before the common stockholders. In addition, a variety of other provisions relating to voting, redemption, and preference to assets in case of dissolution are usually included in a preferred stock contract. A preferred stock is a hybrid form that combines the features of debt and equity. The prior position, and usually fixed amount of the preferred dividend, make such stock similar to a bond. However, failure to pay the dividend is not considered a default of an obligation; the board of directors has full authority to forego the payment of the preferred dividend. In this respect, the preferred stock is like a common stock. Similarly, preferred dividends, unlike bond interest, cannot be deducted for tax purposes.

The hybrid nature of a preferred stock becomes even more apparent when we attempt to classify it as debt or equity. From the standpoint of the firm's bondholders and other creditors, the preferred stock is equity, providing them with an additional cushion should the firm fail. The creditors have a prior claim to the firm's income and to its assets. On the other hand, adopting the viewpoint of the common stockholder, the preferred stock represents a fixed prior charge much like a bond.

Voting Rights

Voting rights are only of secondary importance to the preferred stockholders, who because of their prior claim to earnings and assets are not usually given the right to vote for directors unless the preferred dividend has been passed for a number of quarters, or if some other provision of the contract has not been fulfilled. Even in such cases, the preferred shareholders typically have the right to elect only a minority of the board.

Cumulative Dividends

cumulative feature
A stipulation that a firm cannot pay a dividend on its common stock until all accumulated preferred dividends in arrears have been paid.

Today almost all preferred issues have a **cumulative feature**. This stipulates that if the preferred dividend is passed for one or more periods, the firm cannot pay a dividend on its common stock until all the accumulated preferred dividends "in arrears" have been paid. The purpose of such a provision is to protect the preferred shareholders. In the absence of a cumulative clause, the company could conceivably pass both the preferred and common stock dividends for a number of years, and then pay the fixed annual preferred dividend, while at the same time declaring a very large dividend on the common stock. On the other hand, this feature does *not* guarantee that the passed preferred dividends will eventually be paid. It is always possible that the company may never again be in a position to pay any dividends—preferred or common.

A numerical example can help clarify the crucial role played by the cumulative dividend provision. Consider a firm that pays a 7% cumulative dividend on its preferred stock of $100 par value—that is, $7 per share. Now assume that the firm skips the preferred and common stock dividends for 2 years. In the absence of the cumulative feature, the firm could resume payment of its dividend on common stock in the third year, as long as it paid out $7 to the preferred shareholders. The cumulative provision requires the firm to pay all of the accumulated preferred dividends in arrears, plus the current year's preferred dividend (a total of $21), before common stock dividends can be resumed.

Now assume a more extreme case in which the preferred dividend has been skipped for 10 years, so that $70 of accumulated preferred dividends are in arrears. To permit the resumption of dividend payments to the common stockholders, the firm might, in such a case, offer the preferred shareholders common stock with a market value equal to the amount of preferred shares, while at the same time resuming the dividend payment on the common shares.

Participating Feature

participating preferred stock
Stock in which the stockholder is given the right to share in a firm's additional earnings beyond the amount stipulated in the preferred contract.

A **participating preferred stock** is one in which the stockholder is given the right to share in the firm's additional earnings beyond the amount stipulated in the preferred contract. For example, our hypothetical 7% cumulative preferred stock might be entitled to participate in any dividends paid to the common stockholders in excess of $7 per share. If a common stock dividend of $8 is declared, the participating preferred shareholders would be entitled to an extra dividend of $1, bringing their total dividend to $8. Such an arrangement is called *full participation,* but many variants are possible.

Retirement Provisions

Preferred stocks have no maturity date, so a firm desiring to avoid permanent financing must make an explicit provision for retirement in the preferred stock contract. Many preferred stock issues, like long-term bonds, have a sinking fund provision that provides for the orderly retirement of the stock. In the case of preferred stock, a sinking fund appears to be of considerably more significance, since in its absence a preferred stock is a *perpetuity.* In effect, the sinking fund provision is tantamount to issuing redeemable preferred shares, and depending on an investor's expectations regarding the course of future interest rates, such a feature may or may not be desirable. The importance of the sinking fund feature has declined somewhat today, since almost all firms issuing preferred stock now add a *call provision.*

Tax Advantage for Corporations

Much of the recent interest in preferred stock was generated by corporations seeking to take advantage of an interesting tax feature. Before 1986, a corporation that invested in short- or long-term debt had to pay a relatively high corporate income tax. A firm that was in the 46% marginal tax bracket could keep only 54 cents on each dollar of its interest income. However, corporations that purchased certain preferred stocks could exclude 85% of dividend income from their taxable income, thereby reducing the effective corporate tax rate to 7% ($0.15 \times 0.46 = 0.069 = 6.9\%$). The 1986 Tax Reform Act reduced the corporate tax rate to 34% and the exclusion to 80%

of preferred dividends received (see Chapter 2). However, the effective corporate tax rate on the preferred dividends remains approximately 7% (0.20 × 0.34 = 6.8%).

The tax advantage of preferred stock to investing corporations meant that a lower dividend yield was required than for a similar grade bond's interest yield. The preferred stock was often *issued* by firms that were not paying taxes themselves, since for such firms the fact that interest is tax deductible, while dividends are not, is not a consideration. However, many of the opportunities to exploit this particular tax exemption have been closed by the tax authorities.

Floating-Rate Preferred Stock

Since corporations typically invest their liquid reserves for short periods of time, they are especially vulnerable to interest rate risk. Consider, for example, a corporate money manager who wants to invest surplus cash for 6 months, after which it will be used to finance part of a plant expansion. In order to minimize risk, the manager probably will avoid anything but very high grade short-term bonds, or their equivalent. The "infinite" duration of a typical preferred stock would seem to exclude these securities from the money manager's menu.

floating-rate preference share
A share of preferred stock having adjustable interest rates and priced according to a formula pegged to the highest Treasury rates.

To get around the problem posed by preferred stocks' infinite duration, the **floating-rate preference share** was introduced. Adjustable-rate preferreds are often priced according to a formula pegged to the highest of the 90-day, 10-year, or 20-year Treasury rates, with the rate reset quarterly. But the pricing structure also includes a **collar rate** above and below which the yield cannot go. The collars can present a problem, as investors will "bail out" of low collars into high ones.

collar rate
A rate in floating-rate preference shares above and below which the yield cannot go.

Floating-rate preferreds are usually issued by banks or other corporations which are not subject to corporate tax, or are able to shelter their dividend payments. (Recall that dividends are *not* tax deductible to the issuing corporation, whereas interest is.) Figure 13–2 shows the tombstone advertisement for Citicorp's issue of 1 million shares of cumulative price-adjusted preferred stock. Note that the dividend is adjusted quarterly to the movements of the yield on Treasury bills. The link to the short-term interest rate provides an effective floor to the fall in the shares' price should the required market yield on preferred stock rise. This innovative capital market instrument made the otherwise long-term security of Citicorp an appropriate outlet for the temporary investment of corporations' excess funds.

SUMMARY

The fixed income securities are long-term debt and preferred stock. From the firm's standpoint, debt financing has the following advantages: (a) relatively low cost, (b) no sharing of control, (c) tax advantage due to the deductibility of interest, and (d) greater flexibility. The principal disadvantages

NEW ISSUE

February 3, 1984

1,000,000 Shares

CITICORP ✚

Price Adjusted Rate Preferred Stock

(Preferred Stock, Fourth Series)
(without par value)

Dividends are cumulative from the date of issue and are payable quarterly on March 31, June 30, September 30 and December 31 of each year, beginning on March 31, 1984. The dividend rate for the initial dividend period ending March 31, 1984 will be 8% per annum (which is 86.5%, the Applicable Percentage for the initial dividend period, of the bond equivalent of the three-month U.S. Treasury bill secondary market discount rate immediately prior to the offering of the Preferred Stock). The Dividend Rate for each subsequent dividend period, determined in advance of such period, will be the product of (a) the Index Rate times (b) the Applicable Percentage. The Index Rate for any subsequent dividend period will be equal to the arithmetic average of the two most recent three-month U.S. Treasury bill secondary market discount rates (expressed on a bond equivalent basis) as published during the fourteen days prior to the last ten days of the preceding dividend period. The Applicable Percentage for each subsequent dividend period is the Applicable Percentage for the immediately preceding dividend period times the Market Price Adjustment Ratio, which is $100 divided by the Market Price of the Preferred Stock.

Price $100 Per Share

plus accrued dividends from the date of original issue

Copies of the Prospectus may be obtained in any State in
which this announcement is circulated only from such of the
undersigned as may legally offer these securities in such State.

The First Boston Corporation

Merrill Lynch Capital Markets

Lehman Brothers Kuhn Loeb
Incorporated

Goldman, Sachs & Co.	**Morgan Stanley & Co.** Incorporated	**Salomon Brothers Inc**
Bear, Stearns & Co.	**A. G. Becker Paribas** Incorporated	**Blyth Eastman Paine Webber** Incorporated
Donaldson, Lufkin & Jenrette Securities Corporation	**Drexel Burnham Lambert** Incorporated	**Keefe, Bruyette & Woods, Inc.**
Prudential-Bache Securities	**L. F. Rothschild, Unterberg, Towbin**	**M. A. Schapiro & Co., Inc.**
Shearson/American Express Inc.		**Smith Barney, Harris Upham & Co.** Incorporated
Wertheim & Co., Inc.		**Dean Witter Reynolds Inc.**

FIGURE 13–2   Tombstone Advertisement for Citicorp Issue

of the use of debt are: (a) increase in financial risk, (b) increased probability of bankruptcy, and (c) restriction on management's freedom of action.

The long-term debt of corporations often takes the form of a bond issue. The document which stipulates the detailed provision of the bond issue is called the *indenture*. The interests of the bondholders are represented by a *trustee* (usually a large bank); the trustee is responsible for insuring that all provisions of the bond indenture are carried out.

The riskiness to investors of a particular bond issue can be mitigated by including a *pledge of assets* clause in the indenture, such as a mortgage on specific corporate assets which gives the bondholders priority over other creditors in case of liquidation. Risk can also be reduced by means of a *negative pledge*, which places limitations on management's freedom to incur additional debt during the life of the bond issue.

Most bond issues also include some sort of sinking fund provision, which stipulates that the firm will make periodic sinking fund payments for the purposes of retiring the bond issue. The bond indenture may include a *call provision*, which gives the company the right to repurchase the bonds at a stipulated call price during all, or part, of the bond's lifetime.

Since most investors are unable to make an independent assessment of a bond's default risk, *bond ratings* are published regularly by agencies such as Moody's and Standard and Poor's. Bond issues are rated from "gilt edge" (bonds of minimal default risk) to "speculative" (bonds that are already in default or have a significant probability that the obligations will not be met in the future). Institutional investors are very sensitive to the bond ratings, since many of them are precluded by law or by custom from holding low-grade securities.

Financial managers who are concerned with predicting or monitoring the ratings on their bonds can employ the tools of financial ratio analysis. The two best-known measures of bond quality are the *times interest earned ratio (TIE)* and the *burden coverage ratio:*

$$\text{TIE} = \frac{\text{earnings before interest and taxes (EBIT)}}{\text{total bond interest}}$$

$$\text{burden coverage ratio} = \frac{\text{earnings before interest and taxes (EBIT)}}{\text{interest} + \text{principal}/(1 - T)}$$

where T = the appropriate corporate tax rate.

The capital market offers a wide variety of corporate bonds. Some of the most popular forms of bond financing are:

☐ *Mortgage bonds.* The debt is secured by a lien on specific assets. Bonds that have a secondary claim to the same asset are called *second mortgage bonds.*

☐ *Equipment trust certificates.* These represent a first lien against the equipment, but the title to the equipment remains with the trustee, who in turn leases the equipment to the corporation.

☐ *Debentures.* These are bonds which are *not* secured by a direct pledge of specific property.

☐ *Subordinated debentures.* These bonds have a *secondary* claim, relative to other debtors, to the firm's assets.

☐ *Income bonds.* These are the weakest form of debt a corporation can issue. The interest on such bonds is payable only if earned.

☐ *Floating rate bonds.* The interest rate on such bonds is pegged to the Treasury bill rate, usually every 6 months.

☐ *Index bonds.* These are bonds whose interest and principal are tied to some index of the general price level.

☐ *Zero coupon bonds.* These are an extreme form of a *deep discount* bond in which no interest coupon exists. The yield on such a bond results solely from the difference in value between the redemption value and the discounted purchase price.

Corporations also raise long-term debt capital by means of term loans from financial institutions. The principal term lenders to corporations are commercial banks, insurance companies, pension funds, the Small Business Administration, commercial finance companies, and equipment manufacturers. The term loan offers corporate borrowers a fast, flexible, and relatively cheap method of raising long-term debt.

Preferred stock is a hybrid form of capital that combines features of debt and equity. From the bondholder's standpoint, preferred stock is equity which has a claim to dividends and assets *after* all debt obligations have been met. For the common stockholders, the preferred stock has a *prior* claim to both earnings and assets.

In the following chapter, we turn to the firm's basic financing strategy—how to set the best possible debt-equity mix. In Chapter 20 we return to debt financing and discuss some additional variants: convertibles, warrants, options, and leasing.

REVIEW EXERCISE

Circle the correct word(s) to complete the sentences; see p. 344 for the correct answers.

13.1 A limitation on the creation of additional debt is called a *positive/negative* pledge.

13.2 By introducing a number of protective provisions into the bond indenture, the issuing company can enhance the *quality/durability* of its bonds.

13.3 The call feature gives the company the right to *sell/repurchase* its securities at a given call price.

13.4 The call price is invariably fixed *below/above* par.

13.5 The call privilege is *advantageous/disadvantageous* to the investor.

13.6   A lower bond rating, which signifies high default risk, translates itself into *lower/higher* interest costs.

13.7   "Baa" is *sheep in a good mood/a Moody's rating.*

13.8   A high agency rating at time of issue *does/does not* constitute a guarantee that the bonds will retain their initial investment quality until redemption.

13.9   A popular measure of "ability to pay" is the coverage ratio, which *multiplies/divides* EBIT by total bond interest.

13.10   The senior mortgage bondholders must be *partly/fully* compensated before the holders of junior mortgage bondholders can be compensated.

13.11   A closed-end mortgage stipulates that additional bonds, secured by the same property, *can/cannot* be offered.

13.12   Debentures are bonds that *are/are not* secured by a direct pledge of specific property, and are often issued by firms whose creditworthiness *is/is not* especially strong.

13.13   An income bond is the *weakest/strongest* form of debt a corporation can issue.

13.14   When uncertainty regarding the purchasing power of money becomes very great, investors may become *willing/unwilling* to acquire fixed-income-bearing securities.

13.15   Term loans have *lower/higher* costs than comparable bond issues.

13.16   If the default trigger will induce bankruptcy, the loan is *usually/rarely* recalled.

13.17   The holders of preferred stock have a right to receive dividends *before/after* common shareholders and *before/after* all creditors have received their payments.

13.18   Failure to pay the preferred dividend *does/does not* constitute the default of an obligation.

13.19   Today almost all preferred issues have a cumulative feature which stipulates that if the preferred dividend is passed for one or more periods, the firm *can/cannot* pay a dividend on its common stock.

13.20   The cumulative feature *does/does not* guarantee that the passed preferred dividend will eventually be paid.

13.21   Preferred stock has *a/no* maturity date.

QUESTIONS

13.1   Define the following terms:
  a. Mortgage bond
  b. Sinking fund
  c. Investment grade
  d. Debenture
  e. Zero coupon bond
  f. Participating preferred stock
  g. Floating-rate preferred stock
  h. Serial bond
  i. After-acquired property clause
  j. Delayed settlement basis
  k. "Cocktail" bond

13.2   List and explain the advantages and disadvantages of debt financing over equity financing.

13.3 "The goal of management is to maximize shareholders' wealth." If this is so, why would anyone invest in bonds?

13.4 What precludes a firm that is facing bankruptcy from selling off all its assets and distributing them as dividends to its shareholders, thereby leaving the bondholders out in the cold?

13.5 What is a call provision? When might a corporation wish to call its bonds? Explain.

13.6 "The coverage ratio is always greater than the burden coverage ratio." Do you agree with this statement?

13.7 During the last few years so-called junk bonds, which offer very high interest rates, have appeared on the market. How do you account for the high interest rates on such bonds?

13.8 List the types of bonds you know in decreasing order of riskiness.

13.9 "Zero coupon bonds are the best deal around! They are much, much cheaper than an interest-paying bond with the same maturity and face value." Comment on this statement.

13.10 What advantages does SEC Rule 415 give a company?

13.11 How can you account for the fact that many creditors do *not* call in a loan when a debtor is in financial difficulties, even though they have the right to do so?

13.12 How can the following be expected to affect an investor's "valuation" of a call feature?
   a. He expects future interest rates to fall.
   b. He expects future interest rates to rise.

PROBLEMS

13.1 Coverage ratios.   Boulder & Co. is financed in part by $2,000,000 of senior debt at 6% interest and a $1,000,000 junior debt with 8% interest. The senior bonds are redeemed in yearly instalments of $100,000, the junior bonds in instalments of $66,666 per year. Earnings before interest and taxes are $850,000, and the corporate tax rate is 34%.
   a. Compute the appropriate TIE ratios.
   b. Compute the appropriate burden coverage ratios.

13.2 Preferred stock.   In addition to the senior and junior bonds, Boulder has 300,000 preferred shares outstanding (par value $10). The preferred dividend is 10% per year. Recompute your answers to problem 13.1.

13.3 Index bonds.   An investor is offered a 9% 1-year $1,000 bond with both interest and principal linked to the cost of living index. Assume the consumer price index is expected to rise this year from 130 to 195 points.
   a. How much will the investor receive at the end of the year?
   b. What is the *real* interest rate on the bonds?
   c. How do your answers change if only the principal is linked to the cost of living index?

13.4 Liquidation.   John Smythe & Co. has gone bankrupt. The company had

$600,000 straight debentures and $100,000 subordinated debentures on its books. It also had $300,000 trade credits outstanding. John Smythe's assets are auctioned off for $700,000.

a. Who gets what?

b. How does your answer change if the proceeds of the auction are $900,000?

13.5 Cumulative preferred stock.   The Rafer Corporation wants to distribute $500,000 as dividends. There are 50,000 preferred shares at $100 par value carrying a $5 cumulative dividend, and 100,000 shares of common stock outstanding. Last year's preferred and common dividends were skipped.

a. What dividends will the holders of each share of common stock receive?

b. How does your answer change if Rafer wants to distribute $700,000 as dividends?

13.6 Cumulative preferred dividends in arrears.   Filbers & Co. pays a 6.5% cumulative dividend on its 100,000 shares of preferred stock of $60 par value. There are also 100,000 shares of common stock outstanding. Filbers has not paid any dividends during the last four years. This year Filbers has net after-tax earnings of $1,750,000. What is the maximum dividend Filbers can pay to its common stockholders?

13.7 Zero coupon bonds.   You are offered the choice between buying a zero coupon bond for $370, which has a face value of $2,000 and will mature in 25 years, or a 7% bond which also has a face value of $2,000 and matures in 25 years. Interest is paid on the last day of the year. Which bond do you prefer?

13.8 Inflation and alternative bond investments.   John Brown has the option of buying one of these three bonds: (a) A 9% unlinked bond with 15 years to maturity and $2,000 face value. (b) A 7% bond whose principal and interest are linked to the rate of inflation, with 15 years to maturity and $1,000 face value. (c) An unlinked zero coupon bond with 15 years to maturity and $3,000 face value. All three bonds sell for $1,000. Inflation is expected to run at 5% annually during the coming 15 years. Which bond should John Brown choose?

13.9 Term loan.   Joseph Luton, the lending manager of Green Grass Bank, is computing the cash flow of a 10-year loan of $12,000 that was extended to Dick Bogle, a store owner. The terms are as follows: The interest rate is 9%; during the first 3 years only interest needs to be paid. Starting in the fourth year, a certain amount must be paid annually, such that all interest and the principal will have been paid at the end of the tenth year.

a. Help Joseph Luton figure the cash flow for this loan.

b. What is the *real* cash flow of the loan, if we assume that the rate of inflation for the next 10 years will run at 3% annually?

SAMPLE PROBLEMS

SP13.1 The Barrow Corporation has earnings before interest and taxes of $70,000, and the following interest obligations: annual interest on senior bonds:

$100,000, annual interest on junior bonds: $40,000. Annual principal repayments amount to $80,000 for the senior bond, and $25,000 for the junior bonds. The corporate tax rate is 34%.

a. Compute the appropriate interest coverage (TIE) ratios.

b. Compute the burden coverage ratios.

SP13.2 Consider the case of a firm that is liquidated for $1,500,000 but has outstanding $800,000 of straight debentures, $700,000 of bank loans, and $500,000 of subordinated debentures.

a. Who receives what?

b. How does your answer change if only $1,200,000 had been realized upon liquidation?

c. How does your answer change if $1,800,000 had been realized upon liquidation?

Solutions to Sample Problems

SP13.1 a. The times interest earned ratio for the senior bonds is defined as "earnings before interest and taxes" divided by "interest on the senior bonds". Hence:

$$\text{TIE ratio of senior bonds} = \text{EBIT/interest}$$
$$= 700{,}000/100{,}000 = 7$$

For the junior bonds we have to compute the TIE ratio on the *cumulative* combination of senior and junior bonds. Hence:

$$\text{TIE ratio for the junior bonds} = \text{EBIT/interest on both bonds}$$
$$= 700{,}000/(100{,}000 + 40{,}000)$$
$$= 700{,}000/140{,}000 = 5$$

b. For the burden coverage ratio, we must include the after-tax cost of principal repayment in the denominator. Hence,

burden coverage ratio of senior bonds
$$= \text{EBIT/(interest + principal repayment } [1/1 - T])$$
$$= 700{,}000 / (100{,}000 + 80{,}000 [1/1 - .34])$$
$$= 700{,}000 / (100{,}000 + 121{,}216) = 700{,}000/221{,}216$$
$$= 3.16$$

For the junior bonds we must compute the coverage ratio for the cumulative combination of senior and junior bonds:

burden coverage ratio of junior bonds
$$= \text{EBIT/(interest + principal repayment } [1/1 - T])$$
$$= 700{,}000 / (100{,}000 + 105{,}000[1/1 - .34])$$
$$= 700{,}000 / (100{,}000 + 159{,}091) = 700{,}000/259{,}091$$
$$= 2.70$$

SP13.2 Each group is entitled to a share of the proceeds from liquidation in proportion to its share in the total debt:

	Outstanding Claims	
Straight debentures	$ 800,000	40%
Bank loans	$ 700,000	35%
Subordinated debentures	$ 500,000	25%
Total	$2,000,000	100%

a. If the firm's assets are liquidated for $1,500,000, the debtors share in the proceeds as follows:

	Share in Liquidation
Straight debentures	$ 800,000
Bank loans	$ 525,000
Subordinated debentures	$ 175,000
Total	$1,500,000

In this case the holders of the straight debentures receive $800,000 (600,000 plus 200,000 from the share of the subordinated debentures), the banks receive $525,000, and the holders of the subordinated debentures receive $175,000 (375,000 minus 200,000).

b. If the liquidation of the firm's assets yields only $1,200,000, the debtors receive the following:

	Share in Liquidation
Straight debentures	$ 780,000
Bank loans	$ 420,000
Subordinated debentures	—
Total	$1,200,000

In this case the holders of the straight debentures receive $780,000 (480,000 plus 300,000 from the share of the subordinated debentures), the banks receive $420,000, and the holders of the subordinated debentures receive nothing.

c. If the firm's assets are liquidated for $1,800,000, the debtors receive the following:

	Share in Liquidation
Straight debentures	$ 800,000
Bank loans	$ 630,000
Subordinated debentures	$ 370,000
Total	$1,800,000

In this case, the holders of the straight debentures again receive their entire $800,000 (780,000 plus 20,000 from the share of the subordinated debentures), the banks receive $630,000, and the holders of the subordinated debentures receive $370,000 (450,000 minus 80,000).

Answers to Review Exercise							
13.1 negative	**13.2** quality	**13.3** repurchase	**13.4** above
13.5 disadvantageous	**13.6** higher	**13.7** a Moody's rating
13.8 does not	**13.9** divides	**13.10** fully	**13.11** cannot
13.12 are not, is	**13.13** weakest	**13.14** unwilling	**13.15** lower
13.16 rarely	**13.17** before, after	**13.18** does not	**13.19** cannot
13.20 does not	**13.21** no

SUGGESTIONS FOR FURTHER READING

The classic study of the factors affecting risk premiums on bonds is that of Lawrence Fisher, "Determinants of Risk Premiums on Corporate Bonds," *Journal of Political Economy*, June 1959. Calvin M. Boardman and Richard W. McEnally generalize this approach to include the effects of sinking fund provisions, exchange listing, industry and bonds' beta risk, in "Factors Affecting Seasoned Corporate Bond Prices," *Journal of Financial and Quantitative Analysis*, June 1981. See also Michael G. Ferri, "An Empirical Examination of Bond Yield Spreads," *Financial Management*, Autumn 1978.

The effects of the downgrading of bond ratings are discussed by W. B. Hickman, *Corporate Bond Quality and Investors' Experience* (New York: National Bureau of Economic Research, 1958); George Pinches and J. Clay Singleton, "The Adjustment of Stock Prices to Bond Rating Changes," *Journal of Finance*, March 1978; and Morton Backer and Martin L. Grossman, "The Use of Financial Ratios in Credit Downgrade Decisions," *Financial Management*, Spring 1980.

The significance of the call option on a bond is discussed in greater detail by Zvi Bodie and Benjamin Fried-man, "Interest Rate Uncertainty and the Value of Bond Call Protection," *Journal of Political Economy*, February 1978.

The advantages of income bonds for the issuing firm are examined in J. J. McConnell and G. G. Schlarbaum, "Returns, Risks, and Pricing of Income Bonds, 1956–1976," *Journal of Business*, January 1981.

Innovations in bond financing and markets are analyzed by James C. Van Horne, "On Financial Innovations and Excesses," *Journal of Finance*, July 1985.

The hybrid nature of preferred stock is critically examined by J. Clay Singleton and Daniel E. Vetter, "Factors Affecting the Pricing of Listed, Industrial Preferred Stocks," *Journal of the Midwest Finance Association*, Vol. 12, 1983; and Eric H. Svenson and Clark A. Hawkins, "On the Pricing of Preferred Stock," *Journal of Financial and Quantitative Analysis*, November 1981.

Adjustable-rate preferreds are examined by Bernard J. Winger, Carl R. Chen, John D. Martin, Jr., J. William Petty, and Stephen C. Hayden, "Adjustable Rate Preferred Stock," *Financial Management*, Spring 1986.

14 | Leverage and Capital Structure

In the preceding two chapters the principal characteristics of debt and equity were examined. This chapter is devoted to the tradeoff between these two types of corporate strategies. We shall attempt to isolate and explain the impact of the financing mix on the return earned by the firm's shareholders and on the risk level of its common stock. The economic factors which affect a firm's choice of long-term financing strategy are examined. These include tax considerations, bankruptcy costs, level and stability of assets, and the probable impact on dividend policy.

In the discussion of capital budgeting, we assumed that the firm's risk-return profile could be changed only by altering its investment program. In this chapter we deal with an alternative means of influencing earnings and risk—changing the firm's financial mix. Here we take the firm's investment program and its business risk as given, and seek to determine the influence of changes in its capital structure on the market value of the owners' equity. The objective is to find the particular combination of debt and equity that provides the best expected risk-return combination.

FINANCIAL LEVERAGE AND EARNINGS

What effect does the introduction of fixed-interest-bearing debt (or preferred stock) have on the return to the firm's shareholders and on the risk level of its common stock? To answer this question, we start by considering a new company that faces a decision regarding its initial capital structure—a decision with respect to the best debt-equity mix with which to finance its operations. For simplicity, assume that there are only two mutually exclusive alternatives: (a) financing the firm with 100% equity, and (b) financing the firm with equal amounts of stock and bonds. We also assume that taxes are not levied on either the firm's income or that of the shareholders.

Table 14–1 shows the relevant data for these two alternatives. Since we are discussing two alternative financial plans for the same company, the net operating income (net earnings *before* interest) is the same in both cases. Note also that the distribution of the operating income, and therefore the degree of business risk attached to these earnings, must be the same in both cases. The net income in alternative B declines from $1,000 to $750, since (by assumption) 5% interest must be paid on the $5,000 of capital raised via bonds. But as fewer shares are issued in alternative B, earnings per share of common stock (EPS), which are one of the key inputs for shareholders' wealth maximization, rise in alternative B from $1.00 to $1.50. The change in EPS caused by the use of fixed payment securities to finance a company's operations is called **financial leverage.** The bonds in our example serve as a lever, so to speak, which raises EPS for a given **net operating income (NOI).** The reason for this is not hard to find. Although the company pays out 5% interest on the bonds, it earns a return of 10% on its assets, thereby raising the return to the common shareholders. And since we are considering a case without taxes, substitution of a 5% preferred share for the bonds has the same leverage effect as the bonds.

If we introduce corporate taxes[1] (at the rate of 34%), net income will be reduced in both examples: EPS (after taxes) becomes $0.66 and $0.99 in alternatives A and B, respectively. The general line of reasoning remains the same. Although the firm pays out 5% on the bonds, the effective cost in terms of after-tax income is only $(1 - T)r$, where T denotes the corporate tax rate and r the rate of interest. This reduction in the cost of debt follows directly from the tax deduction afforded by the interest payments. In our

financial leverage
The change in EPS caused by the use of fixed payment securities to finance a company's operations.

net operating income (NOI)
A firm's net earnings before deducting interest.

TABLE 14–1 Selected Data for Two Alternative Financing Strategies

	Alternative A (100% Equity) ($)	Alternative B (50% Bonds, 50% Equity) ($)
Net operating income (NOI)	1,000	1,000
Interest (5% on bonds)	—	250
Net income (NI)	1,000	750
Capitalization:		
Stock	10,000	5,000
Bonds	—	5,000
Total stocks and bonds	10,000	10,000
Number of shares	1,000	500
Earnings per share (EPS)	**1.00**	**1.50**

[1] To simplify the presentation, any positive effects of leverage on the price of a firm's shares are ignored, in the tables below, when calculating the number of shares issued. See H. Levy and R. Brooks, "Financial Break-Even Analysis and the Value of the Firm," *Financial Management,* Autumn, 1986.

example, the after-tax cost of the debt is $(1 - 0.34)\,0.05 = 3.3\%$. Since the firm earns a net *after-tax* return of 6.6% on its assets, the leverage effect again results from the difference between the effective (after-tax) rate of outlay on the bonds, 3.3%, and the (after-tax) rate of return earned by the company on the total capital invested, 6.6%. Note, however, that in the after-tax example, substituting a 5% preferred stock creates a much smaller leverage effect because the dividend paid on preferred stock is *not* tax-deductible. The after-tax "cost" of the preferred dividend is 5%, compared with the after-tax cost of 3.3% in the case of the bonds. If the preferred dividend were exactly 6.6%—that is, just equal to the company's after-tax rate of return on assets—the EPS would remain constant; there would be no leverage effect from using preferred stock.

FINANCIAL LEVERAGE AND RISK

favorable leverage
A situation in which EPS rises as a result of the introduction of debt into the capital structure.

unfavorable leverage
A situation in which EPS falls as a result of debt introduced into the capital structure.

In the previous example we saw that the introduction of fixed-interest-bearing securities into a firm's capital structure can raise EPS as long as the firm earns more on its assets than it pays out to the bondholders. However, upon reflection, leverage might, in certain circumstances, also lower EPS. This happens if the rate of interest on the debt exceeds the rate of return on the firm's assets. We will refer to the first scenario, in which EPS rises as a result of the introduction of debt into the capital structure, as **favorable leverage,** and one in which EPS falls as **unfavorable leverage.** Thus, the use of debt financing potentially can increase a firm's profitability, but it also introduces an additional element of risk. In "good" years financial leverage will most likely be favorable; however, the leverage effect may reduce EPS in relatively bad years.

One of the crucial tasks of management is to attempt to evaluate the risks of leverage by forecasting the relative probability of "good" versus "bad" economic conditions. This task can be facilitated by using a special version of that well-known management tool, *breakeven analysis,* in order to simulate the impact of financial leverage on EPS for varying levels of output and sales—or alternatively, for different levels of net operating income.

Table 14–2 shows the earnings per share for the two alternative financing plans (A = 100% equity and B = 50% equity and 50% bonds) over a wide range of possible levels of future net operating income. (For simplicity, we again assume the absence of taxes.) A glance at the data in Table 14–2 shows that the leverage is "favorable", that is, it raises EPS when net operating income is greater than $500. It decreases EPS when net operating income is less than $500. The leverage is neutral (leaves EPS unchanged) for the case in which NOI = $500. Hence, the "breakeven" point in this example is $500.

For levels of NOI above $500, the firm earns a rate of return on total assets in excess of the 5% paid to the bondholders, thereby raising the EPS to its common shareholders. Conversely, should net operating earnings fall

TABLE 14–2   Earnings per Share for the Alternative Financing Plans

Alternative A: 100% Equity

Net operating income	1,500	1,250	1,000	750	500	250	0	−500
Interest	−	−	−	−	−	−	−	−
Net income	1,500	1,250	1,000	750	500	250	0	−500
Number of shares	1,000	1,000	1,000	1,000	1,000	1,000	1,000	1,000
Earnings per share	1.50	1.25	1.00	0.75	0.50	0.25	0	−0.50

Alternative B: 50% Shares, 50% Bonds

Net operating income	1,500	1,250	1,000	750	500	250	0	−500
Interest	250	250	250	250	250	250	250	250
Net income	1,250	1,000	750	500	250	0	−250	−750
Number of shares	500	500	500	500	500	500	500	500
Earnings per share	2.50	2.00	1.50	1.00	0.50	0	−0.50	−1.50

below $500, the firm will earn less than 5% on its assets, and the bondholders can be compensated only at the "expense" of the shareholders, which reduces EPS.

The differential impact of financial leverage is illustrated in Figure 14–1, which graphs EPS as a function of NOI. The dashed line ZZ which goes through the breakeven point divides the chart into two sections. All points to the right of this line represent favorable leverage (+), and all points to the left represent unfavorable leverage (−).

**FIGURE 14–1
Impact of Financial
Leverage: Break-
even Analysis**

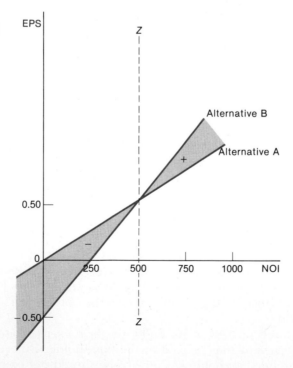

Since risk is associated with the degree of variability, the graph shows that the financial risk associated with the mixed capital structure (alternative B) is greater than that of the all-equity structure (alternative A). The greater riskiness is reflected in the *steeper slope* of line *B;* for each per-unit change in NOI, the induced change in EPS is greater in the case of the leveraged capital structure. Despite the identical business risk (we are making alternative assumptions about the financing of the same company), the introduction of leverage magnifies the fluctuations of EPS, increasing the risk associated with the investment in common stock. It follows that the riskiness of an investment in the shares of a company with a levered capital structure exceeds the risk associated with the same shares when the capital structure is unlevered.

This relationship can be seen more clearly from Figure 14–2, which plots the hypothetical fluctuations of EPS over time. The solid line, labeled *A,* represents the assumed fluctuations when the company is financed solely by common stock. The dashed line, marked *B,* represents the fluctuations in EPS for the same operating incomes when the firm is financed by equal proportions of bonds and stock. Note that the introduction of leverage magnifies the variability of the income stream to the shareholders in both directions. Once again, the leverage breakeven point is given by NOI = 500, which corresponds to the point EPS = 0.50 on the vertical axis of Figure 14–2. (The guideline marked "NOI = 500" has been added to identify the critical breakeven point.) Note also that when the firm is financed solely by stock, it never suffers an operating loss. (We assume zero profits in only one

FIGURE 14–2
Impact of Financial Leverage: Time Series Analysis

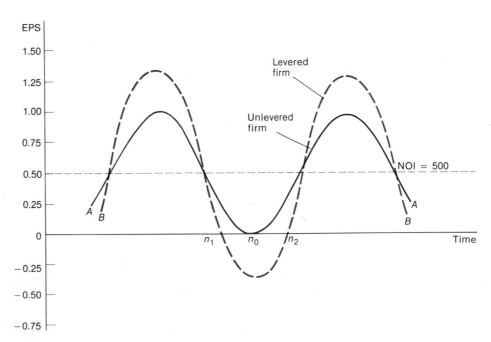

year, point n_0 on the horizontal axis.) However, when leverage is introduced, losses are incurred during the period between n_1 and n_2.

Business Risk vs. Financial Risk

A firm's business risk reflects the industry to which it belongs and general economic conditions. It reflects uncertainty regarding the future prices of inputs and outputs, as well as possible changes in technology, competition, and tastes. The business risk of public utilities is usually significantly less than that of most manufacturing firms. This reflects the smaller fluctuations in the demand for the services provided by utilities. The demand for the products of industrial firms tends to be more unstable. This instability may reflect changes in fashion, fluctuations in the real incomes of consumers, or perhaps overseas competition.

Even if firms never issue debt, we would still expect to find a higher variability in the earnings per share of industrial firms than in the EPS of utilities. This is what is meant by the statement that industrial firms have a greater **business risk** than public utilities. Since business risk depends on general economic conditions, it is not related to the firm's financial structure. Therefore, the variability of net operating income (NOI per share), which reflects the firm's net earnings *before* interest payments are deducted, is an appropriate measure of such risk.

business risk
Risk that depends on the industry to which a business belongs and on general economic conditions.

As we have previously noted, financial leverage intensifies the variability of EPS. We shall denote the additional variability of earnings induced by leverage as **financial risk.** The decision of a firm to enter a particular line of economic endeavor, or undertake a particular investment program, affects its business risk; the decision to finance the investment (partially or completely) with debt determines its financial risk. Clearly, the company's shareholders are concerned with total risk—with the firm's business as well as its financial risk.

financial risk
The additional variability of earnings induced by leverage.

To illustrate the impact of leverage on risk, Table 14–3 shows a firm's expectations regarding future operating earnings; in this particular example, an equal chance of earning $1,000 or $250. (For simplicity we again assume a world without taxes.) As can be seen from Table 14–3, introducing debt into the capital structure increases the *expected value* of earnings per share from $0.625 to $0.75. But leverage also has an impact on risk. If the net operating income turns out to be $1,000, leverage increases the EPS from $1.00 to $1.50; however, there is also a 50% likelihood of a less favorable result—that is, of a net operating income of only $250. Should this occur, the use of debt will *decrease* the EPS from $0.25 to zero.

In general, we must take both the bad and the good into account if the financial decision is to reflect the actual underlying uncertainties of business life. We are concerned with the variance (or standard deviation) of EPS, and not just with its expected value. The variance of alternative A, which represents a case of pure equity financing, is 0.14. The variance of the unlevered earnings measures the firm's *business risk*. Alternative B gives the results for the same firm should it decide to introduce 50% debt. The variability of the

TABLE 14–3   Example of Impact of Financial Leverage on Risk

	Alternative A (100% Equity) Probability		Alternative B (50% Bonds, 50% Equity) Probability	
	½	½	½	½
	$	$	$	$
Net operating income (NOI)	1,000	250	1,000	250
Interest (5% on bonds)	—	—	250	250
Net income (NI)	1,000	250	750	0
Capitalization				
Stock	10,000	10,000	5,000	5,000
Bonds	—	—	5,000	5,000
Total shocks and bonds	10,000	10,000	10,000	10,000
Number of shares	1,000	1,000	500	500
Earnings per share (EPS)	1.00	0.25	1.50	0
Expected EPS*	**0.625**		**0.75**	
Variance of EPS*	**0.14**		**0.56**	

* The expected value of EPS of firm A is given by ½ × 1.00 + ½ × 0.25 = $0.625 and its variance is calculated as follows: ½ (1.00 − 0.625)² + ½ (0.25 − 0.625)² = 0.14. Similarly, the expected value and variance of the EPS of firm B are given by ½ × 1.50 + ½ × 0 = $0.75 and ½ (1.50 − 0.75)² + ½ (0 − 0.75)² = 0.56, respectively.

EPS in the latter case is higher, 0.56. In this instance, the variance reflects the business *and* the additional financial risk. Only the 0.14 variance is due to business risk; the additional 0.42 is generated by the financial risk incurred from the use of debt.

OPERATING LEVERAGE

operating leverage
The degree to which a business's costs are fixed and do not decline when sales fall.

As we have already noted, business risk depends, among other things, on fluctuations in the demand for a firm's output. It also depends on fluctuations in costs. A firm's **operating leverage** deals with this aspect of business risk. Operating leverage reflects the extent to which the firm's costs are fixed. When a high percentage of costs are fixed, and therefore do not decline when sales fall, there is less flexibility, and so the firm is exposed to a high degree of business risk.

When it establishes its financial strategy, each firm is confronted with a difficult decision regarding the total amount of risk it is willing to undertake. In this context, we should recall that any given level of total risk reflects both the financing mix (financial leverage) and the firm's cost structure (operating leverage). Given a specific target for the level of total risk, we expect a firm with a large proportion of fixed costs to adopt a relatively conservative capital structure.

Figure 14–3 presents operating leverage charts for two firms which differ only in the composition of their costs. Both firms sell the same prod-

**FIGURE 14–3
Operating
Leverage Break-
even Charts**

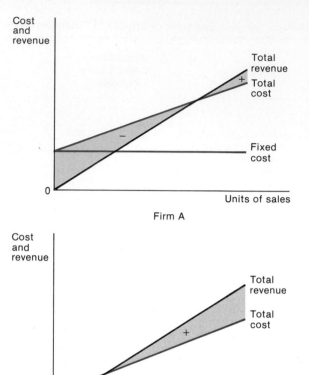

Firm A

Firm B

uct at the same price, and therefore have the same total revenue. However, firm A has a higher operating leverage: its variable costs are lower, and its fixed costs are higher, than those of firm B. The fact that firm A has *lower* variable costs is reflected in the smaller slope of its "total cost" function, which for diagrammatic simplicity is assumed to be linear.

Clearly, the *operating breakeven* points of the two firms are not identical. Moreover, a per-unit shift of sales induces a relatively greater change in the profit (or loss) of firm A. This follows from our assumption that the difference in the slopes of the "total cost" and the "total revenue" lines of firm A is greater than the difference between the slopes of the relevant cost and revenue lines of firm B. Firms with relatively high fixed costs (operating leverage) are characterized by relatively high variability of operating earnings. Such firms can reach the desired total risk level by adopting a relatively conservative debt policy. Conversely, firms with lower operating leverage might conceivably reach the same target risk level with a far larger debt-equity ratio. Their willingness to undertake the additional financial risk reflects in this instance the greater stability of the underlying operating earnings.

The tradeoff between operating and financial leverage is illustrated by a numerical example in Table 14–4. In actual practice, of course, these two strategies are not perfect substitutes, as the simplified example might seem to imply. However, both do affect the variability of earnings per share in the same direction.

In the example we have assumed that there is an equal probability that sales will turn out to be 100,000 or 500,000 units. Each unit is sold for $1; therefore the total revenue is either $100,000 or $500,000. Firm A has a larger operating leverage, since its fixed cost is $50,000, as compared with only $35,000 for firm B. However, firm A is a pure equity company; the firm issued 100,000 shares at $5 each, so its total equity is $500,000. Firm B, on the other hand, issued only 80,000 shares for $5 each, and an additional $100,000 worth of bonds paying interest at the rate of 5%. The variable cost of firm A is assumed to be 50 cents per unit, while the variable cost of firm B (with the low fixed cost) is higher—60 cents per unit. Taking all these data into account, the earnings per share of both firms will be zero or $1, depending on which of the two sales forecasts is used.

The two firms thus offer the same variability of earnings to stockholders. This goal is achieved in the case of firm B by the use of more intensive financial leverage; and in firm A by a combination of a higher operating leverage with a lower level of debt financing. But choosing between financial and operating leverage is not as simple as it might seem. In many cases, the firm has only limited discretion regarding its plant and equipment. The limited objective of this numerical exercise is merely to point out that the firm must consider the impact of *both* kinds of leverage when deciding on its financial strategy. A good rule to keep in mind is this: The higher the operating leverage, the more risky the recourse to financial leverage.

TABLE 14–4 **The Tradeoff Between Operating and Financial Leverage**

	Firm A		Firm B	
	Bad Year	Good Year	Bad Year	Good Year
	$	$	$	$
Sales	100,000	500,000	100,000	500,000
Fixed cost				
(not including interest)	50,000	50,000	35,000	35,000
Interest	—	—	—	—
Total fixed cost	50,000	50,000	40,000	40,000
Variable cost	50,000	250,000	60,000	300,000
Total cost	100,000	300,000	100,000	340,000
Net earnings before tax	0	200,000	0	160,000
Corporate tax	0	100,000	0	80,000
Net earnings after				
corporate tax	0	100,000	0	80,000
Number of shares	100,000	100,000	80,000	80,000
Earnings per share	**0**	**$1.00**	**0**	**$1.00**

THE RISK-RETURN TRADEOFF

In a fanciful world of no risk, in which the future volume of sales, prices, costs, and hence profits are known with absolute certainty, the use of financial leverage presents no particular difficulty. Given these unrealistic assumptions, management would know in advance the exact point on the horizontal axis of Fig. 14–1 that denotes a future year's NOI. If the leverage is favorable, the firm would use a maximum of debt to finance its investments. In such a case, the greater the leverage, the higher the EPS. On the other hand, if we knew *with certainty* that the NOI is located to the left of the breakeven point, the optimal solution would be to finance the firm with 100% equity.

These two extreme cases really have no practical significance. The actual problem facing the financial manager is to choose a financial strategy (capital structure) in a realistic setting in which future sales prices, costs, and hence net operating income are all uncertain. That is to say, the manager does not know in advance if the future NOI will lie to the right or to the left of the breakeven point. Consequently, the firm cannot be certain that the financial leverage will be favorable.

The impact of financial leverage, given the realistic assumption that uncertainty prevails, can be reduced to three alternatives:

1. Situations in which leverage increases risk, but at the same time decreases expected EPS.
2. Neutral situations in which the increase in risk following the introduction of leverage leaves expected EPS unchanged.
3. Situations in which the introduction of leverage increases expected EPS and risk simultaneously.

These situations are shown schematically in Figure 14–4. The three solid curves in the diagram describe the EPS probability distributions of a firm financed by 100% equity; these curves provide a pictorial description of the firm's expected profit and business risk. Future EPS is not known with certainty, and the solid curves present the probabilities of occurrence for various alternatives of EPS.

The dashed curves in the same diagram represent the probability distribution of EPS when debt is used. In all three cases leverage increases the variability of earnings; that is, leverage increases shareholders' risk. The dashed curves are flatter, which reflect the fact that leverage *increases* variability (risk). However, the three dashed curves in Figure 14–4 differ with respect to the degree of impact leverage has on expected (mean) EPS.

Figure 14–4a depicts a situation in which leverage *increases* risk, but *decreases* expected EPS. This can occur if the mean post-tax unlevered rate of return on assets is less than the post-tax interest cost. In such a case we

FIGURE 14–4
**Financial Leverage
and Uncertainty.**

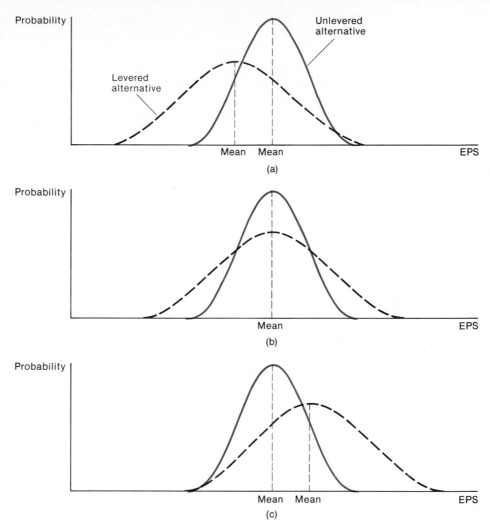

would expect the firm to adopt an *unlevered* financial strategy. The second alternative is illustrated in Figure 14–4b. In this case, introducing leverage *increases* the variability of the EPS, but the mean EPS is *unaffected*. This can occur if the unlevered post-tax rate of return on assets is just equal to the after-tax interest cost. Again, the optimal strategy is to forego the use of leverage, since introducing debt does not raise profitability, but it does increase risk.

   Although the first two cases could occur in real life, they are relatively uninteresting; in both instances the firm would simply forego debt financing. The only relevant, and by far the most challenging, situation confronting financial managers is the third alternative in which the use of leverage increases both EPS and risk. This is depicted in Figure 14–4c, where the introduction of leverage increases expected EPS and risk simultaneously. In this instance, the expected unlevered after-tax rate of return on assets exceeds the after-tax interest cost; hence any increase in the degree of leverage increases expected profitability. In terms of Figure 14–4c, the mean of the levered alternative (dashed curve) lies to the right of the mean of the unlevered distribution. Again the increase in variance is reflected by the relative flatness of the dashed curve. Unfortunately, finding the optimal solution to the financing problem in this case, which incidentally characterizes almost all firms, is neither straightforward nor simple.

EPS VS. STOCK PRICES

The situation depicted in Figure 14–4c, which is the typical case, shows that the levered alternative is characterized by both a higher expected EPS and a higher variance—that is, greater variability of earnings. This result confronts financial managers with the difficult problem of finding a way to weigh and compare the advantages and disadvantages of leverage. A first step in this direction is to recall that the goal of the firm is to maximize the value of shareholders' equity—that is, to seek the highest stock price. Since leverage increases both risk and return, striving to reach the highest possible (mean) EPS may not, and often is not, compatible with achieving the maximum market value of the firm's equity. After a point, the capital market may penalize the increase in risk and as a result, the stock price will fall.

This is illustrated in Figures 14–5a and 14–5b. Because leverage is assumed to be favorable, expected EPS rises continually as more debt is added to the firm's capital structure. After a point, however, the capital market reacts to the increased risk and demands higher interest rates on the firm's debt, reducing the degree of positive leverage. Finally, the leverage becomes unfavorable and expected EPS begins to fall. As can be seen from Figure 14–5a, EPS is maximized when the firm adopts the capital structure denoted by the debt-equity ratio, L^*.

The increase in risk also has an impact on stock prices; see Figure 14–5b. Leverage increases EPS, but it also increases the market's required capitalization rate because of the additional risk. The question is, which of the two effects will dominate. As debt is introduced into the capital structure, investors translate the increase in expected EPS into increases in the value of the firm's equity by bidding up the price of its shares. But as more and more debt is used the increase in risk becomes dominant, and the rise of the market capitalization rate accelerates. After a point, the price of the firm's shares begins to fall. The optimal financing mix; that is, the debt-equity ratio that maximizes share price, is denoted by L^{**} in Figure 14–5b. It lies considerably to the left of the debt-equity ratio that maximizes EPS.

**FIGURE 14–5
Relationship
Between Expected
EPS, Stock Price,
and Degree
of Leverage**

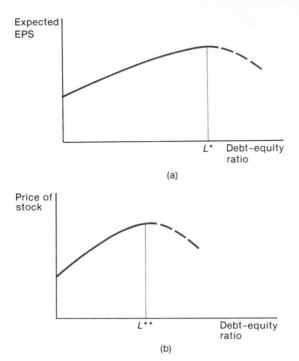

(a)

(b)

**Taxes
and
Bankruptcy
Costs**

Two factors account for the pattern by which leverage first causes stock prices to rise and then to fall. This pattern largely reflects the impact of the tax deductibility of interest payments and the costs of bankruptcy.

Since interest is tax-deductible while dividends are not, the tax laws have created a bias in favor of the use of debt. And other things being equal, the higher the corporate tax rate, the greater the potential advantage of using debt financing. On the surface, the existence of such a tax shelter seems to lead to the conclusion that firms should always use maximum leverage. But as we have already noted, you can have too much of a good thing! Tax deductibility enhances the positive impact of leverage on expected EPS, but the additional debt also increases the probability of default and possible bankruptcy, which causes the market capitalization rate to increase.

Bankruptcy risk is one risk which financial managers and investors are not likely to ignore. The negative impact of bankruptcy risk on share prices reflects the fact that the **costs of bankruptcy** are not trivial. These costs include legal fees, accountants' fees, administrative expenses, and other *direct* costs paid out during the liquidation and reorganization process. To these we must add the often considerable *indirect* bankruptcy costs, the loss of earnings from foregone sales. One recent study has estimated the indirect bankruptcy cost alone at more than 17% of the firm's market value (see Appendix 14A).

costs of bankruptcy
*Legal fees,
accountants' fees,
administrative
expenses, and other
direct and indirect
costs incurred during
liquidation and
reorganization.*

The combined impact of taxes, the rise in the market capitalization rate, and bankruptcy costs on the market value of the firm is illustrated in Figure 14–6. The diagram assumes that up to the capital structure denoted by L_1, the present value of the tax shelter from debt increases stock prices and therefore the market value of the firm. From that point on, however, the probability of incurring bankruptcy costs becomes significant, so that additional leverage increases the value of the firm (stock price), but at a *decreasing* rate. If the debt-equity ratio is increased beyond L_2, potential bankruptcy costs outweigh the tax benefits, and the additional leverage reduces the value of the firm because stock prices fall.

target capital structure
A combination of debt and equity that maximizes the price of a firm's stock.

The capital structure that maximizes the price of the stock represents the *optimal* mix of debt and equity. We will refer to this combination of debt and equity as the firm's **target capital structure.**

ECONOMIC FACTORS AFFECTING THE CHOICE OF FINANCIAL STRUCTURE

In Chapter 15 we will examine the relationship between a firm's capital structure and its cost of capital. But first we briefly review some economic factors which in addition to taxes and bankruptcy costs can also affect long-term corporate financing strategy.

Level of Earnings

The willingness of a firm to accept the increased risks of financial leverage depends on the distribution of its earnings. Other things being equal, the

FIGURE 14–6 Relationship of Value of Firm to Leverage, With and Without Bankruptcy Costs

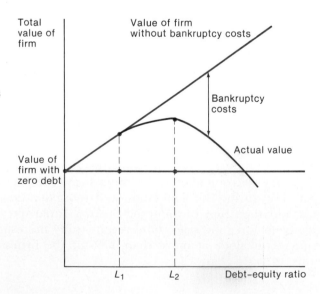

lower the probability of unfavorable leverage, the greater should be its use of financial leverage. Thus, firms with relatively high rates of operating profit are in a better position to undertake the risk of greater leverage. Financial leverage, on the other hand, can become a dangerous strategy when employed by a firm with an inadequate operating profit base. Despite this, we often find such firms, out of desperation, using high degrees of financial leverage. Once again, management is confronted by the fact that the old adage "To him that has, is given" tends to hold with almost frustrating persistence in the world of finance.

Stability of Sales and Earnings

Another key factor that determines the range of earnings, and hence the amount of debt the firm borrows, is the stability of sales. The latter, in turn, influences the stability of operating earnings. Generally speaking, the more stable the earnings, the better the chances that the firm can meet its fixed charges and obligations. Thus we expect firms with relatively stable earnings to finance a larger proportion of their investments with debt.

Structure of Assets

The firm's use of leverage also depends on its assets and borrowing power. For example, firms with high percentages of fixed assets often cannot shift risk as easily as those which are more liquid. Some firms can sell off part of their assets in order to meet debt charges more easily than others. This also enhances the collateral value of such assets, thereby increasing the firm's borrowing power as well. Other firms hold relatively large cash reserves. In general, the greater the firm's liquidity, either from holding cash assets or from the convertibility of its other assets to cash, the smaller its vulnerability to bankruptcy, and the greater will be the willingness of such firms to undertake the risks of leverage.

Dividend Policy

Although the analysis of a firm's dividend policy is deferred to Chapter 16, it is noteworthy that almost all firms attach great importance to achieving an "unbroken" dividend record—one in which the dividend payment is never skipped or even temporarily reduced. The implications of such an objective for financial policy are straightforward. Given the dividend rate, higher leverage ratios increase the chance that the firm will be unable to meet its dividend payments out of current operating income.

The relationship between leverage and dividend policy is illustrated in Figure 14–7, which shows the financial breakeven chart for a hypothetical firm, assuming three alternative financing strategies: pure equity, 25% debt, and 50% debt. Two alternative dividend policies—cash dividends of 45 cents or $1 per share—are also portrayed. Figure 14–7 shows that the higher the leverage ratio, the greater the chance of not meeting the cash dividend out of operating earnings. For example, under the pure equity option, the 45-cent dividend will not be covered if NOI falls in the range labeled *OA;* how-

FIGURE 14–7
Relationship
of Leverage
and Dividend
Policy

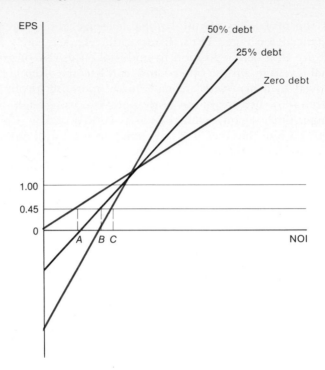

ever, as debt financing is successively increased to 25% and 50%; larger operating incomes are required to ensure dividend coverage. In the case of 25% leverage, NOI must exceed *OB;* should a 50% leverage ratio be adopted, the NOI must lie to the right of point *C.* Similarly, a higher dividend payout, say $1 per share, also shifts each "dividend coverage point" to the right.

Control   In some cases, firms may resort to the use of intensive leverage to retain effective control over the corporation. A loss of control might occur, for example, should the company issue additional shares to the public. Such a firm might well prefer to use additional debt rather than issue equity, even though the debt increases the risk beyond what otherwise might be considered a critical maximum.

Agency Costs   Since the capital structure decision reflects judgment and the assessment of a highly uncertain future, management's degree of risk aversion may also affect the firm's financing policy. In the extreme case of Henry Ford, all capital structures were optimal so long as they contained no debt! This, of course, is the financial counterpart of his more famous marketing dictum: "You can buy a Model T Ford in any color so long as it's black!" In this instance, the firm's owner and its manager were one and the same. However, in general, a clear distinction should be made between management and the firm's stockholders.

The separation of ownership from management gives rise to so-called **agency costs.** These costs reflect the monetary losses to stockholders when management does not act in the shareholders' best interests. This occurs when a firm's managers make decisions that are not motivated by the maximization of the market value of the owners' equity.

agency costs
Costs that reflect the divergence of interests between owners and managers.

Consider, for example, the case of a manager who is evaluating the purchase of a new executive jet (or executive dining room, or some similar management perk) versus the declaration of a dividend to the shareholders. Agency considerations can also affect a firm's financing policy. Suppose the stockholders (and the market as well) consider a capital structure with 60% debt to be optimal, but managers realize that with this level of leverage, the firm could also suffer a sequence of losses which in turn might cost them their jobs. As a result, they may prefer a safer degree of leverage, say 40%, even though 60% is the debt level that would maximize the value of the firm. If managers feel that they are exposed to a greater risk, (loss of job), this may lead them to prefer a more conservative debt policy than the shareholders might prefer.

To put it somewhat differently, the income bonuses to top management that reward extraordinarily high profits fall short of the penalties involved when the firm is in the red. The latter may cost managers their jobs. Hence, top management may be more risk-averse than stockholders would like.

ACTUAL MANAGEMENT CONSIDERATIONS

This chapter has examined a number of elements that affect corporate debt policy. Table 14–5 lists the factors that managers actually consider to be the important determinants of the long-term debt level. The sample consists of the largest firms whose stock is listed on the New York Stock Exchange. In contrast to some of the academic theories, it seems that most managers consider the level of long-term debt to be an important issue. In actual practice, capital structure does matter!

The two most important considerations affecting the debt level are credit ratings and the need for investment funds. (These factors were mentioned by 85% and 78% of the respondents, respectively). As we noted in Chapter 13, the credit rating is an index of default risk. A lower agency rating is an indicator of a higher probability of bankruptcy. As a result, the firm is required to pay higher interest on its future debt issues, or in extreme cases might be unable to borrow at all. Since potential investors are influenced by the bond ratings, it is not surprising that most managers consider this factor to be dominant in determining the level of long-term debt. Managers, when polled, attached greater importance to credit ratings than

TABLE 14–5   Important Considerations in Establishing the Level of Long-Term Debt*

	Very Important	Moderately Important	Not Important
1. Level of current and prospective profitability	49.0%	46.9%	4.1%
2. Stability of profits	40.8	53.1	6.1
3. Continuity of dividends	26.5	44.9	28.6
4. Need for investment funds	78.0	16.0	6.0
5. Tax considerations	28.6	55.1	16.3
6. Stockholder and creditor attitudes	58.0	40.0	2.0
7. Mangement attitudes	44.9	49.0	6.1
8. Credit ratings	85.7	12.2	2.1

*Percentage of total number of respondents.
SOURCE: M. E. Blume, I. Friend, and R. Westerfield, *Impediments to Capital Formation,* Rodney White Center for Financial Research, Wharton School, University of Pennsylvania, December 1980.

to "management attitudes"—their own perception of the firm's appropriate debt policy.

The results of this survey are consistent with the emphasis given to bankruptcy risk in this chapter. An increase in the proportion of debt may induce an increase in the firm's expected profit, which of course is desirable. However, leverage also increases the firm's default risk, which is reflected in its credit rating. Indeed, managers see this increase in risk as a key factor affecting the firm's long-term financing decision.

SUMMARY

Financial leverage is a two-edged sword: If the leverage is favorable, the rise of debt raises expected EPS; however, if the return on assets is less than the interest rate, expected EPS falls. Although in general we may assume that leverage increases EPS, the use of debt also enhances the fluctuations of EPS, thereby increasing financial risk. As a result, financial managers are confronted with the difficult task of weighing the advantages and disadvantages of leveraging the firm's financial structure. To this end, it is convenient to differentiate a firm's business risk from its financial risk. The former is related to the industry to which a company belongs and to the general conditions prevailing in the economy. The variability of the firm's net operating income (NOI) is an appropriate measure of its business risk. Financial risk is associated with the firm's use of leverage. An appropriate measure of this element of risk is the *additional* variance of per share earnings (EPS) induced by leverage.

There is a tradeoff between financial and operating leverage. Although the two strategies are not substitutes—many firms find it difficult to alter their operating leverage—both affect the variability of EPS, and therefore risk, in the same direction. As a result, a high degree of instability of earnings due to operating leverage has a mitigating effect on the firm's willingness to undertake the additional financial risk inherent in a high debt-equity ratio.

The firm's *optimal* or *target* capital structure is defined in terms of the impact of leverage on the value of the firm to its owners (stock price). Bankruptcy risk appears to be the chief factor affecting the optimal amount of debt a firm can use, but a complete analysis of this thorny problem requires consideration of a number of economic factors:

☐ *Level of earnings.* Other things being equal, the use of leverage is inversely related to the probability that the leverage will reduce future EPS.

☐ *Stability of sales and earnings.* The more stable a firm's sales and earnings, the greater the probability that it will be able to meet its fixed charges out of operating income. Hence we expect such a firm to finance a relatively larger proportion of its assets out of debt.

☐ *Asset structure.* The higher a firm's liquidity, the smaller will be its vulnerability to bankruptcy, and therefore the greater will be its willingness to undertake higher degrees of leverage.

☐ *Taxes.* Since interest is tax-deductible and dividends are not, the corporate tax system encourages the use of debt.

☐ *Dividend policy.* The strong desire of many firms never to skip or reduce a regular dividend payment is a deterrent to the use of leverage. Since leverage increases the variability of EPS, higher leverage ratios increase the probability that the firm will be unable to cover its dividend payments out of current operating revenues.

☐ *Control.* The desire to retain effective control of a company could conceivably lead owners to adopt a higher debt ratio than would otherwise be desirable in order to avoid issuing additional voting stock.

☐ *Agency costs.* Because managers tend to be more risk-averse than shareholders, they may prefer a more conservative debt policy; that is, a *lower* debt ratio, than that which the shareholders might consider optimal.

APPENDIX 14A | Leverage, Financial Failure, and Bankruptcy

The modern theory of capital structure stems from a series of pioneering articles by Modigliani and Miller.[1] The M & M analysis leads to the extreme proposition that the firm's optimal capital structure is comprised of nearly 100% debt. This reflects the deductibility for tax purposes of interest payments. It can readily be seen by examining M & M's equilibrium relationship, which states that:

$$V_L = V_U + TB$$

[1] The first of these is Franco Modigliani and Merton H. Miller, "The Cost of Capital, Corporation Finance and the Theory of Investment," *American Economic Review*, June 1958.

where

V_U = the market value of the unlevered firm

V_L = the market value of the same firm with leverage

T = the corporate tax rate

B = the amount of debt in the firm's capital structure

Clearly the higher the amount of debt *(B)*, the greater the value of the firm (V_L).

This unrealistic result reflects, among other things, the fact that the M & M analysis ignores bankruptcy. In practice, a firm is confronted with steeply rising interest rates beyond fairly low levels of the debt-equity ratio, since lenders and borrowers are sensitive to the possibility of "gamblers' ruin," or bankruptcy. The latter, as we have already noted, is ruled out in the M & M analysis. The actual degree of leverage used will reflect the particular firm's ability to absorb the financial risk inherent in the use of debt, without incurring a penalty from the financial community in the form of higher interest rates and/or a fall in the price of its stock.

THE NATURE OF FINANCIAL FAILURE

Broadly speaking, we denote by the term **economic failure** a firm whose net rate of return, adjusted for risk, is significantly lower than the prevailing rate of interest. A corporation is a *legal failure* if its assets are not sufficient to meet the legally enforceable claims of creditors. These two concepts of business failure are not identical: The former measures success or failure in terms of earnings on invested capital; the latter uses a corporation's ability to meet its legally enforceable liabilities as the benchmark of performance.

Two other terms are commonly used with respect to financial failure:

1. **Technical insolvency.** This refers to a state in which a firm finds itself unable to meet its current obligations, even though its total assets exceed its total liabilities.
2. **Bankruptcy** (or insolvency in an equity sense). A firm is bankrupt or insolvent in an equity sense when its total liabilities exceed a fair valuation of its total assets.

For convenience, we will use the word "failure" to include both aspects of the problem.

CHAPTER 11 OF THE BANKRUPTCY CODE

Under **Chapter 11** of the federal Bankruptcy Code, a company can operate with court protection from creditor lawsuits while it works out a plan to pay its debts. Thus, a firm that misses interest payments to its creditors may file for court protection under Chapter 11. This protection allows the firm to attempt to raise money to pay its obligations, thereby avoiding bankruptcy.

For example, in 1984 it was reported that Reliable Investors Corporation had missed three consecutive semi-annual interest payments to debenture holders. The company had reported losses since 1980, and it was predicted that in October 1984 the company would be insolvent. The company suggested that its creditors swap the outstanding debt for a new issue of debentures. The creditors did not agree and threatened to initiate bankruptcy court proceedings. In August 1984, Reliable Investors, in turn, filed for court protection from its creditors under Chapter 11 of the Bankruptcy Code.

Underlying Causes of Failure

The usual "causes" given for financial failure, such as lack of capital, faulty accounting, or poor planning, are more often not causes but rather rationalizations or excuses. The underlying cause of most failures can best be summarized by the term *management incompetence*. It is the lack of managerial skills which appears to be the fundamental cause of business failure, independent of the size or nature of the business undertaking. Business success or failure ultimately depends on the quality of human management.

Scope of Financial Failure

As we have already noted, the extreme solution implied by the M & M analysis must be rejected because it does not reflect the essential properties of the capital structure decision, and therefore fails to "explain" (account for) the behavior patterns of actual firms. The source of much of this distortion of economic reality can be traced to the failure of the M & M model to reflect the risks and costs associated with the possibility of financial failure. The significance of this omission can be gauged by examining the data on corporate failures.[2]

From 1925 to 1982, the failure rate of corporations ranged from a low of 4 per 10,000 during World War II to a high of 154 per 10,000 during the Great Depression of the 1930s. If, for illustrative purposes only, we take the average failure rate during the decade of the 1970s, which was slightly more than 35 per 10,000, it suggests a probability of 1/2% that a firm chosen at random will go bankrupt during the year. If we apply the average failure rate for the period as a whole, this probability rises to 1%. Clearly, even a relatively small probability of such a disaster as financial failure will be a cause of great concern to management and therefore will affect the financial decision-making process.

BANKRUPTCY RISK AND OPTIMAL CAPITAL STRUCTURE

Now let us turn to the question of how the probability of bankruptcy can be expected to affect the firm's financial structure decision. Clearly, the probability of going bankrupt depends on many economic factors; however, the two most important, for our purposes, are the firm's business and financial risks. Business risk is associated mainly with the industry to which the firm belongs and general economic conditions. Even competent management can do very little to reduce this risk, once the underlying decision regarding the type of economic activity to be pursued is taken. Financial risk, on the other hand, is subject almost completely to the discretionary control of management. By reducing the use of leverage, the firm can decrease the variability of earnings, thereby decreasing the probability of not being able to meet fixed charges (interest and redemptions) during a series of consecutive years. Conversely, by increasing its use of leverage

the firm also increases its financial risk, and thereby the probability of financial failure.

LIQUIDATION COSTS

Even with the possibility that the firm may go bankrupt, it can be shown that given certain restrictive assumptions, the relationship between the value of the firm and its leverage, as proposed by M & M, still holds. The most restrictive and unrealistic assumption necessary for this result is that bankruptcy be *costless*.

In order to better understand the assumption, recall that bankruptcy is the financial state bondholders may choose to precipitate should the firm fail to meet the interest and principal payments on its debt. If the firm's failure to meet its cash obligations results in the bondholders suing for the interest and principal owed them, a state of *bankruptcy* is entered: The firm's assets are liquidated, the fees of lawyers representing both sides are paid, and the residual funds obtained from the liquidation are distributed among security holders, with bondholders having prior claim. Thus, bankruptcy involves costs. Direct liquidation costs have been estimated to comprise anywhere from 30% to 70% of the assets' going-concern value.

Moreover, the *indirect* costs of bankruptcy, such as loss of sales and profits, are also substantial, and must be added to the direct costs (lawyer fees, administrative expenses, and so on) when estimating total bankruptcy costs. A recent study by Altman[3] estimated such indirect costs at 17.7% of the value of the firm, on average, for a sample of seven large bankrupt firms in the period 1980–1982. Clearly cost considerations of such a magnitude vitiate the M & M proposition about the relationship between leverage and the value of the firm. In the real world firms do not adopt extremely leveraged positions that increase the possibility of bankruptcy beyond acceptable levels. Moreover, even if bankruptcy were costless, the managers would still tend to lose their jobs once bankruptcy occurs, which again implies that firms normally will not willingly take on the extreme amount of debt implied by the M & M theorem.

---

[2] The data were taken from the *Statistical Abstract of the United States.*

[3] Edward I. Altman, "A Further Empirical Investigation of the Bankruptcy Cost Question," *Journal of Finance,* September 1984.

REVIEW EXERCISE

Circle the correct word(s) to complete the sentence; see p. 372 for correct answers.

14.1 The change in earnings per share (EPS) induced by the use of fixed-interest-bearing debt is often referred to as *portfolio diversification/financial leverage*.

14.2 The use of debt financing *can/cannot* increase a firm's profitability.

14.3 The introduction of fixed-interest-bearing securities in a firm's capital structure can raise EPS as long as the firm earns a *higher/lower* rate of return on its assets than it pays out to the bondholders.

14.4 Leverage decreases EPS if the rate of interest on the debt *exceeds/is less than* the rate of return on the firm's assets.

14.5 The introduction of leverage *diminishes/magnifies* the fluctuations of EPS, thereby *decreasing/increasing* the risk associated with the investment in common stock.

14.6 Since business risk depends on general economic conditions, it *is/is not* related to the firm's financial structure.

14.7 The variance of the unlevered operating earnings measures the firm's *business/financial* risk.

14.8 The additional *variability/secular growth* of earnings generated by financial leverage is called financial risk.

14.9 The variance of the levered earnings per share reflect the firm's *business/business and financial* risk.

14.10 The higher the proportion of the firm's costs which are fixed, the *lower/higher* is its operating leverage.

14.11 When a high percentage of costs are fixed and hence do not decline when sales fall, the firm is exposed to a *low/high* degree of business risk.

14.12 Given a specific target for the level of total risk, we expect a firm with a large proportion of fixed costs to adopt a relatively *aggressive/conservative* capital structure.

14.13 A good rule to remember is this: the higher the operating leverage, the *more/less* risky the recourse to financial leverage.

14.14 If leverage increases the variability of EPS, but expected EPS is unaffected, the optimal strategy is to *use/forego the use* of leverage.

14.15 Since leverage increases risk as well as return, achieving the highest possible EPS often *is/is not* compatible with the goal of achieving the highest possible market value for the firm's stock.

14.16 As leverage rises, risk *decreases/increases* and the capital market may react by demanding *lower/higher* interest rates on the firm's debt.

14.17 The capital structure that maximizes the *price of the stock/EPS* represents the optimal mix of debt and equity.

14.18 The optimal debt-equity ratio is considerably *lower/higher* than the debt-equity ratio that maximizes EPS.

14.19 Lower corporate tax rates *decrease/increase* the advantage of using debt.

14.20 Other things being equal, the lower the probability of unfavorable leverage, the *lower/greater* will be the use of financial leverage.

14.21 We expect firms having relatively stable earnings to finance a *lower/larger* proportion of their investment with debt.

14.22 In general, the greater the firm's liquidity, the *lower/greater* will be its willingness to undertake the risks of leverage.

14.23 Higher leverage ratios *increase/decrease* the chance that the firm will be unable to meet its dividend payment.

14.24 In some cases, a closely held firm may resort to the use of *more/less* debt in order to retain control over the corporation.

14.25 Risk-averse managers may prefer a debt-to-equity ratio that is *lower/higher* than the optimal ratio.

QUESTIONS

14.1 Define the following terms:
- **a.** Financial leverage
- **b.** Operating leverage
- **c.** Debt-equity ratio
- **d.** Financial breakeven point
- **e.** Favorable leverage
- **f.** Business risk
- **g.** Financial risk
- **h.** Agency costs

14.2 Give a numerical example which shows that EPS increases with leverage in good years, and decreases with leverage in bad years.

14.3 In a financial breakeven chart, what is the significance of the intersection between the lines denoting levered and unlevered capital structure? What happens to the left of this point? What happens to the right of this point?

14.4 Why must the line denoting the unlevered capital structure in the breakeven chart go through the origin?

14.5 Depict graphically the payment of dividends out of current earnings on the breakeven chart. What can you infer from such a chart?

14.6 Evaluate the following statement: "We don't know what degree of leverage to use: Depending on the debt-equity ratio, we obtain different breakeven points."

14.7 How do you think the following firms will rank in terms of debt-equity ratios? Explain.
- **a.** National Lumber (a lumber yard)
- **b.** Inventions 'n Things (builders of better mousetraps)
- **c.** Philadelphia Electric (a public utility)
- **d.** Food 'n Stuff (chain of supermarkets)
- **e.** Softy House (a computer software firm)

Hint: Put yourself in the position of a banker who has to decide on a loan to each of these firms.

14.8 Why do many new companies typically lease machines instead of purchasing them, subcontract instead of producing in-house, and use outside consultants rather then hiring full-time staff?

14.9 List the alternative scenarios of what can happen to expected EPS and variability of EPS due to increased leverage. What policy would you adopt in each case?

14.10 "If NOI is higher than the breakeven NOI, expected EPS will increase with leverage. Therefore it is in the shareholders' best interest to increase debt as much as possible." Comment on this statement.

14.11 How do tax laws favor the use of debt? What does a higher tax rate imply for the debt-equity ratio?

14.12 List the factors you can think of which affect the choice of financial structure. In which direction do they influence the debt-equity ratio?

14.13 Give some examples of managerial decisions that are subject to agency costs.

PROBLEMS

14.1 **EPS.** The Zytex Company has earnings before interest and taxes of $250,000. Its balance sheet shows a $2 million debt at 6% interest and 500,000 shares outstanding (at $1 per value), and $500,000 of retained earnings. The corporate tax rate is 34%.

   a. What are net earnings per share?

   b. Assume now that Zytex is financed completely by equity, that is, 1,500,000 shares are outstanding. What are net earnings per share?

14.2 **Expected EPS.** Both the Cyder Corporation and Lutex Company have a 60% probability of earning $40,000 and a 40% probability of earning $70,000. Cyder is financed by $200,000 of equity, with 50,000 shares outstanding. Lutex has a $120,000 debt on its balance sheet and equity of $80,000, with 20,000 shares outstanding. Lutex pays 10% interest on its debt. The corporate tax rate is 34%. What are Cyder's and Lutex's earnings per share, and variances in expected EPS?

14.3 **Expected EPS.** Compute the mean EPS of the following two companies, which are identical in every respect except that the Albert Corporation is financed by 150,000 shares of common stock, at $15 par, while the Bretton Corporation is financed by 125,000 shares of common stock ($15 par value) and a $375,000 debt on which it has to pay 7% interest. The probability distribution of NOI is $34,000 with a 45% probability, $52,000 with a 30% probability, and there is also a 25% chance that NOI will be $68,000. (Assume no taxes.)

14.4 **Financial leverage.** Eddie's Food Store is 100% equity financed. Super-Mart has a debt-equity ratio of 1:1, pays 11% interest on its debt, and has 5,000 shares outstanding. The two firms are identical in everything else, and the capitalization of both is $100,000. The par value of Eddie's shares is the same as that of SuperMart's shares. Net operating income could be anywhere between $70,000 and $160,000. Show the EPS for both firms in increments of NOI of $10,000. (Assume no taxes.)

14.5 **Financial leverage.** Assume now that NOI for Eddie's Food Store and for SuperMart could be $70,000, $80,000, . . . $150,000 or $160,000 each, with a 10% probability. What are the expected EPS and the variance in EPS? Should Eddie try to emulate SuperMart's debt-equity ratio? (Assume no taxes.)

14.6 **Operating leverage.** The Ryder Corporation sells a product for $100. The production of each unit requires $80 of variable costs. Furthermore, $1,200 of fixed costs are incurred per year. Sales are expected to be 800 or 1,200 units per year (each occurrence is equally likely). Ryder's balance sheet shows $50,000 debt at 6% interest and $300,000 equity with 100,000 shares outstanding. Solvent & Co. sells the same product for the same price. However, it uses a different production system, which requires $60 of variable costs per unit and $20,000 fixed costs per year. Sales are expected to be identical to Ryder's, and the same amount of capital is needed. Debt can be raised at 6% interest per year. How much debt must Solvent use to offer the same expected earnings per share? What is the resulting variance in earnings per share? (Assume no taxes.)

14.7 Expected EPS, variance. The AAA Company estimates sales for next year at $600,000, $800,000, or $1,000,000. All three figures are equally likely. Cost of goods sold and all other expenses amount to 80% of sales; the corporate tax rate is 34%. Compute the expected EPS and the variance in EPS under the following conditions:

a. AAA is financed by $500,000 in bonds at 8% interest and $500,000 in equity, with 100,000 shares outstanding.

b. AAA is financed by $100,000 in bonds (with an interest rate of 8%), and $900,000 in equity, with 180,000 shares outstanding.

14.8 Operating leverage, financial leverage. Major Motion Picture and Captain Movies are movie producers. Major owns most of its equipment, while Captain uses rented equipment. As a result, Major has $5,000,000 of fixed costs per year, compared to Captain's $1,500,000. On the other hand, variable costs per movie are $800,000 for Captain, but only $300,000 for Major. All movies gross $1 million. Major's capital structure is comprised of 500,000 shares with a $10 par. Captain has 300,000 shares with a par value of $10, and $2,000,000 of debt on which it pays 8% interest.

a. What is the EPS for both producers if they expect to produce 10 movies each?

b. What are the expected EPS and variance if Major and Captain are faced with the following distribution: 10 movies with a 50% probability, 8 movies with a 25% probability, 12 movies with a 25% probability.

14.9 Financial leverage. Nancy Barton wants to start a company. She expects to earn an NOI of $1,500,000. The capital needed is $10,000,000, which could be raised through a share issue ($10 par) and/or by 12% bonds. Assume a corporate tax rate of 34%.

a. If Ms. Barton wants to pay a dividend of $1.80, how much debt can she take on?

b. If Ms. Barton finances her company solely by equity, what is the minimum NOI required to meet the dividend payment?

14.10 Computer problem. For the following companies, compute the financial breakeven point, the minimum NOI that permits the payment of dividends, and the NOI below which EPS becomes negative. Assume a tax rate of 34%.

Company	Total Capitalization	Debt-to-Equity Ratio	Interest Rate	Book Value	Dividends
A	$ 583,600	0:1	18.05%	$24.00	$3.25
B	1,258,641	1:3	8.38	43.50	4.35
C	6,007,900	2:1	9.52	19.00	2.15
D	994,050	1:4	6.08	36.70	4.05

QUESTIONS AND PROBLEMS: APPENDIX 14A

14A.1 Explain how the removal of the "no bankruptcy" assumption affects the M & M conclusion regarding leverage and valuation.

14A.2 Distinguish between economic failure and legal failure.

14A.3 Give a numerical example of a firm that is bankrupt or insolvent in an equity sense.

14A.4. What is the purpose of Chapter 11 of the U.S. Bankruptcy Code?

SAMPLE PROBLEMS

SP14.1 What is the expected (mean) EPS of the following two companies, which are identical in everything except that company A is financed by 3,000 shares of common stock at $50 par, and company B is financed by 2,500 shares of common stock at $50 par, and a $25,000 debt on which it has to pay 8% interest. NOI can be $4,000 with a 60% probability and $5,000 with a 30% probability; there is a 10% chance that NOI will be $14,000.

SP14.2 The Galton Company has a $1,000,000 debt on which it pays 6% interest, and 400,000 shares (par value $10) of common stock outstanding. Assume there are no corporate taxes and that the market price of the shares is also $10.

a. What is the minimum NOI Galton needs to earn in order to be able to meet its interest payments out of current income?

b. Draw the line depicting EPS as a function of NOI.

c. What is the minimum NOI Galton needs to earn in order to be able to cover a dividend of $1 per share?

d. For what range of NOI is leverage positive? When is it negative?

Solutions to Sample Problems

SP14.1 Company A has no debt, and hence no interest payments. Therefore, we have:

Company A			
NOI	4,000	5,000	14,000
Interest	0	0	0
Net income	4,000	5,000	14,000

Since company A has 3,000 shares, EPS is net income divided by 3,000:

EPS	1.33	1.66	4.67

Company B has a $25,000 debt on which it pays 8% interest; total interest comes to $2,000 per year, and we have

Company B			
NOI	4,000	5,000	14,000
Interest	2,000	2,000	2,000
Net income	2,000	3,000	12,000

Company B has 2,500 shares outstanding, and EPS is net income divided by 2,500:

EPS	0.80	1.20	4.80

To compute the expected (mean) EPS, we compute the weighted average of EPS for each company:

Company A:

$$\text{expected EPS} = (60\% \text{ of } 1.33) + (30\% \text{ of } 1.66) + (10\% \text{ of } 4.67)$$
$$= 1.76$$

Company B:

$$\text{expected EPS} = (60\% \text{ of } 0.80) + (30\% \text{ of } 1.20) + (10\% \text{ of } 4.80)$$
$$= 1.32$$

SP14.2 Galton has capital of $5,000,000, of which $1,000,000 is debt, and $4,000,000 is equity.

a. Interest payments amount to $60,000 (6% on $1,000,000); if Galton earns less than that, EPS is negative, and Galton could not pay the interest out of current NOI.

b. Because of (a) above, the line depicting EPS as a function of NOI crosses the x axis at $60,000. Any amount over the $60,000 must be divided by the number of shares outstanding to arrive at EPS. For example, if NOI is $500,000, then the excess over the interest payment of $60,000 is $440,000, which must be divided by 400,000, to arrive at EPS of $1.10. So the straight line that describes Galton's EPS as a function of NOI goes through the two points ($60,000, $0) and ($500,000, $1.10). The equation for Galton's EPS as a function of NOI is

$$\text{EPS} = (\text{NOI} - 60,000) \div 400,000$$

c. To pay dividends of $1 per share, Galton first needs to pay the interest on its debt ($60,000), and must also earn at least $1 for each share outstanding, i.e., $400,000. Hence NOI must be at least $460,000 in order for Galton to cover a dividend of $1 per share. Alternatively, this result could have been read off the graph: Galton's EPS as a function of NOI is $1 when NOI = $460,000.

d. In order to determine when leverage is positive, we compare the levered alternative with a hypothetical unlevered alternative; that is, with a capital structure comprised of $5,000,000 of equity and no debt. In this alternative, the firm would have 500,000 shares outstanding (500,000 shares with a par value of $10 = $5,000,000). Hence, the EPS line goes through the origin (0,0) and then rises at the rate of $1 EPS for each additional $500,000 NOI. Therefore, we get the following equation:

$$EPS = NOI/500,000$$

Leverage is positive whenever Galton's EPS line lies above the EPS line of the unlevered company—that is, whenever

$$(NOI - 60,000)/400,000 > NOI/500,000$$

Solving this inequality for NOI, we find

$$NOI > \$300,000$$

Thus leverage is positive whenever NOI is greater than $300,000.

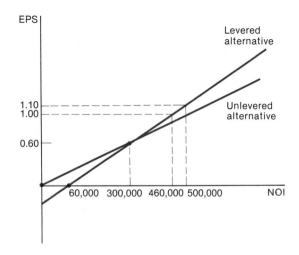

Answers to Review Exercise

14.1 financial leverage   **14.2** can   **14.3** higher   **14.4** exceeds
14.5 magnifies, increasing   **14.6** is not   **14.7** business   **14.8** variability
14.9 business and financial   **14.10** higher   **14.11** high
14.12 conservative   **14.13** more   **14.14** forego the use   **14.15** is not
14.16 increases, higher   **14.17** price of the stock   **14.18** lower
14.19 decrease   **14.20** greater   **14.21** larger   **14.22** greater
14.23 increase   **14.24** more   **14.25** lower

SUGGESTIONS FOR FURTHER READING

The impact of leverage on the value of the firm is examined in much greater detail by Haim Levy and Marshall Sarnat, *Capital Investment and Financial Decisions,* 3rd ed. (Englewood Cliffs, NJ: Prentice-Hall, 1986).

Under a set of restrictive assumptions, Merton Miller has shown that when corporate and personal taxes are considered, capital structure "does not matter." See his "Debt and Taxes," *Journal of Finance,* May 1977. However, when these assumptions are relaxed and a realistic model that incorporates bankruptcy risk and uncertainty is introduced, debt strategy once again becomes a crucial corporate decision variable affecting the value of the firm.

The significance of bankruptcy risk for financial decision-making is discussed by Edward I. Altman in *Corporate Bankruptcy in America* (Lexington, MA: Lexington Books, 1971).

For an interesting comparison of leverage in the United States and Japan, see W. Carl Kester, "Capital and Ownership Structure: A Comparison of United States and Japanese Manufacturing Corporations," *Financial Management*, Spring 1986.

Additional insights into the relationship between financial and operating leverage can be found in James M. Gahlon and James A. Gentry, "On the Relationship between Systematic Risk and the Degrees of Operating and Financial Leverage," *Financial Management*, Summer 1982.

Agency costs were introduced into finance by Michael C. Jensen and William H. Meckling, "Theory of the Firm: Managerial Behavior, Agency Costs and Ownership Structure," *Journal of Financial Economics*, October 1976.

Economic evidence pertinent to the use of leverage is given by Robert M. Bowen, Daley A. Lane, and Charles C. Huber, Jr., "Evidence on the Existence and Determinants of Inter-Industry Differences in Leverage," *Financial Management*, Winter 1982; David F. Scott, Jr., and D. J. Johnson, "Financing Policies and Practices in Large Corporations," *Financial Management*, Summer 1982; A. K. Gehr, Jr., "Financial Structure and Financial Strategy," *Journal of Financial Research*, Spring 1984; J. M. Harris, R. L. Rosenfeldt, and P. L. Cooley, "Evidence of Financial Leverage Clienteles," *Journal of Finance*, September 1983; and Marshall E. Blume, Irwin Friend and Randolph Westerfield, *Impediments to Capital Formation* (Philadelphia: Rodney L. White Center for Financial Research, The Wharton School, University of Pennsylvania, December 1980).

15

The Cost of Capital

To this point we have tried to avoid a direct confrontation with the concept of the *cost of capital*. In those chapters devoted to the analysis of investment decisions under certainty and uncertainty, we assumed that the problem of the cost of capital was solved, thereby permitting the use of a given "riskless" or "risky" discount rate, as the problem required. Questions relating to the definition of the cost of capital and its measurement were carefully swept under a by now bulging carpet. However, postponement of the discussion should *not* be interpreted as an indication that the cost of capital has a secondary impact on financial decision-making. On the contrary, it is crucial, since the discount rate serves as one of the direct determinants of the acceptability of a firm's capital investments. Postponement of the discussion simply reflects our hope that you will be better prepared to handle this controversial subject now that you have acquired the fundamental tools of financial analysis.

In this chapter we will spell out the economic logic underlying the definition of the cost of capital, and then go on to examine several practical methods of estimating the firm's required rate of return (cost of capital) for new investments.

COST OF CAPITAL: THE FIRM VS. INDIVIDUAL PROJECTS

The cost of capital and the discount rate are two concepts that are used interchangeably throughout the book. However, there is an important distinction between the *firm's* cost of capital (discount rate) and a *specific project's* cost of capital (discount rate).

firm's cost of capital
The discount rate applied to a firm's average cash-flow.

specific project's cost of capital
The discount rate used when a project's risk profile differs significantly from that of the firm.

1. The firm's cost of capital is the rate employed to discount its average cash flow, thereby deriving the value of the firm. It is also, as we will see below, the *weighted average cost of capital (WACC)*. The weighted average, however, should be used for project evaluation (calculating the NPV) *only* if the risk profile of the new project is a carbon copy of the risk profile of the firm.

2. The specific project's cost of capital is the discount rate to be used when the risk profile of the individual project differs significantly from that of the firm. In such cases, an adjustment must be made if the discount rate is to reflect this deviation from the average risk (see Chapter 11). To illustrate, suppose the firm's WACC is 20% and the risk-free interest rate is 10%. The firm should discount the project's average cash flows at the 20% discount rate. However, consider a case in which the firm faces a project whose cash flow is *perfectly certain*. What is the minimum required rate of return on this project? In this instance, it is clearly the 10% rate that reflects the opportunity cost, or the alternative return the firm could earn by investing its money in other equally safe assets. Conversely, if the project under consideration is very risky, the 20% discount rate (the weighted average) may be insufficient, and a higher discount rate should be employed.

The following general formula for a project's required rate of return, or cost of capital, has been developed.[1] Here we spell out its implications for project analysis:

$$\text{project's cost of capital} = k + \Delta k + \frac{\Delta k}{I_0} v_0 \qquad (15.1)$$

where

k = the firm's *average* cost of capital *before* the investment
Δk = the increase in the cost of capital due to this project's riskiness
I_0 = the project's initial investment outlay
v_0 = value of the firm *before* the investment.

From Eq. 15.1 we can see that the cost of capital will vary from project to project, depending upon its riskiness. However, if the new project does not materially change the firm's overall risk, and therefore, $\Delta k = 0$, the appropriate discount rate is k, which we will see in the next section is the firm's weighted average cost of capital (WACC).

Although academics and practitioners agree in principle that each project has its own risk profile and hence its own discount rate, it is often difficult to estimate discount rates for each and every project. Due to uncertainty, the future variability of a potential project's cash flow is unknown;

[1] The derivation of this general formula for the cost of capital is given in Haim Levy and Marshall Sarnat, *Capital Investment and Financial Decisions*, 3rd ed. (Englewood Cliffs, NJ: Prentice-Hall International, 1986).

hence, Δk is also unknown. Therefore, it is common practice to estimate the firm's WACC as an initial benchmark. In many cases (where Δk is close to zero), the WACC is the appropriate discount rate. However, when management considers a project to be relatively risky ($\Delta k > 0$), an additional risk premium is added to the WACC. Similarly, if a project is less risky than the firm's average riskiness ($\Delta k < 0$), a "safety premium" is deducted from the firm's WACC. Although various statistical methods are available to estimate the cost of capital, estimating the additions or reductions due to a project's specific risk profile remains an art, often based on intuition and experience rather than on formal statistical methods.

THE WEIGHTED AVERAGE COST OF CAPITAL (WACC)

weighted average cost of capital (WACC)
A discount rate that reflects the costs of individual sources of financing, weighted by their share in the firm's optimal capital structure.

In this chapter, unless otherwise specified, we will assume that the project in question has the same risk profile as the firm ($\Delta k = 0$, or is very small). Given this assumption, the **WACC** is the *appropriate discount rate,* keeping in mind that for some projects adjustments may be needed to reflect specific risk profiles.

For simplicity, assume that all new investments have the *same risk profile* as that of the firm, and that they are financed in the exact proportions of debt and equity given by the firm's target (optimal) financial structure. Given these assumptions, what is the appropriate discount rate for evaluating a new project? Table 15–1 illustrates the case of a firm which has adopted a long-run strategy of financing investments with 40% debt and 60% equity, presumably on the assumption that this capital structure is optimal (maximizes the market value of the owners' equity). Thus, its initial capital structure (column 1 of Table 15–1) is comprised of $6,000,000 of common stock and $4,000,000 of bonds, on which it pays 5% interest. Ignoring corporate taxes for the moment, we assume that the firm earns $1,100,000 on its $10,000,000 of assets, paying out $200,000 (5% × $4 million) as interest to

TABLE 15–1   Capital Structure and Cash Flows Before and After the New Investment

	Before the New Investment ($)	New Investment ($)	After the New Investment ($)
Capital structure:			
Bonds (5%)	4,000,000	400,000	4,400,000
Stock	6,000,000	600,000	6,600,000
Total	10,000,000	1,000,000	11,000,000
Cash flows:			
Net operating income	1,100,000	110,000	1,210,000
Interest	200,000	20,000	220,000
Dividends	900,000	90,000	990,000

bondholders. Hence, the rate of return on the existing equity is 15% ($900,000 ÷ $6,000,000 = 15%). To simplify the discussion, we assume that the firm always distributes *all* its net earnings ($900,000) as dividends; hence the stockholders' required rate of return (for the given capital structure) is equal to the dividend yield.

Column 2 of Table 15–1 shows the expected results of a proposed new investment that requires an outlay of $1,000,000. The firm decides to raise 40% of this sum by issuing 5% bonds and the remaining 60% by issuing additional common stock in order to preserve its existing debt-equity ratio. What is the *minimum required rate of return* on the new investment—that is, the rate of return that will leave the value of the existing shareholders' equity unchanged? To answer this question, we begin by examining the cost of each element of the financing mix. Clearly one component of the required return consists of the $20,000 (5% × $400,000 = $20,000) the firm must pay the new bondholders. In addition, the firm must also earn an additional $90,000 to avoid a reduction in the dividends (earnings) on the existing equity (column 2 of Table 15–1). This $90,000 represents a 15% return on the new equity ($90,000 ÷ $600,000 = 15%) which allows the firm to pay a 15% dividend to the new shareholders *without* affecting the old shareholders' dividends. In other words, the new investment must earn $110,000 if the value of the existing equity is to remain unchanged by the new investment. If the operating returns are less than $110,000, the investment should be rejected. If the investment yields more than $110,000 it should be accepted, because the position of the existing shareholders will be improved; they will receive a higher return for the same risk.

This contention can be illustrated using the data in column 3 of Table 15–1, which gives the firm's capital structure and cash flows *after* the new investment has been accepted, under the explicit assumption that the critical breakeven amount ($110,000) is earned on the new project. As can be seen, the $110,000 is just sufficient to leave the old stockholders' position unchanged. The amount of earnings available for dividends for all shareholders is $990,000 which represent an unchanged dividend (earnings) yield of 15% ($990,000/$6,600,000 = 15%). Should the firm earn less than this amount on the new investment—say, only $44,000 rather than $110,000—the earnings available for dividends, after interest is paid, will be only $924,000 ($900,000 + 24,000). As a result, the dividend (earnings) yield will decline from 15% to 14% ($924,000/$6,600,000 = 14%). Similarly, should the return on the new investment be more than $110,000—say, $176,000—the existing stockholders will be better off. In this case, the firm again pays $20,000 to the new bondholders, leaving $156,000 as the contribution of the new investment to the firm's shareholders. Thus, the total earnings available for distribution to the stockholders is $1,056,000 ($900,000 + $156,000 = $1,056,000), and the new dividend (earnings) yield rises to 16% ($1,056,000/$6,600,000 = 16%).

What is the discount rate this firm should apply when evaluating an investment proposal's NPV? For the sake of convenience, we assume a project that involves an initial outlay of $1,000,000 and generates a perpetual cash flow of $110,000 per year. Denoting the appropriate discount rate by k, the NPV calculation is reduced to

$$NPV = \frac{110,000}{k} - 1,000,000$$

To be consistent with our previous analysis, we must make the further stipulation that for the case in which $110,000 is earned, the existing shareholders will be *indifferent* to the project; hence the NPV must be zero. Imposing this condition, we have

$$NPV = \frac{110,000}{k} - 1,000,000 = 0$$

The discount rate that equates the NPV to zero is given by

$$k = \frac{110,000}{1,000,000} = 11\%$$

In this example, the appropriate *cost of capital* is 11%. If the annual cash flow of the new project is greater than $110,000, the NPV (at 11%) will be positive, and the firm should accept the project. If the annual cash flow is less than $110,000, the NPV using the 11% discount rate will be negative, and the project should be rejected. These results are consistent with the previous analysis, and confirm our conclusion that for earnings in excess of $110,000 the existing stockholders are better off; for earnings below $110,000 they are worse off; and for earnings exactly equal to $110,000 they are indifferent to the proposal. This relationship between the interests of existing shareholders and the NPV calculation of project acceptability can be ensured in our example *if and only if* the discount rate is set at 11%.

DEFINING THE WACC

How should the 11% discount rate be interpreted? An examination of Table 15–2 shows that the 11% rate is a *weighted average* of the required rates of return of the individual sources of financing, with each type of financing being given its proportional weight in the firm's long-run target capital structure. (Market values, rather than book values, should be used as the weights when calculating the WACC; see Appendix 15A.) Alternatively, the 11% can be viewed as the weighted average of the individual cost components. Since debt accounts for 40% of the firm's total financing mix, the contribution of the debt component to the cost of capital is 2% (0.40 × 0.05 = 0.02 = 2%). Similarly, the contribution of the equity component is 9% (0.60 × 0.15 = 0.09 = 9%). Combining the two components gives a *weighted average cost of capital (WACC)* of 11%. The justification for using a

TABLE 15–2   Weighted Average Cost of Capital (WACC)

	Amount Raised ($) (1)	Proportion of Total Money Raised (2)	Cost of the Specific Components (3)	Contribution to the Cost of Capital (4) = (2) × (3)
Debt	400,000	0.40	5%	0.40 × 5% = 2%
Stocks	600,000	0.60	15%	0.60 × 15% = 9%
				WACC 11%

discount rate (cost of capital) that reflects the costs of the individual sources of financing, weighted by their share in the firm's optimal (target) capital structure, is straightforward. The WACC ensures that the value of the existing owners' equity will be maximized. Setting a lower discount rate, as our numerical example showed, would induce the firm to accept projects that are not in the existing shareholders' best interest. Setting the discount rate above the WACC, on the other hand, would lead the firm to reject projects whose implementation would increase the value of the existing shareholders' equity.

FINANCING A NEW PROJECT IN PRACTICE

We have assumed up to now that all projects have the same risk profile, and that the firm finances each project in the same proportion as its optimal (target) capital structure. However, in practice firms do not issue stocks and bonds simultaneously every time a need for additional long-term financial resources arises. This is especially true when the firm raises relatively small amounts of money. As we noted in Chapter 12, it is often not economical to split such sums by raising part of it by a bond issue and the rest by a stock issue. Even a firm that has a set target financial structure will tend to deviate from this optimal mix from time to time.

Figure 15–1 illustrates the financing policy of a hypothetical firm with a target capital structure of 40% debt and 60% equity. As can be seen from the graph, the proportion of debt decreases in both 1984 and 1985. This does not necessarily mean that the firm issued common stock in these years; the decline in the share of debt in the total financing mix might reflect an increase in retained earnings during the same years, or the retirement of part of the firm's outstanding debt. In 1986, the firm "corrects" for these deviations from its target capital structure by issuing bonds, restoring the proportion of debt in the capital structure to 40%.

This financing mix is retained in 1987; however, due perhaps to un-usually favorable market conditions, the firm raises additional debt in 1988. As a result, the proportion of debt temporarily rises above the 40% target.

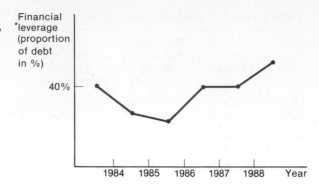

**FIGURE 15–1
Financial Policy
of Hypothetical
Firm**

In the future, the firm will have to meet its financial requirements by raising additional equity, if the long-run target capital structure is to be restored. So even though the firm has set a specific debt policy, it will often deviate from its target debt-equity ratio in the short run. Practical considerations (flotation costs, market considerations) make the alternative of raising capital each year by issuing a financing package in fixed proportions of debt and equity undesirable.

Does the fact that firms tend to deviate from their long-run optimal financial structure change the conclusion that the WACC is the appropriate discount rate for evaluating new investments? To answer this question, let us once again turn to the numerical example given in Table 15–1, in which the cost of the debt component is assumed to be 5%, the cost of the equity component is 15%, and the firm's target financial structure has been set at 40% debt and 60% equity. As noted in Figure 15–1, the firm does not issue bonds and stock each year, and as a result it tends to deviate temporarily from its optimal financial structure. Now suppose the firm considers a project whose internal rate of return is 7% and which will be financed by a bond issue. Should the project be accepted? If we compare the project's internal rate of return (7%) with the cost of the debt component (5%), the project is clearly acceptable. However, if the internal rate of return is compared with the WACC of 11% (see Table 15–2), the project will be rejected. The question remains: Which of the two, 5% or 11%, is the appropriate discount rate?

We can again easily show that the WACC (11%) is the appropriate discount rate. If the WACC is used as the discount rate, the 7% project will be rejected. To clarify the line of reasoning that underlies this decision, recall that financing this particular project with low-cost debt capital will tend to raise the proportion of debt in the firm's capital structure above the target level of 40%. This, in turn, implies an undesirable increase in risk. The firm will have to finance projects in future years with relatively expensive equity capital if the optimal debt level is to be restored. Should the firm use the specific interest cost, rather than the WACC, it might conceivably accept a project with an internal rate of return of 7% in the years in which bonds are issued, while a project with a 14% rate of return might be rejected in a year in which equity capital is raised. This is an undesirable strategy if the value of the firm is to be maximized.

To avoid such a dilemma, *firms should ignore transitory deviations from their target debt-equity ratios,* and concentrate on their long-term targets. Increasing the proportion of debt this year *implies* that the firm will have to issue additional equity in the future. Therefore, both sources must be taken into account when evaluating a new project, even if only one of the sources is currently used. With the WACC, the firm can avoid situations in which relatively low-return projects are accepted, while at other times high-return projects are rejected, solely because of timing. In our example, using the 11% WACC as the discount rate, the project with a 7% rate of return will be rejected even though it is financed by debt. But the project with a 14% internal rate of return will be accepted even though the firm finances it with high-cost equity. To sum up: The individual types of financing constitute a *joint product* that must not be split into its individual components if the firm is to optimize its investment decisions.

LEVERAGE AND THE COST OF CAPITAL

So far we have tried to show that when individual projects have broadly similar risk profiles, the firm should employ the WACC as its cutoff rate for new investment. However, *these individual costs are neither constant over time nor independent of the firm's overall financial strategy.* In general, all the component costs tend to rise as leverage is increased. Bondholders settle for a fixed annual income, but for intensive degrees of leverage, the risk of bankruptcy rises. The bondholders may lose all or part of their interest income and/or principal. Hence, the larger the risk of bankruptcy, the higher will be the interest rate required to compensate the bondholders for incurring the greater risk. Even relatively small firms, who do not ordinarily influence money market rates, will be confronted by an upward-sloping supply curve for loans. The higher the proportion of debt, the higher the risk from the bondholders' point of view, and therefore the higher the required interest rate. By an analogous argument, we also expect the cost of preferred stock to rise with leverage. The higher the risk of bankruptcy, the higher the required return, and hence the higher the specific cost of preferred stock. Similarly, as we pointed out in Chapter 14, the variability of per-share earnings increases with leverage. Since most stockholders are risk-averse, *the greater the variability of the earnings stream, the higher the average required return on equity.* And needless to add, common stockholders are the most vulnerable to bankruptcy risk as well, so we also expect the cost of equity to rise with leverage.

In general, the larger the risk, the larger the required return, and therefore the higher the firm's financing cost. However, remember that financial leverage is only one of the risk factors which affect the cost of capital. A second factor is the firm's business risk. Each specific cost component reflects the riskless interest rate (representing the time value of money) plus a risk premium. This risk premium, in turn, is determined by the firm's business risk (which exists even when financial leverage is zero) plus its financial risk. Thus the cost of each specific source can be expressed as follows:

$$
\boxed{\begin{array}{c} \text{cost} \\ \text{of} \\ \text{component} \end{array}} = \boxed{\begin{array}{c} \text{riskless} \\ \text{interest} \\ \text{rate} \\ (R_F) \end{array}} + \boxed{\begin{array}{c} \text{business} \\ \text{risk} \\ \text{premium} \\ \text{(BRP)} \end{array}} + \boxed{\begin{array}{c} \text{financial} \\ \text{risk} \\ \text{premium} \\ \text{(FRP)} \end{array}}
$$

in symbols:

$$
k_i = R_F + \text{BRP} + \text{FRP} \tag{15.2}
$$

where k_i denotes the cost of component i.

Does the analysis imply that the firm's WACC must also increase with leverage? As can be seen from Table 15–3, the firm's cost of capital can have U-shaped properties even when the cost of each individual component is assumed to increase with leverage. This reflects the fact that the cost of capital is a *weighted average* of the individual sources. Up to a point (40% debt in our hypothetical example), the inclusion of relatively low-cost debt in the capital structure reduces the average cost; however, for highly levered financing structures, the cost of both debt and equity rises sharply. These factors combine to reverse the favorable impact of the inclusion of additional debt in the capital structure.

TABLE 15–3   Relationship Between Cost of Capital and Leverage

Capital Structure		Cost of Debt Component (%) (3)	Cost of Equity Component (%) (4)	Weighted Average Cost of Capital % (5) = (1) × (3) + (2) × (4)
Debt (1)	Equity (2)			
0.1	0.9	5.0	15.0	14.00
0.2	0.8	5.0	16.0	13.80
0.3	0.7	6.0	17.0	13.70
0.4	0.6	7.0	18.0	**13.60**
0.5	0.5	8.0	20.0	14.00
0.6	0.4	9.0	22.0	14.20
0.7	0.3	10.0	25.0	14.50
0.8	0.2	12.0	28.0	15.20
0.9	0.1	15.0	35.0	17.00

The numerical example of Table 15–3 is illustrated in Figure 15–2, which graphs the relationship between the cost of capital and financial leverage. Although both debt and equity costs are assumed to rise with leverage, the firm's WACC is U-shaped. It initially decreases up to a leverage ratio of 40%, and then rises. Since the goal of the firm is to minimize its cost of capital, thereby maximizing the value of the firm, 40% debt represents the *optimal* financial leverage (see Chapter 14).

FIGURE 15–2
Graphical Relationship Between Cost of Capital and Leverage

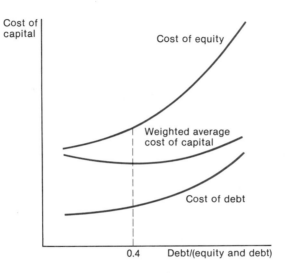

CHANGES IN LONG-TERM FINANCIAL POLICY

Earlier in this chapter, we distinguished between a firm's long-run optimal financial strategy and temporary deviations around this target ratio (see Figure 15–1). Although purely transitory deviations can properly be ignored, the firm should reexamine its long-term financial policy from time to time. Capital market conditions, government policy, and the tax structure can and do change over time, often generating significant changes in the relative cost of alternative sources of finance. The need for such a reevaluation of financial policy is illustrated in Table 15–4, which reproduces the data of Table 15–3 with one difference: We now assume that the interest rate has *fallen* by two percentage points. As a result, the weighted average costs of capital given in Table 15–4 are lower than those of Table 15–3. Moreover, we can also see that the proportion of debt in the optimal capital structure changes as well. Before the fall in interest rates, the optimal proportion of debt was 40%; following the change in interest rates, the optimal debt-equity mix rises to 50%. This illustrates the fact that changes in the required rates of return

TABLE 15—4   Relationship Between Cost of Capital and Leverage After the Fall in Interest Rates

| Capital Structure | | Cost of Debt Component (%) | Cost of Equity Component (%) | Weighted Average Cost of Capital (%) |
Debt (1)	Equity (2)	(3)	(4)	(5) = (1) × (3) + (2) × (4)
0.1	0.9	3.0	15.0	13.80
0.2	0.8	3.0	16.0	13.40
0.3	0.7	4.0	17.0	13.10
0.4	0.6	5.0	18.0	12.80
0.5	0.5	5.5	20.0	**12.75**
0.6	0.4	6.0	24.0	13.20
0.7	0.3	7.0	28.0	13.30
0.8	0.2	10.0	30.0	14.00
0.9	0.1	13.0	35.0	15.20

on debt and equity not only change the absolute size of the cost of capital, but the optimal proportions of debt and equity in the firm's capital structure as well. Similarly, economic, social, and political forces that significantly affect the character of a firm's operations, thereby altering its business risk, can also affect its long-term financing strategy. All these considerations suggest the danger of getting locked in to a particular financial policy, and the need for periodic reassessment of the firm's overall financial strategy.

DEFINING THE COST COMPONENTS

Having examined the logic underlying the use of the WACC as the firm's discount rate, we turn now to the definition of the individual cost components. Here we focus on the preliminary stage in which the costs of the individual components that make up the weighted average are estimated. To avoid any confusion, note that these specific costs must not be used as the cutoff rate in project evaluation; they are employed solely for the purpose of calculating the WACC. It is this weighted average which constitutes the appropriate cutoff point (discount rate) for the evaluation of investments. Thus, the specific costs of debt and equity are the appropriate costs that enter the calculation of the WACC; they are not appropriate, as we have just seen, for the analysis of changes in the financing mix.

The specific cost of each component is the *minimum rate of return required* by the suppliers of the capital. For example, the specific cost of the bond component is the yield to maturity (YTM) required by the bondholders. Clearly, paying interest *without* reducing earnings per share implies that the firm must earn at least this rate on its investment. It is this minimum rate of return, which ensures shareholders' earnings against dilution, that constitutes the "specific cost" of debt or the "cost of the debt component." A similar definition is used for the equity component.

COST OF DEBT

The **specific cost;** that is, the required minimum rate of return for the **debt** component, is the *after-tax yield to maturity:*

$$(1 - T)\, k_d \qquad\qquad (15.3)$$

where

> T = the corporate tax rate
> k_d = the bond's yield to maturity

To clarify this concept, let's suppose that a firm raises $1,000,000 by issuing 1,000 bonds at a unit price of $1,000 and with an interest rate of 8%; that is, the firm pays the holder of each bond $80 interest at the end of each year. Also assume that the corporate income tax rate is 34% and that these bonds will be redeemed after 10 years. At the end of the tenth year the firm pays the bondholder $80 interest plus an additional $1,000 to retire the principal. The rate of interest on these bonds, defined as the *yield to maturity,* is the internal rate of return of the cash flow to the bondholder:

$$1,000 = \frac{80}{1 + k_d} + \frac{80}{(1 + k_d)^2} + \ldots + \frac{1,080}{(1 + k_d)^{10}}$$

The discount rate, k_d, which solves this equation is exactly 8%.

dilution
Reduction in EPS due to increase in number of shares outstanding.

What is the minimum return required to meet the interest payments without any **dilution** (reduction) in shareholders' earnings? Column 1 of Table 15–5 gives the firm's financial position *before* the bond issue. Although we assume that the firm earns 10% on its assets, the rate of return on invested capital, *after taxes,* is only 6.6%, compared with the pretax return of 10%. This reflects, of course, the 34% corporate tax rate. Column 2 of Table 15–5 isolates the changes in the financial figures generated by the new $1 million bond issue on the assumption that, for the moment at least, the firm has not yet invested the proceeds of the bond issue. As a result, operating income remains unchanged at $1,000,000. However, because the firm must pay interest on the debt, earnings after interest are reduced by $80,000 to $920,000. Since interest payments are tax-deductible, the firm's tax bill is only $312,800, and the after-tax rate of return on existing equity falls from 6.6% to about 6.1%.

How can we account for the fact that although the firm pays $80,000 interest to the bondholders, its post-tax flow is reduced by only $52,800? Do the bondholders get interest of only $52,800? Although the bondholders actually receive $80,000 each year as interest, only $52,800 is payable out of

TABLE 15–5   Firm's Financial Position Before and After the Bond Issue

	Before the Bond Issue (1)	After the Bond issue but Before the Investment (2)	After the Bond Issue and Investment (3)
	$	$	$
Total investment	10,000,000	10,000,000	11,000,000
Operating income	1,000,000	1,000,000	1,080,000
Interest	—	80,000	80,000
Earnings after interest	1,000,000	920,000	1,000,000
Corporate Tax (34%)	340,000	312,800	340,000
Net after-tax earnings	660,000	607,200	660,000
Existing investment	10,000,000	10,000,000	10,000,000
New debt	—	1,000,000	1,000,000
After-tax rate of return on equity	6.6%	6.1%	6.6%

the firm's net profits; the remaining $27,200 comes from the reduction in corporate tax. The firm pays the bondholders $52,800 and the Internal Revenue Service, so to speak, pays the other $27,200 because of its willingness to recognize corporate interest payments as a tax-deductible expense.

If we denote the annual pretax interest payment by C and the corporate tax rate by T, the annual *after-tax* interest payment is only $(1 - T)C$. The specific *after-tax* cost of the debt component is given by that rate of discount k_d^* which equates the after-tax cash flow generated by the bond with its initial price:

$$1,000 = \frac{(1 - T)80}{(1 + k_d^*)} + \frac{(1 - T)\,80}{(1 + k_d^*)^2} + \ldots + \frac{(1 - T)80}{(1 + k_d^*)^{10}} + \frac{1,000}{(1 + k_d^*)^{10}}$$

Assuming $T = 34\%$, the discount rate that solves the equation is 5.28%. If the proceeds of the bond issue are invested to yield either 8% on a pretax basis *or equivalently* 5.28% on an after-tax basis, the firm's return on equity will remain unchanged. This is illustrated in column 3 of Table 15–5. Hence the after-tax cost of the debt component is 5.28%, or

$$\text{cost of debt component} = k_d^* = (1 - T)k_d \qquad (15.4)$$

Other things being equal, the higher the corporate tax rate, the lower the actual cost of using debt, since the Internal Revenue Service will cover a larger share of the total interest cost. Consequently, note that it is the *after-tax* cost of debt financing which is relevant to the firm and its shareholders. On occasion, we employ pretax or no-tax examples, but this is for illustrative purposes only. In actual practice, a firm cannot afford to ignore the tax implications of its investment and financing policies.

FLOTATION COSTS

When issuing a new security of any type a firm incurs flotation costs that reflect the administrative expenses, registration and legal fees, and risks associated with the raising of the funds, as well as the need to underprice the issue relative to outstanding securities (see Chapter 12). Flotation costs reduce the proceeds to the firm, increasing the specific cost of the capital raised. Using our previous example of an 8% bond issue whose specific after-tax cost is 5.28%, we now assume that $38,600 of flotation costs are incurred. This sum includes all the costs (including any underpricing) necessary to float the bond issue. The net proceeds available for investment are thus reduced from $1,000,000 to $961,400. How does this affect the cost of the bonds to the firm? The after-tax specific cost is now given by the following formula:

$$961.4 = \frac{(1 - T)80}{(1 + k_d^*)} + \frac{(1 - T)\,80}{(1 + k_d^*)^2} + \ldots + \frac{(1 - T)80}{(1 + k_d^*)^{10}} + \frac{1,000}{(1 + k_d^*)^{10}}$$

and k_d^* rises to 5.8%. Thus the after-tax cost of the bond component rises. This reflects the need to cover the expenses incurred by the bond issue. In general, the higher the flotation costs, the higher the specific component cost, because the firm must cover the costs of flotation in addition to providing the required rate of return to the purchasers of the new securities.

COST OF PREFERRED STOCK

A preferred stock is a hybrid security in the sense that it has some properties of bonds and others that are similar to equities (see Chapter 13). Like bondholders, preferred shareholders typically receive a *fixed* annual income, in this instance the preferred dividend; but as is true of common stock, failure to pay the preferred dividend will not cause bankruptcy.

specific cost of preferred stock
Preferred dividends divided by net proceeds.

For the purposes of calculating the WACC, the **specific cost of the preferred stock** component, k_p, will be defined as follows:

$$\text{cost of preferred stock component} = \frac{\text{preferred dividends}}{\text{net proceeds}}$$

in symbols:

$$k_p = \frac{D}{P\,(1 - FC)} \qquad (15.5)$$

where D denotes the annual dividend and $P(1 - FC)$ is the *net* issuing price after deducting flotation costs *(FC)*. Assuming a net price of $95 and a dividend of $10, the specific cost of the preferred stock is 10.53%:

$$k_p = \frac{10}{95} = 10.53\%$$

Because a preferred stock represents a greater risk to the investor than a bond, the required dividend yield on preferred stocks will usually be greater than the interest yield on long-term bonds. This gap is even greater from the viewpoint of the firm because dividends, unlike interest, are not *tax-deductible*. Ignoring flotation costs, the *after-tax* cost of an 8% bond is only 5.28%; the after-tax cost of a 10% preferred share remains 10%. The firm must earn 10% *after tax* to meet its obligation to the preferred shareholders. Dividends, unlike interest, must be paid out of net after-tax profits. Hence the cost to the firm of the preferred stock component of the WACC is significantly higher than the cost of the debt component. Once again we caution you that neither the after-tax cost of the debt component, nor that of the preferred stock component, should be used as the cutoff rate for new investments. The latter is the appropriate *weighted average* of both components, combined with the cost of equity.

COST OF EQUITY

A firm's equity includes both common stock and retained earnings. We define equity to *exclude* preferred stock. Hence a firm can increase its equity by selling additional common stock or by retaining part of its current profits. But note that here the term *retained earnings* refers to that part of current earnings which is reinvested in the business rather than being paid out as dividends, and *not* to the accumulated surplus of the balance sheet.

These two modes of finance are for all practical purposes two components of the *same* financing source—owners' equity. However, due to flotation costs, the actual cost of raising new equity capital in the market is somewhat higher than that of retained earnings. Nevertheless, the principle remains the same. In both cases, we must estimate the opportunity cost of using the firm's own capital resources, and as is true of bondholders and preferred shareholders, we will base the **cost of equity** on the *rate of return shareholders require on the firm's common stock*. For simplicity, we initially consider the cost of retained earnings, since this does not require an adjustment for flotation costs.

cost of equity
The rate of return shareholders require on a firm's common stock, adjusted for flotation costs.

Methods Used in Practice

In their survey of the largest firms whose stocks are listed on the NYSE, Blume, Friend, and Westerfield included a question regarding the method employed by the firm in estimating the cost of equity. Their study shows that many firms use more than one method[2] (see Table 15–6). However, the dominant method is the dividend growth model. Twenty percent of the firms surveyed rely solely on this method, and more than 14% use this method along with the CAPM. Only 2% rely solely on the CAPM. Many firms still employ rough rules of thumb to estimate the cost of equity. Twelve percent of the responding firms used a simple variant of the price/earnings approach; another 10% added a risk premium to the bond yield. Finally, 12% of the firms used historical returns on equity to estimate the cost of equity.

TABLE 15–6   Percentage of Respondent Firms Using Different Methods of Estimating Cost of Equity Capital

Model	Percentage
1. Dividend growth model	20%
2. Capital asset pricing model and dividend growth model	14
3. Earnings to current market price ratio	12
4. Bond yield plus risk premium	10
5. Accounting return on equity	8
6. Historical common stock return	4
7. Capital asset pricing model	2
8. Other (Including judgmental and no response)	30
9. Total	100%

SOURCE: M. E. Blume, I. Friend, and R. Westerfield, *Impediments to Capital Formation*, Philadelphia: Rodney L. White Center for Financial Research, The Wharton School, Dec. 1980.

DIVIDEND GROWTH APPROACH

In Chapter 7 we derived the dividend valuation model for common stock. With only a minor change to allow for flotation costs when necessary, this model can be used to estimate the specific cost of the equity component of the WACC.

---

[2] See M. E. Blume, I. Friend, and R. Westerfield, *Impediments to Capital Formation* Rodney L. White Center for Financial Research, The Wharton School, University of Pennsylvania, (Philadelphia: December 1980).

The adjusted net present value (APV) approach, a sophisticated method advocated by some finance professors, does not appear to be in use in actual practice. According to this approach, there are two steps in evaluating projects: (1) Calculate the project's NPV by assuming that it is financed purely by equity, and use the firm's cost of equity as the discount rate. (2) Adjust the NPV by adding (or subtracting) to it any benefit the project induces. For example, if the project is relatively safe and allows the firm to borrow more money, one should credit to the project the interest tax shield due to the potential borrowing power created by the project's cash flows. In principle, this method should lead to a correct decision, but it is difficult to implement. This approach requires the firm to be able to specify in great detail the risk level attached to each project and its "borrowing power"—namely, how much the firm can borrow due to the new project without increasing its risk. This task is not simple, and in practice would have to be determined mainly by relying on experience and intuition, and not on any quantitative method.

Constant Growth   If, for simplicity, we assume that earnings (and dividends) are expected to grow at a constant rate of g percent per year, the price of a share of common stock (P) can be expressed by the formula:

$$P = \frac{D}{k_e - g}$$

where: D = the expected first year dividend, g = the constant growth rate, and k_e = the cost of equity. Rearranging terms, the cost of equity, k_e, becomes:

$$k_e = \frac{D}{P} + g \qquad (15.6)$$

Thus, for the case of constant growth, the cost of retained earnings is equal to the dividend yield (D/P) *plus* the constant growth rate.

The cost of the *new issue component* of equity uses the same formula, but replaces the observed market price, P, with the *net proceeds* from the new issue, $P(1 - FC)$, where FC denotes flotation costs:

$$P(1 - FC) = \frac{D}{k_e - g}$$

and therefore:

$$k_e = \frac{D}{P(1 - FC)} + g \qquad (15.7)$$

Growth for a Limited Period   Using the formula $k_e = D/P + g$ to estimate the firm's cost of equity may, on occasion, lead to paradoxical results; that is, to an unreasonably high estimate of the cost of equity. Consider, for example, the case of Xerox Corporation. Suppose that one wanted to estimate the firm's cost of equity at the end of 1969, using the earnings per share for the years 1960–1969 to estimate the growth rate g. The decade of the sixties was a golden period for Xerox, and its EPS rose at a compounded annual rate of 53%! Since its dividend yield at the end of 1969 was about 1%, Xerox's cost of equity (ignoring flotation costs) was 54%. Does a 54% cost of equity make sense, even for this supergrowth firm? Since the required return on equity consists of the riskless interest rate plus a risk premium, such a high equity cost is reasonable only if the risk of default is very high. Obviously this is not the case for many supergrowth firms, and it was certainly not true for Xerox.

The apparent paradox can be resolved if we note that a firm cannot earn extraordinarily high profits *forever*. As new firms enter a highly profitable industry, extraordinary profits will tend to disappear after a few years. Even in the case of a firm that earns extraordinary profits due to an invention, patents have finite lives. Hence we must consider the possibility of a reduction in future growth, and not rely solely on past data when applying the dividend growth formula to high-flying firms.

Chapter 7 presented a formula to handle situations in which extraordinary growth is not expected to last forever:

$$P = \boxed{\begin{array}{l} \text{present value} \\ \text{of dividends} \\ \text{during the} \\ \text{supergrowth period} \end{array}} + \boxed{\begin{array}{l} \text{present value} \\ \text{of dividends} \\ \text{during the normal} \\ \text{growth period} \end{array}}$$

Assume, for example, that dividends (and earnings) are expected to grow at a "supergrowth" rate g_1 for $n - 1$ years, after which they will continue to grow at some normal rate, g_2. The following equation can be used to estimate k_e:

$$P = \sum_{t=1}^{n} \frac{D(1 + g_1)^{t-1}}{(1 + k_e)^t} + \frac{D(1 + g_1)^{n-1}}{(1 + k_e)^n} \times \frac{1 + g_2}{k_e - g_2} \qquad (15.8)$$

The first term of the right-hand side of Eq. 15.8 is the present value of the dividends during the supergrowth period; the product of the last two terms equals the present value of the dividend streams during the normal growth period. The same equation can be used to estimate the cost of equity by solving for the rate of return k_e, using the method of trial and error (or an appropriate computer program).

To sum up, the dividend model must be based on a realistic estimate of *future growth rates*. For many mature firms that have reached a stable development, the past growth rate serves as a good estimate of future growth in profits and dividends. For supergrowth firms, those with temporary monopoly power or patents, analysis based solely on past growth may lead to a gross overestimate of the true cost of equity.

CALCULATING THE WACC USING THE DIVIDEND GROWTH MODEL

Having examined the theoretical underpinnings of the WACC, we turn now to the question of its practical application. Can the procedures outlined in the previous sections be applied by actual business firms? The question of application is crucial. As we have tried to emphasize throughout the book, a theory or analytical apparatus which is "good in theory but bad in practice" is simply a bad theory! The ultimate test of the theory of corporate finance is not its formal elegance, but rather our ability to apply the theoretical concepts to actual corporate decisions. To this end, we will illustrate the calculation of the WACC (using the dividend growth approach) for a well-known firm, General Foods (GF).

As a first step, we estimate the specific cost of equity capital for GF at the end of 1983. As we have already noted, this requires the estimation of the future growth of earnings (dividends). For the purpose of this analysis, the growth rate has been estimated by means of regression analysis, using historical data on earnings per share over the period 1969–1983. Using this approach, the annual growth rate of per share earnings was estimated to be 8.44%. Given GF's 1983 dividend of $2.40 and a market price at the end of 1983 of $51.375, the specific cost of equity is 13.11% (for simplicity, we ignore flotation costs throughout):

$$k_e = \frac{D}{P} + g = \frac{2.40}{51.375} + .0844 = 13.11\%$$

Since the per-share earnings used to estimate the growth rate have been calculated *net* of corporate taxes, 13.11% represents the estimate of GF's *after-tax* specific cost of equity. The after-tax specific cost of debt, $(1 - T)k_d$, was estimated to be 5.39% at the end of 1983.

Table 15–7 shows the specific costs of debt and equity and the market value of each source of financing (number of shares outstanding times their market price). Assuming that the observed capital structure constitutes GF's target financing mix, its after-tax weighted average cost of capital is approximately 11%. *The latter should be used as the cutoff rate for evaluating investment projects.*

A word of caution is in order. The calculation of GF's WACC is only illustrative. In particular, the all-important growth rate was estimated solely on the basis of historical earnings data. Presumably the company's financial analysts and economists would use additional sources of information, drawn from general economic, industry, and company forecasts, when estimating future patterns of earnings and dividends.

TABLE 15–7   General Foods Corporation: Weighted Average Cost of Capital, 1983

	Capital Structure		After-tax Specific Costs (%) (3)	Contribution to the Weighted Average Cost of Capital (%) (4) = (2) × (3)/100
	($ million) (1)	(%) (2)		
Debt*	963.6	26.51	5.39	1.430
Common equity†	2,671.5	73.49	13.11	9.635
	3,635.1	100.00		11.065%

*Based on book values.
†Based on market values.

THE CAPM APPROACH

We now apply the capital asset pricing model (CAPM), which was described in Chapter 8, to the problem of estimating the WACC. As we have already noted, a firm's cost of equity can be split into two components: the risk-free interest rate and a risk premium. This premium, in turn, depends on the firm's risk level. The higher the risk, the greater the required rate of return on equity. Clearly, a firm's business risk as well as the intensity of its financial leverage have a direct impact on the size of the risk premium. Following this approach, we can estimate the cost of the equity component using the capital asset pricing model (CAPM). This approach takes into account not only a firm's own earnings variability, but also the relationship of its returns to those of the market in general. The CAPM assumes that investors in the stock market hold a portfolio of stocks of many firms. Even though the variability of a firm's own earnings may be relatively high, its stock might still be considered relatively safe due to low or negative correlation with the other securities in the portfolio.

In the CAPM, only *nondiversifiable* risk is relevant (see Chapter 8). The beta coefficient is an index of this risk, and the required return (specific cost) of the firm's common stock, k_e, is given by:

$$k_e = R_F + (E_m - R_F) \beta_i \qquad (15.9)$$

where

R_F = the risk-free interest rate
E_m = the expected rate of return on the market portfolio
k_e = the required rate of return on the firm's equity
β_i = beta, an index of the firm's systematic risk.

Table 15–8 presents estimates of the cost of equity, based on the CAPM, for the five "aggressive" and five "defensive" stocks whose betas were

TABLE 15–8   Estimates of the Cost of Equity Using the CAPM

	(1) Systematic Risk β_i	(2) Risk Premium $0.1412 \times (1)$	(3) Specific Cost of Equity $k_e = 3.31 + (2)$
Abbott Laboratories	0.42	5.93	9.24
General Telephone	0.60	8.47	11.78
Greyhound Corporation	0.62	8.75	12.06
R.H. Macy Corporation	0.65	9.18	12.43
Union Carbide Corporation	0.92	12.99	16.30
Bethlehem Steel	1.37	19.49	22.65
Hooper Chemical	1.43	20.19	23.50
Cerro Corporation	1.67	23.58	26.89
Medusa Portland	1.86	26.26	29.57
Conalco, Inc.	3.44	48.57	51.88

estimated in Chapter 8. The analysis covers a 20-year period. During this period, the average rate of return on the market portfolio was 17.43% and the average risk-free interest rate (on Treasury bills) was 3.31%. Substituting the observed values for E_m and R_F in (15.9), we derive the following equation:

$$k_e = 0.0331 + (0.1743 - 0.0331)\beta_i$$
$$= 0.0331 + (0.1412)\beta_i$$

This formula is applied to each of the 10 companies in Table 15–8. Column 2 shows the risk premium for each firm; the specific cost of equity is given in column 3. The cost of equity for "defensive" stocks ranged from a low of 9.24% for Abbott Laboratories to 16.3% for Union Carbide. (Note that the required return on Union Carbide stock was very close to the return on the market as a whole, since its beta was close to 1). The minimum required rates of return (specific costs of equity) for aggressive stocks were all greater than 20%.

In a similar fashion, the cost of the other components of the weighted average, preferred stock and debt, can be calculated by estimating the *beta risk* of the preferred shares and bonds, and then using these estimates to calculate the specific cost (required return) for each component. Alternatively, their costs can be estimated directly from their observed yields, as before. Finally, the individual costs are combined to form the weighted average cost of capital (WACC).

Now let's take a closer look at how the calculations are carried out in practice, using the cost of the equity component as our example:

STEP 1: The riskless interest rate (R_F) is estimated, usually using the annualized rate paid on 30-day Treasury bills as a proxy for the riskless return.

STEP 2: The expected return on the market (E_m) is estimated using the historical returns or some broad index of securities such as the New York Stock Exchange Index, the S&P 500, or the CRSP Market Index published by the University of Chicago.

STEP 3: Estimate the firm's beta risk coefficient (see Chapter 8).

STEP 4: Compute the cost of equity (retained earnings) by applying the formula

$$k_e = R_F + (E_m - R_F)\,\beta_i$$

For example, if we let $R_F = 6\%$, $E_m = 10\%$, and $\beta_i = 0.05$, the cost of equity is 8%.

$$k_e = 6\% + (10\% - 6\%) \times (\tfrac{1}{2})$$
$$= 6\% + 2\% = 8\%$$

STEP 5: Estimate the cost of new issues of common stock by adjusting the cost of retained earnings for flotation costs.

STEP 6:   Calculate the specific cost of each of the other components (preferred stock, debt).

STEP 7:   Calculate the weighted average cost of capital using the specific cost for each component, weighted by its proportion in the firm's target capital structure.

CALCULATING THE WACC USING THE CAPM APPROACH

In this section we will use the CAPM to estimate the cost of capital for General Motors Corporation (GM), using for this purpose a corporate tax rate of 45% and data on GM and the market over the period 1964–1983.

STEP 1:   Using the average annual return on Treasury bills, the risk-free rate of interest was estimated at 6.8% ($R_F = 6.8\%$).

STEP 2:   Using the average annual rate of return on the S&P 500 index, the expected return on the market portfolio was estimated at 8.41% ($E_m = 8.41\%$).

STEP 3:   Using the regression technique of Chapter 8, GM's beta risk coefficient was estimated to be 1.533 ($\beta_i = 1.533$).

STEP 4:   GM's cost of equity was estimated at 9.27%:
$k_e = 6.8 + (8.41 - 6.8)\ 1.533 = 9.27\%$.

STEP 5:   For simplicity only, flotation costs are ignored throughout the analysis.

STEP 6:   The specific cost of debt, k_d, was calculated as follows:

$$k_d = \frac{\text{interest payment}}{\text{debt}}\ (1 - \text{corporate tax rate})$$

$$= \frac{530}{4,777}\ (1 - 0.45) = 6.10\%$$

The specific cost of preferred stock was calculated as follows:

$$k_p = \frac{\text{preferred dividend}}{\text{preferred stock}} = \frac{12.9}{283.6} = 4.54\%$$

STEP 7:   Table 15–9 estimates GM's cost of capital, using the CAPM approach, as 8.752%. This is the after-tax discount rate to be used in project valuation when projects do not deviate significantly from GM's average risk level.

TABLE 15–9   General Motors: Cost of Capital, 1983

Capital Structure	Amount ($ millions)	(%)	Specific Cost	Contribution to the Weighted Average Cost of Capital
Common equity	$26,786.1	0.8411	9.27	7.797
Preferred stock	283.6	0.0089	4.54	0.040
Debt	4,777.0	0.1500	6.10	0.915
	$31,846.7	1.0000		8.752

THE COST OF CAPITAL: U.S. INDUSTRIAL FIRMS

Now let's check our estimates of individual firm's costs of capital against some independent empirical evidence. Table 15–10 shows the costs of various sources of funds as supplied by a sample of large U.S. industrial firms. The data are taken from managers' responses to a survey conducted by Blume, Friend, and Westerfield. The cost of new common stock equity is 17.2%; the cost of retained earnings is a bit lower, 16.6%, presumably due to the saving of flotation costs. The after-tax cost of debt is 6.4%, and the after-tax weighted average cost of capital is 12.4%.

TABLE 15–10   Average Costs of Capital for Plant and Equipment Expenditure Programs Supplied by Largest NYSE Corporations

	All Industry Groups Combined (%)
1. After-tax cost of new common equity	17.2
2. After-tax cost of retained earnings	16.6
3. Before-tax cost of debt	12.5
4. After-tax cost of debt	6.4
5. After-tax cost of capital	12.4

SOURCE: Blume, Friend and Westerfield, *op cit.*

SUMMARY

The economic logic underlying the definition of the cost of capital; that is, the required rate of return for new investments, is as follows: If the new project does not materially change the firm's overall risk profile, the appropriate discount rate is the *weighted average of capital (WACC)*. However, if a project's risk is significantly different from the firm's average riskiness, an adjustment of the individual project's discount rate must be made.

The WACC is an average of the required rates of return of the individual sources of financing, with each source being given its proportional weight in the firm's target (optimal) capital structure. Using the WACC as the discount rate for investments insures that the value of the owners' equity will be maximized. Setting a lower (higher) discount rate would lead the firm to accept (reject) projects that decrease (increase) the market value of the firm.

The cost of capital is sensitive to risk. In general, the greater the risk, the higher the required rate of return. Hence each specific cost component of the WACC reflects the riskless interest rate (the time value of money) plus a risk premium. This premium, in turn, is determined by the firm's business risk and financial risk. The latter reflects the impact of the use of financial leverage:

$$k_i = R_F + \text{BRP} + \text{FRP}$$

where

k_i = the cost of component i
R_F = the riskless interest rate
BRP = the business risk premium
FRP = the financial risk premium

The specific cost of each component (the cost used in the calculation of the WACC) is defined as the minimum rate of return required by the suppliers of the capital.

1. *Cost of Debt Component:* The cost of debt is the *after-tax* required yield to maturity, adjusted for flotation costs:

$$k_d^* = (1 - T)\, k_d$$

where

k_d^* = the after-tax cost of the debt component
T = the corporate tax rate
k_d = the yield to maturity, after taking flotation costs into account

In general, higher flotation costs imply higher costs of capital, since the firm must cover these costs in addition to providing the required rate of return to the suppliers of the capital.

2. *Cost of Preferred Stock.* The after-tax cost of the preferred stock component is given by:

$$k_p = \frac{D}{P(1 - FC)}$$

where

k_p = the after-tax cost of preferred stock
D = the preferred dividend
P = the issue price
FC = the flotation cost, so that $P(1 - FC)$ represents the net proceeds to the firm

3. *Cost of Equity.* Two methods for estimating the cost of the equity component of the WACC are given: the dividend growth approach, and the CAPM approach. Using the dividend growth model, the after-tax cost of retained earnings is defined as:

$$k_e = \frac{D}{P} + g$$

where

k_e = the after-tax cost of equity
D = the expected first year dividend
g = the (constant) growth rate

The cost of new issues of equity is the same except for an adjustment for flotation costs:

$$k_e = \frac{D}{P(1 - FC)} + g$$

The after-tax cost of equity, using the CAPM, is given by:

$$k_e = R_F + (E_m - R_F)\,\beta_i$$

where

E_m = the return on the market portfolio
β_i = the index of the firm's undiversifiable risk
R_F = the riskless interest rate

The CAPM model can also be used to estimate the cost of the debt and preferred stock components.

The operational method for estimating the weighted average cost of capital (WACC) uses either the dividend growth model or the CAPM. Necessary adjustments to reflect corporate taxation and flotation costs must be made, as the estimates of WACC for General Foods and General Motors, as well as for a sample of large U.S. industrial firms, illustrate.

APPENDIX 15A | Market Value vs. Book Value

A firm's weighted-average cost of capital (WACC) can be calculated on the basis of book (accounting) values or on the basis of market values. Considerable confusion can be avoided if we emphasize from the very outset that market values should be used when calculating the cost of each specific component, and market weights should be used for calculating the weighted average. Perhaps the easiest way to justify the reliance on market rather than accounting values is to consider a simplified yet not unrealistic example. Consider the case of a firm which a number of years ago issued a $100 bond bearing 5% interest. For the sake of simplicity we shall assume zero corporate taxes and flotation costs, and that the bond (like the consols issued by Britain at the time of Napoleon) is a perpetuity. The interest yield of the debt therefore is 5%:

$$100 = \frac{5}{1 + k_d} + \frac{5}{(1 + k_d)^2} + \ldots = \frac{5}{k_d}$$

and

$$k_d = \frac{5}{100} = 5\%$$

where k_d denotes the interest yield.

Now assume that inflation induces a sharp rise in interest rates. To be specific, assume that the interest rate on bonds of similar risk and duration doubles to 10%. Given these circumstances, what do you expect the *market* price of the old bond to be? Clearly, it must now provide investors a return of 10% rather than 5%, or no one will hold them. However, since the firm's annual interest payment is fixed at $5 per bond, the only way this can be achieved is by fall in the bond's market price to $50. In a free and competitive security market, bondholders will try to sell the bonds as long as the price is over $50 (and the yield below 10%), but no investor will buy them until the price falls to $50 (and the yield equals the going market rate of 10%).

What impact does the price change above have on the cost of debt? If we use historical accounting book values, the issue price remains $100 and therefore the yield remains 5% as before. However, if we use the new market price of $50, the cost rises to 10%:

$$50 = \frac{5}{1 + k_d} + \frac{5}{(1 + k_d)} + \ldots = \frac{5}{k_d}$$

and

$$k_d = \frac{5}{50} = 10\%$$

Which of these two calculations is appropriate for our purposes? Recall that we defined the cost of capital in the text as the minimum required rate of return on investment, or the discount rate to be used when evaluating new capital investment projects. Assuming for a moment a hypothetical world in which *all investment is financed by debt,* the use of accounting values suggests that investments should be accepted if they earn a return of more than 5%. The market value approach would stipulate 10% as the cutoff rate. Clearly, only the latter is correct. The firm can always earn more than 5% simply by repurchasing *two* of its own bonds in the market for $100, since their market price is now $50. As a result, the firm saves $10 in interest payments— that is, earns a rate of return of 10%. The cost of the debt component cannot be less than its opportunity cost to the firm, which in this case is 10%. Historical accounting costs and prices are simply irrelevant.

An analogous argument can readily be found to support the use of market prices when evaluating preferred and common stocks. Since market values are used in calculating each cost component, market weights should be used in calculating the WACC. Note that market values rather than accounting values should be used *even if the firm does not plan a new issue.* Retirement of existing debt, or the repurchase of its own securities, always represent alternative investment options. Although market values are the only conceptually correct figures to use, it would be uneconomic and impractical to revise the calculation of the cost of capital daily, after every change in the market price of a firm's securities. A compromise with reality is required in which the *average* market price or trend is used as a benchmark. Temporary deviations around the trend line can, and should, be ignored.

REVIEW EXERCISE

Circle the correct word(s) to complete the sentence; see p. 406 for the correct answers.

15.1   The specific project's cost of capital must be used when the risk profile of the individual project *is similar to/differs from* the average risk of the firm.

15.2 If a project is risky, a risk premium must be *deducted from/added to* the WACC.

15.3 If a project has the same risk profile as the firm, the *riskless rate of interest/ WACC* is the appropriate discount rate.

15.4 When computing the WACC, each type of financing must be given *an equal/ a proportionate* weight in the firm's long-run target capital structure.

15.5 The WACC ensures that the value of the existing *owners' equity/bondholders' stake* will be maximized.

15.6 Setting a discount rate lower than the WACC would induce the firm to *accept/reject* projects which are not in the existing shareholders' best interest.

15.7 In practice, firms usually *issue/do not issue* stocks and bonds simultaneously.

15.8 A decrease in the proportion of debt in the firm's capital structure *does/does not* necessarily mean that stocks were issued.

15.9 Firms *should/should not* ignore transitory deviations from their target debt-equity ratio.

15.10 In general, the costs of all components of the WACC tend to *fall/rise* when leverage is increased.

15.11 The WACC *does/does not* always rise with increasing leverage.

15.12 The specific cost of each component is the *minimum/maximum* rate of return required by the supplier of the capital.

15.13 The cost of debt is the *before-tax/after-tax* yield to maturity.

15.14 The higher the tax rate, other things being equal, the *lower/higher* the cost of using debt.

15.15 The cost of equity is based on the rate of return shareholders require on the firm's *common/preferred* stock.

15.16 The dividend valuation model *can/cannot* be used to estimate the cost of equity.

15.17 The specific cost of *all components/equity only* can be computed using the CAPM.

QUESTIONS

15.1 Define the following terms
    a. WACC   **b.** Target financial structure
    c. Flotation costs

15.2 The capital structure of the Prudent Corporation currently contains more debt than is considered optimal. What courses of action are open to Prudent to correct this deviation?

15.3 What is the effect on corporate decisions of using too low a discount rate? Be specific.

15.4 "Our company has a very strict policy concerning the debt-equity ratio. We never deviate from it, even when we raise new capital." What does such a policy imply? Is it a desirable policy? Explain.

15.5   Why should a firm ignore transitory deviations from its long-term target debt-equity ratio?

15.6   "Since the costs of the individual components of the WACC rise with leverage, one should never use any debt at all if one wants to minimize the cost of capital." Evaluate this statement.

15.7   Why should a firm's long-term financial policy be reevaluated periodically?

15.8   Why must the *after-tax*, rather than the *before-tax*, cost of debt be used to compute the WACC?

15.9   "Whenever the interest on debt and the preferred dividend are equal, we prefer preferred shares to debt, since we are at liberty not to pay the preferred dividend." Evaluate this statement.

15.10   Comment on the following statement by the president of a large corporation: "We are going to acquire a company in the Midwest. All the funds needed will be provided by a 6% bond issue. Therefore, the minimum required rate of return on this investment is 6%."

15.11   What assumption regarding the future must be made when computing the cost of equity using the standard dividend growth model? When is this assumption unrealistic, and how can one correct for this?

PROBLEMS

15.1   **WACC.**   Based on market values, Rupert & Co. is financed by 30% debt and 70% equity. The debt consists of bonds on which it pays 6% interest; the cost of equity is 11%. Assume there are no taxes.
a. What is Rupert's WACC?
b. What is Rupert's WACC if the corporate tax rate is 34%?

15.2   **WACC.**   Rupert & Co. is financed as in the previous question. However, the debt consists of two different types of bonds, on one of which the firm has to pay 6% interest, and another on which it has to pay 6.5%. The amounts of funds raised by each of the two bonds is equal.
a. Compute the WACC assuming a 34% corporate tax rate.
b. How does your answer change if the corporate tax rate is assumed to be 45%?

15.3   **WACC.**   Shulten & Co. is financed by $2.5 million of 4% bonds, $3.25 million of 5% bonds, $2.75 million of 7% preferred stock which sells at par, and common stock whose market value is $1.5 million. The after-tax cost of equity is 9%. Assume a corporate tax rate of 34%, and compute Shulten's WACC.

15.4   **WACC.**   The following information on the Burton Corporation is available:

☐   Long-term debt: $4,300,000
☐   Preferred stock outstanding: 60,000 shares at $35 par value
☐   Common stock outstanding: 1,000,000 shares
☐   Retained earnings: $6,500,000

The interest on the long-term debt is 6.5%. The preferred shares have an 11% dividend. Next year's expected dividend on common stock is $2.80 per share, and is expected to grow at the rate of 2% per year. The common stock sells on the market for $22, preferred stock for $40. The corporate tax rate is 34%. Compute the WACC, and ignore flotation costs.

15.5　Cutoff rate.　Sutton Corporation is financed by 50% debt and 50% equity, which represents Sutton's target capital structure, given its risk-return profile. Sutton pays 6% interest on its debt, and the after-tax cost of equity is 14%. A new project yielding an 8% return on investment is under consideration. All the funds needed can be raised by a bond issue on which Sutton has to pay 6% interest. The corporate tax rate is 34%.

a. Should Sutton undertake the project?

b. Sutton is considering another project that yields 12%, but for which the capital must be raised by equity. Should Sutton undertake this project?

c. Explain the logic underlying your answer to parts (a) and (b).

15.6　Flotation costs and the cost of debt.　A company decides to raise $1 million by issuing a 5-year bond on which it has to pay 6% interest. Flotation costs amount to $21.30 per $1,000 bond, and the corporate tax rate is 34%. What is the cost of this debt?

15.7　Flotation costs and the cost of preferred stock.　A company decides to raise $1 million by issuing preferred stock. Flotation costs amount of $4.50 per $100 share, and the company pays a $7 preferred dividend. The corporate tax rate is 34%.

a. What is the cost of the preferred shares?

b. How does your answer change if the preferred shares are cumulative?

15.8　Cost of equity: dividend growth model.　A company's expected dividend next year is $5 per $100 of common stock. Earnings (and dividends) are expected to grow by 40% per year thereafter.

a. What is the cost of equity?

b. After 3 years of growth, the company's earnings (and dividends) stabilize, and no longer grow. How does your answer change?

15.9　Cost of debt.　A firm wants to raise $2 million by issuing bonds at an interest rate of 7.5%. Assume a corporate tax rate of 34%.

a. How much must the firm earn on the additional capital in order to preserve the return on equity?

b. What is the after-tax cost of the bonds?

15.10　Minimum required return.　Assume a firm with an initial capital structure comprised of $15 million of common stock yielding 18% in dividends, and $5 million of bonds on which it pays 6% interest. Assume also that the firm distributes all its net earnings as dividends, and answer the following questions, ignoring corporate taxes:

a. How much is the net operating income?

b. Suppose the firm needs $2 million to finance new investments but desires to preserve its existing debt-equity ratio. What is the minimum required net operating income on new investment?

15.11　WACC.　Consider the following financial statements of the Gamma Corporation:

Balance Sheet

Assets		Liabilities	
Cash	20,000	Bonds ($1000 par value)	60,000
Inventories	180,000	Short term-loan	10,000
Plant and equipment	50,000	Common stock ($1 par)	180,000
Total	250,000		250,000

Income Statement

Earnings before interest and taxes	100,000
Operating expenses	60,850
Operating income	39,150
Interest payments	3,150
Net income	36,000
Taxes (34%)	12,240
Net after-tax income	23,760
Earnings per share (EPS)	$0.132

The market price of a share of stock is $1.25, and the market price of a bond is $750. Suppose Gamma distributes *all* its earnings as dividends (and the growth rate is zero). The specific cost of debt is equal to after-tax interest/market price of the bonds.

a. Should the firm accept a project whose after-tax internal rate of return is 7%?

b. Should the project is accepted if the firm's long-term target capital structure is 30% debt and 70% equity?

15.12 Cost of retained earnings: dividend growth model. Abell & Co.'s dividend per share was $0.50 this year and is expected to grow by 3% per year forever. The share sells for $8. What is the cost of retained earnings?

15.13 Cutoff rate. The Larbo Corporation's target debt-equity ratio is 1:4. The interest rate on long-term debt is 9%, the tax rate is 34%, and the cost of equity is 16%. A new project has an IRR of 14%, but will be financed exclusively by debt. Should Larbo accept this project?

15.14 CAPM. The Zyton Corporation wants to compute its weighted average cost of capital using the CAPM to determine the cost of equity. The following facts are known:

- ☐ The 30-day T-bill rate is 4%.
- ☐ The rate of return on the market portfolio is 12%.
- ☐ Zyton's beta risk coefficient has been estimated at 1.5.
- ☐ Bonds yield 9%
- ☐ The corporate tax rate is 34%.

Zyton's capital structure consists of $4 million bonds and $6 million of equity ($4 million of retained earnings and $2 million of common stock).

a. What is the cost of equity? What is the WACC?

b. How do your answers change if beta = 0.5?

15.15 WACC, computer problem.

Compute the WACC for firms A, B, and C, for which the following facts are given (assume there are no flotation costs):

Debt

	Number of Bonds Outstanding	Face Value ($)	Coupon Rate (%)	Market Price ($)
A	200,000	1,500	6.380	1,326
B	125,500	1,000	7.125	1,043
C	63,600	2,200	8.365	2,261

Preferred Shares

	Number of Shares Outstanding	Preferred Dividend ($)	Market Price ($)
A	21,500	12.00	131.50
B	9,580	4.35	49.80
C	49,950	0.85	12.25

Common Shares

	Number of Shares Outstanding	Market Price ($)	Last Dividend ($)	Growth of Dividends
A	1,200,350	16.55	2.20	5%
B	840,230	83.95	11.35	zero
C	450,500	45.45	4.85	2%

	Retained Earnings ($)	Tax rate
A	5,435,980	34%
B	1,234,675	34%
C	2,321,555	34%

SAMPLE PROBLEM

SP15.1 The following information for the Aston Corporation is available:

- ☐ Long-term debt: $1,100,000
- ☐ Preferred stock outstanding: 10,000 shares (par value = $50)
- ☐ Common stock outstanding: 200,000 shares
- ☐ Retained earnings: $2,500,000

The interest on the long-term debt is 7%. The preferred shares have a 12% preferred dividend. The expected dividend on common stock is $4.80 per share, and is expected to grow at the rate of 3% per year. Common stock sells on the market for $40, preferred stock for $60. The corporate tax rate is 34%. Compute the WACC, ignoring flotation costs.

Solution to Sample Problem

SP15.1 First of all, let us determine what the total capital of the corporation is: Debt amounts to $1,100,000. Preferred stock sells for $60, and there are 10,000 shares outstanding; hence they have a market value of $600,000 (remember, book value is not relevant). There are 200,000 shares of common stock outstanding, which sell at $40 on the market. Thus the market value of the common shares is $800,000. Aston has $2,500,000 of retained earnings.

	Capital Structure	
	($)	(%)
Debt	1,100,000	22
Preferred shares	600,000	12
Common stock	800,000	16
Retained earnings	2,500,000	50
Total	5,000,000	100

The pretax cost of debt is 7%, as stated in the question. With a 34% tax rate, the after-tax cost of debt is $(1 - T) \times 7\% = (0.66) \times 7 = 4.62\%$. The preferred dividend is 12% of par value, i.e., $6 per share. With a current market value of $60 per preferred share, the cost of preferred stock is $6/$60 = 10%. Common dividends next year are expected to be $4.80 per share, the shares sell for $40, and the growth rate is 3%. Hence the cost of common shares is given by the formula:

$$\frac{D}{P_0} + g$$

which in this case is

$$\frac{4.80}{40} + 0.03 = 15\%$$

The cost of retained earnings, ignoring any flotation costs, is the same as the cost of common stock, 12%.

The weighted cost of capital can now be computed:

	Specific Cost (%) (1)	Weight (2)	(1) × (2)
Debt	4.62	0.22	1.02
Preferred shares	10.00	0.12	1.20
Common stock	15.00	0.16	2.40
Retained earnings	15.00	0.50	7.50
		WACC:	12.12

Answers to Review Exercise

15.1 differs from   15.2 added to   15.3 WACC
15.4 a proportionate   15.5 owners' equity   15.6 accept
15.7 do not issue   15.8 does not   15.9 should   15.10 rise
15.11 does not   15.12 minimum   15.13 after-tax
15.14 lower   15.15 common   15.16 can   15.17 all components

SUGGESTIONS FOR FURTHER READING

The weighted average cost of capital has been the subject of numerous articles; see, for example: Fred D. Arditti and Haim Levy, "The Weighted Average Cost of Capital as a Cutoff Rate: A Critical Examination of the Classical Textbook Weighted Average," *Financial Management*, Fall 1977; Kenneth J. Boudreaux and Hugh W. Long; John R. Ezzell and R. Burr Porter; Moshe Ben-Horim; and Alan C. Shapiro, "The Weighted Average Cost of Capital: A Discussion," *Financial Management*, Summer 1979; and Alan C. Shapiro, "In Defense of the Traditional Weighted Average Cost of Capital as a Cutoff Rate," *Financial Management*, Summer 1979.

An alternative approach is presented by Richard Brealey and Stewart C. Myers in *Principles of Corporate Finance*, 2nd ed. (New York: McGraw-Hill, 1984).

Applications of the CAPM to capital budgeting can be found in John Lintner, "The Valuation of Risk Assets and the Selection of Risky Investments in Stock Portfolios and Capital Budgets," *Review of Economics and Statistics*, February 1965; Dan J. Laughhun and C. Ronald Sprecher, "Probability of Loss and the Capital Asset Pricing Model," *Financial Management*, Summer 1976; and

Stylianos Perrakis, "Capital Budgeting and Timing Uncertainty within the Capital Asset Pricing Model," *Financial Management*, Autumn 1979.

The cost of equity is discussed by Myron J. Gordon and Lawrence I. Gould, "The Cost of Equity Capital: A Reconsideration," *Journal of Finance*, June 1978; Glenn V. Henderson, Jr., "Shareholder Taxation and the Required Rate of Return on Internally Generated Funds," *Financial Management*, Summer 1976; and Aril K. Makhya and Howard E. Thompson, "Comparison of Alternative Models for Estimating the Cost of Equity Capital for Electric Utilities," *Journal of Economics and Business*, February 1984.

For empirical evidence on the estimation of the cost of capital in practice, see Marshall E. Blume, Irwin Friend, and Randolph Westerfield, *Impediments to Capital Formation* (Philadelphia: Rodney L. White Center for Financial Research, The Wharton School, University of Pennsylvania, December 1980); Lawrence J. Gitman and Vincent A. Mercurio, "Cost of Capital Techniques Used by Major U.S. Firms: Survey and Analysis of Fortune's 1,000," *Financial Management*, Winter 1982.

16

Dividend Policy

As we have already seen, the firm is continually faced with two crucial and interrelated problems: capital investment and long-term financing decisions. Along with its investment and financing strategy, the firm must also decide on its dividend policy—that is, the proportion of earnings that should be distributed to shareholders as cash dividends. In this chapter we focus on a question that has occupied leading financial analysts: Why do firms almost universally pay out a substantial portion of their earnings as cash dividends? The key to this problem can be found in the answer to an additional, but closely related, question: Does dividend policy affect the market price of a firm's common stock? Essentially this question asks whether dividend policy is significant in determining the market value of the shareholders' equity. Dividend policy has been (and remains today) a subject of considerable controversy, and operational solutions are far from perfect. Qualitative and judgmental factors, the so-called intangibles of financial decisions, are often crucial in determining dividend policy. The purpose of this chapter is to clarify some of the more important issues so that an intelligent choice can be made between alternative dividend strategies.

WHAT IS A DIVIDEND?

Perhaps more than any other financial decision, a firm's dividend policy is influenced by legal, institutional, and other nonquantifiable factors. The payment of a dividend is a distribution to the firm's shareholders of assets that already belong to them in their capacity as owners of the corporation. Although we often associate the term with a payment of cash (*The Random House Dictionary of the English Language*, for example, defines a *dividend* as "a sum of money paid to shareholders of a corporation out of earnings"), any asset can serve as a dividend. At one time or another, real property, or the stock of another corporation, have been distributed as dividends. A well-known example of the latter is the distribution of General Motors' stock that was made by Dupont to its shareholders. Perhaps the most striking distribution of real property as dividends is provided by the "whiskey dividends" (literally a liquid asset!) distributed to shareholders by some distillers during World War II.

How Dividends Are Declared

Authority to decide on the payment of dividends rests with the board of directors. However, the board's discretion in declaring a dividend distribution is subject to several important restrictions:

1. Although the board has the final authority to declare, or not to declare, a dividend, the dividend payment to all members of a particular class of shareholders must be the same.
2. Dividends can only be paid out of current earnings, or out of accumulated past earnings that have been retained in the firm.

declaration date
The date on which a dividend is announced.

record dates
Quarterly dates on which dividends are credited to shareholders of record.

ex-dividend date
The date on which the right to receive a particular dividend payment is detached from the stock.

date of payment
The date on which dividend checks are mailed to stockholders of record.

Constraints on the board's freedom of action may also be imposed by the corporation's creditors or bondholders in order to minimize the possibility of insolvency. For example, the firm may be restricted by a debt contract or bond indenture to the payment of dividends out of current (and future) earnings, and *not* out of accumulated surplus. In some cases, even the proportion of earnings that can be declared as dividends may be stipulated. Similarly, the payment of cash dividends on a firm's common stock is often contingent on the corporation's preferred stock not being in arrears.

The procedure for declaring a dividend is as follows: On a given date, the **declaration date,** the board may decide, subject to any restrictions, to pay a dividend. Typically, dividends are paid quarterly to the shareholders of record on March 31, June 30, September 30, and December 31 (the **record dates**). The date on which the right to receive a particular dividend payment is "detached" from the stock is called the **ex-dividend date.** Finally, the date on which the dividend checks are mailed to the stockholders of record is called the **date of payment.** Thus, we can identify four pertinent dates: declaration date, date of record, ex-dividend date, and the payment date.

Stock Prices on Ex-Dividend Dates

The payment of periodic cash dividends to shareholders raises a technical question relating to the fluctuations of a stock's market price on these payment dates. Failure to recognize the need for a price adjustment as the stock goes ex-dividend can lead to serious misinterpretation of the impact of dividends on a security's performance.

Consider, for simplicity, a firm which pays a $10 cash dividend at the end of each year. Since the shares' market price reflects the *discounted value* of *all* future dividends (see Chapter 7), we would expect the market price of such a stock to rise gradually during the year, dropping off again at the end of the year when the dividends are paid. If we assume, for the moment, the absence of taxes and any growth potential, and an initial share price of $100, the expected price movements of the hypothetical share are illustrated in Figure 16–1. Its price rises gradually, in this case from $100 to $110, during the year, returning to the initial price of $100 as the stock goes *ex-dividend*— that is, when the dividend is detached from the stock.

In practice, we expect share price to drop by less than the full amount of the pretax dividend, since many investors must pay tax on their dividend income. However, the empirical evidence is somewhat mixed. Typically, the differences between the observed drop in market price, as a stock goes ex-dividend, and the full pretax dividend was not as large as one might have expected, given the marginal tax rates of many investors.

FIGURE 16–1
Price Movements of Hypothetical Share

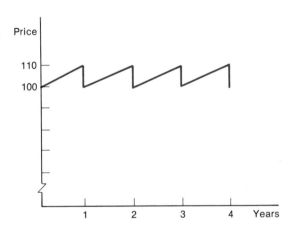

SHARE REPURCHASE

Repurchase by the firm of part of its outstanding common stock is one alternative to the payment of cash dividends. The actual repurchase may be made in a number of ways:

1. Buying the stock on the open market. To avoid any possibility of "insider" manipulation, stock repurchases are carefully regulated by the Securities and Exchange Commission.
2. Direct purchase from a large private or institutional shareholder.
3. Buying by tender offer to the shareholders or a particular group of shareholders.

The shares obtained are rarely canceled, and are usually held as treasury stock (see Chapter 4) to be issued in the future should the firm require additional funds.

The motivation for share repurchase is not always simple. Before the 1986 Tax Reform Act, the repurchase of shares, instead of paying a dividend, allowed stockholders to be taxed at lower rates. The dividends were subject to marginal personal tax; any gain on the repurchase was taxable at the lower capital gains rate. But this consideration was eliminated by the 1986 tax act, which stipulates that capital gains are to be taxed at regular rates. But even in the absence of a tax motive, some firms may repurchase their shares because they feel that, at a particular point of time, the shares are undervalued in the market. In such circumstances, repurchase becomes an attractive investment opportunity. For example, in the 2 days following the October 1987 stock market crash corporate buybacks were estimated at $9.2 billion.[1]

An alternative reason for repurchase is provided by Pioneer Corporation, which announced the repurchase of about 12% of its outstanding common stock in September 1984. The company said it was repurchasing the shares because it was the best use of its excess cash. Pioneer had the cash on hand, but did not have sufficiently profitable investment projects. So instead of taking on projects that would yield less than the return on its shares, the firm simply repurchased its own stock.

STOCK DIVIDENDS AND SPLITS

stock dividend
An accounting transaction in which part of current or retained earnings is allocated to the shareholders' equity account of the balance sheet.

Since a dividend is defined as a "transfer of assets" from the company to its shareholders, a **stock dividend** is not really a dividend at all. A stock dividend represents an accounting transaction in which part of current or retained earnings is allocated to the shareholders' equity account of the balance sheet. No actual transfer of assets occurs. For example, take a look at Table 16–1, which shows the balance sheet of the ABC Company before and after a 10% stock dividend. Ten percent means that the company allocates one new share for every 10 shares outstanding. For simplicity, assume that the stocks' fair market value (as evidenced by recent price quotations) was $10. In this particular case, retained earnings are decreased by $100,000, which is the full amount of the shares' market value. The amount to be transferred from retained earnings is calculated as follows:

$$\text{amount transferred} = \binom{\text{total shares}}{\text{outstanding}} \times \binom{\text{stock dividend}}{\text{in percent}} \times \binom{\text{market value}}{\text{of a share}}$$

or in the case of ABC:

$$\$100,000 = 100,000 \times 10\% \times \$10$$

[1] *Business Week*, November 2, 1987, p. 28.

TABLE 16–1   Balance Sheet of the ABC Company Before and After the Stock Dividend ($000)

Before the Stock Dividend			
Assets	1,000	Liabilities	300
		Capital	
		(100 shares of $1 par value)	100
		Capital surplus	100
		Retained earnings	500
		Total net worth	700
Total assets	1,000	Total liabilities and net worth	1,000
After the Stock Dividend			
Assets	1,000	Liabilities	300
		Capital	
		(110 shares at $1 par value)	110
		Capital surplus	190
		Retained earnings	400
		Total net worth	700
Total assets	1,000	Total liabilities and net worth	1,000

The $100,000 transferred from retained earnings are reallocated in the balance sheet in the following proportions:

Capital: + $10,000 (the new shares' par value)

Capital surplus: + 90,000 (the difference between par and market values)

Comparing the balance sheets "before and after" the stock dividend confirms that *no change* in total assets or total net worth has taken place. The stock dividend merely represent the book allocation of earned surplus to the capital accounts.

A **stock split** is similar to a stock dividend in its effects. In a split, the shares' par value is reduced; the retained earnings and other capital accounts remain unchanged. Assume, for example, that the ABC Company decides on a 2 for 1 split instead of a 10% dividend. The par value of its shares is reduced from $1 to 50 cents, and each shareholder receives an additional new share. Table 16–2 shows the firm's net worth *before* and *after* the split. The effect of the 2 for 1 stock split is very similar to that of a 100%

stock split
A technical device in which the number of shares is increased but total assets and total net worth remain unchanged.

TABLE 16–2   The ABC Company's Capital Accounts Before and After the Stock Split ($000)

Before the Split		After the Split	
Capital		Capital	
(100 shares of $1 par value)	$100	(200 shares of $0.50 par value)	$100
Capital surplus	100	Capital surplus	100
Retained earnings	500	Retained earnings	500
Total net worth	$700	Total net worth	$700

stock dividend. The number of shares is doubled, but total assets and total net worth remain unchanged by the bookkeeping transaction.

Stock dividends and splits do not involve additional flows of funds from the firm to its shareholders; both are technical devices that change the market price of a share of stock by increasing the number of shares outstanding. The stock dividend, however, also changes the internal structure, *but not the total* of the net worth section of the balance sheet. In addition, stock dividends must be paid out of current or retained earnings; a split can be made even if the firm has no past or present earnings.

Impact of Stock Dividends and Splits on Share Price

The price effects of a split or stock dividend are similar, because both result in a larger number of shares outstanding. Let's look at a firm which declares a 10% stock dividend. Assume the market price of its shares *before* the stock dividend was $11, and that 1 million shares were outstanding. Hence, the total market value of its shares was $11,000,000. Following the stock dividend, the new price of a share can be calculated as follows:

$$\text{new price} = \frac{\text{firm's market value}}{\text{new number of shares}} = \frac{11,000,000}{1,100,000} = \$10$$

The formula reflects the fundamental proposition that an accounting transaction per se should not change the market value of the firm's equity unless there is a change in expected profits. An investor who had 100 shares prior to the stock dividend gets 10 new shares, but as the market price is expected to fall from $11 to $10 on the *ex-stock dividend* date, the investor neither gains nor loses from the transaction:

Value of investment before
   stock dividend: $100 \times \$11 = \$1,100$

Value of investment following
   stock dividend: $110 \times \$10 = \$1,100$

In general, the expected market price of a share after a stock dividend or split can be calculated from the following formula:

$$\text{expected price} = \frac{\text{old price}}{\text{one plus percentage stock dividend (split)}}$$

or in symbols

$$P_x = \frac{P_c}{1 + q}$$

where
    P_x = the ex-stock dividend (ex-split) share price
    P_c = the price of a share before the stock dividend (split)
    q = the percentage stock dividend (split).

Reasons for Stock Dividends or Splits

Since stock dividends and stock splits are technical accounting devices that by themselves do not affect the value of the firm, it is not clear why a firm should use them. It will help matters somewhat if we distinguish between stock dividends and splits. Usually when a firm declares a stock dividend it *does not* make a compensating change in the annual cash dividend. Since the investor holds more shares as a result of the stock dividend, the total cash dividend to which he or she is entitled increases. Some firms use a stock dividend as a "signaling" device to announce an increase in future cash dividends. In such cases, stock dividends convey information to the shareholders. This explains the often-noted tendency for share prices to rise when a stock dividend is declared. But these price rises reflect the implied dividend increase, and not the technical accounting transaction per se.

The reason why a firm splits its shares is often quite different. Here the firm usually *does* adjust its cash dividend rate following the split. For example, suppose ABC Company pays a cash dividend of $1 per share. Now assume further that the firm declares a 2 for 1 split—that is, a 100% stock split. Following the split, the dividend is adjusted downward to $0.50 per share so that the total cash dividend remains unchanged. In such a case, the informational content argument is not relevant in explaining the motive for a split.

One possible explanation for the split is that the firm seeks to increase the marketability of its shares. The lower price per share can help increase the extent of share ownership. Consider, for example, a company whose shares are selling for $90, which then splits the stock 2 to 1. Other things being equal, the price will fall to $45 per share. Given the structure of stock exchange commissions, a significant saving accrues to investors who buy **round lots;** that is, 100 shares or multiples of 100 shares. Before the split, the minimum investment required to buy a round lot was $9,000 (100 × $90 = $9,000); following the split $4,500 is sufficient (100 × $45 = $4,500). Of course, relatively large stock dividends (say 25% and over) or a series of smaller stock dividends may also have a significant influence on the marketability of the shares. And in fact the New York Stock Exchange views all stock dividends of more than 25% as splits.

round lots
Stock transactions of 100 shares or multiples of 100 shares.

Do Stock Dividends Dilute Earnings?

One question that often confuses investors is whether or not stock dividends and splits dilute earnings. Obviously, a split or stock dividend "reduces" earnings per share, but it should be clear from the discussion so far that the *dilution* is only illusory. Total earnings do not change following a split or stock dividend. A meaningful comparison of earnings per share, before and after a stock dividend (or split), requires an adjustment: The lower per share earnings after the split (stock dividend) must be multiplied by 1 plus the percentage stock dividend or split. For example, if earnings per share prior to a 2 for 1 split (or 100% stock dividend) were $3.00, they fall to $1.50 immediately following the split (stock dividend). This reflects the doubling of the number of shares outstanding, while earnings remain unchanged. However, *adjusted* EPS remains unchanged:

$$\text{adjusted EPS} = 2(\text{EPS})$$
$$= 2(\$1.50) = \$3.00$$

The fall in earnings per share is exactly offset by the increase in the number of shares held by each investor, so that no dilution takes place.

DO CASH DIVIDENDS AFFECT THE VALUE OF THE FIRM?

If a firm operated in a world of perfect certainty, no taxes, and costless efficient capital markets, in which share prices reflect all relevant information, dividend policy would be of only trivial interest.[2] As we have already emphasized, the payment of a dividend is a transfer of part of the firm's assets to its shareholders. Since the stockholders owned the assets *before* the dividend was declared, the dividend payment represents only a change in the form of ownership. It's a little like moving a dollar from your left-hand pocket to the right-hand pocket: You still have the same amount of dollars.

Dividend Policy and Investment

Dividend policy can potentially influence a firm's share price, and thereby its market value, if its investment decisions are affected by its dividend policy. For example, if a decision by the firm to raise dividends induces a parallel reduction in investments, changes in dividend policy can be expected to have a significant impact on the price of the firm's common stock. In such a case, the payment of the dividend has a real cost—the income lost on the foregone investment. However, if we neutralize dividend policy so that it does not affect corporate investment decisions, the shifting of funds between the firm and its owners, in itself, does not affect the value of the firm.

External Financing and an Efficient Capital Market

This can be seen by considering a firm that has fixed its optimal investment program by accepting all proposals with a positive expected NPV. The firm intends to finance part of this investment program out of retained earnings. The remaining portion is to be financed by borrowing. If any funds are left over, they are to be paid out as dividends to shareholders. Now what happens if the firm decides to increase its dividend? Where will it get the money? If it has already reached its desired debt level and does not want to forego profitable investments, it can raise the money for the dividends only

---

[2] The formal proof of the irrelevance of dividend policy in a perfect capital market was given by Merton H. Miller and Franco Modigliani, "Dividend Policy, Growth, and the Valuation of Shares," *Journal of Business*, October 1961.

by issuing new shares. If we assume an efficient capital market, with no flotation costs, transfer costs, or taxes, the shares can be sold at their fair market value. As investments and capital structure have not changed, share price must fall, because there are now a larger number of shares outstanding, while the *total* market value of the firm remains the same. The old shareholders suffer a "capital loss," since the price of their shares has fallen. But this "loss" is exactly offset by the cash dividend they receive. So the change in dividend policy does not affect their net wealth. If they decide to use the cash to buy additional shares, their net wealth is unchanged.

differential taxation
Taxation of capital gains and dividends (current income) at different rates.

The assumptions of no taxes and zero flotation costs are crucial. The shareholders will be indifferent to how they get income—dividends or capital gain on the stock that results from the retention and reinvestment of earnings—only in the absence of **differential taxation,** or if they cannot postpone the tax payment until the capital gain is realized. The firm will be indifferent only if it does not incur flotation costs should it require additional funds to finance investments after the dividend has drained its coffers.

Absence of External Financing

If external sources of financing are not available, the firm's investment decisions are tied to its dividend policy. In such a case, a decision by the firm to raise its dividend does induce a parallel reduction in its investments, and as a result dividend policy affects the value of the firm. Hence, dividend policy is of special significance to a firm that for one reason or another must finance further expansion solely out of retained earnings. In such situations, a proposed increase in dividends must be carefully weighed against the return on the foregone investment.

But even in such a case, dividend policy affects the value of the firm solely through its impact upon investment. This can be seen by applying the dividend valuation model.

Consider the following example of a firm that has no debt and pays out a constant percentage of its earnings as dividends. The value of the company's shares is given by the dividend growth model:

$$P_0 = \frac{(1 - b)E}{k - Rb}$$

where
   E = expected earnings per share
   b = the percentage of retained earnings, so that $(1 - b)E$ denotes the expected dividend
   k = the firm's cost of capital
   R = the internal rate of return on reinvested earnings
   P_0 = the current market price of a share.

To neutralize the effects of investment in this model, we must set the net present value of any new investment at zero. Investment is permitted to change, but only as long as the expected rate of return (R) is just equal to the cost of capital (k).

Given the assumption $R = k$, the valuation equation can be rewritten as

$$P_0 = \frac{(1 - b)E}{k - kb} = \frac{(1 - b)E}{(1 - b)k} = \frac{E}{k}$$

Since b is eliminated from the valuation formula, dividend policy is again irrelevant for valuation, and the price of the firm's stock is independent of its dividend policy.

FACTORS AFFECTING DIVIDEND DECISIONS

Given the assumptions of certainty, no taxes, and perfectly efficient capital markets, dividend policy does not affect share prices. But such assumptions are only intended as a first approximation of reality; real-life capital markets are neither perfect nor riskless. Firms operate in a highly uncertain environment, and taxes are difficult to avoid. We turn now to the many factors which in actual practice can and do influence a firm's dividend policy.

Flotation and Transaction Costs   The irrelevance of dividend policy in a perfect market assumes zero flotation costs. As a result, the firm is indifferent between the financing of new projects out of the retained earnings or from the proceeds of new issues of securities. However, in practice retained earnings and new issues are *not* perfect substitutes. Because of flotation costs, external financing is the more expensive alternative. Other things being equal, the smaller the firm, or the smaller the new issue, the larger the proportion of such costs (see Chapter 12). This is a consideration that favors the use of retained earnings.

Another factor that may favor the use of retained earnings is the existence of transaction costs. Shareholders who want to increase their investment in the firm will prefer to forego cash dividends, thereby increasing the investment in the firm, without the need to pay commissions on share purchases. However, investors who desire to decrease their investment in the firm, say in order to increase current consumption, will by a parallel argument prefer to receive dividends, thereby avoiding the broker's commission that applies to the alternative of selling off some of their shares.

Control   In order to ensure control, some firms operate under a self-imposed constraint that limits the amount of external financing which can be used. Such considerations are prevalent among closely held or family-held firms. New issues of common stock dilute control, while after a point further increases in debt become undesirable or even impossible.

Informational Content of Dividends

informational content of dividends
Changes in the dividend rate that affect investors' expectations regarding a firm's future prospects.

Many researchers place special emphasis on the so-called **informational content of dividends.** In the real world, relevant information regarding a firm's future prospects is neither readily available nor costless. In such a situation, dividends can be (and probably are) important purveyors of information to investors. Shifts in dividend policy may affect investors' expectations regarding a firm's future prospects, thereby affecting its current share price. According to this approach, increases in the dividend rate will be interpreted as an optimistic signal from management regarding the expected level of future profits. Conversely, decreases in the dividend rate will be treated as harbingers of ill tidings. And these two effects need not be offsetting. The negative impact on share prices of a cut in dividends is likely to be greater than the positive effects of a corresponding increase in dividends. This reflects the fact that many current share prices already include a significant premium for some future growth.

Cash Position

A firm's cash position is another important factor that influences long-run dividend policy. Clearly a cash dividend requires that the needed cash balance be on hand, so liquidity can also be a factor affecting the dividend decision. A rapidly expanding and very profitable firm is often plagued by chronic shortages of cash. Such a firm usually prefers to set a relatively low dividend payout ratio and to plow back most of its earnings into financing further growth. The firm could, of course, turn to the capital market for funds. However, the uncertainty caused by rapid expansion often leads to the establishment of a "safe" dividend policy—that is, one that can be maintained should the rate of growth in earnings decline in the future.

Stability of Earnings

In general, the greater the risk of larger fluctuations in future earnings, the greater probability that the firm will adopt a policy of setting a relatively low dividend payout ratio. The line of reasoning that underlines such a policy is as follows:

payout ratio
Proportion of net income that is paid-out as dividends.

1. Most firms are anxious to avoid the negative information content of a decline in cash dividend rates. One way to do this is to set a **payout ratio** that can be maintained even in the face of relatively serious or prolonged declines in earnings.
2. The existence of large fluctuations in earnings also materially increases the risk of default. As a result, a firm with fluctuating earnings will try to avoid too high a proportion of debt in its capital structure. This limits its access to external sources of financing. A parallel policy of paying out a low proportion of earnings as dividends is especially appropriate for such a firm, since it helps provide the relatively large amount of equity capital needed to finance its investment program.

Legal Constraints   There may at times be a legal constraint against declaring cash dividends. For example, bond indentures, or loan contracts, may limit or even preclude the payment of dividends to shareholders (see Chapter 13). Similarly, dividends can be paid only out of earnings; they are usually not permitted if they reduce the firm's paid-in capital.

TAXES AND THE DIVIDEND PUZZLE

To this point we have ignored taxes—a strategy that cannot be recommended (for long) either in theory or practice. The introduction of taxes raises some fundamental questions.

Taxation of Dividends Before 1986   Prior to the Tax Reform Act of 1986, dividend income and capital gains were taxed at different rates. Since the tax rate on capital gains was below the tax rate on dividend income, it is not clear why firms should have paid dividends at all. Dividends were taxed at marginal personal income tax rates, while retained earnings incurred no immediate personal tax liability. Any increase in the value of a firm's shares which stemmed from the reinvestment of income was taxed as a capital gain. This took place only when the shares were sold, and at a rate lower than the marginal personal tax rate. Since many investors were in relatively high personal tax brackets, this could be expected to create a strong preference for capital gains. Despite this, corporations in the United States distributed a substantial part of their real earnings as dividends. Hence the expression **dividend puzzle.**

dividend puzzle
The policy of corporations to pay dividends when capital gains were taxed at a more favorable rate.

The Tax Reform Act of 1986   Under the new tax law, individual (and corporate) capital gains lose their special tax status. From the tax year 1988, there is no longer any distinction between short-term and long-term capital gains. All such gains are taxed at a maximum rate of 28% (unless the taxpayer is subject to a 5% surcharge). Hence, in effect, there is no longer any *differential* taxation of dividend income and capital gains. However, one distinction does remain: Retained earnings still incur no *immediate* personal tax liability. The retention of earnings offers investors the opportunity to defer tax payment until a capital gain is realized on the sale of their shares. Thus, the nagging question of why firms do not eliminate (or at least sharply reduce) their cash dividends still exists. Several, but not necessarily mutually exclusive, ways to resolve the dividend dilemma have been suggested.

Transaction Costs   Investors who desire to receive a steady income stream from their equity holdings might prefer the receipt of periodic dividends to the alternative of selling off a portion of their shares from time to time. This argument could be significant for small investors, and it also holds for some types of institutional investors who prefer to avoid using the proceeds from the sale of investments to finance current expenditures.

The Clientele Effect

Different classes of investors might have differing "tastes" regarding dividend policy. It has been suggested that the differential taxation of capital gains and dividends in the past, or the current ability to postpone the capital gains tax, might lead to a tendency for each corporation to attract a particular "clientele" comprised of investors who have a preference for its dividend policy (payout ratio). Given such a distribution of shareholders among corporations, a firm would be indifferent between alternative payout ratios. However, once a particular dividend policy has been established, the firm would be reluctant to change its payout ratio, because this could lead to clientele shifts, which generate undesirable transactions costs for investors.

Information Signaling

Finally, an intuitively appealing explanation for observed dividend payments can be found by considering some of the implications of the separation of ownership and management. According to this approach, dividends convey information regarding the *sustainable* level of the firm's earnings. In the highly uncertain world confronting investors, the use of dividend changes as a proxy for the trend in earnings is readily understandable and makes good sense. Reported per share earnings can be manipulated by means of "imaginative" accounting (or worse!), even by a firm in dire financial straits. The same cannot be said for cash dividends, which represent a drain on the firm's real resources. And while a firm might conceivably raise dividends, despite declining earnings or even losses, this process cannot continue indefinitely. Investors are likely to treat a rise in reported earnings, which is *confirmed* by a corresponding increase in the dividend rate, with greater confidence. Presumably, they interpret such a dual rise as representing a higher level of *sustainable* earnings, and not just a transitory fluctuation in profits.

UNCERTAINTY AND DIVIDEND POLICY

There is probably some truth in all these explanations, but like financial management in general, dividend policy is a multidimensional activity. Many influences are at work, but once again uncertainty lies at the heart of the problem. In this particular instance, *uncertainty of information* seems to be the key to the puzzle of why corporations pay substantial dividends even though personal tax rates typically exceeded those on capital gains in the past.

DIVIDEND POLICY IN PRACTICE

Now let's examine the actual corporate dividend payments of the Dow Jones Industrial Stocks for the period 1929 to 1985. The fluctuations in earnings were much more pronounced than the fluctuations in dividends during these years. Especially noteworthy is the relatively small magnitude of downturns in dividends per share compared with those of per share earnings. Moreover, in several of the years earnings per share actually fell below dividends. Thus, even in years of losses, firms attempt to avoid a parallel drastic cut in cash dividends.

The Partial Adjustment Hypothesis

The historical pattern of dividends and earnings has fascinated economists and finance specialists for many years. The seminal work in this area is John Lintner's pioneering empirical study,[3] in which he proposed a *partial adjustment* explanation for observed dividend behavior. According to the partial adjustment approach, corporations follow a policy of setting a target dividend payout ratio which they apply to earnings. However, due to the strong bias against dividend cuts, increases in earnings are translated into increases in dividends only gradually to avoid the necessity of future downward revisions. The lag in the adjustment of current dividends to increases in earnings is a sort of safety device designed to make dividends a function of *permanent* income, rather than temporary earnings. This partial adjustment hypothesis is consistent with the theoretical view that emphasizes the importance of the informational content of dividends under uncertainty.

Another argument in favor of regular dividend payments is that such a policy not only enhances the investment position of the company's stock, but also the credit rating of its bonds. A strong dividend record is an important consideration for many institutional investors, and is also one of the factors considered by the bond rating agencies when the firm's bonds are being examined (see Chapter 13).

The Con Edison Experience

The existence of alternative theoretical models would seem to provide little solace for a worried financial executive in a world of inflation and extreme uncertainty. And clearly dividend policy remains one of the most difficult decisions confronting the business firm: Magic answers to management dilemmas do not often jump out of a computer printout. However, recognizing the importance of the information content of unanticipated dividend changes can provide a framework for understanding actual dividend decisions.

A case in point is provided by Con Edison, which in the wake of the oil

---

[3] John Lintner, "Distribution of Incomes of Corporations Among Dividends, Retained Earnings, and Taxes," *American Economic Review*, May 1956.

crisis stunned Wall Street with an announcement that it would not pay any dividend in the second quarter of 1974. The decision marked the first time since the concern was founded in 1881 that the company had failed to make a regular dividend payment. It also served to disprove a favorite Wall Street axiom that utilities *always* pay dividends. The suspension of cash dividend payments reinforced the parallel announcement that Con Edison's operating profits had fallen by 21% in the same quarter. The market's reaction quickly followed. After a delayed opening, the price of Con Edison's shares fell by 32% in a turnover that placed it at the top of the New York Stock Exchange's most active list for the day.

SUMMARY

A number of problems relate to both theoretical and practical aspects of dividend policy. In a world of perfect capital markets in which there are no taxes, no flotation or transaction costs, and no barriers to information, dividend policy would not affect the price of a firm's stock. If the effects of dividend payments on corporate investment decisions are neutralized, share price is *independent* of the time pattern of dividends.

But real-life capital markets are not perfect. The firm is confronted, in practice, by numerous factors that are often neglected in the theoretical models. Flotation and transaction costs, control, the psychological impact of dividend changes on investors' expectations, the instability of earnings, the ability to postpone the payment of taxes until capital gains are realized, and the information conveyed by dividend payments in an uncertain world are all factors that must be given consideration when setting a dividend policy. When all the dimensions of the dividend decision are recognized, establishing a dividend strategy remains one of the most difficult financial decisions confronting the modern business firm.

REVIEW EXERCISE

Circle the correct word(s) to complete each sentence; See p. 425 for the correct answers.

16.1 The payment of a dividend is a distribution of *liabilities/assets* to the firm's shareholders.

16.2 Authority to decide on the payment of dividends rests with the *financial manager/board of directors*.

16.3 Dividends *can only/cannot* be paid out of current or retained earnings.

16.4 On the *record/ex-dividend* date, the coupon is detached from the stock.

16.5 On the ex-dividend date, the stock price tends to *rise/fall*.

16.6 Repurchasing shares instead of paying a dividend allows shareholders to *postpone/accelerate* their tax payments.

16.7 The stock dividend *is/is not* a transfer of assets from the company to its shareholders.

16.8 A stock dividend represents *a cash/an accounting* transaction.

16.9 In a stock split, the shares' par value *is reduced/remains unchanged*.

16.10 The effect of a 2 for 1 split is very similar to a *10%/50%/100%* stock dividend.

16.11 Following the stock dividend, the new price of a share will tend to be *higher/lower* than the old price.

16.12 If a firm declares a stock dividend and makes no compensating change in the annual cash dividend, the total cash dividend *increases/decreases*.

16.13 A stock split or a stock dividend may *increase/decrease* the marketability of a company's shares.

16.14 A stock split or a stock dividend *increases/reduces* earnings per share, but total earnings *also/do not* change.

16.15 Due to flotation costs, some firms may perfer a *high/low* dividend payout ratio.

16.16 Cuts in cash dividends are likely to have a *smaller/greater* impact on share prices than a corresponding increase in dividends.

16.17 Dividends often convey information regarding the *monetary/sustainable* level of the firm's earnings.

16.18 During the period 1929–1985, dividends of major American corporations fluctuated *more/less* than earnings.

16.19 The Tax Reform Act of 1986 *introduced/eliminated* the differential taxation of dividend income and capital gains.

QUESTIONS

16.1 Define the following terms:
   a. Dividends   **b.** Declaration date
   c. Date of record   **d.** Ex-dividend date
   e. Stock dividend   **f.** Stock split

16.2 Why might you expect the market price of a share to drop by substantially less than the amount of the cash dividend?

16.3 What consequences does a share repurchase have for the remaining shareholders?

16.4 What entries must be made in the balance sheet when a stock dividend is declared?

16.5 What entries must be made in the balance sheet when a stock split is declared?

16.6 "After a 2 for 1 stock split, I own twice as many shares as I did before. I love splits." Comment on this shareholder's statement.

16.7 Give some reasons why a firm might decide to declare a stock split or a stock dividend.

16.8 "We never split our stock, since this would decrease EPS. No shareholder wants to receive less per share, so splits are not in their best interest." Evaluate this statement.

16.9 How does the Tax Reform Act's elimination of differential taxation affect shareholders' preferences for cash dividends? Explain.

16.10 "I own shares of Jason & Co., but they never pay any dividends on my shares. I don't have enough voting power to change the company's policy, so there's nothing I can do about it." Is there really nothing that can be done?

16.11 Many professors of finance argue convincingly that dividend policy is irrelevant for valuation and therefore need not be declared, thereby saving a lot of trouble and money. Nevertheless, many companies pay substantial dividends. Why?

16.12 What is meant by the "information content" of dividends?

PROBLEMS

16.1 **Stock dividend.**   The market price of Redson & Co.'s is $36.50. If Redson declares a 20% stock dividend, what is the expected new market price of the shares?

16.2 **Stock split.**   Instead of declaring a stock dividend, Redson decides on a 6 for 5 stock split. What is the expected market price?

16.3 **Stock split.**   The Giles Corporation has 80,000 shares outstanding (par value $24); there is no additional paid-in capital. Giles had decided to split its shares 4 for 3. Earnings per share were $1.20 before the split, of which two-thirds was paid out as dividends. The shares sold for $27 on the market before the split. What changes in the balance sheet will be made after the split? How does the split affect EPS, dividends, and the expected market price of the shares?

16.4 **Stock dividends.**   Part of the Jasmin Company's balance sheet is reproduced below:

Common stock (50,000 shares at $5 par)	$ 250,000
Retained earnings	$1,500,000

This year Jasmin had total earnings of $50,000 and wants to declare a 25% stock dividend. The market price for a share of Jasmin's stock is $7. Show the balance sheet after the stock dividend.

16.5 **Stock split, stock dividend.**   GAT Corporation has 150,000 shares outstanding which sell on the market at $15. Management decides to split the stock 4 for 3. The firm's balance sheet before the stock split is given below:

Liabilities	650,000
Capital (150,000 shares at $3 par)	450,000
Additional paid-in capital	900,000
Retained earnings	1,000,000
Total shareholders' equity	2,350,000
Total liabilities and capital	3,000,000

   a. How does the balance sheet change after the stock split?

   b. How is the balance sheet affected should management decide on a 30% stock dividend instead of the stock split?

16.6 Share price. How are the expected share prices affected by the stock split and the stock dividend of the previous problem?

16.7 Cash dividends. GAT Corporation's cash dividend before the stock split was 60 cents per share.

   a. How much does the owner of a round lot receive in dividends after the stock split? (Assume that GAT does not adjust the cash dividend following the split.)

   b. How much does the owner of a round lot receive in dividends after the stock split if we assume that GAT adjusts the cash dividend following the split?

16.8 Stock prices. Calculate the expected stock prices for the following alternative retention ratios (b) and rates of return (R) using the dividend valuation model. (Assume that earnings per share in the first year, E, are $6 and the discount rate, k, is 15%.)

   a. $R = 20\%$; $b = 0, 15\%, 25\%, 50\%, 60\%$

   b. $R = 10\%$; $b = 0, 15\%, 25\%, 50\%, 60\%$

16.9 Differential taxation. A given share is sold for $30 just before time t_0. If the firm pays a $3 dividend per share, the price will immediately drop to $27. Suppose you own 100 shares. If the firm decides not to distribute the dividends, you would need to sell 10 shares (at $30 a share), since you need to have a $300 cash income. Assume that the shares were originally bought for $20 each.

   a. If both the personal tax rate and the capital gains tax are 28%, what is your after-tax wealth in the two situations?

   b. How would differential taxation affect your answer? (*Hint*: Answer part (a) again, this time assuming that the ordinary income tax is 40%, while the capital gains tax is 25%.)

16.10 Cash dividend. The owners' equity of the Brickles Corporation's balance sheet is given below:

Common stock (15,000 shares at $10 par)	$150,000
Retained earnings	$ 50,000

Total current after-tax earnings amounted to $50,000 this year.

   a. What is the maximum cash dividend per share Brickles can declare?

   b. Show the appropriate balance sheet changes if Brickles declares the maximum allowable dividend.

SAMPLE PROBLEM

SP16.1 The Compton Corporation has 100,000 shares outstanding (par value $12); no additional paid-in capital appears in its accounts. Compton has decided to split its shares 3 for 2. Before the split, earnings per share were $3 and the dividend payout was 50%. The shares sold for $30 on the market. What changes in the balance sheet will be made after the split? How does the split affect EPS, dividends, and the expected market price of the shares?

Solution to Sample Problem

SP16.1 Since 100,000 shares were outstanding at $12 par value, the original entry for "Common stock" in the balance sheet was $1,200,000. After the split there will be 150,000 shares outstanding [(100,000/2) × 3], but the total capital for common stock will stay constant, at $1,200,000, since no additional capital will have been raised. Hence, Compton now has 150,000 shares at $8 par value outstanding (2/3 of $12). Earnings per share, dividends, and the new market price will all be multiplied by 2/3: new EPS is $2 (2/3 of $3), dividends will be $1 (2/3 of $1.50), and the expected market price will be $20 (2/3 of $30).

Answers to Review Exercise

16.1 assets   **16.2** board of directors   **16.3** can only
16.4 ex-dividend   **16.5** fall   **16.6** postpone   **16.7** is not
16.8 an accounting   **16.9** is reduced   **16.10** 100%   **16.11** lower
16.12 increases   **16.13** increase   **16.14** reduces, do not
16.15 low   **16.16** greater   **16.17** sustainable   **16.18** less
16.19 eliminated

SUGGESTIONS FOR FURTHER READING

Dividend policy has been the subject of numerous articles and books, but the flavor of the theoretical debate can be discerned in Merton H. Miller and Franco Modigliani, "Dividend Policy, Growth and the Valuation of Shares," *Journal of Business*, October 1961; Myron J. Gordon, "Optimal Investment Policy," *Journal of Finance*, May 1963; and Michael J. Brennan, "A Note on Dividend Irrelevance and the Gordon Valuation Model," *Journal of Finance*, December 1971.

The definitive work on how corporations actually pay dividends remains that of John Lintner, "Distribution of Incomes of Corporations Among Dividends, Retained Earnings and Taxes," *American Economic Review*, May 1956.

Critical reviews of empirical studies of dividend effects are given by Irwin Friend and Marshall Puckett, "Dividends and Stock Prices," *American Economic Review*, September 1964; and by Thomas E. Copeland and J. Fred Weston, *Financial Theory and Corporate Policy*, 2nd ed. (Boston: Addison-Wesley, 1983).

The effects of stock dividends and splits are analyzed in greater depth by H. Kent Baker, Gail S. Farrelly, and Richard B. Edleman, "A Survey of Management Views on Dividend Policy," *Financial Management*, Autumn 1985.

The question of why corporations pay dividends has been examined by Fischer Black, "The Dividend Puzzle," *Journal of Portfolio Management*, Winter 1975; and by Martin Feldstein and Jerry Green, "Why Do Companies Pay Dividends," *American Economic Review*, March 1983.

The information and signaling aspects of dividend changes are examined by Fred Arditti, Haim Levy, and Marshall Sarnat, "Taxes, Uncertainty and Optimal Dividend Policy," *Financial Management*, Spring 1976; Stephen Ross, "The Determination of Financial Structures: The Incentive Signalling Approach," *Bell Journal of Economics*, Spring 1977; and Sudipto Bhattacharya, "Imperfect Information Dividend Policy and the 'Bird in the Hand' Fallacy," *Bell Journal of Economics*, Spring 1979.

17 Managing Working Capital: Inventories and Receivables

For sheer size alone, few activities can compare in importance with the demand for funds generated by the need to invest in working capital. A firm must provide sufficient working capital to ensure the normal process of purchasing raw materials and other inputs, converting them into finished products, selling them to customers, and waiting for the receipt of payments. Today, increased competition among firms at home, the expansion of many companies into international markets, and the relatively high interest rates engendered by inflation have further enhanced the importance of efficient working capital management. One result has been a tendency on the part of management to pay more attention to working capital. A second has been a pronounced improvement in the techniques (many of them computer-oriented) of working capital management. This chapter provides a brief overview of the basic principles of inventory control and the management of accounts receivable. A third component of working capital, cash and marketable securities, is discussed in Chapter 18. Chapter 19 examines some alternative sources for financing the firm's investment in working capital.

CHARACTERISTICS OF WORKING CAPITAL

As we pointed out in Chapter 4, the main components of current assets are cash, marketable securities, accounts receivable, and inventories. A firm's **current assets** are expected to be realized (turned into cash) within a short period, usually 1 year. The permanent or fixed assets of one firm often are the current assets of another, and vice versa. For example, a newly produced truck is part of Ford's current assets, but becomes a part of the fixed assets

current assets
Cash, securities, accounts receivable, and inventories that are expected to be realized within a year

of the firm which acquires it in order to deliver products. The difference between current and permanent assets depends on their intended economic use, not on their physical characteristics. In both instances, we are talking about the same truck.

In Chapter 4 *net working capital* was defined as the excess of current assets over current liabilities. This is the relatively liquid portion of a firm's total capital, and constitutes a sort of buffer for meeting obligations out of the company's ordinary operating cash flow cycle. The assets comprising a firm's working capital have the following characteristics:

1. *Short life span.* These assets have a short life span, typically less than one year. Exceptions occur in firms whose production cycle is more than a year. For example, tobacco companies that store raw material inventories for as much as 3 years still report them as "current assets."

2. *Rapid transferability into other assets.* The components of working capital are quickly transformed into other asset forms. Thus, for example, cash is used to replenish inventories, the inventories are run down as sales are made and are then transformed into accounts receivable, which again become cash as the receivables are collected. This characteristic of working capital can be visualized by looking at Figure 17–1, which diagrams the firm's cash cycle. Even if the level of working capital is held constant, the components are continuously changing. In our highly simplified example, the production process transforms cash into raw materials and then into finished goods. Credit sales transform the inventories into receivables, and when these accounts are collected we once again have a cash balance—presumably larger than in the beginning, if a profit was made. Thus the size of each component, but not the overall total of working capital, depends on the precise moment of measurement—on the particular stage of the cash cycle.

3. *Synchronization.* Finally, the size of working capital depends on the degree of synchronization between production, sales, and collections. If all these activities occurred instantaneously, with perfect synchronization, the management of working capital would be a trivial pursuit, and this chapter

**FIGURE 17–1
Cash Cycle
of the Firm**

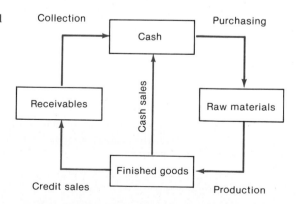

would not be necessary. However, when an element of uncertainty is added to the underlying lack of synchronization among a firm's business activities, the need for careful management of working capital becomes obvious.

THE MANAGEMENT OF WORKING CAPITAL

Effective working capital management implies two closely related types of action. First, basic policy must be set regarding the desired levels for each asset component; second, an administrative framework must be set up for managing and controlling these assets within the policy guidelines. A third facet of working capital management, the financing of the investment in current assets, is postponed until Chapter 19, which discusses the types of credit available to finance a firm's working capital needs.

Because of its quantitative importance, the management of working capital has been the subject of many books and articles on short-term finance, operations research, and applied mathematics. A modern firm's financial management team cannot afford to overlook this important problem, which for many companies represents the largest single use of their financial resources.

Different firms approach the problem of working capital differently. Typically, management relies on the use of ratio analysis, and similar rules of thumb, to determine the efficiency with which short-term resources are allocated (see Chapter 4). The advent of the computer, and the increasing use of financial models, has allowed firms to apply more formal methods to gauge the effectiveness of their working capital strategy. However, whether rules of thumb or formal models, or what is most common, some combination of the two, are used, the goal remains the same. Effective working capital management tries to provide easily implemented rules for routine decisions, as well as a framework for the continuous monitoring and evaluation of policy guidelines.

THE NATURE OF THE INVENTORY PROBLEM

At the end of 1986, total investment in inventory by nonfarm American business firms exceeded $780 billion. This represents a more than threefold increase over the $200 billion invested in such inventories at the beginning of the 1970s. Overall, the investment in inventory in 1986 accounted for about 40% of the total current assets of U.S. firms. However, the level of inventory investment varies greatly among firms. Insurance companies and financial institutions invest very little in inventory; but a large manufacturing firm like General Motors holds inventories well in excess of a billion dollars.

Clearly such corporations are prepared to devote considerable thought and resources to the control of these inventories, by more efficient management, since even a 1% reduction in inventories can save the firm over a million dollars in interest costs alone.

In principle, the investment in inventory is similar to the fixed investment in machinery, equipment, and buildings. In both cases an initial outlay is incurred in expectation of earning a future return. However, the investment in inventory differs from fixed investment in at least two important respects:

1. Typically, the investment in inventory is only one component of a complex project. For example, investing in a new product requires both raw material and finished goods inventories. As a result, it is difficult to measure the direct return on inventory investment. With this in mind, models have been developed to provide for the efficient management of inventory. In other words, the firm does not attempt to maximize the return on its investment in inventory, but rather to *minimize the costs* of holding the inventories.

2. Because inventory decisions are repetitive, the relevant management decisions often relate to *how often,* and by *how much,* inventories should be replenished.

INVENTORY COSTS

Some of the costs involved in holding inventories increase as the amount of inventory held rises, while others tend to fall as the inventory level is increased. Hence, changing the inventory level creates conflicting forces: Some cost components rise, but others are reduced, which is the reason why inventory creates a management "problem."

Costs That Vary Directly with Inventory Levels

One can distinguish six main types of carrying costs which rise when the investment in inventory increases, and fall when the level of inventory is decreased.

1. *Capital costs:* The firm has part of its financial resources tied up in inventory. This component depends on the firm's cost of capital, the size of the inventory investment, and the time period over which the inventory is held. For example, if the appropriate discount rate is 10% and an inventory of $10,000 is held for 6 months, inventory would be charged with $500 of capital costs: $10\% \times 10,000 \times 6/12 = \$500$.

2. *Storage costs:* The capital cost of holding inventories should also reflect the use of buildings and other facilities needed to store the inventory. In cases where space is rented, the rent becomes an important component of total inventory cost. This cost also varies directly with inventory size, on the realistic assumption that the larger the inventory, the more space that must be rented.

3. *Handling costs:* Inventory must be moved from time to time, or delivered to other departments. Hence inventory costs include the costs of labor and mechanical equipment, such as forklifts. It is worth noting that part of this cost varies proportionally with the amount of inventory held. Another part, for example the cost of moving finished goods out of inventory to a firm's retail outlets, depends on the size of sales rather than inventory levels.

4. *Insurance:* Insurance premiums are typically charged on the average value of the inventory in question; hence the higher the level of inventory, the greater the insurance costs.

5. *Property tax:* Property taxes are usually levied as a percentage of the value of the inventory, and therefore they also vary directly with inventory levels.

6. *Depreciation and obsolescence:* Part of an inventory may lose its value over time as a result of spoilage, damage, or obsolescence. The latter is especially serious in cases of fashion goods: A drop in women's hemlines or a shrinking of men's lapels can be potentially disastrous for firms holding large inventories of miniskirts or wide neckties.

Costs That Vary Inversely with Inventory Levels

1. *Ordering costs:* The clerical and administrative work (typing letters, phone calls, and so on) associated with the ordering of inventory are for all practical purposes *fixed per order.* The larger the order, and therefore the larger the average inventory level, the smaller the number of orders placed. This results in *smaller* total annual order costs. Shipping costs, up to a given level, also decline with an increase in order size. When a truck is sent to a firm, per-unit shipping costs will rise by less than 100% if the truck's load is doubled. (We are assuming, of course, that the *same* truck is capable of carrying the additional units.)

2. *Quantity discount loss:* A decrease in average inventory, which means a decrease in order size, may in some instances result in a higher average per-unit price due to the loss of quantity discounts.

3. *Stockout Costs:* When a firm runs out of finished goods, it loses potential revenue and/or consumer goodwill. Stockouts of raw material inventory, on the other hand, often cause serious interruptions and losses in production. Obviously, the larger the inventory, the smaller the probability of running out of stock. Thus, stockout costs also vary inversely with the size of the inventory.

INVENTORY MODELS

Costs that vary in *opposite* directions when the level of inventory is changed lie at the heart of the inventory problem. The purpose of an *inventory model* is to help the firm find the optimal level of inventory—that is, the size of inventory which minimizes total inventory costs. For simplicity, consider a deterministic model which assumes that the demand for the firm's products and the lead time (the time between placing an order and its arrival in stock) are known with certainty.

These assumptions can be relaxed by assuming a probabilistic model in which the demand and/or lead times are subject to a probability distribution. Although probabilistic models describe the realities of business more precisely than their deterministic counterparts, such models are often complicated and difficult to handle. Moreover, experience shows that the greater part of the potential cost savings can usually be secured by using relatively simple deterministic models.

Figure 17–2 illustrates a typical inventory model. On the horizontal axis, inventory size (in units) is measured, while the vertical axis shows the annual costs (in dollars) which are incurred. The curve labeled *A* includes all those cost components which are fixed per order, and therefore vary *inversely* with inventory size—for example, order costs. Since holding a larger inventory implies a smaller number of orders during the year, such costs fall as the level of inventory rises. Costs which vary directly with inventory size (capital costs and insurance) are represented by the rising line *B* of Figure 17–2. Total costs are denoted by the U-shaped curve labeled *T*, which is derived by summing curves *A* and *B*. Since the firm's goal is to minimize the total costs associated with the holding of inventory, point *Q** represents the *optimal* inventory size. Note that at the optimum, the additional "type B" variable costs that would be incurred if the level of inventory is raised by 1 unit is just equal to the decline in "type A" costs.

FIGURE 17–2
A Typical Inventory Model

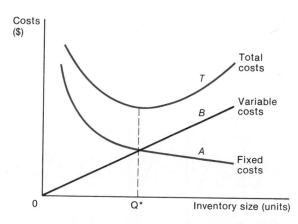

The problem can be clarified further by writing out the cost function that underlies Figure 17–2. In the case of certainty, there are no stockout costs; hence the total annual inventory cost becomes

$$\textbf{total cost} = \textbf{variable cost} + \textbf{fixed cost}$$

in symbols:

$$TC = C_1 \overline{Q} + C_2 N$$

where

TC = the total inventory costs

C_1 = those costs (per unit) which *vary directly* with the inventory level

$\overline{Q}$ = the average inventory held, and $C_1\overline{Q}$ the total variable cost (curve *B* of Figure 17–2)

C_2 = The fixed cost per order

N = the number of orders placed during the year, and $C_2 N$, the total annual fixed costs (curve *A* of Figure 17–2).

Assume that the firm decides to place an order with a supplier for Q units. If the demand for the firm's products is spread evenly over the year, the *average* inventory held during the year will be $Q/2$. The process is illustrated in Figure 17–3. The opening inventory is given by Q—that is, by the initial lot size ordered. Since sales are assumed to take place evenly through the year, the inventory decreases gradually until at point t_1 it is exhausted. But exactly at this point of time, a new shipment of Q units arrives, and the inventory again rises to Q. The process continues, and at points t_2, t_3, and so on, additional orders arrive.

In this type of model, stockouts do not occur. Since the quantity sold by the firm is known with certainty, the precise level of inventory at each point of time is also known. By coordinating the order placements with the information on demand, stockouts can be avoided. For example, suppose that the order lead time is $1/2t$ (see Figure 17–3), and that it is also known

FIGURE 17–3

Size of Inventory with Uniform Demand and Zero Order Lead Time

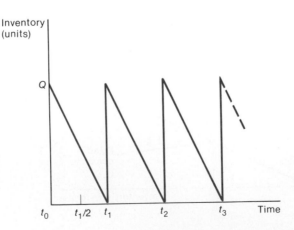

with certainty. As a result, the firm will place its order of Q units at time $1/2t$ so that the shipment will arrive exactly at point t_1. Only in the extreme case of zero lead time would the firm place its order exactly at point t_1.

From the description, you can see that the average inventory held in each period of time, and therefore during the year as a whole, is $Q/2$ units. Inventory declines from Q units at the beginning of each period to zero at the end of the period, which results in an average inventory of $Q/2$.

Given the assumption of certainty, the optimal order size (or optimal lot size as it is also called) can be calculated from the following formula:

$$Q^* = \sqrt{\frac{2SC_2}{C_1}}$$

where

Q^* = optimal order size

S = total quantity (in units) sold during the year

The meaning of the optimal order size formula can be clarified by considering a numerical example. Assume that a firm's annual sales are 100,000 units at a unit price of $10, and that variable inventory carrying costs (as a percent of the sales price) are as follows:

Capital costs	12
Property costs and insurance	5
Handling and other variable costs	3
Total variable costs	20%

Thus variable inventory carrying costs are $2 per unit of inventory. Assuming that the fixed costs per order are $1,000, the optimal order size Q^* can be calculated as follows:

$$Q^* = \sqrt{\frac{2 \times 100{,}000 \times 1{,}000}{2}} = 10{,}000 \text{ units}$$

Since total annual sales are 100,000 units, the firm will place 10 orders of 10,000 units each during the year, and the average inventory will be $Q^*/2 = 5{,}000$ units. Any deviation from these values will increase total inventory costs. Table 17–1 gives the inventory costs for the problem above for a variety of alternative inventory policies. Since annual sales are constant

TABLE 17–1   Inventory Costs for Alternative Inventory Policies

Order size (units)	100	5,000	8,333	10,000	12,500	20,000
Number of orders	1,000	20	12	10	8	5
Average inventory (units)	50	2,500	4,161	5,000	6,250	10,000
Total variable cost ($)	100	5,000	8,333	10,000	12,500	20,000
Total order cost ($)	1,000,000	20,000	12,000	10,000	8,000	5,000
Total cost ($)	1,000,100	25,000	20,333	20,000	20,500	25,000

(S = 100,000 units), changing the order size automatically determines the number of times a year that the firm must place its orders. From the data in the table, we can see clearly that the cost function is U-shaped. For very small orders (such as 100 units), the total inventory holding cost exceeds $1 million. Up to an order size of 10,000 units, increasing the order size leads to a decline in total cost. At an order size of 10,000 units the costs are at a minimum; for order sizes beyond 10,000 units total costs rise, which confirms the result we reached previously using the optimal order size formula.

UNCERTAINTY AND SAFETY STOCKS

In actual practice, demand and order lead times are rarely known with certainty. The purpose of this section is to discuss the problems raised by the existence of uncertainty. Figure 17–4 illustrates an inventory problem in which sales are known with certainty, but order lead times are not. Assume that the firm orders Q units. In periods t_1 and t_2, there is no lag in the lead time, and hence no shortage occurs. However, the third order arrives late, and over the period marked a in Figure 17–4, the firm is out of stock. Conversely, Figure 17–5 illustrates a case in which the shipment comes early, so that the firm's actual inventory exceeds the optimum quantity required. In period t_2, the shipment arrives a days early, and as a result the average inventory held during period t_2 increases.

When sales are uncertain, shortages can occur even if order lead time is known with absolute certainty. This could result if there is a sudden unforeseen increase in the demand for a product. Obviously, in a real-life situation, both the lead time and the demand (sales) are uncertain, so that stockouts can occur from any combination of these two factors. To reduce the risk of stockouts, the firm often holds an extra quantity of inventory as a **safety stock.** The problem that confronts such a firm is how to balance the stockout costs against the cost of carrying the extra inventory.

safety stock
An extra quantity of inventory held to reduce the risk of stockouts.

FIGURE 17–4
Impact of Late Orders on Inventory

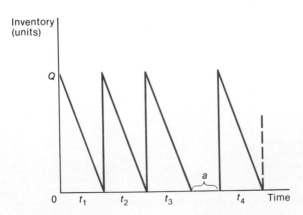

FIGURE 17—5
Impact of Early
Shipments
on Inventory

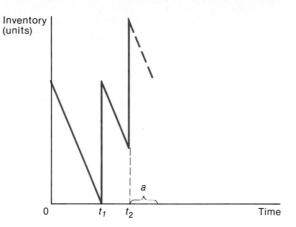

The inventory problem under uncertainty can also be illustrated in Figure 17-6. In the absence of uncertainty, and assuming that the firm knows 162 units will be used with a probability of 1, the firm would order 162 units each period. The existence of uncertainty induces a change in the planned level of inventory. In this case, the firm decides to order an extra 38 units as a *safety stock*. Should the firm decide to suffer possible stockouts, it would order less, and the inventory curve would fall below the horizontal axis.

FIGURE 17—6
Inventory Policy
Under Uncertainty

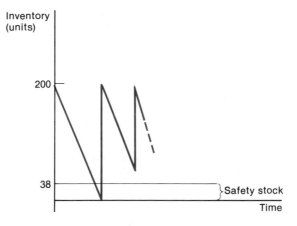

THE TWO-BIN MODEL

Even the simple deterministic inventory model is considered too complicated by some companies. These firms use the so-called two-bin model. This method tells the firm to place an order every time inventory drops below a given level (when one bin is empty). The two-bin method is illustrated in

Figure 17–7. Suppose the firm decides to place an order every time that the inventory falls below Q_0. Hence, t_1, t_2, and t_3 are the order points. It is worth noting that though this method does not guarantee cost minimization, it is an efficient rule of thumb for two cases:

1. Many firms stock thousands of individual items, so it would be prohibitively expensive to apply a sophisticated inventory model to each item. Moreover, a few items often constitute the bulk of the inventory. For example, if 10 items represent 90% of the inventory's value, it would be preferable to use a sophisticated model, based on estimates of the variable and fixed costs, only for those 10 items. The thousands of other items, with a low money value, could be more efficiently controlled using a simple two-bin rule of thumb system.

2. If the ordering points have been adjusted to reflect the firm's past experience, the rule of thumb two-bin system often provides a very close approximation to the optimal inventory policy.

FIGURE 17–7
The Two Bin
Inventory Model

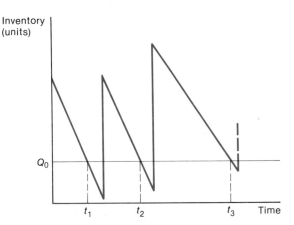

CREDIT POLICY

A firm's credit policy consists of two interrelated activities: *granting credit* and the *collection of receivables*. Both aspects affect the composition of working capital. A more liberal credit policy implies higher levels of credit sales, and as a result, higher levels of accounts receivable. More stringent collection policies imply a reduction in outstanding receivables.

Credit management involves five basic decisions:

1. *Credit period.* This decision relates to the length of time for which the firm is prepared to grant credit to its customers.

2. *Credit instruments.* Having decided to grant credit, the firm must also decide on the legal form it will take. Should a formal IOU be required, or is a simple receipt sufficient?

3. *Credit standards.* Next, credit standards have to be set. This involves the decision as to which customers consitute "good" or "bad" credit risks. It also requires the stipulation of a method for determining their creditworthiness on the basis of past performance, analysis of their financial statements, or external reports of banks and/or credit agencies.

4. *Collection policy.* A policy for monitoring outstanding credits must be established, and a decision must be reached in cases of slow payment.

5. *Incentives.* Finally, the firm must decide on the extent of the financial (or other) incentives that will be offered for prompt payment.

It is clear from the above that credit policy has a twofold purpose. At first glance, it might appear that avoiding credit losses is an end in itself. But this is only part, and not necessarily the most important part, of the credit manager's function. Credit policy also has a direct impact on sales. Easing the terms of credit by lengthening the credit period, offering generous cash discounts, or relaxing credit standards will stimulate sales; the opposite can be expected from a tightening of credit policy. The credit problem affects a firm's overall strategy, because the increase in sales is not without cost. Cash discounts, or a lengthening of the credit period, are equivalent to a reduction in price, and the easing of credit standards can, and often does, lead to bad debts. Hence the additional sales revenue has to be weighed against the additional costs generated by such policies.

There is no fixed rule for locating the credit function within the firm. Different companies have different management styles, and credit management is no exception to this pattern. Depending on the company, we may find credit policy being set in the *finance* department; by *sales* personnel; by *top management;* or, which is becoming increasingly common, by some combination of all three. Since a change in credit policy typically affects sales, production, and the level of accounts receivable, as well as the expense of collections and bad debt losses, there is much to be said for delegating the credit policy to a management committee that includes the vice-presidents in charge of marketing, production, and finance.

THE CREDIT-GRANTING DECISION

The extension of credit is essentially a method of enhancing sales by making it easier for customers to pay for a firm's products or services. It is especially important for customers who find it impossible or inconvenient to borrow.

The key decision, of course, is whether credit should be granted at all, but if the answer is affirmative, the firm must also decide how much credit should be extended. It is at this stage that management discretion is exercised. However, the terms of credit—that is, length of period, size of cash discounts, and so on—are often strongly influenced by industry practice. Significant deviations from accepted standards can lead to reprisals from competitors.

EVALUATING CREDIT RISKS

In reaching a decision on whether or not to extend credit, management must assess the risks involved in the request for credit. Hence the measurement of customer credit quality lies at the heart of the decision.

A popular rule of thumb used by credit managers to evaluate the probability of default is to consider the so-called three Cs of credit:

1. *Character.* This factor attempts to measure the customer's *willingness* to pay. It raises the fundamental question of whether or not the customer will *try* to honor the promise to pay. Most managers consider this issue crucial. If the answer to this question is strongly negative, it is unlikely that credit will be granted.

2. *Capital.* This factor refers to the customer's *ability* to pay. Here an attempt is made to determine whether the customer has sufficient financial resources to meet the proposed obligation. This aspect of the decision is often investigated using the tools of financial statement analysis, with special emphasis on liquidity ratios (current ratio, quick ratio) and risk ratios, such as the debt-equity ratio and interest coverage ratios.

3. *Capacity.* This is a more subjective measure of the customer's *ability to pay.* Here, the previous track record with the firm is crucial.

Two other Cs are sometimes added to the rule of thumb:

4. *Collateral.* This is simply the assets the customer can offer to secure the debt.

5. *Condition.* This is the customer's vulnerability to changes in business conditions, or other specific events.

A credit assessment based on some combination of these five factors requires information drawn from the firm's previous experience, from the analysis of the customer's financial position, or from external sources. The major external sources are *credit reporting agencies* such as Dun & Bradstreet, which collect and sell credit information and, in addition, provide credit ratings based on a customer's ability to pay; *credit associations,* such as the National Association of Credit Management; and local industry associations. Some firms turn to commercial banks to obtain credit references on customers. Although there are no general rules, the subjective weights given to the various sources are usually left to the credit manager's discretion.

To sum up, the credit investigation rests on four principal sources of information: (1) previous experience, if any, with the customer; (2) financial statement analysis; (3) reports of commercial credit-rating agencies; (4) credit references of banks and trade associations. If loss of sales is to be avoided, credit investigations must be carried out quickly. And, as we have already emphasized, the avoidance of credit losses is only part of the management function; the other, and perhaps no less important, function of credit management is the promotion of sales.

CREDIT TERMS

The terms of credit granted to customers affect *sales volume* and the *timing of receipts.* As a result, credit policy has a significant impact on the present value of a firm's revenues. It is reasonably clear why improved credit terms can induce an increase in sales. For all practical purposes, a lengthening of the payment period is, in terms of present value, fully equivalent to a price reduction. Unfortunately, the influence of credit terms on the pattern of customer payments is not as clear-cut.

As we have already noted, the firm has less discretion over the terms of credit. Here the industry practice must be considered if unintended losses are to be avoided. Despite this, some room for maneuver still remains. In many firms, the credit terms offered to customers depend on the outcome of the credit evaluation. For example, very high risk customers may be required to pay cash upon delivery (**C.O.D.**). If they have a credit record which suggests that their checks may be returned due to insufficient funds, they may even be required to pay cash *before* delivery (**C.B.D.**).

C.O.D.
Cash upon delivery; a credit condition imposed on high-risk customers.

C.B.D.
Cash before delivery; a credit condition imposed on customers whose checks are often returned due to insufficient funds.

With respect to credit sales, industry practice is often dominant. The credit period is often dictated by the logic of the business in question; payment terms may reflect the rate of turnover of the customer's inventory. Within these constraints, firms try to control their risk exposure by offering financial incentives for prompt payment. Consider, for example, a firm which requires full payment within 60 days (it offers 2 months credit), but also grants a 2% discount if the account is paid within 30 days. In the jargon of the business world, these terms are written as 2/30 net 60. In essence, the customer is offered the opportunity to earn 2% if it foregoes the second 30 days credit. This is equivalent to an *annual* rate of interest of over 26%.

$$(1.02)^{12} - 1 = 26.8\%$$

Cash discounts in actual practice are often very high. For example, if a cash discount of 5% is offered for early payment—that is, the credit terms are 5/30 net 60—the implicit annual rate of interest is 79.6%:

$$(1.05)^{12} - 1 = 79.6\%$$

In this instance the customer can earn an annual rate of interest of almost 80% simply by foregoing one month's credit.

Numerous examples of cash discounts that imply interest rates of over 100% can be found. For example, the terms of sale 5/10 net 30 permit the customer to earn a 5% discount from the sales price if it pays on the 10th, rather than the 30th day, after the sale. Thus, the customer can earn 5% by foregoing 20 days' credit. At first glance, this seems not unreasonable. Yet this discount is equivalent to an annual rate of interest of almost 144%. Since there are 18.25 20-day periods in a year (365/20 = 18.25), the *annual* interest rate calculation becomes:

$$(1.05)^{18.25} - 1 = 143.6\%$$

The existence of such large discounts for early payment raises a perplexing question. Why do firms offer such large discounts in the first place? It is difficult to imagine a firm with an interest cost of over 100% per year, yet as we have already pointed out, examples of cash discounts which imply such rates can be found. An easy but highly dubious explanation can be found by assuming that such firms' credit managers have never had a course in basic finance, or cannot afford a pocket calculator. A more satisfying explanation can be found by assuming that the firms knowingly offer such discounts as an incentive for early payment in order to control their risk exposure to bad debts. In this view, the firm is prepared to forego part of its real profit in order to avoid slow payments, because the latter have a nagging tendency to evolve into uncollectible debts.

But perhaps a third explanation can be found. In this scenario, the "actual" price of the firm's product is the *discounted* price which, owing to the very liberal payment terms, it expects all its customers to take. The very high rate of foregone interest implicit in the terms of sale can then be considered as a sort of penalty for customers who pay later than the discount period. This approach has plausibility, especially in industries that do not impose a penalty for customers who exceed the period for net payments. Thus, in the case of the terms 5/10 net/30, a customer who succeeds in stretching the payment to 60 days not only adversely affects its ability to get credit in the future, but pays a significant penalty as well. The implicit annual interest rate on the foregone discount is still almost 43% even if an extra 50 days of credit is obtained:

$$(1.05)^{7.3} - 1 = 42.8\%$$

The terms of credit can be changed, within limits, by stipulating the type of credit instrument required. But once again, accepted industry practice must be given strong consideration, especially for good customers. Very

open book account
Credit extended to low-risk customers that may consist only of a sales account entry and a signed receipt upon delivery.

bill of exchange
A written order to pay a sum of money sent by the seller to the customer's bank.

sight draft
A bill of exchange containing an immediate order to pay.

time draft
A bill of exchange containing a delayed order to pay.

banker's acceptance
A time draft in which the customer has secured a bank's guarantee of payment.

conditional sales contract
A contract in which the seller retains legal ownership of equipment until payments are completed.

often domestic sales are made on **open book account**, or **open account**, as it is often called. Here the only evidence of the credit is the entry in the seller's accounts and the receipt signed upon delivery.

The legal standing of the credit can be enhanced if the customer is required to sign a *promissory-note*—that is, the proverbial IOU with which some of us are unfortunately only too familar. But once again, it is difficult, and even unwise, to introduce such a device unless it is accepted industry practice.

In some industries, and in all international transactions, formal methods are available for making explicit the buyer's commitment to pay. The most common of these are **bills of exchange**, which are used in both domestic and international commercial transactions. The seller sends the shipping documents along with an order to pay to the customer's bank. (If the order to pay is immediate, such an order is called a **sight draft**; if payment is delayed, it is called a **time draft**.) The customer then pays (if it is a sight draft) or formally acknowledges the debt by signing and writing "accepted" on the time draft. The bank, in turn, gives the shipping documents to the customer and forwards the payment, or *acceptance*, to the seller, who can hold it until it falls due or use it as collateral for a loan. In order to enhance the quality of the document, the seller may request that the customer secure a guarantee of payment from its bank, in which case the document is call a **banker's acceptance**.

Many other alternatives are available. In international transactions, exporters may require an *irrevocable letter of credit* issued by a bank in the foreign country which guarantees payment by the bank against the delivery of the shipping documents. Where equipment is sent on a time payment basis, the seller may use a **conditional sales contract** in which it retains legal ownership until the payments are completed. The principal advantage of such a contract lies in the fact that it is much easier, and far less costly, to repossess such property if the customer defaults on the payments.

COLLECTION POLICY

As the popular saying reminds us, good intentions are not sufficient to avoid a sentence to Purgatory; similarly, customers' good intentions are often insufficient to ensure the prompt receipt of payments. The "stretching" of payables is an old, if not greatly honored, game, and bad debts can probably never be completely avoided. It is the credit department's responsibility to monitor outstanding debts in order to isolate delinquent accounts, to devise a policy for expediting their collection, and finally to suggest procedures for minimizing such delinquencies in the future.

The *aging* of customers' accounts receivable is a convenient tool for keeping track of the record of payments. A schedule of overdue accounts might take the form of Table 17–2. Customer A has a "clean" account; the

TABLE 17–2   Schedule of Overdue Accounts

	Amount Not Yet Due	1 Month Overdue	2 Months Overdue	More than 2 Months Overdue
Customer A	50,000			
Customer B	20,000	40,000	30,000	
.				
.				
.				
Customer N	—	25,000	25,000	50,000

$50,000 owed is still not due. The second customer, B, is a slow payer; of the $90,000 in credit which it received, it is in arrears in payments by as much as 2 months. Finally, we have customer N, who owes $100,000, all of which is overdue, with $50,000 overdue by more than 2 months. The fact that this customer has no outstanding debt *within* the stated collection period suggests that its credit may have already been cut off.

Procedures have to be devised for handling delinquent accounts, whether it be a strongly worded letter, a telephone call, or both, to the second customer and perhaps turning customer N over to a professional collection agency. However, the continuing nature of the seller-customer relationship implies an additional aspect of the collection process. In most firms, changes in future credit terms are the main device for controlling delinquent accounts and bad debts. Unlike financial institutions, firms rarely collect interest for late payments and usually have no collateral to secure the debt. As a result, the selling firm often turns to more stringent credit terms, or reduction in the amount of credit on future purchases, as a penalty for delinquent payment of current accounts. Legal action is usually taken only in extreme cases.

Credit terms can be tightened in a number of ways. Of course, credit can just be withdrawn. Short of that, the credit period for net payment can be reduced or the amount of credit made available to a late paying customer can be reduced; the remainder can be sold on a C.O.D. basis.

Monitoring accounts is a continuous process, and Table 17–2 also suggests a useful tool for doing this. The firm can compare its average collection period with industry averages, but more important, with its own stated credit terms to see how its credit department is actually operating. Table 17–3 shows the aging schedule of accounts receivable for a hypothetical company. This schedule gives a breakdown of accounts by the length of time they have been outstanding. The interpretation of the data requires some knowledge of the firm's credit terms. For example, if its terms of sale are net 10 days, it may be in deep trouble. If this is the case, 60% of its accounts are overdue. On the other hand, if the firm sells on a 2/10 net/60 basis, almost all of its accounts are on schedule—40% are still within the discount period and fully

TABLE 17–3   Aging Schedule of Accounts Receivable

Age of Accounts (days)	Percent of Total Receivables Outstanding
0–10	40
11–30	30
31–45	10
46–60	10
Over 60	10
	100%

90% are within the 60-day credit period. If this same schedule is for a firm which sells on a 2/10 net 30 basis, the aging of accounts raises some serious questions. In this case, 30% of the accounts are already overdue, and 10% of the accounts are more than a month overdue and perhaps represent potential bad debts.

Finally, a word of caution may be in order. Credit management should not rely solely on mechanical rules of thumb. An overzealous credit manager can lose good customers. One strategy is always to try to find the underlying reason for delinquent payments, especially when a previously good account appears to have gone sour. But no manager should forget the other side of the coin. Profits generated by credit sales are unearned unless the account is collected! Like so many of the firm's activities, credit management is a two-edged sword. A more liberal credit policy implies higher levels of sales, but increases the resources tied up in receivables. More stringent collection policies may reduce receivables and bad debts, but they also tend to reduce sales.

SUMMARY

Two of the principal components of a firm's investment in working capital are inventories and accounts receivable.

The effective management of working capital requires: (a) setting the desired levels for each asset component, and (b) the establishment of an administrative framework for monitoring and keeping these assets within the policy guidelines.

Because of the magnitude of the investment, corporations often expend considerable time and resources on the control and management of the costs of holding inventories. These costs can be divided into two groups:

1. Costs that vary directly with the level of inventory. These include *capital costs, storage costs, handling costs, insurance, property taxes, depreciation,* and *ob-*

solescence. These costs rise when the investment in inventory increases, and fall when inventories are decreased.

2. Costs that vary inversely with the size of inventory—that increase when the inventory level is lower and decrease when inventories are higher. Such costs include *ordering costs, loss of quantity discounts,* and *stock-out costs.*

Simple inventory models can help the firm determine the optimal inventory size. Such models are designed to minimize total inventory costs. One such model, the optimal order size formula, is set out, assuming certainty:

$$Q^* = \sqrt{\frac{2SC_2}{C_1}}$$

where

Q^* = optimal order size
S = total quantity (in units) sold during the year
C_1 = costs (per unit) which vary directly with inventory levels
C_2 = fixed cost per order.

Since the actual pattern of demand and order lead times is rarely known with certainty, the inventory models can be adjusted to reflect the underlying uncertainty. Safety stocks and lagged order points are used for this purpose.

The simple two-bin model provides a rule of thumb solution when inventories are comprised of numerous components. In this model the firm places an order for additional stock whenever the inventory level drops below a given level.

Credit policy involves decisions in five areas: (a) length of credit period, (b) formal legal documents (if any) to be required, (c) setting of credit standards, (d) collection policy, (e) the use of financial (or other) incentives to encourage prompt payment of debts.

Several alternative sources of credit information are available: (a) previous experience with the customer, (b) analysis of the customer's financial statements, (c) reports of commercial credit-rating agencies, (d) credit references of banks and trade associations.

Although the firm has some leeway in setting the terms of credit, industry practice is often a dominant consideration that must be considered if unintended losses of sales are to be avoided. Credit policy is a two-edged sword. Easy credit terms may lead to higher sales, but also tie up the firm's resources in accounts receivable. More stringent collection policies and less liberal terms of credit may reduce receivables and bad debts, but also tend to reduce sales. As is true of many corporate decisions, the optimal strategy usually lies somewhere in the middle.

REVIEW EXERCISE

Circle the correct word(s) in each sentence; see p. 448 for correct answers.

17.1 Working capital is the relatively *liquid/nonliquid* portion of a firm's total capital.

17.2 The assets which comprise a firm's working capital have a *short/long* life span, typically *less than/more than* 1 year.

17.3 The components of working capital can be transformed relatively *slowly/quickly* into other asset forms.

17.4 If production, sales, and collection occurred simultaneously and with perfect synchronization, the management of working capital would be *very complicated/trivial*.

17.5 In order to manage a firm's working capital effectively, basic policy must be set regarding the desired *currencies/levels* for each asset component, and an *administrative framework/overseas office* should be set up for managing and controlling these assets within the policy guidelines.

17.6 Capital costs, storage costs, and handling costs vary *directly/inversely* with the inventory level.

17.7 Per-unit ordering costs and stockout costs vary *directly/inversely* with the inventory level.

17.8 The optimal order size *maximizes revenues/minimizes costs*.

17.9 When sales are uncertain, shortages *can/cannot* occur.

17.10 The two-bin model *does/does not* guarantee cost minimization; it *is/is not* an efficient rule of thumb.

17.11 A firm's credit policy *affects/does not affect* the composition of working capital.

17.12 A more liberal credit policy implies *higher/lower* levels of sales, and *higher/lower* levels of accounts receivables.

17.13 The extension of credit is essentially a method of enhancing *quality/sales*.

17.14 Some firms offer high discounts for early payment in order to control their *exposure/aversion* to risk.

17.15 In international transactions *formal/informal* methods are available for making the buyer's commitment to pay explicit.

17.16 In many firms, *criminal charges/future changes in credit terms* are the main device for controlling delinquent accounts and bad debts.

17.17 More stringent collection policies may *increase/reduce* receivables and bad debts, but can also be expected to have a *positive/negative* impact on sales.

QUESTIONS

17.1 Define the following terms:
    a. Net working capital   **b.** Inventory
    c. Safety stock   **d.** Two-bin model
    e. Credit policy   **f.** C.O.D.
    g. C.B.D.

17.2 What are the principal characteristics of the assets comprising a firm's working capital?

17.3 List the costs which vary directly with inventory levels. List the costs which vary indirectly with inventory levels.

17.4 "We never had and never will have stockouts." What assumptions need to be fulfilled in order for this statement to be correct?

17.5 Which firm do you think holds a larger safety stock (as a percentage of sales), a steel mill or a supermarket? Explain.

17.6 Why would a firm use the two-bin model even though this model may not minimize inventory costs?

17.7 What are the pros and the cons of a liberal credit policy? What are the pros and the cons of a stringent credit policy?

17.8 Which are the five basic decisions that need to be made when a firm decides on its credit policy?

17.9 List and explain the five Cs that credit managers use to evaluate the probability of default.

17.10 Give an example of a cash discount for early payment which implies an interest rate of exactly 100%.

17.11 "Our firm has an interest cost of 15%. Nevertheless, we offer cash discounts that imply interest rates of a multiple of this amount." Why do you think the firm has adopted such a policy?

17.12 "We don't fool around; if a customer is in arrears with a payment, we immediately go to court!" Why is this not necessarily a good policy?

PROBLEMS

17.1 **Optimal order size.**   A drugstore sells 2,500 boxes of a certain very expensive pill per year. The price per box is $100. Variable inventory costs, spoilage, and interest amount to 20% of the price of the box. The fixed cost for every order is $10. How many boxes should be ordered at a time?

17.2 **Optimal order size.**   Pharmacos & Co. uses 10,000 bags of a chemical compound per year which cost $20 each. The fixed cost per order is $208.20. Variable inventory costs are 30% of the price of the bag. What is the optimal order size? At what time intervals will the orders be placed?

17.3 **Optimal order size.**   Your baby daughter needs four disposable diapers per day. A bag that contains 28 diapers sells for $6. Your cost of capital is 10%, and since you have enough space in your garage, there are no inventory storage costs. You estimate the cost of driving to the drugstore and back at $3.90. (The cost of your time is zero.) How often will you make the trip each year?

17.4 **Optimal order size.**   Mr Bunhill, an avid pipe smoker, uses one package of a very rare and expensive tobacco per week. A mail order house offers the tobacco at a price of $20 per pouch, plus a $1 handling fee per order. Mr. Bunhill estimates the cost of postage and of filling out and mailing the order form at $2. His cost of capital is 10.6%. Furthermore, he knows that on average, 5% of the inventory of his tobacco becomes humid and cannot be used. At what time intervals will Mr. Bunhill place his orders?

17.5 **Optimal order size.**   Your local supermarket delivers all purchases to your house for a flat fee of $1.50. You use $100 of goods per week, and 4% of your average inventory is usually lost due to a mouse in your house. Your cost of capital is 8%. How many dollars' worth of goods should you order at a time? How many orders will you place per year?

17.6 **Credit policy.**   Marson & Co. is buying a new typewriter. The terms of payment are 2/15 net 30. What is the implicit interest rate Marson would be charged if it paid only on day 50? (Assume no penalty.)

17.7 **Credit policy.**   Wilson is also buying a new typewriter. The terms of payment which it is offered are 60 days net, or a 2% discount for immediate payment. If Wilson chooses to forego the discount, how high do you think its cost of capital is?

17.8 **Credit policy.**   GTR & Co. have ordered their yearly amount of spare parts. Full payment is required within 30 days, but a 2% discount is offered if the account is settled within 10 days. GTR's cost of capital is 8%. What should it do?

17.9 **Credit policy.**   A mail order firm offers the following payment options: A discount of 1.5% if the invoice is paid upon delivery, or a 1% discount if the account is settled within 15 days. The third option is to pay the net invoice within 40 days.
   a. Your cost of capital is 10%. Which payment option will you prefer?
   b. How does your answer change if your cost of capital is 15%?
   c. How does your answer change if your cost of capital is 16%?

17.10 **Credit policy.**   A firm is offered the following terms: 60 days net, or a 1/2% discount for C.O.D. The firm chooses not to take the discount. Assuming the firm acts rationally, what can you say about its cost of capital?

SAMPLE PROBLEMS

SP17.1 ComputerCity sells 50 home computers per month, at a price of $2,485 each. Capital costs are 8%, insurance is 3%, and warehousing amounts of 6% of the sales price. Whenever an order is placed, a truck has to be sent to the supplier, which costs $220. (The truck can carry at most 150 computers.) What is the optimal order size? At what time intervals will the orders be placed?

SP17.2 The Guthry Corporation sells goods to a customer. The terms Guthry offers are 60 days net, or 1% discount if the bill is settled upon delivery. Guthry knows that the customer's cost of capital is 10%. When can Guthry expect payment?

Answers to Solved Problems

SP17.1 50 computers per month corresponds to yearly sales of 600 units. The variable inventory costs are the cost of capital (8%), insurance (3%), and warehousing (6%), i.e., a total of 17% of the sales price, which is $2,485. The fixed cost per order is the cost of sending the truck, $220. Hence we have

$S = 600$, $C_1 = 17\%$ of the sales price; that is, $C_1 = 17\%$ of $2,485 = 422.40$. And finally, $C_2 = 220$.

Substituting these figures into the formula for the optimal order size, we get

$$Q = \sqrt{2SC_2/C_1} = \sqrt{(2)(600)(220)/422.40} = \sqrt{264,000/422.4} = \sqrt{625} = 25$$

The optimal order size is 25 units, and Computer City will place 24 orders per year (600/25) — that is, 2 orders per month.

SP17.2 The customer can earn 1% by foregoing 60 days credit, which corresponds to 6.2% per year:

$$(1.01)^{365/60} - 1 = (1.01)^{6.08} - 1 = 6.2\%$$

Since this is lower than the customer's cost of capital, the discount will not be taken and Guthry can expect payment only after 60 days.

Answers to Review Exercise

17.1 liquid   **17.2** short, less than   **17.3** quickly

17.4 trivial   **17.5** levels, administrative framework   **17.6** directly

17.7 inversely   **17.8** minimizes costs   **17.9** can

17.10 does not, is   **17.11** affects   **17.12** higher, higher

17.13 sales   **17.14** exposure   **17.15** formal

17.16 future changes in credit terms   **17.17** reduce, negative

SUGGESTIONS FOR FURTHER READING

Overviews of working capital management are given by Dileep R. Mehta, *Working Capital Management* (Englewood Cliffs, NJ: Prentice-Hall, 1974); V. E. Ramamoorthy, *Working Capital Management* (Madras, India: Institute for Financial Management and Research, 1976); and Keith V. Smith, *Guide for Working Capital Management* (New York: McGraw-Hill, 1979).

Inventory management is examined in much greater detail by John F. Magee in a series of articles in the *Harvard Business Review:* "Guides to Inventory Policy: Functions and Lot Sizes," *HBR*, January–February 1956, "Guides to Inventory Policy: Problems of Uncertainty," *HBR*, March–April 1956, and "Guides to Inventory Policy: Anticipating Future Needs," *HBR*, May–June 1956; Keith V. Smith (ed.). *Readings in the Management of Working Capital* (Boulder; Co: West Publishing Company, 1974); and F. C. Wilson, *Short Term Financial Management* (Homewood, IL: Dow Jones–Irwin, 1975).

For a more detailed presentation of the two-bin model, see A. Snyder, "Principles of Inventory Management," *Financial Executive*, April 1964.

Various aspects of credit policy and accounts receivable management are discussed in Moshe Ben Horim and Haim Levy, "Management of Accounts Receivable Under Inflation," *Financial Management*, Spring 1983; R. H. Cole, *Consumer and Commercial Credit Mangement*, 4th ed. (Homewood, IL: Irwin 1972); Gordon S. Roberts and Jeremy A. Viscione, "Captive Finance Subsidiaries: The Manager's View," *Financial Management*, Spring 1981; and Tinlochan S. Walia, "Explicit and Implicit Cost of Changes in the Level of Accounts Receivable and the Credit Policy Decision of the Firm," *Financial Management*, Winter 1977.

18 | Managing Cash and Marketable Securities

"**N**othing is more permanent than the temporary," and in the business world *acting* vice-presidents have a tendency to become *permanent* vice-presidents. Although much of this book has been devoted to the firm's long-term financing and investment decisions, few of the latter are as "permanent" as the decisions to hold reserves of cash and other liquid assets. Cash is one of the firm's key assets. The elements of working capital—the purchase of raw materials, the aquisition of labor and marketing facilities—must all be paid for. Cash is also needed for interest payments, tax obligations, and dividends. And for those firms which find themselves temporarily with excess cash on hand, the availability of a wide variety of marketable short-term securities provides an investment opportunity for such funds. In recent years, inflation and relatively high interest rates have focused attention on the efficient management of the firm's cash and marketable securities. In this chapter we first discuss the motives underlying the holding of these liquid reserves, and then go on to examine some alternative techniques that firms employ to improve the utilization of their cash (and near cash) assets.

THE NEED FOR LIQUIDITY

All firms (and virtually all individuals) hold liquid reserves. On the surface, the holding of cash (or even short-term interest-bearing securities) appears to involve the firm in a loss, because income is foregone on funds that otherwise could have been invested in productive activities. Recognizing this paradox, the English economist John Maynard Keynes explained the holding of liquid assets in terms of three underlying motives: a transactions motive, a precautionary motive, and a speculative motive.

The Transactions Motive

The need for holding cash arises because receipts and expenditures can never be perfectly synchronized. This is the same reason why inventories of any commodity have to be kept, and why a water supply company builds a reservoir. When outflows are not exactly matched in time by inflows, a reservoir is needed to absorb routine fluctuations. The same holds true for the firm; for example, a reserve is needed to meet discrepancies in the daily inflow and outflow of cash, end-of-month bulges, and so on. Similarly, liquid reserves may be accumulated in advance of specific outlays such as dividend payments or the purchase of fixed assets. Finally, the firm needs cash to facilitate payments: when the firm writes a check against its bank, the financial manager must ensure that the funds will be available when the check arrives for collection.

The Precautionary Motive

The precautionary motive reflects the need to hold liquid reserves to allow for unforeseen outflows, and/or unanticipated shortfalls due, for example, to a drop in sales. Although Benjamin Franklin taught us that a man can count on only three reliable friends—a faithful dog, an elderly wife, and money in the bank—a significant interest return can be earned on liquid reserves by investing part of them in short-term securities.

The Speculative Motive

The last, and by far the most volatile, of the three considerations is the speculative motive. This refers to the holding of liquid reserves in anticipation of future profitable investment opportunities. For example, a firm that is planning to acquire the shares of another company may accumulate a liquid reserve because it expects the price of the shares to fall. Another example would be a firm that anticipates the opportunity of developing a new product or process in the near future.

The motives for holding liquid reserves are not mutually exclusive, and in fact it would be difficult and impractical to divide a firm's monetary assets according to the particular purpose for which they are held. Total monetary resources should be regarded as one unit. There is no general rule regarding the division of reserves between cash and marketable securities that can be applied to all firms. The level of monetary assets itself depends on many factors, including the firm's ability to obtain credit from banks and other financial institutions on short notice. Moreover, loan covenants that call for compensating balances may force a firm to increase its liquidity.

RETURN vs. LIQUIDITY

liquidity
The ability to convert an asset to cash quickly and without loss.

Liquidity means the ability to convert an asset to cash quickly and without loss. It is clear from this definition that cash is the perfect liquid asset, but of course its return is zero. Short-term Treasury bills and very high grade commercial paper have no, or almost no, default risk, and very little maturity risk. Even a pronounced shift in market conditions (interest rates) will not affect their price by very much, since they have only a few months left to maturity. This is not true for long-term bonds, whose price fluctuations, and hence the probability of a loss should they be sold before maturity, increase with bond duration. Only very high grade bonds (or notes), with relatively short-term maturities, can be considered liquid assets, if the probability of loss is to be held within tolerable limits.

Since cash and short-term securities account for a significant proportion of many firms' assets, the efficient management of these funds could increase corporate earnings by millions. Recognizing this, many firms have expanded the size of the divisions which deal directly with cash management. In addition, cash management consultants have experienced a boom in their business. To illustrate the importance of the efficient management of liquid reserves, consider the case of IBM, which held *$5,622* million in cash and short-term securities at the end of 1985. Suppose that, on *average,* the firm initially earns 5% on these funds (cash included). IBM's annual interest income would be $281 million. Now suppose that a financial expert (perhaps yourself) is hired and succeeds in increasing the total return by just two-tenths of one percent—from 5 percent to 5.2%, without adversely affecting liquidity. As a result, IBM's interest income rises to $292 million, which represents an increase of $11 million. On the realistic assumption that the cost to the firm of hiring the expert is significantly less than $11 million, it is clear why many firms are actively seeking alert cash managers.

The increase in return on total liquid reserves can be achieved by the investment in securities with higher yields or by a reduction in the proportion of non-interest-bearing cash, or by some combination of the two. But to justify the employment of our expert, the increase in return must be effected without increasing risk beyond some critical level. There are many types of monetary assets. They range from cash, which has a zero return, to long-term high-grade bonds which may yield 10% or more, depending on market conditions. In between there exists a broad spectrum of possible investments with different maturities and different risks (Treasury bills, short-term notes with little or no default risk, and so on.)

As we noted in Chapter 3, liquidity considerations suggest a positive relationship between return and bond duration. This reflects the need to compensate the suppliers of capital with a higher interest rate for giving up liquidity. However, as we saw in Chapter 3, the yield-maturity relationship (term structure of interest rates) is not so simple. It is true that the yield curve is often upward-sloping, that interest rates rise as longer maturities are considered. However, the opposite relationship, a downward-sloping yield curve in which the interest rate on short-term bonds is actually higher (and often much higher) than the return on long-term bonds, has also been observed. On the surface, a downward-sloping yield curve is a windfall for financial managers, who can invest their firm's liquid reserves in high-yielding, but safe, short-term securities.

However, these are the same executives who must also finance the firm's long-term operations, and here the downward-sloping yield curve creates a problem. Essentially it reflects a situation in which interest rates are expected to fall in the future. In such a case, firms may prefer short-term borrowing, even at relatively high interest rates, in the expectation of floating long-term bonds, at even lower rates, in the future. It is this tendency which drives up the current short-term interest rate relative to the long-term rate. This is precisely the situation that characterized the capital markets at the end of the 1970s and beginning of the 1980s.

INVESTING LIQUIDITY RESERVES

The goal of cash management is to reduce the amount of cash on hand, thereby increasing profitability, *without* reducing business activity or exposing the firm to undue risk. Hence the firm must be very selective when investing its liquid reserves. A large number of options are available to a modern financial manager.

Table 18–1 gives a representative sample of the money market instruments available for such short-term investment, with their average yields in 1976, 1981, and May 1986. The striking feature of Table 18–1 is the dramatic rise in interest rates between 1976 and 1981. The 1981 rates were roughly three times their 1976 counterparts, a phenomenon that reflects the

TABLE 18–1   Selected Money Market Instruments and Yields

Type of Security	Maturity When Issued	Average Annual Yields		
		1976	1981	1986*
Treasury bills	90–360 days	4.97	14.65	6.24
Negotiable certificates of deposit (CDs)	Usually 3 months	5.27	16.33	6.72
Eurodollar deposits	Overnight to 1 year	5.58	17.25	6.91
Commercial paper	Up to 270 days	5.24	15.74	6.75
Bankers' acceptances	90 days	5.19	15.75	6.61

* Yields on May 30, 1986.

impact of inflation. In 1976 consumer prices rose, on the average, by less than 6%; by 1981 inflation in the United States was running in the double digits. The return to relative price stability witnessed a sharp fall in interest rates; by 1986, short-term rates were less than one-half of their 1981 levels.

U.S. Treasury Bills

T-bills
Short-term U.S. Treasury securities sold at a discount.

U.S. Treasury issues with maturities ranging from 3 months to 1 year are prime candidates for corporate investment of liquid reserves. These Treasury bills are sold at auction weekly in the case of the 90-day bills, and monthly in the case of the longest maturities. No interest is paid on the bills, which are sold *at discount* from face value. Their yield to investors therefore stems solely from the price appreciation at maturity. The **T-bills**, as they are universally called, can be purchased directly from the Treasury, or in the excellent secondary market provided by dealer firms specializing in government securities.

Agency Securities

Corporate money managers also have the opportunity to purchase an array of short-term obligations of government agencies or government-sponsored corporations. These include the Government National Mortgage Association (Ginnie Mae), the Federal Home Loan Bank, the Federal Housing Administration, the Export-Import Bank, and many others. These securities have a somewhat thinner secondary market and carry a slightly higher interest rate than their government counterparts.

Tax-Exempt Securities

State and local governments also issue short-term notes. Although these securities are more risky and less marketable than T-bills, they have a unique feature that may be attractive to corporate treasurers, depending on the yield structure at the time. The yields on these securities are exempt from federal income taxes. Thus the corporation must compare the "lower" yields on the tax-exempts with the *after-tax* yields on alternative taxable securities.

Certificates of Deposit

certificates of deposit (CDs)
Negotiable money market instruments issued by commercial banks against the time deposits of corporations.

Since the early 1960s, commercial banks in the United States have issued **certificates of deposit** against the time deposits of corporations. The major attraction of these certificates, or CDs, as they are called, lies in their negotiability. There exists a brisk secondary market, through security dealers, for the CDs of the major banks. This greatly enhances their marketability, thereby permitting the safe investment of surplus funds for short periods of time.

Bankers' Acceptances

As we pointed out in Chapter 17, *bankers' acceptances* are instruments used for delayed payments in both international and domestic transactions. They are simply an order to pay against bank deposits, but with the payment at maturity *guaranteed* by the bank. These acceptances are traded in an active secondary market. Since they bear no direct interest, the yield on acceptances, which is similar to that of CDs, is created by the fact that they are traded at a discount from their maturity value.

Commercial Paper

commercial paper
Unsecured promissory notes issued by corporations and financial institutions.

Very large financial institutions and even industrial corporations often bypass the banking system altogether by issuing their own promissory notes, either directly or through security dealers. Maturities vary from a few to 270 days. There is a very limited secondary market for **commercial paper,** which is unsecured except for the financial strength of the issuing firm. The purchase of such paper, and holding it to maturity, has been a relatively popular way to invest excess corporate funds for short periods of time. Their yields (again created by purchasing them at discount) are higher than that of T-bills. However, a good corporate money manager knows that the higher yields reflect the market's assessment that these notes also have a greater risk. This fact was brought home with a vengence in 1970 when about $75 million of the bankrupt Penn Central Railroad's commercial paper could not be redeemed.

Repurchase Agreements

repos
Repurchase agreements; financial transactions in which a corporation buys T-bills from a dealer while entering into an agreement that the dealer will repurchase them at a specified price and time.

Repurchase agreements, or **repos** as they are often called, are simply loans by the corporation to a security dealer, with the latter putting up high-grade securities as collateral. In practice, the corporation buys Treasury securities (often T-bills) from a dealer while at the same time entering into an agreement that the dealer will repurchase the securities at a specified price and time. Repos provide a flexible instrument for investing excess funds overnight, over the weekend, or for longer periods. In addition, there is an active secondary market for the longer repurchase agreements with yields comparable to those of Treasury bills.

INFLATION AND LIQUID RESERVES

The high interest rates that accompanied the rise in inflationary pressures during the 1970s and early 1980s increased the "cost" of holding idle cash balances. As corporate money managers became increasingly sensitive to the earnings lost by holding non-interest-bearing deposits, they became more efficient in the handling of cash balances. They also became more receptive to experimenting with new types of financial instruments. The financial markets responded with a flood of new investment outlets. Some of the more striking innovations designed to enable firms and individuals to maximize their earnings on liquid reserves are money market funds, sweep accounts, NOW accounts, and Eurodollar investments.

Money Market Funds

These funds permit smaller firms to invest indirectly in diversified pools of large-denomination money instruments (commercial paper, negotiable CDs). Most funds permit the withdrawal of money by check or other means, making them a very close substitute for transactions balances.

Sweep Accounts

sweep accounts
A money market arrangement in which a business moves funds automatically out of conventional transaction balances into investment accounts, and vice versa.

Another money market arrangement is the **sweep account**, which permits a small business to move its funds automatically into or out of conventional transaction balances to investment accounts paying market rates of return.

NOW Accounts

NOW accounts
Negotiable Order of Withdrawal accounts; interest-bearing checking accounts.

Prior to 1981, the payment of interest on checking accounts was prohibited. The Monetary Control Act of 1980 authorized the creation of Negotiable Order of Withdrawal (**NOW**) **accounts**. These checkable deposits, at commercial banks and thrift institutions, are interest-bearing.

Eurodollar Investments

Eurodollars
Deposits of U.S. dollars in foreign banks or in foreign branches of U.S. banks.

To improve yields, many corporations have turned to the Eurodollar market. **Eurodollars** are deposits of dollars in foreign banks or in the foreign branches of U.S. banks. These deposits, which are not subject to Federal Reserve regulations, offer slightly higher yields than their domestic counterparts.

   The variety and sophistication of the new money market innovations appear to be limited only by the imagination of the financial community and of corporate money managers. The only thing that is certain is that the process of innovation will continue as existing financial institutions compete to meet the liquidity needs of the business community.

METHODS FOR CONSERVING CASH

As we have seen, the burden of holding liquid reserves can be reduced by seeking investment outlets that offer higher yields without increasing risk beyond tolerable levels. Another way to increase the return on liquid reserves is to minimize the proportion of the reserve kept in cash balances. Many firms can achieve significant savings merely by rearranging their commitments to get a better synchronization of cash inflows and outflows. In this way the firm can reduce its minimum required cash balance and/or avoid costly borrowing. Two principal ways that cash can be conserved are: (a) the speeding up of the firm's collection of accounts receivable; and (b) the slowing down of its own payments to suppliers.

Speeding Collections

Although some customers can be cajoled into making early payments by letters and telephone calls, competition within the industry rarely permits a firm to make significant improvements in the payment habits of its customers. As was pointed out in Chapter 17, it is often more effective to offer credit customers an economic incentive in the form of a cash discount for early payment. However, as we also noted, the *implicit* interest cost of such discounts may be very high. But the firm still has ample room for improving its cash position, independent of the payment policy of customers, by improving the collection of cash. This means finding ways to reduce the delay from the moment the paying firm writes its check to the time the funds become available for use in the recipient firm. At first glance this seems trivial, but a firm receiving payments from a large number of customers spread across the country may find that as much as a week can be lost before the money becomes available.

The left-hand side of Table 18–2 shows a hypothetical example of a customer in California making a payment to the selling firm's home office in Boston. In the case of this out of town customer, 8 working days elapse before the payment becomes available in Boston. The delay reflects the slowness of the mail system and the "many hands" involved in the clearing process. One improvement might be the establishment of regional offices. In such a case, the customer in California would be instructed to make the payment to the Boston firm's California regional office, thereby saving perhaps as much as 2 days. Alternatively, the Boston firm might establish collection accounts at a number of banks in key locations across the country. Customer payment could be received directly in these accounts, thereby sav-

TABLE 18–2   The Check Collection Process

Present System	Elapsed Time	Lock Box System	Elapsed Time
1. California customer writes and mails check.	3 Days	1. Customer writes check and mails it.	1 day
2. Check received at Boston home office.	1 Day	2. Check arrives at lock box in customer's city and is picked up by local bank.	1 day
3. Check deposited in Boston bank.	1 Day	3. Check is cleared locally.	1 day
4. Boston bank sends to Federal Reserve System for clearing.	2 Days	4. California bank wires Boston office that funds are available for use.	
5. If "good," funds are transferred to Boston bank.	1 Day		
6. Money is now available for use.			
	8 working days total		3 working days total

ing additional time, since banks are much more efficient in the transfer of funds than the postal system.

The Lock Box System

lock box system
A device for speeding the collection of cash from customers in which a firm rents Post Office boxes in a number of key cities, which are managed by local commercial banks in its behalf.

The right-hand side of Table 18–2 illustrates what has proved to be the most widely used device for speeding collections—the **lock box system**. Here the Boston firm rents Post Office boxes in a number of key cities, which are managed by local commercial banks acting in its behalf. The local banks monitor the lock boxes around the clock. As soon as the check arrives, it is deposited in the Boston firm's account at the local bank, so that the check clearing process is started immediately. In essence, the lock box reverses the usual order of events. The check is deposited first, and only later is the accounting entry made at the selling firm's Boston office. In Table 18–2, the California paying firm is assumed to be located in San Francisco, a city in which the Boston firm operates a lock box. Since a Federal Reserve Bank is also located in San Francisco, the delay in the receipt of payment is reduced from 8 to 3 working days. Considering the great effort that is being made today to develop improved methods and electronic techniques for the transfer of funds, this delay may well be reduced even more in the future.

Slowing Payments

An alternative strategy for conserving cash is to slow down our own firm's payments to suppliers and other creditors. This might be done in several ways. Just as decentralizing collections can speed up the collection process, making all payments from the corporation's central headquarters allows the firm to take advantage of mailing delays. Alternatively, the corporation might systematically use distant locations when making payments—the New York branch paying the California bills, and so on. Another ploy is to use awkward, difficult to handle, but of course legal, means of payment. For example, bills can be paid using a bank draft drawn by the corporation on itself and payable through a specific bank. In this case, the receiving bank must first present the draft to the issuing firm, and only a day later will the necessary funds become available. The use of bank drafts can be rewarding when the corporation has a large payroll, or is paying dividends to a large number of shareholders. Finally, you might consider delaying payment altogether, but this will cost the firm its cash discount. Moreover, the firm may *receive* the unpleasant letters or phone calls mentioned in Chapter 17.

Playing the Float

float
The difference between the balance shown in a corporation's accounts and its actual balance at the bank.

The name of the game we have been describing is **playing the float**. **Float** is the difference between the balance shown in the corporation's accounts and its actual balance at the bank. Float can be positive or negative. In our lock box example, the Boston firm was suffering from *negative* float—that is, for 5 days the balance of its bank account was lower than that appearing in the bank itself because of the delay in collection. Of course, the other side of the coin is that the California company, due to the delay in the receipt of its payment, benefited from *positive* float—that is, its actual bank balance was

playing the float
Strategies employing lock boxes, distant bank accounts, and other devices by which firms can speed up collections and slow down cash payments.

larger than the balance of its own books during the period of the delay.

The financial manager is, of course, interested in the net collected balance at the bank. And if the managers are quick and knowledgeable, they can take advantage of the existence of the float by making allowance for the expected delay in clearing the check. But it takes two to "play the float." If you are the financial manager of the "buying" firm, you can be certain that across the country your counterpart at the selling firm will be working overtime to reduce your ability to exploit any float to the minimum.

Costs vs. Benefits

Finally, a word of caution to the fledgling financial manager who is about to establish a comprehensive system of 9,000 lock boxes across the country, one in each of the cities or villages in which the firm has a customer. The operation of such a system would cost an awful lot of money! Like any other use of the firm's limited resources, the costs of providing more efficient cash management must be weighed against its benefits. For example, assume that an improved collection system permits the firm *safely* to reduce its cash balance by $100,000, thereby reducing annual interest costs on borrowed funds by $10,000 (assuming a 10% interest rate). In this case, $10,000 is the benefit that must be weighed against the annual cost of operating the system.

THE INVENTORY APPROACH TO CASH MANAGEMENT

The management of cash balances can be facilitated by applying the inventory model described in the preceding chapter. William J. Baumol was the first to apply the inventory principle to the problem of determining the *optimal* size of a firm's cash balance.[1] The *Baumol model* assumes that the size and timing of cash outflows during the period in question are known with certainty (payroll, taxes, and so on). The underlying logic of this approach is best illustrated by a specific example.

Suppose a construction firm is building a power plant for the government. Of the $100 million total cost, the firm receives $75 million in advance. During the construction period, which we assume to be 4 years, the firm will have to make cash payments for raw materials, wages, salaries, and so on. What is the *optimal* amount of cash the construction firm should hold?

The company has two basic options: (a) Hold the entire $75 million in cash, withdrawing from these funds as needed. Such a policy *minimizes* the risk of a cash shortage, but also yields a zero return. (b) Invest the $75 million in short-term securities at *i*% interest, and withdraw *C* dollars every month from this portfolio to meet the cash outflows.

In our example, the time horizon for managing the cash flows is 4 years, during which time the outflows, for simplicity, are assumed to be

---

[1] See William J. Baumol, "The Transactions Demand for Cash, An Inventory Theoretic Approach," *Quarterly Journal of Economics*, November 1952.

known with *certainty*. We denote the total cash flow by the letter T, and assume that the firm holds C dollars in cash at the beginning of the period to meet its wage bill and other expenses. We further assume that when its initial cash holdings are exhausted, the firm withdraws an additional C dollars from its investment portfolio to meet future needs. This process repeats itself until the project has been completed. Figure 18–1 illustrates the withdrawal process. Note that the assumed method of replenishing the cash balance, like the withdrawal of stocks from an inventory, creates a sawtooth pattern with return jumps to level C whenever the cash balance reaches zero.

To find the optimal amount to be withdrawn, denoted as C^*, one must minimize two types of cost. The first is a *fixed cost*, the fixed transactions cost (clerical costs, brokerage fees) associated with converting the securities to cash. In the first option, in which the firm holds the entire $75 million in cash, these costs are zero. The second type of cost is an *opportunity cost*, which reflects the interest income foregone. This cost is at a maximum in the first option. For simplicity, we assume that the income from cash balances is zero.

If the firm's total cash outflow during the four years is T dollars, the *number* of withdrawals of cash from the firm's investment portfolio is given by T/C. The relevant transactions cost is the *fixed cost* per transaction, denoted by the letter F. The total of such costs which are incurred by the firm over the entire planning period is defined as

$$\text{total transactions cost} = \frac{T}{C} \times F$$

where

T is the total dollar amount withdrawn during the period

C is the dollar amount of each withdrawal

T/C is the *number* of transactions

F is the fixed cost per transaction.

The total transactions cost also includes a variable component which depends on the size (dollar amount) of the transaction. But this variable cost

FIGURE 18–1
**The Cash
Withdrawal
Process**

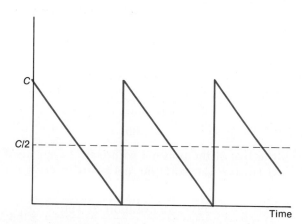

plays no role in determining the desired size of cash balances and is therefore ignored.

The average cash balance held during the period is $C/2$, and therefore the *opportunity cost* of holding this balance is equal to $(C/2)i$, where i denotes the relevant interest rate on short-term securities.

The total cost incurred by the firm for holding this average cash balance is the sum of the opportunity cost and the direct transactions costs of replenishing the cash balance:

$$\text{total cost} = \frac{C}{2} \times i + \frac{T}{C} \times F$$

Using the same approach we used for the inventory problem, the *optimal* size of the periodic cash withdrawal is given by:

$$C^* = \sqrt{\frac{2 \times \text{total fixed transaction cost}}{\text{interest rate}}} = \sqrt{\frac{2TF}{i}}$$

where C^* denotes the *optimal* size of the cash withdrawal, and therefore $C^*/2$ is the *optimal average* cash balance.

The optimal cash balance varies directly with the fixed transaction cost, F, and inversely with the interest rate, i. Thus, if the fixed cost per transaction is very high, a firm will wish to decrease the number of transactions by which it replenishes its cash balance, thereby increasing the size of its average cash balance. Conversely, if the interest rate is high, the firm will tend to decrease the size of each transaction. This tends to decrease the proportion of reserves held as cash—the size of the average cash balance.

The application of the Baumol formula can be illustrated by considering a few numerical examples. For simplicity, assume that during the first 3 years of the project above total outlays are $25 million per year ($T = \$25$ million); the current short-term interest rate is 5% per annum; and the fixed transaction cost is $100. Applying the inventory model, the optimal size of cash withdrawals is $316,228:

$$C^* = \sqrt{\frac{2 \times \$25 \text{ million} \times 100}{.05}} = \$316,228$$

As we have already noted above, the firm will decrease the number of transactions (thereby increasing the size of periodic withdrawals) if the fixed transactions cost rises. For example, should the transaction cost rise to $150, the optimal size of withdrawals increases to $387,298:

$$C^* = \sqrt{\frac{2 \times \$25 \text{ million} \times 150}{.05}} = \$387,298$$

Conversely, the size of the optimal withdrawal *decreases* if the relevant interest rate rises. In our last example, a rise in interest rates to 6% implies a reduction of the optimal withdrawal to $353, 553:

$$C^* = \sqrt{\frac{2 \times \$25 \text{ million} \times 150}{.06}} = \$353,553$$

CASH BUDGETING

The high opportunity cost of holding excess cash balances has induced firms to put considerable effort not only into the calculation of the optimal levels of their liquid assets, but into the *planning and control* of cash flows as well. The goal of this particular aspect of management is to ensure the availability of needed cash while at the same time permitting the firm to earn a maximum return on idle balances.

High interest rates provide an eloquent argument on behalf of careful forecasting and periodic budgeting. In too many instances, large cash balances are a substitute (and an expensive one at that) for the systematic planning of the firm's cash needs. But the potential benefits of cash budgeting often go beyond the direct saving of lost interest income. Budgeting future cash needs allows management to *pretest* the financial impact of its plans before making a binding commitment. Moreover, careful budgeting may uncover idle balances that can be profitably invested.

Cash budgeting is usually carried out by the treasurer's office. However, because almost all of the firm's activities affect the flow of funds, cash budgeting requires comprehensive and accurate data on the firm's prospective operations. Hence, the financial officer responsible for collecting the required data must rely on the cooperation of other operating departments if the budgeting process is to be effective. Cash forecasting is easiest for firms that plan their operations to achieve preset profit targets. Here the budgeting process is facilitated, since the operational plans, which are usually set out in terms of accounting income and expenses, can easily be restated as cash flows. But even when a firm does very little formal planning of operations, cash budgeting can still be an effective management tool.

Difficulties can arise, especially in firms which are in relatively unstable lines of business. In such cases, the cash budgeting process can be amended: (a) to include greater allowances for error; (b) to reflect alternative assumptions regarding key variables; and (c) to allow for more frequent revisions. Finally, if cash forecasting becomes very difficult and uncertain, the firm may simply decide to plan on holding a larger cash balance.

The major planning tool is the *cash budget,* which is essentially a tabulation of the firm's plans in terms of their impact on cash receipts and expenditures during future periods. It seeks to predict when, and in what quantities, cash will flow into the firm, and when, and in what quantities, cash payments will have to be made. The cash budget includes all receipts, even if they are not income. For example, the proceeds from the sale of assets or securities and the taking of loans are part of the budget. Similarly, all payments, even if they are not expenses, should be included in the firm's cash budget. Taxes and loan repayments, as well as wages, rent, and purchases of materials, are included. On the other hand, the cash budget does not include expenses which do not require a cash outlay—for example, depreciation or an allowance for bad debts.

The cash budget can be prepared for any period, but even when an annual budget is decided upon, it is usually broken down to show the timing of cash flows by months. And in fact if the cash flows within a month are very uneven, it may be necessary to define the budget in terms of weeks or days. One method to handle such situations is to budget the coming month by weeks or days, and the remainder of the year by months. The following year might be budgeted by quarters. Such a procedure meets the need for very detailed information in the immediate future. As the planning period recedes into the future, the need for detail is diminished, so the use of monthly or quarterly forecasts is adequate.

Preparing the Cash Budget

Three principal steps can be identified in the cash budgeting process:

STEP 1:   Determine the probable patterns of cash inflows and outflows.

STEP 2:   Try to change the timing of inflows and outflows by postponing payments and/or accelerating receipts.

STEP 3:   Compare the costs and benefits of alternatives to holding cash balances—for example, the substitution of a bank loan for the building up of a required balance.

The preparation and use of the cash budget can be illustrated by a specific example. To focus on the logic of the budgeting process, rather than on the details, we will use the example of a quarterly budget.

Consider the case of KABLANIM, Inc., a construction company that specializes in medium-cost single-unit dwellings. The company's terms of sale are as follows: 50% of the sales price in cash as a down payment upon the signing of the sales contract; in the next quarter, an additional 40% has to be paid. Upon "delivery" (in the third quarter following the sale), the remaining 10% is paid. Prices for the dwellings are calculated in such a way that the cost of raw materials and labor constitute 80% of the sales price; the remaining 20% represents depreciation, profit, and taxes. Given the way KABLANIM buys materials and pays its labor force, 60% of the costs have to be paid during the first quarter following the signing of the contract. The remaining 40% are paid in the following quarter.

Sales in the housing business are cyclical. It has been KABLANIM's experience that 35% of its annual sales are made in the spring quarter, 30% in the summer quarter, 25% in autumn, and 10% in the winter. The sales forecast for next year is $1,000,000.

KABLANIM's financial manager has been having a hard time lately computing NPVs, IRRs, and depreciation rates and is trying to convince management to buy a minicomputer that costs $75,000, to be paid in three quarterly instalments of $10,000, $35,000, and $30,000. In the winter quarter, $40,000 in taxes will have to be paid.

A few years ago, KABLANIM had some serious financial difficulties and, in fact, almost went bankrupt because some large bills could not be met. Since that time, it has been company policy never to allow the quarterly cash

TABLE 18–3 KABLANIM: Worksheet for Cash Budget ($000)

	Winter	Spring	Summer	Autumn
Total sales	100	350	300	250
Receipts from sales:				
Winter	—	40	10	—
Spring	50	175	140	35
Summer	30*	—	150	120
Autumn	100*	25*	—	125
Total receipts	180	240	300	280
Outlays for labor and materials				
Winter	48	32	—	—
Spring	—	168	112	—
Summer	—	—	144	96
Autumn	80*	—	—	120
Total cash outlays	128	200	256	216
Taxes	40			
Purchase of computer	10	35	30	—
Total outlays	178	235	286	216
Receipts less outlays	2	5	14	64
Cash at start of quarter	20	22	27	41
Cash balance	22	27	41	105
Minimum required	30	30	30	30
Surplus (deficit)	(8)	(3)	11	75

* From previous quarters.

balance to fall below $30,000. However, due to a planning mistake, cash on hand at the beginning of the planning period is only $20,000.

Table 18–3 shows the worksheet for next year's cash budget. When the financial manager had finished preparing the budget, he was disappointed. Since the first two quarters showed cash balances below the required mini-

TABLE 18–4 KABLANIM: Condensed Cash Budget ($000)

	Winter	Spring	Summer	Autumn
Total receipts	180	240	300	280
Total cash outlays	128	200	256	216
Taxes	40			
Computer		10	35	30
Total outlays	168	215	291	246
Receipts less outlays	12	40	9	34
Cash at start of quarter	20	22	27	41
Cash on hand	32	62	36	75
Minimum required cash balance	30	30	30	30
Surplus/deficit	+2	+32	+6	+45

mum of $30,000, he realized that he was going to continue doing NPVs and IRRs by hand for a litle while longer. However, as can be seen from Table 18–4, KABLANIM's cash problems can be resolved by simply postponing the purchase of the minicomputer for one quarter. In fact, KABLANIM can have the "best of both worlds." Its financial manager gets his minicomputer and the firm will still be in a position to consider short-term investments in Treasury bills during the spring and autumn quarters.

SUMMARY

Another aspect of the management of working capital is cash and marketable securities. The holding of liquid reserves can be interpreted in terms of three underlying motives: transactions, precautionary, and speculative.

A firm's liquid reserve is comprised of cash and interest-bearing securities. To be considered liquid, an asset must be easily converted into cash *without* loss. Hence only very high grade securities, with relatively short maturities, can be considered appropriate for the investment of a firm's liquid reserves. Among the securities available for this purpose are U.S. Treasury bills, government agency securities, tax-exempt bonds of state and local governments, certificates of deposit, bankers' acceptances, high-grade commercial paper, and repurchase agreements. In addition, a wide variety of money market accounts, sweep accounts, NOW accounts, and Eurodollar investments are also available for this purpose.

The goal of cash management is twofold: (a) to reduce the amount of idle cash on hand without adversely affecting the firm's operations; and (b) to increase the return on the invested reserves without impairing the firm's liquidity. These goals can be facilitated by: (a) speeding collections, (b) use of the lock box system, (c) slowing down payments, and (d) playing the float.

In addition, two formal methods for improving the utilization of a firm's liquid reserves are: (a) the Baumol inventory model, and (b) cash budgeting.

High interest rates have provided an incentive for the further refinement of the techniques employed to control the size of a firm's liquid reserves. In the next chapter we consider the problem of financing the firm's working capital requirements.

REVIEW EXERCISE

Circle the correct word(s) to complete each sentence; see p. 468 for the correct answers.

18.1 The need for holding cash arises because receipts and expenditures can *sometimes/never* be perfectly synchronized.

18.2 *Liquid reserves/common stocks* are also held in anticipation of future profitable investment opportunities.

18.3 Inflation makes the holding of idle cash balances more *profitable/expensive*.

18.4 Liquidity refers to the ability to convert an asset to cash *gradually/quickly* and without loss.

18.5 Only very high grade bonds (or notes) with relatively *short/long* maturities can be considered liquid.

18.6 The goal of the cash manager is to *increase/reduce* the amount of cash on hand without reducing business activity or exposing the firm to undue risk.

18.7 The firm must be very *aggressive/selective* when investing its liquid reserves.

18.8 Treasury bills *pay interest/are sold at a discount*.

18.9 The float is the *sum of/difference between* the balance shown in the corporation's account and its actual balance in the bank.

18.10 The optimal cash balance varies *directly/inversely* with the fixed cost per transaction, and *directly/inversely* with the short-term interest rate.

18.11 Many firms can achieve significant savings merely by rearranging their commitments to get a *closer/weaker* synchronization of inflows and outflows.

18.12 The cash budget is essentially a tabulation of the firm's plans in terms of their impact on *firm strategy/cash receipts and expenditures*.

18.13 Taxes and loan repayments *should/should not* be included in the cash budget; wages, rent, and purchases of material should *also/not* be included.

18.14 The cash budget *does/does not* include depreciation.

18.15 As the planning period recedes into the future, the need for detail in the cash budget *increases/diminishes*.

QUESTIONS

18.1 Define the following terms:
- **a.** Liquidity
- **b.** CD
- **c.** Float
- **d.** Money market funds
- **e.** Sweep account
- **f.** The Baumol model

18.2 What motives can you think of for holding liquid assets?

18.3 "Our firm is quite liquid, since we have large inventories of custom-made suits for overweight men. The only problem would be to find buyers." Evaluate this statement.

18.4 How do you think the following assets rank in terms of liquidity?
- **a.** Treasury bills
- **b.** Grade BBB bonds
- **c.** Inventory of 1/4 inch screws
- **d.** Cash (Australian $)
- **e.** Inventory of women's dresses
- **f.** Cash (American $)

Explain your rankings.

18.5 List at least five suitable investment outlets for liquid reserves.

18.6 What methods can you think of for conserving a firm's cash?

18.7 Explain the lock box system.

18.8 "We use similar methods to decide on the size of our inventory of spare parts, and on our liquidity reserves." Is that possible? Explain.

18.9 "Depreciation is a cost, and therefore must be included in our cash budget." Do you agree? Explain.

18.10 What is meant by the statement "It takes two to play the float"?

PROBLEMS

18.1 T-bills.   A $5,000 U.S. Treasury bill, which matures in 60 days, sells for $4,940. What is its annual yield?

18.2 Yield determination.   A $20,000 U.S. government agency issue pays $600 interest upon maturity in 280 days, and sells for $19,700. What is its annual yield?

18.3 Yield determination.   A $6,000 U.S. government agency issue pays $550 interest upon maturity in 330 days, and sells for $6,100. What is its annual yield?

18.4 Inventory model.   The Farwell Corporation needs $2.6 million per year for cash outlays. The short-term interest rate is 6% and the fixed transaction cost for cash withdrawals is $115.50. What is the optimal size of the cash withdrawal? How often will cash be withdrawn?

18.5 Inventory model.   The Gerten Company needs $1 million cash a month. The cost of the employee's time which is needed to prepare the transaction is estimated at $20. Furthermore, the bank charges $14.80 for each transaction. The interest rate Gerten receives on short-term funds is 6.4%. What is the optimal size of each cash withdrawal?

18.6 Inventory model.   Consider again Gerten's problem in the previous question. Instead of having an employee prepare the transaction every time, a phone call to the bank suffices. The cost comes to 70 cents. How does your answer change?

18.7 Cash budget.   The Melrose Corporation forecasts sales of $600,000 for next year, which are evenly distributed over the four quarters. Assume that receipts are on the first day of the quarter. Cost of goods sold amount to 75% of sales and are incurred on the same day the sale is made. Labor costs amount to 15% and are also incurred on the day the sale is made; $22,000 of taxes are payable on the first day of the second quarter, and a $12,000 debt is due on the first day of the third quarter. Another debt of $16,000 is due on the first day of the fourth quarter. The opening cash balance is $38,000. Prepare Melrose's quarterly cash budget for next year.

18.8 Cash budget.   The Mingoe Company estimates next year's sales at $2,400,000, evenly spread over four quarters. Payments for sales are received on the last day of the quarter. Cost of goods sold come to 60% of sales and are synchronized with sales; they are due on the last day of the quarter. Labor costs come to 25% of sales, and are paid on the first day of the quarter. The last payment ($35,000) for equipment which was bought last year is due on the first day of the first quarter. Taxes in the amount of $60,000 are due on the first day of the second quarter. The beginning balance is $150,000. Prepare Mingoe's quarterly cash budget for next year.

18.9 Cash budget.   The Springer Corporation forecasts sales of $1,200,000, spread evenly over the next 12 months. Assume that receipts are on the first day of the month. Cost of goods sold and labor amount to 95% of sales and are also payable on the first day of the month. Taxes of $20,000 need to be paid on the first day of the second month. The opening cash balance is $5,000. Prepare a monthly cash budget for next year.

SAMPLE PROBLEMS

SP18.1 A $5,000 U.S. non-interest-bearing treasury bill which matures in 60 days sells for $4,970. What is its annual yield?

SP18.2 The P-H Company foresees sales of $1 million for next year, evenly distributed over the four quarters. Assume that receipts are on the first day of the quarter. Cost of goods sold amount to 80% of sales and are incurred on the same day the sale is made. Labor costs amount to 10% and are also incurred on the day the sale is made. $35,000 of taxes are payable on the first day of the second quarter, and an $18,000 debt is due on the first day of the third quarter. Another debt of $30,000 is due on the first day of the fourth quarter. The beginning cash balance is $25,000.

   a. Prepare next year's quarterly cash budget for the P-H Company.

   b. On the assumption that P-H wants to keep a minimum cash balance of $25,000, how much money will be available for investment?

Answers to Sample Problems

SP18.1 The investor earns the difference between the purchase price and the maturity value:

$$\$5,000 - \$4,970 = \$30$$

The total investment required is $4970, so the investor earns:

$$\frac{30}{4,970} = .006$$

Since there are 6.08 sixty-day periods in the year

$$\frac{365}{60} = 6.08$$

the annual yield is

$$(1.006)^{6.08} - 1 = 3.7\%.$$

SP18.2   a. We know that sales are $250,000 each quarter and are received on the first day of that quarter. We also know that cost of goods sold is $200,000 (80% of $250,000) which are payable on the first day of the quarter. Labor costs, which are also payable on the first day of the quarter, amount to $25,000 (10% of $250,000). We are also told that the beginning cash balance is $25,000. In addition, taxes and the two debt repayments are due on the first day of quarters 2, 3, and 4, respectively. We start by preparing the following worksheet:

	Quarter			
	1	2	3	4
Beginning balance	25			
Plus: Sales	250	250	250	250
Less: Cost of goods sold	200	200	200	200
Labor costs	25	25	25	25
Taxes		35		
Debt repayments			18	30

To complete the table, we sum all the outflows and inflows for each quarter and add (subtract) the net inflow (outflow) to the beginning balance. This gives us the cash balance at the end of the quarter, which is also the beginning balance of the following quarter:

	Quarter			
	1	2	3	4
Beginning balance	25	50	40	47
Plus: Sales	250	250	250	250
Less: Cost of goods	200	200	200	200
Labor	25	25	25	25
Taxes		35		
Debt repayment			18	30
Ending cash balance	50	40	47	42

b. The amounts available for investment are derived by deducting the $25,000 minimum cash balance from each quarter's cash balance:

	Quarter			
	1	2	3	4
Ending cash balance	50	40	47	42
Less: Minimum cash balance	(25)	(25)	(25)	(25)
Amount available for investment	25	15	22	17

Answers to Review Exercise

18.1 never   **18.2** liquid reserves   **18.3** expensive   **18.4** quickly

18.5 short   **18.6** reduce   **18.7** selective

18.8 are sold at a discount   **18.9** difference between

18.10 directly, inversely   **18.11** closer

18.12 cash receipts and expenditures   **18.13** should, also

18.14 does not   **18.15** diminishes

SUGGESTIONS FOR FURTHER READING

The two best known applications of formal models to corporate cash balances are those of William J. Baumol, "The Transactions Demand for Cash, An Inventory Theoretic Approach," *Quarterly Journal of Economics*, November 1952; and Merton H. Miller and Daniel Orr, "The Demand for Money by Firms: Extension of Analytic Results," *Journal of Finance*, December 1968.

See also the articles on short-term financial management in Stewart C. Myers (ed.), *Modern Developments in Financial Management* (New York: Praeger, 1976).

The lock box system is analyzed in greater detail by C. A. Batlin and Susan Hinko, "Lockbox Management and Value Maximization," *Financial Management*, Winter 1981; Robert M. Nauss and Robert E. Markland, "Theory and Application of an Optimizing Procedure for Lock Box Location Analysis," *Management Science*, August 1981.

The innovations in bank accounts are discussed in a very readable article by Gillian Garcia and Annie McMahon, "Regulatory Innovation: The New Bank Accounts," *Economic Perspectives*, Federal Reserve Bank of Chicago, March–April 1984.

Alternative strategies for cash management are given by Alfred DeSalvo, "Cash Management Converts Dollars into Working Assets," *Harvard Business Review*, May–June 1972; Lawrence J. Gitman, D. Keith Forrester, and John R. Forrester, "Maximizing Cash Disbursement Float," *Financial Management*, Summer 1976.

The essential features of the U.S. commercial paper market are given in "The Commercial Paper Market Since the Mid-Seventies," *Federal Reserve Bulletin*, June 1982.

19

Financing
The Investment
In Current Assets

By the very nature of their businesses, most corporations require liquid reserves, inventories, and accounts receivable. In the preceding two chapters we examined the firm's need for these current assets. In this chapter we address the question of how these assets are to be financed. But just as there appear to be no universally valid standards of taste or artistic license, there is no universally accepted strategy for financing working capital. Japanese firms often view, and therefore solve, their financing problems very differently from their European or American counterparts. Cigarette manufacturers and steel mills often follow widely differing strategies. Despite these very obvious differences, we shall try to identify and explain the principles that underly most short-term financing policies. We first take a look at the basic relationship between short-term and long-term sources of finance. We then go on to examine, in some detail, alternative sources of short-term finance. Four major types of financing are discussed: trade credits, tax and wage accruals, bank loans, and commercial paper. The comparative costs of these alternatives are analyzed in detail with particular emphasis on short-term borrowing from commercial banks.

FINANCING WORKING CAPITAL: ALTERNATIVE STRATEGIES

Short-term financing strategies usually reflect an attempt to maintain some relationship between the durability of assets and the maturity of the debt used to finance these assets, to reduce to a minimum the impact of interest-rate fluctuations on the value of the firm. One result of this approach is summed up in the well-known dictum, "Never finance fixed investments with short-term capital." The other side of this coin would seem to imply that "Short-term assets should be financed only by short-term sources." But, as we will see below, this is not generally correct. Of course, in an ideal world in which raw materials are acquired at the beginning of the year, processed, and then sold at the end of the year, the expenditure on raw materials would be financed by, say, a 1-year loan from the bank. And if we assume an upward-sloping yield curve (see Chapter 3), so that the 1-year interest rate is less than the long-term rate, such a strategy implies the minimization of capital costs. Figure 19–1 illustrates this simple situation. Resources are acquired at the beginning of the production period, used up during the period, and replenished at the beginning of the next period. This creates the familiar sawtooth pattern we also found in cash and inventory management. Short-term needs are financed by short-term credit; the remaining fixed assets of the firm are financed by long-term capital (long-term debt and equity).

There is much to be said for the matching of assets and liabilities. As we have already noted, using the shortest possible maturity can often lead to significant interest savings. But more important, the matching of maturities minimizes the risk. When long-term assets are financed by short-term debts, say a 1-year loan, the debt must be "rolled over" at the end of the year. It is a rare investment indeed that has a cash flow (profits and depreciation) sufficient to retire the entire debt at the end of the first year of operation! If for any reason the bank does not agree to renew the loan, the firm may face a serious financial problem, even though the underlying investment is sound. Such problems are avoided when investments in fixed plant and equipment are financed by long-term debt. In such a case, interest and capital payments can be paid out of the expected annual cash flow over the lifetime of the investment.

Unfortunately, the real world is not as simple as the example in Figure 19–1 would seem to imply. The uncertainties of business lead the firm to hold precautionary reserves of cash, raw materials, and finished products.

FIGURE 19–1
Financing Working Capital: A Simple Model

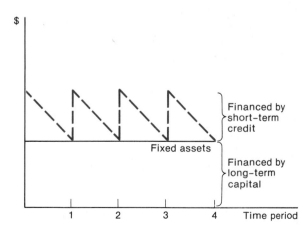

Although these assets are formally listed as "current" in the balance sheet, they are in a sense the "fixed" portion of the firm's current assets. Inventories, for example, are rarely reduced to zero; some slack always remains to cover unforeseen contingencies. Hence a more realistic strategy is to employ long-term sources to finance fixed assets plus the *fixed* portion of current assets. Only those current assets that fluctuate over the firm's operating cycle should be financed by short-term funds (see Figure 19–2).

This financing strategy can also be expressed in terms of the balance sheet. Recall that in Chapter 4 *net working capital* was defined as "the excess of current assets over current liabilities." Put in another way, net working capital can be defined as the component of current assets which is financed out of long-term sources. This can be seen from Table 19–1, which gives Bethlehem Steel's 1985 balance sheet. The company's net working capital, its excess of current assets over current liabilities, was $126.8 million ($1,093.4 − $966.6 = $126.8). From the same balance sheet we can also see that $126.8 corresponds to that part of current assets financed by long-term debt and equity. Net working capital is represented by the shaded part of Figure 19–3, which again shows that the two definitions come to the same thing.

The financing strategy sketched above suggests that the firm will try to make its net working capital approximate its best estimate of the "fixed" component of its current assets. The remaining current assets will be financed out of short-term sources. The principal advantages in "matching" debt maturities to the duration of the assets being financed are as follows:

1. *Flexibility*: The use of short-term debt to finance short-lived assets has the advantage of flexibility. The short-term credit can be scaled to fit the temporary needs of the firm—for example, those which arise because of the seasonal or cyclical nature of its operations.

2. *Risk*: Using long-term credit to finance long-lived assets permits the firm to eliminate the risk of a possible rise in interest rates during the course

FIGURE 19–2
**Financing
Working Capital
Under Uncertainty**

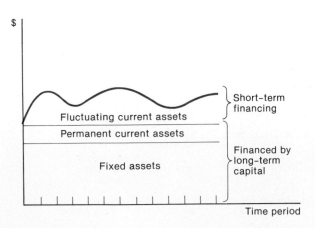

**TABLE 19–1   Bethlehem Steel Corporation
Consolidated Balance Sheet,
Year Ended Dec. 31, 1985
($ millions)**

Assets:

Current assets	1,093.4
Fixed assets	3,649.2
Total assets	4,742.6

Liabilities and Stockholders' Equity:

Current liabilities	966.6
Long-term liabilities	2,764.7
Total equity	1,011.3
Total liabilities and equity	4,742.6

of the project, as well as avoiding the risk that the short-term debt will be difficult to roll over.

With this conceptual framework in mind, we are in a better position to take a closer look at the available alternative sources of short-term financing. In general, they can be classified into one of two categories: *spontaneous sources* which arise out of the firm's operations, such as accounts payable and accrued taxes; and *short-term borrowing* from banks and other financial institutions.

TRADE CREDIT

trade credit
Unsecured credit extended by suppliers to buyers who purchase on a regular basis.

The very existence of many small firms often depends on the availability of trade credit. Many firms would never have gotten started at all if suppliers had insisted on receiving cash upon delivery. **Trade credit** is a "spontaneous" or "self-adjusting" source of finance. When sales expand, purchases (and therefore payables) tend to increase; conversely, when sales decline, purchases (and therefore payables) tend to follow suit.

In one sense, trade credit from suppliers is the other side of the credit the firm offers its own customers. The former creates *accounts payable* (or

**FIGURE 19–3
Net Working
Capital**

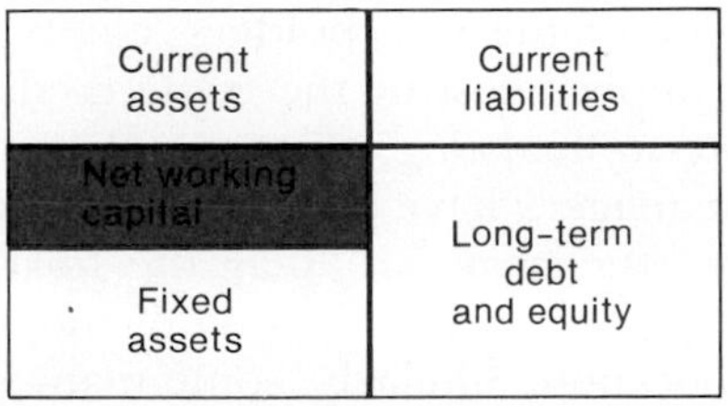

Current assets	Current liabilities
Net working capital	Long–term debt and equity
Fixed assets	

payables
Accounts payable.

receivables
Accounts receivable.

net credit
A firm's trade credit position arrived at by subtracting payables from receivables.

simple **payables**) on the liability side of the balance sheet; the latter creates an asset, *accounts receivable* (or simply **receivables**) in the firm's financial statements. If we look at both sides of the firm's operations, its **net credit** position can be defined as *receivables* minus *payables*. It is positive when the firm is a net supplier of trade credit, and negative when it is a net receiver of trade credit. In general, very large firms tend to be net suppliers, and small firms net receivers, of trade credit. For example, at the end of 1985, IBM had trade receivables totaling $9,757 million and accounts payable of only $1,293 million. The *net credit* position of this giant, therefore, was almost $8.5 billion in that year ($9,757 million less $1,293 million = $8,464 million).

Trade credit has two principal advantages: (1) It is available to almost all buyers who purchase on a regular basis—that is, it is relatively easy to obtain. (2) Often trade credit is made on "open book" (see Chapter 17) and is not secured by a pledge of any specific asset as collateral.

On the surface, accounts payable appear to provide a free source of financing, but as we saw in Chapter 17, the "free lunch" aspect of trade credit should not be exaggerated, because the implied cost of foregone discounts is often extremely high. Consider, for example, a firm that purchases its raw materials on a 2/10 net 30 basis, which means that it is offered a 2% cash discount if it pays it invoices within 10 days. The gross bill is due at the end of 30 days. Now suppose our firm foregoes its cash discount, thereby acquiring 20 days of additional credit. What is the cost of the additional credit? In this particular case, the annual interest rate on the additional credit is over 43%. Since there are 18.25 20-day periods in a year (365/20 = 18.25), the interest calculation is as follows:

$$(1.02)^{18.25} - 1 = 43.5\%$$

What would be the effect of a lower cash discount, say only 1%?

$$(1.01)^{18.25} - 1 = 19.9\%$$

The lower rate reduces the cost of foregoing the cash discount to 19.9%, which is still rather high. And in fact, given the terms of sale in many industries, extending the trade credit period by foregoing cash discounts is one of the most, *if not the most*, expensive source of short term credit.

Although the trade credit decision depends on the particular firm in question, and its alternative means of financing, two rules can be applied to all firms: (1) Always take advantage of the full discount period. In our example, paying *before* 10 days does mean foregoing a "free lunch," and this can only reduce the value of the stockholders' equity. (2) Forego the cash discount *only* when the implicit cost of the trade credit is lower than alternative sources of short-term financing.

Finally, financial managers have been known to push the credit term to the limit. Here again, the firm can "play the float" by taking the cash discount and then mailing the check at the end of the tenth day—preferably to the farthest possible location. Similarly, some managers try to extend the net period beyond the 30-day limit by paying the *net* invoice on, say, the

45th day. If the original terms of sale were 2/10 net 30, such a practice (if you can get away with it) is equivalent to changing the effective terms of sale to 2/10 net 45. This reduced the cost of foregoing the cash discount from 43.5% to 22.9%. Since there are 10.43 35-day periods in a year, the formula becomes:

$$(1.02)^{10.43} - 1 = 22.9\%$$

These, and other variations on the same theme, make for good conversation at lunch, but remember that the supplier has a financial manager (who has also read Chapter 17), so this game can be played only so far. An additional cost of stretching trade credit to its limits is that your firm may acquire the stigma of being a "slow payer." This can sometimes backfire at a very awkward moment—for example, when you are sitting at the loan desk of your bank!

ACCRUED WAGES AND TAXES

Other balance sheet accruals such as wages and taxes payable also provide spontaneous sources of short-term financing. However, unlike trade credit, management exercises very little discretion over these items. By paying employees at the end of the week or the end of the month, as the case may be, the firm obtains free financing, since employees do not charge interest on these "forced loans." Similarly, taxes are paid quarterly, rather than daily, which is another source of free financing. But before you get carried away and decide to pay your employees once every 3 months and/or to "stretch" your payment to the IRS, it may be prudent to recall that the tax payment dates are fixed by law, and wage and salary payment dates by custom or contract. Ignoring the former can involve the firm in heavy penalties, or worse! Failure to recognize the latter will probably mean a visit from a delegation of employees or the union representative. The only sane rule to follow is this: Exploit accruals to the hilt, but don't try to convert this source of financing into a discretionary decision variable.

SHORT-TERM BORROWING

The second major component of short-term finance is borrowing, from individuals, from other firms, or from financial institutions, especially banks. Borrowing differs from the spontaneous sources in several important respects:

1. Short-term borrowing is planned and negotiated; it does not fluctuate spontaneously with sales.

2. In the case of borrowing, the firm actually receives money ratner than supplies, or the services of employees, in advance of payment.

3. Typically, an individual borrowing transaction tends to be larger than its trade credit counterpart.

4. Borrowing *always* has an explicit cost.

BORROWING FROM BANKS

The most important sources of short-term loans are commercial banks. Despite this, the role of the banker is often misunderstood. Most of us are familiar with the popular saying, "You can get a bank loan only if you prove that you don't need it"! In part, at least, the popularity of this view of a banker's function reflects a basic misunderstanding of the nature of commercial banking.

If there exists one basic principle of banking, it is that the bank is *not* a partner, but a lender. Banks are not a source of venture capital, since they are restricted to a limited return on their loans. As lenders, banks are mainly concerned with three factors: safety, suitability, and profitability. As "consumers" of bank loans, a good corporate financial manager should be knowledgeable about bankers' motives.

Safety.   Traditionally this aspect of lending has received the greatest emphasis, but today the acceptance of some degree of risk is almost inevitable if the bank is to function. However, the amount of risk a bank is willing to take is limited. It depends on general competitive conditions, the bank's willingness and ability to monitor risky loans, and of course the size of the risk premium it charges.

Suitability.   Independent of risk considerations, some loans may simply be considered unsuitable. For example, some banks will not finance gambling activities; others tend to specialize in particular industries.

Profitability.   Financial managers should never forget that banks too are profit-oriented. A reasonable direct, or indirect, financial return on the bank's activities is a must.

Based on these considerations, each individual bank develops its general loan policy which, depending on the case, may be oral or written. A typical set of loan policy guidelines includes:

1. Size of the general loan account

2. Composition of loan portfolio by maturity of loans

3. Diversification of loans among industries

4. Risk policy

5. Policy regarding secured loans—collateral, compensating balances, and so on.

One way to gauge a bank's lending policy is to have a chat with the bank manager or loan officer, but this should always be confirmed by taking a careful look at the bank's actual practice in the past.

CHOOSING A BANK

Unlike most of us, who choose a bank because it is located on campus or around the corner from the house, or has attractive checks, the corporation views the bank as a potential supplier of capital and other services. Often the firm is seeking an *ongoing relationship* that has many facets. The bank's loan policy is just one of a number of criteria the firm will consider when choosing among banks:

1. A first consideration is size. Some firms prefer a relatively small bank in which a personal relationship can be established with the bank's senior officers; others prefer the services of larger banks. However, since the maximum size of a loan a bank can make to an individual customer is generally limited to 10% of the bank's equity capital, one doesn't expect General Motors to be using the services of a small neighborhood bank.

2. The firm must consider the suitability of the bank's general loan policy. One important consideration will be the bank's attitude towards risk and risk diversification. A relatively risky firm that chooses an ultraconservative risk-averse banker may be in for a rough time. The bank's willingness to offer the type of maturities, repayment schedules, and collateral arrangements that fit the firm's needs are other important considerations.

3. Some firms will seek a bank that specializes in its particular type of activity. For example, if the firm is an exporter or importer, the bank's expertise in international trade may be the principal consideration. Conversely, a firm that specializes in commodity trading or oil refining may seek a bank with experience in these particular areas.

4. "Loyalty" is another, somewhat less tangible, characteristic firms often seek. This refers to the bank's willingness to support its customers in difficult times. As we have already noted, the refusal of a bank to renew an outstanding loan can mean serious trouble for the borrower. But this might be a good place to apply the rule of "revealed preference," based on the bank's track record with customers in the past, rather than on the verbal promises made when the bank is recruiting a new customer.

5. With the rapid development of modern banking services, many firms are looking to areas other than loans when choosing a bank. The firm may be interested in the investment advice a large, established, centrally located bank can offer; others may be more concerned with the variety of services offered. For example, some firms require the bank's services for payroll management or collection purposes (such as a lock box arrangement).

In general the banking relationship need not be, and often is not, monogamous. Bigamy or "worse" is perfectly acceptable. On the average, larger firms tend to use more banks than do their smaller counterparts. However, even a relatively small firm which does business on a national basis may seek a relationship with a number of banks across the country to aid in the collection of receivables. A bank that is excellent in one particular area may not be the best choice by some other criterion, so a "portfolio" of banks may be called for. But remember that "loyalty" is a two-way street. A firm that gives one bank its more profitable business while seeking services from another bank, cannot expect the same commitment from the second bank.

NEGOTIATING A BANK LOAN

A strategy that is often helpful to the firm when negotating a loan is to keep the banker's point of view in mind. The firm should be prepared to provide the lending bank with the information it requires to process the loan application.

Background Information.   In the case of a new customer, the bank will require considerable background information. The firm should be prepared to present evidence of its business experience, prospects for the future, and general ability to repay debts. Recall that the bank probably will have obtained much of this information from other sources. And even in the case of an old customer, the financial manager should be ready to present copies of the firm's most recent financial statements, sales forecasts, and cash flow projections.

Size and Purpose of Loan.   The bank will want detailed answers to many questions designed to help it decide on the suitability of the loan: (a) Will the amount of the loan (and other sources) be sufficient for the firm to achieve its stated goal? (b) Has the firm left a sufficient margin of safety to cover unforeseen contingencies? (c) Does the firm have sufficient equity capital, or is it "seeking a partner" for the venture in question? For reasons that we have already emphasized, inadequate equity will deter most bank loan officers on the spot.

Repayment.   Will the firm have sufficient liquid resources to return the loan *after* the loan proceeds have been expended? At this point, most loan officers will appreciate a detailed cash flow forecast for the period the loan will be outstanding.

Security.   The bank may wish to know the amount and type of collateral the firm is prepared to offer to help secure the loan. Here the key consideration is whether or not the collateral is of sufficient value to provide the bank with an acceptable margin of safety in case of default.

promissory note
An IOU; a written promise to pay at a fixed time in the future a sum of money to a specified individual or bearer.

Formal Contract: The Promissory Note.   If the negotiations are successful, a formal loan agreement will be drawn up in the form of a **promissory note**. It specifies the terms of the contract: amount, interest rate, repayment schedule, collateral (if any), and any other additional restrictions.

COST OF BANK CREDIT

The interest rate charged by the bank depends on the general level of interest rates at the time of the loan and the perceived risk level of the borrower. Unlike accruals and some payables, the cost of bank credit is never zero. On the other hand, it rarely reaches the cost of foregoing cash discounts. One rule that should never be forgotten is to calculate the interest cost using only the funds actually available for use. Another is always to express the interest cost as an annual percentage; this greatly facilitates comparison with other sources of financing.

prime rate
The interest rate a bank establishes for low-risk borrowers.

In practice, the bank establishes a **prime rate** for borrowers who because of their size and financial resources are considered "prime," or low risks to the bank. If a firm qualifies, it will be able to borrow at the prime rate. In practice, some creditworthy firms are able to borrow below the prime rate. Other, less creditworthy, firms will be offered loans at the prime rate *plus* a number of percentage points. Because of competition among banks for business, the prime rates set by most banks are identical, and usually follow the rate set by the large money-center banks, which is published regularly in the daily financial press. These banks, in turn, normally set their prime lending rate from 1 to 1.5 points above the "cost of money," as measured by the average rate paid on large negotiable certificates of deposit (CDs) during the preceding week. The difference between the prime rate and the CD rate represents the bank's "spread," which covers its costs and provides the profit from the loan. Table 19–2 gives some representative money market rates (both borrowing and lending) on February 6, 1987. The prime rate on short-term corporate loans was 7.5%; the CD rate on 1-month deposits was 6%. Some idea of the recent volatility of interest rates can be gauged from the fact that at the height of double-digit inflation in 1980, the prime rate reached 21%.

TABLE 19–2

Money Rates

The key annual interest rates below are a guide to general levels but don't always represent actual transactions.

PRIME RATE: 7½%. The base rate on corporate loans at large U.S. money center commercial banks.

FEDERAL FUNDS: 6½% high, 5 15/16% low, 6⅛% near closing bid, 6¼% offered. Reserves traded among commercial banks for overnight use in amounts of $1 million or more. Source: Prebon Money Brokers Inc., N.Y.

DISCOUNT RATE: 5½%. The charge on loans to depository institutions by the New York Federal Reserve Bank.

CALL MONEY: 7% to 7½%. The charge on loans to brokers on stock exchange collateral.

COMMERCIAL PAPER placed directly by General Motors Acceptance Corp.: 6% 30 to 59 days; 5.975% 60 to 89 days; 5.95% 90 to 119 days; 5.925% 120 to 149 days; 5.90% 150 to 179 days; 5.80% 180 to 270 days.

COMMERCIAL PAPER: High-grade unsecured notes sold through dealers by major corporations in multiples of $1,000: 6.025% 30 days; 6% 60 days; 5.95% 90 days.

CERTIFICATES OF DEPOSIT: 6% one month; 6% two months; 6% three months; 6% six months; 6.15% one year. Typical rates paid by major banks on new issues of negotiable C.D.s, usually on amounts of $1 million and more. The minimum unit is $100,000.

BANKERS ACCEPTANCES: 5.99% 30 days; 5.96% 60 days; 5.89% 90 days; 5.88% 120 days; 5.86% 150 days; 5.84% 180 days. Negotiable, bank-backed business credit instruments typically financing an import order.

LONDON LATE EURODOLLARS: 6 3/16% to 6 1/16% one month; 6 5/16% to 6 3/16% two months; 6 5/16% to 6 3/16% three months; 6 5/16% to 6 3/16% four months; 6 5/16% to 6 3/16% five months; 6 5/16% to 6 3/16% six months.

LONDON INTERBANK OFFERED RATES (LIBOR): 6¼% three months; 6¼% six months; 6 5/16% one year. The average of interbank offered rates for dollar deposits in the London market based on quotations at five major banks.

OTHER PRIME RATES: Canada 9.25%; Germany 6.75%; Japan 5.243%; Switzerland 5.75%; Britain 11%. These rate indications aren't directly comparable; lending practices vary widely by location. Source: Morgan Guaranty Trust Co.

TREASURY BILLS: Results of the Monday, February 2, 1987, auction of short-term U.S. government bills, sold at a discount from face value in units of $10,000 to $1 million: 5.58% 13 weeks; 5.59% 26 weeks.

FEDERAL HOME LOAN MORTGAGE CORP. (Freddie Mac): Posted yields on 30-year mortgage commitments for delivery within 30 days. 8.89%, standard conventional fixed-rate mortgages; 6.875%, 2% rate capped one-year adjustable rate mortgages.

FEDERAL NATIONAL MORTGAGE ASSOCIATION (Fannie Mae): Posted yields on 30 year mortgage commitments for delivery within 30 days (priced at par). 8.65%, standard conventional fixed rate-mortgages; 8.55%, 6/2 rate capped one-year adjustable rate mortgages.

MERRILL LYNCH READY ASSETS TRUST: 5.58%. Annualized average rate of return after expenses for the past 30 days; not a forecast of future returns.

SOURCE: *The Wall Street Journal*, February 6, 1987.

ALTERNATIVE METHODS FOR CALCULATING INTEREST

No matter how interest is quoted by the bank, a corporate financial manager must be in a position to understand the method of calculation used by the bank if loans from alternative sources are to be compared. Several methods of calculating bank interest are in general use. We will examine each in turn, assuming a hypothetical case in which Metro Manufacturing borrows

$50,000 for 1 year from its local bank at 8% interest. The relevant cash flows on this loan, using several alternatives, are given in Table 19–3.

Interest Paid at the End of Loan

Under this arrangement, Metro receives $50,000 and the bank, because of Metro's fine credit rating, sets the interest rate at 8%, which at the time was 1 point above the prime rate. At the end of the year Metro repays the bank $54,000. The interest rate on the loan is 8%:

$$\frac{4,000 \text{ interest}}{50,000 \text{ available cash}} = 8\%$$

Discounted Loan

discounted loan
A loan in which the borrower pays the interest in advance.

A second method is a **discounted loan** in which the bank stipulates that Metro pay the interest *in advance*. As can be seen from Table 19–3, the firm receives only $46,000, but repays the full principal of $50,000 at the end of the year. The *effective* annual interest cost of the discount loan is 8.7%:

$$\frac{\$4,000 \text{ interest}}{46,000 \text{ available cash}} = 8.7\%$$

Discounting the loan *raises* the effective interest rate, since Metro has less money available for use while it pays the same dollar amount of interest.

Loan with Compensating Balance

Some banks require borrowers to maintain an average balance in their checking accounts of from 10 to 20% of the face amount of the loan. Such a compensating balance *increases* the effective interest cost of the loan, since not all of the face amount of the loan is available to the firm. The effect of such an arrangement can be illustrated by assuming that the bank requests a 20% compensating balance ($10,000) from Metro on the original loan in question. Table 19–3 gives the relevant cash flow for such an arrangement. Since $10,000 remains in Metro's checking account for the entire period, it

TABLE 19–3   Cash Flows for Alternative Types of Loan

Today	End of Year
A. Interest at End of Year	
$50,000 available to firm	Repay $54,000 to bank
B. Discount Interest	
$46,000 available to firm	Repay $50,000 to bank
C. Loan with Compensating Balance	
$40,000 available to firm	Effective repayment of $44,000 to bank
D. Discount Interest with Compensating Balance	
$36,000 available to firm	Effective repayment of $40,000 to bank

neither affects the amount received and therefore available for use, nor the *effective* repayment. The effective interest cost of the loan to Metro is 10%:

$$\frac{\$4,000 \text{ interest}}{\$40,000 \text{ available cash}} = 10\%$$

Had the compensating balance been higher, say 25%, you can easily verify that the *effective* cost of the loan would be higher—10.7%:

$$\frac{\$4,000 \text{ interest}}{\$37,500 \text{ available cash}} = 10.7\%$$

Conversely, for a 10% compensating balance, the effective interest cost would be *lower*—8.9%:

$$\frac{\$4,000 \text{ interest}}{\$45,000 \text{ available cash}} = 8.9\%$$

In general, the effective rate can be calculated directly from the formula

$$\frac{\text{stated interest rate}}{\text{one minus compensating balance percentage}} = \frac{8}{0.9} = 8.9\%$$

Discounted Loan with Compensating Balance

If in addition to the compensating balance the loan is also discounted, the effective interest cost will reflect the influence of both features. Table 19–3 shows the cash flow for Metro's loan assuming that it is discounted, and that the bank also requires a 20% compensating balance. In this instance, the effective interest cost is 11.1%:

$$\frac{\$4,000 \text{ interest}}{\$36,000 \text{ available cash}} = 11.1\%$$

Line of Credit

line of credit
A loan in which a bank makes available a maximum amount of money and the borrower uses any portion of that amount as it sees fit.

An alternative arrangement that Metro might use is called a **line of credit.** The bank agrees to make available a maximum loan, of say $100,000, during the coming year. Metro, in turn, can use any portion of that amount as it sees fit. Since the firm is charged in one form or another for the *unused* portion of the credit line, failure to utilize the line of credit fully raises the effective interest cost. Assume, for example, that Metro is granted a $100,000 line of credit for the year, but borrows only $50,000. Once again the stated interest rate is set at 8%. Now assume that the agreement with the bank calls for an annual *commitment fee* of 1% on any unused funds. In our case, the unused portion is $50,000. In addition to the 8% interest on the $50,000 actually borrowed, the firm must pay an additional 1% on the unused $50,000. In such a case the total payment to the bank, assuming that all payments are made at the end of the year, would be:

Repayment of principal	$50,000
Interest	4,000
Commitment fee for the year	500
Total payment at end of year	$54,500

The effective interest cost of this loan is 9%:

$$\frac{\$4,500 \text{ interest and fee}}{50,000 \text{ available to firm}} = 9\%$$

revolving credit agreement
A loan arrangement in which a bank offers a firm short-term credit up to a given amount during a specified period.

Numerous alternative arrangements exist but one of the more frequent is a **revolving credit agreement** in which a bank, or a group of banks, offers the firm short-term credit up to a given amount during a specified period, say 3 years. The interest on such future loans is usually stipulated as "prime rate plus," and a commitment fee is charged on any unused balance. Such an arrangement ensures that the firm will have short-term financing available when needed. The variability of the interest rate charge (recall that it follows the fluctuations in the prime rate) insures the bank against unforeseen changes in interest rates.

COMMERCIAL PAPER

As we noted in Chapter 18, some very large firms can bypass the banking system and issue their own promissory notes to lenders directly or via security dealers. Such arrangements are limited to a very small number of firms who, because of their size and the nature of their business, have exceptionally low credit risks. The attraction of the commercial paper market lies in the low cost to the issuing firm. The rate paid on high-grade commercial paper is typically 1 to 1.5 points below the prime rate. For example, on February 6, 1987, the interest rate on 60-day commercial paper was 6%; the prime rate on the same day was 7.5%. Despite the attractiveness of this market for those who qualify, commercial paper is not a substitute for bank loans. There is more to the banker-corporation relationship than can be captured in an effective interest calculation. Few corporations are willing to trade in their banker for the commercial paper dealer if only for the fact that when dark clouds gather, the commercial banker is usually more willing to help a good customer in financial distress.

EFFECTIVE USE OF SECURITY

Given the chance, most corporate financial managers probably would prefer to borrow on an unsecured basis, thereby saving the collateral for future use. The facts of business life, however, are quite different. Many short-term loans are secured by some form of collateral. What accounts for this wide-spread practice?

Borrowers usually offer security to lenders for one of two reasons: (a) For many firms, with only limited equity and an uncertain future, offering security is the only way they can obtain any debt financing. (Recall that the lender is not interested in sharing ownership risk.) (b) Other firms offer security in order to obtain better terms on their loans, such as lower interest rates, longer maturities, more convenient repayment schedules, and so on.

Lenders view the securing of loans primarily as a means of reducing the risk of loss should the firm default on its obligation. The lender seeks to obtain control over assets which are vital to the borrower's business in order to preclude their sale or diversion to other debtors, who would then have priority over their disposal. In case of default, the secured lender has a prior claim on these assets. However, it must be pointed out, in all fairness to the "hardhearted" banker, that the legal right to a particular asset has no more value than the asset itself. And a *secured* position is not synonymous with safety against possible loss.

What assets make good collateral for a loan? In general, an asset can provide a reasonable degree of security if it meets the following three requirements:

1. The lender must be able to secure a *legal* right to the asset.
2. The security arrangement must be such that it can continue in force *without undue expense*.
3. The asset must be one that can reasonably be expected to have realizable value *over the projected life of the loan*.

BORROWING AGAINST RECEIVABLES

Commercial banks and other financial institutions offer a variety of services designed to assist the firm in the management of its accounts receivable or in using them as collateral for short-term loans. The firm may avail itself of one or more of the following types of services:

1. *Credit analysis.* Some firms use their bank or a finance company to check and analyze the creditworthiness of potential customers. This reflects the fact that many financial institutions have greater expertise and experience in making credit appraisals.
2. *Collections.* Some firms adopt the practice of turning the collection of receivables over to a bank or financial institution in the hope of speeding up the collection process and reducing the number of defaults.
3. *Collateral.* Financial institutions are prepared to make loans against the pledge of accounts receivable as collateral.

4. *Transfer of risk of default.* Some financial institutions are prepared to assume the risk of the nonpayment of receivables under a *factoring* agreement.

Of course, the number and types of services the firm utilizes depends on their cost and the particular needs of the firm in question. Here we will take a closer look at two of the most widely used arrangements for securing short-term loans: pledging receivables and factoring.

Pledging Receivables

The simplest type of arrangement is one in which the company pledges its receivables as collateral for a short-term loan. The bank, or financial institution, grants a short-term loan to the firm and holds the receivables as security. The firm collects the receivables itself and makes the payment to the bank. Typically, no additional fee beyond the interest cost of the loan is charged. The bank can secure its position in two ways: (a) It can accept only high-grade receivables of ongoing customers as collateral. For example, in some cases the bank may insist on the receivables of firms having a high credit rating from Dun and Bradstreet or a similar credit rating agency. (b) The bank often requires a "margin of safety"; it demands collateral in excess of the amount of the loan. The size of the margin reflects the creditworthiness of the receivables. Since the financial institution "lends with recourse," the nonpayment of the receivable does not release the company from its obligation to repay the loan. The lending institution does not assume any of the risk of the nonpayment of the outstanding accounts receivable.

Factoring Receivables

factor
A financial institution that specializes in buying receivables.

Factoring refers to the actual sale of the receivables by the firm to a financial institution which specializes in such transactions. As credit sales orders are received, they are forwarded to the financial institution (called the **factor**), which checks the creditworthiness of the customer. If the factor approves, the invoice is assigned to the factor, which immediately transfers most of the money value of the receivable to the firm. The remaining funds are kept as a reserve against possible disputes, and are forwarded when the receivable is actually collected. In this case the assignment of receivables is made *without recourse.* Should the customer default, the factor, and not the firm which made the sale, suffers the loss, except in cases in which the nonpayment reflects a disagreement between seller and customer regarding the quality of the merchandise, order price, and so on.

The factor performs two distinct services. First, it performs a credit-checking and collection service for the firm, while at the same time assuming responsibility for the risk of default. Second, the factor advances the firm money against the future collection of the receivables. The cost of factoring is made up of the payments for these two services. The first has to do with the collection processes and risk of receivables; the second is like a loan.

Consider the following numerical example. Assume that the ABC Corporation enters into a factoring agreement with ACME Factors, Inc., under which ABC sells ACME $100,000 of its receivables. The receivables represent sales that were made on a net 6 months basis. ABC agrees to pay the factor a 2% ($2,000) commission on the face value of the receivables, and a $6,000 anticipation charge, both on a discounted basis. ACME also stipulates that $5,000 will be withheld as a reserve. As a result, ABC receives $87,000 on the date of sale and 6 months later $5,000 (see Table 19–4). The effective interest cost of the loan component of the factoring agreement is 6.9% for 6 months:

$$\frac{\$6,000 \text{ anticipation charge}}{\$87,000 \text{ available to firm}} = 6.9\%$$

Since there are two 6-month periods in a year, the annual interest cost is 14.3%:

$$(1.069)^2 - 1 = 14.3\%$$

If we ignore the 2% commission on the grounds that this is the payment for risk insurance and collection services and therefore must be evaluated against the value to the firm of the services received, the effective cost of the credit received from the factor is reduced to 6.7%:

$$\frac{\$6,000 \text{ anticipation charge}}{\$89,000 \text{ available to firm}} = 6.7\%$$

which comes to 13.9% on an annual basis:

$$(1.067)^2 - 1 = 13.9\%$$

Although factoring is equivalent to the receipt of a loan, no increase in balance sheet liabilities is involved. When a sale is made to a customer under a factoring arrangement, inventories decrease and cash increases. Recall that the firm receives payment directly from the factor. (A small receivable item in the amount of the reserve is also created.) When the firm pledges receivables and takes a loan from the bank, the following accounting entries occur. Upon the sale, inventories are decreased and accounts receivable are created. Following the loan, cash increases and a loan payable liability is created. In an essential sense, however, both variants involve the raising of cash.

TABLE 19–4   Funds Received by the ABC Corporation Under the Factoring Agreement

Face value of receivables	$100,000
Less: Reserve*	(5,000)
Anticipation charge	(6,000)
Commission	(2,000)
Funds available on date of sale	$ 87,000

* To be forwarded to ABC after 6 months.

In addition to its cost, factoring can have several disadvantages:

1. From the firm's point of view, the factor's credit standards may be too stringent.
2. Factoring tends to weaken customer relationships.
3. In some financial circles, factoring carries a bit of a stigma. This reflects the fact that historically such arrangements have been widely used by weaker firms. But even if this was once true, the growing propularity of factoring agreements has all but erased this consideration.

BORROWING AGAINST INVENTORIES

Inventory is another popular vehicle for securing loans. Using inventory as collateral presents two distinct problems, one for the lender and a second for the borrower. The lending institution will want to make sure that the inventory is suitable to serve as security for the loan. The borrower will be concerned to find a way to pledge the inventory without disrupting the business. Ideally, inventory that is to serve as collateral should have the following characteristics:

1. It should *not* be subject to physical deterioration during the course of the loan. If you will forgive the pun, a dairy firm's inventory is likely to go sour before the loan is due.
2. The inventory should be of relatively homogeneous quality.
3. It should have high value relative to bulk.
4. It should have good resale value based on the existence of relative price stability and a broad market.

Of course, depending on the strength of their desire to make the loan, lenders may settle for much less. But clearly cars, trucks, and uncut diamonds make better collateral than an inventory of antique furniture or fresh fruit.

Several methods have been devised for solving the second problem, keeping the firm in business even though its inventory is pledged.

Blanket Lien against Inventory.   Under this method, the lender is given a lien against all the borrowing firm's inventories. Although this gives the lender priority in case of default, it does not prevent the running down of inventories by the firm. As a result, on the day of default the value of the collateral may be badly diminished. In order to protect its interests, the **trust receipt**
A loan against inventory backed by specific assets.
lender may insist on a **trust receipt** in which the loan is backed by specific assets. Although this works in some cases, and automobiles are a good example, the earmarking of specific assets is often impossible or at best clumsy and expensive. A loan agreement has to be made for each asset, and when

it is sold the proceeds are transferred to a trustee who repays the loan. A trust receipt arrangement works well when the inventory items are easily identified (say by serial number) and are relatively expensive, so that the cost of drawing up the individual loan agreement is not prohibitive.

Warehousing.   The disadvantages of trust receipts have led to the search for alternative means of using inventories as collateral. One way is to place the inventory physically out of the control of the borrower by storing it in a warehouse supervised by an independent third party. A cannery provides a good example of this method. Early in the fall, a fruit canner builds up a large investment in inventory and therefore requires a loan to finance it. Under a warehouse arrangement, the lending bank will make short-term loans against the inventory if it is placed in an independent warehouse. Withdrawals from the inventory must be approved by the bank, which of course will insist that the outstanding loan be reduced along with the reduction in inventory, thereby safeguarding its interests. In addition, the bank will normally retain a margin of safety by insisting that the collateral value exceed the amount of the loan at all times.

field warehouse
An arrangement in which a warehouse company rents space in a borrower's plant in order to store inventory used as collateral.

The use of a public warehouse has one principal disadvantage. It is not located on the borrower's premises and therefore may seriously disrupt production or lead to high transportation costs. The establishment of a **field warehouse,** supervised by the warehouse company, is one way to avoid these pitfalls. In such an arrangement, the warehouse company rents space in the borrower's plant for the purpose of storing the collateral. Here too, all withdrawals require the prior approval of the lender.

SUMMARY

There are costs and benefits to using short-term financing. Short-term financing strategies reflect attempts by the firm to maintain some degree of balance between the durability of its assets and the maturities of the debt used to finance these assets. That part of a firm's current assets which, in essence, represents a permanent investment is often financed by long-term sources of finance. In this type of strategy the firm's net working capital represents its best estimate of the fixed portion of its current assets.

There are four major types of short-term financing: trade credit (accounts payable), accruals (taxes and wages), bank loans, and commercial paper. The cost of each of these alternative sources of financing varies, depending on the circumstances.

Trade credit is a self-adjusting source of financing that tends to expand and contract along with sales. For many small firms, trade credit is their primary, and sometimes their only, source of short-term financing. As was emphasized in Chapter 17, the absence of an explicit interest charge for such credit is illusory, and the implicit cost of trade credit (foregone discounts) must be taken into account.

Although balance sheet accruals such as wages or taxes payable provide interim financing, the firm exercises very little discretion over these items.

Commercial banks are the principal source of short-term corporate loans. As lenders, banks are primarily concerned with three factors: safety, suitability, and profitability. With these factors in mind, banks establish general loan policies. Unlike trade credit, bank loans always carry an explicit interest cost, with the rate usually stated in terms of its relationship to the *prime rate*, which is the base rate on corporate loans at large U.S. money-center commercial banks.

One must calculate the cost of the different types of bank loans: interest paid at the end of the loan, discounted loans, loans with compensating balances, discounted loans with compensating balances, and lines of credit.

Very large firms, for example General Motors Acceptance Corporation, issue their own promissory notes to lenders directly or via security dealers. High-grade commercial paper is a very cheap source of financing for firms that are able to qualify for this very selective market. Typically, the interest rate on these notes is significantly below the prime rate.

Working capital (receivables and inventories) may be used as collateral for short-term borrowing:

Pledging receivables is the simplest type of arrangement, in which the company's receivables are used as collateral for a short-term loan. The firm is responsible for the collection of the receivables. Since such loans are usually *made with recourse*, the lending institution does not assume any of the risk of nonpayment of the receivables.

When receivables are factored, the receivables are sold to a *factor*, a financial institution specializing in this type of financing. In this case, the assignment of the receivables is *without recourse* and the factor is responsible for collecting the receivables.

With a blanket lien against inventory, the lending institution is given a general lien against all of the firm's inventories. Alternatively, the lender may demand a *trust receipt* in which the loan is backed by specific assets in the inventory.

In order to protect themselves, lending banks often require that the pledged inventory be placed outside the firm's control—for example, by storing it in a warehouse supervised by an independent third party. To facilitate the borrowing firm's operations, a *field warehouse* is often set up on the firm's premises to avoid delay and transportation costs.

REVIEW EXERCISE

Circle the correct word(s) in each sentence; see p. 493 for correct answers.

19.1 One *should/should not* finance fixed investments with short-term capital.

19.2 When long-term assets are financed by *short-term/long-term* debts, the debt must usually be rolled over at the end of the loan period.

19.3   A realistic strategy is to employ long-term sources to finance *fixed/liquid* assets and the *fixed/fluctuating* portion of current assets.

19.4   Net working capital is that component of *fixed/current* assets which is financed out of *short-/long*-term sources.

19.5   The reason for using short-term debt to finance short-lived assets lies in its *simplicity/flexibility*.

19.6   Trade credits from suppliers create accounts *receivable/payable*.

19.7   A firm *should/should not* consider the bank a partner.

19.8   In general, a firm will do business with *only one/more than one* bank.

19.9   Inadequate equity will *turn off/encourage* most bankers.

19.10 Banks establish a prime rate for borrowers who are considered relatively *high/low* risks; riskier firms will be offered loans at the prime rate *plus/minus* a number of percentage points.

19.11 In a discounted loan, interest is paid *in advance/at maturity*.

19.12 A compensating balance *decreases/increases* the effective interest cost of a loan.

19.13 Failure to utilize the entire line of credit *raises/lowers* the effective cost of credit.

19.14 Factoring refers to the *pledging/actual sale* of receivables by the firm to a financial institution.

19.15 Inventory is not very suitable as collateral to the lending agency if it is of *homogeneous/heterogeneous* quality and has *low/high* value relative to its bulk.

QUESTIONS

19.1   Define the following terms:
  a. Trade credit   **b.** Discounted loan
  c. Compensating balance   **d.** Line of credit
  e. Commercial paper   **f.** Factoring
  g. Field warehouse   **h.** Lending without recourse

19.2   Why is it not advisable to finance fixed investments with short-term capital?

19.3   One definition of net working capital says it is "the excess of current assets over current liabilities." Another defines it as "the component of current assets which is financed out of long-term sources." Do these two definitions describe the same thing? Explain.

19.4   "Our supplier offers a 2% discount if we pay after 10 days instead of after 30 days. Since our cost of capital is 8% per year, we never take the discount." Evaluate the preceding statement.

19.5   What are the factors banks are mainly concerned with when evaluating a loan application?

19.6   What are the factors firms are mainly concerned with when choosing a bank?

19.7   Describe the chief characteristics of the following types of loans:
  a. Loan with interest paid at maturity
  b. Discounted loan

c. Loan with compensating balance

d. Line of credit

19.8 What is the difference between pledging receivables and factoring?

19.9 What two services are performed by factors?

19.10 If you were a banker, what characteristics would you like a firm's inventory to have in order to accept it as security for a loan? Explain.

PROBLEMS

19.1 **Effective interest.** Which would you prefer: a 6-month loan at an annual interest of 5% compounded monthly, or a discounted loan of 5%?

19.2 **Effective interest.** Which would you prefer: a 3-year loan at a straight interest of $r\%$ per year or an interest of $s\%$ per year, compounded monthly? Answer the question for the following pairs of alternatives:

a. $r = 6\%, s = 5.9\%$ **b.** $r = 6.2\%, s = 6\%$

c. $r = 6.1\%, s = 6.1\%$

19.3 **Type of loan.** You need to borrow $10,000 for 3 months. Which do you prefer: a discounted loan at an annual interest rate of 8.75%, or a loan at 8.6% with the interest paid at the end of 3 months?

19.4 **Type of loan.** You would like to borrow $1,000 for 1 year. Your neighborhood bank offers you the following choices:

a. A loan with simple interest of 8% per annum

b. A loan with 7.5% interest, compounded monthly

c. A discounted loan at an interest rate of 7.5%

Which would you choose?

19.5 **Type of loan.** The Norfolk Corporation needs to borrow approximately $280,000 for 6 months. A bank offers a choice of the following three types of loans:

a. Stated interest of 9%, with a required compensating balance of 20%

b. A discounted loan at a stated rate of 8.5%, with a 15% compensating balance

c. A line of credit of $1 million with 0.15% commitment fee, payable in advance on the unused funds, and a stated interest rate of 8%

Which loan should Norfolk choose?

19.6 **Type of loan.** The Soufolk Company needs to borrow approximately $70,000 for 6 months. The bank offers a choice of the following three types of loans:

a. Stated interest rate of 10.5%, with a required compensating balance of 10%

b. A discounted loan at an interest rate of 10%, with a 15% compensating balance

c. A line of credit of $100,000 for a 0.35% commitment fee payable in advance on the unused funds, and a 9.5% interest rate

Which loan should Soufolk choose?

19.7 **Terms of credit.** A firm whose cost of capital is 10% is offered credit terms on a $100,000 purchase of 2/10 net 30. The firm pays on day 7. What does this policy decision cost the firm?

19.8   Factoring. The Wesfolk Corporation enters into a factoring agreement under which it sells its receivables of $50,000, which represent sales that were made on a net 90-day basis. The agreement with the factor stipulates the payment of a 1.5% commission on the face value of the receivables, and a 9% anticipation charge. Furthermore, 12% of the value of the receivables is withheld as a reserve that will be paid only after 90 days. What is the effective interest cost of the "loan component" of the factoring agreement? What is the total cost of the factoring agreement?

19.9   Factoring. Easfolk & Co. enters into a factoring agreement under which it sells its receivables of $250,000, which represent sales that were made on a net 60-day basis. The agreement with the factor stipulates the payment of a 2.5% commission on the face value of the receivables, and a 7% anticipation charge. Furthermore, 20% of the value of the receivables is withheld as a reserve, and will be paid only after 90 days. What is the effective interest cost of the "loan component" of the factoring agreement? What is the total cost of the factoring agreement?

19.10   Type of loan, computer problem. What are the effective yearly interest rates of the following loans:

	Amount	Length (days)	Interest	Discounted	Compensating Balance	Line of Credit	Commitment Fee
A	45,365	125	8.128%	No	16.0%	None	
B	389,003	330	11.050	Yes	12.5	600,000	.24%
C	211,530	189	9.979	Yes	18.3	225,000	.41
D	93,284	36	12.333	No	6.7	100,000	.12

SAMPLE PROBLEM

SP19.1 The Melissa Company needs to borrow approximately $150,000 for 1 year. The bank offers the company a choice of the following three types of loans:

a. Stated interest of 7%, with a compensating balance of 15% of the amount loaned

b. A discounted loan at a stated interest rate of 6.5%, and a 20% compensating balance

c. A line of credit of $250,000 for a 1% commitment fee payable in advance on the unused funds, and a 7% stated interest rate.

Which loan should Melissa choose?

Solution to Sample Problem

SP19.1   a. Here Melissa receives only $127,500 ($150,000 − 22,500), and pays $10,500 in interest (7% × 150,000). Hence, the effective interest rate is:

$$\frac{\$10,500}{\$127,500} = 8.24\%$$

b. In this case Melissa pays $9,750 interest (6.5% × 150,000) in advance, and there is a $30,000 compensating balance on the loan. The available proceeds ($150,000 − 30,000 − 9,750) come to $110,250. Thus the effective interest rate on the loan is:

$$\frac{9,750}{110,250} = 8.84\%$$

c. With this type of loan, Melissa pays $10,500 in interest (7% × 150,000), and also pays a commitment fee on the unused portion of the credit line. The unused portion is $100,000, so the commitment fee is $1,000. Total charges amount to $11,500, and the effective interest rate is:

$$\frac{11,500}{150,000} = 7.67\%$$

Melissa should take the type (c) loan, since it offers the lowest effective interest rate, as well as the option of borrowing an additional $150,000.

Answers to Review Exercise

19.1 should not **19.2** short-term **19.3** fixed, fixed **19.4** current, long

19.5 flexibility **19.6** payable **19.7** should not **19.8** more than one

19.9 turn off **19.10** low, plus **19.11** in advance **19.12** increases

19.13 raises **19.14** actual sale **19.15** heterogeneous, low

SUGGESTIONS FOR FURTHER READING

The financing model presented in the text has been confirmed by Robert Taggert, "A Model of Corporate Financing Decisions," *Journal of Finance*, December 1977, who found empirical support for the hypothesis that firms use long-term debt to finance fixed investment and the permanent portion of inventories, short-term debt being used to finance transitory inventories and liquid assets.

Useful overviews of working capital policy are given by Steven F. Maier and James H. Vander Weide, "A Practical Approach to Short-Run Financial Planning," *Financial Management*, Winter 1978; and Keith V. Smith, *Guide to Working Capital Management* (New York: McGraw-Hill, 1979).

Short-term financing is examined in much greater detail by D. A. Hays, *Bank Lending Policies, Domestic and International* (Ann Arbor: University of Michigan, Bureau of Business Research, 1971); and L. A. Moskowitz, *Modern Factoring and Commercial Finance* (New York: Crowell, 1977).

20 | Convertibles, Warrants, Options, and Leasing

In Chapters 12 and 13 the main features of common stock, preferred stock, and long-term bonds were examined. In this chapter we first take a brief look at two alternative means used by firms to enhance the appeal of their fixed income securities: convertibles and warrants. We then go on to a discussion of options trading, and spell out some of the implications of the use of options for interpreting the salient characteristics of financial assets. Although options are not a source of corporate financing, the existence of an organized market in which options contracts are traded provides a valuable benchmark for evaluating the "contingent claims" embodied in many corporate securities. We conclude our survey with a discussion of the main features of a popular alternative to debt-financing, the long-term leasing of corporate assets.[1] Both the theory and practice of financial management have been influenced by such innovations in the long-term capital market. This chapter gathers together the more important ones: convertibles, warrants, options, and financial leases. Each of these topics deserves a more comprehensive treatment than we are able to give in this chapter. However, with a bit of effort, you should be able to gain some useful insights into the complexities of modern financial management.

CONVERTIBLES

convertible security
A bond or preferred stock that can be exchanged for common stock.

A **convertible security** is a bond or preferred stock that can be exchanged, at the option of its holder, for a given number of shares of common stock.

---

[1] All the topics covered in this chapter are important and deserve more detailed treatment. The interested reader can find a more advanced treatment of leasing and option securities in Haim Levy and Marshall Sarnat, *Capital Investment and Financial Decisions*, 3rd ed. (Englewood Cliffs, NJ: Prentice-Hall International, 1986).

Convertible securities are a source of long-term funds when they are sold to the public. However, their conversion into common stock subsequent to their issue does *not* provide additional capital to the firm. Upon conversion, debt (or preferred stock) is replaced by common stock. But the reduction in leverage such a swap implies improves the firm's debt-equity ratio, thereby paving the way for additional debt financing.

Some Basic Definitions

The number of shares of common stock which a convertible security can be exchanged for is called the *conversion ratio (CR)*. A closely related concept is the convertible security's *conversion price (CP)*, which is the effective price paid for the common stock received via conversion. The conversion price can be calculated by dividing the convertible security's face value by the conversion ratio:

$$\text{conversion price } (CP) = \frac{\text{face value of convertible security}}{\text{conversion ratio } (CR)}$$

Thus, for example, a $1,000 convertible bond that can be exchanged for 20 shares of common stock has a conversion price of $50 ($1,000/20 = $50). Of course, the essence of convertibles is that the conversion price is set *above* the current market price of common stock at the time of issue.

The security's *conversion value (CV)* is defined as the market value of the common stock received by converting the security. At any point in time the conversion value can be calculated by multiplying the conversion ratio (number of shares to be received via conversion) by the current market price of the shares. Thus, in the case of our convertible bond with $CR = 20$ shares, its conversion value depends on the market price of the shares. For example, if share price is $60, the bond's conversion value will be $1,200 (20 × $60 = $1,200).

Figure 20–1 reproduces the tombstone advertisement for MCI Communications Corporation's issue of convertible bonds. The bonds had a face value of $1,000, a conversion ratio of 38.99 shares of common stock for each $1,000 of principal. Hence their conversion price was $25.65 per share:

$$\text{conversion price} = \frac{\$1,000}{38.99} = \$25.65$$

The special feature of this issue, therefore, is that should the market price of MCI common rise significantly above the conversion price (above $25.65), the conversion value of the bond will also increase.

Market Value of Convertibles

For convenience, let's consider the specific case of a convertible bond. Its market price depends on its value as a "straight" bond, i.e., its value *without* the conversion option, and on its conversion value. The latter is the current market value of the shares which are received if the bond is converted. In effect, the price of the convertible bond has two *lower bounds*. First, compe-

**FIGURE 20–1
Tombstone
Advertisement
for MCI**

This announcement is neither an offer to sell nor a solicitation of an offer to buy any of these securities.
The offer is made only by the Prospectus.

MCI

$100,000,000

MCI Communications Corporation

10¼% Convertible Subordinated Debentures due August 15, 2001

Interest Payable February 15 and August 15

The Debentures are convertible into shares of MCI Common Stock at $25.65
per share (equivalent to a conversion rate of 38.99 shares of Common Stock
for each $1,000 principal amount of Debentures), subject to certain adjustments.

Price 100%

(Plus accrued interest from August 15, 1981)

*Copies of the Prospectus may be obtained in any State from only such of the undersigned
and the other several underwriters as may lawfully offer the securities in such State.*

Shearson Loeb Rhoades Inc.   Drexel Burnham Lambert
                                                        Incorporated

Bache Halsey Stuart Shields   Bear, Stearns & Co.   Dillon, Read & Co. Inc.
        Incorporated

E. F. Hutton & Company Inc.   Kidder, Peabody & Co.   Lazard Frères & Co.
                                            Incorporated

Lehman Brothers Kuhn Loeb   L. F. Rothschild, Unterberg, Towbin
        Incorporated

Salomon Brothers   Wertheim & Co., Inc.   Dean Witter Reynolds Inc.

        Sanford C. Bernstein & Co., Inc.   Hambrecht & Quist tition in the bond market will ensure that the convertible can never sell for a price below its value as a straight bond, which is given by the present value of its cash flow using the appropriate market interest rate. You should note, however, that this floor is flexible: if market interest rates rise subsequent to the issue or if the firm's default risk rises, the straight bond value can fall drastically. Second, the convertible can never sell for less than its conversion value. If it did, investors could gain by converting the bond immediately and selling the shares in the market.

To sum up, the price of the convertible cannot fall below the *higher* of its two lower bounds—its straight bond value or its conversion value. If the firm's performance is poor, the straight bond value provides the effective floor; if its performance is good and share prices rise, the conversion value will be the effective lower bound. However, the actual value of the convertible bond is *higher* than the effective lower bound. This difference reflects the value of the conversion option (see below). Thus, we expect that the actual market price of the convertible will always be higher then its lower bounds—except, of course, at maturity, at which time the option runs out.

Why Firms Issue Convertibles

Firms usually issue convertible bonds (preferred stock) for one of two reasons:

1. Some managers view convertibles as "cheap debt," since the interest coupon on the convertible can be set lower than that of an equivalent straight bond and with fewer restrictive provisions. But as we have already noted, a convertible bond is a package that combines a straight debt with an option. Hence the convertible is cheap *only* if its issue price overvalues the conversion option.

2. Many managers view convertibles as a way of selling common stock at deferred prices.

Convertible bonds are often issued when ordinary bonds require the payment of what appears to the firm to be too high an interest rate. By adding the possibility of future conversion into common stock at a specified price (the conversion price), the company allows investors to share in the firm's future prospects and therefore may be able to set a lower interest rate. The issuing company hopes that investors in the convertible bonds will be willing to accept a lower return on the bonds in exchange for the opportunity to share in the future price appreciation of the stock. However, since the conversion price is set above the current market price of the stock, the purchaser of the convertible cannot benefit from the rise in share prices unless the conversion price is surpassed.

Firms that issue convertibles for the purpose of raising equity view such a security as a device which permits the raising of funds *today* at *tomorrow's* (presumably) higher stock prices. In such cases, management turns to convertibles because there is reason to believe that residual equity capital can be raised *indirectly* on more favorable terms to the issuing corporation than can be obtained via a direct offering of common stock. This is especially true for a firm whose performance is momentarily below normal and that would, under the circumstances, have to offer new shares at an exceptionally low price. But of course, unless share prices rise sufficiently, investors will not convert their bonds, and the firm may end up holding debt. For this reason, a convertible issue is a relatively unreliable method for a firm that feels it needs additional equity.

Another factor affecting the use of convertibles has been the growth of institutional investors to the point where they now represent a dominant force in the capital market. A corporation contemplating a bond or a preferred stock issue must take into account the attitude of institutional investors regarding the attractiveness of the convertible type contract. To the life insurance investor, for example, convertibles offer a contract combining fixed income with some common stock profit potential. Thus, the use of convertibles has the advantage of offering institutional investors a "straddle position" between senior and residual equities. Finally, a particular class of convertibles, convertible preferred stock, is widely used in mergers (see Chapter 21).

Drawbacks of Convertible Financing

As we have just noted, if stock prices do not rise sufficiently, the firm may get stuck with unwanted debt. This is a very serious drawback of convertible bonds for firms that need to raise additional equity. Of course, had it been known with *certainty* that a firm's stock price would not rise, a better strategy might have been to issue stock even if the current price is low, rather than issue convertible bonds that are never converted. But in finance, uncertainty is the name of the game; and hindsight, however sharp, cannot serve as a guide for financial decisions.

Another drawback is the possibility of an *overhang*, the possibility that investors will not convert the bonds even if stock prices do rise. To avoid this, the terms of a convertible security almost always contain a *call provision* (see Chapter 13) which permits the firm to redeem its bonds at a time of its own choosing at a specified price. If share prices rise sufficiently, the firm can force conversion.

Consider the following example: a bond which is convertible into 10 common shares is selling at $1,000 (hence, the conversion ratio is 10 for 1, and the conversion price is $100). The bonds are subject to a *call price* of $1,050. Should the market price of the common stock rise to $110, the firm may call its bonds (the bonds would have to be returned in exchange for $1,050). Since the conversion value of the bonds at a market price of $110 is $1,100, it pays investors to convert their bonds into common stock rather than return them to the firm under the call provision. In this instance, the firm has "forced" the conversion of the debt into equity by "calling" the bonds. This, in turn, gets rid of the overhanging convertibles and paves the way for additional debt financing.

On the surface, it might appear that the use of convertible securities dilutes the equity of the common shareholder. In this context, it should be noted that there is a legal requirement to take into account outstanding warrants and convertibles when reporting earnings. For many investors, earnings per share (EPS) is an important indicator of the desirability of purchasing common stock. However, EPS would be grossly overstated if a sizable amount of convertibles is outstanding. Should conversion occur in large numbers, the available earnings will have to be spread over a much larger number of shares, reducing EPS. As a result, the SEC requires firms to report the *fully diluted EPS*, in addition to ordinary EPS.

To calculate fully diluted EPS, available earnings are divided by the total number of common stock shares, on the assumption that all convertibles are converted and all warrants exercised. However, to offset the charge of dilution, it should be recalled that the corporation typically receives a payment for the conversion option in the form of a higher price (or lower interest rate) on the convertible security. This compensation must be weighed against possible residual equity dilution.

To sum up, convertibles offer the corporation a chance to raise *present* capital in return for a special privilege which may or may not turn out to be profitable. Thus, in one sense convertibles provide cash today in return for a gamble on the future.

WARRANTS

At times, there may be an uneasiness in the market about the economic outlook in general, or about the potential of the firm in question; or the firm may be a young and unknown company with no proven track record, or it may have had a string of bad years. In such cases, financial managers may not be able to issue shares at all, and/or may have a hard time raising money in the bond market at reasonable prices and interest rates. One strategy is to add an extra incentive for investors in the firm's securities in the form of warrants, as a "sweetener," in the hope that investors will consider accepting a lower interest rate on a bond, or a lower dividend yield on a preferred stock. However, since the 1970s, financially strong firms like AT&T have made increasing use of warrants to raise additional capital.

warrant
A piece of paper that gives a purchaser the option to buy a certain number of shares of the company's common stock at a stated price on or before a given date.

A **warrant** is simply a piece of paper, usually attached to a bond, which gives the purchaser of the bond the option to buy a certain number of shares of the company's common stock at a stated price on or before a given date. In most cases the warrants are *detachable*; they can be detached from the bond and sold (and traded) separately. Thus, the investor in the bond is given the option of buying the firm's common stock at a predetermined price. Should the market price of the company's shares rise above this predetermined *exercise price,* he or she can exercise the option to obtain stock, and consequently make a profit.

Warrants are often issued for relatively long periods of time, such as for the life of a long-term bond, so their holders are protected against stock splits and stock dividends by means of an adjustment of the exercise price. On the other hand, holders of warrants are not entitled to receive cash dividends.

Today, virtually all warrants are *detachable,* so their exercise requires a payment of cash that brings in additional capital. The bond to which they were originally attached is not redeemed when the warrant is exercised. Hence, unlike convertibles, warrants represent additional financing, and not a switch of securities. In fact, some firms have raised capital by issuing warrants directly to investors. Warrants have the further advantage of providing equity funds at times when the firm's share prices are rising. This often coincides with periods of corporate expansion in which the need for funds is great. But warrants that never reach their exercise price have no impact on the firm, beyond their influence on the terms of the original bond issue.

Generally speaking, warrants can be exchanged for common stock. However, during times of highly volatile interest rates, some firms sold warrants that gave their holders the option to purchase the firm's *notes* at a given interest rate and price over a fixed period of time.

Valuing Warrants

The way a warrant works can be clarified by looking at the following numerical example:

On January 1, the Acme Company's common stock is selling at $25, and the company sells bonds with detachable warrants which entitle their owners to buy 1 share of Acme stock at a price of $28, on or before December 31. Should the share price rise before December 31, say to $35, bondholders can exercise the right to buy a share at the price of $28. If they then resell immediately, the investors will make a $7 profit on each warrant they exercise. Should the price of the shares fail to rise above $28 during the year, the warrants will expire unexercised. No bondholder will want to purchase a share for $28, since they can be bought for less on the open market.

Share Price on December 31	Investors' Action	Profit	
If $35	Buy at $28	$7	25%
If $27	Do nothing	0	0

Obviously, warrants have an economic value, and this is why they can be and are traded by themselves. In fact, two types of warrant prices can be identified: *theoretical value* (lower bound) and *actual market price*. The theoretical value is the mathematical valuation of the warrant; in our example, the theoretical value on December 31 is $7, since the underlying stock is selling in the market for $35, i.e., $7 more than the exercise price. (If the underlying stock price rises to less than $28, the difference on December 31 would be negative, and the warrants would have no economic value as the theoretical value is zero.)

The term "theoretical value" is used by most financial analysts, but it can be misleading. In essence, the theoretical value constitutes a *lower bound,* a floor below which the price of the warrants cannot fall (see Figure 20–2). The heavy black line of Figure 20–2 is the lower bound. Note that as long as the share price is below the exercise price, the warrants have zero theoretical value; at share prices above the exercise price, the theoretical value of the warrants is positive. This constitutes the lower bound for the price of the warrants; at a lower price, it would pay to buy warrants, to exercise them and sell the stock for an immediate profit.

The actual price of the warrants, before their expiration, lies above the lower bound. This reflects the value to investors of the option to purchase the common stock at the fixed exercise price. However, as the final expiration date approaches, the actual price comes ever closer to the theoretical lower bound. We will return to the valuation of warrants in the section on options below.

Since the actual market price of a warrant usually exceeds its so-called theoretical value, some additional incentive is required to induce investors to exercise their warrants rather than sell them in the market. Three considerations operate to encourage the exercise of warrants: (1) If the warrants have any value (the market price of the stock is above the exercise price), and the warrants are about to expire, they will certainly be exercised; (2) Since the warrants are not entitled to dividends, a rise in dividends provides an incentive to exercise the warrants; (3) Finally, some firms set a rising scale for the exercise price. After a given date, the exercise (like a call price) is raised. Many warrant holders will want to exercise their warrants before the increase in the exercise price.

**FIGURE 20–2
Warrant Valuation
Model**

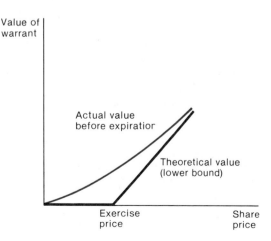

OPTIONS

options
Contracts that give their owners the right to buy or sell a particular stock for a fixed price on or before a given date.

In the last two sections we discussed warrants and convertible securities. Actually, these two financial instruments are just special cases of another financial instrument, **options**. The latter, however, are part of the secondary market for securities (see Chapter 3). The trading of options, unlike the exercise of warrants and the sale of convertible securities, does *not* constitute new financing, nor does the firm have anything to do with the options market. Despite this, options have become increasingly important for corporate decision-making, since many types of financial assets (bonds, warrants, rights) can be analyzed using insights drawn from an option valuation model.

Options are contracts that give their owners the right to buy or sell a particular stock for a fixed price on or before a specified date in the future. Although there are only two basic options types—a *call* and a *put*—the number of possible investment strategies in the options market is quite large and keeps increasing with the introduction of new investment combinations. However, before examining the significance of options for financial management, you should become familiar with the basic terminology of the options market:

- [ ] *Underlying stock* is the common stock involved in the option contract.
- [ ] *Striking price* (or *exercise price*) is the price at which the underlying stock may be bought (in the case of a call option) or sold (in the case of a put option).
- [ ] *Expiration date* (or *maturity date*) is the latest date on which the option can be exercised.
- [ ] *European option* is an option that can be exercised *only* at the maturity date.
- [ ] *American option* is an option that can be exercised at any time *not later* than the maturity date.[2]

Call Options

call option
The right to buy a given number of shares of underlying stock at a given price on or before a given date.

American calls constitute the most prominent type of option. A **call option** is a right (but not an obligation!) to *buy* a given number of shares of the underlying stock at a given price (striking price) on or before a specific date (the expiration date). The interesting feature about call options is that the option buyer does *not* need to exercise his right to buy the underlying stock;

---

[2] Surprisingly, in the absence of dividends, the greater flexibility of the American call has no economic value. It can be shown that it never pays to exercise an American call before the expiration date. Hence the popular dictum that a call option is worth more "alive than dead." The intuitive explanation for this paradoxical result is that the market price for a call option has two components: (a) the immediate profit if exercised, and (b) the additional profit should the price of the stock rise between the present date and the expiration date. If the option is exercised, the investor gets benefit (a) but gives up benefit (b). Hence it never pays to take advantage of the early exercise afforded by American calls.

he may decide to waive his right on the expiration date. When will an investor decide to do so? If the price of the underlying stock on the market is *lower* than the striking price of the option, he will not exercise his right. For example, if he bought an option to buy 100 shares of ABC's stock on or before December 31, at a striking price of $12 per share, and on December 31 the market price of ABC's stock is only $11, he will prefer to buy on the open market, if at all, rather than to exercise his option.

In general, call options are protected against splits and stock dividends, but not against cash dividend distributions. Thus, if a stock dividend reduces the stock price, the striking price of the option is also appropriately adjusted. No such adjustment is made following a cash dividend. In actual practice, the expiration date of an option is the third Saturday of the month, but for simplicity we assume that all options expire at the end of the month.

The logic of a call option can be clarified by considering a specific example. On October 31, 1984, a call on General Motors stock, with an expiration date on the last day of December 1984, and a striking price of $65, traded on the Chicago Board of Options Exchange (CBOE) for $15.50 (line one of Table 20–1). The market price of the underlying stock on that date was $80.25. Thus, the holder of the call option was entitled to buy a share of GM stock for $65 at any time before the end of December 1984. The options are traded in the market, and in our particular example, the price of that call on GM stock was $15.50. The price of the option *plus* the striking price was slightly higher than the market price of the stock ($80.50 compared to $80.25).

On the same day, a November call on Control Data stock, with a striking price of $40, traded for only 25 cents. The market price for the underlying stock was $32.75 on that day. The option's price in this case was very low, since there was only a very small chance that the market price of the stock would rise in the relatively short period of one month to over $40. Recall that a call option is a *right* to buy the underlying stock, but not an obligation. Thus, if the price of the stock remains below $40 until the expiration date, the call value will drop to zero. No rational investor will exercise

TABLE 20–1   Calls on General Motors Corporation Common Stock

Stock Price ($)	Striking Price ($)	Call Prices for Various Expiration Dates ($)		
		December 1984	March 1985	June 1985
80-1/4	65	15-1/2	*r*	*s*
80-1/4	70	10-5/8	10-3/4	11-3/8
80-1/4	75	5-5/8	7-1/8	8-1/4
80-1/4	80	2-1/2	4-3/8	5-3/4
80-1/4	85	15/16	2-3/8	3-1/2

NOTE: *r* means "not traded"; *s* means "no option offered."

SOURCE: *Wall Street Journal*, October 31, 1984.

the option at a striking price of $40 when the stock can be bought in the market for less than $40.

More than one call on the same stock may be traded in the market. For example, on October 31, 1984, 5 different calls on GM stock were traded on the CBOE, as is shown in Table 20–1. Obviously, the market price of the underlying stock is the same for all calls, $80.25. However, the striking price and the expiration date vary from one contract to another. For a given stock price, the lower the striking price, the higher the chance of making a profit by exercising the option. *Hence, for options with the same expiration date, the market price of the call option increases as the striking price decreases.* For example, for options with a December 1984 expiration date, the price of the call option with a $70 striking price was $10-5/8; for a $75 striking price, it was $5-5/8, and so on to only $15/16 for the call with an $85 striking price.

A second interesting phenomenon revealed by the GM example is that *for two call contracts which are identical in all respects except for maturity date, the call with the longer time to expiration will have the higher price* (see Table 20–1). The reason for this is straightforward: Other things equal, the longer the time remaining until expiration, the greater the chance that the price of the underlying stock will move up. This clearly increases the profit potential of the option. This property holds for European as well as American options. Thus, in all cases, investors will be willing to pay more for options with longer maturities.

Since the investor does not have to pay the striking price until he or she decides to exercise the option, the investor receives a sort of free loan. The higher the market rate of interest, and the larger the time to maturity, the greater the worth of the loan. *Hence, the value of an option also increases with the interest rate.*

If the option expires unexercised because the stock price never rises above the striking price, the investor loses *at most* 100% of the investment, which is the price of the call option, no matter how low the price of the stock may fall. On the other hand, the investors' profits from any rise in stock price above the striking price are unlimited. Since the option holder gains from increased variability if prices rise, but does not lose if things go wrong, *the value of an option increases the higher the variance per period of the return on the underlying stock.*[3]

Put Options

put
The right to sell a given number of shares of underlying stock at a specified price on or before a given date.

A **put** is a right (but not an obligation) to *sell* a given number of shares of the underlying stock at a specified price on or before a specific date. The put option differs from the call option in that the word "buy" is replaced with "sell." For example, on January 7, 1982, the price of the put written on Alcoa stock was $2 for a July 1982 expiration date. The striking price was

---

[3] The relationships above provide the foundation of the Black-Scholes option valuation formula. See Fischer Black and Myron Scholes, "The Pricing of Options and Corporate Liabilities," *Journal of Political Economy*, May 1973.

$25, while the market price of Alcoa stock on that day was $25.50. The put holder had the right to sell one share of Alcoa for $25 at any time before the end of July 1982. As long as the price of Alcoa remains above $25 the put will not be exercised, since it is more profitable to sell the stock at the higher market price. Unlike a call option, other things being equal, the *higher* the striking price, the *higher* is the put price. To understand this, recall that with put options the investor *sells* the stock at the striking price rather than buying it. Thus, for a given market price of the underlying stock, the profit potential is greater for a higher striking price. As with the call option, however, the longer the time remaining to expiration, the higher the put price, since the investor is allowed a longer period of time over which to exercise the put.

These two properties of a put option can be confirmed by looking at the CBOE data on Boeing puts in Table 20–2. The Boeing put figures reveal the following: (a) for a given maturity, the higher the striking price, the higher the option market price; (b) for a given striking price, the longer the time remaining until the expiration date, the higher the put price.

Option Trading   For each investor buying a call (put), there must be an investor who sells the call (put). Sellers of options are known in the financial world as *writers* of calls or writers of puts. Unlike the option buyers, option writers (sellers) do have the obligation, and not just the right, to fulfill their contracts. Thus, the writer of a call option agrees to sell the underlying stock to the buyer of the call option at a specified time and price; conversely, the writer of a put option agrees to buy the underlying shares at the conditions specified in the option contract.

The transactions in options are not carried out directly between sellers and buyers. All options are bought or written on the exchange through the Option Clearing Corporation. The anonymity of the participants in the transactions creates a current market for options which allows each investor to buy or sell an option in the market at any time. Normally the option contracts are in units of 100 shares. Thus, if the published quotation of a call is, say, $2 and the striking price is $30, the holder of the call will have

TABLE 20–2   Puts on Boeing Stock

Stock Price ($)	Striking Price ($)	Put Prices for Various Expiration Dates		
		January 1982	April 1982	July 1982
22-3/4	20	5/16	7/8	1-3/8
22-3/4	25	2-1/2	3	3-7/8
22-3/4	30	7-1/2	r	s
22-3/4	35	r	s	s

NOTE: *r* means "not traded"; *s* means "no option offered."

SOURCE: *Wall Street Journal*, January 7, 1982.

to pay $30 × 100 = $3,000 for 100 shares of the underlying stock when the option is exercised, and the market price of the call entitling the buyer to this privilege is $2 × 100 = $200.

FINANCIAL ASSETS AS OPTIONS

Much of the significance of options for corporate financial management reflects the fact that many financial instruments can be analyzed in terms of the options they explicitly (or implicitly) offer investors. In this section we mention only a few examples. In actual day to day decision-making, corporate managers face many financial transactions which can be usefully analyzed as options.

Warrants　Let's take another look at warrants, this time using the option approach. Warrants are similar to call options in the following respect: As we have already seen, the holder of a warrant has the right to exercise it on or before the expiration date, at some predetermined exercise price. However, unlike call options, warrants are issued by business corporations and thus involve cash flows between corporations and investors, and not between two investors, as with call or put contracts. Also warrants can have maturities of several years; options usually expire in less than 12 months. The differences between call options and warrants can be summarized as follows:

1. The maturity of warrants is usually longer.
2. In general, it is the issuing corporation that receives the proceeds from the sale of the warrants.
3. On exercise, the holders of warrants pay the corporation the exercise price for its stock.
4. When a warrant is exercised, the corporation issues stock and the number of outstanding shares goes up. The corporation gets back the warrant and hence the number of outstanding warrants decreases, vanishing completely if all investors exercise their warrants.

Thus, warrants are a financial instrument for raising money by corporations. Unlike calls and puts, which are negotiated directly between investors, warrants have an impact on corporate cash flows and capital structures. From the investor's point of view, however, a warrant is an investment some of whose characteristics are very similar to a call option, since the warrants will be exercised if and only if the stock price is higher than the exercise price.

Convertible Bonds

As we have seen, the holder of a convertible bond owns a straight bond plus a call option on the firm's stock. Thus, the value of the convertible is equal to its bond value plus its conversion value. The degree to which the price of the convertible exceeds its conversion value reflects the value of the call option on the underlying stock.

Rights

Many firms raise additional equity by issuing rights (see Chapter 12). In a right's issue, the subscription price, P_s, is normally set below the market price of the stock. An allocation ratio, N, is fixed. If, for example, N is 5, this means that a holder of 5 shares is entitled to buy, during a given period of time (usually a few weeks), one new share at price P_s; that is, at a discount. Since these rights are traded daily in the market up to their expiration date, the value of a right can be analyzed as a call option on the stock with striking price of P_s.

Insurance

Suppose that you own a house. If it is not insured and fire breaks out, what is left is the salvage value. Thus, the future value of your house is uncertain. Now assume that you buy a fire insurance contract which guarantees that you can always obtain a value A (the insured value) no matter what the market value of your house actually is—whether fire breaks out or not. In this case, buying an insurance policy is like buying a put option on the house with a striking price equal to A.

Callable Bonds

Suppose that the 20-year interest rate is 10%, and a firm would like to issue 20-year bonds. However, the firm would also like to protect itself against a possible decline in the interest rate. To achieve this goal, the firm issues a bond, say for $100, but which is callable, say at $105. If the interest rate should fall, the firm can call its bonds and issue new bonds at the lower rate. Thus, the firm has a call option to buy back the bonds at a striking price of 105. Here again option models can be used to evaluate the callability property of a bond.

LEASING

lease
A contract in which the lessor grants to the lessee the use of the property's services for a specified period of time.

Throughout the book we have assumed that the firm acquires needed assets by purchasing them. But for many years, the leasing of assets has been a significant alternative to outright ownership. In general, a **lease** can be defined as a contractual relationship in which the owner of the asset or property *(the lessor)* grants to a firm or person *(the lessee)* the use of the property's services for a specified period of time. In a lease contract, the firm is able to use the leased assets without assuming ownership. Although the idea that leasing can provide an alternative to the use of long-term debt to acquire assets has been around for many years, it was not until the early 1950s that the leasing of capital equipment became a generally accepted method. At present, industrial leasing companies are prepared to offer almost any type of asset. The use of land, warehouses, manufacturing facilities, retail stores, jet engines, computers, trucks, or even beer kegs all can be acquired by lease.

sale and leaseback
An arrangement in which an institutional investor buys an asset from a firm and then leases it back to the firm on a long-term basis.

A popular variant is the so-called **sale and leaseback**—an arrangement in which an institutional investor, such as an insurance company or university endowment fund, buys an asset from a firm (or builds a new one to the firm's specifications) and then leases it back to the firm on a long-term basis (20 years or more).

Some idea of the magnitude of the leasing industry can be had from an examination of the rental revenues of International Business Machines, the world's leading lessor of computers. During the second half of the 1970s, income from rentals and services amounted to $57 billion and accounted for over 60% of IBM's total operating income. In 1985, IBM generated over $15 billion of income in leasing arrangements.

Aggregate data on the leasing industry are difficult to obtain, but in a survey[4] conducted by the American Association of Equipment Lessors (AAEL), members reported a total leasing volume of over $10 billion in 1980, and since the AAEL accounts for only 55% of the activity of leasing companies, this would indicate that the annual volume of the leasing industry was around $20 billion in that year. To this figure must be added the volume of car leasing (estimated at $15 billion annually) and the direct leasing activities of giant manufacturers such as IBM and the Xerox Corporation.

TYPES OF LEASES

operating lease
A contract in which an asset, usually equipment, is leased for a short period of time.

In general, the types of leases offered in the market today can be classified into two categories: *operating leases* and *financial leases*. An **operating lease** is not financial in nature and is written for a short period of time, usually for a period substantially shorter than the equipment's useful life. Durations of this type of lease run typically from a few months to a few years; some, however, run for as short as a few hours. Under an operating lease, the lessor assumes most or all of the responsibilities of ownership, including maintenance, service, insurance, liability, and property taxes. The lessee can cancel an operating lease on short notice. Thus, the operating lease does not involve the long-term fixed future commitment of the financial lease, and is

---

[4] 1981 Survey of Accounting and Business Practices, American Association of Equipment Lessors.

similar to renting. A good example of this type of lease is provided by the rental of an office copying machine.

financial lease
A contract by which the lessee agrees to pay the lessor a series of payments whose sum equals or exceeds the purchase price of the asset.

A **financial lease**, on the other hand, is a contract by which the lessee agrees to pay the lessor a series of payments whose sum equals or exceeds the purchase price of the asset. Typically, the total cash flows from the lease payments, the tax savings, and the equipment's residual value will be sufficient to pay back the lessor's investment and provide a profit.

Most financial leases are *net* leases: The fundamental ownership responsibilities such as maintenance, insurance, property and sales taxes are placed upon the *lessee*. And since the agreement entered into with the lessor is a long-term one, financial leases are not cancellable by either party. Some contracts, however, provide that in case of unforeseen events, the contract can be canceled but the lessor imposes a substantial prepayment penalty which will assure the return of its investment and a profit. Upon termination of the financial lease the equipment is returned to the lessor, or in some cases, the lessee is given the option to purchase the asset. In the remainder of this chapter, we devote our attention to the analysis of the long-term financial lease. Given the character of such contracts, the emphasis will be on the analysis of leasing as a "financial decision"—as a substitute for long-term debt–financing.

TAX TREATMENT OF LEASES

The tax status of a lease is crucial. To this end, the contract must be of a form which the Internal Revenue Service will accept as a genuine lease, and not simply an instalment loan called a lease. A lease having the following characteristics is likely to be approved by the IRS, thereby permitting the deduction for tax purposes of the full amount of the annual lease payment:

1. The lease term should not exceed 75% of the property's estimated economic life.
2. The terms of the lease must provide the lessor with a reasonable rate of return.
3. The contract must contain a bona fide renewal option, and this requirement can best be met by granting the lessee the prior option to meet an equal bona fide outside offer.
4. There should be no repurchase offer, but if there is, the lessee should not be given more than parity with equal outside offers.

The reason for the Internal Revenue Service's concern is clear. Without any restrictions, "lease" contracts could be drawn up which permit very rapid payments, all of which would be considered tax deductions. In effect, this would permit firms to use such arrangements to depreciate equipment over a much shorter period than its useful life. By increasing the tax deductions in early years, the firm would be receiving an interest-free loan from the IRS. And of course the firm's gain on such a transaction is the IRS's loss!

ACCOUNTING TREATMENT OF LEASES

capitalizing a lease
An accounting procedure in financial leases in which firms report lease payments as a fixed asset, and the present value of future lease payments as a liability.

The lease has been called "off the balance sheet" financing, because in the past many lease contracts permitted a firm to ignore both the asset and the lease liability in its balance sheet. Consider, for example, two identical firms, both of which have 50% debt, and whose balance sheets appear in Table 20–3. Now assume that both firms acquire the same asset, but firm A finances its purchase by a loan, while firm B acquires the use of the asset under a long-term financial lease. The proportion of debt rises in firm A from 50% to 67%, but in the case of firm B, the assets remain unchanged and the proportion of debt in its capital structure also stays unchanged at 50%. This is unacceptable, since the fixed lease payments may be considerably higher than the loan payments. In such a case, the enhanced leverage *implicit* in the lease may actually increase the firm's financial risk by even more than the loan. But whatever the size of the lease payments, they certainly do affect the firm's financial risk.

To correct this situation, the Financial Accounting Standards Board (FASB) issued, in November 1976, its Statement of Accounting Standards No. 13, *Accounting for Leases*. Statement 13 requires firms who enter into financial (capital) leases to report the leased payments as a fixed asset, and the present value of future lease payments as a liability. Firms that do not comply with Statement 13 will not receive an *unqualified* auditor's report. The procedure, which is usually called **capitalizing the lease**, eliminates the balance sheet differences between firms such as A and B of Table 20–3.

The logic underlying Statement 13 is straightforward and conforms

TABLE 20–3   Effect of Leasing on the Balance Sheet

Before the Increase in Assets

		Firms A and B	
		Debt	50
Total		Equity	50
Assets	100		100

After the Increase in Assets

Firm A (which borrows and buys)				Firm B (which leases)			
		Debt	100			Debt	50
		Equity	50			Equity	50
Total assets	150		150	Total assets	100		100

with the analysis of leverage in Chapter 14. An agreement to make a series of fixed payments under a lease contract is no less binding than a debt contract, and *both* increase the firm's financial leverage. But as we have already seen in Chapter 14, the increased leverage also increases the firm's financial risk. Recognizing this increase in riskiness, the FASB reasoned that failure to report the lease on the firm's balance sheet could mislead shareholders and potential investors by understating the firm's effective leverage, thereby understating its true risk. In the absence of the FASB requirement, we would conclude that firm A, which borrowed to purchase its asset, has a greater risk than firm B, which leased the same asset (see Table 20–3). But this is not true! Both firms are essentially in the same position, once we realize that the fixed lease payments can be (and should be) restated as an equivalent debt obligation.

From the standpoint of the lessee, Statement 13 defines a financial (capital) lease, which must be capitalized, as a contract that contains at least *one* of the following conditions:

1. Ownership of the property is transferred to the lessee by the end of the term of the lease contract.
2. The lessee is offered the option of buying the property *below* its true market value upon expiration of the lease.
3. The term of the lease is 75% or more of the property's estimated economic life.
4. The present value of the lease payments is equal, or greater, than 90% of the property's fair value at the beginning of the lease.

Leases that do not meet at least one of the above requirements are classified by Statement 13 as *operating leases*, and are also subject to very strong disclosure rules. However, in the case of an operating lease, the disclosure of the terms of the lease obligation appears as a footnote rather than in the balance sheet itself. But given the sophistication of today's financial analysts, such disclosure is likely to be sufficient to prevent anyone from being deceived by lease financing. In particular, it is not very likely that the use of leases in place of debt allows the firm to increase its optimal (target) capital structure.

ADVANTAGES OF LEASING

Many reasons are given for leasing rather than purchasing assets, but not all of them can be substantiated. The following are some of the chief claims that have been made on behalf of leasing.

Shift of Ownership Risk. At first glance, the lease appears to allow the firm to avoid the substantial risk of owning obsolete equipment. Thus, if the firm leases a computer and the agreement contains a cancellation clause, the risk of obsolescence is passed back to the lessor. However, the lessor obviously includes an estimate of the cost of obsolescence when calculating the rental payment. But the cost of "insuring" the lessor against the risk of obsolescence may be significantly lower than the comparable cost to the lessee, especially in cases where the leased equipment has alternative uses in other firms or industries. Moreover, like an insurance company, the lessor can spread the risk of obsolescence over many contracts.

Flexibility.   Relatively short-term operating leases permit the firm to acquire the use of equipment as needed. The cost of idle equipment can be avoided by not renewing the lease, so it is often very convenient to utilize a lease arrangement. However, this advantage does not hold for long-term leases in which the firm is obligated to continue its rental payments until the lease is terminated.

Maintenance.   Under a full-service lease the lessor provides maintenance; and in many cases it may be in a better position to provide such service. However, once again, part or all of the benefits of such service will be reflected in the lease payments.

Tax Advantage.   A tax advantage may be gained if the term of the lease is shorter than the depreciation period the tax authorities would allow if the assets were owned, but still meets the IRS lease requirements. In other cases, the lessor may be in a better position than the lessee to use the tax shields generated by the asset. Consider the case of a firm that does not have sufficient income to exploit all the deductions. In such a case, part of the "tax saving" accruing to the lessor may be passed on to the lessee in the form of lower lease payments.

Relief from Debt Restrictions.   Although skilled analysts are quick to recognize the fixed charges implicit in a long-term lease, some relief may be afforded from the restrictions on further borrowing, or on the use of assets, which are often imposed when the assets are financed by a bond issue or term loan (see Chapter 13).

Bankruptcy Risk.   The lease is conceptually similar to borrowing, since it represents an obligation to make a series of fixed rental payments. The impact of these payments on the firm's per share earnings is similar to that of the payment schedule of interest and principal on borrowed money. But there is one further advantage to the lease arrangement: Legal title to the equipment remains with the lessor. In the case of financial difficulty, the leasing company simply takes back the equipment. With a loan, inability to meet the fixed charges may cause bankruptcy, especially in cases where the equipment has only limited marketability.

EVALUATING FINANCIAL LEASES

Clearly these "advantages" have a price, and the degree to which the firm can benefit from them depends on the terms of the lease contract. We now turn to the problem of evaluating the desirability of leasing from the standpoint of the firm which is considering the financing of equipment or property by a lease contract.

The Cash Flow of a Lease We first consider the cash flow of the lease. For convenience, we assume that the lease is for the economic life of the asset, there is no residual value, the firm which leases the equipment pays a rent of L_t in year t, and the firm earns revenue from the sale of the machine's output equal to S_t in year t. The production cost associated with this output is C_t (labor, raw materials, electricity). The firm has no depreciation cost since it does not actually own the machine. Hence the *net* cash flow engendered by the lease can be written as follows:

$$(1 - T) (S_t - C_t - L_t) = (1 - T) (S_t - C_t) - (1 - T)L_t$$

where T denotes the appropriate corporate tax rate.

Thus the annual net after-tax cash flow generated by the lease of an asset is:

net after-tax income from the use of the asset	less	after-tax lease payment

The Cash Flow of a Purchase Suppose now that the firm decides to *buy*, rather than lease, the machine. Assuming a purchase price of I dollars and an annual depreciation allowance of D_t, the relevant cash flow of the purchase option in year t is given by:

$$(1 - T) (S_t - C_t - M_t - D_t) + D_t$$

Note that we first subtract the depreciation expense D_t in order to calculate the corporate tax liability, but then add it back because depreciation is not a cash outflow. We also deduct M_t, which denotes any additional maintenance, insurance, or other costs engendered by the decision to buy rather than lease the machine. For simplicity, we assume that the sum of all these costs (M_t) is zero. Hence the net cash flow in year t of the purchase option reduces to:

$$(1 - T) (S_t - C_t - D_t) + D_t$$

which can be rewritten as:

$$(1 - T)(S_t - C_t) + TD_t$$

Thus the annual after-tax cash flow of the purchase option is:

net after-tax income from the use of the asset	plus	depreciation tax shield

COMPARING ALTERNATIVES

The present value of the income generated by the use of the asset is not relevant for the comparison of the leasing and purchasing alternatives, since it is not affected by the method of acquiring the asset. (We are assuming that the NPV of the operating income generated from the use of the asset is positive, and therefore, we are choosing only the best method of financing the acquisition.)[5]

The *differential* annual cash flow for any year engendered by the decision to buy rather than lease is derived by subtracting the *annual* purchase cash flow from the *annual* lease cash flow:

$$- [(1 - T)L_t + TD_t]$$

Thus, the differential annual cash flow is equal to:

after-tax lease payment	plus	depreciation tax shield

The lease commits the firm to a series of annual fixed after-tax rentals, $(1 - T)L_t$. The purchase option also involves an initial investment outlay of I, but the firm gains an annual tax shield from depreciation, TD_t. Before a meaningful analysis of the two alternatives can be made, risk must be held constant. Only if the risk incurred in the purchase and lease alternatives is equated can their present values be used as a guide for action. However, as we have already seen, the lease option commits the firm to a stream of rental payments, fixed in advance, which implies using up some of the firm's borrowing capacity. In order to neutralize the financial risk differential, the

[5] The present value of the income stream is of course relevant for the decision as to whether or not the asset should be acquired in the first place. But once its NPV has been determined to be positive, the choice of *method of financing* (borrowing to purchase or lease) does not depend on the asset's operational cash flow.

analysis of the purchase alternative requires that it be partially financed by a loan that commits the firm to a stream of fixed payments (principal plus interest) exactly equal to that implied by the lease alternative.

The critical *risk-equating* payments stream on such a loan is equal to the stream of the differential annual cash flows:[6]

$$\sum_{t=1}^{n} [TD_t + (1 - T)L_t]$$

The decision to lease can be evaluated by deducting the present value of this stream of payments from the initial purchase price, I. Since the payments stream is after-tax, the *after-tax cost of debt*, k_d^*, is used as the discount rate:

$$\text{NPV of lease decision} = I - \sum_{t=1}^{n} \left[\frac{TD_t + (1 - T)L_t}{(1 + k_d^*)^t} \right]$$

If the NPV is positive—if the present value of the stream of payments on the implicit loan is less than the purchase price—then the asset should be leased; if it is negative, the equipment should be purchased.

We now apply the lease evaluation formula to a specific numerical example. Assume that the firm has already decided to acquire a given machine, but is considering whether it should be purchased or leased. The price of the machine (I) is \$10,000 and its estimated economic (and accounting) life span (n) is 10 years. The after-tax cost of debt $k_d^* = 5\%$, the corporate tax rate (T) is 34%; the annual straight-line depreciation charge $(D = I/n)$ is equal to \$1,000; and, if leased, the annual rental payment (L_t) would be \$1,500. For simplicity we assume a zero salvage value.

Should the firm buy or lease the machine? The annual differential cash flow is given by:

$$TD_t + (1 - T)L_t = 0.34 \times 1000 + 0.66 \times 1,500$$
$$= 340 + 990 = 1,330$$

And its present value over the 10-year period, at 5%, is given by:

$$DFA_{5\%,10} \times 1,330 = 7.722 \times 1,330 = 10,270$$

Plugging this into the NPV formula, we get

$$\text{NPV} = 10,000 - 10,270 = -270$$

Since the present value of the differential cash flow exceeds the purchase price, the NPV is negative and the machine should be purchased rather than leased.

Suppose the firm is offered the same leasing arrangement at a lower

---

[6] The proof that this payments stream neutralizes the differential riskiness of the two alternatives is given in Haim Levy and Marshall Sarnat, "On Leasing, Borrowing and Financial Risk," *Financial Management*, Winter 1979.

cost, for example for an annual lease payment of only \$1,000. In this case, the annual differential cash flow is

$$TD_t + (1 - T)L_t = 0.34 \times 1,000 + 0.66 \times 1,000$$
$$= 340 + 660 = 1,000$$

And the present value of the 10-year cash flow is

$$DFA_{5\%,10} \times 1,000 = 7.722 \times 1,000 = 7,722$$

The purchase price now exceeds the present value of the differential cash flow. Hence, the NPV is positive (2,278), and therefore the machine should be leased rather than purchased:

$$NPV = 10,000 - 7,722 = +2,278$$

THE LOGIC OF THE LEASE OR BORROW APPROACH

The "lease or buy" decision really comes down to "lease or borrow." If leasing represents a better financing alternative than borrowing, it becomes the preferred alternative. Underlying this approach is the idea that the implicit additional debt financing generated by the lease must be compared not simply with the purchase of the asset, but with the relevant alternative of borrowing rather than leasing. If the present value of the differential implicit fixed payments generated by the lease $[(1 - T)L_t + TD_t]$ is greater than the initial purchase price of the property (I), the NPV will be negative and the asset should be purchased. In this case, the implicit annual cash flow generated by the decision to lease (the after-tax lease rentals plus loss of the depreciation tax shield) would be sufficient to borrow an amount greater than the purchase price, I. Thus, the purchase could be financed by an *equivalent* loan, and the firm would still have money left over. Conversely, if the present value of the differential cash flow is less than I so that the NPV is positive, the lease option represents the better alternative. In this case, the present value of the implicit annual payments stream is smaller than that of an equivalent loan.

LEVERAGED LEASES

leveraged lease
An arrangement in which the lessor borrows a substantial part of the purchase price of the asset that is to be leased.

Until relatively recently only two parties, the lessor and the lessee, were involved in lease contracts. Today a new type of lease, the so-called **leveraged lease**, has come into widespread use. A leveraged lease is an arrangement in which the lessor borrows a substantial part of the purchase price of the asset which is to be leased. Such a lease can best be explained in terms of a simple diagram (See Figure 20–3).

Essentially there is no basic difference between leveraged leases and the

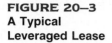

**FIGURE 20–3
A Typical
Leveraged Lease**

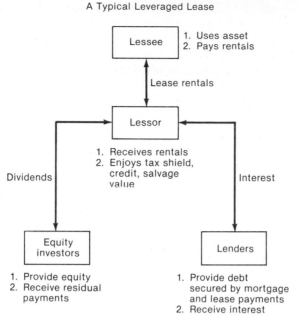

A Typical Leveraged Lease

financial lease contracts we have been discussing. Strictly speaking, the lessor always obtains the asset to be leased with a combination of debt and equity, but a third party is not involved. In the leveraged lease, lenders (other than the lessor) provide debt capital, usually secured by a first mortgage on the leased asset; in addition, the lease payments are usually assigned to the lender (or a trustee). The lender deducts interest and the instalment on the loan principal and then sends the balance to the provider of equity. Once again, the equity may be provided by the lessor or indirectly by third parties. The lessor has the benefits of the depreciation tax shield, any salvage value, the deductibility of interest payments on the loan, and the return to equity if it also provides the equity.

The leveraged lease can be a useful tool in the case of very large transactions, and/or when one company is not in a position to exploit all the possible tax benefits from the transaction. The leveraged lease provides a flexible tool for dividing the risk and tax benefits among a group of investors, no one of which could, or would, be willing to effect the transaction by itself.

The classic and often quoted example of the leveraged lease was Anaconda's decision to finance most of a new $138 million aluminum plant through lease arrangements. The company had previously suffered a $365 million tax-deductible loss when its Chilean copper mines were expropriated. Anaconda was not in a position to take advantage of the investment tax credit (which then existed) or the depreciation tax shields from the new investment. As a result, a leveraged lease of over $110 million was arranged, with the First Kentucky Trust Company acting as lessor. A number of banks and financial institutions put up $38.7 million of equity and received the lease payments (net of debt service payments); three insurance companies put up an additional $72 million of debt capital secured by a mortgage on the new plant and a prior claim to the lease payments. However, it was a *nonrecourse* loan; it was not secured by the lessor or by the equity holders. If Anaconda had defaulted, the lender's only claim was against the value of the mill (first mortgage) and a general claim against the company's other assets.

SUMMARY

Although warrants and convertibles are well-established financial instruments, options are relatively new. But interest in options among academics and practitioners has been growing steadily since the establishment of the Chicago Board of Options Exchange.

A *warrant*, usually attached to a bond or preferred stock, gives its owner the right to buy a certain number of shares in the company at a stated price. Warrants represent additional financing to the firm, since the security to which the warrant was originally attached is not redeemed when the warrant is exercised. The lower bound theoretical value of a warrant is equal to the market price of the underlying stock less the exercise price, and constitutes a floor below which the warrant's price cannot fall. However, since warrants contain a call option on the firm's common stock, the actual price of the warrant exceeds its lower bound by the value of the option.

A convertible security (bond or preferred stock) is one that can be *exchanged* for a given number of common shares under specific conditions. Unlike warrants, conversions represent a switch of securities rather than new financing. From the firm's viewpoint, convertibles are usually issued for one of two reasons: (a) as a "sweetener" to bolster an otherwise weak security; (b) as an indirect method for raising needed common equity.

Strictly speaking, *options* are really part of the secondary market, since trading options is not connected with the raising of additional capital for the firm. However, options offer important insights into many types of financial assets.

The firm also faces the problem of evaluating financial leases. The decision to lease is a type of capital budgeting problem requiring the application of present value techniques. It also has tax implications, and the relevant after-tax cash flows of the lease and purchase alternatives must be set out with great care. The correct solution requires a comparison of the present value of the loan payments implicit in a lease with the alternative of borrowing funds to purchase the equipment.

REVIEW EXERCISE

Circle the correct word(s) to complete each sentence: See p. 522 for correct answers.

20.1   A convertible security can be exchanged at the option of the *issuer/holder* for a given number of shares of common stock.

20.2 The conversion *does/does not* provide additional capital for the firm.

20.3 The conversion *increases/reduces* leverage.

20.4 The conversion price is set *above/below* the current market price of common stock at the time of *issue/conversion*.

20.5 If a firm's performance is poor, the *straight bond value/conversion value* is the lower bound on its value.

20.6 Fully diluted EPS is *higher/lower* than EPS.

20.7 If the market price of a firm's common stock *falls below/rises above* the exercise price of a warrant, a profit can be made.

20.8 The exercise of a warrant *does/does not* provide additional capital to the firm.

20.9 When the share price is below the exercise price, the warrant's theoretical price is *one/zero*.

20.10 A warrant's actual price lies *below/above* its theoretical price.

20.11 A rise in dividends provides *an incentive/a disincentive* to exercise the warrants.

20.12 A European option has *fewer/more* restrictions than an American option.

20.13 If the market price of the underlying stock is higher than the striking price of a call option, the right to buy the shares *will/will not* be exercised.

20.14 For two call contracts identical in all respects except for the maturity date, the call with the longer time to expiry will have the *lower/higher* price.

20.15 Sellers of options, known as "writers," have the *right/obligation* to fulfill their contracts.

20.16 Lease payments *can/cannot* be deducted from income for tax purposes.

20.17 If the present value of the stream of payments on the implicit loan $[TD_t + (1 - T)L_t]$ is less than the purchase price, the asset should be *bought/leased*.

QUESTIONS

20.1 Define the following terms:
  a. Convertible security
  b. Conversion ratio
  c. Call provision
  d. Fully diluted EPS
  e. Warrant
  f. Call option, put option
  g. Striking price
  h. Financial lease

20.2 Why can a convertible bond never sell for a price below its value as a straight bond?

20.3 Why can a convertible bond never sell for a price below its conversion value?

20.4 Give two reasons why firms might want to issue convertible bonds.

20.5 "I never invest in convertible bonds because the interest they yield is always lower than what I could get on regular bonds." Comment on this statement.

20.6 Why is a convertible issue an unreliable method for the raising of equity?

20.7 Why would a firm want to force conversion?

20.8 Explain the main differences between a convertible bond and a bond with an attached warrant.

20.9 "There's a value for everything. Therefore it's good to have warrants, since you can always sell them for a price." Do you agree?

20.10 Why is the actual price of a warrant higher than the theoretical price?

20.11 Explain the underlying reason why the value of an option increases with the market interest rate.

20.12 List some characteristics a lease contract should have so that the IRS will approve it as a genuine loan.

20.13 Explain the term "off the balance sheet financing," and give a numerical example.

20.14 What are the advantages of leasing compared to purchasing equipment?

20.15 Who are the parties to a leveraged lease, and what are their roles?

PROBLEMS

20.1 **Convertibles: conversion price.** A $500 convertible bond can be exchanged for 15 shares of common stock. What is the conversion price?

20.2 **Convertibles: conversion value.** The current market price of one share of common stock of the previous question is $37.50. What is the conversion value?

20.3 **Convertibles: lower bounds.** A 10 year convertible bond has yearly interest coupons of $100 and a maturity value of $800. It can be exchanged for 20 shares of common stock, which currently sell for $42 on the market. Long-term interest rates are 10%. Compute the two lower bounds on the price of this convertible bond.

20.4 **Convertibles: conversion.** A $1,200 convertible bond can be exchanged for 45 shares of common stock. Current market price of one share of common stock is $26.65. What is the conversion price? Will conversion take place?

20.5 **Convertibles: call provisions.** A $600 convertible bond can be exchanged for 12 shares of common stock. The bonds are subject to a call price of $660. The price of a share of common stock has just risen to $58. When the issuing company calls its bonds, what will happen, and why?

20.6 **Warrants.** One share of Bessel's common stock is selling at $83, and the company issues bonds with detachable warrants that entitle their owners to buy one share of Bessel's stock at a price of $96 on or before July 31.
   a. To what level must the share price rise so that the warrants will be exercised?
   b. What is the theoretical price of the warrant if Bessel's shares rise to $101?
   c. On July 1, Bessel's shares stand at $98. What can you say about the actual price of the warrant?
   d. How does your answer change if the price of Bessel's shares is still $98 on July 31?

20.7 **Options.** The call and the put options for the stock of Zeta Corporation sell for $5 each. The striking price for both options is $50. What is the cash flow on the combination of writing a call and buying a put?

20.8 **Options.** The call and the put options for the stock of Etha Corporation sell for $6.50 each. The striking price for both options is $78. What is the cash flow on the combination of writing a call and buying a put?

20.9 **Options.** On July 19, 1987, an investor holds stock of Allen & Company priced at $86-5/8. He buys a put option and sells a call option on the stock with 90-day maturities at prices of $8 and $4-1/2, respectively. The exercise price of both the put option and the call option is $85. What is the value of his portfolio, as a function of the stock price?

20.10 Leasing.   Alsop & Co. is considering acquiring a next-generation computer for $150,000. The computer's economic (and accounting) life is 5 years. The after-tax cost of debt is 4%, and the tax rate is 34%. Depreciation is computed on a straight-line basis. If leased, the annual charges are $36,000. Should Alsop buy or lease the computer?

20.11 Leasing.   Jones, Smith and Kaplan, Inc., a medium-sized law firm, is considering the acquisition of a photocopying machine that costs $6,000. The economic (and accounting) life of the copier is 12 years. The after-tax cost of debt is 8%, and the corporate tax rate is 34%. Depreciation is computed on a straight-line basis. If leased, the annual charges are $650. Should the law firm buy or lease the copier?

20.12 Leasing: breakeven point.   Consider again the "lease vs. buy" decision of Problem 20.11. How high would the annual lease charges have to be to leave the firm indifferent between leasing and buying?

20.13 Leasing, computer problem.   Consider the "lease vs. buy" decisions in the following table.

   a. Give a recommendation for each case. (Depreciation is computed on a straight-line basis.)

   b. What is the "breakeven" lease payment in each case—the annual lease payment for which the decision-maker will be indifferent between leasing and purchasing?

	Initial Investment	Economic and Accounting Life	After-tax Cost of Debt	Tax Rate	Annual Lease Payments
a.	$ 45,500	6	6.65%	34%	$ 9,900
b.	132,650	14	4.85	26	10,844
c.	7,250	3	8.33	34	2,870
d.	66,340	6	5.83	34	11,002

SAMPLE PROBLEMS

SP20.1 A $1,500 convertible bond can be exchanged for 40 shares of common stock. The price of one share of common stock is currently $39. What are the conversion price and the conversion value?

SP20.2 Bolsen & Co. is considering acquiring a new spinning machine for $260,000. The machine's economic (and accounting) life is 13 years. The after-tax cost of debt is 5%, and the tax rate is 34%. Depreciation is computed on a straight-line basis. If leased, the annual charges are $25,000. Should Bolsen buy or lease the spinning machine?

SP20.3 The call and the put options for the stock of Theta Corporation sell for $2.50 each. The striking price for both options is $36. What is the cash flow on the combination of writing a call and buying a put?

**Solutions
to Sample
Problems**

SP20.1 The conversion price is defined as the value of the bond divided by the conversion ratio; conversion price = $1,500/40 = $37.50. The conversion value is defined as the market value of the shares, multiplied by the conversion ratio: conversion value = $39 × 40 = $1,560.

SP20.2 The differential annual cash flows are $TD_t + (1 - T)L_t$, where T is 34%, L_t is $25,000, and the yearly depreciation is $20,000 ($260,000/13 years). Hence

$$TD_t + (1 - T)L_t = .34(20,000) + (1 - .34)25,000 = 6,800 + 16,500$$
$$= 23,300$$

and the present value of 23,300 for 13 years when discounted at 5% is

$$23,300 \times 9.394 = \$218,880$$

The NPV of the lease decision is

$$I - PV \text{ (differential cash flow)} = \$260,000 - \$218,880 = \$41,120$$

Since the last number is positive, the spinning machine should be leased.

SP20.3 If the stock price on the expiration date, S, is less than the striking price (E), then the buyer of the call will let the option expire, and the writer of the call will have earned the amount which the buyer paid him at the beginning of the transaction—namely, $2.50. If the stock price on the expiration date is greater than the striking price, then the buyer of the call will exercise his option: The writer must purchase the stock on the market and sell it to the buyer for the striking price ($36). The writer's profit in this case is $C - S + E = 2.50 - S + 36 = 38.50 - S$. The buyer of a put pays $2.50 to the writer of a put. Then, if S is greater than E on the date of expiration, he lets his option expire. If S is smaller than E on the date of expiration, he will buy the stock for S on the open market and use his option to sell it for S, thereby making a profit of $-2.50 - S + E = -2.50 + 36 - S = +33.50 - S$.

To summarize:

	Profit From		
	Writing the Call	**Buying the Put**	**Total**
If $S < E$	+2.50	−33.50 + S	−31 + S
If $S > E$	+38.50 − S	−2.50	36 − S

Hence, if the stock price on the date of expiration lies between $31 and $36, the investor will make a profit; at any other stock prices, he will make a loss.

**Answers
to Review
Exercise**

20.1 holder   **20.2** does not   **20.3** reduces   **20.4** above, issue
20.5 straight bond value   **20.6** lower   **20.7** rises above
20.8 does   **20.9** zero   **20.10** above   **20.11** an incentive
20.12 more   **20.13** will   **20.14** higher   **20.15** obligation
20.16 can   **20.17** leased

SUGGESTIONS FOR FURTHER READING

The pioneering study on the evaluation of options is that of Fischer Black and Myron Scholes, "The Pricing of Options and Corporate Liabilities," *Journal of Political Economy*, May 1973.

For a comprehensive review of the application of the option model to corporate assets and liabilities, see Scott P. Mason and Robert C. Merton, "The Role of Contingent Claims Analysis in Corporate Finance," in *Recent Advances in Corporate Finance* (Homewood, IL: Irwin, 1984).

For a comprehensive discussion of options trading and the implications of options pricing for financial theory, see Richard M. Bookstaber, *Options Pricing and Strategies in Investing*, (Boston: Addison-Wesley, 1981); John C. Cox and Mark Rubenstein, *Option Markets*, (Englewood Cliffs, NJ: Prentice-Hall, 1985); and Dan Galai, Robert Geske, and Steven Givot, *Options Markets: Theory and Evidence* (Boston: Addison-Wesley, forthcoming).

A more detailed examination of the lease or buy decision is given in Haim Levy and Marshall Sarnat, *Capital Investment and Financial Decisions* (Englewood Cliffs, NJ: Prentice-Hall, 1986), Chapter 21.

21 | Growth By Merger

The 1980s have witnessed a flood of corporate mergers many of which have been actively opposed by the management of the "targeted" company. These merger battles raise a number of perplexing questions. What leads a firm in the prime of life to seek the assets of its neighbor? What do *greenmail*, *golden parachutes*, and *white knights* have in common? What are the underlying motives for corporate takeovers? And who, if anyone, benefits from them? In short, how can we explain the "urge to merge" that characterizes some very stout middle-aged dowager companies as well as high-flying conglomerates.

Clearly, two of the prime objectives of business activity—profitable growth and risk diversification—can be achieved either internally, by means of capital investments, or externally, through the acquisition of existing productive and marketing facilities of other firms. Parts IV and V of the book have been devoted to internal growth. They examined the way a firm allocates its physical and financial resources. In this chapter, we take a long look at the alternative strategy of achieving growth by means of the acquisition of another firm.

TYPES OF MERGERS

For the purposes of our discussion, mergers, consolidations, and acquisitions will be treated as synonyms, although the term *merger* is often restricted to corporate combinations in which one of the combining firms loses its corporate existence. *Consolidation* often refers to the formation of an entirely new company—that is, a combination in which both combining firms lose their separate corporate identities. Three types of mergers can be usefully distinguished:

horizontal merger
A merger in which the assets of two companies engaged in similar lines of activity are combined.

Horizontal Merger. In a **horizontal merger**, the assets of two companies engaged in similar lines of activity are combined. The Great Trusts which were establish at the turn of the century (for example, the American Tobacco Company) provide examples of such mergers. Economies of scale in production, research, and management are often cited as the underlying motives for this type of merger. However, the enhancement of market power, following the elimination of competing firms, appears to have been a primary motive for many horizontal mergers in the past.

Sometimes it is expedient to distinguish a special type of horizontal merger, the so-called *circular combination.* These are mergers in which firms whose products use the same channels of distribution are combined. General Foods and Standard Brands are among the better-known examples of this type of merger.

vertical merger
A merger in which a firm acquires the sources of its supply of raw materials or other inputs of the productive process, or acquires control over the sales outlets for its products.

Vertical Merger. A **vertical merger** is one in which a firm acquires the sources of its supply of raw materials, or other inputs of the productive process, or alternatively, acquires control over the sales outlets for its products. Such combinations represent the replacement of part of the market allocation mechanism by internal organization and control within the firm. And as is true of horizontal mergers, vertical integration also raises perplexing questions with respect to the possible creation of market power and restriction of competition.

Conglomerate Merger. In this type, firms whose economic activities are relatively unrelated are combined. Such mergers often appear to have the diversification of risk, rather than the achievement of scale economies, as their primary objective. These mergers created a new type of company, the so-called conglomerate firm. Textron, Litton Industries, Ling-Temco-Vought, Gulf & Western, International Telephone & Telegraph, and Teledyne are examples of conglomerate firms.

TRENDS IN MERGER ACTIVITY

At one time or another the U.S. economy has witnessed periods of accelerated merger activity of all types. Three distinct historical merger waves can easily be identified; a fourth and most recent wave of merger activity is still going on.

Turn of the Century

From 1893 to 1904, a wave of horizontal mergers, motivated by the desire to acquire monopoly power, swept the United States. This merger wave created many of the now familiar corporate giants: U.S. Steel Corporation, the original Standard Oil Company, the American Tobacco Company, and many others. This was the golden age of the Great Trusts, and while scale economies played a role, monopolization and promoters' profits were the prime movers behind many of the most famous and largest of the mergers. In many ways, this was the most important of the merger movements for it shaped the structure that characterizes much of U.S. industry to this day. Prior to 1890, many of the nation's more important industries were made up of many small and medium-sized firms; subsequent to the mergers, they were transformed into industries dominated by a single firm or small group of large enterprises. This early wave of merger activity was brought to an end by the Supreme Court's Northern Trust decision, which clearly prohibited the creation of monopoly power through mergers and acquisitions.

The 1920s   Following World War I, the consolidation process was given a further boost by a renewed wave of mergers. If the first wave represents an attempt at monopolization, the mergers of the 1920's have been characterized by Nobel Prize laureate George Stigler as "mergers for oligopoly." These combinations attempted to restore the concentration that had become diluted over the years in many industries. However, only rarely did the percentage of the market controlled by the new firm approach that of the first wave, in which the leading firms seldom merged less than 50% of an industry's output. The Great Depression of the 1930s and World War II brought an effective end to merger activity, but not before government had intervened to discourage increases in concentration and the creation of market power.

Mid-1950s to 1970   Merger activity continued to increase during the 1950s, and by the middle of the decade had again reached the level of the 1920s. But it was in the second half of the 1960s that a virtual explosion of mergers and acquisitions (over 8,000) took place. This is about double the number of mergers during the first half of the decade.

From the standpoint of financial management, considerable interest attaches to this wave of mergers, which also ushered in the "age of the conglomerate." Motivated by the Celler-Kefauver Merger Act of 1950, which had an adverse effect on horizontal combinations, and perhaps by the theory of risk diversification (see Chapter 8), the bulk of the acquired assets during this period are accounted for by conglomerate mergers. This merger wave came to an end in 1970, which coincides with the stock market decline.

Late 1970s to 1980s   The most recent merger wave began at the end of the 1970s and has continued on into the 1980s. This latest wave has not been as widespread as its predecessor of the 1960s, but it has produced a number of very large combinations. Although many of the mergers of this period have again been of the conglomerate type, it also marks the reappearance of horizontal and vertical mergers. Two significant changes in government policy have sparked the latest increase in merger activity: (1) The removal, in 1982, of the antitrust rule against vertical mergers, and the relaxing of the U.S. Justice Department's rule against horizontal mergers in the same year, and again in 1984. (2) The deregulation of specific industries since 1978. For example, the deregulation of the banking, transportation, and communications industries has permitted a greater combination of assets than had hitherto been possible. As a result, recently deregulated industries accounted for a significant share of merger and acquisition activity during the first half of the 1980s.

Both changes reflect the Reagan administration's view that "big is not necessarily bad." As can be seen from Table 21–1, which lists the seven largest mergers of all time, the mergers of this period have involved a lot of money. As a result, financial managers often devote considerable time and resources searching for, and analyzing the economic value of, suitable candidates for aquisition. Similarly, as a result of the recent wave of hostile takeovers, some firms also devote considerable time to worrying about the possibility that some other company may attempt to acquire them.

MOTIVES FOR MERGER

As we have already noted, external growth via merger is a substitute for growth generated internally by the firm's own capital investment projects. However, a merger differs from the typical capital investment. More often than not it represents a strategic decision to enter a new market over a prolonged period of time. What are the corporate motives for choosing the option of external growth via acquisition?

Numerous reasons for seeking a merger are often cited in the financial literature; these include desire to grow, integration of production process, acquisition of marketing facilities, and so on. Although all are legitimate goals for management, it should be noted that a merger may not be a necessary condition for their fulfillment. In principle, these objectives can be achieved via the alternate route of internal expansion. If the firm decides to expand via a merger, it should do so because the acquisition of the existing enterprise is more attractive than alternative methods of achieving the de-

TABLE 21–1   The Largest Mergers, 1981–1985

Acquiring Company	Target Company	Value ($ million)	Date
Chevron Corp.	Gulf Corp.	$13,300	June 1984
Texaco, Inc.	Getty Oil	10,125	Feb. 1984
Du Pont	Conoco	6,924	Aug. 1981
U.S. Steel	Marathon Oil	6,150	March 1982
Mobil Corp.	Superior Oil	5,700	Sept. 1984
Royal Dutch/Shell Group	Shell Oil	5,670	June 1985
R.J. Reynolds	Nabisco Brands	4,904	Sept. 1985

sired expansion. For example, despite the often lengthy and tedious legal negotiations necessary to conclude a merger, the acquisition of productive and marketing facilities, via merger, may still be considerably faster than trying to produce them from scratch. This can be of major importance when a firm desires to take advantage of market opportunities.

Motives cannot be observed and measured, and as a result, a wide variety of explanations for choosing the merger path have been put forth. The motivation for merger can be divided into four major categories: efficiency, managerial considerations, undervaluation, and taxes (see Table 21–2).

Efficiency   The quest for efficiency is perhaps the most general and straightforward of all merger motives. But its very generality poses a problem. Clearly profit-seeking firms, other things being equal, will always prefer efficiency to inefficiency. It is therefore our task to differentiate that subset of efficiencies which can best be achieved by a merger rather than by internal growth.

For many firms, management and other specialized personnel constitute its limiting resource. Acquisition of another firm's management or production team, therefore, is often a primary motive for a merger. If the level of efficiency of the combined firm, after the merger, rises, such a merger represents a gain both to the firm and the economy as a whole.

Alternatively, mergers can, in some instances, be viewed as a way of eliminating bad management when the takeover is accompanied by corporate reorganization. In such a case, the merger represents a sort of "civilized alternative to bankruptcy." It is a kind of voluntary liquidation that transfers assets from a weaker, failing firm, to a stronger and more efficient one.

TABLE 21–2   Merger Motives

1. Efficiency	*Managerial Efficiency*
	Acquire more efficient management
	Replace inefficient management
	Operating synergy
	Scale economies
	Acquire technical knowhow
	Exploitation of markets
	Reduction of risk
	Improved liquidity
	Financial synergy
	Reduction of debt costs
	Increase in debt capacity
	Market power
2. Managerial	Agency considerations:
	Managerial risk diversification
	Executive compensation
	Power, size, and growth
3. Target undervaluation	Better analysis
	Insider information
4. Tax considerations	Loss carryovers
	Dividends vs. acquisitions

synergy
A hypothesis that the combined value of merged firms is greater than the sum of the two parts.

Synergy, or the "two plus two equals five" hypothesis, as it is sometimes called, concerns motives based on the claim that a merger may create a net gain to the merged firm. As a result, the combined value of the merged firm is greater than the sum of the two parts. *Operating synergy* refers to operating economies which may result in horizontal and vertical mergers. This type of synergy, to the degree that it exists, usually stems in horizontal mergers from some sort of economies of scale. More efficient utilization of capacity after the merger, cost savings from the elimination of duplicate facilities, better organization, and so on have all been mentioned as possible sources of operating synergy.

In a vertical combination, the source of the operating synergy may be more efficient coordination of the different levels of operation following the merger. Finally, by definition, we do not expect operating synergy from a conglomerate merger. The possibility of financial synergy will be examined in the section on conglomerate mergers below.

Managerial Motives

It has been suggested that managers may be motivated by a desire to increase the size of the firm because they believe their compensation will rise as a result. In this context it should be noted that executive compensation is significantly correlated to profitability and not to size per se. On the other hand, managers may well have a desire to diversify their own employment risk by means of mergers that diversify the firm's activities, thereby stabilizing the corporation's income stream and reducing bankruptcy risk. From this viewpoint, the corporate managers' principal asset is their own human capital and reputation. Since no market exists in which the risk attaching to such human capital can be diversified, managers may be motivated to diversify the firm by means of conglomerate mergers.

Target Undervaluation

If stock prices are sufficiently depressed, the acquisition of existing plant and equipment by merger may constitute a bargain relative to the alternative of investing in new facilities. In terms of capital budgeting, the net present value of the acquisition of existing facilities is higher than that of the investment in new plant and equipment, and therefore the merger should be preferred. This argument hinges on the existence, over a significantly long period of time, of imperfections in the capital market. Alternatively, such bargains can result when the assets of a firm with inefficient management are acquired through merger and later replaced.

Tax Benefits

Corporate income taxes and inheritance taxes have often provided the underlying motive for a merger. A firm with a large tax loss carryforward is ripe for a merger with a firm with sufficient current profits to ensure that the tax benefits will not expire due to insufficient earnings. Similarly, the anticipated need to pay inheritance taxes may lead a profitable but closely held family firm to seek a merger with a larger firm that has more easily marketable common stock. After the merger, the owners of the family-held firm typically will hold the larger firm's stock, which can be more readily sold when the need arises. Finally, some recent mergers reflect the fact that a firm without profitable internal investment outlets for its surplus funds may prefer using surplus cash to acquire another company to the alternative of paying an enlarged *taxable* dividend to its shareholders. This is especially the case if it feels that the repurchase of its stock, solely to avoid paying a dividend, might be challenged by the IRS (see Chapter 16).

In 1984, a sample of firms was surveyed on their willingness to expand by means of the acquisition of existing companies rather than the purchase of new assets. The proportion of firms preferring the merger route was over 40%. The surveyed firms were also asked to indicate the factors that influenced the choice between the two methods of expansion (see Table 21–3). The firms indicated that the most important reason to acquire control of another firm rather than purchase new plant and equipment was for expansion into new markets and technology. Potential synergies due to economies of scale were next in importance, followed by undervaluation of the targeted firms by the general market.

RISK DIVERSIFICATION AND CONGLOMERATE MERGERS

The rapid rise of the interindustry conglomerate giant raises questions that are difficult to answer within the traditional framework of merger theory. That horizontal and vertical mergers potentially can produce real

TABLE 21–3   Factors Considered in Acquisitions

	Degree of Importance*		
	Very Important	Moderately Important	Not Important
1. Tax considerations	23.9%	52.1%	18.5%
2. Opportunity to increase profitability through changes in management	21.2	46.7	27.4
3. Expansion into new markets and technology	66.8	20.1	8.1
4. Undervaluation of the prospective firm by the general market	40.9	47.1	8.1
5. Synergies due to economies of production	52.5	35.1	8.1
6. Increased market share	36.3	43.2	15.1
7. Diversification	26.6	37.5	31.3

* The percentages across an industry or size group may not add up to 100% because of nonresponse to this question.

SOURCE: Marshall E. Blume, Irwin Friend, and Randolph Westerfield, "Factors Affecting Capital Formation," Rodney L. White Center for Financial Research, The Wharton School, University of Pennsylvania, December 1984.

economic gains is nowhere denied; in fact, the central problem of anti-trust policy stems from the possible existence of economies strong enough to offset the socially unacceptable features of some of these mergers. Expansion by means of such mergers may create significant economies of scale in production, research, distribution, and management; the case for a conglomerate merger is less clear. The traditional analysis relating to the possible creation of economies of scale is not relevant for the *pure* conglomerate.

The portfolio diversification and valuation model presented in Chapter 8 provides a convenient vehicle for analyzing the potential gains from conglomerate growth. The essence of the portfolio approach is that a merger between *unrelated* firms can help stabilize overall corporate income because the variability of the combined income streams will be reduced following the combination of statistically independent or negatively correlated income streams. At first glance, it would seem that the pooling of unrelated income streams as a result of a conglomerate merger should produce an improved risk-return position for investors. In an efficient capital market, however, these same advantages of risk diversification can be achieved by means of individual stockholder portfolio diversification. Thus, the diversification argument depends on the existence of some sort of imperfection in the capital market.

Real-life capital markets are not perfectly efficient. For example, substantial economies of scale exist in the new issues market (see Chapter 12). Large firms have better access to the capital markets and also enjoy significant cost savings when securing their financial needs. These cost savings presumably reflect, at least in part, the reduction in bankruptcy risk achieved through diversification. If we assume that in any given year (or run of years) there exists for each individual firm some positive probability of suffering losses large enough to induce financial failure, it can be shown that the joint probability of such an event is reduced by a conglomerate merger. The possibility that the critical level of losses will occur simultaneously for each of the component companies making up the merger is less (and often very much less) than the individual probabilities.

In this instance, the diversification can be expected to create a true economic gain to the shareholders. The combination of the financial resources of the two firms making up the merger reduces bankruptcy risk, whereas combining each of the individual shares of the two companies in investors' portfolios does not. Since in this case capital market diversification is *not* a perfect substitute for corporate diversification, the merger provides a source of potential gain to investors.

A parallel argument on behalf of conglomerate mergers can be made in terms of enhanced borrowing power. The lowering of the firm's bankruptcy risk following the merger permits an increase of the firm's borrowing capacity—that is, an increase in the optimal debt-equity ratio. Thus the combined firm can increase the degree of leverage employed beyond what was possible before. As we saw in Chapter 14, this will increase the market value of the firm's shares.

VALUATION IN MERGERS

Assuming that for any of the above-mentioned reasons two firms have decided upon a merger, several formal conditions must be fulfilled. Obviously the proposed merger must be approved by the respective boards of directors; perhaps less obviously, it must also be ratified by the stockholders (usually by a two-thirds majority) of both firms. This clears the way for putting through the proposal. However, even at this late stage the Antitrust Division of the Department of Justice or the Federal Trade Commission can seek an injunction against the merger under Section 7 of the Clayton Act on the grounds that it lessens competition.

Two alternatives are open to the merging firms: One can purchase the assets of the second, or alternatively, it can assume responsibility for both the assets and the liabilities of the acquired firm by purchasing its stock. Only in the latter instance does the acquired company necessarily cease to exist as a separate corporate entity. In either case, payment by the acquiring company can be made in cash or in securities. The advantage of the latter form of payment lies in the deferment of taxes until the securities are sold.

Assume that for tax purposes, or for any other reasons, firm A acquires firm B by exchanging its stock for the stock of B. This establishes a *ratio of exchange*—that is, the price of B's stock in terms of the stock of A. Several different benchmarks have been suggested at one time or another to help the firm's management in such negotiations.

Net Asset Value

One possibility would be to measure a firm's value by net asset value per share, or book value as it is usually called. But the use of book values has some very serious drawbacks as a measure of value. Since accounting values depend on assets' historical costs, inflation makes their use all but meaningless. The sole remaining function of this approach apparently is to serve as a convenient straw man to be killed off periodically by the writers of textbooks. A more sophisticated approach would be to estimate the current **replacement value** of the firm's assets, deduct the liabilities, and thereby derive a book value figure that has been adjusted for changes in price levels. But even such a procedure is unsatisfactory. Not all the assets listed in the balance sheet have value, and conversely not all the firm's valuable assets appear in its balance sheet. For example, the adjusted book value approach may overstate the true value of the firm by including assets that may become obsolete after the merger. On the other hand, it may understate value by excluding all intangible assets for which original cost is nil—for example, mineral deposits, business connections, management knowhow, and so on.

replacement value
Adjusting the book value of a firm's assets according to changes in asset prices.

Earnings per Share

Another possibility would be to examine the impact of the merger on the earnings per share (EPS) of the acquiring company. For simplicity, consider the following example of firm A, which is considering the acquisition of the stock of firm B:

	Firm A	Firm B
Current earnings ($)	10,000,000	1,000,000
Number of shares	5,000,000	1,000,000
EPS ($)	2.00	1.00
Stock price ($)	30.00	10.00
Price-earnings ratio	15	10

What is the maximum price firm A can offer for firm B's shares without incurring an *initial dilution* of per share earnings of the merged firm? If firm A offers $12 per share (that is, a 20% premium over B's current market price), the exchange ratio will be $12/$30, which is 0.4 shares of A for each share of B. Hence A will issue 400,000 new shares to the former stockholders of B. Assuming no change in earnings of the combined firm, earnings per share of the merged company become:

Total earnings	$11,000,000
Number of shares	5,400,000
EPS	$2.04

Thus the EPS of the combined firms rises to $2.04 at the expense, so to speak, of company B's shareholders, each of whom receives 0.4 shares of stock of A for every share of B formerly held. As a result, the EPS of these stockholders falls following the merger from $1.00 to $0.82 (0.4 × 2.04). Should firm A offer $20 per share for the stock of B, the opposite result occurs. In this case the exchange ratio is $20/30, or about 0.667 shares of A for every share of B; hence 667,000 shares of A must be issued in payment for the shares of B, and initial earnings per share of the combined firm become:

Earnings	$11,000,000
Number of shares	5,667,000
EPS	$1.97

In this case, the EPS of the combined firm falls from $2.00 to $1.97, this time at the expense of the shareholders of firm A. No dilution for either party takes place when A offers the shareholder of B a price compatible with its own price/earnings ratio, in our example $15. At this price, 500,000 new shares are issued, and the earnings per share before and after the merger remain the same for all parties.

Despite the popularity of such calculations in practice, the impact of a merger on current earnings per share is a *very poor* guide for managerial action:

1. As we have emphasized throughout the book, *future* earnings, and not current earnings, should be considered in the valuation of a firm's stock.

2. Concentration on the merger's initial impact on EPS tacitly assumes that a merger is a purely additive process. This can be very misleading in cases where complementarities are expected to lead to *synergistic* growth; that is, the sum of the parts following the merger is expected to be greater than the sum of the individual contributions.

3. By far the most important deficiency stems from the fact that EPS comparisons tacitly assume that the earnings of the two firms are of the same quality; that is, they have the same risk. But this is often not the case.

Market Price Comparisons

A straightforward solution to the problems would be to compare the market prices of the two firms' stocks, since these prices presumably reflect the market's evaluation of the shares' future growth potential and risk. In our numerical example, the exchange ratio, using the market price rule, would be set at $10/30, and each shareholder in firm B would receive 1/3 of a share of the stock of company A for every share of B held. But once again, difficulties are encountered. The prices of the two firms' shares may not be strictly comparable if the one is traded in a thin market, say over-the-counter, while the other is traded on a large national exchange. Technical problems also arise regarding which particular price should be used—that of a particular day, an average over a particular month, and so on. Once again, the prices of the individual firms' shares may not reflect the full extent of the potential increases in the combined market value of the two companies following the merger. Clearly much room remains for negotiation, and as a rule the buying firm will have to offer the sellers a premium over current market price to induce them to enter the merger.

Present Value Analysis

Merger is one subject for which market values may not be a reliable indicator of value. For example, the value of the target as a separate entity can be significantly different from its value in a merger. This, of course, is the source of the *premium* over market price buying firms are often willing to pay to acquire the target firm.

One way to handle this dilemma is to treat the acquisition of another firm by merger as a special type of capital budgeting problem. From the standpoint of the acquiring firm, this requires the estimation of the merger's impact on the cash flow of the combined firm. If the present value of the benefits exceeds the price paid to the target firm's shareholders, the merger is desirable. The target company's shareholders, of course, will accept the merger offer if they deem that the proposed price exceeds the present value of the cash flows that will be generated by the target company *without the merger*.

On the surface, the present value approach appears relatively simple, but in practice this is not the case. In order to reach a correct evaluation of the target, the acquiring firm must solve a number of problems:

1. Operating synergies, which are often the motivating force for the merger, are difficult to estimate.

2. Similarly, the full impact of the replacement of inefficient managers is also hard to gauge in advance.

3. A tendency exists for buyers to overstate the value of the target's assets. For example, not all its inventories may be actually salable, nor all its receivables collectible.

4. It is difficult to tell just how the target's key personnel will adapt to the acquiring firm's management style. Moreover, a postmerger decision to trim excess staff may evoke opposition, or even a strike.

5. Even if the cash flow is assessed correctly, its riskiness must still be estimated in order to arrive at the appropriate discount rate.

MERGER TACTICS

friendly merger
A merger in which the managements of an acquiring firm and a target firm work out suitable terms that are agreed to by both firms' stockholders.

Up to this point, we have assumed a simple scenario in which one of the parties to a merger (the acquiring firm) decides to acquire another firm, which we have called the target firm. We have been assuming a **friendly merger.** In such cases, the acquiring company approaches the target firm with a proposal to merge. The two firms' managements then sit down to try and work out suitable terms. If they succeed, the plan is submitted to both firms' stockholders along with managements' recommendation that the merger be approved. If the stockholders, in turn, approve the merger, the acquiring firm buys the target firm's shares (in accordance with the terms of the agreement), paying for them with its own securities (shares or bonds) or with cash.

This description no longer characterizes the "merger mania" of the 1980s. More and more frequently, target companies have attempted to fight off attempts at acquisition, either because they feel the merger is not in the best interests of the shareholders, or perhaps out of fear for their own jobs. Whatever the motivation, we shall denote such a situation as a **hostile merger.** Since a joint working out of the merger terms is not possible in such cases, the acquiring company will usually make a *takeover bid* to the target firm's shareholders.

hostile merger
A merger that a target company resists.

Takeover Bids   Since negotiation between managements (and boards of directors) of the interested firms is not possible in a hostile merger, the acquiring firm can circumvent the target company's management by appealing directly to its

takeover bid
An acquiring firm's offer to purchase a target firm's shares.

stockholders. Such an appeal is known as a **takeover bid** or *tender offer*. Usually, it takes the form of one company approving, with great publicity, its offer to purchase the shares of the target company for a price that involves a substantial premium over the prevailing market price. Alternatively, the acquiring company might offer a package of its own securities in return for the target stock. Of course, the target company's management, if it objects, can use counter tactics.

two-tier offer
A takeover bid that provides a cash price for sufficient shares to obtain control of a firm and securities for the remaining stock.

In some cases, the acquiring firm may make a so-called **two-tier offer.** This is a takeover bid that provides better terms to shareholders who tender their shares earlier. A two-tier takeover bid might provide a cash price for sufficient shares to obtain control of the corporation, and a lower noncash (securities) price for the remaining stock. In the U.S. Steel Corporation's bid for Marathon Oil (see Table 21–1), a cash price was offered for 51% of the stock on a first-come basis. The remaining stock could be exchanged only for bonds, which presumably induced many shareholders to offer their stock immediately to ensure the receipt of cash. Similarly, in the summer of 1981 DuPont offered Conoco's shareholders cash for 40% of the outstanding shares plus 1.7 shares of DuPont for the balance.

Partial Takeovers

The hostile mergers of the 1980s led to an additional phenomenon—the *partial stock buyout.* In a partial buyout, an investor or group of investors buys a sizable stake in a company they consider undervalued and therefore a good candidate for a takeover. If they guess right and a takeover bid with a significant premium over the target stock's market price is forthcoming, the group stands to make a substantial profit. This type of speculation has been called **risk arbitrage.** But at least one of the principal practitioners of this art decided to take the risk out of risk arbitrage by obtaining information in advance of impending mergers. The use of such insider information is illegal under U.S. security laws, and in November 1986 Ivan Boesky, one of Wall Street's leading risk arbitrageurs, agreed to pay a $100 million fine to the SEC for the abuse of insider information obtained from an investment banker.

risk arbitrage
A form of speculation in which investors buy a sizable stake in a company that is considered a candidate for a takeover.

Merger Defenses

The merger wars that swept the United States in the 1980s consumed enormous amounts of time, cash, and corporate resources. Embattled managements, trying to avoid takeovers, created a virtual maze of defenses. They also created a new lexicon—the "language of takeovers." With the help of outside advisors (investment bankers and law firms specialzing in mergers), many target firms in an unfriendly merger scenario attempted to fight off the takeover by recourse to so-called **shark repellents.** These are anti-takeover corporate charter amendments, such as supermajority requirements for approving a nonuniform two-tier takeover bid that has not been approved by the board of directors.

shark repellants
Antitakeover corporate charter amendments.

greenmail
An antitakeover tactic in which a target firm pays a premium to an acquiring firm or investor in exchange for its own shares.

Another policy that has been used frequently is so-called **greenmail.**

lockup defense
An antitakeover strategy in which management gives a third party the right to buy the firm's assets.

crown jewel
A target firm's most valued asset.

Pac-Man defense
An antitakeover strategy in which a target firm tries to buy up the acquiring firm's stock.

white knight
A partner solicited by the management of a target firm to help fight off a takeover attempt.

poison pill
An agreement that gives shareholders of a firm not involved in a takeover the right to buy a target firm's securities at a favorable price.

golden parachute
Provisions in executives' contracts that call for severance pay or other compensation should they lose their jobs as a result of a hostile takeover.

This is the premium paid by a target firm to an acquiring firm (or individual) in exchange for its own shares. Alternatively, the acquiring firm may pay a premium to another competing acquiring firm (or individual) to buy back its holdings of the target firm's shares. Thus, for example, in the Texaco-Getty merger (see Table 21–1), Texaco bought the Bass Brothers' immense holdings of Texaco stock at a 20% premium over market price, apparently out of a fear that the Bass Brothers might attempt to gain control of Texaco. Many analysts consider this purchase to have amounted to the payment of greenmail by Texaco's management.

Another antitakeover tactic is the **lockup defense.** In this strategy, management gives a third party the right to buy the firm's assets in order to persuade the acquiring firm to drop its bid. This ploy is particularly effective when the targeted company offers for sale its **crown jewel**, the target firm's most valued asset.

Yet another tactic is the **Pac-Man defense** in which a targeted company tries to buy up its attacker's stock. Thus, for example, after Bendix made an "unfriendly" attempt to take over Martin Marietta, the latter counterattacked by buying up Bendix stock. This case is of special interest because a third party, Allied Corporation, came to Bendix's defense by buying enough Bendix stock to preclude Martin Marietta's gaining control of Bendix. In the language of takeovers, this made Allied a **white knight**, a partner solicited by the management of a target firm to help fight off the attempted takeover.

The targeted firm can also employ a **poison pill.** This gives shareholders of a firm not involved in the takeover the right to buy the target firm's securities at a favorable price if the takeover goes through.

But even if management gives up the fight, managers can still award themselves **golden parachutes.** These are provisions in the executives' employment contracts that call for the payment of severance pay, or other compensation, should they lose their jobs as a result of a successful takeover.

WHO GAINS FROM MERGERS?

Mergers in general, and the merger mania of the 1980s in particular, are a controversial subject. Greenmail, corporate raiding, shark repellents, and the time wasted on short-term merger and antimerger strategies have all come under attack at one time or another. Moreover, the insider trading abuses that have accompanied the latest merger wave have been the subject of government litigation. On the positive side, takeovers seem to promote a more efficient use of resources in target firms, thereby contributing to the efficiency of capital markets.

The quantitative measurement of the impact of mergers is very difficult, but the following generalizations can be supported by the available empirical evidence:

1. The market value of target firms tends to rise in takeover attempts. Selling shareholders almost always receive a substantial premium over market price. Thus, it is the shareholders of the acquired firm who stand to gain in a merger.

2. The evidence is less clear with respect to the buyers. But even if we assume that they do gain from the mergers, their gain is proportionately much less than that of the sellers.

3. The empirical evidence suggests that attempts to fight off a takeover attempt by means of shark repellents has a depressing effect on stock prices.

FINANCING CORPORATE MERGERS WITH CONVERTIBLES

In the previous sections we have often assumed that if a merger is effected by means of an exchange of securities, the target firm's stockholders receive the stock of the surviving corporation in payment. Clearly this need not be the case. The deferment of taxation, inherent in an exchange of common stock, can also be realized when other types of securities are offered in payment. One popular expedient has been the use of convertible bonds or convertible preferred stock to finance corporate mergers. The use of a convertible fixed income security has several advantages:

1. It permits a reconciliation of divergent dividend policies of the acquiring and acquired firms. For this purpose it is sufficient to consider the case of an acquiring firm that pays no dividends and an acquired firm whose shareholders wish to continue to receive their regular dividend payment after the merger.

2. Convertible debentures can also be used to avoid the dilution of earnings that occurs, after the merger when the earnings per share of one of the firms falls. However, as we noted in Chapter 20, the Securities and Exchange Commission requires companies to report their "fully diluted earnings"—that is, the EPS—assuming that all outstanding convertible securities are converted to common stock.

SOME ACCOUNTING CONSIDERATIONS

As is so often the case in finance, mergers also have some implications for the firm's accounting staff. In general, two alternative accounting treatments are available. The combination of the two firms in a merger can be handled as a *pooling of interests* or as a *purchase*. In the latter case, any payment beyond the tangible book value of the acquired firm must be shown as goodwill in the balance sheet and written off over a reasonable period of time. Since the depreciation of goodwill is not deductible for tax purposes, further net income will be reduced as the goodwill is amortized. This constitutes a psychological and perhaps an economic disadvantage of this type of treatment. A pooling of interests, on the other hand, avoids this disadvantage by combining the balance sheets of the two firms; the assets and liabilities are simply added together. In this approach neither goodwill, nor charges against future income, are created. Unfortunately, this type of accounting treatment has led to some abuse; in particular, so-called *dirty pooling*, the altering of asset value at the time of merger. As a result of such abuses, the pooling of interests method has been legally restricted to mergers of firms of roughly the same size in which both managements continue to function in the merged firm.

DIVESTITURES, GOING PRIVATE, AND SPINOFFS

To this point we have examined situations in which one firm decides to acquire the productive assets of another. Divestitures, spinoffs, and "going private" are reverse merger phenomena in which a firm is interested in getting rid of some of its assets.

divestiture
A firm's sale of a division or subsidiary to another firm in exchange for cash or notes.

A **divestiture** is a sale by the firm of a division or a subsidiary to another firm, usually in exchange for cash and notes. In one sense, a divestiture can be thought of as a sort of partial merger in which a part of the selling firm has been merged into the buying firm. The sale by International Paper of its Canadian subsidiary to Canadian Pacific, and U.S. Steel's sale of part of its coal facilities to Standard Oil of Ohio, are two examples of corporate divestitures.

Many motives have been suggested for corporate divestitures:

1. An important motive for many divestitures is the desire to generate cash for other purposes. The selling firm may wish to reduce its debt to expand into other lines of activity, to build a warchest for a contemplated takeover bid, or even to build up a cash reserve in order to fight off a hostile takeover.

2. Some companies are motivated by a desire to divest themselves of an unprofitable line of business activity, or a business that does not fit their long-run strategic design.

3. Some firms feel they are undervalued by the market. The sale of part of their assets at true market value is designed to induce the market to recognize this error and raise the firm's stock price.

going private
The purchase of a firm from its public stockholders by a group of private investors.

Going private refers to the purchase of a company from its public stockholders by a group of private owners which may include the firm's existing managers. After the transaction, the shares are delisted and public trading in the stock ceases. Going private enables a firm to avoid listing costs, which can be significant for a small firm. By concentrating ownership, more effective monitoring of managerial performance becomes possible, and this can be expected to have a positive impact on management performance.

leveraged buyout (LBO)
A divestiture in which management and other investors take loans to buy a firm from its public stockholders.

Considerable interest has been generated by a special type of managerial buyout—the so-called **leveraged buyout (LBO).** An LBO is a type of divestiture in which existing management joins with other investors to buy a firm from its public stockholders, using loans to finance the purchase. Following the buyout, public trading in the stock ceases, although the new owners can again "go public" at some later date. The key feature of LBOs has been the extremely high degree of leverage employed. A classic example of such an LBO is provided by RCA's sale of Gibson Greeting Cards to a group of investors which included Gibson's own management team for $81 million. The purchasers put up only $1 million in cash; the remaining $80 million was raised by bank loans. This particular scenario had a "happy ending"—at least for Gibson's buyers, if not for RCA. A year after the LBO, Gibson went public, and the purchasing group's original equity investment of $1 million was worth more than 100 times its original cost in the market.

spinoff
A divestiture in which the divested division is given to the shareholders of the parent firm.

A **spinoff** is a special type of divestiture in which no cash is involved and there is no shift in ownership. In a spinoff, the divested division is given to the shareholders of the parent firm. The parent corporation issues shares to its present stockholders, who remain the owners of both the parent and its offspring. The newly created entity is operated as a separate corporation with its own board of directors, officers, and so on.

The motivation for a spinoff is not always clear. Some may be undertaken to avoid certain regulatory or institutional constraints. Setting up the separate entity may also improve owners' ability to assess managerial performance, thereby providing a positive incentive to management.

HOLDING COMPANIES

holding company
A firm whose purpose is to hold a controlling interest in one or more other corporations.

In addition to the three types of company mergers, a frequently encountered form of corporate organization is the holding company. A **holding company** is simply a firm whose purpose is to hold a controlling interest in one or more other corporations, known as its **subsidiaries.** The controlling interest need not be 51% of the outstanding stock. Given the dispersion of ownership of most large modern firms, holding as little as 10% of the voting stock often provides effective control.

subsidiaries
Corporations, the controlling interests of which are owned by the same holding company.

In many respects, a holding company shares both the advantages and disadvantages of other large-scale operations, such as mergers, consolidations, or a large single company with multiple national divisions. However, the holding company is unique in several aspects. On the positive side, it permits a high degree of leverage through fractional ownership; isolation of risk due to the preservation of legal distinctions among its subsidiaries; and the ability to gain control of other firms without obtaining formal stockholder or management approval. On the other hand, the holding company is subject to multiple taxation, since dividends received from subsidiaries constitute taxable income; is often more expensive to administer than a single unified corporation; and due to its high leverage, has extremely volatile profitability.

SUMMARY

Three types of business consolidations are: (a) horizontal mergers in which the assets of two or more competing firms are combined; (b) vertical mergers in which one firm acquires control over the sources of its raw materials or over the sales outlets for its final products; and (c) conglomerate mergers in which otherwise economically unrelated firms are consolidated.

At one time or another the U.S. economy has witnessed waves of mergers of all three types, horizontal, vertical, and conglomerate, but in the mid-1960s conglomerate forms of combination became dominant. The absence in a pure conglomerate merger of the traditional economies of scale in production, research, distribution, and management raises doubts about the potential gains from such acquisitions. And in fact in a *perfectly efficient* security market the risk diversification created by a conglomerate merger would not lead to a true economic gain. However, in practice security markets are not absolutely perfect, and the possibility of gain is restored by considerations relating to the reduction of bankruptcy risk and the economies of scale in the raising of new capital which such a reduction implies.

Many business firms seek profitable growth, risk diversification, integration of productive facilities, and the acquisition of marketing facilities. These objectives, in principle, can be achieved either internally via capital investments or externally by means of the acquisition of other firms. The principal motives for choosing the second alternative are efficiency, managerial considerations, undervaluation, and taxes.

Several methods can be used to help management set a price for the target company's shares: net asset value, earnings per share, comparisons of market prices, and present value of cash flows.

The 1980s have witnessed a flood of "unfriendly" mergers in which the takeover attempts have been actively opposed by the target firms. These merger battles raise serious questions regarding the economic impact of such combinations. They also have created a colorful new language: greenmail, white knights, shark repellents, and so on.

Firms may subtract as well as add or combine through such mechanisms as divestiture, going private, and spinoffs.

REVIEW EXERCISE

Circle the correct word(s) to complete each sentence; see p. 544 for correct answers.

21.1 In a *horizontal/vertical* merger the assets of two companies which are engaged in similar lines of activities are combined.

21.2 Conglomerate mergers usually have the *achievement of scale economies/diversification of risk* for their primary purpose.

21.3 The Supreme Court's Northern Trust decision *permitted/prohibited* the creation of monopoly power through mergers and acquisitions.

21.4 The deregulation of the banking, transportation, and communication industries since 1978 has *permitted/prohibited* a greater combination of assets than had previously been possible.

21.5 External growth via mergers is a *necessary condition/substitute* for internal growth.

21.6 Synergy means that the combined value of two firms is *less/greater* than the sum of the two parts.

21.7 A merger between *related/unrelated* firms can help stabilize overall corporate income.

21.8 Following a conglomerate merger, the firm may be able to *increase/decrease* the degree of leverage beyond what was possible before.

21.9 A proposed merger *must/must not* be ratified by the stockholders.

21.10 The Antitrust Division can seek an injunction against the merger on the grounds that it *furthers/reduces* competition.

21.11 Payment by the acquiring company can be made *in cash only/in cash or in securities*.

21.12 Net asset value, or book value, *is/is not* a good measure of a firm's value.

21.13 Concentration on the merger's initial impact on EPS tacitly assumes that a merger is a purely *additive/multiplicative* process.

21.14 For mergers, market value *is/may not be* a reliable indicator of value.

21.15 Selling shareholders almost *always/never* receive a premium over market price.

21.16 If a firm purchases another firm, any payment beyond the tangible book value of the acquired firm must be shown as *inventories/goodwill*.

21.17 In a leveraged buyout, *cash is/loans are* used to finance most of the purchase.

21.18 A holding company *manages/holds a controlling interest in* one or more other corporations.

QUESTIONS AND PROBLEMS

21.1 Define the following terms:
- **a.** Horizontal merger
- **b.** Vertical merger
- **c.** Conglomerate merger
- **d.** Synergy

     e. Hostile merger   **f.** Leveraged buyout
     g. Greenmail   **h.** Poison pill
     i. Divestiture   **j.** Spinoff
     k. White knight

21.2 What are the differences between a horizontal and a vertical merger?

21.3 Why doesn't a pure conglomerate merger produce operating synergy?

21.4 Comment on the following statement: "If I were the owner of the largest firm in the industry, I would buy numbers two and three, in order to control the industry."

21.5 "Nobody would want to buy a firm with a large loss carryforward, since this is an indication of an unprofitable business." Evaluate the statement.

21.6 What synergies exist in
     a. Horizontal mergers   **b.** Vertical mergers
     c. Conglomerate mergers

21.7 "Our conglomerate simply buys firms whose stock is undervalued." What implicit assumptions are necessary to make this a reasonable strategy?

21.8 "In order to improve the risk-return position of investors, companies should merge into conglomerates." Under what conditions is this statement incorrect?

21.9 Why might a conglomerate pay lower interest rates than one of its individual components?

21.10 How can a conglomerate firm use its enhanced borrowing power to increase the market value of its shares?

21.11 How are the EPS of Jones & Co. and of Smythe & Co. affected in the following case: Jones offers 1 share of its common stock for each of Smythe's common stock. The following information is also given:

	Jones & Co.	Smythe & Co.
Current earnings	2,400,000	360,000
Number of shares	1,000,000	200,000
Stock price	24	9

21.12 What ratio of exchange will leave the EPS after the merger unchanged?

	Acquiring Company	Target Company
Current earnings	7,800,000	1,350,000
Number of shares	2,600,000	300,000
Stock price	36	18

21.13 What problems arise when present value analysis is used for the valuation of a merger candidate?

21.14 Why would an acquiring firm make a two-tier offer?

21.15 What defenses can the management of a target company employ to avoid a takeover?

21.16 Can a golden parachute be employed to defend against a hostile takeover?

21.17 Is it possible for the shareholders of a target company's stock to receive less than the stock's current market value?

21.18 Define and list the potential advantages of "going private."

Answers to Review Exercise

21.1 horizontal   **21.2** diversification of risk   **21.3** prohibited
21.4 permitted   **21.5** substitute   **21.6** greater   **21.7** unrelated
21.8 increase   **21.9** must   **21.10** reduces   **21.11** in cash or in securities
21.12 is not   **21.13** additive   **21.14** may not be   **21.15** always
21.16 goodwill   **21.17** loans are   **21.18** holds a controlling interest in

SUGGESTIONS FOR FURTHER READING

Two very useful collections of articles on mergers are available, see *Midland Corporate Journal*, Winter 1983 and Summer 1986.

Detailed and thought-provoking summaries of the empirical evidence on mergers can be found in Dennis C. Mueller, "The Effects of Conglomerate Mergers: A Survey of the Empirical Evidence," *Journal of Banking and Finance*, September 1977; and Thomas E. Copeland and J. Fred Weston, *Financial Theory and Corporate Policy*, 2nd ed. (Boston: Addison-Wesley, 1983).

The economic impact of the merger mania of the 1980s is examined by Mack Ott and G. J. Santoni, "Mergers and Takeovers—the Value of Preditors' Information," *Federal Reserve Bank of St. Louis Review*, December 1985.

A comprehensive analysis of the pros and cons of vertical integration is given by Oliver E. Williamson, "The Vertical Integration of Production: Market Failure Considerations," *American Economic Review*, May 1971.

The earliest merger wave also played a crucial role in fostering the development of the New York Stock Exchange; see Ralph L. Nelson, *Merger Movements in American Industry: 1895–1956* (Princeton, NJ: National Bureau of Economic Research, Princeton University Press, 1959).

22 International Financial Management

International financial management differs from the domestic treatment of finance because of currency, tax, and capital market variations between currencies that do not exist within a country. These differences reflect the unique cultural heritage of individual countries, which have shaped their values and attitudes toward business enterprise. Indeed, if all countries used the same currency, the same tax system, and had perfectly integrated capital markets, international finance would simply be an extension of the domestic model.

Although fluctuations in foreign exchange rates have always been a source of potential financial risk, in the two decades prior to 1970 the exchange rates of highly developed nations were relatively stable. Because the exchange rates of most major trading countries were expected to remain fixed vis-à-vis the dollar, there was little need for diversification of foreign currencies even for multinational firms. However, since that time, firms' financial managers have been faced with increasing difficulties. Fluctuations in the external value of the dollar can no longer be ignored, and exchange risk, if anything, can be expected to increase during the forseeable future. This chapter takes a look at some of the peculiarities of the international financial community and the options available to a corporation that wishes to avoid, or at least contain within manageable levels, exposure to the risk of change in the exchange rates of foreign currencies. We will try to see how the international environment can be exploited, and how the firm can protect itself from the increased risk and complexities of "going international."

INTRODUCTION TO EXCHANGE RATES

Foreign currency is a good, just like wheat, gold, or Toyotas. The demand for foreign currency reflects the need to acquire that currency to finance the

exchange rate
The price of a unit of foreign currency in terms of a domestic currency.

purchase of goods, or to make investments, in the country in question. Like any other good, foreign currency has a price, which is called its **exchange rate**.

The *exchange rate* for a foreign currency is the price of a unit of the foreign currency in terms of the domestic currency. Just as one might quote the price of wheat at $4 per bushel, one might quote the price of a British pound as $2 per British pound. The exchange rate for wheat is $4 per bushel, and the exchange rate for British pounds is $2 per British pound. Onions may cost $0.40 per pound, while one German mark (DM) is $0.50 per DM. The exchange rate for onions is $0.40 per pound, and the exchange rate for German marks is $0.50 per DM.

direct quote
The exchange rate that divides the amount of dollars required to purchase foreign currency by one unit of the foreign currency.

Calculating exchange rates in this manner is called a **direct quote**. It divides the amount of dollars required to purchase foreign currency by one unit of the foreign currency:

$4/BU of wheat $2/British pound

$0.40/lb onions $0.50/DM

Prices of any commodity can also be quoted the other way. For example, the price of wheat can be quoted as one-quarter bushel per dollar, rather than $4 per bushel. Similarly, the price of a British pound can be quoted as 0.50 British pounds (= 50 pence) per dollar, or the German mark can be quoted as 2DM per dollar. This type of exchange rate is called an **indirect quote**:

indirect quote
The amount of foreign currency required to buy one U.S. dollar.

1/4 BU wheat/$ 0.50 British pounds/$

2.5 lb onions/$ 2 DM/$

Foreign currency quotations are a bit difficult to understand. Most of us make them only when traveling in Europe on vacation. Moreover, in essence, the price of foreign exchange, as we have just seen, involves *two currencies*. In a direct quote, foreign currency (British pounds, German marks) is priced in terms of dollars; U.S. dollars are the unit of account. In an indirect quote, dollars are being priced in terms of foreign currency; British pounds or German marks serve as the unit of account.

One easy rule to remember is to always give the unit of account first; the unit of currency being priced comes last. For example, in the direct quote for German marks, $0.50/DM, the unit of account is the U.S. dollars and the currency priced is the German mark. Hence we can say the German mark is selling for half a dollar. Alternatively, in the case of an indirect quote, 2DM/$, the unit of account is the German mark and it is the U.S. dollar which is being priced. Hence, we can also say a U.S. dollar is selling for 2 German marks.

Exchange rates are published daily in the leading newspapers all over the world. Table 22–1 gives some sample quotations on March 20, 1987. Column (1) gives the *direct quotation*, the amount of U.S. dollars required to

TABLE 22–1   Exchange Rates as of March 20, 1987

	Direct Quotes U.S. Dollars per Unit of Foreign Currency	Indirect Quotes Foreign Currency per U.S. Dollar
Australia (dollar)	0.6865	1.4566
Austria (schilling)	0.0777	12.8700
Belgium (franc)	0.0262	38.1250
Britain (pound)	1.5977	0.6259
Canada (dollar)	0.7627	1.3110
Denmark (krone)	0.1451	6.8875
France (franc)	0.1639	6.1000
Germany (mark)	0.5461	1.8310
Greece (drachma)	0.00744	134.2500
Hong Kong (dollar)	0.1281	7.8015
India (rupee)	0.777	12.8700
Israel (shekel)	0.6172	1.6200
Italy (lira)	0.000769	1300.7500
Japan (yen)	0.00659	151.6000
Netherlands (guilder)	0.4831	2.0698
Norway (kroner)	0.1444	6.9250
Saudi Arabia (rial)	0.2666	3.7502
South Africa (rand)	0.4807	2.0800
Sweden (krona)	0.1563	6.3975
Switzerland (franc)	0.6518	1.5342

SOURCE: *USA Today*, March 21, 1987.

buy 1 unit of foreign currency. (The names of each country's currency unit are given in parentheses.) Column (2) gives the *indirect quotation* for the same day, the amount of foreign currency per U.S. dollar.

It is now almost the universal practice in the foreign currency markets to quote all exchange rates on an indirect basis, in which the dollar is priced in terms of foreign currency. There is one notable exception to this rule. It is an accepted convention to quote the British pound on a direct basis, as dollars per pound.

Cross-Currency Quotes

All exchange rates are quoted in terms of dollars. Even if you are a German interested in trading marks to buy British pounds, the exchange rate will be quoted to you in terms of dollars. If you wish to find the number of British pounds (£) that you can get for a German mark (DM), you multiply the rates out as follows:

$$\text{cross rate} = \frac{\text{pounds}}{\text{dollars}} \times \frac{\text{dollars}}{\text{DM}} = \frac{\text{pounds}}{\text{DM}}$$

Using the exchange rate for the British pound in column (2) of Table 22–1 and that of the German mark in column (1) of the same table, we get

$$\text{cross rate} = 0.6259 \times 0.5461 = .3418$$

cross rate
An exchange rate in which one currency is quoted in terms of another, when neither currency is the U.S. dollar.

Thus the price of a German mark in terms of British pounds is £0.3418. This sort of exchange rate, where one currency is quoted in terms of another, and neither currency is the dollar, is called a **cross rate**. Since the exchange rates of all currencies are quoted in terms of the dollar, all the cross rates can easily be computed in this manner.

Pricing Foreign Goods

The exchange rates of Table 22–1 can be used to find the cost of an American product in terms of a foreign currency. Assume that a German wants to buy a U.S. computer that costs $5,000. What is its equivalent price in German marks—how many DM will the German purchaser have to pay for the computer? The exchange rate for the dollar was DM 1.8310 per dollar (see Table 22–1). Hence the cost of the computer in German marks is DM9,155:

$$\$5,000 \times DM1.8310/\$ = DM9,155$$

Now, how many U.S. dollars would have to be paid to acquire a British sports car that costs 10,000 pounds? Again, using the exchange rates of Table 22–1, we calculate the dollar price as $15,977:

$$£10,000 \times \$1.5977/£ = \$15,977$$

The key to ensuring that the answer is correct is to make certain that the units cancel correctly. In the first case, the $ in the numerator cancels with the $ in the denominator, leaving German marks (DM). In the second example, the British pounds (£) cancel, leaving dollars.

Appreciation and Depreciation of Exchange Rates

If the value of domestic currency declines in terms of foreign currency, it is said to have depreciated. When the value of the domestic currency declines, it takes more of that currency to purchase a unit of the other currency. Conversely, it takes less of the other currency to buy one unit of the depreciated domestic currency. For example, if the dollar exchange rate goes from $0.5/DM to $0.6/DM, the dollar has depreciated relative to the German mark. Whereas one used to be able to buy a German mark for 50 cents, it now takes 60 cents. The dollar has thus depreciated by about 20%. Conversely, in terms of the indirect quote, the exchange rate has gone from DM2/$ to DM1.66/$. It used to take 2 marks to buy a dollar; it now takes only 1-2/3 marks.

The effect of a currency depreciating relative to another currency is the same as the currency depreciating relative to the price of goods. If the price of onions goes from $0.40/lb to $0.50/lb, then the dollar has depreciated relative to onions. There has been price inflation in the goods market for onions—it takes more dollars to buy a given amount of onions. The depreciation of the dollar relative to foreign currencies means that there has been inflation in the dollar relative to other currencies—it takes more dollars to buy a unit of any given foreign currency.

EXCHANGE RATE DETERMINATION

As we have seen, the exchange rate is nothing more than the price of a foreign currency in terms of the domestic currency. If we treat the foreign currency like any other good, its price will be determined by the supply and demand for the foreign currency. If there is more of the currency being supplied than is being demanded at the going price (if there is excess supply for the currency), then the price of the foreign currency will fall in terms of the domestic currency until demand and supply are equated. This drop in price means that the foreign currency will depreciate relative to the domestic currency. This decline in the value of the foreign currency is the same as the decline in the value of beef if there are more steers produced. If the supply of beef increases and the demand for beef stays unchanged, the only way the beef market will clear is if the price of beef drops.

If the exchange rate is treated as the price that clears the market for a given currency, then we must ask what determines the supply and demand of the currency. The traditional approach to exchange rate determination using the supply and demand framework views the exchange rate as the price that equilibrates the demand and supply for domestic currency in exchange for foreign currency. These "demands and supplies" reflect, in turn, international transactions in goods, services, and financial assets.

International Trade and Exchange Rates

When the United States buys goods from Germany, it pays for them in currency or in barter. If it exports as much to Germany as Germany exports to the United States, the balance of trade between the two countries is in equilibrium, and no further currency transactions are needed. But if the United States exports less than it imports, it must make up for the deficit by paying in currency. If Germany will accept dollars as payment, then the United States can pay the difference between its imports and exports with dollars. The larger the deficit, the greater the supply of dollars that finds its way into the German market. But the Germans only have a demand for so many dollars. As the United States gives them more and more dollars to meet its deficit, an excess supply of dollars is created and the dollar must *depreciate* relative to the mark.

If Germany does not want all the dollars, it can sell them to another country that has an excess demand for dollars. Such an excess demand will occur if that country imports more from the United States than it exports, and therefore, the dollars are needed to make up the difference. Germany will sell its excess of dollars at whatever price the market for dollars will bear. The world price for dollars will be determined by the net world demand for dollars compared with the net world supply of dollars. If the United States is faced with a trade deficit with all countries, then all countries will eventually find that they are holding more dollars than they want at the going exchange rate. For example, Germany may try to sell its dollars to Britain, only to find that Britain also has more dollars than it wants. The only way Germany can get rid of its excess supply of dollars is to sell them at a discount. Instead of trading them to Britain at the going rate of, say, $1.50 per pound, it must sell them at, say, $1.60/£. In such a case, the dollar has also depreciated relative to the British pound.

The exchange rate for the dollar will depreciate until supply and demand are equated. If the United States continues to finance its trade with dollars rather than with exports of goods and services, then it will continue to increase the supply of dollars abroad and the dollar will continue to depreciate.

The Monetary Approach

The *monetary approach* to exchange rate depreciation emphasizes the role of financial transactions in producing exchange rate changes. In this view, exchange rates fluctuate as a result of the willingness of individuals to hold the outstanding stock of money, rather than as a result of the flow of payments due to international trade. The monetary model emphasizes the effects of three variables on exchange rate depreciation: (1) inflation, (2) the real interest rate, and (3) aggregate income.

Inflation.   The depreciation or appreciation of a currency is closely linked to the rate of inflation. This link comes about through a relationship called **purchasing power parity**, or **PPP**. Assume, for example, that Germany and the United States both produce a compact car. The cars are identical, and are recognized by most consumers as being identical. This implies that the two cars must sell for the same price in the market, or else one of the two will take away the market from the other.

purchasing power parity (PPP)
An argument that states that identical goods produced in two countries must sell for the same price in the market.

Suppose that last year the U.S. car was selling for $4,000 in the United States, the German car was selling for DM8,000 in Germany, and the exchange rate between the two currencies was $0.5/DM. Hence, the two cars were also selling for the same price in each of the two countries:

U.S. car: $4,000
German car: DM8,000 × $0.5/DM = $4,000

Now assume that the inflation rate over the next year was higher in the United States than in Germany—say 10% in the United States and 5% in Germany. As a result, the price of the U.S. car will rise to $4,400 and the price of the German car will rise to DM8,400. If the exchange rate stays at $0.5/DM, the new price of the two cars in the U.S. market will be

U.S. car: $4,400
German car: DM8,400 × $0.5/DM = $4,200

Thus the German car will be cheaper in the U.S. market. It is also easy to see that the U.S. car will be more expensive than the German car in the German market:

U.S. car: $4,400 × DM2/$ = DM8,800
German car: DM8,400

The net effect will reduce demand for the U.S. car, both at home and abroad, and increase demand for the German car at home and abroad. In order to keep the two markets competitive, the exchange rate must change. Specifically, it must change to equate the price of the two cars given the shift in the relative inflation rates. That is, we must have the new exchange rate, X_1, such that

$$DM8,400 × \$X_1/DM = \$4,400$$

This implies a new rate of $0.5238/DM. Thus the dollar will depreciate relative to the DM.

The purchasing power parity argument generalizes this relationship. It states that the required change in the exchange rate is related to the ratio of the relative change in the price levels of the two countries:

$$(1 + \% \text{ change in exchange rate}) = \frac{(1 + h_d)}{(1 + h_f)}$$

where

h_d = the inflation rate in the domestic country
h_f = the inflation rate in the foreign country

Plugging in the inflation rates and the exchange rate change, it is easy to verify this formula from the example above:

$$\frac{0.5238}{0.5} = \frac{1.10}{1.05}$$

This, then, is the *purchasing power parity* argument. It states that the country with the higher inflation rate will experience depreciation in its currency, and that the change in exchange rates is equal to the difference between the rates of inflation in the two countries. However, the PPP argument has some very serious shortcomings:

1. It applies only to traded goods. Haircuts, housing, and other goods that are not easily imported are exempt from this argument, since they cannot be substituted from abroad.

2. It is a *long-run* argument. As inflation makes the domestic goods relatively more expensive, there will be an incentive to substitute the less expensive foreign goods for the domestic ones. But this will take time: time to recognize the price difference, to evaluate the relative quality of the good, to make marketing arrangements, and to increase the foreign production of the good for export. As a result, large and prolonged deviations from PPP have persisted.

Decreasing the Interest Rate.   If the real interest rate in the United States is lowered, investment money will leave the country. Foreigners and U.S. citizens will invest elsewhere, since their return will be higher. This capital out-flow will cause an increase in the supply of dollars abroad, as investors try to cash in their dollars for the currency of a country with more attractive investments. This will cause the dollar to depreciate relative to the other currencies.

Increase in Aggregate Income.   If the aggregate income in the United States increases relative to the income of other countries, the United States will import more from abroad since the demand for all goods, both foreign and domestic, will increase in the United States. But the demand abroad for U.S. goods will not increase by an equal amount, because the income in these other countries has not increased. As a result, the U.S. trade deficit will rise, leading to a depreciation in the dollar.

To sum up, three relationships can lead to a depreciation of the home currency:

1. Having a higher rate of inflation
2. Having its (real) interest rate fall relative to that of the foreign country
3. Having its income grow faster

One point worth noting is that it is the *relative* changes that are impor-tant. If both countries have the same rates of inflation, or if both countries experience the same shift in income or in real interest rates, an adjustment in the exchange rate will not be necessary.

THE INTERNATIONAL MONETARY SYSTEM

It is difficult to think of another area in which change has been so dramatic as the emergence of the "new economic order" during the 1970s and 1980s. These two decades have witnessed a veritable revolution of the international monetary system.

Gold Standard

gold standard
A currency system in which the par value of paper money is defined in terms of gold and in which currency can be redeemed, upon demand, for gold.

For almost five thousand years, from the time of the ancient Greeks and Romans to the outbreak of World War I, gold served as an almost univer-sally accepted standard of international value. Gold coins were used as a medium of exchange and store of value. However, because carrying gold was inconvenient, the major trading countries in the nineteenth century used paper money whose par value was defined in terms of gold and which could be redeemed, upon demand, for gold. One of the last countries to adhere to the **gold standard** was the United States, which did not go on the gold standard until 1879.

The gold standard virtually fixed exchange rates between countries.

(Deviations beyond the cost of transporting gold bullion could be arbitraged away.) However, in effect the gold standard was actually a *sterling standard*. Prior to World War I, London was the world's financial center and receivables, bills of exchange, and so on were usually denominated in British pounds. This was convenient because the pound was almost universally used as the standard of account, and moreover was fully convertible to gold at the Bank of England. However, few traders spoke of convertibility. After all, as the historians have put it: In the nineteenth century there was nothing "better" into which the pounds could be converted.

Modified Gold Standard

World War I destroyed the old economic order and the gold (or sterling) standard as well. During the war and the early 1920s, currencies fluctuated both in terms of gold and in terms of each other. Several unsuccessful attempts were made during the 1920s to restore the gold standard, but the Great Depression of the 1930s led most of the major trading countries to abandon the gold standard completely. The chief exception was the United States, which in 1934 established a *modified gold standard*: Gold was priced at $35 an ounce, but was traded only with official central banks and not with private citizens. From the mid-1930s to the end of World War II, all the major currencies floated against the U.S. dollar, which was convertible into gold.

Gold Exchange Standard: 1944–1971

Bretton Woods Agreement
A monetary agreement reached in 1944 between the United States and its European allies in which all member countries fixed the par value of their currencies in gold, with only the U.S. dollar being convertible into gold upon demand at $35 an ounce.

devaluation
An official announcement that a country is reducing the value of its currency relative to other countries.

In 1944, representatives of the allied powers met in Bretton Woods, New Hampshire, to establish a so-called gold exchange standard. The Bretton Woods Conference also created the *International Monetary Fund (IMF)* and the *International Bank for Reconstruction and Development (World Bank)*. Under the **Bretton Woods Agreement**, all member countries were required to fix the par value of their currencies in terms of gold; however, there was no obligation to convert the various currencies into gold upon demand. The exception was the U.S. dollar, which was convertible to gold at the official price of $35 per ounce. In practice, each country decided on the rate of exchange to the dollar and then calculated the gold par value of its currency which would result in the desired dollar exchange rate. It was also agreed that all other currencies would be permitted to deviate from their gold par values within a very narrow band of plus-minus 1%. Responsibility for maintaining the exchange rates was placed on each country's central bank, which would buy or sell foreign exchange or gold as needed. Larger deviations required the approval of the IMF.

In 1959, the major trading nations returned to the full convertibility of their currencies, but not all the countries could maintain their exchange rates within the 2% band. In 1967, the United Kingdom was forced by its growing trade deficit to devalue the pound. France followed in 1969 with a devaluation of the franc. A **devaluation** is the official announcement that a country is reducing the value of its currency relative to other countries. For example, the 1967 devaluation of the British pound reduced its value (exchange rate) from $2.80 per pound to $2.50 per pound. This made British exports cheaper abroad while raising the cost of imports, thereby reversing the trade deficit. Conversely, countries with very strong currencies could revalue their currencies. A **revaluation** is the official announcement that a country is raising the value of its currency relative to other countries. This was done by Germany during the 1960s.

revaluation
An official announcement that a country is raising the value of its currency relative to other countries.

The net result of the Bretton Woods system was that the exchange rates of the major trading nations were relatively stable. Changes due to devaluation or revaluation were large, but infrequent.

The Financial Crisis of 1971

In 1971, Bretton Woods came to an end. Inflation, plus a weakening of the dollar's acceptability as an international currency, led to a massive attack on the dollar and a large-scale outflow of gold from the United States. On August 15, 1971, President Nixon suspended the dollar's convertibility to gold. This effectively brought the gold exchange standard to an end. The system of pegged exchange rates that had been established at Bretton Woods could not be maintained, and the exchange rates of the leading trading nations were allowed to float against the dollar.

Numerous attempts were made to restore the old economic order. A series of international agreements were negotiated for the purpose of reintroducing a measure of exchange rate stability.

Smithsonian Agreement. In December 1971, the world's leading industrial nations, the so-called *Group of Ten*, reached an agreement: (a) They agreed to revalue their currencies upward with respect to the dollar. (b) The trading band around the new par values was expanded from 2 to 4.5%; maximum movements of 4.5% relative to the dollar were permitted before the central bank's intervention. (c) The United States devalued the dollar, in terms of gold, to $38 per ounce.

snake
The European Joint Float Agreement of 1972, under which the currencies of member countries were restricted a narrow trading band with each other and a wider one when trading relative to the U.S. dollar.

The Snake. In the spring of 1972, the members of the European Economic Community (EEC), along with the prospective members (Denmark, Ireland, Norway, and the United Kingdom) entered into the European Joint Float Agreement, popularly known as the **snake**. Under this agreement: (a) Members' currencies were restricted to a 2.25% trading band vis-à-vis one another; (b) jointly, they were allowed to trade relative to the dollar within the Smithsonian 4.5% band. This rather complex arrangement was referred to as *the snake within the tunnel*. But subsequent to the agreement, some countries, notably the United Kingdom, withdrew.

European Monetary System (EMS)
A monetary agreement reached in 1979 that restricts the fluctuations of EEC countries' currencies among themselves.

The EMS. In March 1979, the nine members of the EEC launched a new experiment—the **European Monetary System (EMS)**—which replaced the old snake. The EMS is more flexible than the snake, and has proved more durable. Its major features are these: (a) A new "composite currency," the

European Currency Unit (ECU)
A composite currency established by the EMS in 1979, the value of which is based on a weighted average of the value of individual currencies.

European Currency Unit (ECU), was created. The ECU is not a circulating currency; it exists only on the books of the EMS members, and is used to settle accounts among member countries. Its value is based on a weighted average of the value of individual member countries' currencies, with the weights reflecting the volume of trade and size of GNP. (b) Each country values its currency in terms of the ECU. (c) Deviations from these par rates are permitted within a band which is not the same for all countries. Beyond these limits, members intervene to restore the old rates. (d) However, if the deviation is extreme, the country in question must take action to correct the situation and/or devalue (or revalue) its currency's ECU value.

The Floating Exchange Rate System

All efforts to restore the fixed exchange rate system failed. By 1973, the United States was again forced to devalue the dollar to $42.22 per gold ounce, and the fixed trading bands could not be held in the face of massive speculative pressures. Worldwide inflation and the oil crisis of 1973 sounded the final death knell of the fixed exchange rate system.

In 1976, the IMF meeting in Jamaica laid down the rules for a new agreement. The main provision was that floating exchange rates were officially accepted and member countries were no longer required to maintain fixed bands around their par values. However, they were permitted to intervene in trading in order to offset unwarranted fluctuations caused by speculation. Under the present **floating rate system**, exchange rates are determined by the forces of demand and supply and fluctuate daily against one another. But it is also a *managed* floating system. Although exchange rates are no longer restricted by international agreements regarding permissible trading bands, central banks can, and often do, intervene to influence trading. Hence, the expression "managed float," or in popular slang, "dirty float." Moreover, the current floating system still retains "regional" agreements, such as the EMS, which restrict the fluctuations of member countries' currencies among themselves.

floating rate system
An agreement reached by the IMF in 1976 under which exchange rates are determined by supply and demand and fluctuate daily, subject to the intervention of central banks.

The forces of supply and demand, and therefore exchange rate fluctuations, are strongly influenced by world events. The major events since the 1976 Jamaica agreement were the following:

1. The dollar crisis in 1977–78 and the sharp increase in U.S. interest rates by the Carter administration. During this period the dollar lost about 10% of its value relative to major European currencies.
2. The oil crisis of 1979. The Organization of Oil Exporting Countries (OPEC) reacted to the weakness of the dollar by doubling the price of oil, which triggered a new worldwide recession. In addition, the Iran-Iraq war in the 1980s has further affected oil production and prices.
3. In the second half of the 1980s, exchange rates have been strongly influenced by the growing U.S. trade deficit. This led to a sharp decline in the value of the dollar relative to the major European currencies, and especially relative to the Japanese yen.

THE MARKET FOR FOREIGN EXCHANGE

Like a stock exchange, the foreign exchange market is not a meeting place for the ultimate suppliers and demanders of the currency in question. Typically, transactions are carried out by an intermediary; in this case, often a bank. Nor is the foreign exchange market a physical place. Today, the foreign exchange market spans the globe. And like the British Empire in the nineteenth century, the sun literally never sets on foreign exchange trading. Trading starts each morning in the Far East, moves west to Europe, from there to New York, and from there to the U.S. West Coast. Among the major trading centers are Tokyo, Sidney, Hong Kong, Singapore, Frankfurt, Paris, London, and New York. Moreover, modern communications technology connects these centers by telephone, telex, and on-line computers. Thus, the foreign exchange market is not a physical place, like the New York Stock Exchange, but a highly sophisticated communications network that connects the major market participants.

Market Participants

The market is comprised of four major categories of participants:

1. Banks and nonbank *dealers* in foreign exchange who buy and sell foreign exchange for their customers. They earn their profit from the difference between the "bid" price at which they buy the currency and the slightly higher "ask" price at which they sell the currency. By their willingness to buy and sell foreign exchange, these dealers "make the market."

2. Individuals and firms who use the market to facilitate commercial or financial transactions, or as we shall see below, to "hedge" their foreign exchange risks. This group includes exporters, importers, international portfolio investors, multinational firms, and tourists.

3. Speculators and arbitrageurs who profit from trading in the market itself. The former seek their profits by anticipating a change in exchange rates, while the arbitrageur tries to profit from the existence of simultaneous differences in the price quotation for a given currency in different markets.

4. Central banks that buy and sell currencies in order to influence the exchange rates of their own currency. It is their presence which led the market to coin the phrase "dirty float." Thus, for example, should the mark rise too sharply, the Bundesbank, which is Germany's central bank, might intervene by using marks to buy dollars. Conversely, it might sell dollars should the mark fall below the level it deems desirable. The central banks are not profit-motivated; they seek to influence exchange rates in order to promote the economic interests of their citizens.

Trading in the Foreign Exchange Market

A key to understanding foreign exchange trading is to remember that, with the exception of speculation and arbitrage, foreign exchange transactions are derived from transactions in commodity and investment markets. Trade in currencies is needed because people want to trade in commodities and assets. Thus, the American importer of Mercedes cars buys German marks in order to pay for the cars. If you want to buy shares in Daimler Benz, rather than the cars, you have to buy German marks in the foreign exchange market in order to pay for your purchase of stock on the Frankfurt Stock Exchange. A second point to remember is that you *cannot* be a demander of one currency in the foreign exchange market without being the supplier of another. Thus, in our example above, the U.S. importer and investor are both suppliers of dollars and demanders of German marks in the $/DM market.

spot transaction
A transaction in which foreign currency is purchased for delivery and payment on the second following business day.

Foreign exchange transactions are made on both a spot and forward basis. A **spot transaction** is one in which foreign currency is purchased for delivery and payment on the second following business day. (Same-day deliveries are possible at slightly different prices.) A **forward transaction** is one which stipulates the delivery of a specific amount of one currency on a specified date in the future, at an exchange rate fixed in advance. The contract is signed today, but future payment and delivery are effected at a known exchange rate. Such contracts, as we will see below, can eliminate uncertainty regarding the future course of exchange rates.

forward transaction
A transaction that stipulates the delivery of a specific amount of one currency on a given date at a fixed exchange rate.

Table 22–2 shows a typical array of spot rates and forward rates of the dollar relative to seven major foreign currencies. A glance at the forward rates for the German mark, Swiss franc, and Japanese yen shows that these three currencies were expected to rise against the dollar over the year. Thus, for example, the one-year forward rate for the Swiss franc was SF 1.70 to one dollar, as compared with the spot rate of SF 1.79 per dollar, which represents a market expectation that the value of the franc would rise over the year. Hence, the Swiss franc, German mark, and Japanese yen were selling at a *premium*; their spot rates (indirect quotes) were greater than their forward rates. Conversely, the forward rates for the other four currencies

TABLE 22–2   Forward Exchange Rates*

	German Mark	Swiss Franc	Japanese Yen	Canadian Dollar	French Franc	British Pound	Italian Lira
Spot	2.23	1.79	229	1.19	5.64	.5361	1,189
Three-Month	2.21	1.77	225	1.20	5.69	.5372	1,216
Six-Month	2.19	1.76	222	1.21	5.74	.5373	1,239
One-Year	2.15	1.70	214	1.22	5.84	.5372	1,286

* Foreign units per U.S. dollar as of November 10, 1981.

(Canadian dollars, French francs, British pounds, and Italian lire) were at a *discount* relative to their spot rates; the spot rates for these four currencies were *less* than their forward rates.

FOREIGN EXCHANGE RISK

As we have already noted, the system of pegged exchange rates which was established during World War II under the Bretton Woods Agreement was replaced in the mid-1970s by a regime of floating exchange rates. Today, all the major currencies are free to fluctuate (at least to some extent) against the dollar. Figure 22–1, which graphs the monthly percentage change in the exchange rates of eight major currencies (British pounds, Swiss francs, Italian lire, French francs, Japanese yen, German marks, Dutch guilders, and Belgian francs), clearly shows the dramatic change in the variability of exchange rates. For example, up to 1967 the exchange rate between the U.S. dollar and the British pound was completely stable; however, since November 1967, when the pound sterling was officially devalued, the exchange rate has fluctuated significantly. Thus if an American firm (or investor) holds pounds or some other financial asset denominated in pounds, and the exchange value of the pound rises against the dollar, an *exchange profit* is made. Conversely, should the pound fall relative to the dollar, an *exchange loss* will be incurred. Figure 22–1 clearly shows that these potential gains and losses from the holding of foreign currencies can be very large.

exchange risk
The risk entailed by the holding of foreign currencies because of large fluctuations in the exchange rate.

The net result of these greatly enhanced exchange rate movements has been to increase both the potential gains and losses from international transactions. Today, exporters, importers, and multinational corporations are exposed to a new type of risk—**exchange risk**. Table 22–3 quantifies the cumulative profit or loss on the holding of non-interest-bearing foreign currencies for selected subperiods during the years 1959–1982. The two early subperiods 1959–1961 and 1966–1968 illustrate the argument that,

TABLE 22–3   Total Gain or Loss (in %) to a U.S. Investor from the Holding of Non-Interest-Bearing Foreign Currencies, Selected Periods, 1959–1982

Currency	Feb. 1959– Dec. 1961	Jan. 1966– Dec. 1968	Jan. 1971– July 1973	Aug. 1973– Dec. 1973	Jan. 1971– Dec. 1973	Jan. 1974– Jan. 1980	Jan. 1980– Aug. 1981	Aug. 1981– Jan. 1982
Belgian francs	0.44	1.00	38.49	−13.90	20.22	34.01	−45.86	4.50
French francs	0.00	−1.01	33.72	−12.32	17.25	20.82	−48.12	2.61
German marks	4.50	0.25	55.10	−12.99	34.96	38.04	−45.10	8.36
Italian lire	0.13	0.19	6.50	−3.78	2.48	−21.83	−54.57	1.36
Japanese yen	−0.50	0.89	35.76	−5.91	27.73	20.41	1.79	3.89
Dutch guilders	4.72	0.00	38.40	−7.97	27.37	34.57	−46.00	9.57
Swiss francs	−0.23	0.47	50.59	−11.65	33.05	51.57	−36.05	14.99
UK pounds	0.00	−14.29	4.98	−7.55	−2.95	−0.57	−19.65	3.72

SOURCE: Calculated from data in IMF *International Financial Statistics*, various issues.

FIGURE 22–1 Monthly percentage change in exchange rate relative to the dollar.

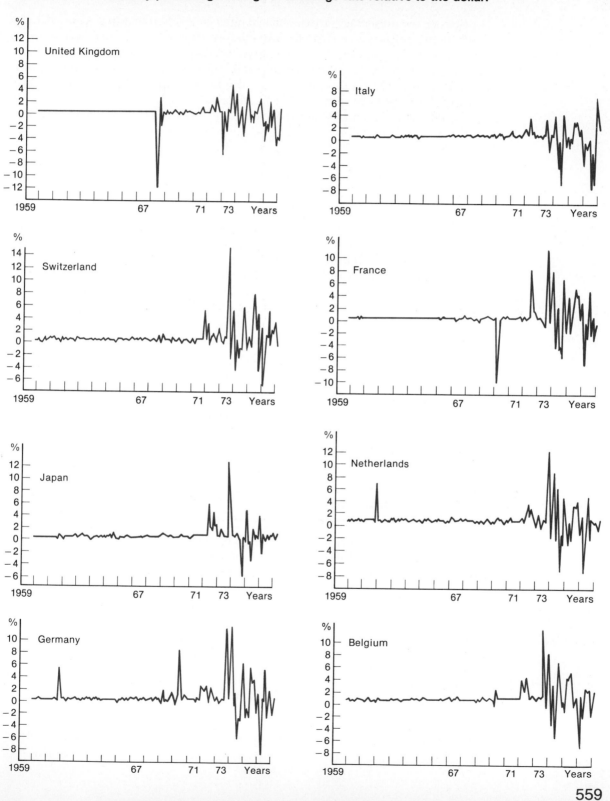

prior to the monetary crisis, the changes in exchange rates were of only secondary importance. On the other hand, during the 2-year period from 1971 to 1973, American firms or investors could have earned a significant profit by holding all but one of the eight foreign currencies included in our sample. In the last 5 months of 1973, the holding of foreign currencies produced a loss relative to the dollar in all cases.

The fluctuations in foreign exchange rates did not abate after 1973; indeed, the uncertainty regarding both the magnitude and the direction of exchange rate fluctuations has continued to be a significant factor in international investment and trade. For example, from 1974 to 1979, the foreign currencies included in our sample, with the exception of the United Kingdom, rose in value relative to the dollar—but these gains were more than wiped out in 1980 and the first half of 1981. The sharp fall in the dollar in recent years again made the holding of foreign currencies attractive. Table 22–4 shows the gain to U.S. firms and investors from holding foreign currency during the month of January 1987. The gain is impressive: The Belgian franc rose by 5.68% relative to the dollar in that month alone. The relevant figures for the German mark and British pound were 4.95% and 2.12%, respectively. The magnitude of the potential gains and losses can be gauged if we convert the monthly figures to compounded annual rates. Thus, the monthly rise in the Belgian franc represents a 94% return on an annual basis:

$$(1.0568)^{12} - 1 = 94\%$$

And even the 2.12% gain on the holding of pounds in January corresponds to an annual rate of 29%. And, of course, the other side of this coin is comprised of the equivalent losses suffered by European and Japanese firms and investors who held U.S. dollars during this same period.

MANAGING EXCHANGE RISK

Almost all firms view foreign exchange management as a form of risk management. Few will condone the undertaking of foreign currency transactions that are unconnected with operations; that is, they do not permit outright speculation. But that is about the extent of the agreement. Each firm tends to develop its own management style with respect to the central questions of exchange risk:

1. How should exchange risk exposure be defined?
2. To what extent should exchange risks be hedged?
3. If hedged, what particular strategy should be adopted?

A firm's answers to these questions depend on its overall corporate philosophy, the structure of its business, and the goals it sets for its foreign operations.

TABLE 22—4 **Monthly Gain to U.S. Investors from Holding Non-Interest-Bearing Foreign Currencies in January 1987 (%)**

Belgian francs	5.68%
French francs	4.44
German marks	4.94
Italian lire	2.69
Japanese yen	3.03
Dutch guilders	5.13
Swiss francs	4.37
U.K. pounds	2.12

SOURCE: *IMF Survey*, March 9, 1987.

Defining Exchange Risk

economic exposure
The risk that a change in exchange rates will affect the NPV of a firm's expected cash flow.

translation (accounting) exposure
The risk that translating foreign revenues and assets into a home currency will lower consolidated earnings.

transaction exposure
The risk stemming from an agreement to make or receive a future payment denominated in a foreign currency.

Foreign exchange exposure relates to the potential impact of a change in exchange rates on the firm's cash flows, profitability and market value. Three principal types of foreign exchange exposure can be identified: economic exposure, translation exposure, and transaction exposure.

Economic exposure reflects the possibility that a change in exchange rates may affect the net present value of the firm's expected cash flows. The change in NPV can be positive or negative depending on the effect of the exchange rate change. For example, consider a U.S. firm that exports to Germany. How will a fall in the German mark affect its operations? This depends on the economic analysis of the impact of the devaluation of the mark. The devaluation of the mark discourages U.S. exports to Germany by making them more expensive in terms of marks. Hence the competitiveness of U.S. exports to Germany is reduced.

Translation exposure, or *accounting exposure* as it is also called, stems from the need to report income from foreign operations according to accepted accounting principles. Consider, for example, a multinational U.S. firm with subsidiaries operating in a number of foreign countries. Each country requires the subsidiary corporation to report its income and expenses in local currency. However, in order to prepare the consolidated financial statements of the parent corporation, the local currency accounts of each subsidiary must be "translated" to U.S. dollars.

Accepted accounting practice requires U.S. corporations to include the profit (loss) from changes in the value of foreign currency in their reported earnings per share. The method for carrying out the translation is set out in *Statement of Financial Accounting Standards Number 52 (FASB # 52)*. Translation is a controversial subject, but one thing is clear. Firms with international operations (export, import, foreign subsidiaries) are exposed to very significant translation risks—that is, to the possibility that the method of translation of foreign revenues and assets to the home currency may have a pronounced negative impact on reported consolidated earnings.

Transaction exposure arises when a firm agrees to make a payment or receive a payment denominated in a foreign currency. For example, suppose a U.S. firm exports its products to France on open book account for 5 million French francs, payable in 60 days. If at the end of 60 days the franc *appreciates* by 10% relative to the dollar, the U.S. firm will gain; the 5 million francs will be converted into more dollars than could be obtained at the current exchange rate. Conversely, should the exchange rate for the franc fall, the 5 million francs will be converted into fewer dollars than could be obtained in the spot market at the current exchange rate.

What Exposures Should Be Covered?

cover
A strategy to eliminate or reduce the exchange risk of an exposed position.

Once the firm's risk exposure has been defined and estimated, it still must decide which (if any) of the exchange rate risks should be covered. **Cover** refers to a strategy by which exchange risk embodied in an exposed position is eliminated or reduced. Covering foreign exchange risks is something like insurance. At first glance, it seems as if all risks should be covered. After all, we assume firms to be risk-averse. But coverage, like insurance, has its price, and the benefits of coverage must be weighed against the costs. This again is a controversial subject, but many firms limit their coverage decisions to transaction exposure, preferring not to expend real resources to offset accounting risks.

ALTERNATIVE METHODS FOR ELIMINATING EXCHANGE RISK

Many of the risks created by the instability of foreign exchange rates can be avoided if the firm (or investor) foregoes any chance of gain. But like insurance contracts, the institutional arrangements for avoiding exchange risk are not costless.

Hedging in the Forward Market

forward contract
A contract under which a firm agrees to deliver a certain amount of a foreign currency in exchange for U.S. dollars at a future date at a specified price.

Exchange rate risk can be hedged, at a cost, by recourse to the forward market; the cost of the cover depends on the difference between the spot rate and the spread between the relevant "bid" and "ask" prices. Hence, modern financial risk management requires a working knowledge of the **forward contract.** Consider, for example, a firm that invests part of its liquid resources in short-term Japanese bonds which yield 8.74%. The firm must first acquire the yen through a spot purchase at the prevailing exchange rate for the yen. But by the time the bond matures the value of the yen may have changed. To hedge against this possibility of changing exchange rates, assume that the firm, when it acquired the yen, also sold a forward contract which stated that the firm would deliver a certain amount of yen in exchange for dollars at a future date at a specified price. This is what is meant by "selling yen forward." The forward transaction, in this case, allows the firm to eliminate the uncertainty of any future change in the exchange rate. No matter what happens to the yen's value, the firm is completely *hedged* against this risk and receives, as a result, an 8.74% return on the Japanese utility bond, *less* the cost of the forward transaction.

If the firm had expected a rise in the yen's value *and was willing to take the risk*, it could have abstained from hedging with a forward contract or might have covered only a proportion of the total amount instead. A hedge that covers only part of the exposure is called a **variable hedge.** The latter permits a firm to bear as much risk as it sees fit.

variable hedge
A hedge against changing exchange rates that covers only part of a firm's exposure.

To see how a forward market works, consider the following simplified example. A U.S. manufacturer purchases electronic components from a Japanese electronics firm for 229 million yen. Assuming a current spot exchange rate of 229 yen per dollar, the U.S. importer's cost is equal to $1 million (229 million ÷ 229 = 1 million). The invoice is payable (in yen) in 180 days. If the importer takes advantage of the trade credit and waits 3 months, it must bear the transaction risk. Should the yen appreciate in value relative to the dollar to an exchange rate of 200 yen per dollar, the U.S. importer will have to pay $1,145,000 at the new spot price in order to acquire the 229 million yen. The additional cost of $145,000 might conceivably wipe out the entire profit on the transaction. If the importer is sufficiently worried about such a possibility, it can purchase 229 million yen on the forward market for delivery in 180 days, say at a rate of 225 yen per dollar. Thus, the dollar cost will be $1,017,778 (229 million ÷ 225 = 1,017,778) no matter what the spot exchange rate happens to be 3 months later. This is what is meant by covering a transaction exposure (in this case a trade payable) by a **hedge in the forward market.**

hedge in the forward market
A hedge against a foreign currency's appreciation in value that involves purchasing a forward contract at the present lower spot exchange rate.

Until recently, forward contracts were unavailable for periods greater than 1 year. A corporation that wanted to hedge its exchange rate over a longer period had to find another firm or financial institution willing to participate in a currency exchange, usually called a **swap** or **back-to-back loans.** But finding such a partner was both cumbersome and expensive. Today, many large banks offer forward contracts for periods extending up to 5 years for U.S. and Canadian dollars, German marks, British pounds, and Swiss francs. As a result, the long-term forward market has tended to replace swaps in these currencies. However, swaps remain an important hedging device for lesser traded currencies and for transactions extending beyond 5 years.

swap (back-to-back) loans
Exchange of currencies between firms or institutions.

Currency Future Markets

Forward contracts are typically created by banks and serve the purposes of many large international corporations. Access to the forward market is limited to these firms who have a regular banking relationship with the banks who offer forward contracts. Smaller firms, or those firms and investors who wish to speculate in the market, are largely excluded from this market. However, this type of investor can turn to the **futures market.**

futures market
Trading contracts in foreign currencies for small firms and individual investors available on the International Money Market.

Futures trading in foreign currencies was introduced by the Chicago Mercantile Exchange, which in 1972 established the *International Monetary Market (IMM)* as an alternative to the regular forward contracts offered by commercial banks. On the IMM, contracts are available in the leading trading currencies and other financial instruments. Unlike the forward market, trading on the IMM takes place in an organized exchange. The IMM clearinghouse guarantees performance of the contract even if one party defaults. To this end, the IMM requires participants to deposit a required margin.

Local Currency Borrowing

Exposure to foreign exchange risk can be offset by borrowing the needed money directly in the local currency market of the country in question, or by lending (purchasing a security in that country's money market). Large multinationals achieve a similar effect by intercompany transactions.

"Leads and Lags"

This is the practice followed by some firms of accelerating their payments of accounts payable which are denominated in a strengthening currency ("leads"), while delaying for as long as possible payments of accounts in terms of a weakening currency ("lags").

Numerous variants of these methods are available. For example, some firms are able to manipulate the "invoicing" currency for their transactions; others attempt to manage their balance sheets to achieve a balance of assets and liabilities by currency denomination.

INTERNATIONAL FINANCIAL MARKETS

International financial activity is concentrated in certain cities that can be identified as international financial centers. London and New York are the most important of these, but Amsterdam, Geneva, Paris, Tokyo, and Zurich have also emerged as important centers for international finance. Since the end of the 1950s, another important international marketplace has evolved. This is the Eurocurrency market, which today plays a significant role in both the money and the long-term capital markets.

Eurocurrency Market

Eurodollars
U.S. dollars deposited in banks outside the borders of the United States.

The Eurocurrency market is an international money and capital market that deals in currencies outside their countries of origin. **Eurodollars** are U.S. dollars deposited in banks outside the borders of the United States. An example would be the deposit of dollars with a London bank or the London branch of an American or German bank. Originally the dollar was virtually the only currency used in the Euromarket. Today, all major Western currencies are represented in the Eurocurrency market. A Euro-DM is created by the deposit of German marks in banks outside the Federal Republic of Germany, and Euro-yen are Japanese yen deposited outside Japan.

Most Eurocurrency deposits are placed with the bank for a specific maturity and at a fixed interest rate. The maturities range from overnight funds to maturities of up to 5 years. The remaining deposits take the form of a negotiable certificate of deposit. The advantage of, say, a London Eurodollar deposit stems from its geographical location. Since it is held outside the United States, the Eurodollar deposit is not subject to control and regulation by U.S. monetary authorities. This reduces the cost of such funds to the bank, which in turn permits the payment of interest rates higher than their equivalent U.S. rates. These higher interest rates have proved a major attraction for corporations and public institutions that wish to hold part of their liquid assets in dollar-dominated deposits.

LIBOR (London Inter-Bank Offer Rate)
The interest rate paid by the largest London banks on Eurodollar loans and deposits.

Loans offered on the Euromarket range from 24 hours to 1 year. Longer-term loans of up to 5- or 10-year maturities are also available. Both interest rates on Eurodollar loans and deposits are tied to a standard rate, in this case **LIBOR**—the *London Inter-Bank Offer Rate*. This is the rate of interest paid to large banks on their deposits with the largest London banks.

International Bond Market

foreign bond
A bond floated by a foreign borrower, but denominated in the currency of another country and sold principally in that country.

Yankee bonds
Foreign bonds sold in the United States.

Samurai bonds
Foreign bonds sold in Japan.

Eurobond issue
A bond issue sold in countries other than the one in whose currency the bonds are denominated.

An international bond issue is one that is sold outside the country of the borrower. International bonds are foreign bonds or Eurobonds.

A **foreign bond** issue is one floated by a foreign borrower, but denominated in the currency of another country and sold principally in that country. Foreign bonds sold in the United States are often called **Yankee bonds;** foreign bonds sold in Japan are sometimes called **Samurai bonds.**

A **Eurobond issue** is sold in countries other than the one in whose currency the bonds are denominated. Thus, for example, a Eurodollar bond of a multinational U.S. corporation will be sold simultaneously in several different national capital markets, but not in the United States.

One important feature of the Eurobond market is its relative freedom from governmental controls. For example, disclosure requirements in the Eurobond market are far less stringent than those of the SEC for new issues in the United States.

THE PORTFOLIO APPROACH TO INTERNATIONAL FINANCIAL MANAGEMENT

The sharply increased exchange rate fluctuations of the 1970s and 1980s have prompted many American firms to reconsider their policy of holding all their liquid balances in U.S. dollars. Unfortunately, some financial institutions were tempted by the new monetary situation and tried to make a quick profit by speculating in foreign currency; but obviously this new opportunity, which reflects the underlying international monetary instability, is a two-edged sword; one bank, the eighth largest in the United States, collapsed. For firms as well as individuals, the exchange fluctuations provide a new, albeit risky, vehicle of investment, but nonetheless one with important potential if properly understood and managed.

Under the Bretton Woods system of pegged exchange rates, the markets for foreign currency tended to be inefficient, in the sense that economically unrealistic rates were often maintained by central banks, or by direct exchange controls, over relatively long periods of time. Although central banks still intervene in the market, and hence the popularity of the terms "managed" or "dirty" float, the weight of empirical evidence strongly suggests that today's foreign exchange markets are efficient. Thus, it appears reasonable to assume that the observed exchange rates reflect all relevant information, and as a result the structure of interest rates across countries will prevent firms or other investors from systematically exploiting past information on exchange rate trends to increase their return. Similarly, the empirical evidence also supports the notion that the forward exchange markets are efficient. Thus, the return on a domestic security (say a Treasury bill) and the return on a fully hedged foreign treasury bill (or its equivalent) should be the same.

In such a market, a firm cannot "gain" in expected return from hedging exchange risk, but it can achieve a more efficient risk-return balance (in the sense of Chapter 8) by applying the portfolio principle to the management of its liquid reserves. The portfolio approach to the management of foreign currencies provides a way, for those who are heavily exposed to this new type of risk, to mitigate (but not completely eliminate) losses (and gains) due to fluctuations in exchange rates.

Cash Management and Diversification in Practice[1]

"Companies are no longer looking at a bank balance, they are looking at a portfolio." This statement by Geoffrey Bell, senior advisor to the J. Henry Schroeder Bank & Trust Company and head of its Reserve Asset Management Group, accurately describes the new approach of many corporations to cash management. Up to the early seventies, firms held their liquid reserves in bank accounts, short-term government securities, and so on. However, since that time fluctuations in the value of the dollar against many foreign currencies have led many firms, especially those with international dealings, to view their cash assets in terms of a portfolio consisting of foreign currencies and securities. Although in doing so firms rarely apply a precise formal model to determine the optimal diversification of their cash reserves, they clearly apply what can be termed as the portfolio principle to cash management problems.

The global outlook for cash management which is implied by the portfolio approach is not the figment of some overworked academic's imagination. The unsettling events that rocked the international financial structure

---

[1] The following review of actual business practice draws on the survey of corporate financial managers reported in "Cash Management," *Business Week*, March 13, 1978, pp. 62–68.

during the 1970s and 1980s have left a permanent imprint on corporate strategy and practice. Many firms have sought new and more aggressive ways to invest their cash, more often than not turning to foreign currencies, foreign certificates of deposit, and even maturing high-grade foreign bonds. One such company, National Cash Register, in 1978 held 20% of its cash reserves in domestic commercial paper (mostly 90-day maturities), 20% in domestic certificates of deposit, and 60% in the Euromarket and the Caribbean offshore market, where interest rates were generally higher than in the United States. These outside investments were well diversified; the firm maintained about 100 different positions of $2 to $3 million each. The company's treasurer, Robert C. James, explained: "Our thought is that whatever the risk is, if we ever lose anything, we won't lose a big hunk." Reflecting this approach, NCR's policy vis-à-vis foreign holdings was never to have more than $50 million invested in any one country.

Another firm that diversified its cash balances among foreign currencies is Litton Industries. In 1978, Litton invested one-third of its cash portfolio in foreign certificates of deposit; at the time, the certificates were yielding more than those available in the United States. Another third of its funds was invested in time deposits denominated in German marks and Swiss francs yielding only 4.6 and 1.37%, respectively. Litton's treasurer, Charles Black, explained that even though the interest rate was low, investing in "strong" currencies such as marks and Swiss francs offset risks associated with investing in "weak" currencies such as U.S. and Canadian dollars. Clearly Litton expected an exchange gain, relative to the dollar, from the holding of marks and Swiss francs that would materially enhance the low interest yield on the foreign time deposits.

Another firm that pursued an even more aggressive policy is Dow Chemical, which invested in a levered portfolio of foreign currencies, sometimes borrowing in the United States to back the investments. The idea behind the strategy is that any unforeseen cash needs can be met by short-term borrowing in the United States, while cash funds should seek the highest yield. Dow did not hedge its investment in the forward market, thereby bearing a higher risk, but also enjoying the possibility of a higher return on investment.

Even this brief review of cash management practices clearly underscores the fact that traditional methods are giving way to a more aggressive form of investment with a broader perspective. Firms have learned the value of diversification and now hold investments in many currencies, as opposed to the traditional notion of holding cash assets in the home (base) currency only. Some firms use the forward market extensively to further reduce or eliminate their exposure to risk of exchange rate fluctuations and hence seek only interest-rate differentials among different countries. More aggressive firms expose themselves to some of the inherent risks of exchange rate fluctuations, speculating that the gains will overshadow the losses. Such firms mitigate these risks by holding a portfolio of "naked" or uncovered foreign currency investments.

SUMMARY

This chapter has been devoted to international financial management in the turbulent atmosphere of volatile exchange rate fluctuations. The decades of the 1970s and 1980s have witnessed a remarkable change in the international economic order. The Bretton Woods System of fixed exchange rates was replaced by freely or semifreely fluctuating exchange values. Today, all the major currencies are free to fluctuate, at least to some extent, against the dollar. This shift has not only created additional risks, but has also confronted corporate financial managers with a challenge in the form of new investment opportunities.

The exchange rate for foreign currency is the price of a unit of the foreign currency in terms of the domestic currency. Several alternatives can be identified:

A direct quote is one which divides the amount of dollars required to purchase foreign currency by one unit of the foreign currency, e.g., 50 cents per German mark.

An indirect quote is one which divides the amount of foreign currency required to purchase one dollar, e.g., 2 German marks per dollar.

A cross-currency quote, or cross rate, is one in which one currency is quoted in terms of another, and neither is the dollar, e.g.,

$$\text{Cross Rate} = \frac{\text{Pounds}}{\text{Dollars}} \times \frac{\text{Dollars}}{\text{German Marks}} = \frac{\text{Pounds}}{\text{German Marks}}$$

The exchange rate, like any other price, is determined by the forces of demand and supply for the foreign currency in question. These demands and supplies, in turn, reflect a multitude of influences:

1. If the United States imports more than it exports to a particular country the supply of dollars will increase (in order to pay for the import surplus) and the exchange rate for the dollar will depreciate.

2. In the long run purchasing power parity will tend to make exchange rates adjust so as to reflect the differential rates of inflation between countries.

3. If the *real* interest rate in the U.S. falls relative to other countries, investors will seek outlets abroad. This tends to increase the supply of dollars and leads to a depreciation of the dollar.

4. If aggregate income in the U.S. grows at a relatively fast rate, the increased demand for imports will lead to a depreciation of the dollar.

Currencies are traded in the foreign currency market. This market is comprised of four major categories of participants:

1. Dealers who buy and sell foreign exchange for their customers.

2. Individuals and firms who are in the market to facilitate their international commercial or financial transactions.

3. Speculators and arbitrageurs who profit from trading in the market itself.

4. Central banks who buy and sell currencies in order to influence their country's exchange rates.

Several types of foreign currency transactions can be identified:

A spot transaction is one in which foreign currency is purchased for delivery and payment on the second following business day.

A forward transaction stipulates the delivery of a specific amount of one currency on a specific date in the future, at an exchange rate fixed in advance.

Because of the volatile fluctuations in exchange rates, almost all firms view foreign exchange management as a special case of risk management. Three principal types of exchange risk can be identified:

Economic exposure which reflects the possibility that a change in exchange rates may affect the NPV of the firm's expected cash flow.

Translation (accounting) exposure stems from the legal requirement to report income derived from foreign subsidiaries according to accepted accounting principles. The method for carrying out the translation from foreign currencies to dollars is set out in the *Statement of Financial Accounting Standards Number 52 (FASB #52)*.

Transactions exposure arises when a firm agrees to make, or receive, a future payment denominated in a foreign currency.

There are several alternative methods for avoiding exchange risk:

Exchange risk can be hedged in the forward market by entering into an appropriate forward contract, by participating in a currency swap, or by transactions in the futures market.

Exchange risk can also be offset by borrowing (or lending) in the currency market of the country in question.

The chapter also examines the structure of the international financial markets. International financial activity is concentrated in financial centers such as New York, London, and Tokyo. Another important market is the Eurocurrency market, an international money and capital market that deals in currencies outside their country of origin.

The chapter concludes with a discussion of the portfolio approach to international financial management.

REVIEW EXERCISE

Circle the correct word(s) to complete each sentence; see p. 572 for correct answers.

22.1   Fluctuations in the external value of the dollar *can/cannot* be ignored.

22.2   Foreign currency *is/is not* a good, just like wheat.

22.3   In a *direct/indirect* quote, foreign currency is priced in terms of the dollar.

22.4   When one currency is quoted in terms of another and neither currency is the dollar, the exchange rate is called a *forward/cross* rate.

22.5 If the value of the domestic currency rises in terms of the foreign currency, it is said to have *depreciated/appreciated*.

22.6 According to the traditional approach to exchange rate determination, if the USA exports less from a country than it imports to that country, it must make up for the *deficit/surplus* by paying in currency.

22.7 If the United States exports less to the rest of the world than it imports from the rest of the world, the price of the dollar will *rise/drop*.

22.8 According to the "purchasing power parity" argument, the country with the lower inflation rate will experience *appreciation/depreciation* of its exchange rate.

22.9 If the real interest rate falls relative to that of a foreign country, the home currency will *appreciate/depreciate*.

22.10 The official announcement that a country is reducing the value of its currency is called *depreciation/devaluation*.

22.11 Devaluation of a country's currency makes its exports *more expensive/cheaper* abroad.

22.12 If the forward rate is at a premium relative to the spot rate, this represents the expectation that the currency's value will *rise/fall*.

22.13 Each country requires the subsidiaries of a U.S. corporation to report income and expenses in *dollars/local currency*.

22.14 Firms try to accelerate the payment of accounts payable which are denominated in a *weakening/strengthening* currency.

22.15 Eurodollars are U.S dollars deposited in banks *inside/outside* the borders of the USA.

22.16 The portfolio approach to the management of foreign currencies provides a way to *eliminate/mitigate* gains and losses due to fluctuations in exchange rates.

QUESTIONS

22.1 Define the following terms:
- **a.** Exchange rate
- **b.** Direct quote
- **c.** Cross rate
- **d.** Depreciation
- **e.** Purchasing power parity
- **f.** Gold standard
- **g.** Devaluation
- **h.** European currency unit (ECU)
- **i.** Spot transaction
- **j.** Forward transaction
- **k.** LIBOR

22.2 What is the mathematical relationship between a direct and an indirect quote?

22.3 The exchange rate of the Japanese yen changes from 145 per dollar to 153 per dollar. Which of the currencies has appreciated?

22.4 What variables determine the exchange rate according to the monetary approach?

22.5 Explain why a country's currency appreciates if the real interest rate rises in that country.

22.6 List the main points of the Bretton Woods Agreement.

22.7 How does a devaluation affect imports and exports? Why?

22.8 What is the value of the ECU based on?

22.9 What factors determine the value of a currency under a floating rate system?

22.10 What are the principal types of foreign exchange exposure?

22.11 Explain how the risk inherent in the foreign exchange rates can be avoided by hedging in the forward market.

22.12 Why can the interest paid on Eurodollars be higher than the interest paid on similar dollar accounts in the United States?

PROBLEMS

22.1 **Direct and indirect quotes.** Compute the corresponding direct quotes from the following indirect quotes:
  a. 1.55 Swiss francs per dollar   **b.** 6.07 French francs per dollar
  c. 1299 Italian lira per dollar   **d.** 6.83 Norwegian krone per dollar
  e. 145 Japanese yen per dollar

22.2 **Cross quotes.** Use the data of the previous problem to compute the following cross rates:
  a. Swiss franc per French franc   **b.** Japanese yen per Italian lira
  c. Italian lira per Japanese yen   **d.** Norwegian krone per Swiss franc.

22.3 **Pricing foreign goods.** A French textile manufacturer wants to buy a Swiss weaving machine that costs 84,500 Swiss francs. Use the data given in problem 22.1 to compute how much the manufacturer has to pay in terms of local currency.

22.4 **Pricing foreign goods.** An American importer buys 2,000 men's suits from a Japanese firm at a cost of 17,000 yen per suit, payable in dollars. Use the data of problem 22.1 to compute how much the importer has to pay.

22.5 **Purchasing power parity.** The exchange rate between the English pound and the U.S. dollar is 0.60 dollars per pound in 1987. Assume that inflation will amount to 3.5% in the USA and 7.6% in England during 1988. What do you expect the exchange rate to be after 1 year, if the purchasing power parity hypothesis holds?

22.6 **Purchasing power parity.** On March 1, one Swiss franc sells for 1.10 German marks. One year later, the rate is 1.20 marks per Swiss franc. In Switzerland there was no inflation during that year. According to the PPP theorem, what was the rate of inflation in Germany?

22.7 **Return on foreign currency.** On January 15, the exchange rate of the Belgian franc to the dollar was 37.78. On February 15, the rate was 38.21. What was the exchange profit (converted to an annual basis)?

22.8 **Return on foreign currency.** On April 5, the exchange rate of the U.S. dollar to the Canadian dollar was $1.02. On June 5, the rate was $0.98. What exchange profit (converted to an annual basis) was made by the holder of which currency?

22.9 **Hedging in the forward market.** A German automobile producer sells 500 cars to a U.S importer at a price of $4,000 each. The invoice is payable in 90 days, in dollars. The spot rate is 2 German marks per dollar, and the forward rate is 1.95 marks per dollar. What transactions will take place, should the German firm want to hedge in the forward market?

22.10 Hedging through borrowing. The German automobile producer of the previous problem now wants to cover its exchange risk by borrowing. The yearly interest rates are 6.4% in Germany and 9.5% in the United States. What transactions will be made?

SAMPLE PROBLEMS

SP22.1 One "Jovi" sells for 283 "Misus," while 68 "Misus" buy 2.5 "Gefis." How many Jovis does it take to buy a Gefi?

SP22.2 The exchange rate between the "Mupa" and the U.S. dollar is 17 Mupas per dollar. Inflation in Mupania is expected to reach 7% during the coming year, while it is 4% in the United States. What will the exchange rate be a year from now, under the assumption of purchasing power parity?

Solutions to Sample Problems

SP22.1 The cross rate is computed as follows:

$$\frac{\text{Jovi}}{\text{Gefi}} = \frac{\text{Jovi}}{\text{Misu}} \times \frac{\text{Misu}}{\text{Gefi}}$$

Substituting the numerical data given in the problem (1 J per 283 M, 68 M per 2.5 G), we obtain

$$\frac{\text{Jovi}}{\text{Gefi}} = \frac{1}{28} \times \frac{68}{2.5} = 0.035336 \times 27.2 = 0.096$$

Hence 0.096 Jovis buy 1 Gefi. Alternatively, 10.4 Gefis buy 1 Jovi (1/0.096 = 10.4).

SP22.2 According to the purchasing power parity hypothesis, next year's exchange rate is calculated as:

$$\text{current exchange rate} \times \frac{1 + \text{inflation in Mupania}}{1 + \text{inflation in the USA}}$$

Substituting the numbers, we get

$$17 \times \frac{1.07}{1.04} = 17.49 \text{ Mupas per U.S. dollar}$$

Answers to Review Exercise

22.1 cannot	**22.2** is	**22.3** direct	**22.4** cross
22.5 appreciated	**22.6** deficit	**22.7** drop	**22.8** appreciation
22.9 depreciate	**22.10** devaluation	**22.11** cheaper	**22.12** rise
22.13 local currency	**22.14** strengthening	**22.15** outside	**22.16** mitigate

SUGGESTIONS FOR FURTHER READING

A number of excellent textbooks in international finance are available: David K. Eiteman and Arthur I. Stonehill, *Multinational Business Finance*, 3rd ed. (Boston: Addison-Wesley, 1982); Maurice Levi, *International Finance: Financial Management and the International Economy* (New York: McGraw-Hill, 1983); Rita M. Rodriguez and E. Eugene Carter, *International Financial Management*, 3rd ed. (Englewood Cliffs, NJ: Prentice-Hall, 1984).

For useful collections of articles on various aspects of international financial management, see Richard J. Herring (ed.), *Managing Foreign Exchange Risk* (New York: Cambridge University Press, 1983); David A. Ricks, *International Dimensions of Corporate Finance* (Englewood Cliffs, NJ: Prentice-Hall, 1978); Marshall Sarnat and Giorgio P.

Szego (eds.), *International Finance and Trade*, Vols. I and II (Lexington, MA: Ballinger, 1979).

In addition, the *Midland Corporate Finance Journal* devoted a recent issue to international financial management; see *MCFJ*, Fall 1986.

For empirical evidence on the efficiency of the foreign exchange markets, see Robert Z. Aliber, *The International Money Game*, rev. ed. (New York: Basic Books, 1981); Ian Giddy and Gunter Dufey, "The Random Behavior of Flexible Exchange Rates," *Journal of International Business Studies*, Spring 1975; Dennis E. Logue and George S. Oldfield, "Managing Foreign Assets When Foreign Exchange Markets Are Efficient," *Financial Management*, Summer 1977.

A | The Crash of '87

The stock market plays a crucial role in the theory of finance; stock prices are a key determinant of the cost of capital, and thereby affect corporate investment decisions. Moreover, as we have emphasized throughout the book, common stock prices also provide a benchmark for evaluating the performance of management. Clearly, this does *not* mean that daily fluctuations in stock prices should be permitted to influence our analysis; however, the events of October 1987 were so pronounced that some of their implications need to be spelled out explicitly.

BLACK MONDAY

On Monday, October 19, 1987, America's longest-lived bull market came to an abrupt and unprecedented end. In one frantic day of trading, the Dow Jones Stock average dropped by 22%, and a half a trillion dollars of stock values were wiped out. The following day stock prices plunged on major stock exchanges around the world. One market, the Hong Kong Stock Exchange, closed shop for the week. When the smoke cleared, the old saying that "the sun never sets on the British Empire" required revision. In the electronic world of the 1980s, it's the world capital market that never goes to sleep. As trading closes in the United States it moves across the Pacific to Tokyo and the new international financial centers of Hong Kong and Singapore. From there, trading again moves westward to the major financial centers of Europe: London, Frankfort, and Paris.

Hindsight is always clearer than foresight and numerous candidates for the "cause" of the crash were immediately mentioned. The one thing that is clear, however, is that a financial collapse of this magnitude must reflect a combination of factors, operating together, to undermine investors' confidence. Among these factors we find:

☐ Stock prices had risen in the United States almost continuously since 1982, with the rise being especially pronounced in the nine months prior to the fall. This invoked the old stock market rule that what goes up must eventually come down.

☐ The United States budget deficit had reached record levels, and its financing posed a major problem

☐ Similarly, the United States was running a large deficit in its balance of trade, i.e., imports to the United States greatly exceeded American exports. As a result, the value of the dollar against major foreign currencies had been falling.

☐ The persistence of the gap in the U.S. balance of trade, and the need to attract foreign capital to finance the budget deficit, induced expectations of rising interest rates and the possibility of economic recession.

☐ The "globalization" of stock trading and the rapid transfer of stock market trends from market to market as well as technological and financial innovations, such as the widespread use of computers and the interaction between futures and spot trading, was viewed by some analysts as destabilizing.

☐ And of course the politicians came in for their share of the responsibility with the U.S. Treasury Secretary and the German Finance Minister being singled out for criticism for their public pronouncements (and policies) prior to the crash.

THE STOCK MARKET CRASH AND REAL ECONOMIC ACTIVITY

The importance of the stock market lies in its connection with real economic activity. Stock prices reflect expectations about future corporate profits as well as changes in the rate at which these future earnings should be discounted. As a result, the stock market is one of the better statistical indicators of the business cycle. Almost all of the economic recessions during the past 40 years in the United States have been accompanied by substantial declines in stock prices.[1] However, as we pointed out in Chapter 5, forecasting is a very dangerous business. As Groucho Marx put it, no one trusts forecasts, especially forecasts about the future. And who amongst us can forget Irving Fisher's immortal statement on the eve of the 1929 financial collapse, "Stock prices have reached what looks like a permanently high plateau."[2]

THE STOCK MARKET CRASH AND FIRMS' COST OF CAPITAL

As we have already noted, transitory fluctuations in stock prices are not usually allowed to affect the analysis of corporate investment behavior. However, a 22% drop in the stock market average in *one day* cannot be ignored.

[1] See Geoffrey Moore, *Business Cycles, Inflation, and Forecasting*, Cambridge MA: Ballinger, 1983.
[2] See John Kenneth Galbraith, *The Great Crash*, Boston: Houghton, Mifflin, 1955, p. 75.

In particular, we must address the question of the impact of such a change on real economic activity. For example, what does the sharp fall in stock prices imply for the firm's investment in new plant and equipment? The answer to this question lies in the stock market's impact on the firm's cost of capital.

To simplify the discussion, consider a hypothetical firm which finances its investments solely out of equity.[3] Assume further that the company in question has 100 shares outstanding and *stable* annual earnings of $100, all of which are distributed as dividends. Hence earnings per share (EPS) are $1. If the share price is assumed to be $10, the firm's cost of capital is 10% (see Chapter 15). Now let's assume that the firm is considering the possibility of issuing an additional 100 shares to finance a new investment project. What is the minimum required return on the new project? Recalling the discussion in Chapter 15, and ignoring any flotation costs, you can easily verify that the required return, i.e., the firm's cost of capital, is 10%. The company raises an additional $1,000 of equity (100 shares at a price of $10 per share). A 10% cost of capital implies that the new project, if it is to be acceptable, must earn a profit of *at least* $100 per year. At this minimum rate of profit there is no dilution of earnings: the EPS after the investment remains $1 ($200/200 = $1). Thus, by definition, the firm's cost of capital is 10%.

Now assume that due to the stock market crash, the price of the firm's shares falls from $10 to $6. If the firm can sell the 100 new shares for only $6, it will have only $600 to invest (100 shares × $6 = $600). Since the firm must earn $100 on these additional shares to avoid the dilution of earnings, its cost of capital has risen sharply to 16.7% ($100/$600 = 16.7%). And other things being equal, this will have an inhibiting effect on new investment.

How does our analysis change if the firm in the preceding example does *not* intend to raise additional equity? Will its cost of capital rise even in the absence of new equity financing? Although it may not be intuitively obvious we can again show that the cost of capital following the fall in stock price is 16.7%, *independent* of the firm's financing decisions. Recall that, in the specific example above, EPS is $1 and the stock price (after the crash) is assumed to be $6. Should the firm decide to repurchase one of its shares for $6 the remaining shareholders will "earn" 16.7% ($1/$6 = 16.7%). Hence, the firm should accept projects only if they offer a return of at least 16.7%. Thus, even without additional financing, the firm's cost of capital rises to 16.7%.

The logic underlying this result can be clarified by a simple example. Assume for simplicity that there are only two shareholders in the firm in question, one of whom sells his shares to the firm at a price of $6 per share. The second shareholder retains his shares. Thus the second shareholder gives up $6 out of the firm's cash inflow, which is used to repurchase the

---

[3] The inclusion of debt financing complicates the analysis but does not change the conclusions.

shares. However, he gains an annual earnings stream of $1 per share which otherwise would go to the first shareholder. Hence, the return to the remaining shareholder on the repurchase is 16.7% ($1/$6 = 16.7%).

THE STOCK MARKET CRASH AND SHARE REPURCHASE

We are now in a position to understand the flood of corporate repurchases which occurred following the crash (see Chapter 16). Among the firms which announced their intention to buy back their own shares we find USX, Citicorp, IBM, Honeywell, United Technologies, and many others. Their decision reflects the underlying belief that the outlook for future corporate earnings does not justify the fall in share price. Hence, the higher return on share repurchase represented an attractive investment opportunity. This implies that the firms in question either did not expect future corporate profits to fall as a result of the crash, or at worse, expected that any decline in future earnings would be smaller than the fall in share price.

The Dividend Growth Model This conclusion can be clarified further by applying the dividend growth model which sets out the firm's cost of capital as:

$$k = \frac{D}{P} + g$$

where:

k = the cost of capital
D = the expected dividend
P = current market price of a share
g = the expected growth rate of earnings and dividends.

If we assume the following values:

$$D = \$5$$
$$P = \$100$$
$$g = 7\%$$

the cost of capital is 12%:

$$k = \frac{\$5}{\$100} + .07 = 12\%$$

Now if there is a sudden fall in share price to say $60, but expectations regarding future earnings remain unchanged, the cost of capital, as we pointed out in the previous example, will rise sharply:

$$k = \frac{\$5}{\$60} + .07 = 15.3\%$$

However, if the fall in stock price is accompanied by a downward revision of expectations regarding future corporate profits (and therefore growth rates) the change in the cost of capital becomes ambiguous and depends on the relationship of the fall in stock price to the decline in the expected growth rate.

The Capital Asset Pricing Model (CAPM)   Finally, we can also examine the behavior of corporations following the stock market decline within the context of the CAPM, which estimates the firm's cost of capital as follows:

$$k_i = R_F + (R_m - R_F) \beta_i$$

where:

k_i = the cost of capital
R_F = the riskless interest rate
R_m = the return on the market portfolio
β_i = the firm's beta (systematic) risk.

If we asume that there was *no* meaningful change in the risk-free interest rate the only variables affecting the cost of capital are the systematic risk (β_i) and the expected return on the market portfolio.

Since β_i measures the *relative* deviation of the individual stock's return (price) to deviations in the market as a whole, a *general decline* in the market cannot be expected to change these relative deviations. Of course a specific β_i may change, but on average the betas can be expected to remain the same. This is clear if we recall that the average of all individual betas must always be equal to 1 no matter what happens to the absolute level of stock prices. Once again expected corporate profits provide the key variable affecting the firm's cost of capital. If expected corporate profits do not change, the fall in stock prices will raise the expected return on the market portfolio, R_m, and the individual firm's cost of capital k_i will increase thereby making the re-purchase of its shares attractive.

B | Financial Tables

TABLE A-1 Present Value of $ 1

Periods	1%	2%	3%	4%	5%	6%	7%	8%	9%	10%
1	0.990	0.980	0.971	0.962	0.952	0.943	0.935	0.926	0.917	0.909
2	0.980	0.961	0.943	0.925	0.907	0.890	0.873	0.857	0.842	0.826
3	0.971	0.942	0.915	0.889	0.864	0.840	0.816	0.794	0.772	0.751
4	0.961	0.924	0.888	0.855	0.823	0.792	0.763	0.735	0.708	0.683
5	0.951	0.906	0.863	0.822	0.784	0.747	0.713	0.681	0.650	0.621
6	0.942	0.888	0.837	0.790	0.746	0.705	0.666	0.630	0.596	0.564
7	0.933	0.871	0.813	0.760	0.711	0.665	0.623	0.583	0.547	0.513
8	0.923	0.853	0.789	0.731	0.677	0.627	0.582	0.540	0.502	0.467
9	0.914	0.837	0.766	0.703	0.645	0.592	0.544	0.500	0.460	0.424
10	0.905	0.820	0.744	0.676	0.614	0.558	0.508	0.463	0.422	0.386
11	0.896	0.804	0.722	0.650	0.585	0.527	0.475	0.429	0.388	0.350
12	0.887	0.788	0.701	0.625	0.557	0.497	0.444	0.397	0.356	0.319
13	0.879	0.773	0.681	0.601	0.530	0.469	0.415	0.368	0.326	0.290
14	0.870	0.758	0.661	0.577	0.505	0.442	0.388	0.340	0.299	0.263
15	0.861	0.743	0.642	0.555	0.481	0.417	0.362	0.315	0.275	0.239
16	0.853	0.728	0.623	0.534	0.458	0.394	0.339	0.292	0.252	0.218
17	0.844	0.714	0.605	0.513	0.436	0.371	0.317	0.270	0.231	0.198
18	0.836	0.700	0.587	0.494	0.416	0.350	0.296	0.250	0.212	0.180
19	0.828	0.686	0.570	0.475	0.396	0.331	0.277	0.232	0.194	0.164
20	0.820	0.673	0.554	0.456	0.377	0.312	0.258	0.215	0.178	0.149
21	0.811	0.660	0.538	0.439	0.359	0.294	0.242	0.199	0.164	0.135
22	0.803	0.647	0.522	0.422	0.342	0.278	0.226	0.184	0.150	0.123
23	0.795	0.634	0.507	0.406	0.326	0.262	0.211	0.170	0.138	0.112
24	0.788	0.622	0.492	0.390	0.310	0.247	0.197	0.158	0.126	0.102
25	0.780	0.610	0.478	0.375	0.295	0.233	0.184	0.146	0.116	0.092
26	0.772	0.598	0.464	0.361	0.281	0.220	0.172	0.135	0.106	0.084
27	0.764	0.586	0.450	0.347	0.268	0.207	0.161	0.125	0.098	0.076
28	0.757	0.574	0.437	0.333	0.255	0.196	0.150	0.116	0.090	0.069
29	0.749	0.563	0.424	0.321	0.243	0.185	0.141	0.107	0.082	0.063
30	0.742	0.552	0.412	0.308	0.231	0.174	0.131	0.099	0.075	0.057
40	0.672	0.453	0.307	0.208	0.142	0.097	0.067	0.046	0.032	0.022
50	0.608	0.372	0.228	0.141	0.087	0.054	0.034	0.021	0.013	0.009

TABLE A–1 (contd.) **Present Value of $ 1**

Periods	11%	12%	13%	14%	15%	16%	17%	18%	19%	20%
1	0.901	0.893	0.885	0.877	0.870	0.862	0.855	0.847	0.840	0.833
2	0.812	0.797	0.783	0.769	0.756	0.743	0.731	0.718	0.706	0.694
3	0.731	0.712	0.693	0.675	0.658	0.641	0.624	0.609	0.593	0.579
4	0.659	0.636	0.613	0.592	0.572	0.552	0.534	0.516	0.499	0.482
5	0.593	0.567	0.543	0.519	0.497	0.476	0.456	0.437	0.419	0.402
6	0.535	0.507	0.480	0.456	0.432	0.410	0.390	0.370	0.352	0.335
7	0.482	0.452	0.425	0.400	0.376	0.354	0.333	0.314	0.296	0.279
8	0.434	0.404	0.376	0.351	0.327	0.305	0.285	0.266	0.249	0.233
9	0.391	0.361	0.333	0.308	0.284	0.263	0.243	0.225	0.209	0.194
10	0.352	0.322	0.295	0.270	0.247	0.227	0.208	0.191	0.176	0.162
11	0.317	0.287	0.261	0.237	0.215	0.195	0.178	0.162	0.148	0.135
12	0.286	0.257	0.231	0.208	0.187	0.168	0.152	0.137	0.124	0.112
13	0.258	0.229	0.204	0.182	0.163	0.145	0.130	0.116	0.104	0.093
14	0.232	0.205	0.181	0.160	0.141	0.125	0.111	0.099	0.088	0.078
15	0.209	0.183	0.160	0.140	0.123	0.108	0.095	0.084	0.074	0.065
16	0.188	0.163	0.141	0.123	0.107	0.093	0.081	0.071	0.062	0.054
17	0.170	0.146	0.125	0.108	0.093	0.080	0.069	0.060	0.052	0.045
18	0.153	0.130	0.111	0.095	0.081	0.069	0.059	0.051	0.044	0.038
19	0.138	0.116	0.098	0.083	0.070	0.060	0.051	0.043	0.037	0.031
20	0.124	0.104	0.087	0.073	0.061	0.051	0.043	0.037	0.031	0.026
21	0.112	0.093	0.077	0.064	0.053	0.044	0.037	0.031	0.026	0.022
22	0.101	0.083	0.068	0.056	0.046	0.038	0.032	0.026	0.022	0.018
23	0.091	0.074	0.060	0.049	0.040	0.033	0.027	0.022	0.018	0.015
24	0.082	0.066	0.053	0.043	0.035	0.028	0.023	0.019	0.015	0.013
25	0.074	0.059	0.047	0.038	0.030	0.024	0.020	0.016	0.013	0.010
26	0.066	0.053	0.042	0.033	0.026	0.021	0.017	0.014	0.011	0.009
27	0.060	0.047	0.037	0.029	0.023	0.018	0.014	0.011	0.009	0.007
28	0.054	0.042	0.033	0.026	0.020	0.016	0.012	0.010	0.008	0.006
29	0.048	0.037	0.029	0.022	0.017	0.014	0.011	0.008	0.006	0.005
30	0.044	0.033	0.026	0.020	0.015	0.012	0.009	0.007	0.005	0.004
40	0.015	0.011	0.008	0.005	0.004	0.003	0.002	0.001	0.001	0.001
50	0.005	0.003	0.002	0.001	0.001	0.001	0.000	0.000	0.000	0.000

TABLE A-1 (contd.) Present Value of $ 1

Periods	21%	22%	23%	24%	25%	26%	27%	28%	29%	30%
1	0.826	0.820	0.813	0.806	0.800	0.794	0.787	0.781	0.775	0.769
2	0.683	0.672	0.661	0.650	0.640	0.630	0.620	0.610	0.601	0.592
3	0.564	0.551	0.537	0.524	0.512	0.500	0.488	0.477	0.466	0.455
4	0.467	0.451	0.437	0.423	0.410	0.397	0.384	0.373	0.361	0.350
5	0.386	0.370	0.355	0.341	0.328	0.315	0.303	0.291	0.280	0.269
6	0.319	0.303	0.289	0.275	0.262	0.250	0.238	0.227	0.217	0.207
7	0.263	0.249	0.235	0.222	0.210	0.198	0.188	0.178	0.168	0.159
8	0.218	0.204	0.191	0.179	0.168	0.157	0.148	0.139	0.130	0.123
9	0.180	0.167	0.155	0.144	0.134	0.125	0.116	0.108	0.101	0.094
10	0.149	0.137	0.126	0.116	0.107	0.099	0.092	0.085	0.078	0.073
11	0.123	0.122	0.103	0.094	0.086	0.079	0.072	0.066	0.061	0.056
12	0.102	0.092	0.083	0.076	0.069	0.062	0.057	0.052	0.047	0.043
13	0.084	0.075	0.068	0.061	0.055	0.050	0.045	0.040	0.037	0.033
14	0.069	0.062	0.055	0.049	0.044	0.039	0.035	0.032	0.028	0.025
15	0.057	0.051	0.045	0.040	0.035	0.031	0.028	0.025	0.022	0.020
16	0.047	0.042	0.036	0.032	0.028	0.025	0.022	0.019	0.017	0.015
17	0.039	0.034	0.030	0.026	0.023	0.020	0.017	0.015	0.013	0.012
18	0.032	0.028	0.024	0.021	0.018	0.016	0.014	0.012	0.010	0.009
19	0.027	0.023	0.020	0.017	0.014	0.012	0.011	0.009	0.008	0.007
20	0.022	0.019	0.016	0.014	0.012	0.010	0.008	0.007	0.006	0.005
21	0.018	0.015	0.013	0.011	0.009	0.008	0.007	0.006	0.005	0.004
22	0.015	0.013	0.011	0.009	0.007	0.006	0.005	0.004	0.004	0.003
23	0.012	0.010	0.009	0.007	0.006	0.005	0.004	0.003	0.003	0.002
24	0.010	0.008	0.007	0.006	0.005	0.004	0.003	0.003	0.002	0.002
25	0.009	0.007	0.006	0.005	0.004	0.003	0.003	0.002	0.002	0.001
26	0.007	0.006	0.005	0.004	0.003	0.002	0.002	0.002	0.001	0.001
27	0.006	0.005	0.004	0.003	0.002	0.002	0.002	0.001	0.001	0.001
28	0.005	0.004	0.003	0.002	0.002	0.002	0.001	0.001	0.001	0.001
29	0.004	0.003	0.002	0.002	0.002	0.001	0.001	0.001	0.001	0.000
30	0.003	0.003	0.002	0.002	0.001	0.001	0.001	0.001	0.000	0.000
40	0.000	0.000	0.000	0.000	0.000	0.000	0.000	0.000	0.000	0.000
50	0.000	0.000	0.000	0.000	0.000	0.000	0.000	0.000	0.000	0.000

TABLE A–1 (contd.)   **Present Value of $ 1**

Periods	31%	32%	33%	34%	35%	36%	37%	38%	39%	40%
1	0.763	0.758	0.752	0.746	0.741	0.735	0.730	0.725	0.719	0.714
2	0.583	0.574	0.565	0.557	0.549	0.541	0.533	0.525	0.518	0.510
3	0.445	0.435	0.425	0.416	0.406	0.398	0.389	0.381	0.372	0.364
4	0.340	0.329	0.320	0.310	0.301	0.292	0.284	0.276	0.268	0.260
5	0.259	0.250	0.240	0.231	0.223	0.215	0.207	0.200	0.193	0.186
6	0.198	0.189	0.181	0.173	0.165	0.158	0.151	0.145	0.139	0.133
7	0.151	0.143	0.136	0.129	0.122	0.116	0.110	0.105	0.100	0.095
8	0.115	0.108	0.102	0.096	0.091	0.085	0.081	0.076	0.072	0.068
9	0.088	0.082	0.077	0.072	0.067	0.063	0.059	0.055	0.052	0.048
10	0.067	0.062	0.058	0.054	0.050	0.046	0.043	0.040	0.037	0.035
11	0.051	0.047	0.043	0.040	0.037	0.034	0.031	0.029	0.027	0.025
12	0.039	0.036	0.033	0.030	0.027	0.025	0.023	0.021	0.019	0.018
13	0.030	0.027	0.025	0.022	0.020	0.018	0.017	0.015	0.014	0.013
14	0.023	0.021	0.018	0.017	0.015	0.014	0.012	0.011	0.010	0.009
15	0.017	0.016	0.014	0.012	0.011	0.010	0.009	0.008	0.007	0.006
16	0.013	0.012	0.010	0.009	0.008	0.007	0.006	0.006	0.005	0.005
17	0.010	0.009	0.008	0.007	0.006	0.005	0.005	0.004	0.004	0.003
18	0.008	0.007	0.006	0.005	0.005	0.004	0.003	0.003	0.003	0.002
19	0.006	0.005	0.004	0.004	0.003	0.003	0.003	0.002	0.002	0.002
20	0.005	0.004	0.003	0.003	0.002	0.002	0.002	0.002	0.001	0.001
21	0.003	0.003	0.003	0.002	0.002	0.002	0.001	0.001	0.001	0.001
22	0.003	0.002	0.002	0.002	0.001	0.001	0.001	0.001	0.001	0.001
23	0.002	0.002	0.001	0.001	0.001	0.001	0.001	0.001	0.001	0.000
24	0.002	0.001	0.001	0.001	0.001	0.001	0.000	0.000	0.000	0.000
25	0.001	0.001	0.001	0.001	0.001	0.000	0.000	0.000	0.000	0.000
26	0.001	0.001	0.001	0.000	0.000	0.000	0.000	0.000	0.000	0.000
27	0.001	0.001	0.000	0.000	0.000	0.000	0.000	0.000	0.000	0.000
28	0.001	0.000	0.000	0.000	0.000	0.000	0.000	0.000	0.000	0.000
29	0.000	0.000	0.000	0.000	0.000	0.000	0.000	0.000	0.000	0.000
30	0.000	0.000	0.000	0.000	0.000	0.000	0.000	0.000	0.000	0.000
40	0.000	0.000	0.000	0.000	0.000	0.000	0.000	0.000	0.000	0.000
50	0.000	0.000	0.000	0.000	0.000	0.000	0.000	0.000	0.000	0.000

TABLE A–2 Present Value of Annuity of $ 1

Periods	1%	2%	3%	4%	5%	6%	7%	8%	9%	10%
1	0.990	0.980	0.971	0.962	0.952	0.943	0.935	0.926	0.917	0.909
2	1.970	1.942	1.913	1.886	1.859	1.833	1.808	1.783	1.759	1.736
3	2.941	2.884	2.829	2.775	2.723	2.673	2.624	2.577	2.531	2.487
4	3.902	3.808	3.717	3.630	3.546	3.465	3.387	3.312	3.240	3.170
5	4.853	4.713	4.580	4.452	4.329	4.212	4.100	3.993	3.890	3.791
6	5.795	5.601	5.417	5.242	5.076	4.917	4.767	4.623	4.486	4.355
7	6.728	6.472	6.230	6.002	5.786	5.582	5.389	5.206	5.033	4.868
8	7.652	7.325	7.020	6.733	6.463	6.210	5.971	5.747	5.535	5.335
9	8.566	8.162	7.786	7.435	7.108	6.802	6.515	6.247	5.995	5.759
10	9.471	8.983	8.530	8.111	7.722	7.360	7.024	6.710	6.418	6.145
11	10.368	9.787	9.253	8.760	8.306	7.887	7.499	7.139	6.805	6.495
12	11.255	10.575	9.954	9.385	8.863	8.384	7.943	7.536	7.161	6.814
13	12.134	11.348	10.635	9.986	9.394	8.853	8.358	7.904	7.487	7.103
14	13.004	12.106	11.296	10.563	9.899	9.295	8.745	8.244	7.786	7.367
15	13.865	12.849	11.938	11.118	10.380	9.712	9.108	8.559	8.061	7.606
16	14.718	13.578	12.561	11.652	10.838	10.106	9.447	8.851	8.313	7.825
17	15.562	14.292	13.166	12.166	11.274	10.477	9.763	9.122	8.544	8.024
18	16.398	14.992	13.754	12.659	11.690	10.828	10.059	9.372	8.756	8.204
19	17.226	15.678	14.324	13.134	12.085	11.158	10.336	9.604	8.950	8.362
20	18.046	16.351	14.877	13.590	12.462	11.470	10.594	9.818	9.129	8.511
21	18.857	17.011	15.415	14.029	12.821	11.764	10.836	10.017	9.292	8.649
22	19.660	17.658	15.837	14.451	13.163	12.042	11.061	10.201	9.442	8.772
23	20.456	18.292	16.444	14.857	13.489	12.303	11.272	10.371	9.580	8.883
24	21.243	18.914	16.936	15.247	13.799	12.550	11.469	10.529	9.707	8.985
25	22.023	19.523	17.413	15.622	14.094	12.783	11.654	10.675	9.823	9.077
26	22.795	20.121	17.877	15.983	14.375	13.003	11.826	10.810	9.929	9.161
27	23.560	20.707	18.327	16.330	14.643	13.211	11.987	10.935	10.027	9.237
28	24.316	21.281	18.764	16.663	14.898	13.406	12.137	11.051	10.116	9.307
29	25.066	21.844	19.188	16.984	15.141	13.591	12.278	11.158	10.198	9.370
30	25.808	22.396	19.600	17.292	15.372	13.765	12.409	11.258	10.274	9.427
40	32.835	27.355	23.115	19.793	17.159	15.046	13.332	11.925	10.757	9.779
50	39.196	31.424	25.730	21.482	18.256	15.762	13.801	12.233	10.962	9.915

TABLE A-2 (contd.)   **Present Value of Annuity of $ 1**

Periods	11%	12%	13%	14%	15%	16%	17%	18%	19%	20%
1	0.901	0.893	0.885	0.877	0.870	0.862	0.855	0.847	0.840	0.833
2	1.713	1.690	1.668	1.647	1.626	1.605	1.585	1.566	1.547	1.528
3	2.444	2.402	2.361	2.322	2.283	2.246	2.210	2.174	2.140	2.106
4	3.102	3.037	2.974	2.914	2.855	2.798	2.743	2.690	2.639	2.589
5	3.696	3.605	3.517	3.433	3.352	3.274	3.199	3.127	3.058	2.991
6	4.231	4.111	3.998	3.889	3.784	3.685	3.589	3.498	3.410	3.326
7	4.712	4.564	4.423	4.288	4.160	4.039	3.922	3.812	3.706	3.605
8	5.146	4.968	4.799	4.639	4.487	4.344	4.207	4.078	3.954	3.837
9	5.537	5.328	5.132	4.946	4.772	4.607	4.451	4.303	4.163	4.031
10	5.889	5.650	5.426	5.216	5.019	4.833	4.659	4.494	4.339	4.192
11	6.207	5.938	5.687	5.453	5.234	5.029	4.836	4.656	4.486	4.327
12	6.492	6.194	5.918	5.660	5.421	5.197	4.988	4.793	4.611	4.439
13	6.750	6.424	6.122	5.842	5.583	5.342	5.118	4.910	4.715	4.533
14	6.982	6.628	6.302	6.002	5.724	5.468	5.229	5.008	4.802	4.611
15	7.191	6.811	6.462	6.142	5.847	5.575	5.324	5.092	4.876	4.675
16	7.379	6.974	6.604	6.265	5.954	5.668	5.405	5.162	4.938	4.730
17	7.549	7.120	6.729	6.373	6.047	5.749	5.475	5.222	4.990	4.775
18	7.702	7.250	6.840	6.467	6.128	5.818	5.534	5.273	5.033	4.812
19	7.839	7.366	6.938	6.550	6.198	5.877	5.584	5.316	5.070	4.843
20	7.963	7.469	7.025	6.623	6.259	5.929	5.628	5.353	5.101	4.870
21	8.075	7.562	7.102	6.687	6.312	5.973	5.665	5.384	5.127	4.891
22	8.176	7.645	7.170	6.743	6.359	6.011	5.696	5.410	5.149	4.909
23	8.266	7.718	7.230	6.792	6.399	6.044	5.723	5.432	5.167	4.925
24	8.348	7.784	7.283	6.835	6.434	6.073	5.746	5.451	5.182	4.937
25	8.422	7.843	7.330	6.873	6.464	6.097	5.766	5.467	5.195	4.948
26	8.488	7.896	7.372	6.906	6.491	6.118	5.783	5.480	5.206	4.956
27	8.548	7.943	7.409	6.935	6.514	6.136	5.798	5.492	5.215	4.964
28	8.602	7.984	7.441	6.961	6.534	6.152	5.810	5.502	5.223	4.970
29	8.650	8.022	7.470	6.983	6.551	6.166	5.820	5.510	5.229	4.975
30	8.694	8.055	7.496	7.003	6.566	6.177	5.829	5.517	5.235	4.979
40	8.951	8.244	7.634	7.105	6.642	6.233	5.871	5.548	5.258	4.997
50	9.042	8.304	7.675	7.133	6.661	6.246	5.880	5.554	5.262	4.999

TABLE A–2 (contd.)   Present Value of Annuity of $ 1

Periods	21%	22%	23%	24%	25%	26%	27%	28%	29%	30%
1	0.826	0.820	0.813	0.806	0.800	0.794	0.787	0.781	0.775	0.769
2	1.509	1.492	1.474	1.457	1.440	1.424	1.407	1.392	1.376	1.361
3	2.074	2.042	2.011	1.981	1.952	1.923	1.896	1.868	1.842	1.816
4	2.540	2.494	2.448	2.404	2.362	2.320	2.280	2.241	2.203	2.166
5	2.926	2.864	2.803	2.745	2.689	2.635	2.583	2.532	2.483	2.436
6	3.245	3.167	3.092	3.020	2.951	2.885	2.821	2.759	2.700	2.643
7	3.508	3.416	3.327	3.242	3.161	3.083	3.009	2.937	2.868	2.802
8	3.726	3.619	3.518	3.421	3.329	3.241	3.156	3.076	2.999	2.925
9	3.905	3.786	3.673	3.566	3.463	3.366	3.273	3.184	3.100	3.019
10	4.054	3.923	3.799	3.682	3.571	3.465	3.364	3.269	3.178	3.092
11	4.177	4.035	3.902	3.776	3.656	3.543	3.437	3.335	3.239	3.147
12	4.278	4.127	3.985	3.851	3.725	3.606	3.493	3.387	3.286	3.190
13	4.362	4.203	4.053	3.912	3.780	3.656	3.538	3.427	3.322	3.223
14	4.432	4.265	4.108	3.962	3.824	3.695	3.573	3.459	3.351	3.249
15	4.489	4.315	4.153	4.001	3.859	3.726	3.601	3.483	3.373	3.268
16	4.536	4.357	4.189	4.033	3.887	3.751	3.623	3.503	3.390	3.283
17	4.576	4.391	4.219	4.059	3.910	3.771	3.640	3.518	3.403	3.295
18	4.608	4.419	4.243	4.080	3.928	3.786	3.654	3.529	3.413	3.304
19	4.635	4.442	4.263	4.097	3.942	3.799	3.664	3.539	3.421	3.311
20	4.657	4.460	4.279	4.110	9.954	3.808	3.673	3.546	3.427	3.316
21	4.675	4.476	4.292	4.121	3.963	3.816	3.679	3.551	3.432	3.320
22	4.690	4.488	4.302	4.130	3.970	3.822	3.684	3.556	3.436	3.323
23	4.703	4.499	4.311	4.137	3.976	3.827	3.689	3.559	3.438	3.325
24	4.713	4.507	4.318	4.143	3.981	3.831	3.692	3.562	3.441	3.327
25	4.721	4.514	4.323	1.147	3.985	3.834	3.694	3.564	3.442	3.329
26	4.728	4.520	4.328	4.151	3.988	3.837	3.696	3.566	3.444	3.330
27	4.734	4.524	4.332	4.154	3.990	3.839	3.698	3.567	3.445	3.330
28	4.739	4.528	4.335	4.157	3.992	3.840	3.699	3.568	3.446	3.331
29	4.743	4.531	4.337	4.158	3.994	3.841	3.700	3.569	3.446	3.332
30	4.746	4.534	4.339	4.160	3.995	3.842	3.701	3.570	3.447	3.332
40	4.760	4.544	4.347	4.166	3.910	3.846	3.703	3.571	3.448	3.333
50	4.762	4.545	4.348	4.167	3.910	3.846	3.703	3.571	3.448	3.333

TABLE A–2 (contd.)   **Present Value of Annuity of $ 1**

Periods	31%	32%	33%	34%	35%	36%	37%	38%	39%	40%
1	0.763	0.758	0.752	0.746	0.741	0.735	0.730	0.725	0.719	0.714
2	1.346	1.331	1.317	1.303	1.289	1.276	1.263	1.250	1.237	1.224
3	1.791	1.766	1.742	1.719	1.696	1.673	1.652	1.630	1.609	1.589
4	2.130	2.096	2.062	2.029	1.997	1.966	1.935	1.906	1.877	1.849
5	2.390	2.345	2.302	2.260	2.220	2.181	2.143	2.106	2.070	2.035
6	2.588	2.534	2.483	2.433	2.385	2.339	2.294	2.251	2.209	2.168
7	2.739	2.677	2.619	2.562	2.508	2.455	2.404	2.355	2.308	2.263
8	2.854	2.786	2.721	2.658	2.598	2.540	2.485	2.432	2.380	2.331
9	2.942	2.868	2.798	2.730	2.665	2.603	2.544	2.487	2.432	2.379
10	3.009	2.930	2.855	2.784	2.715	2.649	2.587	2.527	2.469	2.414
11	3.060	2.978	2.899	2.824	2.752	2.683	2.618	2.555	2.496	2.438
12	3.100	3.013	2.931	2.853	2.779	2.708	2.641	2.576	2.515	2.456
13	3.129	3.040	2.956	2.876	2.799	2.727	2.658	2.592	2.529	2.469
14	3.152	3.061	2.974	2.892	2.814	2.740	2.670	2.603	2.539	2.478
15	3.170	3.076	2.988	2.905	2.825	2.750	2.679	2.611	2.546	2.484
16	3.183	3.088	2.999	2.914	2.834	2.757	2.685	2.616	2.551	2.489
17	3.193	3.097	3.007	2.921	2.840	2.763	2.690	2.621	2.555	2.492
18	3.201	3.104	3.012	2.926	2.844	2.767	2.693	2.624	2.557	2.494
19	3.207	3.109	3.017	2.930	2.848	2.770	2.696	2.626	2.559	2.496
20	3.211	3.113	3.020	2.933	2.850	2.772	2.698	2.627	2.561	2.497
21	3.215	3.116	3.023	2.935	2.852	2.773	2.699	2.629	2.562	2.498
22	3.217	3.118	3.025	2.936	2.853	2.775	2.700	2.629	2.562	2.498
23	3.219	3.120	3.026	2.938	2.854	2.775	2.701	2.630	2.563	2.499
24	3.221	3.121	3.027	2.939	2.855	2.776	2.701	2.630	2.563	2.499
25	3.222	3.122	3.028	2.939	2.856	2.777	2.702	2.631	2.563	2.499
26	3.223	3.123	3.028	2.940	2.856	2.777	2.702	2.631	2.564	2.500
27	3.224	3.123	3.029	2.940	2.856	2.777	2.702	2.631	2.564	2.500
28	3.224	3.124	3.029	2.940	2.857	2.777	2.702	2.631	2.564	2.500
29	3.225	3.124	3.030	2.941	2.857	2.777	2.702	2.631	2.564	2.500
30	3.225	3.124	3.030	2.941	2.857	2.778	2.702	2.631	2.564	2.500
40	3.226	3.125	3.030	2.941	2.857	2.778	2.703	2.632	2.564	2.500
50	3.226	3.125	3.030	2.941	2.857	2.778	2.703	2.632	2.564	2.500

TABLE A–3   Future Value of $ 1

Periods	1%	2%	3%	4%	5%	6%	7%	8%	9%	10%
1	1.010	1.020	1.030	1.040	1.050	1.060	1.070	1.080	1.090	1.100
2	1.020	1.040	1.061	1.082	1.102	1.124	1.145	1.166	1.188	1.200
3	1.030	1.061	1.093	1.125	1.158	1.191	1.225	1.260	1.295	1.331
4	1.041	1.082	1.126	1.170	1.216	1.262	1.311	1.360	1.412	1.464
5	1.051	1.104	1.159	1.217	1.276	1.338	1.403	1.469	1.539	1.611
6	1.062	1.126	1.194	1.265	1.340	1.419	1.501	1.587	1.677	1.772
7	1.072	1.149	1.230	1.316	1.407	1.504	1.606	1.714	1.828	1.949
8	1.083	1.172	1.267	1.369	1.477	1.594	1.718	1.851	1.993	2.144
9	1.094	1.195	1.305	1.423	1.551	1.689	1.838	1.999	2.172	2.358
10	1.105	1.219	1.344	1.480	1.629	1.791	1.967	2.159	2.367	2.594
11	1.116	1.243	1.384	1.539	1.710	1.898	2.105	2.332	2.580	2.853
12	1.127	1.268	1.426	1.601	1.796	2.012	2.252	2.518	2.813	3.138
13	1.138	1.294	1.469	1.665	1.886	2.133	2.410	2.720	3.066	3.452
14	1.149	1.319	1.513	1.732	1.980	2.261	2.579	2.937	3.342	3.797
15	1.161	1.346	1.558	1.801	2.079	2.397	2.759	3.172	3.642	4.177
16	1.173	1.373	1.605	1.873	2.183	2.540	2.952	3.426	3.970	4.595
17	1.184	1.400	1.653	1.948	2.292	2.693	3.159	3.700	4.328	5.054
18	1.196	1.428	1.702	2.026	2.407	2.854	3.380	3.996	4.717	5.560
19	1.208	1.457	1.754	2.107	2.527	3.026	3.617	4.316	5.142	6.116
20	1.220	1.486	1.806	2.191	2.653	3.207	3.870	4.661	5.604	6.727
21	1.232	1.516	1.860	2.279	2.786	3.400	4.141	5.034	6.109	7.400
22	1.245	1.546	1.916	2.370	2.925	3.604	4.430	5.437	6.659	8.140
23	1.257	1.577	1.974	2.465	3.072	3.820	4.741	5.871	7.258	8.954
24	1.270	1.608	2.033	2.563	3.225	4.049	5.072	6.341	7.911	9.850
25	1.282	1.641	2.094	2.666	3.386	4.292	5.427	6.848	8.623	10.835

TABLE A–3 (contd.)   **Future Value of $ 1**

Periods	11%	12%	13%	14%	15%	16%	17%	18%	19%	20%
1	1.110	1.120	1.130	1.140	1.150	1.160	1.170	1.180	1.190	1.200
2	1.232	1.254	1.277	1.300	1.322	1.346	1.369	1.392	1.416	1.490
3	1.368	1.405	1.443	1.482	1.521	1.561	1.602	1.643	1.685	1.728
4	1.518	1.574	1.630	1.689	1.749	1.811	1.874	1.939	2.005	2.074
5	1.685	1.762	1.842	1.925	2.011	2.100	2.192	2.228	2.386	2.488
6	1.870	1.974	2.082	2.195	2.313	2.436	2.565	2.700	2.840	2.986
7	2.076	2.211	2.353	2.502	2.660	2.826	3.001	3.185	3.379	3.583
8	2.305	2.476	2.658	2.853	3.059	3.278	3.511	3.759	4.021	4.300
9	2.558	2.773	3.004	3.252	3.518	3.803	4.108	4.435	4.785	5.160
10	2.839	3.106	3.395	3.707	4.046	4.411	4.807	5.234	5.695	6.192
11	3.152	3.479	3.836	4.226	4.652	5.117	5.624	6.176	6.777	7.430
12	3.498	3.896	4.335	4.818	5.350	5.936	6.580	7.288	8.064	8.916
13	3.883	4.363	4.898	5.492	6.153	6.886	7.699	8.599	9.596	10.699
14	4.310	4.887	5.535	6.261	7.076	7.988	9.007	10.147	11.420	12.839
15	4.785	5.474	6.254	7.138	8.137	9.266	10.539	11.974	13.590	15.407
16	5.311	6.130	7.067	8.137	9.358	10.748	12.330	14.129	16.172	18.488
17	5.895	6.866	7.986	9.276	10.761	12.468	14.426	16.672	19.244	22.186
18	6.544	7.690	9.024	10.575	12.375	14.463	16.879	19.673	22.901	26.623
19	7.263	8.613	10.197	12.056	14.232	16.777	19.748	23.214	27.252	31.948
20	8.062	9.646	11.523	13.743	16.367	19.461	23.106	27.393	32.429	38.338
21	8.949	10.804	13.021	15.668	18.822	22.574	27.034	32.324	38.591	46.005
22	9.934	12.100	14.714	17.861	21.645	26.186	31.629	38.142	45.923	55.206
23	11.026	13.552	16.627	20.362	24.891	30.376	37.006	45.008	54.649	66.247
24	12.239	15.179	18.788	23.212	28.625	35.236	43.297	53.109	65.032	79.497
25	13.585	17.000	21.231	26.462	32.919	40.874	50.658	62.669	77.388	95.396

TABLE A–3 (contd.)   Future Value of $ 1

Periods	21%	22%	23%	24%	25%	26%	27%	28%	29%	30%
1	1.210	1.220	1.230	1.240	1.250	1.260	1.270	1.280	1.290	1.300
2	1.464	1.488	1.513	1.538	1.563	1.588	1.613	1.638	1.664	1.690
3	1.772	1.816	1.861	1.907	1.953	2.000	2.048	2.097	2.147	2.197
4	2.144	2.215	2.289	2.364	2.441	2.520	2.601	2.684	2.769	2.856
5	2.594	2.703	2.815	2.932	3.052	3.176	3.304	3.436	3.572	3.713
6	3.138	3.297	3.463	3.635	3.815	4.002	4.196	4.398	4.608	4.827
7	3.797	4.023	4.259	4.508	4.768	5.042	5.329	5.629	5.945	6.275
8	4.595	4.908	5.239	5.590	5.960	6.353	6.768	7.206	7.669	8.157
9	5.560	5.987	6.444	6.931	7.451	8.005	8.595	9.223	9.893	10.604
10	6.727	7.305	7.926	8.594	9.313	10.086	10.915	11.806	12.761	13.786
11	8.140	8.912	9.749	10.657	11.642	12.708	13.862	15.112	16.462	17.922
12	9.850	10.872	11.991	13.215	14.552	16.012	17.605	19.343	21.236	23.298
13	11.918	13.264	14.749	16.386	18.190	20.175	22.359	24.759	27.395	30.288
14	14.421	16.182	18.141	20.319	22.737	25.421	28.396	31.691	35.339	39.374
15	17.449	19.742	22.314	25.196	28.422	32.030	36.062	40.565	45.587	51.186
16	21.114	24.086	27.446	31.243	35.527	40.358	45.799	51.923	58.808	66.542
17	25.548	29.384	33.759	38.741	44.409	50.851	58.165	66.461	75.862	86.504
18	30.913	35.849	41.523	48.039	55.511	64.072	73.870	85.071	97.862	112.455
19	37.404	43.736	51.074	59.568	69.389	80.731	93.815	108.890	126.242	146.192
20	45.259	53.358	62.821	73.864	86.736	101.721	119.145	139.380	162.852	190.050
21	54.764	65.096	77.269	91.592	108.420	128.169	151.314	178.406	210.080	247.065
22	66.264	79.418	95.041	113.574	135.525	161.492	192.168	228.360	271.003	321.184
23	80.180	96.889	116.901	140.831	169.407	203.480	244.054	292.300	349.593	417.539
24	97.017	118.205	143.788	174.631	211.758	256.385	309.948	374.144	450.976	542.801
25	117.391	144.210	176.859	216.542	264.698	323.045	393.634	478.905	581.759	705.641

TABLE A–3 (contd.)   Future Value of $ 1

Periods	31%	32%	33%	34%	35%	36%	37%	38%	39%	40%
1	1.310	1.320	1.330	1.340	1.350	1.360	1.370	1.380	1.390	1.400
2	1.716	1.742	1.769	1.796	1.822	1.850	1.877	1.904	1.932	1.960
3	2.248	2.300	2.353	2.406	2.460	2.515	2.571	2.628	2.686	2.744
4	2.945	3.036	3.129	3.224	3.322	3.421	3.523	3.627	3.733	3.842
5	3.858	4.007	4.162	4.320	4.484	4.653	4.826	5.005	5.189	5.378
6	5.054	5.290	5.535	5.789	6.053	6.328	6.612	6.907	7.213	7.530
7	6.621	6.983	7.361	7.758	8.172	8.605	9.058	9.531	10.025	10.541
8	8.673	9.217	9.791	10.395	11.032	11.703	12.410	13.153	13.935	14.758
9	11.362	12.166	13.022	13.930	14.894	15.917	17.001	18.151	19.370	20.661
10	14.884	16.060	17.319	18.666	20.107	21.647	23.292	25.049	26.925	28.925
11	19.498	21.199	23.034	25.012	27.144	29.439	31.910	34.568	37.425	40.496
12	25.542	27.983	30.635	33.516	36.644	40.037	43.717	47.703	52.021	56.694
13	33.460	36.937	40.745	44.912	49.470	54.451	59.892	65.831	72.309	79.371
14	43.833	48.757	54.190	60.182	66.784	74.053	82.052	90.846	100.510	111.120
15	57.421	64.359	72.073	80.644	90.158	100.713	112.411	125.368	139.708	155.568
16	75.221	84.954	95.858	108.063	121.714	136.969	154.003	173.008	194.194	217.795
17	98.540	112.139	127.491	144.804	164.314	186.278	210.984	238.751	269.930	304.913
18	129.087	148.024	169.562	194.038	221.824	253.338	289.048	329.476	375.203	426.879
19	169.104	195.391	225.518	260.011	299.462	344.540	395.996	454.677	521.532	597.630
20	221.527	257.916	299.939	348.414	404.274	468.574	542.514	627.454	724.930	836.683
21	290.200	340.449	398.919	466.875	545.769	637.261	743.245	865.886	1007.653	1171.356
22	380.162	449.393	530.562	625.613	736.789	866.674	1018.245	1194.923	1400.637	1639.898
23	498.012	593.199	705.647	838.321	994.665	1178.677	1394.996	1648.994	1946.885	2295.857
24	652.396	783.023	938.511	1123.350	1342.797	1603.001	1911.145	2275.611	2706.171	3214.200
25	854.638	1033.590	1248.220	1505.289	1812.776	2180.081	2618.268	3140.344	3761.577	4499.880

TABLE A—4 Future Value of an Ordinary Annuity of $1 for n Periods

n	1%	2%	3%	4%	5%	6%	7%	8%	9%	10%
1	1.000	1.000	1.000	1.000	1.000	1.000	1.000	1.000	1.000	1.000
2	2.010	2.020	2.030	2.040	2.050	2.060	2.070	2.080	2.090	2.100
3	3.030	3.060	3.091	3.122	3.152	3.184	3.215	3.246	3.278	3.310
4	4.060	4.122	4.184	4.246	4.310	4.375	4.440	4.506	4.573	4.641
5	5.101	5.204	5.309	5.416	5.526	5.637	5.751	5.867	5.985	6.105
6	6.152	6.308	6.468	6.633	6.802	6.975	7.153	7.336	7.523	7.716
7	7.214	7.434	7.662	7.898	8.142	8.394	8.654	8.923	9.200	9.487
8	8.286	8.583	8.892	9.214	9.549	9.897	10.260	10.637	11.028	11.436
9	9.368	9.755	10.159	10.583	11.027	11.491	11.978	12.488	13.021	13.579
10	10.462	10.950	11.464	12.006	12.578	13.181	13.816	14.487	15.193	15.937
11	11.567	12.169	12.808	13.486	14.207	14.972	15.784	16.645	17.560	18.531
12	12.682	13.412	14.192	15.026	15.917	16.870	17.888	18.977	20.141	21.384
13	13.809	14.680	15.618	16.627	17.713	18.882	20.141	21.495	22.953	24.523
14	14.947	15.974	17.086	18.292	19.598	21.015	22.550	24.215	26.019	27.975
15	16.097	17.923	18.599	20.023	21.578	23.276	25.129	27.152	29.361	31.772
16	17.258	18.639	20.157	21.824	23.657	25.672	27.888	30.324	33.003	35.949
17	18.430	20.012	21.761	23.697	25.840	28.213	30.840	33.750	36.973	40.544
18	19.614	21.412	23.414	25.645	28.132	30.905	33.999	37.450	41.301	45.599
19	20.811	22.840	25.117	27.671	30.539	33.760	37.379	41.446	46.018	51.158
20	22.019	24.297	26.870	29.778	33.066	36.785	40.995	45.762	51.159	57.274
21	23.239	25.783	28.676	31.969	35.719	39.992	44.865	50.422	56.764	64.002
22	24.471	27.299	30.536	34.248	38.505	43.392	49.005	55.456	62.872	71.402
23	25.716	28.845	32.452	36.618	41.430	46.995	53.435	60.893	69.531	79.542
24	26.973	30.421	34.426	39.082	44.501	50.815	58.176	66.764	76.789	88.496
25	28.243	32.030	36.459	41.645	47.726	54.864	63.248	73.105	84.699	98.346
30	34.784	40.567	47.575	56.084	66.438	79.057	94.459	113.282	136.305	164.491
40	48.885	60.401	75.400	95.024	120.797	154.758	199.630	259.052	337.872	442.580
50	64.461	84.577	112.794	152.664	209.341	290.325	406.516	573.756	815.051	1163.865

TABLE A—4 Future Value of an Ordinary Annuity of $1 for n Periods (cont.)

n	11%	12%	13%	14%	15%	16%	17%	18%	19%	20%
1	1.000	1.000	1.000	1.000	1.000	1.000	1.000	1.000	1.000	1.000
2	2.110	2.120	2.130	2.140	2.150	2.160	2.170	2.180	2.190	2.200
3	3.342	3.374	3.407	3.440	3.472	3.506	3.539	3.572	3.606	3.640
4	4.710	4.779	4.850	4.921	4.993	5.066	5.141	5.215	5.291	5.368
5	6.228	6.353	6.480	6.610	6.742	6.877	7.014	7.154	7.297	7.442
6	7.913	8.115	8.323	8.535	8.754	8.977	9.207	9.442	9.683	9.930
7	9.783	10.089	10.405	10.730	11.067	11.414	11.772	12.141	12.523	12.916
8	11.859	12.300	12.757	13.233	13.727	14.240	14.773	15.327	15.902	16.499
9	14.164	14.776	15.416	16.085	16.786	17.518	18.285	19.086	19.923	20.799
10	16.722	17.549	18.420	19.337	20.304	21.321	22.393	23.521	24.709	25.959
11	19.561	20.655	21.814	23.044	24.349	25.733	27.200	28.755	30.403	32.150
12	22.713	24.133	25.650	27.271	29.001	30.850	32.824	34.931	37.180	39.580
13	26.211	28.029	29.984	32.088	34.352	36.786	39.404	42.218	45.244	48.496
14	30.095	32.392	34.882	37.581	40.504	43.672	47.102	50.818	54.841	59.196
15	34.405	37.280	40.417	43.842	47.580	51.659	56.109	60.965	66.260	72.035
16	39.190	42.753	46.671	50.980	55.717	60.925	66.648	72.938	79.850	87.442
17	44.500	48.883	53.738	59.117	65.075	71.673	78.978	87.067	96.021	105.930
18	50.396	55.749	61.724	68.393	75.836	84.140	93.404	103.739	115.265	128.116
19	56.939	63.439	70.748	78.968	88.211	98.603	110.283	123.412	138.165	154.739
20	64.202	72.052	80.946	91.024	102.443	115.379	130.031	146.626	165.417	186.687
21	72.264	81.698	92.468	104.767	118.809	134.840	153.136	174.019	197.846	225.024
22	81.213	92.502	105.489	120.434	137.630	157.414	180.169	206.342	236.436	271.028
23	91.147	104.602	120.203	138.295	159.274	183.600	211.798	244.483	282.359	326.234
24	102.173	118.154	136.829	158.656	184.166	213.976	248.803	289.490	337.007	392.480
25	114.412	133.333	155.616	181.867	212.790	249.212	292.099	342.598	402.038	471.976
30	199.018	241.330	293.192	356.778	434.738	530.306	647.423	790.932	966.698	1181.865
40	581.812	767.080	1013.667	1341.979	1779.048	2360.724	3134.412	4163.094	5529.711	7343.715
50	1668.723	2399.975	3459.344	4994.301	7217.488	10435.449	15088.805	21812.273	31514.492	45496.094

TABLE A–4 Future Value of an Ordinary Annuity of $1 for n Periods (cont.)

n	21%	22%	23%	24%	25%	26%	27%	28%	29%	30%
1	1.000	1.000	1.000	1.000	1.000	1.000	1.000	1.000	1.000	1.000
2	2.210	2.220	2.230	2.240	2.250	2.260	2.270	2.280	2.290	2.300
3	3.674	3.708	3.743	3.778	3.813	3.848	3.883	3.918	3.954	3.990
4	5.446	5.524	5.604	5.684	5.766	5.848	5.931	6.016	6.101	6.187
5	7.589	7.740	7.893	8.048	8.207	8.368	8.533	8.700	8.870	9.043
6	10.183	10.442	10.708	10.980	11.259	11.544	11.837	12.136	12.442	12.756
7	13.321	13.740	14.171	14.615	15.073	15.546	16.032	16.534	17.051	17.583
8	17.119	17.762	18.430	19.123	19.842	20.588	21.361	22.163	22.995	23.858
9	21.714	22.670	23.669	24.712	25.802	26.940	28.129	29.369	30.664	32.015
10	27.274	28.657	30.113	31.643	33.253	34.945	36.723	38.592	40.556	42.619
11	34.001	35.962	38.039	40.238	42.566	45.030	47.639	50.398	53.318	56.405
12	42.141	44.873	47.787	50.895	54.208	57.738	61.501	65.510	69.780	74.326
13	51.991	55.745	59.778	64.109	68.760	73.750	79.106	84.853	91.016	97.624
14	63.909	69.009	74.528	80.496	86.949	93.925	101.465	109.611	118.411	127.912
15	78.330	85.191	92.669	100.815	109.687	119.346	129.860	141.302	153.750	167.285
16	95.779	104.933	114.983	126.010	138.109	151.375	165.922	181.867	199.337	218.470
17	116.892	129.019	142.428	157.252	173.636	191.733	211.721	233.790	258.145	285.011
18	142.439	158.403	176.187	195.993	218.045	242.583	269.885	300.250	334.006	371.514
19	173.351	194.251	217.710	244.031	273.556	306.654	343.754	385.321	431.868	483.968
20	210.755	237.986	268.783	303.598	342.945	387.384	437.568	494.210	558.110	630.157
21	256.013	291.343	331.603	377.461	429.681	489.104	556.710	633.589	720.962	820.204
22	310.775	356.438	408.871	469.052	538.101	617.270	708.022	811.993	931.040	1067.265
23	377.038	435.854	503.911	582.624	673.626	778.760	900.187	1040.351	1202.042	1388.443
24	457.215	532.741	620.810	723.453	843.032	982.237	1144.237	1332.649	1551.634	1805.975
25	554.230	650.944	764.596	898.082	1054.791	1238.617	1454.180	1706.790	2002.608	2348.765
30	1445.111	1767.044	2160.459	2460.881	3227.172	3941.953	4812.891	5873.172	7162.785	8729.805
40	9749.141	12936.141	17153.691	22728.367	30088.621	39791.957	52570.707	69376.562	91447.375	120389.375
45	25294.223	34970.230	48300.660	66638.937	91831.312	126378.937	173692.875	238384.312	326686.375	447005.062

TABLE A–4   Future Value of an Ordinary Annuity of $1 for *n* Periods (cont.)

n	31%	32%	33%	34%	35%	36%	37%	38%	39%	40%
1	1.000	1.000	1.000	1.000	1.000	1.000	1.000	1.000	1.000	1.000
2	2.310	2.320	2.330	2.340	2.350	2.360	2.370	2.380	2.390	2.400
3	4.026	4.062	4.099	4.136	4.172	4.210	4.247	4.284	4.322	4.360
4	6.274	6.362	6.452	6.542	6.633	6.725	6.818	6.912	7.008	7.104
5	9.219	9.398	9.581	9.766	9.954	10.146	10.341	10.539	10.741	10.946
6	13.077	13.406	13.742	14.086	14.438	14.799	15.167	15.544	15.930	16.324
7	18.131	18.696	19.277	19.876	20.492	21.126	21.779	22.451	23.142	23.853
8	24.752	25.678	26.638	27.633	28.664	29.732	30.837	31.982	33.167	34.395
9	33.425	34.895	36.429	38.028	39.696	41.435	43.247	45.135	47.103	49.152
10	44.786	47.062	49.451	51.958	54.590	57.351	60.248	63.287	66.473	69.813
11	59.670	63.121	66.769	70.624	74.696	78.998	83.540	88.335	93.397	98.739
12	79.167	84.320	89.803	95.636	101.840	108.437	115.450	122.903	130.822	139.234
13	104.709	112.302	120.438	129.152	138.484	148.474	159.166	170.606	182.842	195.928
14	138.169	149.239	161.183	174.063	187.953	202.925	219.058	236.435	255.151	275.299
15	182.001	197.996	215.373	234.245	254.737	276.978	301.109	327.281	355.659	386.418
16	239.421	262.354	287.446	314.888	344.895	377.690	413.520	452.647	495.366	541.985
17	314.642	347.307	383.303	422.949	466.608	514.658	567.521	625.652	689.558	759.778
18	413.180	459.445	510.792	567.751	630.920	700.935	778.504	864.399	959.485	1064.689
19	542.266	607.467	680.354	761.786	852.741	954.271	1067.551	1193.870	1334.683	1491.563
20	711.368	802.856	905.870	1021.792	1152.200	1298.809	1463.544	1648.539	1856.208	2089.188
21	932.891	1060.769	1205.807	1370.201	1556.470	1767.380	2006.055	2275.982	2581.128	2925.862
22	1223.087	1401.215	1604.724	1837.068	2102.234	2404.636	2749.294	3141.852	3588.765	4097.203
23	1603.243	1850.603	2135.282	2462.669	2839.014	3271.304	3767.532	4336.750	4989.379	5737.078
24	2101.247	2443.795	2840.924	3300.974	3833.667	4449.969	5162.516	5985.711	6936.230	8032.906
25	2753.631	3226.808	3779.428	4424.301	5176.445	6052.957	7073.645	8261.273	9642.352	11247.062
30	10632.543	12940.672	15737.945	19124.434	23221.258	28172.016	34148.906	41357.227	50043.625	60500.207
35	41028.887	51868.563	65504.199	82634.625	104134.500	131082.625	164818.438	206998.375	259680.313	325394.688

Index